Using
Liferay Portal

A Complete Guide

THE LIFERAY DOCUMENTATION TEAM
Richard Sezov, Jr.
Jim Hinkey
Stephen Kostas
Jesse Rao
Cody Hoag
Russell Bohl
Nicholas Gaskill
Michael Williams

Liferay Press

Using Liferay Portal 6.2
by The Liferay Documentation Team
Copyright ©2015 by Liferay, Inc.

ISBN 978-0-578-15433-6

CONTENTS

PREFACE

Welcome to the world of Liferay Portal! This book was written for anyone who has any part in setting up, using, or maintaining a web site built on Liferay Portal. For the end user, it contains everything you need to know about using the applications included with Liferay. For the administrator, you'll learn all you need to know about setting up your site with users, sites, organizations, and user groups, as well as how to manage your site's security with roles. For server admins, it guides you step-by-step through the installation, configuration, and optimization of Liferay Portal, including setting it up in a clustered, enterprise-ready environment. Use this book as a handbook for everything you need to do to get your Liferay Portal installation running smoothly, and then keep it by your side as you configure and maintain your Liferay-powered web site.

What's New in the Second Edition

Liferay Portal visually changed a lot in the 6.2 release. This is reflected in all the updated screenshots in this book. Of course, everything from the old book has been updated to reflect the release of Liferay Portal 6.2. We also have complete coverage of Liferay's new features, such as web content folders, the Recycle Bin, Audience Targeting, Application Display Templates, and more.

There is, of course, coverage of Liferay Marketplace as well as the Plugin Security Manager. Mobile devices are first-class citizens in Liferay Portal 6.2, and we cover how to serve sites to mobile devices, using responsive layouts and mobile device rules. We cover the new, split Control Panel UI, which is much more convenient, especially for those who want to grant access to content functionality, but not administration of the overall portal. We also cover the enhancements to staging and the many new settings for sites, including membership management, site hierarchies, and more.

The new release is feature-packed, and so the documentation must be also: we have over 44,000 more words of goodness awaiting you in these pages than we had the last time around.

Conventions

The information contained herein has been organized in a way that makes it easy to locate information. The book has two parts. The first part, *Using Liferay Portal*, describes how to configure and use a freshly installed Liferay Portal. The second part, *Deploying Liferay Portal*, is for administrators who want to install Liferay Portal and optimize its performance.

Sections are broken up into multiple levels of headings, and these are designed to make it easy to find information.

Source code and configuration file directives are presented monospaced, as below.

```
If source code goes multi-line, the lines will be \

separated by a backslash character like this.
```

Italics are used to represent links or buttons to be clicked on in a user interface.
`Monospaced type` is used to denote Java classes, code, or properties within the text.
Bold is used to describe field labels and portlets.
Page headers denote the chapters and the section within the chapter.

Publisher Notes

It is our hope that this book is valuable to you, and that it becomes an indispensable resource as you work with Liferay Portal. If you need any assistance beyond what is covered in this book, Liferay offers training, consulting, and support services to fill any need that you might have. Please see http://www.liferay.com/services for further information about the services we can provide.

It is entirely possible that some errors or mistakes made it into the final version of this book. Any issues that we find or that are reported to us by the community are documented on the Liferay Developer Network website.[1]

As always, we welcome any feedback. If there is any way you think we could make this book better, please feel free to mention it on our forums or in the feedback on the Liferay Developer Network site. You can also use any of the email addresses on our Contact Us page.[2] We are here to serve you, our users and customers, and to help make your experience using Liferay Portal the best it can be.

---

[1]https://dev.liferay.com
[2]http://www.liferay.com/contact-us

Part I

Using Liferay Portal

## CHAPTER 1

WHAT IS LIFERAY?

Let's attempt some mind reading: you're reading this because you need to build a website. You're thinking about using Liferay Portal for your site, or you've already decided to use it and you want to learn all about it. Either way, you've come to the right place. What you'll find here is that Liferay Portal is the right decision, and we'll be happy to tell you all the reasons why. But since you might be in a rush, we'll give you all the reasons in a nutshell right here, and then you can read the details in the rest of the chapter.

The reasons to use Liferay Portal for your website are simple: it provides a robust *platform* to serve your site to all clients, be they desktop, mobile, or anything in between; it provides all the standard *applications* you need to run on your site; and it provides an easy to use development *framework* for new applications or customization. In addition to this, Liferay Portal is developed using an open source methodology, by people from around the world. The code base is solid, and has been proved to be reliable and stable in mission critical deployments in diverse industries.

But don't just take our word for it. Let us *show* you how Liferay does all this. Probably the first thing you want to do after you install Liferay Portal to manage your site is to get your content published. Let's dive right in and see how Liferay Portal handles that task.

1.1 Building a site with Liferay Web Content

When you log into Liferay and look at its default screen, one thing should jump out at you right away: it's built for all clients that access the web, not just desktop browsers.

Another thing to notice is that all the page controls are right there for you. For example, to add something, you click the + button, and then you can add any kind of content Liferay supports. The interface—particularly in Liferay 6.2—has been designed to get out of your way and let you do your work.

Liferay WCM scales to work for the tiniest of sites all the way up to the largest of sites. For example, you can click that *Add* button, choose *Web Content Article*, and immediately start typing content into a WYSIWYG editor, in place. Or you can set up Liferay Portal to host many different web sites, all with their own domain names. Each site can take advantage of a separate staging server, where content and pages are created by teams of people using structures and templates, and updates to the production server are published on a schedule, only after having gone through a multi-step approval process.

That's powerful.

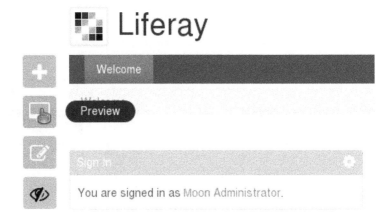

Figure 1.1: When designing pages, Liferay includes a preview that lets you see how it would look when displayed at resolutions for computers, tablets, and phones.

By default, Liferay Portal starts with a single site that has a single page. You can build any website you wish out of this, complete with multi-nested page hierarchies, as the figure below shows.

Figure 1.2: Liferay's page hierarchies are easy to create, using a tree structure that's familiar to anyone who has used a file manager.

These pages can have any layout you like: Liferay Portal ships with several built-in, and you can create your own custom layouts and deploy them easily. Pages can be added, removed, or reordered any time, and you have the full flexibility of all the HTML page attributes, such as meta tags and robot file declarations, that you need.

Pages are also integrated with Liferay's powerful permissions system, so it's easy to restrict access to certain portions of your site. You can give individual users sites of their own, with public pages that have their content and blog, and private pages that contain their calendars and email.

If you're running a large website that has lots of different sub-sites for individuals and groups, you can use page templates and site templates. The former enables you to set up templates of pages with predefined layouts and applications already on them, and the latter enables you to create a whole site made up of multiple, predefined pages.

There's even more. If you have a very large site, you might need multiple people to work on it. And you certainly don't want the live site changing before your users' eyes. For that reason, Liferay Portal provides a feature called *staging* that lets you place your changes in a holding area while they're being worked on. You can have a local staging server, where the staged site resides on the same server as the live site, or you can have a remote staging server, where all web content work happens on a separate server from your live site. In either case, when you're ready, site changes can be pushed to the live site, either manually or on a schedule.

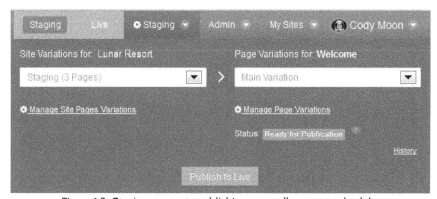

Figure 1.3: Staging supports publishing manually or on a schedule.

Liferay Portal's web content creation tools are easy and intuitive to use at all levels. If you need only basic content management capabilities for your site, you can jump right in. You can add the Web Content Display application anywhere in your page layout and enter content in place. It's easy to go from this basic level of content management to more sophisticated levels of functionality.

For example, suppose you wanted to build a news-oriented site. Most of the content you'll publish is an article of some kind. Liferay's web content management system lets you create a *structure* for this, so that you can capture all the information from your writers that you'd need in an article. The figure below shows what this structure might look like to a journalist who'd be entering his or her article into the system.

As you can see, you can use structures to make sure writers provide the title of the story, what type of story it will be, and the byline (i.e., the writer's name). You've made sure that all the relevant information for the story is captured in the system.

Web content is one example of an *asset*. Assets can have meta-data attached to them, and that meta-data is used to aggregate similar assets together in searches or as published content. One way to do this in the example above is to tag and categorize stories so they can be found more easily by users.

This is just one example, of course. But the concept is applicable to any kind of site you'd want to build. For example, if you were building a site for a zoo, you could use web content structures to help users enter data about animals in the zoo, such as their common names, their scientific names, their species, their locations in the wild, and more.

When it comes time to publish content, structures are combined with *templates*. Templates are instructions for how to display structures, written most of the time in Freemarker or Velocity—both of which are well-known templating languages used for mixing HTML

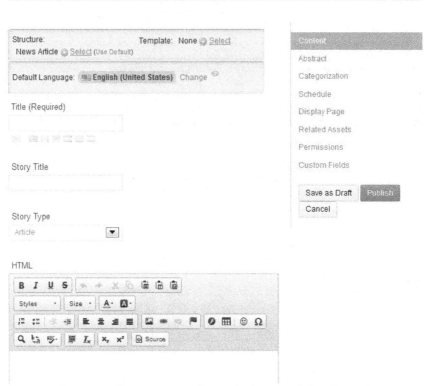

Figure 1.4: Structures allow you to specify exactly the type of data that makes up your content. You can also include tooltips to help your users understand what each field is for.

with programmatic elements. Because of this, they're very easy to write and can help you ensure that your site has a consistent look and feel.

There is much more to web content. You can create abstracts, schedule when content is published and when it should be taken down (or reviewed), define related assets, and more.

This is just the web content portion of Liferay's content management system. Liferay Portal is also great at managing file-based content.

Keeping track of documents, images, video, and more

It's rare to find in an open source project a full-featured content management system. Most of the time, you'll find web content management systems and file-based content management systems as separate projects. Liferay Portal, however, provides you with both. As shown above, the web content management system is as robust as any other you'll find, and its file-based content management system is the same.

Liferay Portal keeps the UI of its file-based content management system in an application called *Documents and Media Library*. This application resides on the Site Administration page or can be added to any page, and, as shown below, looks very much like the file manager that you're already familiar with from your operating system.

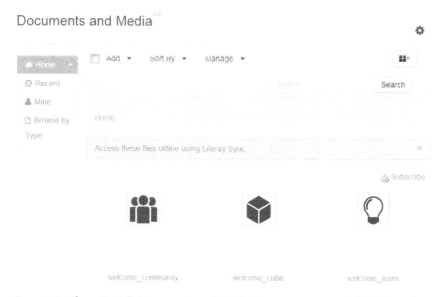

Figure 1.5: Liferay Portal's Documents and Media library was purposefully designed to be familiar to anyone who uses a computer.

Like a file manager, you can browse files and folders in nested hierarchies. You can also mount other repositories that you might have in your environment, such as Documentum (enterprise subscribers only) or any system that implements Content Management Interoperability Services (CMIS). It provides previews of just about every document type you can think of. And, like a file manager, you can upload, copy, and move files between folders by dragging and dropping them. Of course, if you still want to use your operating system's file manager, you can, because Liferay's Documents and Media library supports WebDAV, using the same credentials you use to log in to Liferay.

Liferay Portal's Documents and Media library, however, is much more robust than a file manager is, because it's a full content management system. You can define ways of classifying files that may be of different types, but are meant for the same, overarching purpose.

For example, *metadata sets*, are groups of fields describing attributes of a file. One that ships with the product is called *meeting metadata*, and it contains fields such as Meeting Name, Date, Time, Location, Description, and Participants. This is a generic set of fields that go together and that you'd want to use as a group. You can create as many of these as you want.

For files, you can define *document types*. They provide a more natural way of working with files. For example, you might create a document type called Meeting Minutes. The file format doesn't matter: whether it's a Microsoft Word document, an HTML file, or a text file, the document contains meeting minutes. Once you've created the document type, you can attach the Meeting Metadata set that contains many of the fields you'd want, and you can also add extra fields, such as a field for action items. When users want to add files containing their notes for meeting minutes, they can also add all the relevant metadata about the meeting (such as the time, location, and action items). This captures the context information that goes with the document, and it provides a much more natural way of working with documents than just dumping them into a shared file system.

Of course, the system goes much further than this. Folders can be set so that only certain document types can be added to them. Workflow rules can also be added to folders to run files through an approval process that you define. In short, Liferay's file-based content management system gives you all the features you need to manage and share files in a group.

Many Liferay Portal users see it as a robust content management system, and they use it primarily for that purpose. Now, hopefully, you can see why. We'll cover the system in-depth in the body of this book, but for now we need to look at some of the other ways you can use Liferay Portal, starting with its fantastic collaborative tools.

1.2   Using Liferay Portal as a collaborative platform

Many sites have grown organically. You may have grown your community by using separate tools: first a forums application, and then a wiki for collaborative documentation, and maybe even a chat application. It can be hard (and error-prone) to integrate all these applications so your users can use them seamlessly. Thankfully, Liferay includes a suite of collaborative applications, and they're all integrated together.

Liferay Portal offers every standard collaborative application that's available. These applications range from personal productivity applications like a calendar and email, to community-building applications like message boards, polls, and wikis.

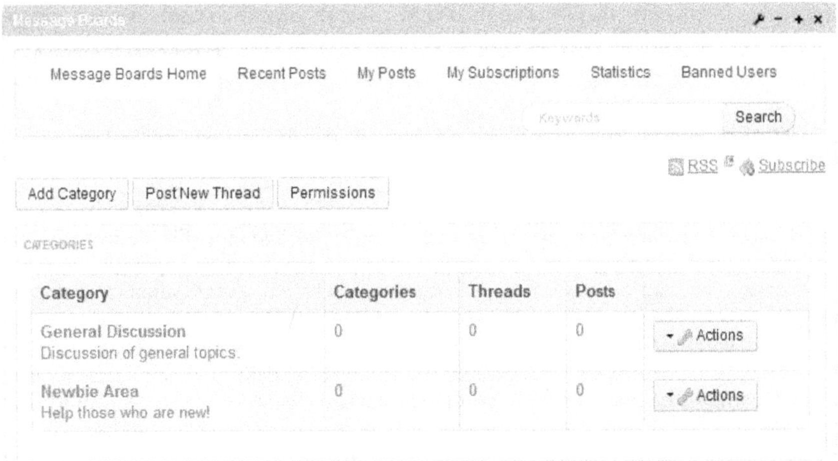

Figure 1.6: Liferay Portal's message boards are as fully featured as any standalone forum application, with the added benefit that they're integrated with the rest of the system.

This is a suite of integrated applications with all the features of similar, standalone applications. For example, Liferay Portal's message boards include categories and subcategories, message threads, captcha, RSS feeds, email notification, posting via email, and much more. But more than this, the applications are integrated with the rest of Liferay Portal's framework. Users log in, and their profiles are used automatically by the message boards and all the other collaborative applications. And as we'll see later, functionality from the built in applications can be added to your own to provide features like comments in your own software, and you don't have to write any code to do it.

Liferay Portal's wiki is another example of a full-featured collaborative application. It has support for authoring pages in a WYSWYG editor, or more advanced users can use the easy-to-learn standard Wiki Creole syntax. Users can comment on wiki articles, and it keeps a full history of every change that's been made, allowing users to revert back to any change. It also supports RSS feeds (just about every Liferay application does) so you can subscribe to see new articles as they are posted. Each site can have one or more wikis, and each wiki can have one or more top-level nodes.

One important feature of all the collaborative applications—as well as web content and documents—is the Recycle Bin. If users delete content that needs to be restored later, you don't have to find it in your backups: it's in the Recycle Bin.

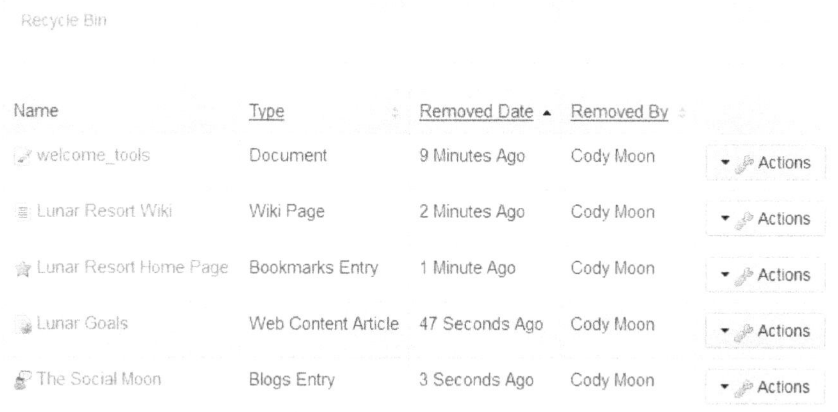

Recycle Bin

Name	Type	Removed Date ▲	Removed By	
welcome_tools	Document	9 Minutes Ago	Cody Moon	▾ Actions
Lunar Resort Wiki	Wiki Page	2 Minutes Ago	Cody Moon	▾ Actions
Lunar Resort Home Page	Bookmarks Entry	1 Minute Ago	Cody Moon	▾ Actions
Lunar Goals	Web Content Article	47 Seconds Ago	Cody Moon	▾ Actions
The Social Moon	Blogs Entry	3 Seconds Ago	Cody Moon	▾ Actions

Figure 1.7: The Recycle Bin can hold any kind of content.

We could go through all of Liferay Portal's collaborative applications, but let's save that for the body of the book. Liferay Portal's suite of collaborative applications includes a blog (complete with blog aggregation features so you can publish multiple users' blog entries in one place), a chat application for users who are online at the same time, message boards, a wiki, a knowledge base that you can use to publish a library of technical articles, a polling system you can use to have users vote on certain questions, and personal productivity applications like a calendar and email.

Liferay Portal includes every application you'll need to enable users to collaborate. Next, we'll see how you can use Liferay Portal as a social platform.

1.3   Using Liferay as a social platform

Whether you plan to build a social network or enable social applications as part of your overall user experience, Liferay Portal has the tools to make those features work for you. Starting with a suite of applications—including a profile summary, activities feeds, social requests, a wall, and more—and rounding things out with an API to handle relationships between users as well as publish their activities to each other, Liferay Portal helps you implement common features of social networks.

Social relationships in Liferay Portal are ideally suited for everything from public social networks to enabling social features in your corporate Intranet. Users can form relationships with one another, allowing them to see updates from those whose activity they need to track. That's far more powerful than having them subscribe to multiple individual RSS feeds or visit multiple profiles, because the system keeps track of the updates from those with whom you have a relationship, automatically.

More than this, however, Liferay is a great integration platform for social applications. It fully supports the OpenSocial framework. You can publish gadgets you find online, or you can use Liferay Portal's built-in OpenSocial gadget editor to create and serve your own OpenSocial gadgets.

Figure 1.9: Liferay Portal's OpenSocial gadget editor lets you rapidly create social applications that can be served across the web to any other OpenSocial container.

Liferay Portal also supports the creation of Facebook applications; in fact, no additional coding is necessary to publish your Liferay applications on Facebook (you would, of course, need to use Facebook's API to use Facebook-specific features like posting on users' time-lines). All you need to do is get an API key and canvas page URL from Facebook.

As you can see, Liferay Portal is built with social applications in mind. It's highly likely, however that you also have your own application you need to run on your website. The Liferay Portal platform is ideal for the web application you're considering writing. In addition to this, Liferay Portal is easily configured to be used as a shared hosting platform for multiple web sites. Let's look at the benefits you can reap by using Liferay Portal in these ways.

1.4   Using Liferay as a web platform

We can't even begin to imagine what you're thinking of building, but whatever it is, you're going to put your heart and soul into it. Building it on Liferay's web platform can give you a leg up. It provides everything you need to support your application, so you can concentrate solely on what *you're* building, and not the rest of the features your users expect will come along with it.

Imagine your application for a moment. Does it require users to register on your site? Can users comment on content contained in your application? Is there something that users can tag or categorize? If you think about the layout of the application, would it benefit from modularization? Could you make use of a rich JavaScript framework with many components built into it? How about security—will you need to make information available to some users, but not to all users? Liferay Portal has all of this and more available to developers.

Liferay Portal's development framework is a great help when you're building a web application. While the framework itself is covered in other resources such as the *Liferay Developer Network* or *Liferay in Action*, the strengths of Liferay as a platform are also apparent once you've finished writing your application.

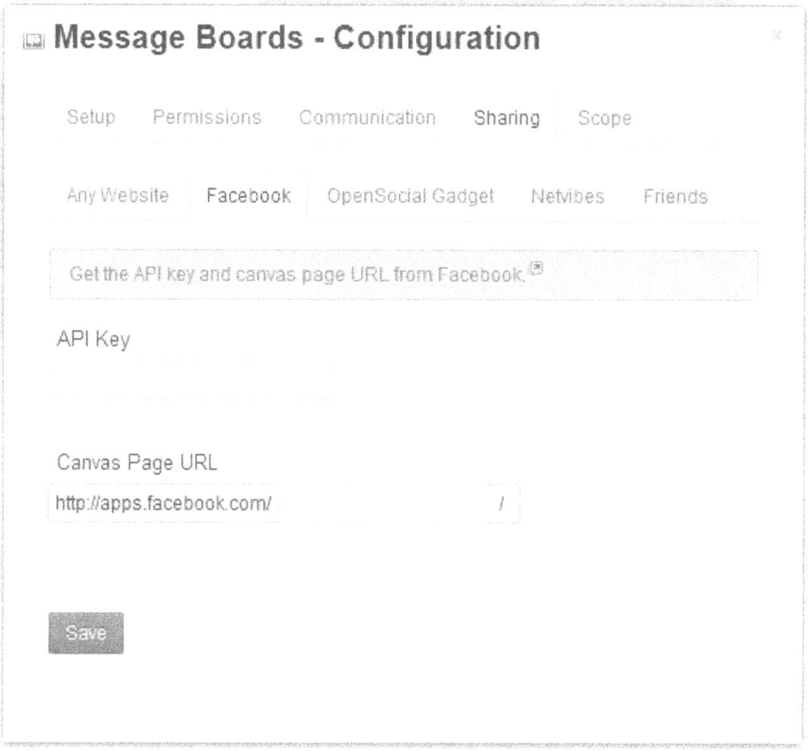

Message Boards - Configuration

Setup   Permissions   Communication   **Sharing**   Scope

Any Website   **Facebook**   OpenSocial Gadget   Netvibes   Friends

Get the API key and canvas page URL from Facebook.

API Key

Canvas Page URL

http://apps.facebook.com/

Save

Figure 1.10: Any Liferay application can be published to multiple social networks with a few clicks.

For example, bug fixes to your applications are easy to apply, because Liferay applications are hot deployed to the running server. Liferay's Marketplace gives you a ready-made shopping center for your applications. And Liferay's web services and JSON architecture make it easy for you to share data from your applications with other systems running on different platforms.

You get all this—not to mention the automatic Facebook and OpenSocial integration mentioned above—with Liferay's development platform. It's a very powerful platform, and certainly worth your investigation.

A great integration platform

If you're building an enterprise system, portals were designed in the first place to be a single point of entry to your users' applications and content. Since Liferay Portal integrates well with user directories such as LDAP and Active Directory, and single sign-on systems such as SAML and OpenSSO, it fits well into your enterprise systems. This allows you to use it as an integration platform for existing applications.

Liferay Portal, since it adheres to the JSR standard for portlets, was designed from the ground up for application integration. You can add any application installed on the system to any page in the portal. You can make use of APIs provided by other systems to integrate their data into an application window in Liferay. And applications you create with Liferay's Service Builder API are web service-enabled from the start.

Hosting multiple sites on Liferay Portal

Liferay Portal excels as a multi-site hosting platform. You can use it to host multiple sites under the same overall architecture, or you could host several completely different websites based solely on Liferay's ability to serve multiple instances of itself from the same physical installation.

In the first scenario, Liferay Portal's Sites architecture lets you create multiple, different websites that have public and/or private sets of pages and as many pages within those sets as you'd like. Users can join and leave open sites with one click. Some sites can be defined as restricted or private, and users can't access those unless they're added by site administrators. All of these sites can have canonical domain names such as baseballcards.liferay.com or progrock.liferay.com.

Using this construct, you can build anything from Facebook, to Yahoo Groups, to Source-Forge, to the now-defunct-but-once-loved Geocities. There is no limit to the number of sites you can have: some Liferay installations have only one or two, but others have many thousands. For those larger installations, Liferay Portal contains a complete site membership management framework that lets administrators manage automatic site members for groups of users. It really is built to scale to the size you need.

In the second scenario, Liferay Portal lets you create completely separate instances of itself from the same installation. Users, groups, organizations, sites, and roles from each instance are kept completely separate. If a user registers for a user id on one instance, he or she would have to register as a new user on another instance as well.

This lets you host many different, separate websites from one Liferay Portal installation. Users of each instance have access to the same powerful content management, collaboration, social, and web development platform that they'd have if they were operating from a single, standalone installation.

Okay, so maybe this still isn't enough for you. Let's see how you can customize Liferay Portal so that it looks and operates exactly the way you've envisioned for your site.

1.5   Extending and customizing Liferay for your own needs

Beyond using Liferay as a development platform for new applications, Liferay Portal has also been designed to be extended and modified. As an open source project, its source code is available, but Liferay Portal's developers have designed the product to make it easy to build whatever you want out of it.

The first (and easiest) way of customizing parts of Liferay Portal is with Application Display templates. These let you change the way built-in applications look. For example, if you don't like the Documents and Media Library's file manager view with large icons, you can create an Application Display template that shows documents in a list view. If you don't like the layout of the Blogs portlet, you can change it so that it has the look you want.

Liferay Portal goes far beyond this, though. Special software components called *hook* and *ext* plugins enable developers to change any aspect of Liferay's interface and behavior—without having to modify any of Liferay Portal's source code. This provides you all the benefits of building your site from scratch, but without all the effort to actually build from scratch. If you want to make a change to the user registration screens, add support for a proprietary single sign-on mechanism that you've written, add a feature to the message boards application, or anything else, you can make those customizations. And if you're a developer, we're sure you know that it's a whole lot easier to customize something that almost does things exactly the way you want than it is to write that feature from scratch. With Liferay Portal, you *can* have your cake and eat it too.

1.6 Summary

So what is Liferay? As you can see, it's hard to describe, because it does so much. What we've essentially done is say it's a totally awesome content and document managing, user collaborating, socially enabling, application developing, corporate integrating, completely customizable platform for building the Internet. If we'd said that up front, you'd probably have doubted us. Hopefully now, you can see that it's true.

If you're interested in using Liferay Portal for *your* product, continue reading. We'll go through all of these features (and more that we couldn't mention) throughout the rest of the book.

## CHAPTER 2

WEB CONTENT MANAGEMENT

Liferay's Web Content Management system allows non-technical users to publish content to the web without having advanced knowledge of web technology or programming of any sort. Liferay WCM empowers you to publish your content with a simple point and click interface and it helps you to keep your site fresh. You'll find yourself easily creating, editing and publishing content within just a few minutes of being exposed to its features. But Liferay WCM doesn't sacrifice power for simplicity. If need be, you can use your developer skills to create complex presentation layer templates that make your content "pop" with dynamic elements. Once these templates have been deployed into the portal, your non-technical users can manage content using these templates as easily as they would manage static content. All of this makes Liferay WCM an appropriate choice both for sites with only a few pages and for sites with gigabytes of content.

Nearly all Liferay users use Liferay's Web Content Management system (WCM). After all, all every web site has content that needs to be managed. Liferay's WCM empowers you to manage all the content on your site quickly and easily within your browser. Beyond managing existing content, Liferay's WCM lets users easily create and manage everything from simple articles containing text and images to fully functional web sites. Web publishing works alongside Liferay Portal's larger collection of applications, which means you can add shopping cart functionality, visitor polls, web forms, site collaboration tools and more. Everything is done with our collection of easy-to-use tools with familiar rich-text editors and an intuitive interface.

In Liferay, you can create multiple sites within a single portal instance. Each site can have distinct sets of users, content, and application data. Once set up, non-technical users can administer a site. Liferay's fine-grained permissions system ensures that your content and applications can be accessed only by appropriate sets of users. To manage a site, no programming is required. With Liferay's WCM, you have the ability to create, edit, stage, approve, and publish content with easy-to-learn yet powerful tools. Liferay's WCM streamlines the content creation process for end users. It's much faster to use Liferay's WCM than it would be to create all the content for your site in HTML. WCM is integrated with Liferay's services so advanced template developers can use them to query for data stored elsewhere in Liferay. In this chapter, we'll cover the following topics:

- Leveraging Liferay's multi-site capabilities to create and administer sites
- Creating pages and selecting page types and layout templates
- Creating and publishing web content

- Exporting and importing content
- WCM workflow
- Site memberships and permissions
- Page and content permissions

By the time we're done, you should be able to apply all these concepts to your own content. To demonstrate Liferay's Web Content Management features, we'll create and manage content on the portal for the ambitious (and fictitious) *Lunar Resort* project. The Lunar Resort project specializes in facilitating lunar vacations. It provides space shuttle transportation from the Earth to Moon and back, offers the use of a state-of-the-art recreational facility enclosed by a large, transparent habitat dome, and even rents out lunar rovers. Once you're familiar with Liferay WCM, you'll wonder how the Lunar resort's portal could ever manage without it!

2.1   Touring Liferay Portal's User Interface

Liferay Portal's user interface is designed to be simple and intuitive. Across the top is what's known as the *Dockbar*, a series of links that appear based on the permissions of the logged-in user. There are four sections in the Dockbar: *Admin, My Sites, Notifications*, and the *User* section.

The Admin section gives you access to Liferay Portal's Site Administration interface, as well as to the Control Panel. Both of these are explained in more detail later in this book. Site administration in particular can be done directly on the page as well, as will be described.

Figure 2.1: The Dockbar provides convenient access to Liferay Portal's functions.

The My Sites section provides a list of the sites which the logged-in user can access. These appear as a drop down list. Next are Notifications. The Notifications icon shows the unread notifications you have. You are notified upon receiving a private message, an invitation to join a site, a social connection request, or an event reminder. Alerts and announcements created via the Alerts or Announcements applications are accessible via the Notifications icon.

Finally, the user section shows the users name and provides links to the user's profile (his or her publicly-accessible pages), dashboard (his or her private pages), account settings, and a sign out link.

On the left side of the page are three icons: one for add, one for previews, and one to show or hide the edit controls if you have administrative access to the page. All of these are explained later in this chapter.

Anything else you see on the page is provided by the theme that is installed. This includes site navigation and application windows, called *portlets*. Let's jump in and start creating the site we'll use for this book.

2.2   Setting up the Lunar Resort Example Portal

Suppose that you've been assigned the task of building a web site for an innovative new company called Lunar Resort, Inc. You've decided to take advantage of Liferay Portal and its rapid deployment features as well as its ability to get a fully functional, content-rich web site with integrated social features up and running in little time. We can get you started. We'll walk you through the creation of the Lunar Resort's web site, starting by creating and publishing some simple content using Liferay's built-in WYSIWYG editor. In the next chapter, we'll take advantage of Liferay's robust structure editor. Then we'll use templates to display the content and then explore some of the advanced publishing features such as the built-in workflow and Asset Publisher.

First, a little housekeeping. If we're going to be the Lunar Resort, our portal should also be called *Lunar Resort*. To set general information about your portal like the name and mail domain, go to the Control Panel and select *Portal Settings* under the Configuration heading. You could set up the configuration for the Lunar Resort as follows.

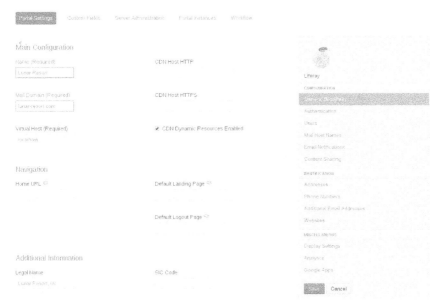

Figure 2.2: You can change the portal settings by navigating to the Control Panel and selecting *Portal Settings*.

You can also customize the logo in the top left corner of every page by selecting *Display Settings* under the *Miscellaneous* tab on the panel to the right. Once you've made the changes, we can begin creating pages. With most products, you would learn what the software can do in terms of setting up your users and security model and then start building your system. You'd design your infrastructure and get your server environment up and running while your developers write the applications that live on your web site. With Liferay Portal, however, you start farther ahead. Liferay Portal is more than just a *container* for applications with a robust security model. It already includes many of the applications you'll need, out of the box. These applications are ready to go and are integrated with the rest of Liferay's user management and security features.

2.3 Leveraging Liferay's Multi-site Capabilities

As stated in chapter 1, a site is a set of pages that can be used to publish content or applications. Sites can be independent or they can be associated with an organization and serve as the website for that organization. With Liferay, you can create as many different sites as you like within the context of a single portal.

You can use sites in Liferay to build many different kinds of websites. Whether you're building a large corporate website, a company intranet, or a small site designed to facilitate collaboration among team members, Liferay's framework provides all the tools you need. To support different kinds of collaboration and social scenarios, Liferay's sites provide three membership types:

- Open: Users can become members of the site at any time. Users can join sites from the *My Sites* portlet.

- Restricted: Users can request site membership but site administrators must approve requests in order for users to become members. Requests can be made from the *My Sites* portlet.

- Private: Users are not allowed to join the site or request site membership. Private sites don't appear in the *My Sites* portlet. Site administrators can still manually select users and assign them as site members.

In addition to these memberships, when a site is associated with an organization, all the users of that organization are automatically considered members of the site.

Members of a site can be given additional privileges within the site by using Liferay's permission settings. It is also possible to assign different roles within the site to different members. This can be done through *site roles* which are defined equally for all sites or *teams* which are unique for each site.

As of Liferay 6.2, sites can be organized hierarchically, just like organizations. The difference between sites and organizations, of course, is that sites are used to organize pages, content, application data, and users (via site memberships) whereas organizations are only used to group users. Content sharing is available for sites within the same hierarchy. For instance, if a parent site has a document called *Lunar Goals and Objectives* and would like for all its subsites to have a copy, the parent site's administrator can enable content sharing to automatically share the document with its subsites, instead of having to send each site the document individually. Also, content sharing privileges can be set to let every site administrator share content across sites they manage.

Please refer to the Sites Admin Portlet section of Liferay's `portal.properties` file for a list of relevant configurable properties. For example, the `sites.content.sharing.with.children.enabled` property allows you to disable content sharing between sites and subsites, disable it by default while allowing site administrators to enable it per site, or to enable it by default while allowing administrators to disable it per site.

The Sites Directory portlet is a configurable portlet that can allow users to view a hierarchy of sites and subsites. It enables users to navigate to any of the displayed sites. To use this portlet to display site hierarchies, add it to a page, open its Configuration window, and under Display Style, select *List Hierarchy*. The Site Map portlet is another configurable portlet that's intended to help users navigate among pages within a site. When configuring this portlet, a site administrator can select a root page and a display depth. Just as sites can be organized hierarchically, so can the pages within a site. The display depth of the Site Map portlet determines how many levels of nested pages to display.

Liferay's sites have two categories of pages called page sets. There are two kinds of page sets: public pages and private pages. A site can have only public pages, only private pages or both. Private pages can only be accessed by site members. Public pages can be accessed by anyone, including users who haven't logged in. It's possible to restrict access to pages at the page set level or at the level of individual pages through the permission system. Public pages and private pages have different URLs and can have different content, applications, themes, and layouts.

Building a corporate intranet is a typical use case for Liferay sites. A corporate intranet could have sites for all the organizations in the company: Sales, Marketing, Information Technology, Human Resources and so on. But what about the corporate health and fitness

Figure 2.3: The Site Directory portlet can allow users to navigate between sites organized hierarchically. The Site Map portlet can allow users to navigate among pages of site organized hierarchically.

center? That's something everybody in the company, regardless of organization, may want to join. This makes it a good candidate for an open and independent site. Similarly, the home page for a corporate intranet should probably be placed in an open independent site so any member of the portal can access it.

> **Tip:** Prior to Liferay 6.1, there were two ways of creating sites: organizations and communities. This has been simplified to provide more ease of use and allow for more flexibility. The main role of organizations is still to organize the users of the portal in a hierarchy but they can also have associated sites. Communities can still be created through independent sites but the new name reflects the fact that sites can be used for many different purposes besides communities.

For other kinds of web sites, you may want to use independent sites to bring users together who share a common interest. If you were building a photo sharing web site, you might have independent sites based on the types of photos people want to share. For example, those who enjoy taking pictures of landscapes could join a Landscapes site and those who enjoy taking pictures of sunsets could join a Sunsets site.

Liferay always provides one default site, which is also known as the main site of the portal. This site does not have its own name but rather takes the name of the portal. By default the portal name is *liferay.com* but this value can be changed through the simple configuration of the setup wizard. The portal name can also be changed at any time through the Control Panel within *Portal Settings*.

Creating and Managing Sites

Sites can be created through the Control Panel by a portal administrator. Liferay's Control Panel provides an administrative interface for managing your portal. There are four main sections of the Liferay's Control Panel: Users, Sites, Apps, and Configuration. In this chapter, we'll learn how to use the Control Panel to manage sites. In the next chapter, we'll learn about using the Control Panel to manage site templates and page templates. For information about the Apps, Users, and Configuration sections of the Control Panel, please see chapters 14, 16, and 17 of this guide.

Tip: Prior to Liferay 6.2, the Control Panel included interfaces both for site administration and for portal administration. In Liferay 6.2, these interfaces have been separated. If you're signed in as an administrator, you can access the Liferay 6.2 Control Panel by clicking *Admin →Control Panel*. To manage a single site, navigate to the site by clicking on *My Sites* and clicking on the site's name. Then click on *Admin →Site Administration*. The Site Administration interface allows to configure site settings and manage the pages, content, and users of the site.

To add a site, click on *Sites* under the Sites section of the Control Panel and then click *Add*. If there is at least one site template available, a dropdown menu appears. Site templates provide a preconfigured set of pages, portlet applications, and content that can be used as the basis of a site's public or private page set. To create a site from scratch, select *Blank Site*. Otherwise, select the name of the site template you'd like to use. If you opt to create a site from a site template, you have to choose whether to copy the site template's pages as your new site's public or private page set. If other site templates are created, they will appear in the Add menu as they become available. The following figure shows the form that needs to be filled when creating a *Blank Site*.

Name: is the name of the site you wish to create.

Description: describes the site's intended function.

Active: determines whether a site is active or inactive. Inactive sites are inaccessible but can be activated whenever a site administrator wishes.

Membership Type: can be open, restricted or private. An open site appears in the My Sites portlet and users can join and leave the site whenever they want. A restricted site is the same except users must request membership. A site administrator must then explicitly grant or deny users' requests to join. A private site does not appear in the My Sites portlet and users must be added to it manually by a site administrator.

Allow Manual Membership Management: determines whether to allow or disallow users to be manually added or removed from the site. By default, manual site membership management is enabled. This allows administrators to manually assign users to the site. It also allows users to join open sites or request membership from restricted sites using the My Sites portlet. For organization sites, manual site membership management is disabled, by default. This causes organization members to be automatically assigned membership following the organization's membership policy. Also, because manual membership management is disabled for organization sites, by default, the *Users* section of *Site Administration* is unavailable. To activate the *Users* functionality for your organization site, you'll need to check *Allow Manual Membership Management* after creating the organization site by navigating to its *Site Settings* menu.

It's possible for site memberships to be handled automatically by a membership policy. The membership policy can check various pieces of information from each user, such as their first names, last names, birthdays, job titles, organizations, and user groups. Using this information, the site membership policy can automatically assign members to the site. If your site will implement a membership policy, your site administrators can disallow manual membership management for their site. When the Allow Manual Membership Management option is disabled, the *Users* section of *Site Administration* (Site Memberships and Site Teams) is hidden, even from administrators.

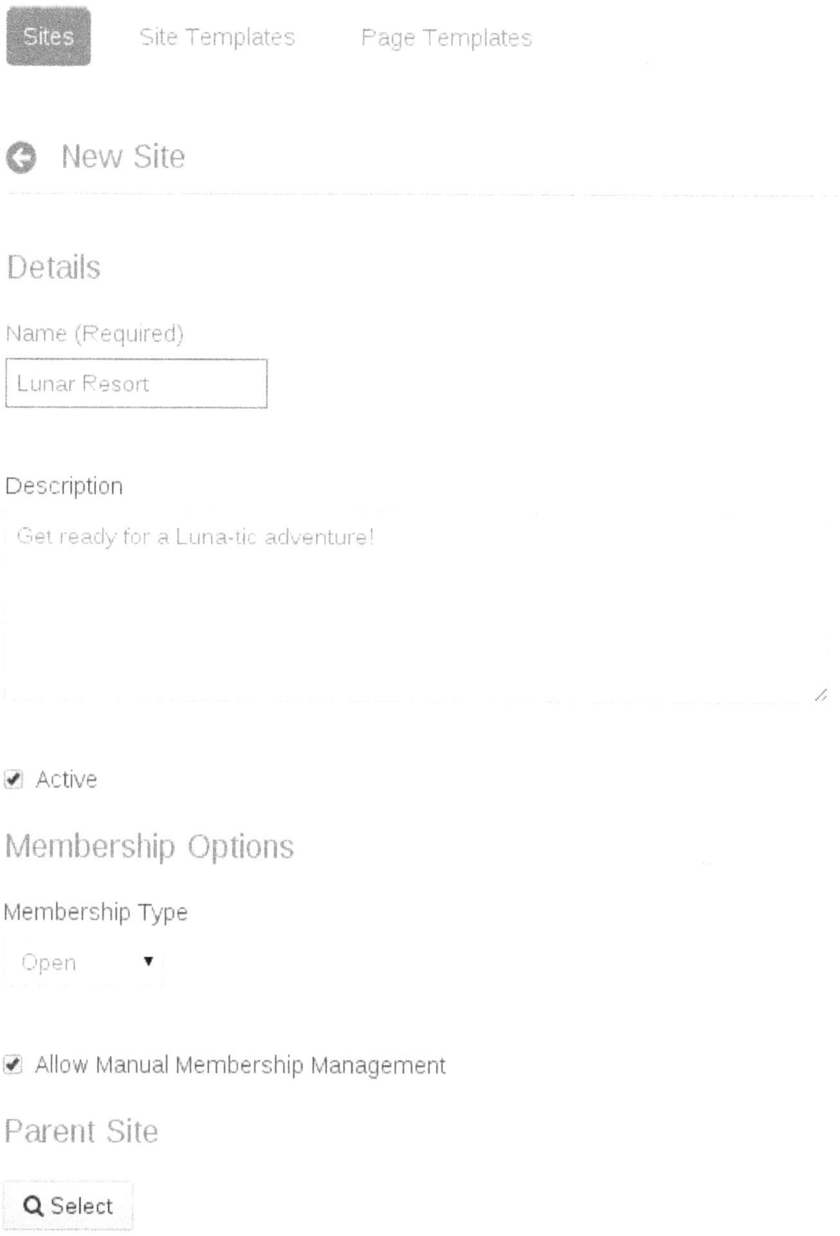

Sites   Site Templates   Page Templates

← New Site

Details

Name (Required)

Lunar Resort

Description

Get ready for a Luna-tic adventure!

☑ Active

Membership Options

Membership Type

Open ▼

☑ Allow Manual Membership Management

Parent Site

Q Select

Figure 2.4: The New Site window aids in your new site development.

Directory Indexing Enabled: allows site administrators to browse the site's documents and media files and folders. For example, a site administrator of a site called *Lunar Resort* can browse documents at http://localhost:8080/documents/lunar-resort if this option is enabled.

Parent Site: lets you select a parent site for the site that's being created. As of Liferay 6.2, sites can be organized hierarchically. Using hierarchical sites provides a simplified way to manage site memberships and site content sharing. For organizations that have attached sites, the organization hierarchy should match the site hierarchy. When you select a parent site, an additional option appears: *Limit membership to members of the parent site*. If this option is enabled, the site's membership policy performs a check so that you can only assign members to the current site if they're already members of the parent site.

Once you've created a site, it appears in the Sites page of the Control Panel. Once the site has been created you can specify more details about the site using three categories: Basic Information, Search Engine Optimization, Advanced, and Miscellaneous. We'll go into more detail for your site's settings in the *Site Settings* section later in the chapter.

When creating a site from a site template, the initial form provides a new option that lets you decide if you want to copy the pages from the template as public pages or as private pages. By default, the site is linked to the site template and changes to the site template propagate to any site based on it. A checkbox appears that allows users to unlink the site template if the user has permission to do so.

Now that our new site is created, lets learn how to create and manage its pages.

Creating and Managing Pages

You have a few options for accessing and configuring your site's page editing interface. There are three interfaces to be aware of: *Site Pages*, *Page*, and *Edit Page*. These interfaces all deal with your site's pages, however, each interface is configurable in a different place and completes different objectives.

From the Site Administration page, your site pages can be accessed and configured. If you're already on your desired site, you can reach the Site Administration page by navigating to the *Admin* tab in the Dockbar and selecting *Site Administration*. If you're not currently on the site you'd like to edit, go to *My Sites* in the Dockbar and select your desired site. Once you're on the Site Administration page, select *Site Pages* (if necessary) under the Pages tab from the left panel. You can also use the *Pages* shortcut which is also listed under the Admin tab.

To add new pages to your site, click the *Add* icon from the left palette and select the *Page* tab. This is the *Page* interface, which offers a plethora of options for your new page including name, site layout, and site template.

To manage the specific page of the site you've navigated to, click the *Edit* icon from the left palette. This will only edit the specific page you're currently on.

Site Pages is an interface to view existing pages, create new pages, view pages and export or import pages using Liferay Archive (LAR) files. Note that you can switch between managing a set of pages and managing a single page using the left-hand side navigation menu. Click on *Public Pages* or *Private Pages* to manage the group or click on an individual page to manage just that one. Switching views like this changes the list of available tabs to the right. By default, liferay.com, which we renamed to lunar-resort.com, contains a single public page called *Welcome*.

Liferay's page groups are always associated with sites. Even users' personal pages are part of their personal sites. All pages belong to one of two types of page sets: public pages and private pages. By default, public pages are accessible to anyone, even non-logged in users (guests). Private pages are accessible only to users who are members of the site which owns the pages. This means the private pages of an organization's site would only be viewable by site members and members of the organization.

Figure 2.5: The *Site Pages* interface allows you to edit your site pages as a whole.

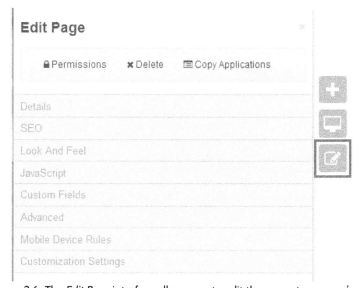

Figure 2.6: The *Edit Page* interface allows you to edit the current page you're on.

Regardless of whether the pages are public or private, Liferay uses the same interface to manage them. Let's look at this interface more closely.

More Page Management Tools

From the Site Pages interface in Site Administration, you can add a page to the site by clicking the *Add Page* button. Because *Public Pages* is selected on the left, clicking *Add Page* here adds a top level page next to the Welcome page. You can, however, nest pages as deeply as you like. To create a sub-page under the Welcome page, select the *Welcome* page first and then create your page. If you later decide you don't like the order of your pages, you can drag and drop them in the list to put them in whatever order you want. Let's go ahead and add another top level page and name it *Community*. We'll use this page for the Recent Bloggers and Wiki portlets.

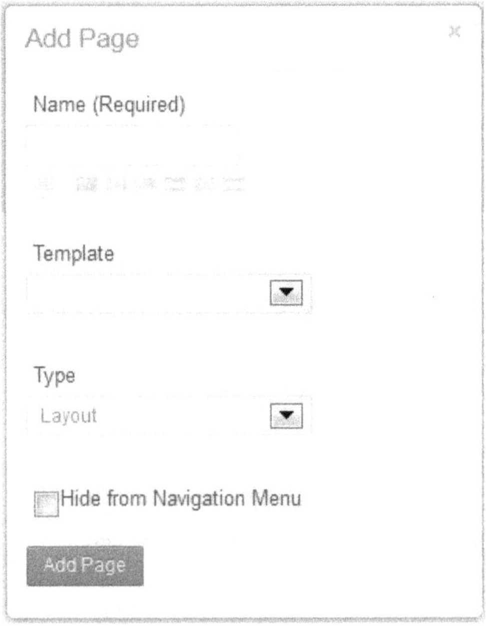

Add Page

Name (Required)

Template

Type

Layout

Hide from Navigation Menu

Add Page

Figure 2.7: You can add a page to your site by giving it a name, page template, and page type.

When you create a new page, you can create either a blank page or a page prepopulated with portlets from a page template. When you're entering the name of the page, you can select from a list of page templates that are currently available. To view the pages once you add them, click the *View Pages* button. This is how you'd populate your pages with content and applications. This is covered in succeeding chapters. Page types include **Layout**, **Panel**, **Embedded**, **Link to URL**, and **Link to a Page of This Site**. By default, all pages are created as portlet pages but in some situations you might want to use one of the other options.

Layout: the pages we're usually talking about. They have a layout which you can drag and drop portlets into. Most of the pages you create will be layout pages.

Panel: can have any number of portlets on them, as selected by an administrator, but only one will be displayed at a time. Users select which portlet they want to use from a menu on the left side of the page and the selected portlet takes up the entire page.

Embedded: display content from another website inside of your portal. An administrator can set a URL from in the page management interface and that page will appear in the context and within the navigation of your Liferay portal.

Link to URL: are just redirects to any URL specified by an administrator. You can use URL pages to create links to pages belonging to other sites of your portal or to pages of an external site. Use URL pages cautiously since blind redirects create a poor user experience.

Link to a Page of This Site: creates a portal page which functions as an immediate redirect to another page within the same site. You can select which page to link to from a dropdown in the page management interface. You could use a *Link to a Page of This Site* to place a deeply nested page in the primary navigation menu of your site, for example.

To use the Edit Page interface to modify an existing page, navigate to the left palette and select the *Edit* icon. Notice that it's not possible to add a new page. This is because you're only managing the current page.

Once you've created pages and populated them with content, Liferay provides a way for you to back them up to separate files. Let's see how that works.

Backing up and Restoring Pages   Next to the *Add Page* button on the Site Pages screen, there are two buttons labeled *Export* and *Import*. The Export button allows you to export the your site's data as a single file, called a LAR (Liferay Archive) file. When importing data into a site, it's best to use a newly created site to avoid potential conflicts between the existing site data and the data about to be imported. When exporting site data, you can specify exactly what data should be included in the LAR:

- Site pages (you can select exactly which ones)
- Page settings
- Theme
- Theme settings
- Logo
- Application configurations
- Application content
- Archived setups
- User preferences

Once you've created a LAR file, you can import it into a site on another Liferay server. The data included in the LAR file, including all the site pages, will be imported into the site. Exporting and importing LARs is a great way to take content from a site in one environment (say, a development or QA environment) and move it all in one shot to a site on another server. You can use LARs to import data onto production servers, but you should not make this a regular occurrence. If you want to regularly move pages from one server to another, you should use Liferay's staging environment, which we discuss in chapter 3.

LARs can be a good way to back up your site's content. You can export them to a specific location on your server which is backed up. If you ever have to restore your site, all you need to do is import the latest LAR file. However, please be careful! If there's any content that exists both in the LAR and in the site that's importing the data, there may be a conflict, and data could be corrupted. If you'd like to restore a Liferay site using a LAR file, it's best to delete the site entirely, create a new site with the same name as the old one (i.e., recreate the site), and then import the LAR file into the new site. This way, there's no chance for there to be a data conflict.

Liferay can handle some kinds of naming collisions when importing a LAR file into a site. For example, suppose you're importing a LAR file into a site and the LAR file has a page with a certain friendly URL. If an existing page in the site has the same friendly URL there will be a collision. Liferay resolves the collision by adding a number to the end of the friendly URL and incrementing until there's no collision. This behavior takes place for friendly URL translations as well. Similarly, if importing a LAR into a site causes a category name collision, Liferay renames the imported categories.

 Note: LAR files are version dependent. You can't import a LAR file that was exported from one version of Liferay into a Liferay server that's running a different version of Liferay. Also, note that periodically exporting LARs is *not* a complete backup solution; please refer to chapter 18 of this guide for information on backing up Liferay.

Let's be good administrators and export a LAR file for backup purposes. Click on the *Export* button and then name the file lunarresortv1.lar. Use the check boxes to determine what you'd like to export. For this initial export, select everything. Note that if you select one of the *Choose* radio selectors or *Change* links, you're given checkboxes for options to choose. The applications' content can also be selected for export, including the Documents and Media Library, Message Boards, and Web Content assets. You can even export the theme you're using!

Once you click *Export*, your browser prompts you to save the file. Once you have the file, you can copy it to a backup location for safekeeping or import it into another installation of Liferay Portal. If you must rebuild or wish to revert back to this version of your site, you can import this file by clicking the *Import* button from the Site Pages dialog box, browsing to it and selecting it.

Next, we'll look at the options on the right side menu, starting with Look and Feel.

Customizing the Look and Feel of Site Pages   When you open *Site Pages* from within Site Administration, it defaults to the Look and Feel tab. On this tab, you're presented with an interface that allows you to choose a theme for the current site. Themes can transform the entire look of the portal. They are created by developers and are easily installed using the Liferay Marketplace. Since we don't have any themes beyond the default one installed yet, we'll use the default theme for our pages.

Many themes include more than one color scheme. This allows you to keep the existing look and feel while giving your site a different flavor. Change the color scheme from blue to green by selecting *Dark* under *Color Schemes*. If you now go back to the site (by clicking the left arrow in the top left corner of the Dockbar), you'll see some parts of the page are now tinged with a darker hue.

If you apply a color scheme to a set of public or private pages, it is, by default, applied to each page in the set. If, however, you click the *Edit Page* button from the left palette of a specific page, you can select *Define a specific look and feel for this page* from the *Look and Feel* tab to make the color scheme apply to this page only. You can use this feature to choose a different color scheme for a particular page than the one defined for the set of public or private pages to which it belongs.

There are a few more configurable settings for your theme. You can switch the bullet style between dots and arrows and you can choose whether or not to show portlet borders by default.

Starting in Liferay 6.2, WAP related technologies have been deprecated. In particular, the ability to modify themes for regular browsers and mobile devices can now only be accomplished using Mobile Device Rules, which can be found in the right menu. You can learn more about using Mobile Device Rules in the *Advanced Content Management* chapter. You can enable the WAP functionality for your portal's Look and Feel section by opening/creating your portal-ext.properties file in your ${LIFERAY_HOME} directory and setting mobile.device.styling.wap.enabled=true. WAP functionality will be completely removed from Liferay in the next release.

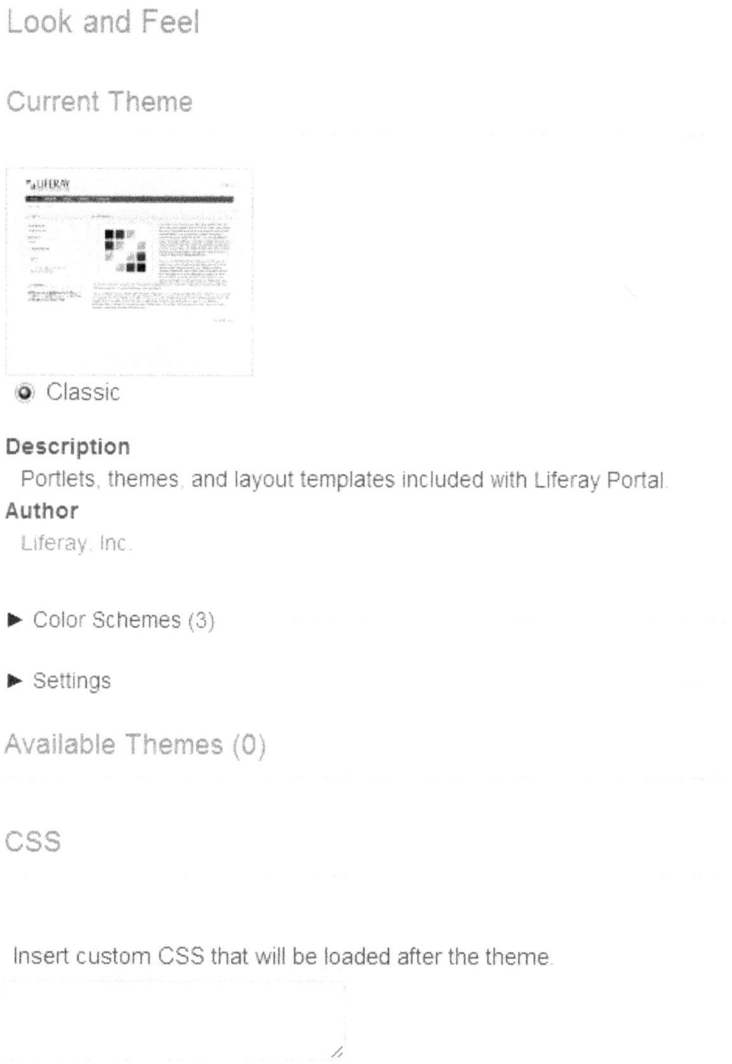

Look and Feel

Current Theme

⊙ Classic

Description
Portlets, themes, and layout templates included with Liferay Portal.
Author
Liferay, Inc.

▶ Color Schemes (3)

▶ Settings

Available Themes (0)

CSS

Insert custom CSS that will be loaded after the theme.

Figure 2.8: The Look and Feel interface allows you to choose a theme for the current site.

The *CSS* section allows you to enter custom CSS that will also be served up by your theme. In this way, you can tweak a theme in real time by adding new styles or overriding existing ones.

The next option configures the logo that appears for your site.

Using a Custom Logo for a Site   By default, the Liferay logo is used for your site pages' logo. If you want to use your own logo for a specific site, use the *Logo* tab. Adding a custom logo is easy: select the Logo tab from the Site Pages interface and browse to the location of your logo. Make sure your logo fits the space in the top left corner of the theme you're using for your web site. If you don't, you could wind up with a site that's difficult to navigate, as other page elements are pushed aside to make way for the logo.

In the logo tab, you can also choose whether or not to display the site name on the site. If you check the box labeled *Show Site Name* the site name will appear next to the logo. This option is enabled by default and cannot be disabled if the *Allow Site Administrators to set their own logo* option is disabled in *Portal Settings*. Removing the site name is not available for the default site—only newly created sites and user pages have the option to have the name display.

JavaScript   If you click on *JavaScript* from the Site Pages interface for a page set (either Public Pages or Private Pages), you'll find a window where you can enter JavaScript code the will be executed at the bottom of every page in the site. If your site's theme uses JavaScript (as is usually the case), it's best to add custom JavaScript code to the theme and *not* in this window. This way, all of your site's JavaScript code remains in one place.

Using the JavaScript window of your site's Site Pages interface may be useful if your site's theme does *not* use JavaScript. In this case, the JavaScript window of your site's Site Pages interface will contain *all* of your site's JavaScript and you can add some dynamic features to your site's pages.

Next, let's look at an advanced feature of the Site Pages interface: merging the current site's pages with the pages of the default site.

Advanced   If you click on *Advanced* from the Site Pages interface for a public page set, you'll find an option to merge the public pages of your portal's default site with the public pages of the current site. If you enable this option, the pages of the default site appear in the current site's navigation bar, along with the current site's pages. Also, the pages of the current site appear in the navigation bar of the default site, along with the default site's pages. This "merging" of pages only affects the list of pages in the default site's and the current site's *navigation bars*. This allows users to more easily navigate from the current site to the default site, and vice versa. This option can be enabled for the public pages of both personal sites and regular sites.

Note that this "merging" of pages is not a "hard merge". For example, suppose that the site administrators of twenty different sites on your portal all enabled the *Merge default site's public pages* option. Would the pages of all these different sites be merged into each site's navigation bar? No, that would make a mess! Instead, the portal keeps track of the current scopeGroupId (the ID of the current site) and the previous scopeGroupId (the ID of previously visited site). If the *Merge default site's public pages* option is enabled for either the current site or the previous site, the pages of the default site are merged in the pages of the other site.

For example, suppose that your portal has three sites: the default site, site A, and site B. All three sites have some public pages. Site A has the *Merge default site's public pages* option enabled, site B does not. When a user first logs in, he's directed to the default site. The scopeGroupId is that of the default site and there is no previous scopeGroupId, so no additional pages appear in the default site's navigation bar. Then suppose the user navigates to site A. Site A has the *Merge default site's public pages* option enabled, so the default site's pages are added to site A's navigation bar. Now if the user goes back to the default site, site A becomes the previous site so site A's pages are added to the default site's navigation bar. If the user navigates to site B, no additional pages appear in site B's navigation bar because site B does not have the *Merge default site's public pages* option enabled. And if the user navigates back to the default site, site B becomes the previous site, and, again, since site B does not have the *Merge default site's public pages* option enabled, no additional pages are added to the default site's navigation menu.

Next, let's examine how to configure individual pages.

Changing Options for Individual Pages

When you use the *Edit Page* interface for a single page, some different options appear. Let's look at what these do.

Details: lets you name the page for any localizations you need, set whether the page is hidden on the navigation menu, set an easy to remember, friendly URL for the page, and select the page type. Plus you can specify how portlets are arranged on a page. Choose from the available installed templates to modify the layout. It's very easy for developers to define custom layouts and add them to the list. This is covered more thoroughly in both the *Liferay Developer Network* and in *Liferay in Action*.

SEO: provides several means of optimizing the data the page provides to an indexer that's crawling the page. You can set the various meta tags for description, keywords and robots. There's also a separate Robots section that lets you tell indexing robots how frequently the page is updated and how it should be prioritized. If the page is localized, you can select a box to make Liferay generate canonical links by language. If you want to set some of these settings for the entire site, you can specify them from the Sitemaps and Robots tabs of the Manage Site Settings dialog box (see below).

 In previous versions of Liferay, it was possible that a single page could be indexed multiple times. In Liferay 6.1, all URLs that direct to the same page will only create one entry in the index. Previously, the simple URL *http://www.lunar-resort.com/web/guest/blog/-/blogs/themoon* and different versions of the URL which provided additional information about the referring page had different entries in the index. As of Liferay 6.1, each asset (web content article, blog entry, etc.) has a unique URL. From the search engine's point of view, this will make your pages rank higher since any references to variations of a specific URL will all be considered references to the same page.]

Look and Feel: lets you set a page-specific theme.

JavaScript: gives you the ability to paste custom JavaScript code to be executed on this page.

Custom Fields: If custom fields have been defined for pages (which can be done from the *Custom Fields* page of the Control Panel), they appear here. These are metadata about the page and can be anything you like, such as author or creation date.

Advanced: contains several optional features. You can set a query string to provide parameters to the page. This can become useful to web content templates, which you'll see in the next chapter. You can set a target for the page so that it either pops up in a particularly named window or appears in a frameset. And you can set an icon for the page that appears in the navigation menu.

Mobile Device Rules: allows you to apply rules for how this page should be rendered for various mobile devices. You can set these up in the *Mobile Device Rules* section of Site Administration.

Embedded Portlets: only appears if you have embedded one or more portlets on the page. To embed a portlet on a page, first look up its portlet name in Liferay's WEB-INF/-

portlet-custom.xml file. Portlet names in portlet-custom.xml are sometimes referred to as portlet IDs. What we usually mean by "portlet names," portlet-custom.xml refers to as "display names". Next, add a web content display content to the page, create a new web content article, switch to source, and paste in the following:

```
<runtime-portlet name="" />
```

Then add the portlet name (ID) inside of the quotation marks, publish the web content article, and select the article in the web content display portlet. Once you've selected the new web content article, the embedded portlet appears on the page.

 Usually, you don't want the web content display portlet that you're using to embed a portlet to be visible. To make the web content display portlet invisible, click on the gear icon of the web content display portlet, select *Look and Feel*, set *Show Borders* to *No*, and click *Save*. Once you've refreshed the page, only the embedded portlet will be visible.

Customization Settings: lets you mark specific sections of the page you want users to be able to customize.

Next, we'll run practice modifying page layouts!

Modifying Page Layouts

Page layouts allow you to arrange your pages so the content appears the way you want it to. Liferay comes with many layouts already defined. Developers can create more and they can be deployed to your portal for your use.

To prepare for the portlets we'll soon be adding, let's change the layout of the Collaboration page. To access layouts, select the *Edit* icon from the left palette and click the *Details* tab (if necessary).

Now, select the 2 *Columns (70/30)* layout and click *Save*. Once saved, you'll return to the page and it'll seem as though nothing has happened. Once we start adding portlets, however, you'll notice the page is now equally divided into two columns. You can stack portlets on top of each other in these columns. There are, of course, more complicated layouts available and you can play around with them to get the layout you want.

Sometimes a particular layout is *almost* what you want but not quite. In this case, use the Nested Portlets portlet to embed a layout inside another layout. This portlet is a container for other portlets. It lets you select from any of the layouts installed in Liferay, just like the layouts for a page. This gives you virtually unlimited options for laying out your pages.

The next option we'll explore is page customizations.

Page Customizations

With page customizations, any user with the appropriate permissions can create personalized versions of any public page. Before users can create personalized versions of pages, customizations must first be enabled by an administrator. Administrators can activate or deactivate customizations for any row or column on any page. When users customize a page, they have the option to use either their version or the default version of a page. Users can't see alternate versions of pages other than their own.

To activate page customizations, click the *Edit Page* button from the left palette and select the *Customization Settings* tab. Then select *Show Customizable Sections* to view and modify sections on your page.

When an administrator activates page customizations for a page, any portlets that are in a *Customizable* row or column can be moved around the page or removed from the page.

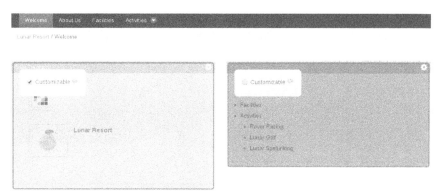

Figure 2.9: During page customization, individual columns change colors to indicate whether they are selected or not.

Users can add new portlets of their own choosing to these columns of the page and can also customize portlet configurations. If at any time users determine they don't like their customizations, they can click *Reset My Customizations* to revert their pages back to the default. For more information about page customizations, please refer to the Page Customizations section of chapter 6.

Now that you know how to enable page customizations, let's look at the settings for the site as a whole.

Configuring Site Settings

As with Site Pages, you can access Site Settings by navigating to Site Administration and clicking *Site Settings* from the Configuration section on the left panel. You can also select the Site Administration sub-tab *Configuration* from the *Admin* drop-down.

You'll find options to specify details and metadata about your site, set up friendly URLs and virtual hosts, configure search engine optimization settings, turn staging on or off and specify a Google Analytics ID. Let's take a closer look.

Details: allows an administrator to change the description and membership type of a site and also to specify tags and categories for the site. The membership type can be set as open, restricted or private based on the privacy needs of the site. Users can join and leave an open site at will. To join a restricted site, a user has to be added by the site administrator. A user can also request to be added through the Sites section of the Control Panel. A private site is like a restricted site but doesn't appear in the Sites section of the Control Panel for users who aren't members.

Categorization: allows you to apply categories and tags to the site.

Site URL: Set a friendly URL and/or a virtual host for your site here. The *Friendly URL* option lets you manage the path to your site in the portal's URL. Friendly URLs are used for both public and private pages. For public pages, the friendly URL is appended to http://localhost:8080/web. For private pages, the friendly URL is appended to http://localhost:8080/group. Each friendly URL needs to be a unique name, of course. Having a human-readable friendly URL assists indexing bots and is critical to good search engine optimization.

For example, suppose you were creating a portal for a bank called the Best Bank. If you set the friendly URL of your portal's default site to /best-bank, the URL of your default site's public home page would change to http://localhost:8080/web/best-bank/home. If your portal's default site had private pages, the URL of the default private home page would change to http://localhost:8080/group/best-bank/home.

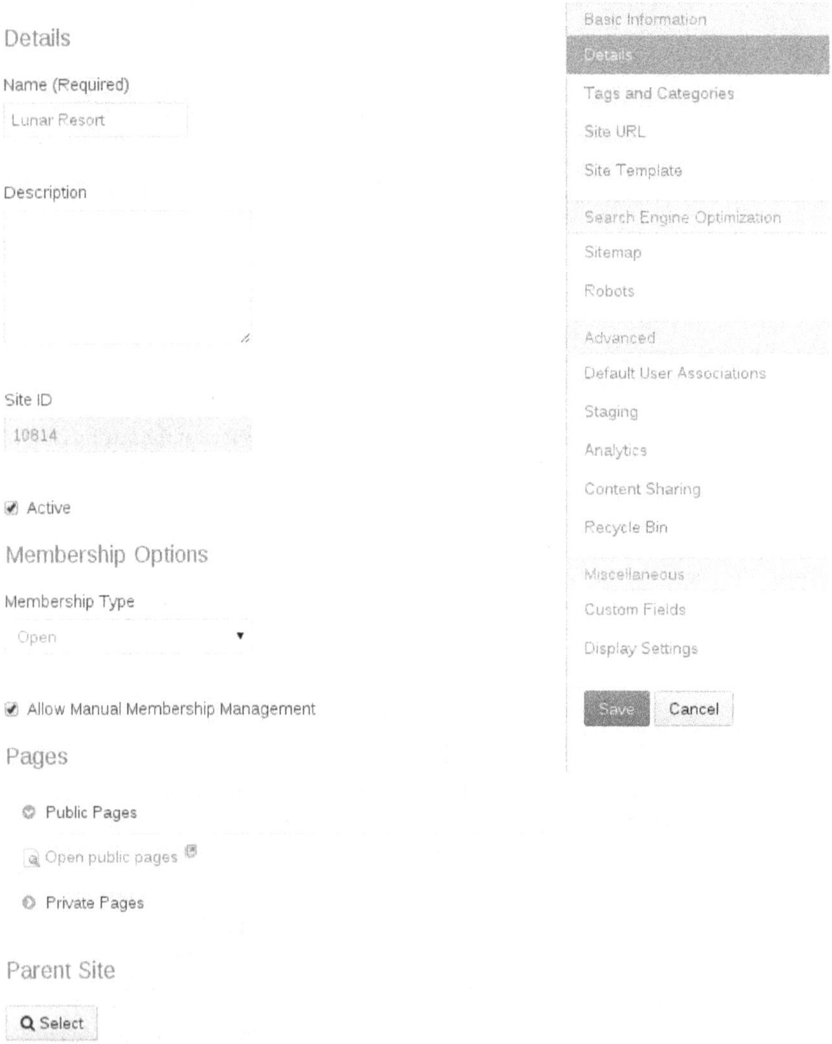

Details

Name (Required)

Lunar Resort

Description

Site ID

10814

☑ Active

Membership Options

Membership Type

Open ▼

☑ Allow Manual Membership Management

Pages

⊘ Public Pages

⊙ Open public pages

⊙ Private Pages

Parent Site

🔍 Select

Basic Information

Details

Tags and Categories

Site URL

Site Template

Search Engine Optimization

Sitemap

Robots

Advanced

Default User Associations

Staging

Analytics

Content Sharing

Recycle Bin

Miscellaneous

Custom Fields

Display Settings

Save Cancel

Figure 2.10: The Site Settings window offers a plethora of options for your site.

Note that if you're adding a friendly URL for your portal's home page, you should update your portal's Home URL field so that page requests to http://localhost:8080 redirect properly. To do this, navigate to the Portal Settings page of the Control Panel and find the Home URL field in the Navigation section. For our bank example, we would enter /web/best-bank/home into the Home URL field. Once you've entered this setting, page requests to localhost:8080 will redirect to the friendly URL of your portal's new homepage: http://localhost:8080/web/best-bank/home.

Virtual Hosts make web navigation much easier for your users by connecting a domain name to a site. This tab allows you to define a domain name (i.e., www.mycompany.com) for your site. This can be a full domain or a subdomain. This enables you to host a number of web sites as separate sites on one Liferay server.

For instance, if we set this up for the Lunar Resort's development network, users in that site could use *developers.lunar-resort.com* to get to their site, provided that the Lunar Resort portal's network administrators created the domain name and pointed it to the Liferay server.

To set this up, the DNS name *developers.lunar-resort.com* should point to your portal's IP address first. Then enter *http://developers.lunar-resort.com* in the Virtual Host tab for the Developers site. This helps users quickly access their site without having to recall an extended URL.

Site Template: If you've created the site from a site template, this section displays information about the link between the site template and the site. Specifically, you can see which site template was used and whether or not it allows modifications to the pages inherited from it by site administrators. If you're not using site templates for this site, you can safely ignore this section.

Sitemap: lets you send a sitemap to some search engines so they can crawl your site. It uses the sitemap protocol, which is an industry standard. You can publish your site to Yahoo or Google and their web crawlers will use the sitemap to index your site. Liferay Portal makes this very simple for administrators by generating the sitemap XML for all public web sites.

By selecting one of the search engine links, the sitemap will be sent to them. It's only necessary to do this once per site. The search engine crawler will periodically crawl the sitemap once you've made the initial request.

If you're interested in seeing what is being sent to the search engines, select the *Preview* link to see the generated XML.

Robots: If you're using virtual hosting for this site, you can configure robots.txt rules for the domain. The Robots page gives you the option to configure your robots.txt for both public and private pages on a site. If you don't have Virtual Hosting set up, this tab is rather boring.

Default User Associations: lets you configure site roles and teams that newly assigned site members will have by default. If you'd like to learn more about creating roles and/or teams, visit the *Advanced Web Content Management* chapter.

Staging: enables you to edit and revise a page behind the scenes, then publish changes to your site once they have been completed and reviewed. For a full explanation of Staging, see chapter 3: *Advanced Web Content Management*.

Analytics: allows you to integrate your pages with Google Analytics. Liferay provides seamless integration with Google Analytics, allowing you to place your ID in one place, then it will get inserted on every page. This enables you to focus your efforts on building the page, rather than remembering to put the code everywhere. Google Analytics is a free service which lets you do all kinds of traffic analysis on your site so you can see who visits, where visitors are from and what pages they most often visit. This helps you tweak your site so you can provide the most relevant content to your users.

Content Sharing: lets you configure whether sub-sites can display content from this site. Even if you initially allowed content sharing between the parent site and its sub-sites, you're able to deselect this option and immediately revoke content sharing from all subsites.

Recycle Bin: provides the option to enable/disable the Recycle Bin for your site. You can also regulate the age (in days) for which content is able to be stored in the Recycle Bin until it is permanently deleted. For a full explanation of the Recycle Bin, see the *Configuring Liferay Applications* chapter.

Custom Fields: lets you edit the custom fields you already have configured for the *Site* resource. If you don't have any custom fields configured for the Site resource, you can navigate to the Control Panel →*Custom Fields* located under the *Configuration* tab.

Display Settings: lets you configure the language options for your site. You have options to use the default language options or define a new default language.

Pages: From Site Settings, click on *Public Pages* or *Private Pages* to manage some basic features of the pages on a site. If no pages have been defined yet, you can set site templates for the public or private pages. If pages already exist, links are provided to view them. You can also change the site's application adapter, which is a special type of hook plugin that customizes out of the box functionality for specific sites.

Site Hierarchy: New to Liferay 6.2 is the ability to organize sites into hierarchies. At the bottom of the Site Settings page is the *Parent Site* section. This feature allows you to select the parent site for the site you're currently on. After selecting a parent site, you have a checkbox option to limit membership to members of the parent site. For more information on site hierarchies, navigate to the *Leveraging Liferay's Multi-site Capabilities* section.

Now that you know how to configure sites, let's look at page templates and site templates.

Page Templates and Site Templates

Page Templates and *Site Templates* are invaluable tools for building similar pages on larger portals. As you continue to add pages to sites in your portal, you'll notice repeatable patterns in the designs of those pages. Page templates enable you to preconfigure a single page and then apply it to any new page you create. Site templates allow you to do the same thing but on the scale of a site—if you have multiple sites that use a similar structure of pages, you can create a single site template and use it to create as many sites as desired. For more information on page templates and site templates, see the *Advanced Web Content Management* chapter.

Site Content

Liferay 6.2 separates Web Content management from the Control Panel by placing it on the *Admin* →*Site Administration* page. From Site Administration, you'll notice the Content heading where all your portal's content can be managed, including web content.

For details about Liferay's social collaboration suite, see chapter 10.

> **Note:** The *Web Content List* and *Recent Content* plugins were deprecated in Liferay 6.2 and are disabled by default. To activate a disabled plugin, navigate to the Control Panel *Plugins Configuration* and scroll through the list of portlets until you find the plugin. Select the plugins name and click the *Active* checkbox. Then click *Save*. Both plugins will be removed in Liferay 7.0.
>
> The Web Content List portlet will be migrated to the Asset Publisher for 7.0, and configured to only display web content with the category matching the type.

Next, let's learn more details about creating pages.

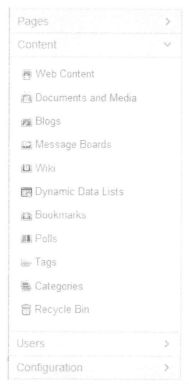

Figure 2.11: Your site's content resides on the Site Administration page.

Creating Pages

There are a lot of other things you can do beyond placing portlets on a page. So let's start working on the Lunar Resort site. You can do this by going up to the Dockbar and clicking *My Sites →Lunar Resort*.

We'll use the *Community* page you created earlier in the chapter. Navigate to the *Community* page and select the *Add* button from the left palette and then the *Page* tab.

This screen's options should look familiar to you from previous sections, but let's briefly go through how to create a new page:

The Page interface allows you to:

- Give the name of the page
- Hide the page from the theme navigation
- Choose the page template
- Link to another website
- Link to another page in the current site
- Copy an existing page

When you select *Add Page* at the bottom of the menu, your new page will appear on the navigation menu of your site. You can drag the page names to their correct order as you see fit.

You can also create new pages from the Site Pages interface. Navigate to Site Administration →*Site Pages*. If you navigate to *Public Pages* or *Private Pages* on your site hierarchy, you'll notice the *Add Page* button, which we discussed earlier in the chapter. If you navigate to a specific site, you'll notice the *Add Child Page* button.

The *Add Child Page* lets you create child pages underneath the page you've selected. You can nest pages as deep as you like but for every page below the top level hierarchy you must provide navigation to it via a Navigation or Breadcrumb portlet, at least with most themes (including the default). Developers can create themes which have cascading menu bars which show the full hierarchy. Some examples of that are in Liferay's plugin repositories.

For now, click the back arrow. You should be able to define and manage pages in Liferay at this point so let's look at what you'd put on a page.

Adding Portlets to a Page

As we discussed earlier, Liferay Portal pages are composed of portlets. All of your site's functionality, from blogs to shopping, is composed of portlets. Even static web content can be displayed through Web Content Display portlets. To add a portlet to a page, just click the *Add* button from the left palette and select the *Applications* tab. You can either browse through the categories of available portlets until you find the one you're looking for or you can search for portlets by name. Once you've found a portlet, click the *Add* button to add it the current page. Once it's been added to the page, you can drag it to a new position. Alternatively, you can drag the portlet directly from the Applications menu to a specific location on the page. Let's add some portlets to the Collaboration page of the Lunar Resort site.

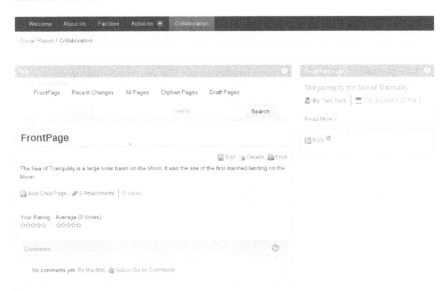

Figure 2.12: Yeah, we're showoffs. But as you can see, your page layout options are virtually limitless.

1. From the left palette, select *Add →Applications*.
2. In the menu that appears, expand the *Collaboration* category.
3. Drag the *Blogs Aggregator* portlet off the Add Application window onto the right column of our page.

4. Next, drag the *Wiki* portlet to the *left column*.

See how easy it is to add applications to your pages? We've added the Wiki portlet and Blogs Aggregator portlet to the Community page.

It's easy to make your pages look exactly the way you want them to. If the default layout options provided aren't enough, you can even develop your own. To find more information about developing custom layout templates, please refer to the Liferay Developer Network.[1]

Page Permissions

By default, public pages are just that: public. They can be viewed by anybody, logged in or not logged in. And private pages are really only private from non-members of the site. If someone has joined your site or is a member of your organization, that person can see all the private pages. You can, however, modify the permissions on individual pages in either page group so only certain users can view them.

Let's say we wanted to create a page only for administrators to see. We can do this with the following procedure:

1. Go to the Dockbar and select *Admin* → *Site Administration*.
2. Click the *Site Pages* link (if necessary).
3. Click the *Private Pages* tab to switch to the Private Pages. Remember, these pages by default are viewable only by members of the site.
4. Create a page called *Admin Tips*.
5. Click on the page in the tree on the left and then click *Permissions*.
6. Uncheck the *View* and *Add Discussion* permissions next to the Site Member role.
7. Click the *Save* button.

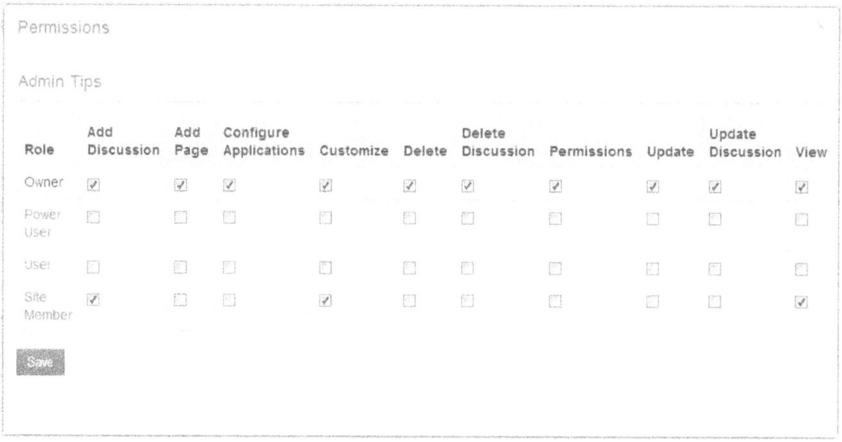

Role	Add Discussion	Add Page	Configure Applications	Customize	Delete	Delete Discussion	Permissions	Update	Update Discussion	View
Owner	✔	✔	✔	✔	✔	✔	✔	✔	✔	✔
Power User	☐	☐	☐	☐	☐	☐	☐	☐	☐	☐
User	☐	☐	☐	☐	☐	☐	☐	☐	☐	☐
Site Member	✔	☐	☐	✔	☐	☐	☐	☐	☐	✔

Figure 2.13: The Permissions offer a plethora of options for each role.

Congratulations! You've just changed the permissions for this page so only site administrators can view it. Any users you add to this role can now see the page. Other users, even members of this site, won't have permission to see it.

Pages in Liferay are as flexible as pages you'd create manually without a portal. Using a point and click interface, you can define your site any way you want. You can create and

---

[1] https://dev.liferay.com

remove pages, export and import them, set their layouts, define how they are indexed by search engines and more. You've also been introduced to Liferay's concept of sites. Again, using a point and click interface, you can create multiple web sites and define how users can access them, whether they are linked to a domain name and create all of their pages.

You now understand how to manage pages in Liferay Portal. It's time to move on to adding content to those pages. Liferay's Web Content Management (WCM) is a highly powerful, yet flexible, set of tools that enables you to successfully manage your web site.

You'll soon discover that Liferay's WCM is easy to learn and highly configurable. If you already have experience with WCM, you'll see some new features and improvements to old ones. If you're new to Liferay's WCM, then you'll be surprised at how fast you will be adding, editing and scheduling content on your site. Once you're familiar with portlets such as Web Content Display and Asset Publisher, your ability to manage an immense site with a large amount of content will simply amaze you.

We'll be using Liferay's WCM to publish simple pieces of content, develop templates to define how content is to be displayed, set up a workflow for content to be approved, schedule when content is to be published and much, much more.

2.4   Features of Liferay's WCM

Liferay's WCM offers a host of features that makes managing the content of your site easier:

- **WYSIWYG Editor:** A complete HTML editor that allow you to modify fonts, add color, insert images and much more.

- **Structure Editor:** Easily add and remove fields you want available to content creators and then dynamically move them around. This editor includes an entire suite of form controls you can drag and drop onto your structure.

- **Template Editor:** Import template script files that inform the system how to display the content within the fields determined by the structure.

- **Web Content Display:** A portlet that allows you place web content on a page in your portal.

- **Asset Publisher:** A portlet which can aggregate different types of content together in one view.

- **Scheduler:** Lets you schedule when content is reviewed, displayed and removed.

- **Workflow Integration:** Run your content through an approval or review process.

- **Staging:** Use a separate staging server or stage your content locally so you can keep your changes separate from the live site.

Liferay's Web Content Management is a powerful and robust tool for creating and organizing content on your web site. Let's begin by examining some basic concepts involving sites and pages.

As you'll see, Liferay's WCM is a full-featured solution for managing your web site. We'll start with an overview of what it has to offer and then we'll dive down into its features. Note that web content is just one kind of asset on Liferay. Other types of content (blog posts, wiki articles, message board posts, etc.) are also considered assets. Liferay provides a general framework for handling assets that includes tags, categories, comments, ratings, and more. Please see chapter 5 for more information on Liferay's asset framework.

Creating (Basic) Content

As we've already discussed, content is the reason web sites exist. Liferay Portal has made it easier than ever to get content published to your site. Because Liferay Portal is so flexible, you can use basic authoring tools right away or take advantage of the more advanced features. It's adaptable to your needs.

We'll begin by creating some simple content using Liferay's WYSIWYG editor. Then we'll publish it to the home page of the Lunar Resort's web site. This is a fast and straightforward process that demonstrates how easy it is to create and publish content on your Liferay Portal instance. Let's learn about the Web Content section in Site Administration so we can create and publish our first pieces of content.

When you manage web content from the Site Administration page, you can select the location where the content resides. For instance, you can add content that's available to a specific site or globally across the portal. If you're on the site you wish to add content to, simply navigate to the *Admin* tab on the Dockbar and select *Site Administration*. Conversely, if you need to switch sites or would like to add content globally, navigate to the Control Panel and select *Sites*. From this window, you can change the scope of where you'd like to view, edit, or create content.

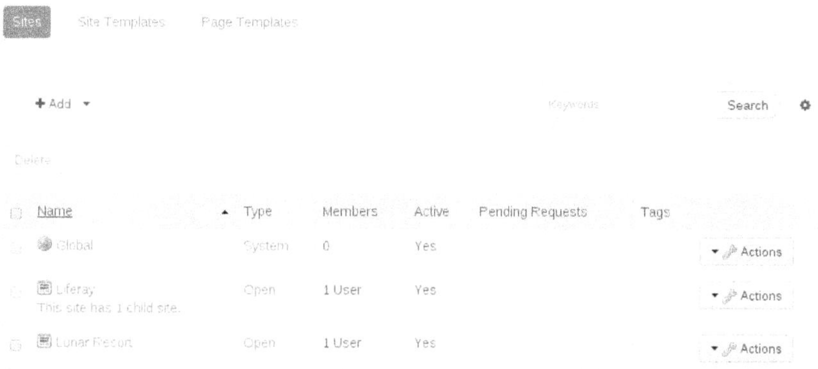

Figure 2.14: You can choose where to create content by navigating to the Control Panel and selecting *Sites*.

Once you have the Lunar Resort site selected, click on the *Web Content* link in Site Administration. You'll see a folder structure containing all of the web content articles that exist in the currently selected scope (the Lunar Resort site). You can click *Add Folder* to create a new folder. For sites with lots of content and web content articles, it can be very useful to use folders to group certain kinds of web content articles together. Click *Add Basic Web Content* to create a new web content article.

Existing web content structures also appear in the *Add* menu. This provides users with shortcuts for creating specific kinds of web content articles. For example, if a web content structure called *FAQ* has been created for Frequently Asked Questions articles in your currently selected scope, you can create a new FAQ article by clicking *Add →FAQ*.

Click *Manage →Structures* to view a list of web content structures that have already been created in your chosen scope. You can add new web content structures here. Web Content templates are always associated with a particular web content structure, so you can click *Actions →Manage Templates* to view the web content templates associated with a structure or add a new template to a structure. In the next chapter, we'll cover advanced features such as structures, templates, and content scheduling in detail.

Figure 2.15: Click *Add* →*Basic Web Content* to create a new simple web content article. To create a new web content article based on an existing web content structure, click *Add* and then click on the name of the structure you'd like to use.

Rich, WYSIWYG Editing

Once you've clicked *Add* →*Basic Web Content*, you'll find a highly customizable form that by default has two fields: a title and a powerful WYSIWYG editor. We could customize this form to contain whatever fields our content needs but we'll keep things simple for now. If web content structures have already been created in your currently selected scope, you can select one for your new web content article by clicking *Select* next to the *Structure* heading. We discuss web content structures and templates in detail in the next chapter.

Type the words *Welcome to the Lunar Resort* in the *Name* field. Notice that content can be localized in whatever language you want. If you click on the *localize* checkbox, two select boxes appear which allow you to pick the language you're working in and the default language. You can enter translations of your content for any language in the list. The figure below shows this interface but for now, we won't be using it, so you can leave it unchecked. In the content field, add a short sentence announcing the web site is up and running.

Getting a new web site up and running is an exciting step for anyone, whether it is a large corporation or a small non-profit charity. To celebrate this momentous achievement at the Lunar Resort, let's give our announcement some of the pomp and circumstance we think it deserves!

Using the editor, select all the text and then change the style to *Heading 1* and the color to *Navy*. You could insert an image here or even more text with a different style, as demonstrated in the screenshot below. You can also add bullets, numbering, links to another site or custom images. You can even add an emoticon. Go ahead and add a smiley face to the end of your announcement.

The WYSIWYG editor is a flexible tool that gives you the ability to add text, images, tables, links and more. Additionally, you can modify the display to match the purpose of the content. Plus it's integrated with the rest of Liferay Portal: for example, when you upload an image to be added to a page, that image can be viewed and manipulated in the Documents and Media portlet.

If you're HTML savvy, Liferay WCM doesn't leave you out in the cold. You can switch from the WYSIWYG view by clicking the *Source* button. From the Source view, you can view the HTML content of your web content. If you wish, can edit the HTML directly.

You can integrate Liferay with external services to enable additional functionality. For example, if you navigate to the Control Panel, click on *Server Administration* and then on *External Services*, you can install and enable Xuggler. Enabling Xuggler allows you to embed audio and video files in web content. Installing and enabling Xuggler is easy; you can do it right from the Control Panel. Please refer to chapter 17 of this guide for more details.

Figure 2.16: View your content changes directly in the editor.

Once Xuggler has been installed and enabled, embedding audio or video files in a web content is easy. From the Dockbar, navigate to *Site Content →Web Content* and click *Add →Basic Web Content*. Look for the buttons on the CKEditor toolbar with audio and video icons. Click on either the audio or video button and then click *Browse Server* to browse to the audio or video file's location on your portal's documents and media repository. When you find the appropriate file, click *Choose*. If you haven't already uploaded the audio or video file to the portal, you can do so by clicking on the *Upload* button. Select the file and then check that the audio or video component appears in the web content. Excellent! When your web content is published, users can view or listen the embedded multimedia!

The right side of the New Web Content form provides options for customizing your web content.

Abstract: lets you to create a brief summary of the web content. You can also pair the text with a small image.

Categorization: specifies the content type from a list of options. They are *Announcements*, *Blogs*, *General*, *News*, *Press Release*, and *Test*. You can also create tags to make the content easier to find in a search. Note that these categories are defined by a property in the properties file; see the `journal.article.types` property in chapter 20 for further information.

> **Note:** The Web Content Type portlet, located within the Categorization menu, is deprecated for Liferay 6.2 and will be removed in Liferay 7.0. The portlet will be migrated to a vocabulary with categories.

Schedule: customizes the date and time your content publishes and/or expires.

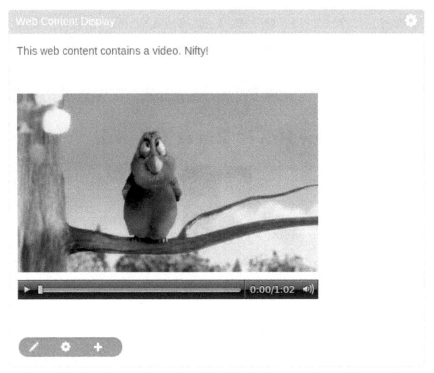

Figure 2.17: If you've installed and enabled Xuggler from the *Server Administration* →*External Tools* section of the Control Panel, you can add audio and video to your web content!

Display Page: lets you determine where the web contents are displayed when linked from other pages. The Canonical URL can be used here. The Canonical URL is unique for articles that redirect the visitor to the article's default display page.

Imagine you have a newspaper with a sports section and a technology section. You add a Sports page and a Tech page to your site, each one with a specific banner and look and feel. You want the articles to appear in the appropriate pages, but you know in Liferay articles are not related to pages. You can add an article as often as you like in different web content display portlets or in configured Asset Publishers. But if you have a *View in context* link, where will you show your article? This is where you'd use a default display page. Articles that have a default display page defined are shown with other related articles in the same display page.

Imagine you have 100 sports articles and 100 tech articles. In previous versions of Liferay you'd need to create a page for each article to show it. Now with only one sports page and one tech page, you can show all articles in one place in a consistent fashion.

Creating a Display Page

There are two ways of creating a display page. You can use a *Content Display Page* template, which automatically creates everything you need, or you can create one manually. The Content Display Page template is found under *Page Templates* in the Sites section of the Control Panel.

Figure 2.18: New web content can be customized in various ways using the menu on the right.

To create a display page manually, add an Asset Publisher to a page. Then make it the Default Asset Publisher for the page. This defines this Asset Publisher as the one that displays the content if several Asset Publishers are on the same page. Set this up by clicking *Configuration* on your Asset Publisher. Under the *Setup* tab, navigate to *Display Settings* and check the checkbox labeled *Set as the Default Asset Publisher for This Page*.

Once you've given an article its default display page, links to the article redirect the user to its default display page. To see how this works, add an Asset Publisher to another page, like the Home page of the newspaper, and configure it to *View in a Specific Portlet*. This setting is found in the *Asset Link Behavior* menu under Display Settings. If you click on the link, you'll be redirected to the Default Display Page of the article.

You now see that the link looks something like this:

```
www.lunar-resort.com/lunar-article
```

This is an example of a canonical URL, and it's a nice enhancement for Search Engine Optimization (SEO) because the article's URL becomes the page URL. To a search engine that's crawling your site, this means that the location of your article never changes. And if you decide to use the content on another page in the future, the article is still available at this URL. This feature is used in search results, in related assets and in Asset Publishers. For more information on Liferay's Display Pages, see chapter 5.

Related Assets: enables you to connect any number of assets within a site or across the portal, even if they don't share any tags and aren't in the same category. You can connect your content to a Blogs Entry, Message Boards Message, Web Content, Calendar Event, Bookmarks Entry, Documents and Media Document, and a Wiki Page.

You'll learn how to publish links to related assets using the Related Assets portlet in the *Defining content relationships* section of chapter 5.

Permissions: customize who has access to the content. By default, content is viewable by Anyone (Guest Role). You can limit viewable permissions by selecting any Role from the drop-down or in the list. Additionally, Liferay Portal provides the ability to customize permissions in more detail. Select the *More Options* link next to the drop down button and you'll find the different activities you can grant or deny to your web content.

Custom fields: customize metadata about the web content. The fields can represent anything you like, such as the web content's author or creation date. If custom fields have been defined for web content (which can be done from the *Custom Fields* page of the Control Panel), they appear here.

For more information on Custom Fields see the Custom Fields section in chapter 16.

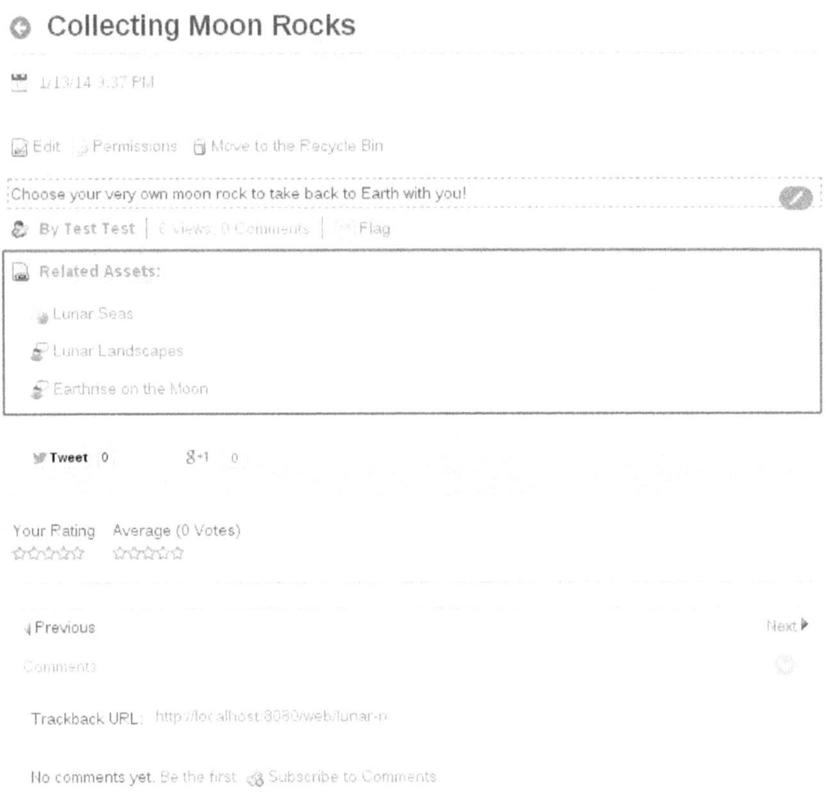

Collecting Moon Rocks

1/13/14 9.37 PM

Edit   Permissions   Move to the Recycle Bin

Choose your very own moon rock to take back to Earth with you!

By Test Test | 0 Views, 0 Comments | Flag

Related Assets:

Lunar Seas

Lunar Landscapes

Earthrise on the Moon

Tweet 0   g+1   0

Your Rating   Average (0 Votes)
☆☆☆☆☆   ☆☆☆☆☆

◄ Previous   Next ►

Comments

Trackback URL: http://localhost 8080/web/lunar-r

No comments yet. Be the first. Subscribe to Comments

Figure 2.19: This blog entry has links to three Related Assets: one web content and two message board entries.

For this piece of web content, we don't need to change anything. After you're finished with permissions, click *Save as Draft*. This saves the content in draft form. Once you're satisfied with your changes, select *Publish*. This makes the content available for display, but we still have some work to do to enable users to see it. In Liferay WCM, all content resides in a container, which is one of two portlets: Web Content Display or Web Content List. By far the most frequently used is the *Web Content Display* portlet. Let's look at how it works.

Publishing (Basic) Content

Now that we've created and published our first piece of web content for the Lunar Resort, it's time to display it. First, add the *Web Content Display* portlet to our Welcome page by selecting the *Add* button from the left palette and selecting the *Applications* tab.

Once the portlet appears, drag it to the position on the page where you want your content to appear. You can have as many Web Content Display portlets on a page as you need, which gives you the power to lay out your content exactly the way you want it.

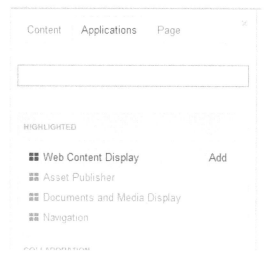

Figure 2.20: Adding the Web Content Display Portlet

To add existing web content, click the *Select Web Content* button on the lower left of the portlet. You will see the message *Please select a web content from the list below*. You have several options here.

Naturally, if your content appears in the list, you can simply select it. If there is lots of published content available, you could search for the content by name, ID, type, version, content and site (click the *Advanced* gear to see all the options). You can also show the available locales for your content. If you're working on the page for a particular language, you can select the translation of your content that goes with your locale.

If you have enabled OpenOffice.org integration with your portal, you can also enable document conversion for your content. This gives your users the ability to download your content in their format of choice. This is especially handy if you are running a research or academically oriented site; users can very quickly download PDFs of your content for their research projects.

Note that you also have other options, such as enabling a Print button, enabling ratings so users can rate the content, enabling comments and enabling ratings on comments.

The Print button pops the content up in a separate browser window that contains just the content, without any of the web site navigation. This is handy for printing the content. Enabling ratings shows one of two ratings interfaces Liferay has: five stars or thumbs up and thumbs down. This can be set globally in the portal-ext.properties file. See chapter 12 for further information about this.

Enabling comments creates a discussion forum attached to your content which users can use to discuss your content. Enabling ratings on comments gives your users the ability to rate the comments. You may decide you want one, some or none of these features, which is why they're all implemented as simple check boxes to be enabled or disabled at need.

If you click the *Supported Clients* tab, you'll see you can choose the type of client to which you want to expose content. This lets you target the large screens of users' computers for expansive graphics and lots of special effects or target the small screens of mobile devices with pertinent information and a lightweight page. For now, leave both checked and click the *Save* button. You can now close the configuration window.

To publish new content, select the *Add* button on the lower left of the portlet. This launches the same full-featured editor you've already seen in the Control Panel, which lets you add and edit content in place as you are working on your page.

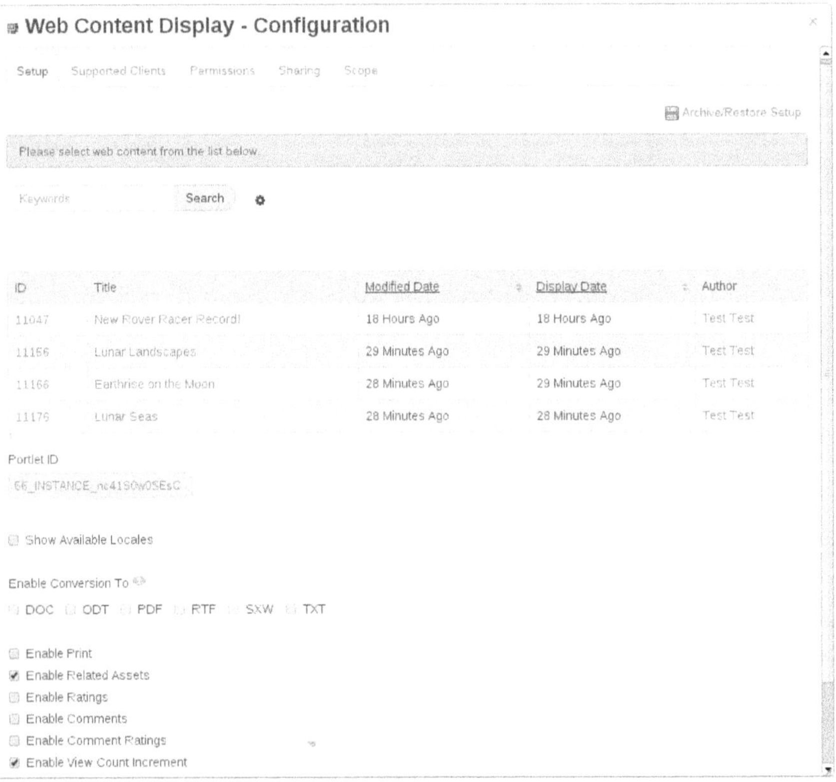

Figure 2.21: Publishing web content is a snap. At a minimum, you only have to select the content you wish to publish. You can also enable lots of optional features to let your users interact with your content.

This is another example of the flexibility that Liferay Portal offers. At times, you may want to add content directly into the Web Content Display portlet of the page you're managing, especially if you are in the process of building the page. At other times, you may want to navigate to Site Administration to create content, because at that moment you're more concerned with the creation of the content and not where the content will later be displayed. Liferay WCM supports both processes.

Editing content that's already been published is just as easy as creating new content is. You'll use the same exact tools.

Editing Content

Once the content is displayed—whether you've selected content or created it in the Web Content Display portlet—you can edit the content directly from the Web Content Display portlet or from the Control Panel. To edit it from the Web Content Display portlet, select the *Edit* button to the lower left of the portlet. This launches the WYSIWYG editor and from there you can make any necessary changes.

When you publish updates to a web content that's already being displayed somewhere on your portal (e.g., in a Web Content Display portlet or an Asset Publisher portlet), the content is immediately updated (unless, of course, you have a workflow enabled, which

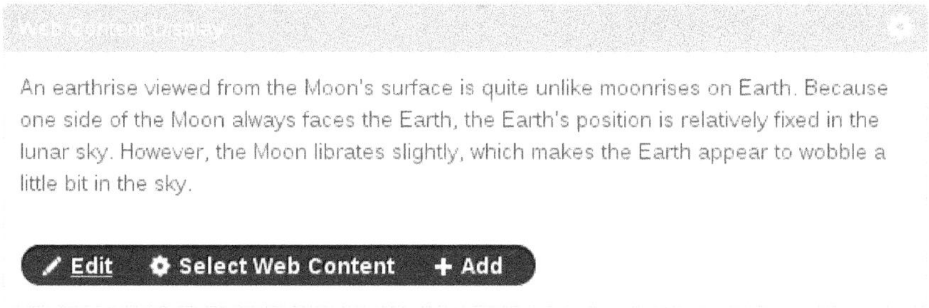

Figure 2.22: The *Edit*, *Select Web Content*, and *Add* buttons appear when hovering over their icons.

we'll discuss below). It makes no difference whether you edit it from a Web Content Display portlet, from the Asset Publisher, or from the Site Administration interface.

Note: if you want to view your page the way your users will see it (i.e., without all those portlet controls and icons), go up to the left palette and select the *Edit Controls* icon. This makes all those extra controls you see as a portal administrator disappear. You'll also notice the green "eye" transforms into an orange "eye". If you need to use those controls again, just select *Edit Controls* to return to the original format.

That's pretty much all there is to simple content creation. Whole sites have been created this way. But if you want to take advantage of the full power of Liferay's WCM, you'll want to use structures and templates found in chapter 3. Next, let's see how you can manage your content with an approval process called workflow.

2.5   Using Liferay's Workflow with WCM

Workflow is essentially a predetermined sequence of connected steps. In Liferay WCM, workflow is designed to manage the creation, modification and publication of web content. You can set up a workflow so content can't be published without going through an approval process you design. In this way, content is published to the site only after it has been reviewed and approved.

Liferay's workflow engine is called Kaleo workflow and it ships with Liferay CE. If you have uninstalled it or are using EE, it needs to be installed and configured separately. This is covered in chapter 6. Since we have somewhat of a "What came first—the chicken or the egg?" problem, for now, we'll assume it's installed and look at how you can take advantage of workflow in getting your content through any approval steps between creation and publication.

You may have noticed something appears to be missing from the staging process discussed above. In particular, you might be asking the question, "How do I reject changes?" Staging is integrated with Liferay's Workflow engine. To have a review process for staged pages, you need to make sure you have a workflow engine configured and you have staging set up in the workflow. To do this, select the workflow definition desired for page revisions in the Workflow Configuration.

When using a workflow, clicking *Submit for Publication* submits the staged pages into the workflow. Once all necessary approvals have been completed, the page status is marked as ready for publication. The *Publish to Live Now* and *Schedule for Publication* options publish the last version of the selected pages marked as ready for publication.

To enable workflow for Web Content, navigate to the Control Panel and select *Workflow Configuration*. From there, select a workflow that has been deployed to Liferay.

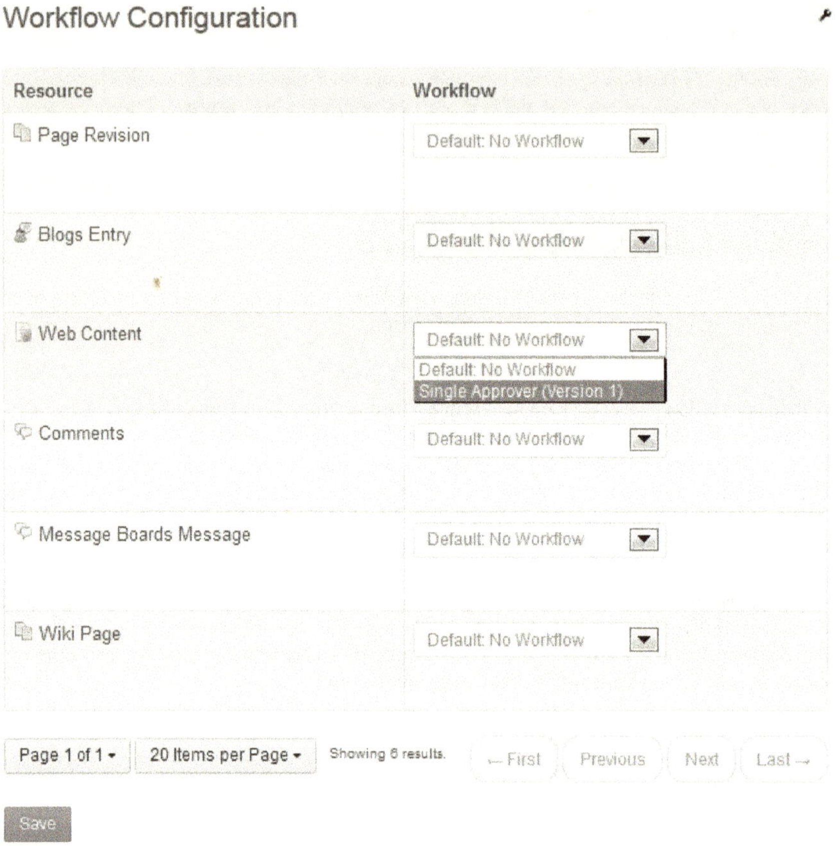

Workflow Configuration

Resource	Workflow
🗐 Page Revision	Default: No Workflow ▼
🗐 Blogs Entry	Default: No Workflow ▼
🗐 Web Content	Default: No Workflow ▼ Default: No Workflow Single Approver (Version 1)
🗐 Comments	Default: No Workflow ▼
🗐 Message Boards Message	Default: No Workflow ▼
🗐 Wiki Page	Default: No Workflow ▼

| Page 1 of 1 ▼ | 20 Items per Page ▼ | Showing 6 results. | ← First | Previous | Next | Last → |

Save

Figure 2.23: You can select the pre-made *Single Approver* workflow to experiment with workflow management.

As you'll discover in chapter 10, you can design workflows to suit your organization's approval process. For the Lunar Resort's implementation we'll use the *Single Approver* workflow which ships with the product.

Defining Workflows for Web Content

Let's set up Liferay's Workflow for the Lunar Resort web site. You must have the Kaleo workflow plugin installed in order for the workflow categories to appear in the Control Panel. Liferay's Kaleo workflow engine ships with CE versions of Liferay. For installation instructions for Liferay EE, please see chapter 10.

1. Go to the Site Administration page and select *Workflow Configuration* from the *Configuration* section.

2. From the select box, choose *Single Approver* for Web Content. Click *Save*. Note that you can add workflow to many of Liferay's portlets.

That's all it takes to set up workflow for web content. Now that workflow is enabled, publishing content works a little bit differently. Let's go through the process of publishing details for new class offerings at the Lunar Resort. Return to the home page and click the *Add Web Content* icon on the Web Content Display portlet. Call the new content *Course Offerings* and enter some content. Notice that the Publish button is now gone. In its place is a *Submit for Publication* button. Go ahead and click it.

Next, go to the *Workflow Tasks* in Site Administration and select *My Workflow Tasks*. You will see the option to Review Content for Sales Goals. It shows because you are logged in as an Administrator. There is also a Content Approvers role which is defined by this workflow and anyone in this role can approve content as well.

To approve the content, you must first take ownership of it. Click on the task. You should see the screen below.

Taking ownership of, reviewing and approving content is very easy:

1. Click the *Assign to Me* button. Alternatively, you could assign it to someone else in the Content Approvers role or create / update a due date for the content's approval.
2. Once you've assigned it to yourself, buttons allowing you to approve or reject the content appear. Click *Approve*.
3. You're asked to submit a comment. You'd have to do this for either *Approve* or *Reject*. Add a comment and click *Save*.
4. The content is now approved.

In a real world situation, you obviously wouldn't want the person who created the content to be the one who approves it. Instead, you would have one or more roles designed for users who will be creating content and you would have specific users assigned to one or more roles for approving content. Our example was of a very straightforward workflow, as it has only a single approver. Kaleo workflow allows you to design workflows that go through as many steps as you need to conform to your business processes. We look at Kaleo workflow in more detail in chapter 6.

2.6 Summary

This chapter has provided an introduction to Liferay site management and web content management. We've learned how you can use Liferay to create multiple sites with different membership types. We've seen how easy it is to create and manage sites and to create and manage pages within a site in Liferay. We've also seen how easy it is to create and edit web content using Liferay's rich WYSIWYG editor. This powerful tool enables users who don't have much experience with HTML and CSS to easily create and style web content of any type that you'd like to publish on the web.

Liferay WCM also includes a powerful workflow engine, allowing you to set up custom publishing rules to fit your organization. You can set up custom approval processes for different sites as well as for different kinds of content within a site. We'll examine sites in more detail in chapter 3. We'll also cover some more advanced web content management tools such as web content structures and templates, page templates and site templates, staging, and mobile device rules.

ADVANCED WEB CONTENT MANAGEMENT

In the previous chapter you learned some basic ways you can use Liferay to handle your web content. In this chapter you'll delve deeper into slightly more complex web content management techniques. But don't be alarmed, it's not too intense. We'll cover the following topics:

- Web content structures and templates
- RSS Feeds
- Site templates and page templates
- Localization
- Allowing users to customize site pages
- Scheduling Web Content
- Staging
- Creating teams to allow for flexible management of site permissions
- Mobile device rules
- Monitoring with Google Analytics

You'll examine how web content structures and templates provide additional power and flexibility to the web content management system you saw previously. You'll also learn how easy it is to set up and administer multiple sites in Liferay. Next, we'll learn how you can empower your users to create personal customizations of site pages. You'll also examine how you can use staging to manage the publication of pages and content on your site. You'll conclude with sections on creating teams and rules for presenting site pages to mobile devices.

3.1 Advanced Content with Structures and Templates

If you've ever launched a web site, you know that as it grows, you can experience growing pains. This is the case especially if you've given lots of people access to the site to make whatever changes they need to make. Without preset limitations, users can display content in any order and in any manner they desire (think huge, flashing letters in a font nobody can read). Content can get stale, especially if those responsible for it don't maintain it like they should. And sometimes, content is published that should never have seen the light of day.

Thankfully, Liferay WCM helps you handle all of those situations. You can use *Structures* to define which fields are available to users when they create content. These can be coupled with *Templates* that define how to display that content. Content won't get stale, because you can take advantage of the *Scheduling* feature to determine when content is displayed and when it's removed. Additionally, you can configure Liferay's built-in *Workflow* system to set up a review and publishing process so only what you want winds up on the live site. Liferay Portal gives you the management tools you need to run everything from a simple, one-page web site to an enormous, content-rich site.

All of this starts with structures.

Using Structures

Structures are the foundation for web content. They determine which fields are available to users as they create new items for display. Structures not only improve manageability for the administrator, they also make it much easier for users to quickly add content.

For example, say you're managing an online news magazine. All your articles need to contain the same types of information: a title, a subtitle, an author and one or more pages of text and images that comprise the body of the article. If Liferay only supported simple content as has been described above, you'd have no way to make sure your users entered a title, subtitle, and author. You might also get articles that don't match the look and feel of your site. If titles are supposed to be navy blue but they come in from your writers manually set to light blue, you need to spend time reformatting them before they are published.

Structures give you the ability to provide a format for your content so your users know what needs to be entered to have a complete article. Using structures, you can provide a form for your users which spells out exactly what is required and can be formatted automatically using a template.

You create a structure by adding form controls such as text fields, text boxes, text areas (HTML), check boxes, select boxes and multi-selection lists. Also you can add specialized, Liferay-specific application fields such as an Image Uploader and Documents and Media right onto the structure. Furthermore, you can move the elements around by dragging them where you want them. This makes it easy for you to prototype different orders for your input fields. Additionally, elements can be grouped together into blocks which can then be repeatable. Template writers can then write a template which loops through these blocks and presents your content in innovative ways, such as in sliding navigation bars, content which scrolls with the user and more.

Let's look at how we can create and edit structures through the Manage Structures interface.

Editing Structures

Go back to the Site Administration page and select *Web Content* from the Content section. The first way to access the Manage Structures interface is simply by clicking *Manage →Structures*. This opens a popup showing all the web content structures that exist in your currently selected scope. Here, you can add new web content structures, edit existing ones, manage the templates associated with a structure, edit the permissions of a structure, and copy or delete structures.

Copying web content structures can be useful if you'd like to create a new web content structure that's similar to an existing one, but you don't want to start from scratch. Liferay generates a unique portal ID for the copied structure, but every other attribute of the copied structure, including the name, is the same as that of the original. Once you've copied a web content structure, you should enter a new name for it to avoid confusing it with the original. When you copy a web content structure, you'll be prompted to choose whether to copy any detail templates or list templates associated with the structure. For information on detail templates and list templates, please refer to chapter 11 on *Using Web Forms and Dynamic Data Lists*.

Figure 3.1: You can access the Manage Structures interface by clicking *Manage* →*Structures* from the Web Content page.

The second way to access the Manage Structures interface is directly from the web content article WYSIWYG editor. Click *Add Basic Web Content* from the Web Content page to add another piece of content to your portal. Instead of going right for the content, this time we'll first create a structure. To access the Manage Structures interface, simply click on *Select* next to the *Structure* heading near the top of the page. To create a new structure in your chosen scope, simply click on the *Add* button in the Manage Structures popup.

It's very easy to create and edit structures: all you have to do is drag elements into the structure and then give them names. For instance, select the *Text* element and drag it onto the structure. You can do the same with any of the elements. To remove it from the structure, simply select the *Delete* icon (trash can) in the upper right corner of the element. You also have the ability to duplicate the element, which can be done by selecting the *Duplicate* (addition sign) button. We'll explain the *Configuration* button later.

Web content structures also have the capability of inheriting characteristics from other structures. When a parent structure is configured, the child structure inherits the parent's fields and settings. Using this feature is helpful when you want to make a similar structure to one that already exists. For example, if you'd like to create an in-depth Lunar Resort sports article in addition to a regular Lunar Resort sports article, you can simply inherit the characteristics of the regular article and only add additional fields to the more in-depth article. When the in-depth article is configured, it will display its parent's fields in addition to its own fields.

For Liferay 6.2, the WebDAV URL feature was introduced for web content structures and templates so users could upload and organize resources from both a web interface and the file explorer of their desktop operating system. With the WebDAV URL, site administrators are capable of adding, browsing, editing, and deleting structures and templates on a remote server. After you complete your structure, you can access the WebDAV URL by re-opening the structure or template and clicking the *Details* section. If you'd like the see WebDAV in action, visit the *Document Management* chapter's *WebDAV access* chapter.

Note: Some operating systems require a WebDAV server to be class level 2 (i.e., to support file locking) before allowing files to be read or written. For Liferay 6.2, the Documents and Media library was upgraded to class level 2 but Web Content structures and templates were not. This means that Liferay 6.2's Document and Media library supports WebDAV file locking but Web Content structures and templates do not. However, on operating systems which require WebDAV servers to be class level 2, it's possible to avoid the restriction by using third-party WebDAV clients (e.g., Cyberduck).

Another method to edit your structure is switching to *Source* mode and manually customizing your structure by editing its XML file. You'll notice by default the *View* mode is selected. Click the *Source* tab to switch to Source mode. This method is for the more experienced developers.

Take a moment to add, delete, and rearrange different elements.

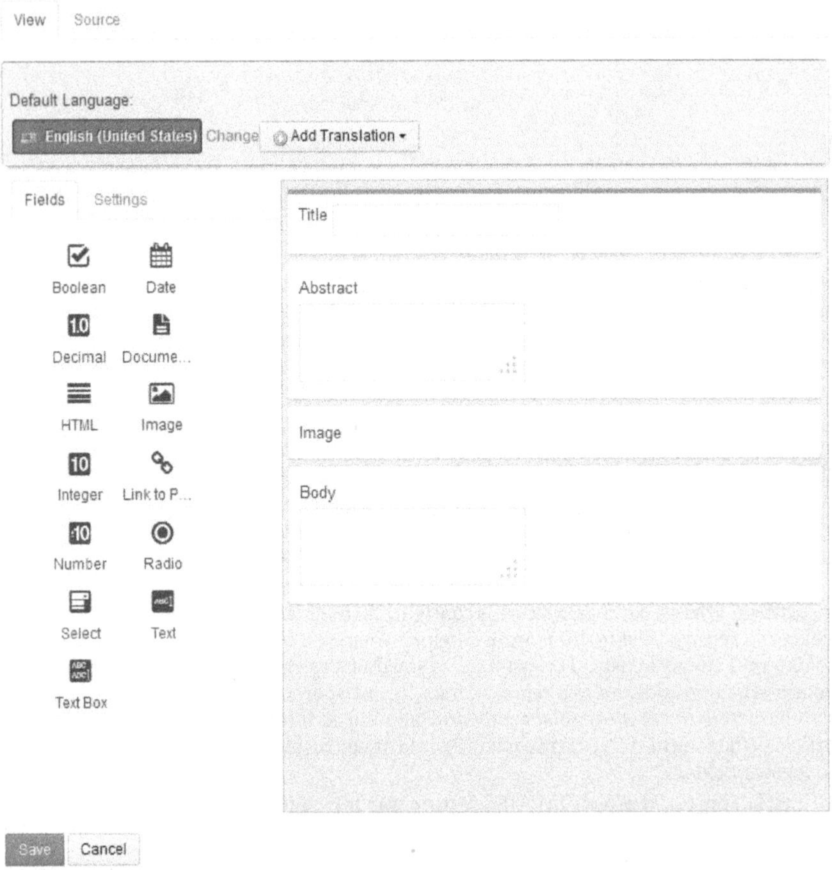

Figure 3.2: The structure editor gives you many options to customize your Web Content.

Liferay supports the following fields in structures:

Boolean: Adds a checkbox onto your structure, which stores either true (checked) or false (unchecked). Template developers can use this as a display rule.

Date: Adds a preformatted text field that displays a convenient date picker to assist in selecting the desired data. The format for the date is governed by the current locale.

Decimal: Similar to *Number*, except that it required a decimal point (.) be present.

Documents and Media: Adds an existing uploaded document to attach to the structure. Also has the ability to upload documents into the Document Library.

HTML: An area that uses a WYSIWYG editor to enhance the content.

Image: Adds the browse image application into your structure.

Integer: Similar to *Number*, except that it constrains user input to non-fractional numbers.

Link to Page: Inserts a link to another page in the same site.

Number: Presents a text box that only accepts numbers as inputs, but puts no constraints on the kind of number entered.

Radio: Presents the user with a list of options to choose from using radio button inputs.

Select: Presents a selection of options for the user to choose from using a combo box. Can be configured to allow multiple selections, unlike *Radio*.

Text: Used for items such as titles and headings.

Text Box: Used for the body of your content or long descriptions.

These fields provide all you need to model any information type you would want to use as web content. Liferay customers have used structures to model everything from articles, to video metadata, to databases of wildlife. You're limited only by your imagination. To fire that imagination, let's look more closely at field settings.

Editing Field Settings

When creating a new structure, it is essential that you set variable names. Template writers can use these variables to refer to elements on your form. If you don't set variable names, Liferay generates random variable names and these can be difficult for a template writer to follow. For example, consider a field called *Author*. You might create this field in your form but the underlying variable name in the structure might look something like `TextField4882`. The template writer needs to create markup for your structure and place the Author field in a certain spot in the markup. How will he or she know which field is Author when they're all named randomly?

To solve this problem, all you need to do is set a variable name for each field as you add it to your structure. Let's do this now. In your structure, add an element *HTML*. To change its field label and variable name, you'll need to access the field's settings. Hover over the field and select the wrench icon that appears in the upper right corner. Change the *Field Label* value to *Instructions* and the *Name* value (variable name) to `Steps`. Now your template writer has a variable by which he or she can refer to this field.

Here's a list of all the configurable settings available for a structure's fields:

Type: Lists the type of field placed in the definition. This is not editable but is available to reference from a template.

Field Label: Sets the text that can be displayed with the field. This is the human-readable text that the user sees.

Show Label: Select *Yes* to display the Field Label.

Required: Select *Yes* to mark the field required. If a field is required, users must enter a value for it in order to submit content using this structure.

Name: The name of the field internally, automatically generated. Since this is the variable name that you can read the data from in a template, you should give a more memorable name here.

Predefined Value: Specifying predefined values for structure forms is a way to specify defaults. When a user creates a new web content article based on a structure that has predefined values for various fields, the predefined values appear in the form as defaults for those fields.

Tip: Each field can have a small help icon, with a tooltip attached that displays helpful information. If you would like to provide text for the tooltip you may enter it here.

Indexable: Select *Yes* to enable Liferay to index your field for search.

Repeatable: Select *Yes* to make your field repeatable. Your users can then add as many copies of this field as they like. For example, if you're creating a structure for articles, you might want a repeatable Author field in case you have multiple authors for a particular article.

Width: Changes the width of the field. The field width can be *small, medium,* or *large* (not available for Boolean, Documents and Media, Image, Radio, and Select).

Multiple: Select *Yes* to enable a multi-selection list (only available for Select).

Options: Changes the options available for selection. You're able to add and remove options as well as edit each individual option's display name and value (only available for Radio and Select).

For the Lunar Resort structure, type something in the *Tip* field that helps users know what to put into the Body element (example: *This is an HTML text area for the body of your content*). Now, when users hover over the Help icon near your title, your tip is displayed.

Structure Default Values   Structure Default Values allow you to create one structure that uses common data from multiple articles.

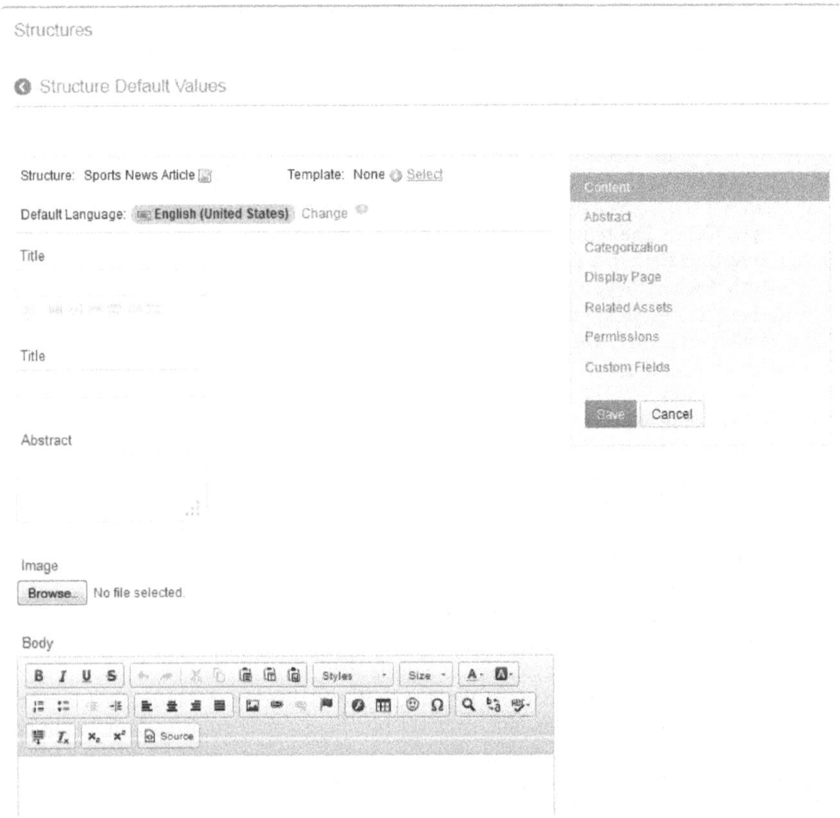

Figure 3.3: You can edit default values via the *Actions* button of the Manage Structures interface.

Returning to our newspaper scenario again, let's say you want all sports articles to have the same display page (sports page), the same categories, or the same set of tags. Instead of adding them for each article or wondering if your users are adding them to every web content, you can add these characteristics once for every sports article by creating default values for the structure. Creating default values is not part of creating a new structure, so make sure you have an existing structure.

To edit a structure's default values, go to *Web Content* in the Content section of the Site Administration page and click *Manage →Structures* to see the structures list. Find the *Actions* button for the desired structure and select *Edit Default Values* from the menu to view a window like the one below. This form allows you to manage the structure settings.

Every new web content you create with this structure is preloaded with the data you inserted. Next, let's demonstrate assigning permissions.

Assigning Permissions

Setting permissions on structures is done using the same procedure as permissions everywhere else in Liferay. Most users should not have the ability to edit structures. Structures are coupled with templates, which require some web development knowledge to create. This is why only trusted developers should be able to create structures and templates. Users, of course, should be able to view structures. The *View* permission enables them to make use of the structures to create content.

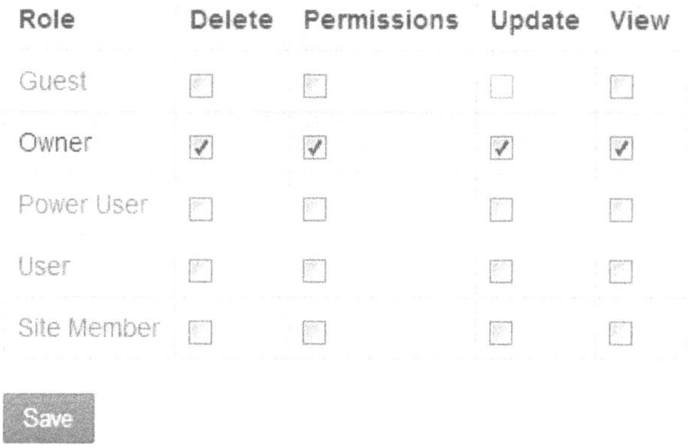

Role	Delete	Permissions	Update	View
Guest	☐	☐	☐	☐
Owner	✔	✔	✔	✔
Power User	☐	☐	☐	☐
User	☐	☐	☐	☐
Site Member	☐	☐	☐	☐

Save

Figure 3.4: You're able to assign structure permissions via the *Actions* button.

You can grant or deny permissions based on Roles and this is the recommended way to handle permissions for structures.

Now that you understand what structures are used for, you need to understand the other half of Liferay's web content management system: templates.

Using Templates

Developers create templates to display the elements of the structure in the markup they want. Content can then be styled properly using CSS, because markup is generated consistently by the template when structured content is displayed. In essence, templates are scripts that tell Liferay how to display content in the structure. Any changes to the structure require corresponding changes to the template, because new or deleted fields produce errors on the page. If users enter content into a structure, it *must* have a matching template. However, you have options for whether you want your template to be permanently linked to your structure. Generic templates are templates that are not tied to a structure, which allows for reusable code that can be imported into other templates. Without a template, the portal has no idea how to display content which has been created using a custom structure.

Let's look more closely at the types of templates Liferay supports.

Template Types (FTL, VM, and XSL)

Liferay supports templates written in three different templating languages, to support the skill sets of the largest number of developers. This increases the chances you can jump right in and use whichever one you've already used before. If you haven't yet been exposed to any of them, your best bet is FreeMarker or Velocity, as they are less "chatty" than XSL and extremely simple to understand.

FTL (FreeMarker Template Language): Freemarker is a templating language which could be considered a successor to Velocity. It has some advantages over Velocity for which it sacrifices some simplicity, yet it is still easy to use. If you haven't used any of the template languages before, we recommend using FreeMarker: you'll get up to speed the fastest.

VM (Velocity Macro): Velocity is a scripting language that lets you mix logic with HTML. This is similar to other scripting languages, such as PHP, though Velocity is much simpler.

XSL (Extensible Style Sheet Language): XSL is used in Liferay templates to transform the underlying XML of a structure into markup suitable for the browser. While it may not be as clean and compact as Velocity or FTL, it's widely used for transforming XML into other formats and it's very likely your developers have already been exposed to it.

Adding Templates

Liferay WCM makes it easy to create structures, templates, and content from the same interface. Let's go through the entire flow of how you'd create a structure, link it to a template and then create content using them both. We'll use FreeMarker for our template and we'll lay out the structure fields systematically to go along with the format we've defined for our content.

1. Go back to the Web Content section of the Site Administration page and click *Add* →*Basic Web Content*.

2. Click *Select* next to the Structures heading to access the Manage Structures interface.

3. Click on the *Add* button.

4. Name the structure *News Article* and add the following fields:

Field Type	Field Label	Name
Text	Title	title
Text Box	Abstract	abstract
Image	Image	image
HTML	Body	body

5. Click *Save*.

6. In the Manage Structures interface, click *Choose* next to the News Article structure that you created.

7. In the New Web Content form, click *Select* next to the Template heading to access the Manage Templates interface.

8. Click *Add*, enter the name *News Article*, and add a description.

9. Make sure FreeMarker is selected as the script language (it's the default).

10. If you've written the script beforehand, you can select *Browse* to upload it from your machine. Otherwise, you can type the script directly into the script editor window.

11. Click *Save*.

12. Exit the Manage Templates interface and click *Select* next to the Template heading again.

13. Click *Choose* next to the News Article template you created.

14. On the New Web Content form, you'll see the Title, Abstract, Image, and Body fields that you defined for the News Article structure. The News Article template should also be selected.

15. Populate the fields and click *Publish* to publish your News Article.

Below is the template script for this structure. It is written in FreeMarker:

```
<#assign renderUrlMax = request["render-url-maximized"]>
<#assign namespace = request["portlet-namespace"]>
<#assign readmore = request.parameters?is_hash && getterUtil.getBoolean(
    request.parameters.read_more, false)>
<h1>${title.getData()}</h1>
<#if readmore>
<p>${abstract.getData()}</p>
<p>${body.getData()}</p>
<#else>
<p>
<img src="${image.getData()}" border="0" align="right">
${abstract.getData()}</p>
<a href="${renderUrlMax}&${namespace}read_more=true">Read More</a>
</#if>
```

This template is small but accomplishes a lot. First, a portlet URL which maximizes the portlet is created. Once this is done, the template gets the namespace of the portlet. This is important to avoid URL collisions with other URLs that might be on the page.

After this, the template attempts to get a request parameter called read_more. Whether or not this was successful is the key to the rest of the script:

- If the template got the read_more parameter, it displays the abstract and the body below the title (which is always displayed).

- If the template didn't get the read_more parameter, it displays the image, the abstract and the link created above, which sets the read_more parameter.

When this template is rendered, it looks something like Figure 3.5.

New for Liferay 6.2 is the ability to create generic templates that aren't connected to a specific structure. In previous versions of Liferay, each template had to be associated with a structure. Now, you have options for whether to permanently assign a template to a structure or create a generic template and reuse its code for any structure. In other words, generic templates can be embedded in other templates, which allows for reusable code, JS library imports, or macros which will be imported by Velocity or FreeMarker templates in the system.

Suppose you have three different Lunar Resort web content articles and structures with similar aesthetics. Instead of creating three different templates from scratch, you can use the same generic template for all three and build off of it. This creates a smarter and more efficient process when creating a multitude of similar web content articles. Generic templates are created the same way as regular, structure-based templates. The only setting that differs is the *Structure* option, which you'll need to leave blank to create a generic template.

For cases where you're creating your template within Liferay, you can use the template editor. On the left side of the template editor, you'll notice a palette of common variables

Learn More about the Lunar Resort!

We know you'd go to the moon and back for your loved ones, so why not treat them to a relaxing stay
at our exclusive Lunar Resort?

Read More

Liferay's Lunar Resort
"A world away never felt so close!"

Learn More about the Lunar Resort!

We know you'd go to the moon and back for your loved ones, so why not treat them to a relaxing stay at our exclusive Lunar Resort?

Is this your first orbit of our web site? Read here to learn about our exclusive resort and our diverse offerings that will suit even the pickiest travellers. For the adventurous in your party, we offer existing activities like lunar golf, rover races, and hang gliding; those wanting to unwind from their interstellar journey can relax by the Mare Tranquillitatis (Sea of Tranquility) and watch the spectacular earthrise--either way, you'll be blown away by the unique experiences we offer. So come get some lunar dust in your shoes--it's out of this world!

Edit   Edit Te...   Select   Add

Figure 3.5: The initial and expanded views for the Lunar Resort News Article. After
Clicking *Read More*, you're able to read the full text body.

used for making web content templates. This is a great reference when creating your template. To place one of the variables onto the template editor, simply position your cursor where you want the variable placed, and click the variable name. If the variable name doesn't give you sufficient information on the variable's functionality, you can hover your pointer over it for a more detailed description.

The interactive template editor is available for the FreeMarker and Velocity languages. Depending on which language you select, the variable content changes so you're always adding content in the language you've chosen. Another cool feature for the template editor is the autocomplete feature. It can be invoked by typing $\{$ which opens a drop-down menu of available variables. By clicking one of the variables, the editor inserts the variable into the template editor.

After you've saved your template, Liferay provides a WebDAV URL and static URL. These values access the XML source of your structure. You can find these URLs by returning to your template after it's been saved and expanding the *Details* section. For more information on WebDAV and the uses of the WebDAV URL, reference the *WebDAV access* section in the *Document Management* chapter.

Now that you've created a handsome template and know how to use the template editor, it's time to decide who the lucky people are that get to use your new template.

Assigning Template Permissions

Permissions for templates are similar to permissions for structures. As with structures, you only want specific developers editing and creating templates. You may, however, want to make the templates viewable to some content creators who understand the template scripting language but are not directly writing the scripts. You can determine who views and interacts with the template by navigating to *Manage Templates* and selecting *Permissions* from the *Actions* button.

You can grant or deny permissions based on Roles. For instance, you may create a role with the ability to update the template and create a second role that can both update

▼ Script

Script File Browse... No file selected.

Figure 3.6: You can hover your pointer over a variable for a more detailed description.

and delete. Liferay Portal makes it possible to assign permissions based on the roles and responsibilities within your organization.

Now that you understand the role structures and templates play in creating web content, let's look at how to create RSS feeds in Liferay.

3.2 Managing RSS Feeds in Liferay

RSS is a family of web feed formats used to publish frequently updated works such as blog entries and news articles. RSS allows users to stay up-to-date with your site's content without actually having to visit your site! Instead, they can subscribe to your site's RSS feed with an RSS feed reader. Their RSS reader reads your site's RSS feed and displays information about all the web content that's published on your site, such as each article's title and publication date. If one of your site's web content articles grabs their attention, then they can follow their RSS reader's link to the article's full content on your site. Many RSS readers are available today, including web-based readers, ones for the Windows, Mac, and Linux platforms, and ones for mobile devices. Let's see how to create RSS feeds in Liferay.

Managing RSS Feeds from the Control Panel

To manage a Liferay site's RSS feeds, navigate to the Site Administration →Content page of your site and click *Web Content*. Site administrators can use this Web Content administration portlet to manage their site's web content, including web content structures and templates, which we examined above. Site administrators can also use the Web Content administration portlet to manage their site's RSS feeds. Click *Manage* →*Feeds* if you'd like to add, edit, or delete RSS feeds.

Note: The Web Content Feeds portlet is deprecated for Liferay 6.2 and will be removed in Liferay 7.0. The portlet will be migrated to the Asset Publisher portlet.

Feeds

Your request completed successfully.

Keywords   Search   ⚙

Add Feed   Permissions

Delete

☐ ID   Description
☐ 12201   Lunar Resort feed   ▾ 🖉 Actions

Figure 3.7: Clicking *Manage →Feeds* from the Control Panel's Web Content administration portlet opens a popup window which displays your site's RSS feeds. You can add or edit RSS feeds, configure their permissions, or delete them.

Click the *Add Feed* button to add a new feed. You need to enter a name and select a target page for the feed. A feed's target page serves two purposes:

1. The site to which the target page belongs determines which web content articles appear in the feed. For example, if the target page belongs to the Marketing site, only web content articles belong to the Marketing site will appear in the feed.

2. The target page is the page where "orphaned" web content articles will be displayed. "Orphaned" web content articles are articles that have been published in your site but have not been configured to be displayed in specific Web Content Display portlets. Liferay RSS feeds can provide links to any published web content articles, both "orphaned" articles and articles that have been configured to be displayed in specific Web Content Display portlets. For articles that have been configured to be displayed in a specific portlet, the RSS feeds' links point to the portal page of that portlet. For "orphaned" articles, the RSS feeds' links point to the feed's target page. When users click on such links for "orphaned" articles, the full content of the "orphaned" article is displayed on the target page.

To specify a target page, you need to enter the target page's friendly URL. Note that friendly URLs do not include the host name. For example, the friendly URL of a public page called *Welcome* belonging to a site called *Marketing* might look like this: /web/marketing/welcome. Optionally, you can specify a target portlet ID. This would be the portlet ID of a Web Content Display portlet on the target page in which "orphaned" web content should be displayed. The portlet must exist or else the content will not displayed. The URL field contains the address of your RSS feed. It appears after you've actually created the feed by clicking *Save*.

The final two sections of the *Add Feed* form allow you customize which web content articles appear in your feed.

Figure 3.8: To create a new RSS feed, you only need to specify a name and a target page. Of course, you can also configure other features of the feed such as its permissions, web content constraints, and presentation settings.

1. The Web Content Constraints section allows you to select a web content type and a structure with which to filter the articles that appear in your feed. You can select a particular type of web content such as *Announcements*, *News*, or *Press Release*. Only articles of the type you select will appear in your feed. You can also choose for only web content articles that have a particular structure to appear in your feed. This is useful since customized kinds of web content articles are often created using web content structures.

2. The Presentation Settings section allows you to customize additional details about your feed and how articles are displayed in your feed. Leave the Feed Item Content set to *Web Content Description* if you'd just like a description of each article to appear in your feed. Set it to *Rendered Web Content: Use Default Template* if you'd like the full content of each article to appear in the feed. Customizing the Feed Type allows you to choose which web feed language to use for your feed. You can choose *Atom 1.0* (the default), *RSS 1.0*, or *RSS 2.0*. Customize the *Maximum Items to Display* to choose the maximum number of articles should appear in your feed at one time. Leave the Order By Column set to *Modified Date* to have articles arranged in order from the last time they were published or modified. You can set the Order by Column to *Display Date* if you want to have articles arranged in order from the time they were configured to be displayed in a specific Web Content Display portlet. Lastly, you can leave the Order by Type set to *Ascending* to have the oldest articles at the top of the feed or you can set it to *Descending* to have the newest articles at the top of the feed.

When you're done configuring your RSS feed, you can click *Preview* to see how your feed looks. If you're satisfied, click *Save* to create your feed.

Once one or more feeds have been created, they'll appear in a list in the Feeds popup window when you click *Manage →Feeds*. You can edit existing feeds using the same form used for creating them. The main difference is that when you edit an existing feed, the URL field is populated. Copy this URL into a new browser tab or window to test your feed. From the Feeds popup window, you can also customize the permissions of feeds or delete feeds.

It's possible to completely disable RSS feeds at the portal level. You can do this by setting the rss.feeds.enabled property to false. By default, it's set to true. If you keep the default, RSS enabled, you can make several other RSS property customizations. Please refer to the RSS section of your portal.properties file for details.

Using the RSS Portlet

The RSS portlet allows you to display any number of RSS feeds and configure how they are displayed. If you're looking for a web-based RSS reader, look no further: just add the RSS portlet to one your personal site's private pages, and voila! You have your own personal RSS reader. Open the portlet's Configuration popup to select the feeds to be displayed and customize the display. The RSS portlet can also be placed on sites' public or private pages to make feeds available to guests or site members, respectively. In these cases, make sure that only site administrators have permission to customize the RSS portlet and select feeds to be displayed.

Once you've added the RSS portlet to a page, open the portlet's Configuration popup window by clicking on the gear icon at the top right corner of the portlet and selecting *Configuration*.

By default, the RSS portlet displays two feeds. In the Feeds section, click on the green plus sign to add a new feed or on the red minus sign to remove a feed. Enter the URL of the RSS feed to display into the URL field. If you leave the Title field blank, the feed's title appears in the RSS portlet. If you enter a custom title into the Title field, the custom title appears instead of the feed's title.

In the Display Settings section, use the following checkboxes to select the feed details that should be displayed:

- Show Feed Title
- Show Feed Published Date
- Show Feed Description
- Show Feed Image
- Show Feed Item Author

You can also select the number of entries and expanded entries that should be displayed per feed. Expanded entries show more of an article's actual content than regular entries. By default, each feed shows eight entries per feed but only one expanded entry per feed. You can set the feed image alignment to control whether feed images appear to the right or left of the text. By default, the feed image alignment is set to *Right*. Finally, you can select a header web content and/or a footer web content. These are web content articles that appear in the RSS portlet either above all of the feeds or below all of the feeds. You can use these to provide an introduction, description, or footnotes about the feeds that you've selected to be displayed.

Now that we've discussed how to create, manage, and use RSS feeds, let's examine site templates and page templates. Site templates are a powerful tool for managing many similar sites. Let's examine how they work and then we'll look at page templates.

3.3   Using Site Templates

Site Templates can be administered from the Control Panel. They allow portal administrators to create multiple sites with the same default set of pages and content. Site templates

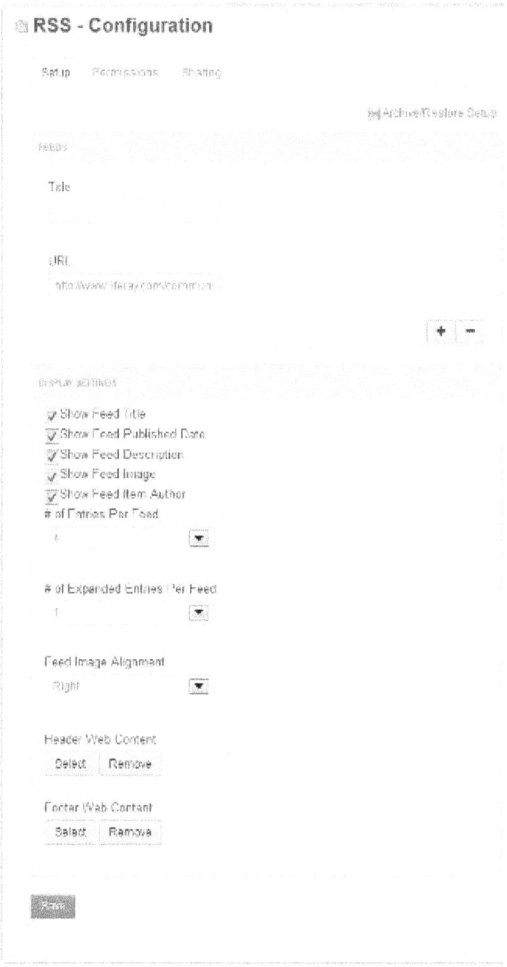

Figure 3.9: The RSS portlet's configuration window lets you choose feeds to be displayed and allows you to customize the display settings.

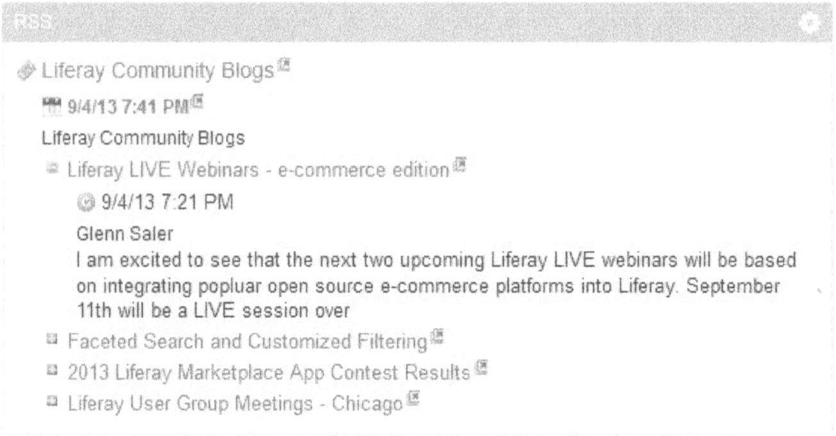

Figure 3.10: By default, the RSS portlet is configured to display feeds from Liferay Community Blogs, Yahoo News, and the New York Times. This image displays what the Liferay Community Blogs feed looks like in the RSS portlet.

can contain multiple pages, each with its own theme, layout template, portlets, and portlet configurations. Site templates can also contain content just like actual sites. This allows administrators to use site templates to create new sites that are each created with the same default pages, portlets, and content. After they've been created, these sites and their pages can be modified by site administrators. Using site templates can save site administrators a lot of work even if each site that was created from a given site template ends up being very different.

To get started, click on *Site Templates* in the Sites section of the Control Panel. Here, you can add, manage, or delete site templates. You can also configure the permissions of site templates. As long as a site is linked to the site template it was created from, changes to the site template's pages, portlets, and portlet configurations are propagated to the site. Changes to a site template's content, however, are not propagated to existing sites that are linked to the site template. We discuss the propagation of changes between site templates and sites in more detail in the section on site templates use cases below.

To manage the pages of a site template, click on *Site Templates* in the Control Panel and then click *Actions* → *Manage*. You're provided a left menu which contains the *Pages*, *Content*, and *Configuration* sections for each site. By default, the Manage Interface begins with the template's *Site Pages*. From here, you can add or remove pages from a site template or select themes and layout templates to apply to the site template. Click on a specific page if you'd like to select a different theme or layout template for that page. To edit the pages themselves, click *Actions* → *View Pages*. You can add specific portlets to each page of a site template and configure the preferences of each portlet. Each page can have any theme, any layout template, and any number of portlet applications, just like a page of a regular site. As with site pages, you can organize the pages of a site template into hierarchies. When you create a site using a site template, the configuration of pages and portlets is copied from the template to the site. By default, all changes made to the site template are automatically copied to sites based on that template.

Tip: If you want to publish a piece of web content to many sites and ensure modifications are applied to all, don't use site template content for that purpose. Instead, place the content in the global scope and then reference it from a *Web Content Display* application in each site.

The Content section offers separate repositories for content related portlets based on your site template. For instance, by clicking *Polls* from the Content section, you can create a poll question that is only available for that specific site template. Assets created within your template's Content section can only be accessed by sites using the template.

Lastly, the Configuration section includes Application Display Template and Mobile Device configuration options for your site template. Also, nested in the Configuration section is the *Site Template Settings*. This option allows you to edit the template's name and description while also offering boolean options for activating your site template and allowing site administrators to modify pages associated with your template.

The following figure displays the form shown when editing the *Community Site* template's settings:

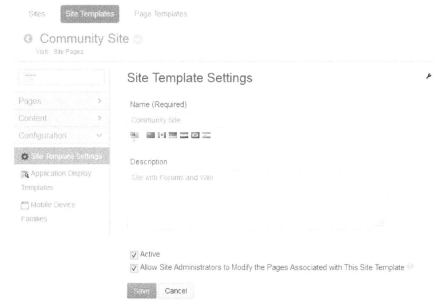

Figure 3.11: Site templates have several configurable options including the option to allow site administrators to modify pages accociated with the site template.

By default, the following site templates are provided:

- **Community Site:** Provides a preconfigured site for building online communities. The Home page of a *community site* provides message boards, search, a display of a poll and statistics of the activity of community members. The site will also be created with a page for a community calendar and a page for a wiki.

- **Intranet Site:** Provides a preconfigured site for an intranet. The Home page displays the activities of the members of the site, search, a language chooser and a list of the recent content created in the intranet. It also provides 3 additional pages for *Documents and Media, Calendar* and external *News* obtained through public feeds.

Now that you know the basics for creating and managing your site templates, let's put your knowledge to the test by completing an example.

Site Templates Example

Suppose we need to create the following three sites for the Lunar Resort's internal use: Engineering, Marketing, and Legal. These should be private sites that are only accessible to members of these respective departments. We could design each site separately but can save ourselves some work if we create a site template to use instead.

To create a site template, navigate to the Control Panel and click *Site Templates*. Then click *Add* and enter a name for your template: we'll use *Department* for our example. Leave the *Active* and *Allow Site Administrators to Modify the Pages Associated with This Site Template* boxes checked. The *Active* box must be checked for your template to be usable. If your template is still a work in progress, you can uncheck it to ensure that no one uses it until it's ready. Checking *Allow Site Administrators to Modify the Pages Associated with This Site Template* allows site administrators to modify or remove the pages and portlets that the template introduces to their sites—if you want the templates to be completely static, you should uncheck this. Click *Save* to create your site template.

From the left menu, select the *Pages* section and click *Site Pages*. Then click on the *View Pages* button to begin adding pages and portlets and configuring the layouts. When you click this button, the site template opens in a new browser tab or window. For our example, we would like our site template to include four pages. First, we'd like a Home page with the Activities, Announcements, and Calendar portlets. Next, we'd like a Documents and Media page with the Documents and Media portlet. Finally, we should create a Wiki page with the Wiki and Tag Cloud portlets and a Message Boards page with the Message Boards and Tag Cloud portlets. When you're done creating and configuring the pages of your site template, just close the browser tab or window that opened when you clicked *View Pages*. Changes to site templates are automatically saved as you make them, so you don't need to return to the Site Templates page of the Control Panel and select *Save*.

Figure 3.12: You can see the name of the site template you're currently editing.

Next, let's use our site template to create our Engineering, Marketing and Legal sites. Go to the Control Panel and click on *Sites*. Then click *Add → Department*. Enter *Engineering* for the site name and set the Membership Type to *Private*. Recall that private sites don't appear in the My Sites portlet so that regular portal users won't even know that the Engineering site exists. Also, the only way users can be added to a private site is via an invitation from a site administrator. Leave the *Active* box checked so that your site can be used immediately. Select the *Copy as Private Pages* option since our Engineering site is intended for internal use only. Leave the *Enable propagation of changes from the site template* box checked so that the Engineering site receives updates if the Department site template is modified. Finally, click *Save* to create your Engineering site.

Repeat these steps to create the Marketing and Legal sites. The new sites have all the pages and portlets you created in the site template. To view the pages of the new sites, click on *Sites* in the Control Panel and then click on *Actions →Go to Private Pages* next to one of your new sites. Using site templates streamlines the site creation process for administrators, making it easy to create sites quickly. Now each department of the Lunar Resort has its own calendar, documents and media library, wiki, and message boards application. Although the pages and portlets of each department's site are the same, each site will quickly be filled with department-specific information as users add and share content within the sites. Also, site administrators can add new pages, portlets, and content to their sites, further differentiating each department's site from the others.

Propagating Changes from Site Templates to Sites

It's possible for site template administrators to add, update, or delete site template pages. Changes made to a site template can be propagated to sites whose page sets are linked to the site template. Such a link is created when you create a site based on a site template and leave the *Enable propagation of changes from the site template* box checked. To disable or re-enable this link for a site, select the site from *My Sites* in the Dockbar. Navigate to *Admin Configuration* to open the *Site Settings* page and uncheck or recheck the *Enable propagation of changes from the site template* checkbox. In this section, we explain the propagation of changes from site templates to sites and discuss the options available to site administrators and site template administrators.

If a site's page set has been created from a site template and the propagation of changes from the site template is enabled, site administrators can add new pages but cannot remove or reorder the pages imported from the site template. If a site has both pages imported from a site template and custom site pages, the site template pages always appear first; custom pages added by site administrators appear after the site template pages. Only site template administrators can remove, reorder, or add site template pages. Site administrators can add or remove custom site pages. They can also reorder custom site pages as long as they're all positioned after the site template pages. Site template administrators cannot add, remove, or reorder custom site pages.

If a site administrator changes a page that was imported from a site template and refreshes the page, the following message appears:

```
This page has been changed since the last update from the site template.
No further updates from the site template will be applied. Click *Reset*
to overwrite the changes and receive updates from the site template.
```

If the site administrator clicks the *Reset* button, changes are propagated from the site template page to the corresponding site page that was imported from the site template. Clicking the *Reset* button makes two kinds of updates to a page. First, changes made by site administrators to the site page are undone. Second, changes made by site template administrators to the site template page are applied to the site page. Note: clicking the *Reset* button only resets one page. If multiple site pages have been modified and you'd like to re-apply the site template pages to them, you'll need to click the *Reset* button for each page.

Site template administrators can set preferences for portlets on site template pages. When a portal administrator creates a site from a site template, the portlet preferences are copied from the site template's portlets, overriding any default portlet preferences. When merging site template and site changes, e.g., when resetting, portlet preferences are copied from site template portlets to site portlets. Only global portlet preferences or local portlet preferences which don't refer to IDs are overwritten.

In some cases, merging site template and site changes fails. For example, if pages from a site template cannot be propagated because their friendly URLs are in conflict, the portal could try to continuously merge the site changes. Instead of entering into an infinite loop of merge fails, Liferay stops the merge after several unsuccessful attempts. However, Liferay doesn't stop there: your merge is temporarily paused, you're given an indication of the current merge fail, and then you have the opportunity to fix your merge conflicts. After you've squared away your conflict, navigate to *Site Administration →Configuration →Site Settings* and click the *Reset and Propagate* button.

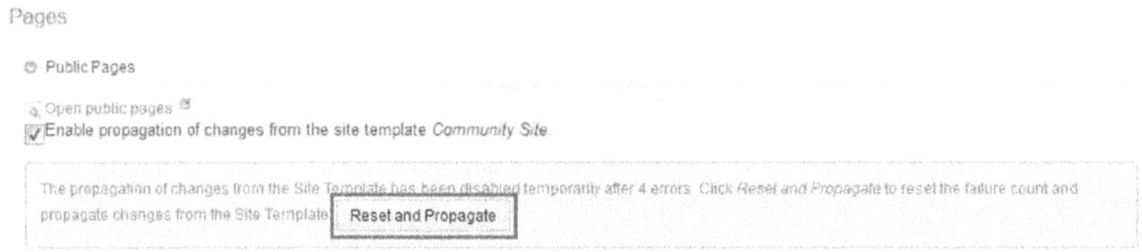

Figure 3.13: You can reset and propagate the merge fail count by navigationg to *Site Settings*.

The *Reset and Propagate* button resets the merge fail count and attempts to propagate your site changes again. This process gives the portal administrator the opportunity to detect and fix a merge fail, when problems arise. This helpful process can also be done with page template merges, which follows similar steps.

Site administrators can also add data to site template portlets. For example, site template administrators can add the Wiki portlet to a site template page and use the Wiki to create lots of articles. When a portal administrator creates a site from a site template, data is copied from the site template's portlets to the site's portlets. The preferences of the site's portlets are updated with the IDs of the copied data. For example, if a site is created from a site template that has a Wiki portlet with lots of wiki articles, the wiki articles are copied from the site template's scope to the site's scope and site's Wiki portlet is updated with the IDs of the copied wiki articles.

Important: Portlet data, related resources, and permissions on resources are only copied from a site template to a site when that site is *first* created based on the template. No changes made in a a template's portlet data, related resources, or permissions are propagated to the site after the site is created. Neither are such changes propagated to a site by *Reset* or *Reset and Propagate* features.

For example, consider a site template administrator who includes a Message Boards portlet as part of a site template. She even creates Message Board categories and configures permissions over the actions of the categories. The first time a site is created based on the site template, the categories (portlet data) and related permissions are copied to the site. If the site template administrator adds, removes, or deletes some categories, however, such changes *aren't* propagated to the site.

Now that we've learned how site templates work, let's discuss how to use page templates.

3.4   Using Page Templates

Click on *Page Templates* in the Control Panel to see a list of page templates. Page templates function similarly to site templates but at the page level. Each page template provides a pre-configured page to reuse. Within a page template, it's possible to select a theme, a layout template, to add portlets to the page and to configure portlet preferences. Both sites and site templates can utilize page templates for creating new pages.

You can edit or delete existing page templates, configure their permissions, or add new page templates. By default, three sample page templates are provided:

Figure 3.14: The Blog page template is already available for use along with the Content Display Page and Wiki page templates.

- **Blog:** provides a page with three applications related to blogging. It has two columns, the main left column contains the blogs portlet and the small right column provides two side portlets, Tag Cloud and Recent Bloggers. The tag cloud application will show the tags used within the site and will allow navigating through the blog entries shown in the main blogs portlet.

- **Content Display Page:** provides a page preconfigured to display content. It has three auxiliary applications (Tags Navigation, Categories Navigation, and Search) and an Asset Publisher. The most significant aspect of this page is that the Asset Publisher is preconfigured to be display any web content associated with this page. This means that you can select any page created from this page template as a *Display Page* for a web content article. You can choose a display page for a web content article when creating a new web content article or when editing an existing one. When you create a new web content article, a unique (canonical) URL for the web content pointing to this page will be assigned to it.

- **Wiki:** provides a page with three applications related to authoring a wiki. It also has two columns, the main left column with the wiki application and two right side portlets to allow navigating through pages by tags and categories.

To add a new page template, click the *Add* button. Then enter a name and description for your template. Leave the *Active* button checked. Click *Save* and then identify your page template in the list. Click its name or use the Actions button to edit the page template. The *Open Page Template* link opens a new browser window which you can use to configure your new page. Any changes you make are automatically saved so you can close the new browser window once you're done.

Note that after a new page template has been created the default permissions are to only allow the creator to use the page template. To give other users access to it, use the actions menu in the list of templates and choose *Permissions*. Once you see the matrix of roles and permissions, check the *View* permission for the role or roles needed to see the page template in the list of available page templates when creating a new page. If you want any user who can create a page to be able to use the page template, just check the *View* permission for the *User* role.

To use your template to create a new page, just navigate to a page over which you have site administrator privileges and select *Add Page* from the left menu. You'll be able to select a page template and type a name for the new page. Alternatively, you can use the Site Administration page. First, make sure you're on your desired site and navigate to *Admin →Site Administration*. Then click on *Site Pages →Add Page*, type a name, select your template from the drop down menu, and click *Add Page* to finish.

Note that by default, when a site administrator creates pages based on a page template, any future changes to the template are automatically propagated to those pages. Site administrators can disable this behavior by unchecking the *Automatically apply changes done to the page template* box. Occasionally, propagation for page templates fails due to unintended errors. To learn how to manage a failed page template propagation, visit the *Propagating Changes from Site Templates to Sites* section of this chapter.

If staging has been enabled, changes to the page template are automatically propagated to the staged page. These changes still need to be approved before the page is published to live. For this reason, the automatic propagation of page template changes to the staged page cannot be turned off and the *Automatically apply changes done to the page template* checkbox does not appear.

We'll discuss staging in more detail later in this chapter. For now let's look at importing and exporting templates.

Exporting and Importing Site Templates and Page Templates

If you want to export a site that uses site or page templates to a different environment (through a LAR file or remote publication), the templates must be exported and imported manually in advance or the import will fail.

To export a Site using a Site Template, use the following process:

1. Go to *Control Panel →Site Templates* and click *Actions →Manage* for the Site Template your site is using.
2. Click *Export* to obtain a LAR file with the content of the Site Template. Be sure to choose the applications and data you want exported.
3. In your target environment, go to *Control Panel →Site Templates* and create a new Site Template.
4. Click *Actions →Manage Pages* for that Site Template and then click *Import*.
5. Upload the LAR file containing your site template's content.

Now the site can be exported and imported normally to this new environment. For page templates, the process very similar:

1. Go to *Control Panel →Page Templates*.
2. Next to the page template you would like to export, click *Actions →Export*. This produces a LAR file you can import later.
3. On the target environment, go to *Control Panel →Page Templates* and create a new Page Template.
4. Next to the new template, click *Actions →Import*.

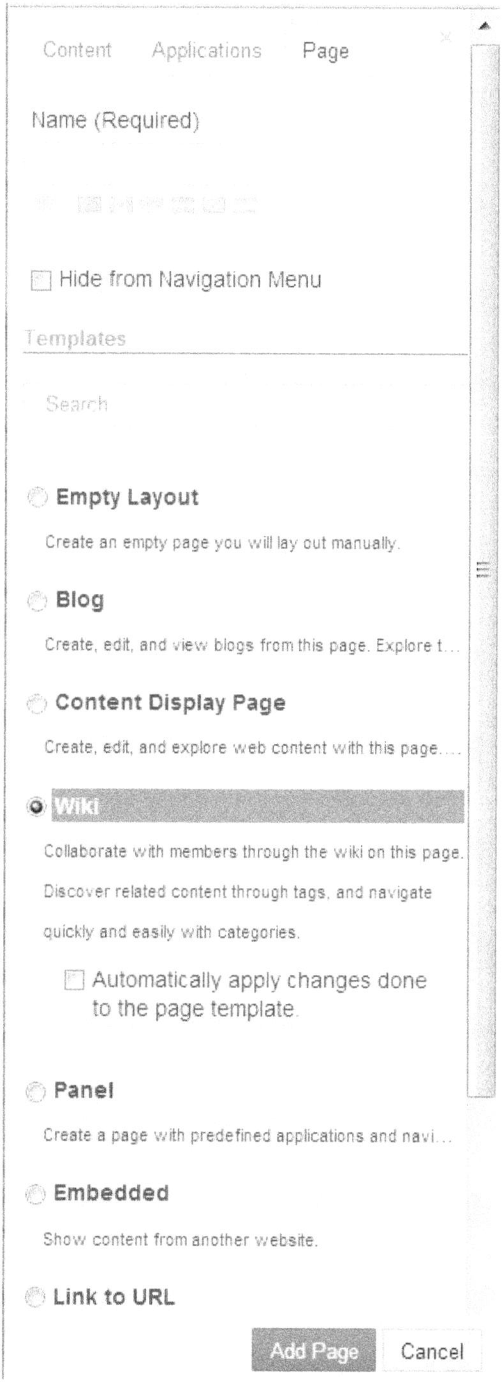

Figure 3.15: When creating a new site page, you're given options for the page template and page type.

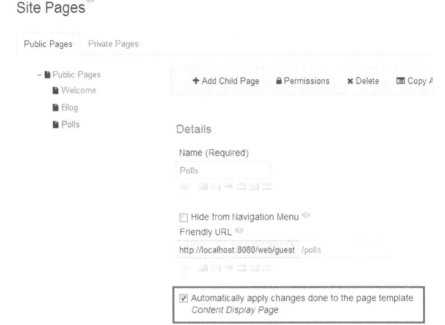

Figure 3.16: You can choose whether or not to automatically apply page template changes to live pages.

5. Upload the LAR file containing the exported page template from step 3.

The page template can now be imported normally to this new environment. Next, let's examine the tools Liferay provides for handling translations.

3.5   Localization

When you create a new piece of Web Content, you have the ability to choose a default language. If you click *Change*, you can select your default language from a large number of languages Liferay supports. Before you can create a translation, you must finish creating the content in your default language and save it. Once you've done that, editing the content provides you with the option to *Add Translation*.

After you click *Add Translation*, you can select a language by scrolling through the list or by entering the language you want to use in the search box. When you select a language, a new window opens within your browser enabling you to translate the original web content into the selected language. Once you are done with the translation, click *Save* and the translation is added to the list of *Available Translations*.

You can modify the language translation list by inserting `locales.enabled=` followed by your preferred languages in your `portal-ext.properties` file. For example, `locales.enabled=ar_SA,nl_NL,hi_IN` offers *Arabic (Saudi Arabia)*, *Dutch (Netherlands)*, and *Hindi (India)*.

The ability to completely delete a translation in one step has also been added. Instead of simply disabling a translation or having to go through a multistep process to remove it, you can now simply open the translation you don't want and click *Remove Translation*.

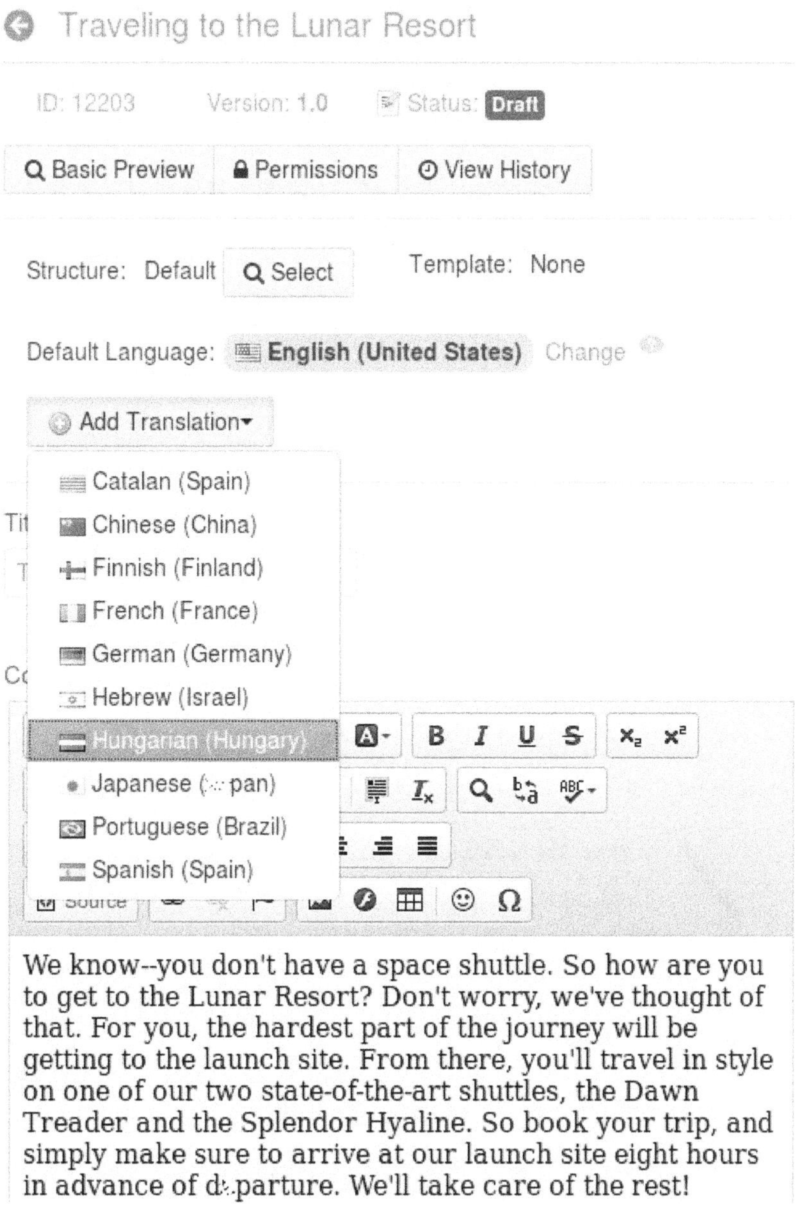

Figure 3.17: You have many translation languages to choose from for your web content.

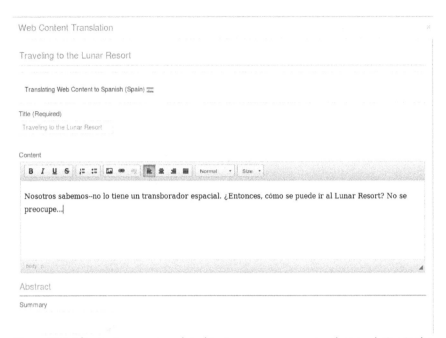

Figure 3.18: After typing your translated text, you can summarize the translation in the *Abstract* section.

When you create a new web content structure, each field you create has a *Localizable* checkbox displayed next to it. This enables you to control what can and can't be changed in the translation process. For example, if you don't want images or content titles to be changed when the content is translated, you can make sure those fields aren't listed as localizable. When you follow the steps above to localize content, only fields within the structure that had the *Localizable* box checked appear within the translation window.

Note: The Localizable checkbox was removed for 6.2 CE GA1 and GA2, and 6.2 EE GA1, SP1, and SP2. However, the Localizable checkbox is now available for Liferay following these versions for web content structure fields. You can view LPS-33161 for more details.

Next, we'll discuss how to let users customize their site pages.

3.6 Allowing Users to Customize Site Pages

As we discussed before, as your site becomes larger and more complex, management of the content becomes more challenging. We've gone over Liferay management tools that help you create content quickly and in an orderly fashion. You created a simple announcement with Liferay's structure editor that allows you to quickly design a structure and prepare it for the template designers. Then you applied a template to the structure. You know how to display content using the Web Content Display portlet. Now, you're ready to take advantage of Liferay's advanced publishing options.

If a web site isn't properly managed, it can quickly become stale and that drives viewers away. If people are finding your site because of search engines, you don't want them presented with outdated (and possibly inaccurate) web content. You also want your content to be found easily by your users. This is done through tags and categories.

Additionally, you may want to create content and send it through an approval and review process weeks before you want it displayed on the web site. Liferay gives you this flexibility with the *Schedule* and *Workflow* features.

3.7 Scheduling Web Content

Liferay's WCM lets you define when your content goes live. You can determine when the content is displayed, expired and/or reviewed. This is an excellent way to keep your site current and free from outdated (and perhaps incorrect) information. The scheduler is built right into the form your users access to add web content. Specifically, it can be found in the right panel listed with several other configurable settings.

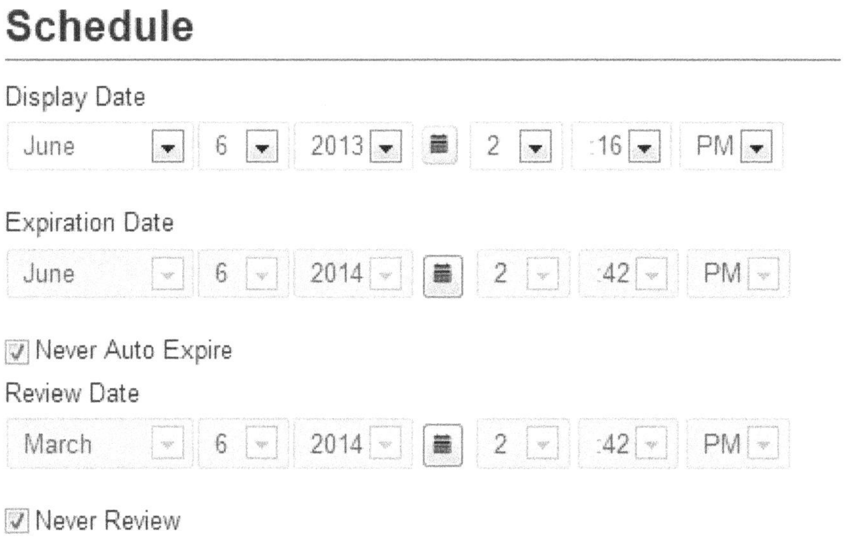

Schedule

Display Date

| June ▼ | 6 ▼ | 2013 ▼ | 🗎 | 2 ▼ | :16 ▼ | PM ▼ |

Expiration Date

| June ▼ | 6 ▼ | 2014 ▼ | 🗎 | 2 ▼ | :42 ▼ | PM ▼ |

☑ Never Auto Expire

Review Date

| March ▼ | 6 ▼ | 2014 ▼ | 🗎 | 2 ▼ | :42 ▼ | PM ▼ |

☑ Never Review

Figure 3.19: The web content scheduler can be easily accessed from the right panel of the page.

Display Date: Sets (within a minute) when content will be displayed.
Expiration Date: Sets a date to expire the content. The default is one year.
Never Auto Expire: Sets your content to never expire.
Review Date: Sets a content review date.
Never Review: Sets the content to never be reviewed.

As you can see, the scheduling feature in Liferay Portal gives you great control in managing when, and for how long, your web content is displayed on your web site. Additionally, you have the ability to determine when your content should be reviewed for accuracy and/or relevance. This makes it possible to manage your growing inventory of content.

Similar to scheduling, Liferay's staging feature also allows you to manipulate time, in a manner of speaking.

3.8   Staging Page Publication

Staging is an important feature of Liferay WCM. The concept of staging is a simple one: you can modify your site behind the scenes and then publish all your updates in one shot. You don't want users seeing your web site change before their eyes as you're modifying it, do you? Liferay's staging environment allows you to make changes to your site in a specialized *staging area*. When you're finished, you can publish all your site changes at once.

Liferay provides site administrators with two different ways to set up staging: Local Live and Remote Live. With Local Live staging, both your staging environment and your live environment are hosted on the same server. When Local Live staging is enabled for a site, a clone of the site is created containing copies of all of the site's existing pages. Portlet data is also copied, depending on which portlets are selected when staging is enabled. The cloned site becomes the staging environment and the original site becomes the live environment.

When Remote Live staging is enabled for a site, a connection is established between the current site and another site on a remote Liferay server. The remote site becomes the live environment and the current site becomes the staging environment—an instance of Liferay Portal used solely for staging. Content creators can use the staging server to make their changes while the live server handles the incoming user traffic. When changes to the site are ready to be published, they are pushed over the network to the remote live server. Whether you enable Local Live or Remote Live staging, the interface for managing and publishing staged pages is the same.

So when should you use Local Live staging and when should you use Remote Live Staging? Local Live staging allows you to publish site changes very quickly, since the staged and live environments are on the same server. It's also easier to switch between the staged and live environments using Local Live staging. However, since the staged content is stored in the same database as the production content, the content isn't as well protected or backed up as with Remote Live staging. Also, you can't install new versions of portlets for testing purposes in a Local Live staging environment since only one version of a portlet can be installed at any given time on a single Liferay server.

With Remote Live staging, your staging and live environments are hosted on separate servers. This allows you to deploy new versions of portlets and content to your staging environment without worrying about interfering with your live environment. With Remote Live staging, you can also use one Liferay instance as the staging server for multiple production servers. However, publishing is slower with Remote Live than with Local Live since data needs to be transferred over a network. And, of course, you need more hardware to run a separate staging server.

Liferay also offers the Page Versioning feature. This feature works with both Local Live and Remote Live staging and allows site administrators to create multiple variations of staged pages. This allows several different versions of sites and pages to be developed at the same time. Variations can be created, merged, and published using a Git-like versioning system. Let's jump in to see how to use staging.

Enabling Local Live Staging

Site administrators can enable Staging for a site via the Site Settings UI. To reach this interface, navigate to the *Site Administration →Configuration* page of your site, make sure *Site Settings* is highlighted in the left menu, and click on *Staging* listed under the Advanced tab. Under Staging Type, select either *Local Live* or *Remote Live* and additional options appear. Staging allows changes to be made in a staging environment so that work can be reviewed, possibly using a workflow, before it's published to a live site. Enabling Local Live staging is easy. Just select *Local Live* and decide whether you'd like to enable page versioning. You can enable page versioning on a site's public pages, private pages, both, or neither. Page versioning allows you to work in parallel on different versions of pages and maintains a history of all page modifications. We discuss page versioning in more detail below.

Enabling Remote Live Staging

When you enable Remote Live staging, the remote site becomes the live environment and the current site becomes the staging environment. The remote (live) Liferay server and the local (staging) Liferay server should be completely separate systems. They should not, for example, share the same the database. When Remote Live staging is enabled, all the necessary information is transferred over the network connecting the two servers.

Before a site administrator can enable Remote Live staging for a site, the remote Liferay server must be added to the current Liferay server's list of allowed servers. The current Liferay server must also be added to the remote Liferay server's list of allowed servers. You also need to specify an authentication key to be shared by your current and your remote server and enable each Liferay server's tunneling servlet authentication verifier. You can make all of these configurations in your Liferay servers' portal-ext.properties files. Your first step should be to add the following lines to your current Liferay server's portal-ext.properties file:

```
tunnel.servlet.hosts.allowed=127.0.0.1,SERVER_IP,[Remote server IP address]
axis.servlet.hosts.allowed=127.0.0.1,SERVER_IP,192.168.0.16,[Remote server IP address]
tunneling.servlet.shared.secret=[secret]
auth.verifier.TunnelingServletAuthVerifier.hosts.allowed=
```

Then add the following lines to your remote Liferay server's portal-ext.properties file:

```
tunnel.servlet.hosts.allowed=127.0.0.1,SERVER_IP,[Local server IP address]
axis.servlet.hosts.allowed=127.0.0.1,SERVER_IP,192.168.0.16,[Local server IP address]
tunneling.servlet.shared.secret=[secret]
auth.verifier.TunnelingServletAuthVerifier.hosts.allowed=
```

Liferay's use of a pre-shared key between your staging and production environments helps secure the remote publication process. It also removes the need to send the publishing user's password to the remote server for web service authentication. Using a pre-shared key allows Liferay to create an authorization context (permission checker) from the provided email address, screen name, or user ID *without* the user's password. You can specify any value for the tunneling.servlet.shared.secret property; the value for your current server just has to match the value of your remote server. Remember to restart both Liferay servers after making these portal properties updates. After restarting, log back in to your local Liferay portal instance as a site administrator. Then navigate to the *Site Administration* →*Configuration* page for your site. Next, click on *Site Settings* in the left menu and then on *Staging* listed under the Advanced tab. Select *Remote Live* under Staging Type and additional options appear.

First, enter your remote Liferay server's IP address into the Remote Host/IP field. If the remote Liferay server is a cluster, you can set the Remote Host/IP to the load balanced IP address of the cluster in order to increase the availability of the publishing process. Next, enter the port on which the remote Liferay instance is running into the Remote Port field. You only need to enter a Remote Path Context if a non-root portal servlet context is being used on the remote Liferay server. Finally, enter the site ID of the site on the remote Liferay server that will be used for the Live environment. If a site hasn't already been prepared for you on the remote Liferay server, you can log in to the remote Liferay server and create a new blank site. After the site has been created, note the site ID so you can enter it into the Remote Site ID field on your local Liferay server. You can find any site's ID by selecting *Actions* →*Edit* next to the site's name on the Sites page of the Control Panel. Finally, it's best to check the *Use a Secure Network Connection* field to use HTTPS for the publication of pages from your local (staging) Liferay server to your remote (live) Liferay server.

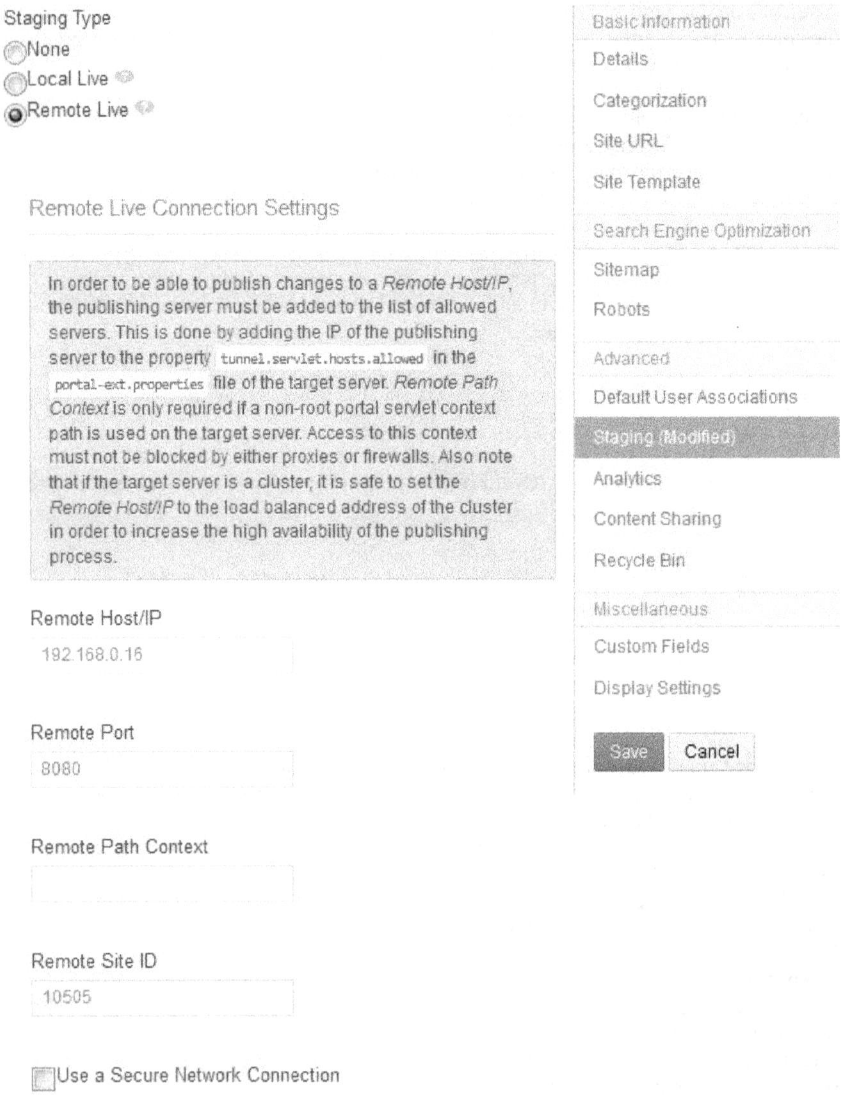

Staging Type

 None

 Local Live

 Remote Live

Basic Information

Details

Categorization

Site URL

Site Template

Search Engine Optimization

Sitemap

Robots

Advanced

Default User Associations

Staging (Modified)

Analytics

Content Sharing

Recycle Bin

Miscellaneous

Custom Fields

Display Settings

Remote Live Connection Settings

In order to be able to publish changes to a *Remote Host/IP*,
the publishing server must be added to the list of allowed
servers. This is done by adding the IP of the publishing
server to the property `tunnel.servlet.hosts.allowed` in the
`portal-ext.properties` file of the target server. *Remote Path
Context* is only required if a non-root portal servlet context
path is used on the target server. Access to this context
must not be blocked by either proxies or firewalls. Also note
that if the target server is a cluster, it is safe to set the
Remote Host/IP to the load balanced address of the cluster
in order to increase the high availability of the publishing
process.

Remote Host/IP

192.168.0.16

Remote Port

8080

Save   Cancel

Remote Path Context

Remote Site ID

10505

Use a Secure Network Connection

Figure 3.20: After your remote Liferay server and local Liferay server have been
configured to communicate with each other, you have to specify a few Remote Live
connection settings.

> **Tip:** In general, remote staging should be enabled for a site as early as possible. It's generally *not* a good idea to add gigabytes of data into Liferay's CMS and then decide to turn on remote staging. There's an existing issue that limits Liferay to less than 2G of data for publishing data to a remote staging server: `http://issues.liferay.com/browse/ LPS-35317`. You can check this issue to see if it's been resolved and to find out which versions of Liferay it affects.

That's all you need to do to enable Remote Live Staging! Note that if you fail to set the tunneling servlet shared secret or the values of these properties on your current and remote servers don't match, you won't be able to enable staging and an error message appears. When a user attempts to publish changes from the local (staging) server to the remote (live) server, Liferay passes the user's email address, screen name, or user ID to the remote server to perform a permission check. In order for a publishing operation to succeed, the operation must be performed by a user that has identical credentials and permissions on both the local (staging) and the remote (live) server. This is true regardless of whether the user attempts to publish the changes immediately or attempts to schedule the publication for later.

If only a few users should have permission to publish changes from staging to production, it's easy enough to create a few user accounts on the remote server that match a selected few on the local server. However, the more user accounts that you have to create, the more tedious this job becomes and the more likely you are to make a mistake. And you not only have to create identical user accounts, you also have to ensure that these users have identical permissions. For this reason, we recommend that you use LDAP to copy selected user accounts from your local (staging) Liferay server to your remote (live) Liferay server. Liferay's Virtual LDAP Server application (EE-only), available on Liferay Marketplace, makes this easy.

Next, you'll learn how to configure your portal to use IPv6 addresses for Remote Live Staging.

Validating IPv6 Addresses If your portal is set up to validate IPv6 addresses, you'll need to configure your Remote Live Connection Settings. Restart your Liferay instance and navigate back to the Staging page. Select the *Remote Live* radio selector and specify the fields for your remote site. The *Remote Host/IP* field should match the host you specified as your `tunnel.servlet.hosts.allowed` property in the `portal-ext.properties` file (e.g., [0:0:0:0:0:0:0:1]). Make sure to include the brackets. Fill in the rest of the information relevant to your site and click *Save*.

To check if the remote site is running on an IPv6 address, add a new portlet to the staged site, and then select *Staging Publish to Remote Live* from the Dockbar. The changes are published to your remote staged site.

Your portal instance now validates the IPv6 address you specified for your remote live site. Great job!

Next, you'll learn how to enable local live staging.

Example: Enabling Local Live Staging

Let's create a Local Live staging environment for the Lunar Resort home page. Before we begin, let's add a new page. Click *Add →Page* from the left side menu in the default site and name the new page *News and Events*. Next, click *News and Events* to view the page. Then add the Alerts and Announcements portlets to the News and Events page.

When you activate staging Local Live staging, Liferay creates a clone of your site. This clone became the staging environment. Because of this, we recommend only activating staging on new, clean sites. Having a few pages and some portlets (like those of the example site we've created) is no big deal. However, if you have already created a large amount of content you might not be able to enable staging on that site. Also, if you intend to use page versioning to track the history of updates to your site, we recommend that you enable it as early as possible, *before* your site has many pages and lots of content. Your site's update history won't be saved until you enable page versioning. Page versioning requires staging (either Local Live or Remote Live) to be enabled.

Now you're ready to activate staging for this site. Go to *Admin   Site Administration →Configuration →Site Settings* and select *Staging* from under the *Advanced* heading. We'll assume you don't have a separate staging server, so select the *Local Live* staging type. If you do have a separate server to use for staging, follow the instructions in the previous section for configuring it and your local server for remote staging. Either way, once you make a selection (either *Local Live* or *Remote Live*), more options become available for page versioning and staged portlets.

Enabling Page Versioning and Staged Portlets

Enabling page versioning for a site allows site administrators to work in parallel on multiple versions of the site's pages. Page versioning also maintains a history of all updates to the site from the time page versioning was enabled. Site administrators can revert to a previous version of the site at any time. This flexibility is very important in cases where a mistake is found and it's important to quickly publish a fix. If you're following the Lunar Resort example, check *Enabled On Public Pages* to enable page versioning for the Lunar Resort site and then click *Save*.

Before you activate staging, you can choose which portlets' data should be copied to staging. We'll cover many of the collaboration portlets listed under the Staged Portlets heading when we come to chapter 8. For now, you just need to be aware that you can enable or disable staging for any of these portlets. Why might you want to enable staging for some portlet types but not others? In the case of collaborative portlets, you probably *don't* want to enable staging since such portlets are designed for user interaction. If their content were staged, you'd have to manually publish your site whenever somebody posted a message on the message boards to make that message appear on the live site. Generally, you'll want web content to be staged because end users aren't creating that kind of content—web content is the stuff you publish to your site. But portlets like the Message Boards or Wiki would likely benefit from *not* being staged. Notice which portlets are marked for staging by default: if you enable staging and accept the defaults, staging is *not* enabled for the collaborative portlets.

Using the Staging Environment

After enabling staging (either Local Live or Remote Live) for a site, you'll notice a colored bar with some new menus on the Dockbar when you navigate to the site. These new menus help us manage staged pages. You'll also notice that most of your page management options have been removed, because now you can't directly edit live pages. You now must use the staging environment to make changes. Click on the *Staging* button to view the staged area. Your management options are restored and you can access some new options related to staging. If you're following along with the Lunar Resort example, navigate back to the News and Events page and click on *Staging* to get your page editing capabilities back.

Add the Bookmarks portlet and then click on *Live* from the Dockbar. Notice that the Bookmarks portlet isn't there. That's because you've staged a change to the page but haven't published that change yet to the live site. Go back to the staged page and click on the *Staging* drop-down menu to look at the options you have available. From here you have many options to choose from to help in your staging conquest.

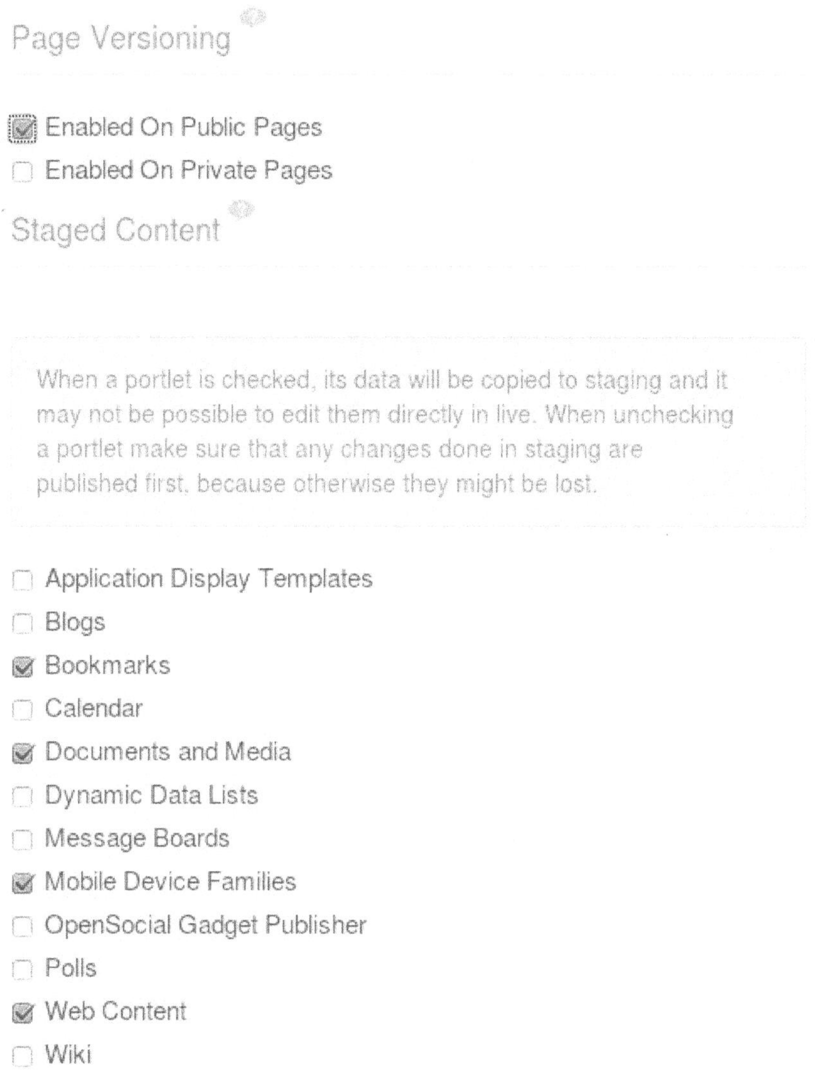

Page Versioning

☑ Enabled On Public Pages

☐ Enabled On Private Pages

Staged Content

When a portlet is checked, its data will be copied to staging and it may not be possible to edit them directly in live. When unchecking a portlet make sure that any changes done in staging are published first, because otherwise they might be lost.

☐ Application Display Templates

☐ Blogs

☑ Bookmarks

☐ Calendar

☑ Documents and Media

☐ Dynamic Data Lists

☐ Message Boards

☑ Mobile Device Families

☐ OpenSocial Gadget Publisher

☐ Polls

☑ Web Content

☐ Wiki

Figure 3.21: You can decide to use versioning and choose what content should be staged.

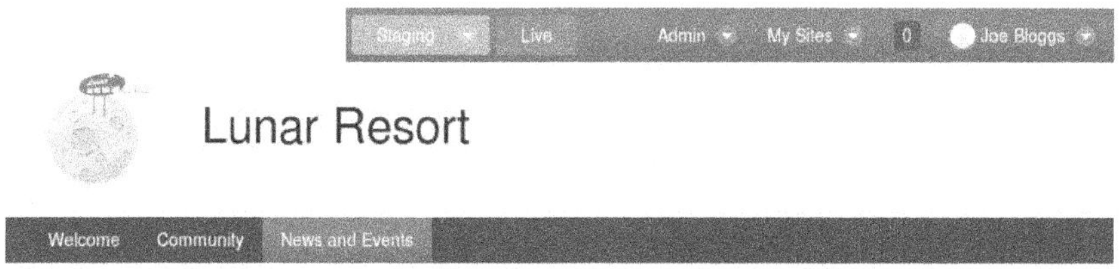

Lunar Resort

Welcome   Community   News and Events

Figure 3.22: You can see the new staging options added to the top of your screen.

Manage Site Pages Variations: allows you to work in parallel on multiple versions of a staged site page. We'll explain this later.

Manage Page Variations: allows you to work in parallel on multiple versions of a staged page. We'll explain this later.

Undo/Redo: allows you to step back/forward through recent changes to a page, which can save you the time of manually adding or removing portlets if you make a mistake.

History: shows you the list of revisions of the page, based on publication dates. You can go to any change in the revision history and see how the pages looked at that point.

Mark as Ready for Publication: After you're done making changes to the staged page, click this button. The status of the page changes from *Draft* to *Ready for Publication* and any changes you've made can be published to the Live Site. When you publish a page to live, only the version which was *Marked as Ready for Publication* is published.

The *Publish to Live* button gives you the option to publish to Live *Now* or *Schedule* a publication to Live.

Now: immediately pushes any changes to the Live Site.

Schedule: lets you set a specific date to publish or to set up recurring publishing. You could use this, for example, to publish all changes made during the week every Monday morning without any further intervention.

The *Publish to Live* button also gives you options to select pages, applications, content, and permissions. Furthermore, you're given the *Current and Previous* and *Scheduled* tabs. The *Current and Previous* tab lets you view past publications along with their authors and create/completion dates. The *Scheduled* tab lets you view what publication processes are scheduled for publishing.

Pages gives you the option to choose which pages to include when you publish. You can see the default settings in the gray text below the header. Click the *Change* button to configure these options to suite your needs.

Application Configuration allows you to select which applications you want to publish. Select the *Choose Applications* radio button to configure the applications and settings to be published.

Content allows you to configure the content to be published. Clicking the *select* option under All Content allows you to delete the portlet metadata before publishing.

Permissions allows you to include permissions for the pages and portlets when the changes are published.

Furthermore, you're given the Current and Previous and Scheduled tabs. The Current and Previous tab lets you view past publications along with their authors and create/completion dates. The Scheduled tab lets you view what publication processes are scheduled for publishing.

Click on *Mark as Ready for Publication*, then click *Publish to Live* →*Now*, and select *Publish* to publish your Bookmarks portlet to the live site.

Content publication can be also controlled using staging. Bookmarks are staged by default (this can be changed in Staging Configuration). If you create a bookmark in the staged site, it isn't visible in the live site until you publish it to the live site following the same steps you just performed (you can select which types of content are published when you publish to the live site). If workflow is enabled for any new resource, the resource needs to go through the workflow process before it can be published to the live site.

Figure 3.23: Ready to publish to the live site.

Web content tends to be frequently updated, often more so than other kinds of content. For some web content articles, this can result in very high numbers of versions, sometimes hundreds. Such high version numbers can make it very slow to publish web content articles. Liferay addresses this issue by allowing site administrators to choose whether or not to publish a web content article's version history when a staged article is ready to be published. To use this feature, staging must be enabled. Edit a web content article that's being displayed in a Web Content Display portlet on one of your pages and then click *Staging ▸ Publish to Live* from the Dockbar. In the popup, expand the Content heading and find the section for Web Content. You can click the *Change* button to select/deselect options to publish dealing with your new Web Content instance.

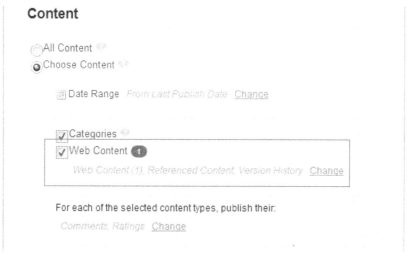

Figure 3.24: Click the *Change* button and uncheck the version history box to only publish the latest approved version of web content articles that have multiple versions.

Liferay 6.2 also added a portal property, `journal.publish.version.history.-by.default`, that sets the default behavior. By default, this property is set to `true` so site administrators have to manually uncheck the *Version History* box mentioned above if they only want to publish the latest approved version of web content articles. If you'd like to change the default behavior, add the following line to your `portal-ext.properties` file:

`journal.publish.version.history.by.default=false`.

One of the most powerful features of staging is page variations. Let's see how to use them to create multiple different variations of your site's pages for different purposes.

Using Site Pages Variations

Let's say you're working on a product-oriented site where you'll have several major changes to a page or a set of pages over a short period of time. Also you need to be working on multiple versions of the site at the same time to ensure everything has been properly reviewed before it goes live. With staging in Liferay 6.2 you can do this using *Page Variations*.

For example, you can create several page variations, enabling the marketing team to give your site a completely different look and feel for Christmas. At the same time, the product management team can work on a different version that will be published the day after Christmas for the launching of a new product. Additionally, the product management team is considering two different ideas for the home page of the site, so they can create several page variations of the home page inside their product launch site.

Variations only affect pages and not the content, which means all the existing content in your staging site is shared by all your variations. In different site page variations you can have different logos, different look and feel for your pages, different applications on these pages, different configuration of these applications and even different pages. One page can exist in just one site page variation or in several of them.

By default, we only have one site page variation which is called *Main Variation*. To create a new one, use the dropdown next to the *Staging* link and click on *Manage Site Pages Variations*. This brings you to a list of the existing site page variations for your site. Click *Add Site Pages Variation* to create a new one. From the *Add Site Pages Variation* screen, you can set a Name, Description, and also set your new variation to copy the content from an existing variation. There are several options to choose in this selector.

All Site Pages Variations: creates a new variation that contains the last version marked as ready for publication from any single page existing in any other variation.

None (Empty Site Pages Variation): creates a new, empty variation.

Main Variation: creates a new site page variation that contains only the last version of all the pages that exist in this variation. The current variation must be marked as ready for publication.

You are also able to rename any variation. For example, edit the Main Variation and change its name to something that makes more sense in your site, such as *Basic*, *Master*, *Regular* and create a variation for Christmas.

You can switch between different variations by clicking on them from the staging menu bar. It's also possible to set permissions on each variation, so certain users have access to manage some, but not all variations.

You can now go to the home page of your Christmas variation and change the logo, apply a new theme, move portlets around, change the order of the pages and configure different portlets. The other variations won't be affected. You can even delete existing pages or add new ones (remember to *Mark as Ready for Publication* when you are finished with your changes).

When you delete a page, it is deleted only in the current variation. The same happens when you add a new page. If you try to access a page which was deleted in the current variation, Liferay informs you this page is not *enabled* in this variation and you must enable it. To enable it, navigate to the *Site Administration →Pages Site Pages* screen. Here all the existing pages for all the variations are shown in a tree. Pages not enabled for the current variation are shown in a lighter color. You can also access Staging options from the Site Pages screen by clicking the *Staging* drop-down menu located above the pages tree.

To publish a variation to the live site, click on *Publish to Live →Publish* in the dropdown next to the variation name. Publications can also be scheduled independently for different variations. For example, you could have a variation called *Mondays* which is published to the live site every Monday and another one called *Day 1* which is published to the live site every first day of each month.

You can also have variations for a single page inside a site page variation, which allows you to work in parallel in different versions of a page. For example, you might work on two different proposals for the design of the home page for the Christmas variation. These page variations only exist inside a site Page variation.

To create a new page variation, click *Manage Page Variations* on the staging toolbar. This brings you to a list of existing page variations for the current page (by default, there is only one called *Main Variation*). You can create more or rename the existing one. You can switch between different page variations using the toolbar containing the page variations below the site pages variations toolbar. When you decide which page variation should be published, mark it as *Ready for Publication*. Only one page variation can be marked as ready for publication and that is the one that gets published to the live site.

For example, we could create a page variation called Thanksgiving for the News and Events page inside of the Christmas variation and another one called Christmas Day to display different content on those particular days.

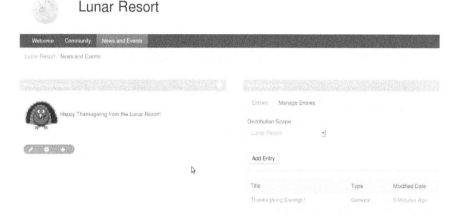

Figure 3.25: This is an example of a Thanksgiving Page Variation.

Another powerful feature is the possibility of *merging* Site Pages Variations. To merge two Site Pages Variations, you need to go to the Manage Site Pages Variations screen. From there, click on *Merge* on the Site Pages Variation you want to use as the base. You will be asked to choose the Site Pages Variation to merge on top of it. Merging works in the following way:

- New pages that don't exist in the base Variation, will be added.
- If a page exists in both Site Pages variations, and at least one version of the page was marked as ready for publication, then the latest version marked as ready will be added as a new Page Variation in the target page of the base Variation. (Note that older versions or page variations not marked as ready for publication won't be copied. However, merge can be executed as many times as needed and will create the needed pages variations in the appropriate page of the base Site Pages Variation).
- Merging does not affect content nor will overwrite anything in the base Variation, it will just add more versions, pages and page variations as needed.

Let's finish our discussion of staging by outlining a few more features.

Wrapping up Staging

You can enable staging on an individual site basis, depending on your needs. This makes it easy to put strict controls in place for your public web site, while opening things up for individual sites that don't need such strict controls. Liferay's staging environment is extremely easy to use and makes maintaining a content-rich web site a snap.

Let's examine teams next.

3.9   Creating Teams for Advanced Site Membership Management

Teams allow site administrators a greater degree of flexibility than was possible using just user groups and roles. They allow site administrators to create various sets of users and permissions for site-specific functions. Teams are the preferred method for collecting permissions within a single site.

If you create a team for one site, the permissions defined for it are not available to any other sites. In contrast, if you assigned a custom role to a user group, the role would be available portal-wide even though the specific permissions defined by it would only apply within the scope of a designated site. Furthermore, team members, unlike user group members, are guaranteed to be members of the desired site.

To create a team within a site, first navigate to the Site Administration page of your site and select *Users →Site Teams*. It's important to note that configuring other site membership groupings, such as *Users*, *Organizations*, and *User Groups* can be found in the *Site Memberships* portlet, which is also located in the Users tab. You can visit the *Management* chapter for more information on how these site memberships. Finally, click the *Add Team* button.

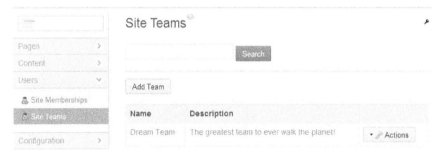

Figure 3.26: Creating teams within your site helps your users demonstrate teamwork and collaboration.

After you've clicked the *Add Team* button and entered a name and a description, click *Save*. Your new team will appear in the list. To add members, simply click on *Actions →Assign Members*.

Permission management for teams is configured by navigating to *Actions →Permissions* for your individual site. Setting permissions for the team assigns every member of the team with equal permissions. Only administrators with the ability to edit/manage the team have the ability to manage team permissions.

That's it! Now your team is ready to perform their functions. Next, let's look at how to configure Liferay for mobile devices.

3.10   Displaying Site Pages to Mobile Devices

Mobile device families allow you to configure sets of rules to alter the behavior of the portal based on the device being used to access Liferay. The proportion of mobile device users browsing the web has been steadily increasing, so it's important to be able to handle different kinds of devices appropriately. For instance, you can configure the look and feel of Liferay pages accessed by smartphone or tablet users differently from those accessed by PC users.

Both sites and individual pages can be configured with any number of mobile device families. A family is designed to describe a group of devices. It can contain one or more rules that describe a category of devices, such as all Android devices or all iOS tablets. You can define as many rules in a family as you need to classify all the devices for which you'd like to define actions. Families can be prioritized to determine which one applies to a given page request.

In order to configure mobile device rules, you need a way to find out the characteristics of the device. While some of the characteristics are provided by the device, most are not. For this reason, there are databases that contain information about thousands of devices. These databases make it possible to learn every detail about a device from the device type, which is included in each request sent to the portal. Liferay's Mobile Device Rules can connect to device databases so that you can use their device characteristics in your rules.

Among the plugins available on Liferay Marketplace, you can find the Device Recognition Provider plugin. This plugin provides out of the box integration with WURFL, an open source database licensed with the AGPLv3 license. Commercial licenses are also available. It's also possible to develop plugins that integrate with other device databases. Even if you don't have a device database, you can still set up mobile device rules. They won't, however, be effective until a database is deployed, because the portal won't have enough information about the devices being used to make page requests.

To configure mobile device rules, you must install the Device Recognition Provider plugin. This plugin uses the WURFL database to enable Liferay to detect which mobile device or operating system is being used for any given request. To install the plugin, navigate to the Store section of the Control Panel, located under the Marketplace heading. Click on the *Utility* section and then on *See All*. Search for the appropriate Device Recognition Provider plugin (CE or EE) and click on it. Finally, click on *Free* to acquire the plugin. Once you've acquired the plugin, you need to download and install it. To do so, navigate to the Purchased section of the Control Panel, find your Device Recognition Provider plugin, and click on *Download* and then *Install*.

Installation Note: If your server doesn't have access to the outside Internet, an error appears in your log:

```
SLF4J: Failed to load class "org.slf4j.impl.StaticLoggerBinder"
```

This occurs because WURFL by default downloads device information from the web. You can provide the same information to WURFL manually by downloading the SLF4J distribution from http://www.slf4j.org/download.html, unzipping the resulting file, copying

```
slf4j-log4j12-[version].jar}
```

to the

```
WEB_APP_HOME/wurfl-web/WEB-INF/lib
```

folder, and restarting your Liferay instance. On some application servers, you'll need to add this .jar file to the wurfl-web.war file first (in the directory noted above) before deploying the file to your server.

You can access the Mobile Device Families administrative page from the Configuration section of Site Administration. Make sure you're on the appropriate site before adding mobile device families via Site Administration. You can also add families for all sites by navigating to the Control Panel →*Sites* →*Global*. The Mobile Device Families administrative page displays a list of defined families and lets you add more. To add rules to a family, select *Actions Manage Classification Rules*, or click on a family to edit it, and then click the *Manage Classification Rules* link.

The rules defined for a family, along with the priorities of the families selected for a particular site or page, determine which family's actions are applied to a given request. From the Manage Classification Rules page for a specific rule set, you can add a rule by

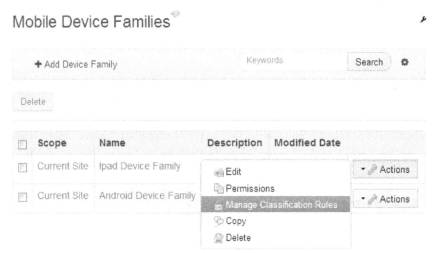

Figure 3.27: You can manage device rules from the Mobile Device Families administrative page.

specifying an operating system, rule type, physical screen size, and screen resolution. Remember that you can add as many rules to a family as you need in order to classify the devices on which you'd like to take actions. You'll notice after saving the classification rule that it's characterized as a *Simple Rule*. By default, only the Simple Rule type is available. The rules are designed to be extensible, and additional rule types can be added by your developers.

Once you've created some mobile device families and added some rules to them, you'll be ready to set up some actions. The actions defined for a family determine what happens to a particular request when the device is detected and the family has been found to apply.

You can add actions to a family from the Site Pages page of Site Administration. Select either the public or private pages and then look for the *Mobile Device Rules* link in the right-hand menu. Use the *Select Device Family* button to select families to be applied either to a site or to a single page. If you select the page group itself from the left-hand menu, the selected family applies to all the pages of the site by default. If, however, you select an individual page and then click the *Select Device Family* button, the families apply only to that page. You can select multiple families for a particular site or page and order them by priority. The families are checked in decreasing order of priority: the actions defined by the first family that applies are executed.

To add actions to a selected rule group, use the *Actions Manage Actions* button and then click *Add Action*. By default, there are four kinds of actions that can be configured for mobile families: layout template modifications, theme modifications, URL redirects, and site redirects. Layout template modifications let you change the way portlets are arranged on pages delivered to mobile devices, and themes modifications let you select a specific look and feel. If it makes more sense for you to create separate mobile versions of certain sites or pages, you can use a redirect to make sure mobile device users get to the right page. To define a URL redirect, you need to specify a URL. To define a site redirect, you need only specify the site name and page name of the page to which you're redirecting. Like mobile device rules, mobile device actions are designed to be extensible. Your developers can define custom actions in addition to the four actions provided by default.

To review, if you'd like to configure an action or actions that take place when mobile device requests are received, take the following steps:

Figure 3.28: You need to install the Device Recognition Provider plugin to populate the OS list.

1. Create a mobile device family to represent the group of devices for which to define an action or actions.

2. Define one or more rules for your family that describe the group of devices represented by your family.

3. Apply your family to an entire page set of a site (all the public pages of a site or all the private pages) or to a single page.

4. Define one or more actions for your family that describe how requests should be handled.

To see how this might work in practice, let's discuss a few examples of how you can use mobile device rules. First, suppose you have a separate version of a site on your portal that's specifically designed for mobile phones running Android or Bada. For our example, we'll make a site called Android/Bada Liferay and we'll configure the default Liferay site to redirect incoming requests from Android or Bada mobile phones to the Android/Bada

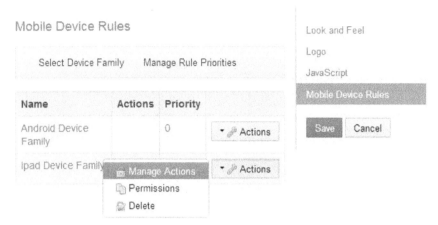

Figure 3.29: You can select a mobile device family to apply for a site or page from the
Site Pages section of Site Administration.

Liferay site. Our first step is to create the Android/Bada Liferay site: go to the Sites page
of the Control Panel and click *Add →Blank Site*. Enter the name *Android/Bada Liferay* and
click *Save*. Then, with Android/Bada selected in the context menu selector, click on *Site
Pages*. By default, the newly created site doesn't have any pages, so click on *Add Page*, enter
the name *Welcome*, and click the *Add Page* button. Now our Android/Bada Liferay site has
a public Welcome page just like our default Liferay site.

Next, select *Liferay* in the *My Sites* tab of the Dockbar, navigate to Site Administration
→Configuration, and click on *Mobile Device Families*. Click on *Add Device Family*, enter the
name *Android and Bada Mobile Phones*, and click *Save*. You'll see the message, *No rules are
configured for this rule group*.

Click the *Manage Classification Rules* link and we'll configure our rule group to apply only
to mobile phones running Android or Bada. Click *Add Classification Rule*, enter *Rule 1* for the
name. Under Operating System, select *Android* and *Bada OS* (hold down Control to make
multiple selections), select *Other Devices* under Tablet since we want our family to apply
only to mobile phones, and click *Save*. Now we just need to define the redirect action for
our family. Navigate to *Pages →Site Pages* and click on *Mobile Device Rules* in the navigation
menu to the right.

Click *Select Device Family* and then click the *Android and Bada Mobile Phones* device family
that you configured. Once you've selected your device family, click on your device family
or *Actions →Manage Actions* next to it. Then click *Add Action*, enter the name *Android/Bada
Liferay Redirect*, and select *Redirect to Site* under Type. Under the Site dropdown menu that
appears, select *Android/Bada Liferay* and under the Page dropdown menu that appears, select the *Welcome* page that you created earlier. Lastly, click *Save*. That's it! Now Android
and Bada mobile phone users are redirected to the Android/Bada Liferay site from the
Liferay site.

Let's look at one more example of using mobile device rules before we move on. Suppose you'd like to create another rule so that when a site is accessed by an Android or iOS
tablet, a different layout is used. To set this up, we need to follow the same four steps described above. First, make sure you're on the Liferay site by checking in the My Sites tab
of the Dockbar. Then navigate to the Mobile Device Families page of Site Administration.
Add a new device family called *Android and iOS Tablets*. Add a classification rule called *Rule
1*, select *Android and iPhone OS* under the *Operating System heading*, select *Tablets* under the
Device Type heading, then click *Save*. As with the previous example, we only need one rule

Figure 3.30: To apply a mobile device family to a page set of a site, click on *Mobile Device Rules*, click *Select Device Family*, and select the desired rule group.

to describe our device family.

Next, click on *Site Pages* in Site Administration, select *Mobile Device Rules*, and select the *Android and iOS Tablets* device family. Notice that you've now selected two rule groups for the Liferay site's public pages and they've been assigned priorities. If a device making a request belongs to both of the device families represented by the rule groups, the priority of the rule groups determines which rule group's actions are executed. Note that in our example, the first rule group contains only mobile phones and the second rule group contains only tablets, so no devices can belong to both rule groups. Now we just need to define an action for our Android and iOS Tablets rule group to use a different layout: On the Site Pages page of Site Administration, click on *Mobile Device Rules*, and then on *Actions* →*Manage Actions* next to Android and iOS Tablets. Click on *Add Action*, enter the name *Layout Template Modification*, and select the *Layout Template Modification* action type. Lastly, select the *1 Column* layout template (or whichever one you like) and click *Save*. Good job! Now the Liferay site's pages are presented to Android and iOS tablet users with the 1 Column layout template.

3.11 Liferay Monitoring using Google Analytics

Liferay includes built-in support for Google Analytics, allowing administrators to make use of Google's tool set for analyzing site traffic data. When you sign up for Google Analytics, a snippet of code is provided which needs to be added to your web pages to allow Google's system to register the page hit. It can be a tedious process to add this code to every page on a site, especially if it's a large site and there is a lot of user-generated content.

This problem can be solved in Liferay by putting Google's code into a custom theme written specifically for the web site on which the portal is running. Doing this, however, requires a theme developer to make specific changes to the theme and it prevents users from using the many themes that are freely available for Liferay "out of the box."

Because of this, support for Google Analytics has been built into Liferay, and can be turned on through a simple user interface. This allows Liferay administrators to make use of Google Analytics on a site by site basis and turn it on and off when needed. You can sign up for Google Analytics at the Google Analytics site here: http://www.google.com/analytics.

To enable Google Analytics support, navigate to *Site Administration* in the Control Panel, expand the *Configuration* area in menu at the left side of the screen, then click on *Site Settings*. Click on *Analytics* and you'll see a very simple form, pictured below.

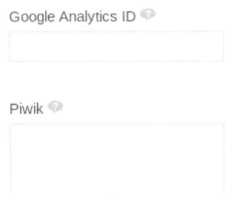

Figure 3.31: Setting up Google Analytics for your site is very easy: sign up for Google Analytics, receive an ID, and then enter it into the Google Analytics ID field.

Enter your Google Analytics ID (which should have been provided to you when you signed up for the service) in the field and click *Save*. All the pages in the site you selected will now have the Google Analytics code in them and will be tracked.

This is a fairly simple procedure, and it gives you the ability to take advantage of some great tools to help you visualize who's coming to your site and from where.

3.12 Summary

This chapter has been your guide to advanced Liferay site management and web content management. We've seen how you can use Liferay to manage both simple content and advanced content with structures and templates. We've also learned how to use page and site templates to simplify the site creation process.

Liferay WCM also includes a powerful staging environment, allowing you to stage content locally on the same server or remotely to another server. You can publish your site when you want it, on the schedule you choose. You can even create different variations of your site that can be worked on simultaneously.

Site administrators can allow users to create personal customizations of site pages. We discussed how site administrators can create teams as a flexible means of delegating site permissions. We also saw how to configure mobile device rules so that site pages are presented differently depending on the device making a page request.

Whether your site is small and static or large and dynamic, Liferay's WCM enables you to plan and manage it. With tools such as the WYSIWYG editor, structures and templates, you can quickly add and edit content. With the Web Content Display and Asset Publisher, you can rapidly select and configure what content to display and how to display it. By using Liferay's integrated workflow, you can set up custom publishing rules to fit your organization. And by using Liferay's staging and scheduling mechanisms, you can manage various branches of pages and content and control when they are published to your live portal instance. You will find that managing your site becomes far easier when using Liferay's Web Content Management system.

## CHAPTER 4

CONFIGURING LIFERAY APPLICATIONS

Just like siblings have common features inherited from their parents, applications that ship with Liferay also share common features. These include look and feel, communication, scoping, sharing, permissions, archive configurations, exporting/importing portlet data, and the Recycle Bin. We'll discuss how these features work together to facilitate information flow within your portal and provide an enhanced experience for your users. So before we get into the nitty gritty of the applications themselves, it's best to cover these common features first, starting with the look and feel configuration options.

4.1 Look and Feel

An administrator can access the look and feel configuration menu of any Liferay portlet by clicking on the gear icon at the top right corner of the portlet and selecting *Look and Feel*. The location of the gear icon may vary, depending on your theme. Liferay portlets' look and feel dialog boxes contain six tabs:

- Portlet Configuration
- Text Styles
- Background Styles
- Border Styles
- Margin and Padding
- Advanced Styling

After making customizations on any tab, remember to click the *Save* button to apply your changes. To see the effect of your changes, you may have to refresh the page. If you don't like the effect of your changes, click the *Reset* button to discard them.

On the Portlet Configuration tab, you can check the *Use Custom Title* box to rename your portlet's title. The value you enter in the Portlet Title box will be displayed at the top of the portlet window on the page. You can also select a language from the Portlet Title drop-down menu. If you've provided a language key translation for the language you select, the your portlet's title will be displayed in the selected language.

If you select a page in the *Link Portlet URLs to Page* drop-down menu, all portlet URLs will point to the page you selected. The current page is the default. Note that you can use the Asset Publisher's View in a Specific Portlet feature and web content articles' Display Page

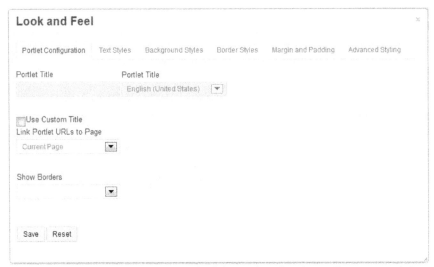

Figure 4.1: The Portlet Configuration tab of the Look and Feel Box allows you to define a custom portlet title, link portlet URLs to a specific page, and select whether or not portlet borders should be displayed.

attribute to achieve a more elegant solution for displaying the full view of web content articles on specific pages. Please see the Display Page section of chapter 5 for details.

 Note: The *Link Portlet URLs to Page* menu is deprecated for Liferay 6.2 and will be removed in Liferay 7.0. The functionality of this menu can also be found in the Asset Publisher.

You can also choose whether or not to display borders around your portlet. By default, borders are displayed. Be careful about turning portlet borders off; some themes assume that portlet borders are turned on and may not display correctly with them turned off.

The Text Styles tab allows you to configure format of the text that appears in the portlet. The fonts you can choose from include Arial, Georgia, Times New Roman, Tahoma, Trebuchet MS, and Verdana. Arial is the default. You can set the text to bold, italics, or both. You can set the font size anywhere from 0.1 em to 12 em, with 0.1 em increments. 1 em is the default. You can set the text color to any six digit hex color code. If you'd like help choosing a color, click on the text box to open the color palette. You can set the text alignment to left, center, right, or justified. (Justified text is both left and right aligned.) You can set an underline, overline, or strikethrough as the text decoration. The default text decoration is none.

You can set the word spacing anywhere from -1 em to 0.95 em, with 0.5 em increments. 0 em is the default. You can set the line height anywhere from 0 em to 12 em, with 0.1 em increments. 0 em is the default. Finally, you can set the letter spacing anywhere from -10 px to 50 px, with 1 px increments. 0 px is the default.

The Background Styles tab allows you to specify the portlet's background color. When you select the text space, you're given a color palette to choose your background color or you can manually enter any six digit hex color code.

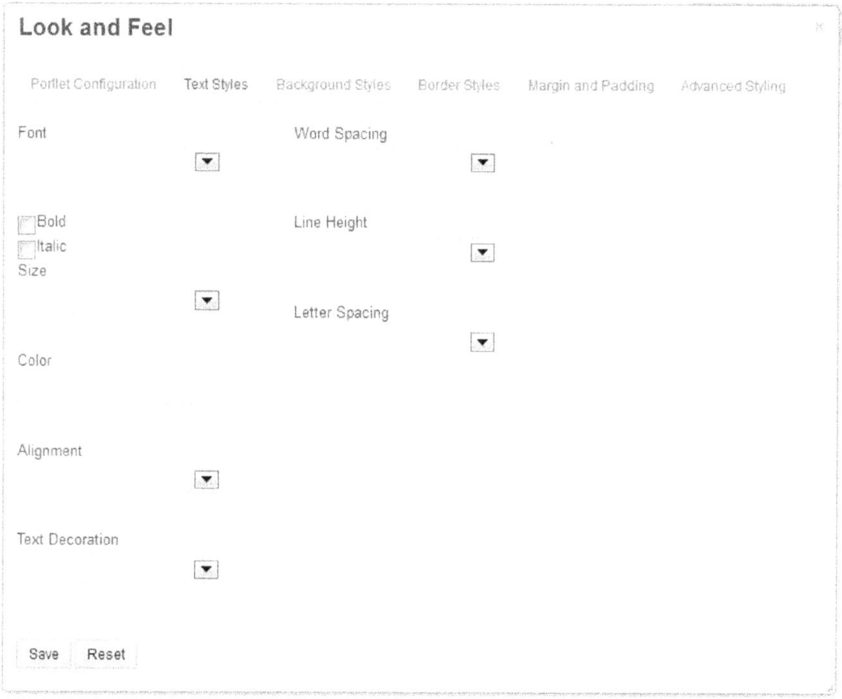

Figure 4.2: The Text Styles tab lets you configure the format of the text that appears in the portlet.

Figure 4.3: The Background Styles tab lets you specify the portlet's background color.

On the Border Styles tab, you can configure your portlet's border width, border style, and border color. For each of these attributes, leave the *Same for All* box checked to apply the same settings to top, right, bottom, and left borders.

Figure 4.4: The Border Styles tab lets you specify a border width, style, and color for each side of the portlet.

For border width, you can specify any % value, em value, or px value. For border style, you can select dashed, double, dotted, groove, hidden, inset, outset, ridge, or solid. For border color, you can enter any six digit hex color code, just like for the text color and background color. You can also use the color palette.

The Margin and Padding tab allows you to specify margin and padding lengths for the edges of your portlet. Just like for border styles, leave the *Same for All* box checked to apply the same settings to each side (top, right, bottom, and left) of the portlet.

For both padding and margin, you can specify any % value, em value, or px value.

The Advanced Styling tab displays current information about your portlet, including your portlet's Liferay ID and CSS classes.

On this tab, you can also enter custom CSS class names for your portlet and custom CSS code. Clicking the *Add a CSS rule for just this portlet* or *Add a CSS rule for all portlets like*

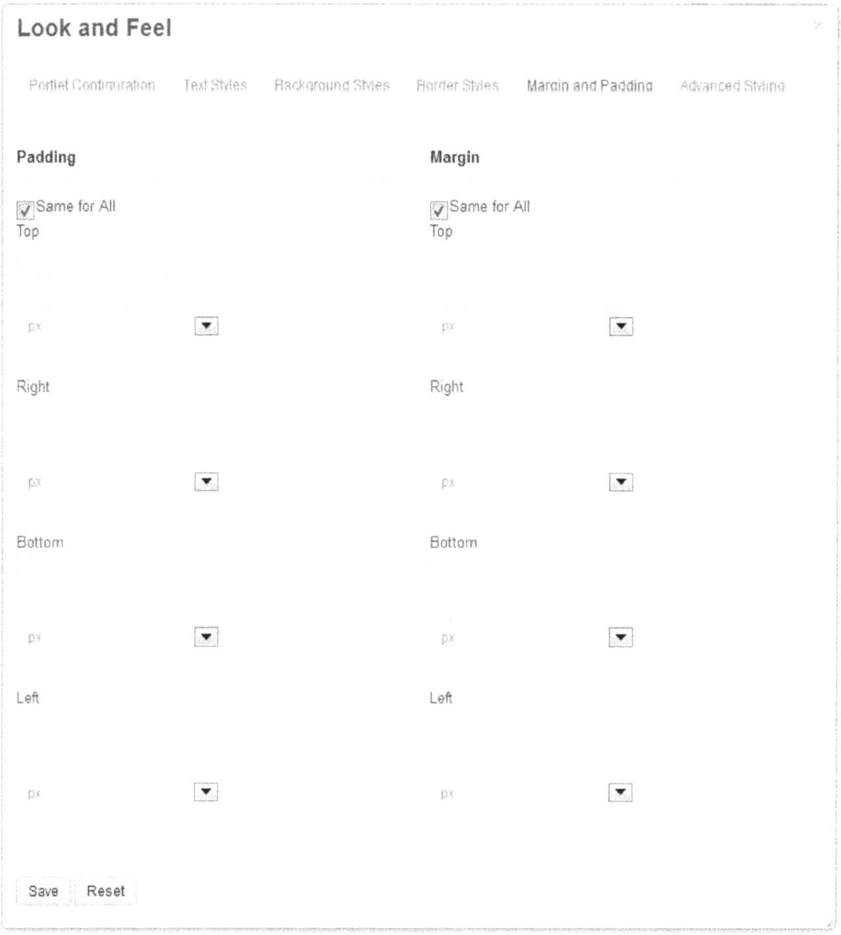

Figure 4.5: The Margin and Padding tab allows you to specify margin and padding lengths for the sides of your portlet.

this one links adds the CSS code shells into your custom CSS text box. If you check the *Update my styles as I type* box, your CSS code will be dynamically applied to your portlet so you can see the effects of your edits.

For Liferay 6.2, the WAP Styling functionality has been deprecated. Liferay Portal uses a new responsive design making WAP Styling configuration unnecessary for your portlet's look and feel. You can enable the WAP functionality for your portal's Look and Feel section by opening/creating your portal-ext.properties file in your ${LIFERAY_HOME} directory and setting mobile.device.styling.wap.enabled=true. WAP functionality will be completely removed from Liferay in the next release.

Next, let's discuss exporting and importing portlet data.

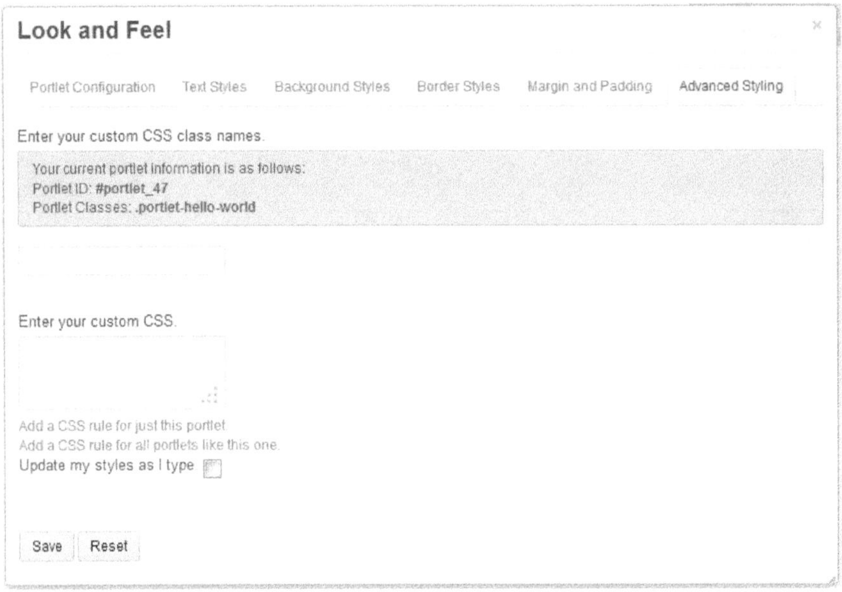

Figure 4.6: The Advanced Styling tab displays your portlet's Liferay ID and allows you to enter CSS code to customize the look and feel of your portlet.

4.2   Export/Import

Some Liferay portlets allow you to export or import portlet data. These include many of Liferay's collaborative applications, such as the Blogs, Wiki, and Message Boards portlets. To export or import portlet data, click on the gear icon of your portlet and select *Export/Import*. Exporting portlet data produces a .lar file that you can save and import into another portlet application of the same type. To import portlet data, you must select a .lar file. Be careful not to confuse portlet-specific .lar files with site-specific .lar files. See the Backing up and Restoring Pages section of chapter 2 for a discussion of exporting and importing data across an entire site. Let's explore the export process first.

First, you can select a *Date Range* of content that you'd like to export. Content that has been added to your portlet within your specified date range is included in the .lar file. You also have options of choosing *All* dates or just the most recently added content, or *Last*.

Next, by checking the *Content* box, you can choose specific content you'd like to export. When you check the *Content* box, more options appear, allowing you to choose specific kinds of metadata to include. For example, if you have a wiki page with referenced content that you don't wish to include, you can simply check the *Wiki Pages* checkbox and uncheck the *Referenced Content* checkbox. Another option in the Content section of the Export/Import window is the selection of content types. Two familiar content types in your portal is *Comments* and *Ratings*. If you wish to include these entities in your .lar file, select *Change* and select them from the checklist.

Lastly, you can choose whether to include permissions for your exported content. The permissions assigned for the exported portlet window will be included if the *Permissions* option is checked. When you check this box, a sub-box called *Permissions Assigned to Roles* appears. If you wish, you can export your portlet's permissions but not the permissions assigned to roles. After you've exported your portlet's data, switch to the *Current and Previous*

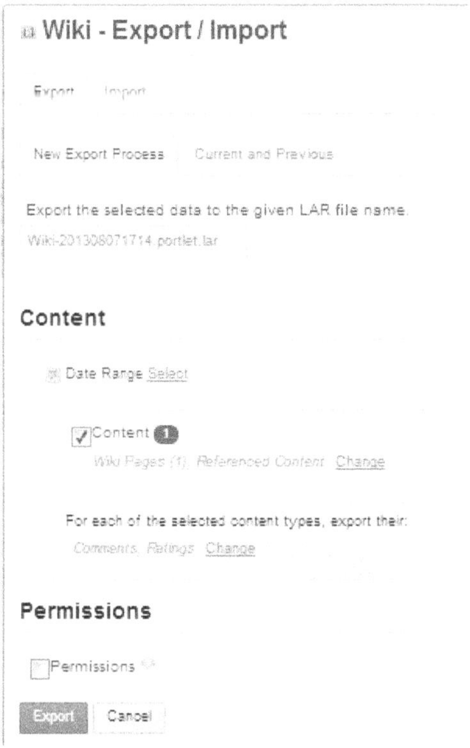

Figure 4.7: When exporting portlet data, you can choose what content to include.

tab to view ongoing export processes and the history of past exports.

To import portlet data, you can select the LAR using your file explorer or by dragging and dropping the file between the dotted lines. After selecting the LAR file, you're given a similar screen to what you'd be offered during export. Select the appropriate content and permissions, and click *Continue*.

The next screen offers options split into two sections: *Update Data* and *Authorship of the Content*. Here's options and descriptions for each section:

Update Data

- *Mirror*: All data and content inside the imported LAR will be created as new the first time while maintaining a reference to the source. Subsequent imports from the same source will update entries instead of creating new entries.
- *Mirror with overwriting*: Same behavior as the mirror strategy, but if a document or an image with the same name is found, it is overwritten.
- *Copy as New*: All data and content inside the imported LAR will be created as new entries within the current site every time the LAR is imported.

Authorship of the Content

- *Use the Original Author*: Keep authorship of imported content whenever possible. Use the current user as author if the original one is not found.
- *Use the Current User as Author*: Assign the current user as the author of all imported content.

Figure 4.8: When importing portlet data, you can choose a LAR file using the file explorer or drag and drop the file between the dotted lines.

Next, let's discuss the concept of a portlet's scope.

4.3 Scope

As we learned earlier, roles can be scoped by the portal, by a site, or by an organization. A role only takes effect within its scope. For example, a Message Boards Administrator role with complete access to the Message Boards portlet has different permissions based on the role's scope. If it's a portal role, members have permission to administer message boards across the entire portal. If it's a site role, members only have permission to administer message boards within the site where they've been assigned the role. For organizations with sites, site roles are automatically assigned to organization members based on the organization roles they have. So for an organization-scoped Message Boards administrator role, members only have permission to administer message boards within the site of the organization that assigned the role to them.

We also use the word *scope* to refer to the data set of a portlet. By default, when a portlet is added to a page in a site, it is *scoped* for that site. This means that its data belongs to that site. If the portlet is added to a page in a different site, it employs a completely different data set. This enables you to place a Message Boards portlet in one site with one set of categories and threads, and place another Message Boards portlet in different site with a different set of categories and threads.

Scoping by site means that you can only have one Message Boards portlet per site. If you add one Message Boards portlet to a page in a site and add another Message Boards portlet to a different page in the same site, the second Message Boards portlet contains exactly the same data as the first. This is because, by default, the Message Boards portlet is scoped by site. Most of Liferay's other portlets also default to being scoped by site.

To avoid this limitation, many Liferay portlets can be scoped by page. In this case, the data sets of page-scoped portlets serve a single page, not an entire site. If you set the scope of a portlet to *page* instead of *site*, you can add any number of these portlets to different pages, and then they have different sets of data. This allows you to have more than one message board per site if you wish. Most portlets, however, default to the "native" configuration, and have their scopes set to the site where they are placed.

Unless otherwise noted, all the portlets in this chapter support scoping by portal (global), site (default), or page. This grants you some flexibility in how you want to set up your portal. You can configure the scope of a portlet with just a few simple steps.

1. Click the *Options* icon in the portlet window (the gear icon).

2. Select *Configuration*.

3. Select the *Scope* tab.

4. Use the drop-down menu to set the scope.

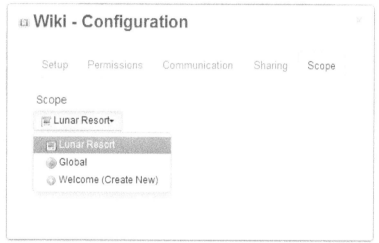

Figure 4.9: You can change the scope of your portlet by navigating to its Configuration menu.

That's all it takes to change the scope for a particular portlet instance. By setting the scope to the current page, you can add as many of these portlets to a site as you want, provided they are all added to separate pages.

Another useful feature of Liferay's portlets is Archived Setups.

4.4 Archived Setups

Once you've configured a portlet, Archived Setups enables you to save those settings in an "archive". If someone goes in and changes the settings of a particular portlet, it then becomes easy to revert those changes back to the original, archived configuration.

To create an archived setup, click the *Configuration* option from the menu in the portlet's title bar. If the current settings of the portlet you're configuring are the ones you want to archive, click the *Archive/Restore Setup* link. If not, change and save the settings until you have the portlet configured the way you want it, and then click the *Archive/Restore Setup* link.

There is only one field to fill out. Enter a name for your archive and click *Save*. You should now see your archive in the list. If you ever need to revert the portlet to these archived settings, you can click *Actions* →*Restore* next to the archived setup you want to restore.

Unless otherwise noted, all of the portlets in this chapter support this feature. This is particularly useful for portlets that have a lot of configuration options, such as the Message Boards portlet.

Next, we'll see how permissions apply to Liferay portlets in general.

4.5 Permissions

All of Liferay's portlets support Liferay's robust, fine-grained permissions system. Some higher level permissions can be configured in the permissions tab of the portlet configuration dialog box. You can grant roles permission to add the portlet to a page, configure the portlet, or view the portlet. To set these permissions, go to the *Configuration* menu and click on *Permissions*. This shows you a table of roles defined in the portal. Use the check boxes to grant certain permissions to different roles. Click *Save* after you've made your selections.

Beyond this, specific permissions are generally defined for specific applications. For example, the message boards portlet contains a *Ban User* permission. This makes no sense in the context of another portlet, say, the blogs portlet. We'll go over permissions for specific applications in the sections for those applications. For now, let's move on to sharing applications.

4.6 Communication

Liferay implements several communication mechanisms across portlets including those specified by the JSR-286 standard: public render parameters and events. Public render parameters are easy to use and can be quite powerful. Some Liferay portlets provide a configuration UI to help you get the most out of this communication mechanism. To access this UI, open your portlet's configuration window by clicking on the gear icon and selecting *Configuration*. Then click on the *Communication* tab.

The screenshot above is for the Wiki portlet, which has six public render parameters: categoryId, nodeId, nodeName, resetCur, tag, title. For each of these parameters, you can configure the portlet to ignore the values coming from other portlets to read the value from another parameter.

Why might it be useful to ignore the values for certain parameters that come from other portlets? Consider a common use case for the Wiki portlet. The Wiki portlet is often used along with the Tags Navigation portlet so that when a user clicks on a tag of the latter, the Wiki portlet shows a list of pages with that tag. In some cases, an administrator may want the Wiki portlet to always show the front page independently of any tag navigation done through other portlets. This can be achieved by checking the *Ignore* checkbox so that the values of the parameter coming from those other portlets are ignored.

Reading the value of a parameter from another portlet is an advanced but very powerful option that allows portlets to communicate with each other even if their developers didn't intend them to. For example, imagine that the Wiki portlet is being used to publish information about certain countries. Imagine further that there's another portlet that allows browsing countries for administrative reasons. The second portlet has a public render parameter called *country* with the name of the country. We'd like the Wiki to show the information from the country that's selected in the administration portlet. This can be achieved by setting the value of the title parameter of the Wiki portlet to be read from the country parameter of the administration portlet. Cool, isn't it?

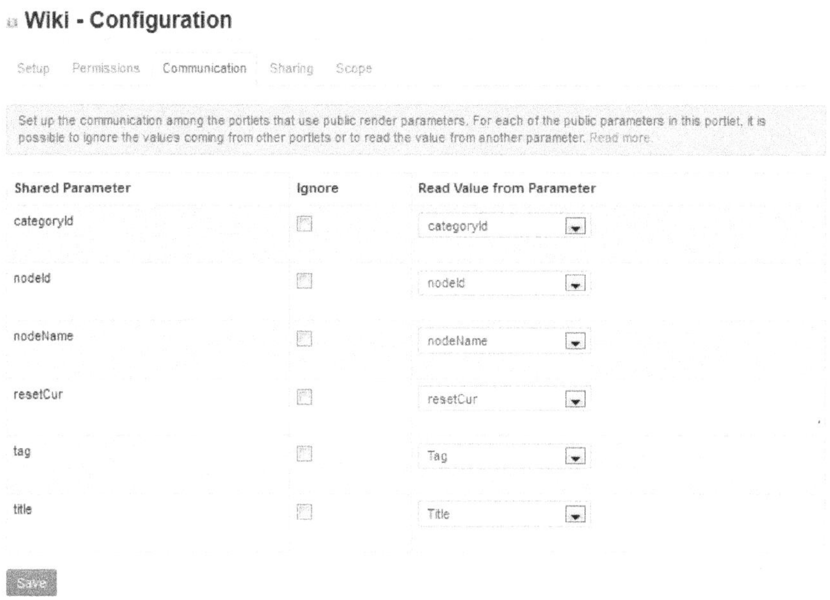

⊕ Wiki - Configuration

Setup   Permissions   Communication   Sharing   Scope

Set up the communication among the portlets that use public render parameters. For each of the public parameters in this portlet, it is possible to ignore the values coming from other portlets or to read the value from another parameter. Read more

Shared Parameter	Ignore	Read Value from Parameter
categoryId	☐	categoryId ▼
nodeId	☐	nodeId ▼
nodeName	☐	nodeName ▼
resetCur	☐	resetCur ▼
tag	☐	Tag ▼
title	☐	Title ▼

Save

Figure 4.10: You can configure portlets to communicate with each other using public render parameters.

4.7 Sharing

The web was once thought of as a number of islands of applications in a vast universe of "cyberspace." Many web sites attempted to make their island the biggest. Some succeeded to a large extent and some failed. More recently, the concept of the web as an application itself has taken hold, and so widgets have become very popular nowadays. This concept is part of the "Web 2.0" concept and is very much enabled by widgets. What is a widget? A widget is a small piece of code which provides a piece of functionality, can be included on any web site, but does not necessarily have to be hosted by that web site. If you have ever embedded a YouTube video on your own web site so that users could watch a video without actually having to visit http://youtube.com, then you've already used a widget.

Liferay supports serving its portlets as widgets. You can embed a particular instance of a portlet running on your site into another site, such as Facebook. This opens up a whole new avenue of exposure to your web site that you would not have had otherwise. In fact, this is how all those Facebook games work.

To share one of your portlets as a widget, open the *Configuration* dialog box from the portlet's title bar and select the *Sharing* tab. There are five sub-tabs under sharing: Any Web Site, Facebook, OpenSocial Gadget, Netvibes, and Friends.

Any Web Site

Copy and paste the provided snippet of JavaScript code into the web site to which you want to add the portlet as a widget. That's all you need to do. When a user loads the page on the other web site, the code will pull the relevant portlet from your site and display it.

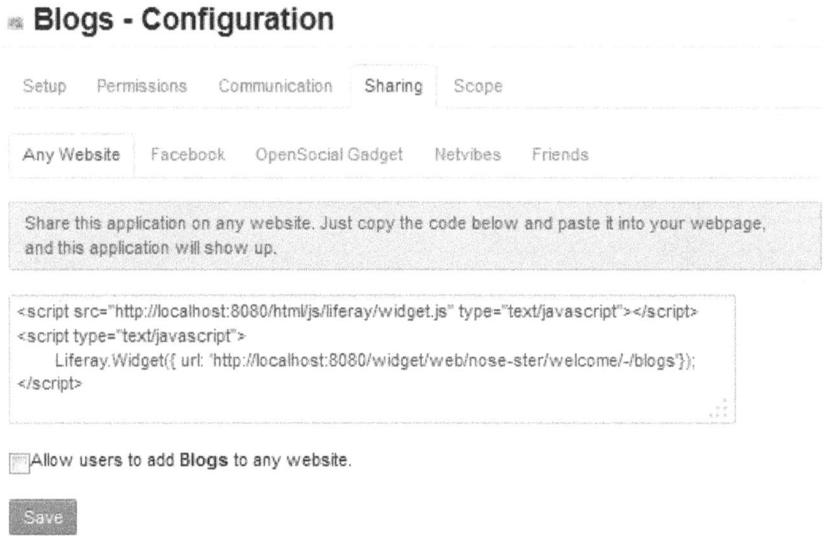

Blogs - Configuration

Setup   Permissions   Communication   Sharing   Scope

Any Website   Facebook   OpenSocial Gadget   Netvibes   Friends

Share this application on any website. Just copy the code below and paste it into your webpage, and this application will show up.

```
<script src="http://localhost:8080/html/js/liferay/widget.js" type="text/javascript"></script>
<script type="text/javascript">
    Liferay.Widget({ url: 'http://localhost:8080/widget/web/nose-ster/welcome/-/blogs'});
</script>
```

Allow users to add **Blogs** to any website.

Save

Figure 4.11: The Sharing tab of the Portlet Configuration Dialog Box allows you to share your portlet in a variety of ways.

Facebook

You can add any Liferay portlet as an application on Facebook. To do this, you must first get a developer key. A link for doing this is provided to you in the Facebook tab. You'll have to create the application on Facebook and get the key and canvas page URL from Facebook. Once you've done this, you can copy and paste their values into the Facebook tab. Your portlet will now be available on Facebook as a Facebook application.

Incidentally, this makes Liferay a fantastic platform upon which to build applications for Facebook. See the *Liferay Developer's Guide* or *Liferay in Action* for more details.

OpenSocial Gadget

OpenSocial comprises a container and a set of APIs for social networking and other web applications. iGoogle is a service provided by Google that lets users create a customizable page and add *Gadgets* to that page. Liferay can serve up portlets to be used as Open Social Gadgets on iGoogle or other OpenSocial-compatible pages.

To serve a Liferay portlet on iGoogle, check the box labeled *Allow users to add [portlet-name] to iGoogle.* Then copy and paste the URL provided into Google's *Add a feed or gadget* feature on the iGoogle configuration page. Your Liferay portal instance will serve that portlet directly onto your iGoogle page. The URL provided is unique to the specific instance of the portlet, so you could serve multiple instances of the same portlet as different Google Gadgets.

You could use this feature to allow users to view what's happening on your portal at a glance, using asset publishers or custom RSS feeds. You could also use Liferay's API to build your own portlet and provide the URL for users to place on their iGoogle pages.

Netvibes

Netvibes offers a similar service to iGoogle—users can log in, create their own personal portal, called a *dashboard,* and add customizable widgets to the dashboard that they cre-

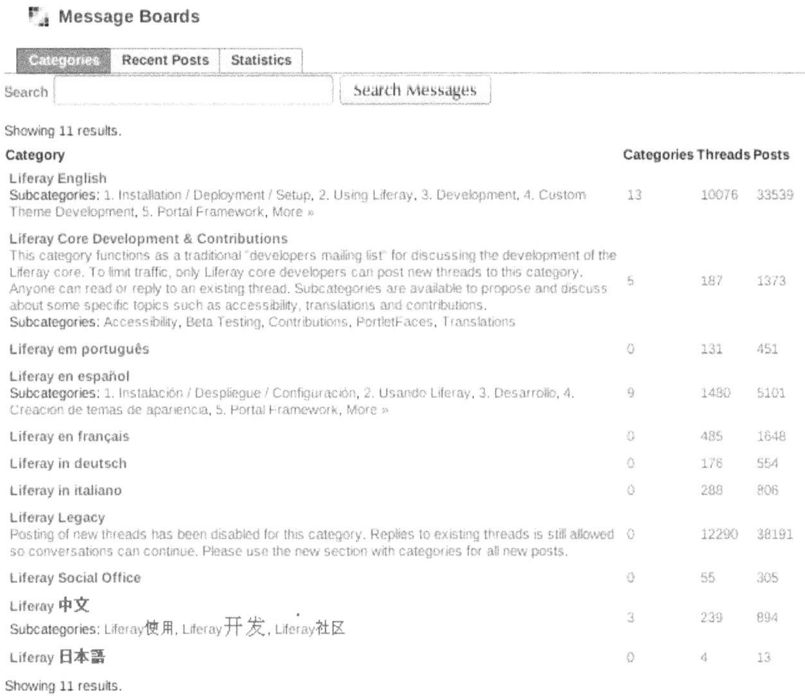

Figure 4.12: Liferay's Forums on Facebook is an example of sharing the Message Boards portlet.

ate. To set up Netvibes support for a particular portlet, check the *Allow users to add [portlet-name] to Netvibes pages* box. You can then use the provided URL to create a custom Netvibes widget based on the instance of the portlet that you're using.

Friends

The final sub-tab of the *Sharing* tab is called *Friends*. This tab has a single check box that allows you to give your friends permission to add the application as a widget to another web site. This could be particularly useful for your blog or calendar if you wish to share them.

Next, let's explore what the Recycle Bin does for your Liferay applications.

4.8 Recycling Assets with the Recycle Bin

Have you ever had that life-altering experience where you deleted an important file and immediately regretted deleting it? The deed is usually followed by a palm to the forehead or a sick feeling. Good news! Liferay is here to turn that frown upside down with the *Recycle Bin* feature. With the Recycle Bin, the *Move to the Recycle Bin* action replaces *Delete* for certain asset types. Content is now temporarily stored in the Recycle Bin. This allows the content to be restored back to its original state. Recycled items can expire after a certain period of time, resulting in their permanent deletion. Before diving into how the Recycle Bin works, let's look at how to configure it.

Configuring the Recycle Bin

To begin using the Recycle Bin, you must enable it where you plan to use it. The Recycle Bin supports portal-wide scope or site-specific scope. The portal-wide scope of the Recycle Bin is set by adding the `trash.enabled` property to your `portal-ext.properties` file. We'll go into more detail for adding this property and several others to your properties file later in the section. First, let's explore the UI and see what the Recycle Bin can do.

First, let's configure the Recycle Bin for site-specific scoping. Choose the site you'd like configure for the Recycle Bin from *My Sites* in the Dockbar. Then click *Admin → Configuration* to navigate to the *Site Settings* page. Next, click *Recycle Bin* on the right-side menu under the Advanced heading. You'll notice a few configurable options:

Enable Recycle Bin: enable and disable settings for the Recycle Bin's site-specific scope.

Trash Entries Max Age: customize the number of days a file is kept in the Recycle Bin until its permanent deletion (default is 30 days).

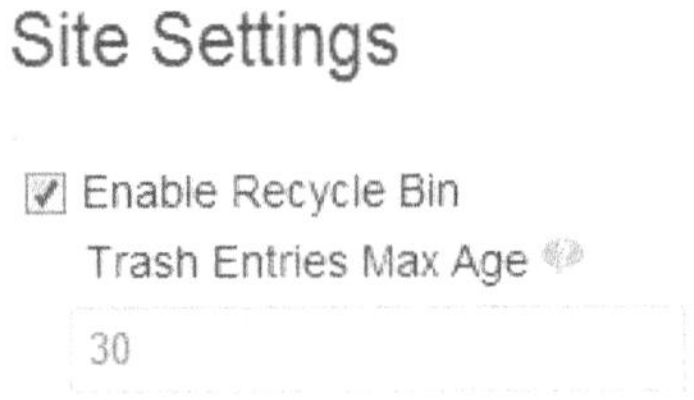

Site Settings

☑ Enable Recycle Bin

Trash Entries Max Age ◆

30

Figure 4.13: The Recycle Bin offers several configurable options for your site.

When you've finished configuring your Recycle Bin settings, click *Save*.

Note: If you disable the Recycle Bin while it's still holding recycled items, the recycled items reappear in the Recycle Bin if it is re-enabled.

You can also configure the Recycle Bin via properties in the `portal.properties` file. Remember that it's a best practice not to edit the `portal.properties` directly, but to create a separate `portal-ext.properties` file containing the properties to override. There are some additional options not available in the GUI that you can set:

`trash.search.limit=500`: set the limit for results used when performing searches in the Recycle Bin (default is 500).

`trash.entry.check.interval=60`: set the interval in minutes for how often the trash handler runs to delete trash entries that have been in the Recycle Bin longer than the maximum age (default is 60).

Also, as we mentioned earlier, there is a property to enable the Recycle bin portal-wide.

`trash.enabled=true`: set this property to true to enable the Recycle Bin for all sites in the portal while allowing site administrators to disable it per site.

Next, you should make sure permissions are set properly for users who can handle/view the assets in the Recycle Bin. Users who had *View* permissions on a document when it was recycled can also view that document in the Recycle Bin. Users who had *Update* or *Delete* permissions on a document when it was recycled can restore the document.

Now that you've successfully configured the Recycle Bin, let's look at how to use it.

Using the Recycle Bin

The Recycle Bin is temporary storage configured for multiple asset types across the portal. Instead of offering a specific Recycle Bin for each asset type, Liferay provides a central master Recycle Bin where different asset types can be stored. This provides an easy search and recovery process.

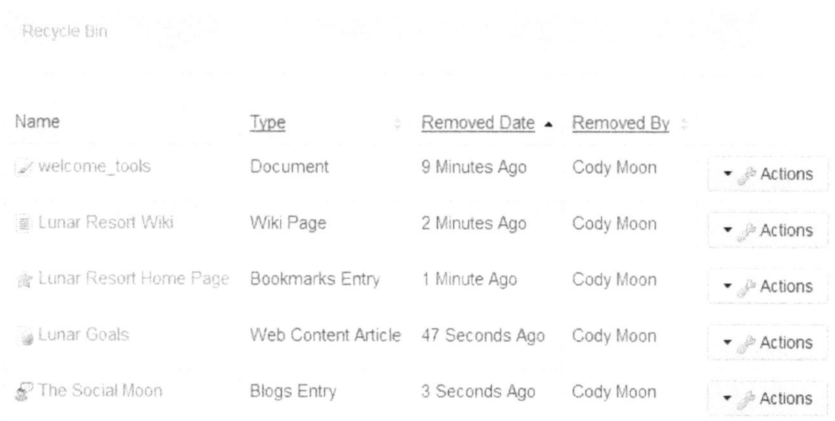

Name	Type	Removed Date ▲	Removed By	
welcome_tools	Document	9 Minutes Ago	Cody Moon	▼ Actions
Lunar Resort Wiki	Wiki Page	2 Minutes Ago	Cody Moon	▼ Actions
Lunar Resort Home Page	Bookmarks Entry	1 Minute Ago	Cody Moon	▼ Actions
Lunar Goals	Web Content Article	47 Seconds Ago	Cody Moon	▼ Actions
The Social Moon	Blogs Entry	3 Seconds Ago	Cody Moon	▼ Actions

Figure 4.14: The Recycle Bin provides a seamless administrative experience for deleting and removing content.

You can recycle several different types of assets, including:

- Blogs
- Bookmarks
- Documents and Media
- Message Boards (and attachments)
- Web Content
- Wiki (and attachments)

For a quick example to show how easy the Recycle Bin is to use, let's send a web content article to the Recycle Bin and then restore it. We'll run through two different methods of restoring the file.

1. Navigate to *Site Administration →Content →Web Content*.

2. Select the *Add* button and click *Basic Web Content*.

3. Enter some text for the Title and Content and click *Publish*.

4. In the top right corner of the web content, select the arrow and click *Move to the Recycle Bin*.

   Note that the *Delete* button is not listed. Liferay avoids the risk of accidental deletion of your files by funneling the content through the Recycle Bin.

5. After deleting the file, a success message appears, offering an *Undo* option. Click *Undo*. The web content is retrieved from the Recycle Bin and stored in its original place.

6. Select the *Move to the Recycle Bin* button again.

7. Navigate back to Site Administration and click the Recycle Bin button from the menu.

8. Find your sample web content and click its *Actions* tab.

9. You can restore or delete the content. Select *Restore*.

Figure 4.15: In the Recycle Bin, you have the option of restoring or permanently deleting the content.

10. Navigate back to the Web Content screen and notice that your sample web content was restored back to its original place.

Congratulations! You now know the two general processes of sending and restoring content to/from the Recycle Bin. For other asset types, the Recycle Bin works similarly.

Some Liferay applications, such as Web Content and Documents and Media, support folders into which their content can be organized. You can also send folders and sub-folders to the Recycle Bin. Keep in mind that this sends the entire folder/sub-folder structure and all files to the Recycle Bin. Folders and sub-folders are restored and deleted the same way as a single file. Also, expired web content can be moved to the Recycle Bin and restored, just like a regular file.

In step 9 of the example, you probably noticed the *Delete* button from within the Recycle Bin. This is the permanent delete button. Once you select this, your file cannot be retrieved and is gone forever. There is also an *Empty the Recycle Bin* button located at the top of the Recycle Bin screen. This permanently deletes all the files from the Recycle Bin. Next, let's discuss how to use the drag and drop feature.

Drag and Drop

A quick and easy way to dispose of your unwanted assets is to drag and drop them into the Recycle Bin. While you're in the Control Panel, you can simply select an asset and drag it to the Recycle Bin portlet located on the Control Panel menu. When you click and begin dragging the asset, a message appears near your cursor notifying you of the amount of files ready to be moved, and the Recycle Bin is highlighted, showing you where the files can be dropped. After you drop the asset onto the Recycle Bin portlet, the asset is removed from its original location and transferred to the Recycle Bin.

Next, let's explore the Recycle Bin's intelligence and behind the scenes support that aids in a seamless recycling experience.

Recycle Bin intelligence and support

Have you ever wondered if it's possible to check the IQ of a software feature? Unfortunately, there is no tangible way to do this; however, if there were, the Liferay Recycle Bin would be at the top of its class. As we've mentioned already, it supports multiple asset types, a drag and drop feature, an Undo option, and many more. Have you ever wondered what happens to file shortcuts if their linked assets are recycled? What if you restore a file that has the same name as another file currently stored in your site/portal? The Recycle Bin already knows how to handle these types of issues for a seamless user experience.

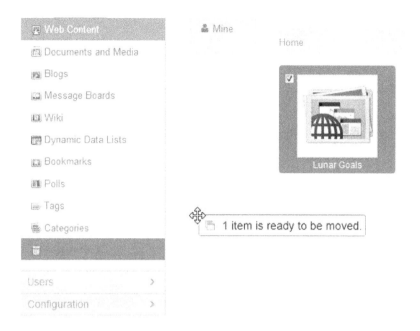

Figure 4.16: A quick and easy way of disposing your items is the drag and drop method.

When documents with shortcuts are moved to the Recycle Bin, the shortcuts are invalidated. This ensures your portal has active links and shortcuts at all times. This cuts down on maintenance time and backtracking after recycling an important asset.

Another important trait is the duplicate name recognition feature. When a file is restored, the Recycle Bin scans the corresponding asset type files currently in the site/portal to check for duplicate file names. If a duplicate file name is found, the Recycle Bin prompts you to overwrite the existing file or rename the file name you're trying to restore.

For example, suppose you have the document file1 stored in the Recycle Bin and you have a separate document you created later with the same name in the document library. If you try to restore the file1 document, the Recycle Bin recognizes duplicate names and prompts you to overwrite the existing document in the document library or rename the document you're trying to restore.

Although the Recycle Bin prohibits the restoration of files that match pre-existing file names in your site/portal, it will store files with matching names.

Have you thought about how the Recycle Bin works during the staging process? Although we stated earlier that there is only one master Recycle Bin, the staging process requires a bit more flexibility with the Recycle Bin to maximize its productivity. Therefore, when staging is enabled, there is a new and separate Recycle Bin: the *Staging* Recycle Bin. The original Recycle Bin, or *Live* Recycle Bin, holding unstaged material is still viewable while in staging; however, it is never used.

During staging, everything you recycle is sent to the Staging Recycle Bin. This prevents staged and unstaged recycled content from mixing. Do you see why this would be a problem? Consider you have an unstaged document currently on your live site. Next, you enable staging and delete that document. If you were to turn staging off and return to the live site, without separate Recycle Bins, the live document would be located on your site and in the Recycle Bin! Because of this, the separate Staging Recycle Bin is necessary and only used during the staging process. Finally, when you publish your staged material to

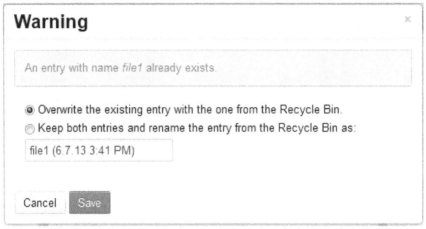

Figure 4.17: The Recycle Bin always scans your site/portal for duplicate file names during the restoration process.

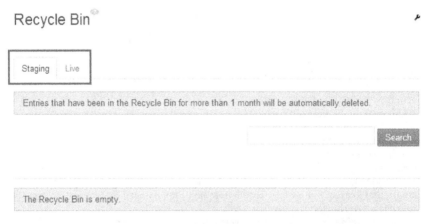

Figure 4.18: During staging, a separate Recycle Bin appears to keep staging and live content separate.

live, the Staging Recycle Bin content is transferred to the Live Recycle Bin.

 Note: The Staging Recycle Bin saves its contents until the staged material has been published to live. This means that you can turn the staging mode on and off without losing your recycled material.

The Recycle Bin saves you time by letting you restore content that's been recycled. Instead of recreating or re-uploading content, you'll be tailoring your Liferay portal to fully leverage its capabilities.

4.9 Summary

In this chapter, we explored the configuration options available for Liferay applications. We showed how to customize your applications, export/import portlet data, take advantage of different scopes, and communicate between portlets. We also examined the different uses of social applications like Facebook and Netvibes for your Liferay applications. Besides the general configuration options, we also explored the Recycle Bin. This feature is a special file directory allowing users to browse, retrieve, or permanently delete recycled content. In all, Liferay gives you an abundance of options to leverage the full capability of your applications.

## CHAPTER 5

DOCUMENT MANAGEMENT

Liferay's Documents and Media library provides a mechanism for storing files online using the same type of structure that you use to store files locally. You can use it to store files of any kind; it serves as a virtual shared drive, and can mount and browse external repositories. Its companion portlet, the Media Gallery, displays selected content from the Documents and Media library. It can display image, audio and video files. Other features in the Documents and Media library include customizable document types and metadata sets, automatic document preview generation, and support for mounting multiple external repositories. The new document types and metadata sets are an addition to, not a replacement for, the portal's system of tags and categories. Let's start exploring how to use the Documents and Media portlet.

5.1 Getting Started with the Documents and Media Portlet

The Documents and Media portlet, like many other of Liferay's portlets, is non-instanceable. This means that each page on your portal can host at most one such portlet. Furthermore, if you add multiple Documents and Media portlets to pages in the same site, these portlets by default share the same data sets since they are scoped by site. However, you can add multiple Documents and Media *Display* portlets to a page. Then you can choose specific subfolders from actual Documents and Media repositories to display. Remember that users, by default, have their own personal sites with public and private pages. They can use their personal sites to host Documents and Media portlets for storing or sharing their own files.

Figure 5.1: The Documents and Media portlet offers a plethora of options to choose from.

The Documents and Media portlet's default view displays the contents of the *Home* folder. The links on the left side of the portlet windows are filters. You can use these filters to choose what you want the main window of the portlet to show. *Recent* displays documents users have recently uploaded, edited or downloaded. *Mine* shows *your* documents; in other words, the documents you have uploaded. *Browse by Type* shows a list of options you can choose to help filter your results. If you click on one of these filters, the main portlet window shows only documents that belong to the selected document type. When you add custom document types, which we discuss below, they are added to the filter list. Next, let's look at how to navigate around Documents and Media.

Navigating the Documents and Media Portlet

In the main window of the Documents and Media portlet, you can click on a document to view details about it. Its version number, version history, status, as well as who uploaded it and who last edited it. Depending on the document, some automatically extracted metadata may also be displayed, such as the document creator, author, title, content type, creation date, and last modification date. In the case of audio or video files, the duration would also be displayed. You can perform several actions on the document here:

Download: lets you download the document.

Get URL: displays the URL of the document on the server.

Get WebDAV URL: displays the WebDAV URL of the document on the server. Specify this URL as the file name when opening the document from Microsoft Office.

Edit: lets you change contents of a document, point it to a different file, change its title, description or document type, or add tags, categories or related assets.

Move: lets you choose a new location in the Documents and Media repository to store the document.

Checkout/Checkin: prevents others from modifying the document while you are working. Other users can still view the current version of the document if they have permission. You can check the document back in when you're done working.

Permissions: allows you to configure file-specific permissions for the document.

Move to the Recycle Bin: lets you remove the document from the Documents and Media library.

If comments are enabled, you can also view comments, add comments, or subscribe to comments about documents. Comments are enabled by default.

The menu at the top of the Documents and Media portlet contains Actions, Add, Sort By and Manage buttons. There are also buttons for switching between icon view, descriptive view, and list view. If there are lots of documents in the Documents and Media library, the search field can help you find the documents you're looking for. If your portlet contains more documents than it can display at once, you can use the navigation tool at the bottom of the portlet window to either switch your view to another page or configure the page to display more documents per page.

When navigating among Documents and Media folders, look for the *Subscribe* link at the top right corner of the folder view. Clicking the *Subscribe* link subscribes you to the folder you're currently viewing so that you'll receive email notifications. You'll be notified about any actions that take place in the folder such as file additions, edits, or deletions.

Actions

The Actions menu will only be displayed if you have selected one or more documents with the check boxes.

Cancel Checkout: lets you check in a document that you had checked out but did not make any changes to. Using this option will prevent the Documents and Media portlet from incrementing the document's version number and saving an identical version of the document.

Figure 5.2: You can click an asset in the Documents and Media portlet to view its options and properties.

Checkin: lets you check in a document that you have edited. Its version number will increment and the previous version will be saved.

Checkout: lets you check out a document that you would like to edit. This option prevents anyone else from modifying it while you are working.

Move: allows you to choose a new location for a document or folder within the portlet's file system. You can move multiple documents and folders at the same time. Moving documents and folders is also possible via drag & drop.

Move to the Recycle Bin: allows you to remove a document or folder from the portlet. You can move multiple documents and folders to the Recycle Bin at the same time.

Add

From the Add button, you can add documents, folders, and shortcuts just like on your local file system.

Folder: lets you create a new location in your portlet's file system.

Shortcut: allows you to create a shortcut to any document that you have read access for. You can set permissions on the shortcut to specify who can access the original document through the shortcut.

Repository: is a new feature of Liferay 6.1. This option allows you to add an entirely new repository to your Documents and Media portlet. To do this you need to specify the

repository type and choose an ID. If you are using the AtomPub protocol you'll also have
to specify the AtomPub URL.

Multiple Documents: allows you to upload several documents at once.

Basic Document: allows you upload a single file that you would like the default document type, "Basic Document," to apply to. By default, basic documents are not described
by any metadata sets.

The remaining items in the Add menu are default document types that are each described by a unique metadata set. When you add a document belonging to a specific document type, you're presented with a form to not only specify the file to upload but also to
fill out the fields defined by the document type's metadata set. We describe the "Contract"
document type by way of example.

Contract: lets you upload a file that you would like the "Contract" document type to
apply to. This document type is intended to be used to describe legal contracts. By default, contracts are described by effective date, expiration date, contract type, status, legal
reviewer, signing authority and deal name fields. Document types are discussed below.

Any custom documents types that have been defined also appear in the Add menu. If a
document type has been created that matches the document you would like to upload, you
can select that document type from the Add menu. This will associate the metadata fields
associated with the document type to your document and you will be asked to fill out the
fields.

Another useful feature for Liferay's Documents and Media portlet is the drag-and-drop
upload feature. Instead of manually uploading an asset via the portlet's menu, you can
select and drag an asset from your desktop and drop it onto your portlet. You can also
drag-and-drop folders full of assets. When you drag the asset onto your browser, the Documents and Media portlet is highlighted blue indicating its compatibility for the drag-
and-drop feature. When the asset is finally dropped on the highlighted region, the asset
is automatically uploaded and available instantly.

Let's move on and discuss the Sort action.

Sort

You can sort the items displayed in the main window of the Documents and Media portlet
using the *Sort By* menu. You can sort by title, create date, modified date, downloads or
size.

Title: lets you alphabetically sort documents by title.

Create Date: lets you sort documents by the time they were created.

Modified Date: lets you sort documents by the last time they were modified.

Downloads: lets you sort documents by the number of times they were downloaded.

Size: lets you sort documents by how much disk space they use.

Let's dive into the Manage action next!

Manage

The Manage menu allows you to view the names of document types and metadata sets, as
well as the last times they were edited.

Document Types: shows you a list of defined document types.

Metadata Sets: shows you a list of defined metadata sets as well as their portal IDs.

Now that we know the basic functionality of the Documents and Media portlet, let's
explore document types and metadata sets.

5.2   Document Types and Metadata Sets

When a user assigns a document type to a document, the user is required to fill out the
fields defined by the metadata set of the document type. This encourages users not to

forget to enter important information about their documents. For example, you could create a *copyrighted* document type and require users to enter a license for all "copyrighted" documents. More importantly, document types and metadata sets can make it easier to find documents. The values that users enter into the fields determined by their document type's metadata set become searchable entities within the portal. You can use Liferay's search portlet to search for these terms. Document types and metadata sets are accessible from the *Manage* button at the top of the Documents and Media portlet window.

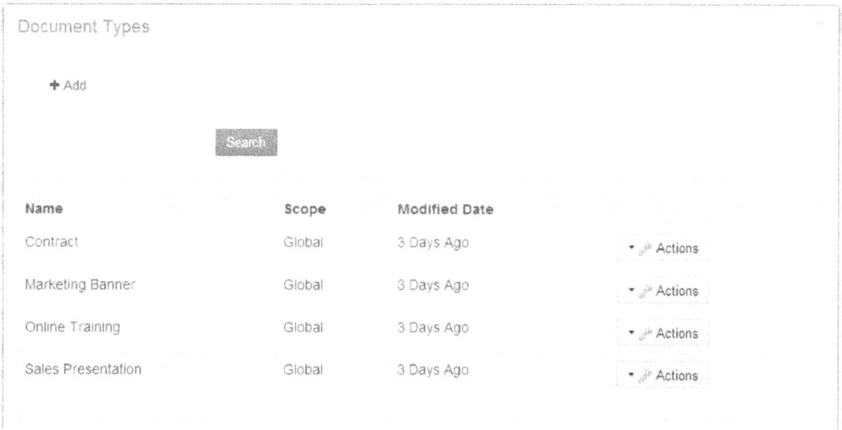

Figure 5.3: Navigate to the Document Types Dialog Box by clicking *Manage* →*Document Types*.

You can add a new document type using the Add button at the top of the dialog box. To do so, you need to define one or more metadata sets to associate with your document type. When creating a new document type, you can define *Main Metadata Fields* or select *Additional Metadata Fields*. Main metadata fields are directly tied to their document type and cannot be made available to other document types. Additional metadata fields, by contrast, can be defined independently and can be used in many different document types. You can differentiate the document types that implement the same additional metadata set by defining different main metadata fields for them. However, additional metadata fields need to be defined and saved before creating a document type that will implement them.

As an example, we could create a document type called *Syllabus* and define a metadata set. What metadata should we associate with syllabi? Let's choose for our syllabi to have course title, professor, semester, course description, and course requirements fields. All syllabi in our portal should maintain entries for these fields. This ensures that a syllabus shows up in a portal search if its course title, professor or semester is searched for. Since we don't want to use our metadata set for any document type other than *Syllabus*, let's create our metadata set under the Main Metadata Fields area. Alternatively, we could create our metadata set independently using *Manage* →*Metadata Sets* →*Add* and then select it as an Additional Metadata Field.

You can view, edit, or add metadata sets from the *Manage Metadata* window. A metadata set consists of a group of fields. If you click the *Add* button, you can use same UI for defining a metadata set that you used in the Add Document Type window.

Make sure the Fields tab is selected on the left. Then, to define a metadata set, just choose fields to use from the area on the left and drag and drop them into the area on the right. The drag and drop interface allows for nested fields so you need to be careful about where you drop the fields. Default values, mouse-over tips, widths, and other settings can be configured for most fields. To configure these settings, just click on a field from the area

Figure 5.4: Adding a New Metadata Set is easier than ever with Liferay's advanced editor.

on the right. This automatically selects the Settings tab on the left. Alternatively, you can access the Settings tab by clicking the fields *Settings* button (wrench). Then double-click on a value to edit. Liferay supports the following kinds of fields for metadata sets:

Boolean: is a checkbox.

Date: lets you enter a date. A valid date format is required for the date field, but you don't have to enter a date manually. When you select the date field a mini-calendar pops up which you can use to select a date.

Decimal: lets you enter a decimal number. The value will be persisted as a double.

Documents and Media: lets you select a file from one of the portal's Documents and Media libraries.

HTML: an area that uses a WYSIWYG editor to enhance the content.

Integer: lets you enter an integer. The value will be persisted as an int.

Link to Page: lets you link to another page in the same site.

Number: lets you enter a decimal number or an integer. The value will be persisted either as a double or an int, depending on the type of input.

Radio: displays several clickable options. The default number is three but this is customizable. Only one option can be selected at a time.

Select: is just like the radio field except that the options are hidden and have to be accessed from a drop-down menu.

Text: lets you enter a single line of text.

Text Box: is just like the text field except you can enter multiple lines of text or separate paragraphs.

Remember that metadata sets created independently are reusable. Once they have been created they can be included in any number of document types as additional metadata sets. Next, let's take a look at tags. Tags can be attached to most forms of web content that can be created in Liferay, including documents.

5.3 Alternative File Repository Options

By default, Liferay stores documents and media files on the file system of the server on which it's running. You can choose a specific location for the document library store's root directory by adding the following property to your `portal-ext.properties` file and replacing the default path with your custom path:

```
dl.store.file.system.root.dir=${liferay.home}/data/document_library
```

You can also use an entirely different method for storing documents and media files. You can use any of the following documents and media library stores with Liferay:

- Advanced File System Store
- CMIS Store (Content Management Interoperability Services)
- DBStore (Database Storage)
- File System Store
- JCRStore (Java Content Repository)
- S3Store (Amazon Simple Storage)

For example, you can store documents and media files in your Liferay instance's database using DBStore. To enable DStore, add the following line to your `portal-ext.properties` file:

```
dl.store.impl=com.liferay.portlet.documentlibrary.store.DBStore
```

Remember to restart your Liferay server after updating your `portal-ext.properties` file in order for your customizations to take effect. Please refer to the Document Library Portlet section of your `portal.properties` file to find a complete list of supported customizations. You can customize features such as the maximum allowed size of documents and media files, the list of allowed file extensions, which types of files should be indexed, etc.

5.4 Using External Repositories

Content Management Interoperability Services (CMIS) is a specification for improving interoperability between Enterprise Content Management systems. Documents and Media allows users to connect to multiple third-party repositories that support CMIS 1.0 with AtomPub and Web Services protocols.

Some of the features supported with third-party repositories include:

- Reading/writing documents and folders
- Document check-in, check-out, and undo check-out
- Downloading documents

- Moving folders and documents within the repository
- Getting revision history
- Reverting to revision

There are some subtle differences in setting up the different kinds of third-party repositories for use in Documents and Media. But there are plenty of similarities too.

Common Liferay configuration steps:

- Adjust the portal properties.
- Add any user accounts required by the repository.
- Add the repository.

Lastly, keep in mind your third-party repository may require installation and deployment of an appropriate Liferay plugin. Plugins for SharePoint and Documentum are available through Liferay's Marketplace.

Let's go through those steps, starting with setting our portal properties.

Adjusting portal properties

The admin must ensure that the same credentials and authentication are being used in Liferay and in the external repository. This is normally synchronized using a mechanism like LDAP. If you don't have LDAP, you need to ensure manually that the credentials and authentication are the same. In order to authenticate with the third-party repository, you need to store passwords for the user sessions. Set the following portal property in your `portal-ext.properties`:

```
session.store.password=true
```

Next, we need to make sure the login and password for Liferay are the same as the external repository. This is easily accomplished by using identical screen names, so in `portal-ext.properties` add the following:

```
company.security.auth.type=screenName
```

Alternatively, configure these properties in the Control Panel under *Portal Settings* → *Authentication*.

Adding required repository users

Once these properties are set, you must create a user in Liferay with a screen name and password matching the administrative user of your external repository. Be sure to assign appropriate roles (e.g. Administrator) to that user. Sign out of Liferay and sign in again as that new user. See sections of the *Management* chapter on adding and managing users.

Adding the repository

You can add new repositories from the UI by clicking the *Add* button from the Home folder. Repositories can only be mounted in the Home folder.

All fields in this form are required, except for *Repository ID*. Leave this field blank, and a repository ID is automatically generated by the system. When finished, the repository is displayed on the left side of the window in the Home folder.

Using this information, we can now add an example repository. As noted previously, there are several repositories that work well with Liferay using CMIS. One that is familiar to many users is SharePoint. In the exercise below, we'll set up SharePoint as a Documents and Media repository.

Figure 5.5: You can add a new repository by navigating to *Add* →*Repository* in the Documents and Media portlet.

Example Repository Setup: SharePoint

With Liferay Portal you can connect to an external SharePoint server and add it as a Documents and Media repository. This lets users collaborate and share documents more easily between both environments. We will mount a SharePoint repository via CMIS AtomPub and SharePoint SOAP web services.

Liferay uses a combination of SOAP and Representational State Transfer (REST), based on the Atom convention, to connect to the SharePoint repository. SharePoint provides various SOAP services for modifying and querying data from its document library. Liferay uses Axis2 to generate SOAP calls to the SharePoint server.

To use SharePoint as a Liferay Documents and Media repository, we'll do the following:

- Configure the CMIS Connector on SharePoint.
- Activate a SharePoint site as a CMIS Producer.
- Acquire your SharePoint document library's repository ID.
- Enable Basic Authentication on the SharePoint host.
- Add SharePoint as a Liferay Documents and Media repository.

Note that this section is geared towards portal system administrators and SharePoint system administrators.

Before you can use SharePoint as an external repository with Liferay portal, you must verify that SharePoint is properly configured. Several services must be set up on the Share-Point server before synchronizing with Liferay.

Configuring the CMIS Connector on SharePoint

SharePoint utilizes a CMIS Connector and a CMIS Producer to interface with Liferay Portal. The Connector is installed with the SharePoint Administrator Toolkit using a solution package called a Windows SharePoint file (.wsp). If you don't have it already, install the SharePoint Administrator Toolkit for its CMIS Connector. Install and deploy the CMIS Connector as a Farm Solution on SharePoint.

The folder Content Management Interoperability Services (CMIS) Connectors contains the spscmis.wsp file. Choose the appropriate deployment settings and deploy that file. When deployment completes, Solution Properties shows the solution is successfully deployed to all target sites. Now it's time to configure the CMIS Producer.

Activating a SharePoint site as a CMIS Producer

The Producer makes SharePoint repositories available through the CMIS Connector. All you have to do is choose the SharePoint site containing the document libraries to be used as document repositories. Every document library in this site is made available as a repository through the CMIS connector.

Go to *Site Actions →Site Settings →Manage Site Features*. Enable the *Content Management Interoperability Services (CMIS) Producer* by clicking *Activate*.

Now any document library created under this site is CMIS enabled. Before we leave our SharePoint console, let's take note of our SharePoint document library's repository ID.

Acquiring the SharePoint document library's repository ID

Acquiring your SharePoint document library's repository ID, or list ID, is important as it must be specified in the AtomPub URL Liferay uses to connect with the external repository. Finding it, however, can be a little confusing. The easiest way to find the repository ID is by accessing the SharePoint repository using a browser such as Mozilla Firefox.

Follow these steps to get the repository ID:

1. In SharePoint, open the desired library.

2. Under Library Tools select *Library*.

3. Click on *Library Settings*, located to the far right.

4. The browser window refreshes displaying the repository ID between curly braces '{' and '}' in the browser's address bar.

Figure 5.6: The repository ID can be found by displaying the repository's URL in a Firefox browser.

The repository ID is highlighted in the figure above. For this example, the repository ID is 6DFDA9–B547–4D1D–BF85–976863CDF533. Therefore, the AtomPub URL you'd use when adding this repository in Documents and Media would resemble this:

```
http://liferay-20jf4ic/CMIS/_vti_bin/cmis/rest/6DFDA9-B547-4D1D-BF85-976863CDF533? \
getRepositoryInfo.
```

Be sure to copy down this URL so you can use it to configure SharePoint as a repository in Documents and Media. Next, let's enable Basic Authentication on the SharePoint host.

Enabling Basic Authentication on the SharePoint host

For the CMIS connector and producer to work, Basic Authentication on IIS must be enabled. This lets Liferay's SharePoint hook authenticate against the SharePoint web services. Enable Basic Authentication on your SharePoint host.

You are now prepared to mount SharePoint as an external repository.

Adding SharePoint as a Liferay Documents and Media repository

With the SharePoint server configured, we now turn our attention to Liferay. As mentioned in the common steps for adding an external repository, be sure to adjust the portal properties and add any user accounts required by the repository.

Here are the steps specific to configuring Liferay to use SharePoint:

1. Download and install the SharePoint Connector EE hook from Marketplace. See the Downloading and Installing Apps section of the *Leveraging the Liferay Marketplace* chapter of this document for more information.

2. Add the Documents and Media portlet to a page, if you haven't done so already.

3. In the Documents and Media portlet click *Add Repository* and enter the following information:

   Name: Enter an arbitrary name for the repository.

   Description: Describe the repository.

   Repository Type: Select *SharePoint (AtomPub)*.

   AtomPub URL: Enter the applicable URL using the format below, substituting the SharePoint server's host name for *[host]* and the SharePoint document library's repository ID for *[repository ID]*:

   ```
   http://[host]/CMIS/_vti_bin/cmis/rest/[repository ID]?getRepositoryInfo
   ```

   Repository ID: Leave this field empty. Liferay searches for the first repository using the given parameters and sets this value to that repository's ID.

   Site Path: Enter data using the format below, the SharePoint server's host information for *[host]* and the SharePoint document library's repository name for *[repository path]*:

   ```
   http://[host]/[repository path]
   ```

4. Click *Save*.

The left navigation panel of your Documents and Media portlet now lists your new repository.

Tip: In the site path example below, notice how the repository path has a folder Shared Documents consisting of two words.

> http://liferay-20jf4ic/CMIS/Shared Docu-
> ments/Forms/AllItems.aspx

The space between the words in the repository name must be accounted for when setting the site path in Liferay. Replace the empty space with the string %20 so the site path value now looks like this:

> http://liferay-20jf4ic/CMIS/Shared%20Documents/Forms/AllItems.aspx

This should be done for any multi-word repository name.

Remember that connecting to an external SharePoint server and adding it as a Documents and Media repository is a great way to give users flexibility for sharing and collaborating on Microsoft Office documents.

Now let's look at configuring the Documents and Media portlet.

5.5   Configuring the Documents and Media portlet

To configure the Documents and Media portlet, click on the gear icon at the top of the portlet window and select *Configuration*. The portlet-specific customizations appear on the Setup tab. To change your Documents and Media portlet's top-level folder, click *Select* below *Root Folder*, browse or create the folder you'd like to be your new top-level folder, and click *Save*. The root folder is the highest-level folder that's accessible from the Documents and Media portlet. For example, suppose you created a folder called *My Documents* in the Documents and Media portlet's default Home folder. If you set the My Documents folder to be your portlet's new root folder, the original Home folder would no longer be accessible.

By default, the Documents and Media portlet contains a search bar to help users quickly find relevant files. If you'd like the search bar not to appear, uncheck the *Show Search* box. The *Maximum Entries to Display* dropdown menu lets you set a limit on how many folders and files can be displayed in the portlet window at once. By default, the Documents and Media portlet contains three display style views: Icon, List, and Descriptive. Icons for each appear in the portlet window, allowing users to select the display style with which they're most comfortable. Under the Display Style Views heading, you can select which display styles users are able to choose and you can arrange the order of the selected display styles. The topmost display style in the list becomes the portlet's default display style.

Related assets are enabled by default for Documents and Media files. Related assets allow users to link assets together even if the assets don't share any tags or categories. To disable related assets for files in your Documents and Media portlet, uncheck the *Enable Related Assets* box. For more information on related assets, see the section on defining content relationships in chapter 6.

Under the Show Columns heading, you can customize which columns appear when your Documents and Media portlet uses the list display style. By default, file names, sizes, statuses, downloads, and actions are displayed. You can also configure the portlet to display files' create dates and modified dates. To add or remove columns from being displayed, move them to the Current box or to the Available box. You can arrange the columns in the Current box to control the order in which the columns appear in the portlet: the topmost column in the box appears as the leftmost column in the portlet.

Ratings and comment ratings are also enabled by default for Documents and Media files. If users decide that a file or certain comment about a file is useful or informative, they can rate it as good by clicking on the thumbs up icon next to the rating. If they think

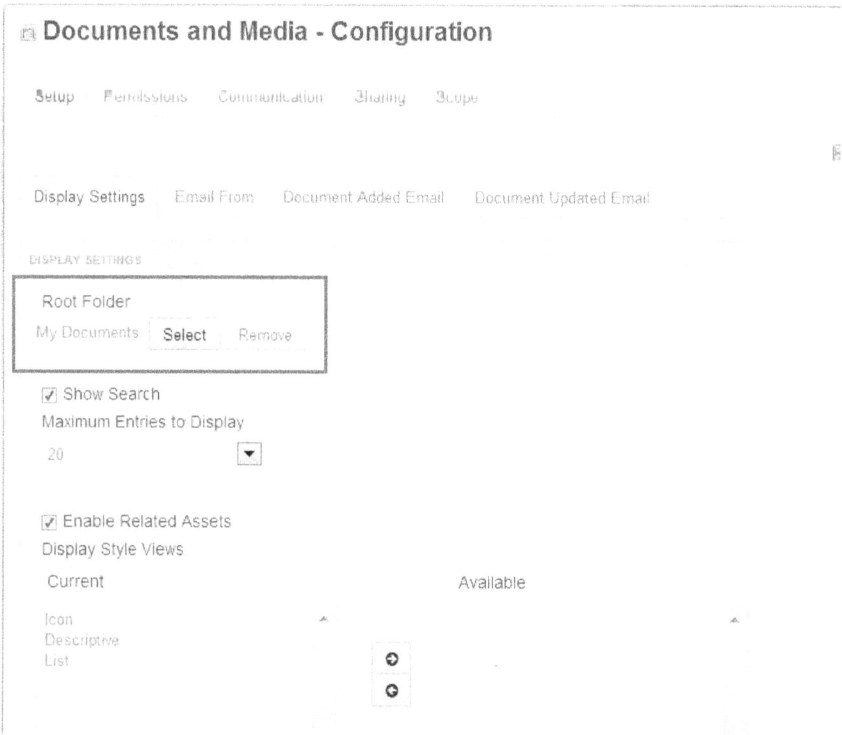

Documents and Media - Configuration

Setup   Permissions   Communication   Sharing   Scope

Display Settings   Email From   Document Added Email   Document Updated Email

DISPLAY SETTINGS

Root Folder
My Documents | Select | Remove

☑ Show Search
Maximum Entries to Display

20   ▼

☑ Enable Related Assets
Display Style Views

Current   Available

Icon
Descriptive
List   ➔

                                ◐

Figure 5.7: To make portlet-specific configurations for Documents and Media, click on the gear icon at the top of the portlet window and select *Configuration*.

the file or comment is unhelpful or misleading, they can click on the thumbs down icon. If you'd like to disable ratings or comment ratings for files, uncheck the *Enable Ratings* or *Enable Comment Ratings* box, respectively.

5.6   Automatic Previews and metadata

Whenever possible, Liferay 6.2 generates previews of documents added to the Documents and Media library. Out of the box, Liferay only ships with Java-based APIs to generate previews for documents. The only tool available that is 100% Java and has a compatible license to be distributed with Liferay is PDFBox. If you upload a PDF file to the Documents and Media portlet, Liferay generates a preview for the PDF in a separate thread. This process may last only a few seconds for a small file. The larger the file, the longer it takes.

The first time you run a conversion like this, look for the following console message:

```
Liferay is not configured to use ImageMagick for generating Document Library
previews and will default to PDFBox. For better quality previews, install
ImageMagick and enable it in portal-ext.properties.
```

While a default implementation of image generation for document previews and thumbnails is provided via PDFBox, you'll need to install and configure some additional tools to harness the full power of Liferay's Documents and Media library. These tools include *OpenOffice* or *LibreOffice*, *ImageMagick*, which requires *Ghostscript*, and *Xuggler*. With these

tools installed and configured, Documents and Media content is displayed using a customized viewer depending on the type of content. Configuring Liferay to use OpenOffice or LibreOffice in server mode allows you to generate thumbnails and previews for
supported file types (.pdf, .docx, .odt, .ppt, .odp, etc.), lets you view documents in your
browser, and lets you convert documents. ImageMagick allows for faster and higher-
quality previews and conversions. Xuggler allows for audio and video previews, lets you
play audio and video files in your browser, and extracts thumbnails from video files. Please
see the *External Services* section of chapter 17 for how to configure Liferay to use these tools.

With the above tools installed and enabled, the Documents and Media library looks like
this:

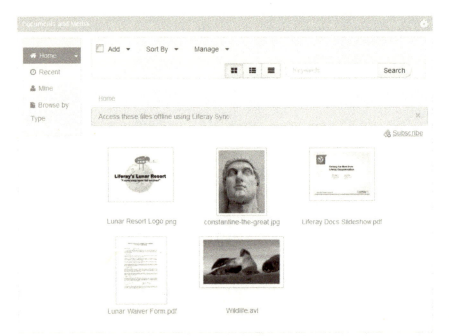

Figure 5.8: After configuring additional tools, previews in the Documents and Media
portlet are more advanced.

You can view a document with a customized viewer that allows you to navigate through
the different pages of the document and read its content. In addition, you can view a
multimedia document (audio or video) and play it online. If the browser supports HTML5,
it uses the native player of the browser. Otherwise it falls back to a Flash player.

Document previews are powerful and help users browse media more successfully to
find what they're looking for.

Automatic extraction of RAW Metadata

When adding new documents or viewing existing documents, a process is triggered automatically that extracts the file's metadata. The library used by this process is TIKA and
it's already included in Liferay out of the box.

You can see the metadata when viewing the document, in the right side of the window.

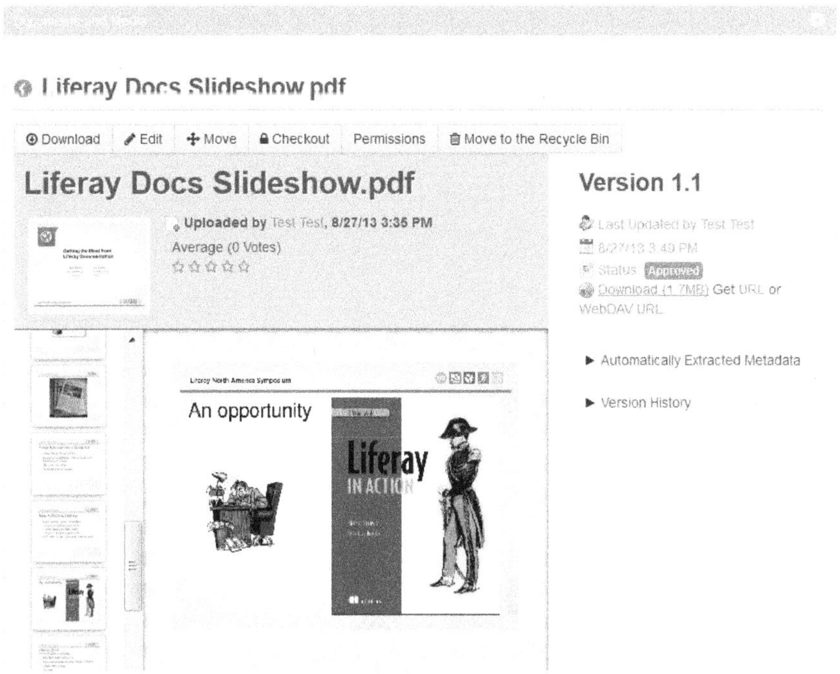

Figure 5.9: You can watch a video clip or even view a slideshow inside Liferay's Documents and Media portlet.

Document type restrictions and workflow per folder

You can force users to add only certain document types to a folder. By default, child folders inherit the restrictions of their parent folder. You can change this behavior by editing the folder and selecting the allowed document types.

If workflow is enabled, you can specify different workflow definitions per folder. Furthermore, you can specify different workflow definitions per document type and per folder. You can set this by editing the folder. Then the UI will look like this:

Document types are a powerful way to enforce rules for documents uploaded by users. Next, we'll see a way to make it incredibly easy for users to access documents stored in Liferay's Documents and Media repositories.

WebDAV access

Wouldn't it be great if you could access documents and folders belonging to Liferay's Documents and Media library from your own machine's file manager? You can, thanks to the Documents and Media library's WebDAV integration. WebDAV stands for Web-based Distributed Authoring and Versioning. It's a set of methods based on HTTP that allows users to create, edit, move, or delete files stored on web servers. WebDAV is supported by most major operating systems and desktop environments, including Linux (both KDE and GNOME), Mac OS, and Windows.

Suppose you've created an *Image Gallery* folder using a Documents and Media portlet and uploaded some images to it. Portal users with the appropriate permissions can access this folder, and the image files it contains, using a browser and Liferay's web interface. WebDAV provides an alternative way to do this using a file manager instead of a web

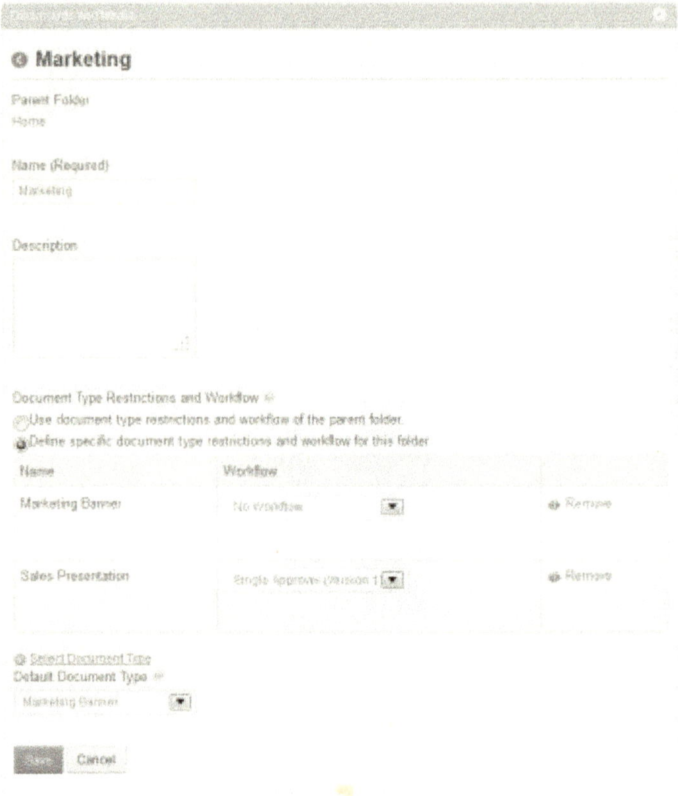

Figure 5.10: Restrict Marketing folder to use specific document types and workflow

browser. To access a folder stored in a Documents and Media portlet on a remote server, you'll need log in credentials for the portal and the WebDAV URL of the folder you'd like to access.

Next, navigate to the Documents and Media portlet hosting the folder you'd like to access. Mouse over the folder (*Image Gallery* for our example) and select *Access from Desktop*.

Copy the WebDAV URL. On Windows, right-click on *Computer* and select *Map Network Drive*. Select an unused drive, paste the WebDAV URL, and click *Finish*. You're prompted to enter your Liferay credentials and then, provided you have the required permissions, the *Image Gallery* folder appears. You can now add, edit, move, or delete files in this directory.

On Mac OS X, select *Go →Connect to Server* in Finder. Then enter the WebDAV URL of the folder you'd like to access in the Server Address field, click *Connect* and you should be prompted for your Liferay credentials.

On Linux, you must slightly modify the WebDAV URL of your folder in your file manager. For KDE's Dolphin, change the URL's protocol so that it says webdav:// instead of http://. For GNOME's Nautilus, change the URL's protocol so that it says dav:// instead of http://. Then press *Enter* and you're prompted for your Liferay credentials.

Note that Liferay increments the version numbers of files edited and uploaded via WebDAV so you don't have to worry that using your file manager will bypass the functionality

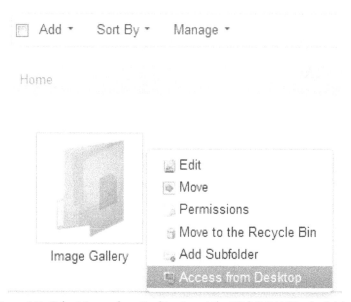

Figure 5.11: Select *Access from Desktop* to get the WebDAV URL of a folder.

of Liferay's web interface. The Documents and Media application is a powerful way to manage any types of files your users need to use. Next, let's look at how you can leverage Liferay Portal's Asset framework.

Now you know just how easy it is to store your files using Liferay's Documents and Media portlet. In the next section, we'll review some ways to organize and manage your assets so you're getting the most out of your content.

5.7 Liferay Sync

Liferay Sync is an add-on product for Liferay 6.1 GA2 CE and EE, and later versions, that synchronizes files between your Liferay server and users' desktop and mobile environments. With Liferay Sync, your users can publish and access shared documents and files from their native environments without using a browser. Windows and Mac OS desktops and Android and iOS-based mobile platforms are currently supported, while Linux users have an unsupported beta they can use. As users add and collaborate on documents and files, Liferay Sync automatically synchronizes them across all configured Sync clients. Liferay Sync is fully integrated into the Liferay Platform so that features such as authentication, versioning, and social collaboration function in the supported environments. Liferay Sync stores files locally so that they're always available, even when you're offline. It automatically synchronizes your files upon reconnection.

How does it work?

Liferay Sync manages documents and site information through Liferay's built-in web services. Clients securely communicate to Liferay using user-supplied credentials such that each users can only access those documents and sites for which they have permission. Changes made through Liferay Sync are immediately available to the rest of the Liferay Platform, including users accessing Liferay through traditional web-based interfaces.

For desktop environments, a new folder structure is created and used for synchroniz-ing files. Files found therein can be treated as any ordinary file. Credentials, sync fre-quency, and other options can be configured in-client. Native desktop notification events keep you abreast of what Sync is doing, and native menu and taskbar integration keep Sync controls within easy reach.

Mobile environments are naturally dependent on the way in which documents are han-dled. For Android and iOS, documents are maintained in a file list, and can be viewed by clicking on the files themselves. External files accessible from other apps can be "opened" using Liferay Sync, thereby dropping them into your Sync folder and synchronizing them across other Sync clients. In iOS devices, "pulling down" on the Sync file list forces a re-fresh. In Android, click on the *Refresh* icon within the menu.

Liferay Sync is designed to work with both Liferay 6.1 GA2 CE and EE, and later ver-sions. Using Sync with Liferay CE limits users to syncing one site. Using Sync with Liferay EE enables users to synchronize documents and files across all the sites they can access.

Liferay Sync is also designed to work with Liferay Social Office. You can sync one site from Social Office CE as well as one site from Liferay Portal CE. If you've installed Social Office CE on Liferay Portal EE, then you can sync any site from Portal, but only one from Social Office. If you've installed Social Office EE on Liferay Portal EE, then you can sync any and all sites.

Installing Liferay Sync

For Windows or Mac OS, visit the Liferay Sync product page Liferay Sync Product Page, and click *Get it Now* (on the right-side navigation menu) to download the client applica-tion for your desktop environment. For Windows, the client application installer should be named `liferay-sync-[version]-[date].exe`. For Mac OS, it should be `life-ray-sync-[version]-[date].dmg`. There is also a Linux beta version available. Fol-low the on-screen instructions of the installer wizard to configure your client to connect to an existing Liferay 6.2 deployment using your Liferay credentials.

Prior to Liferay 6.2, Liferay Portal's Documents and Media services contained all the logic used by Liferay Sync. As of Liferay 6.2, Sync processing has been removed from the portal and been placed in a plugin. Make sure that the Sync plugin has been installed on your Liferay server before trying to connect to your portal via a Liferay Sync client. The Sync plugin's name is *sync-web* and is installed by default in Liferay Portal bundles. The Sync plugin is also available on Liferay Marketplace and can be downloaded and installed on your Liferay server just like any other Marketplace app. To find the app on Market-place, search for *Sync CE* or *Sync EE*, depending on your portal version. To receive new features, optimizations, and bug fixes, make sure to the update your Sync app whenever a new version is available.

Windows

Upon launching the Windows application installer, you'll be prompted to choose an instal-lation location for Liferay Sync. Browse to an appropriate location on your machine and click *Install*. After the installation is complete, you'll need to complete the Liferay Sync setup. Leave the *Run Liferay Sync* button checked to automatically start Liferay Sync after you click *Finish*.

The first time you run Liferay Sync, you'll have to enter some account information. Sync needs to know where you'd like to locally store the files it's supposed to sync with your Liferay server. And, of course, it needs to know your server's URL and the account credentials with which it should authenticate.

The options for the Mac OS application installer are similar.

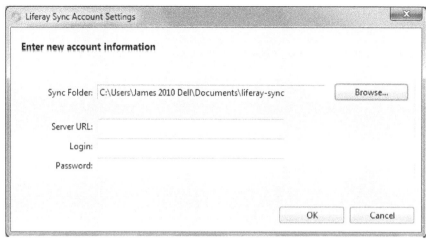

Figure 5.12: The first time you run Liferay Sync, you'll have to tell it how to communicate with your Liferay server.

Mac OS

Liferay Sync for Mac is packaged in a DMG file. Double-clicking on a DMG mounts it as a disk image, and opens a window showing the contents of the image. To install Sync, drag the Liferay Sync icon to the Applications folder. Once it's installed, go to your Applications folder to run it.

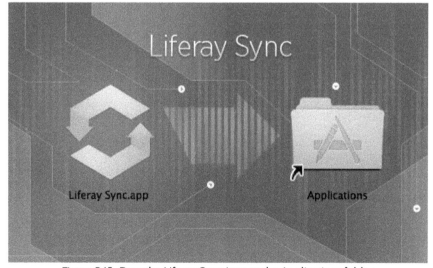

Figure 5.13: Drag the Liferay Sync icon to the Applications folder.

When you launch Liferay Sync, the first thing you need to do is provide it with the URL for the Liferay server that you'll be using Sync with, along with your Liferay credentials. After that, you'll need to run through the brief setup process that was described above for Windows.

Once you've finished your configuration and have clicked *OK*, Liferay Sync starts running in the background, and an icon appears in your top menu bar. If you wish to change any of your settings, click the icon to open the Liferay Sync menu and click on *Preferences*. Note that on Windows, the Sync menu says *Properties*, not *Preferences*.

Mobile

For iOS, visit the App Store, search for Liferay, and install the Liferay Sync App.

For Android, go to Google Play, search for Liferay, and install the Liferay Sync App.

Once the mobile apps are installed, follow the on-screen instructions as below.

Using Liferay Sync on the Desktop

Once installed, you'll see a Liferay Sync icon in your taskbar whenever it's running. A green checkmark means Liferay Sync has a working connection to your Liferay server and is updating the files in your Sync folder according to the interval you specified in the wizard. Click the Liferay Sync icon in your taskbar to bring up the menu. The options availabe from the menu are listed below:

Open Sync Folder opens your Liferay Sync folder in your native file manager.

Open Website provides links to the pages containing the Documents and Media portlets which you have permission to access. By default, you can find links to your personal Documents and Media repository as well as links to the Documents and Media repositories of all the other sites you belong to.

 Note for administrators: If you don't have a Documents and Media portlet anywhere on a site that's been selected for syncing, you'll have to add the portlet. Otherwise, users will get a *The requested resource was not found* error when they try to use the *Open Website* link from their Sync menus.

Recent Files shows a list of recently created or modified files from all the repositories you can access.

Properties (*Preferences*, on Mac OS) lets you change properties like starting on login, desktop notifications, and sync frequency. It also allows you to edit the account information you provided when you started Sync for the first time. For example, you can enter a new URL for your Liferay server and enter a different set of Liferay credentials.

There are three items listed in the *General Settings* section. *Start Liferay Sync on Login* is checked by default. If you don't want Sync to start automatically, uncheck this. *Show Desktop Notifications* is also checked by default. Unless you uncheck this, when a file that you have synced is changed, a small notification will appear in the corner of your screen. The *Check Server For Updates Every:* field enables you to set how frequently it will check to see if anything has changed. This can be set anywhere between 5 seconds and 30 minutes.

Click the *Edit Settings* button in the *Account Settings* section to specify your server's URL and enter your Liferay credentials. Use the *Test Connection* button to make sure Liferay Sync can communicate with the server. Editing your settings also allows you to specify your Sync folder, the folder where Sync will store files on your machine. By default, files are stored in the *liferay-sync* subfolder of your personal Documents folder.

Finally, the *Site Settings* section allows you to choose which sites you wish to sync media from. By default, it will list all of the sites that you are a member of, but you can uncheck any of those sites if you don't want to sync those files.

About displays Liferay Sync version information, copyright information, and a link to Liferay's home page.

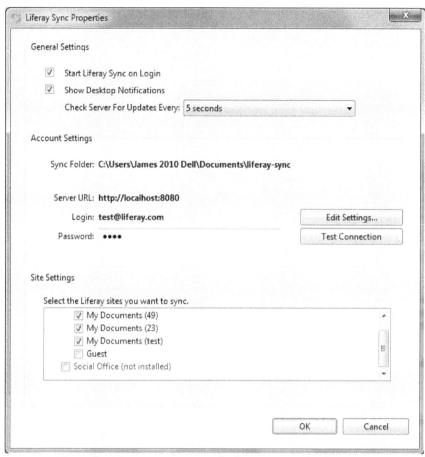

Figure 5.14: Open the Liferay Sync menu and select *Properties* (*Preferences*, on Mac OS) to edit the settings you configured during setup.

Check for Updates checks to see if a new version of Liferay Sync is available from liferay.com and allows you to set whether or not Liferay Sync should automatically check for updates.

Using your Sync folder

Once Liferay Sync has been configured and is running, any files you add to or modify in your Sync folder are automatically detected and uploaded to your Liferay server. Also, changes from other users are downloaded to your Sync folder.

If you delete a file your sync folder, it will only be deleted locally. It will not be deleted on the server. This mechanism prevents users from accidentally deleting shared files. When you delete a file from you Sync folder, Sync will no longer download changes to this file the next time it syncs. If you want to go back to syncing a file, simply restore it from you recycle bin or trash can. Once the file is restored back to the Sync folder, Sync keeps that file in sync by uploading any of your changes and downloading any changes from the server.

You can run through the following exercise to familiarize yourself with how to create,

edit, download, and upload files with Liferay Sync. First, open your Liferay Sync folder
in your file manager (use the *Open Sync Folder* option of the Liferay Sync menu from the
taskbar), and create a new file called README.txt. Edit this file and enter the word *test*.
Next, check that you can access this file from your Liferay site. Open your browser, navigate to your Liferay site, and sign in with your Liferay account credentials. First, make
sure that that you're on the site you want to sync with. Then navigate to *Site Administration*
→*Documents and Media*. You should see your README.txt file listed there.

Download the file (click the small triangle icon at the top right corner of the *README.txt*
icon and select *Download*) to a convenient location on your machine and check that it still
says *test*. Now open the README.txt file in your Sync folder and edit it so that it says *second test*. Once the changes are synced go back to your browser and refresh your Documents
and Media page. Click on the *README.txt* icon, look at the information displayed to the
right, and you'll see that its version number has incremented.

Figure 5.15: Updating a file through Liferay Sync increments the file's version number.
You can view a file's version number through the web interface.

You'll see that it now says *second test*—your edit was uploaded to the server. You can be
confident that this edit was also downloaded by all other Liferay Sync clients connected to
your site.

Demonstrating Liferay Sync Permissions

Liferay Sync uses the default Liferay permissions to determine which files and folders are synced to the user's machine. This means that whatever files a user can access from a certain site are the ones that will be pulled down by Liferay Sync if that site is selected in the Sync client. You can test the functionality of Liferay Sync permissions by performing the following steps. First, create a new file on your desktop called *secret.txt*. Enter the text *classified information* into this file. Then use your browser to log into Liferay and create a new user called *secretagent* with the email address *secretagent@liferay.com* and the password *test*. Also, create a new private site called *Secret Site*. Then assign the *secretagent* user to the *Secret Site* and grant the *Site Administrator* role to this user. There will be no other members of this site unless they are assigned by an administrator. Log in as the *secretagent* and select *Secret Site* from the *My Sites* tab on the Dockbar. Then click on *Documents and Media* and upload the *secret.txt* document.

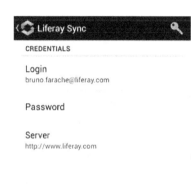

Next, we'll configure our Liferay Sync client to log in with the *secretagent* user's credentials and access the *Secret Site*. Open the Liferay Sync menu from the taskbar and select *Properties*. Click on the *Edit Settings* button, choose a new Sync folder, enter your server's URL, and enter the secret agent's credentials: *secretagent@liferay.com* and *test*. Lastly, uncheck all Liferay sites except the *Secret Site*, and click *OK*. Confirm that the *secret.txt* file that you uploaded to the *Secret Site*, is downloaded to your new Sync folder. Open it and check that it says *classified information*. If you reconfigure your Sync client connect to your Liferay instance using the credentials of another user who doesn't belong to the *Secret Site*, the *secret.txt* will not be downloaded. Congratulations! You've successfully set up a Liferay Sync folder that can only be accessed by the *secretagent* user and your administrators.

Using Liferay Sync Mobile

Once you've installed Liferay Sync on your Android or iOS mobile environment, you'll be able to access the same functionality that's available when using Sync on a desktop environment. However, the interface differs from that of the Sync desktop clients. Let's discuss the usage of Liferay Sync Mobile for Android first.

Figure 5.16: Click the wrench icon to access your Liferay server credentials.

Android

After installing Liferay Sync for Android, an empty screen appears asking you to set up the app. This screen appears whenever preferences are missing. Touch the screen and it displays the *Settings* view. You can always go back to *Settings* by clicking on the wrench icon at the top right corner of the screen.

Enter your Liferay server credentials by filling in your *Login*, *Password*, and *Server* information. Your *Login* is either your user account's email address or screen name. Use the same credentials you use to log in to the portal in a browser. In the *Server* field, enter your portal's URL. In this example, the server URL is *http://www.liferay.com*. Click the key icon on the top right to test your connection and check if everything is correct.

Note for Gingerbread users: If you can't see some of the features described here, click on the menu button to view a list of all possible actions. This includes options to refresh, open the settings menu, upload files, take photos, test your connection, etc. After you have successfully tested your connection, hit the *back* button and you'll see a list of Liferay sites you have access to.

Figure 5.17: Sites

Figure 5.18: Liferay Sync's details view offers several options.

You can browse the files of a site by tapping on any of them. This opens a list of the folders and files belonging to the site that you have permission to view. From here, you can click on a folder and browse deeper into the folder hierarchy or click the *Back* button to navigate back to parent folders up to the initial *Sites* list.

Single-tap on a file to open it. If the file has never been downloaded before, Sync will download it and open after it has finished downloading. You can only view the file's contents if your device has an app installed that can open the file type. For example, in order to open a PDF, you must have at least one PDF viewer app installed. Otherwise, you will see a message informing you that no viewer is available and you need to install an app that can open the file.

Long-press on any folder or file to find a list of actions you can take on it: *Add to Favorites*, *View Details*, *Download*, *Rename* or *Delete*. This actions menu varies depending on which entry type is selected: file or folder.

On Gingerbread, the actions menu appears in the middle of the screen. On Ice Cream Sandwich and above, you can find the action icons and menu at the top right.

Clicking on *Add to Favorites* (Gingerbread) or the gray star (Ice Cream Sandwich) adds the selected file to the *Favorites* list. *Favorites* are special files that can be accessed and viewed even when you are offline (more details below). If a file is already marked as a favorite, you'll see a *Remove from Favorites* or blue star instead. Clicking on it removes the selected file from the *Favorites* list.

Clicking on *View Details* (Gingerbread) or the round icon with the letter "i" (Ice Cream Sandwich) opens the details view, which displays the entry's metadata such as creation date, author, version, description, etc.

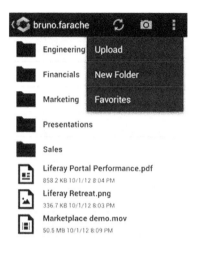

If you click on *Download* (floppy disk icon on Ice Cream Sandwich), it downloads and overwrites the local file copy.

You can rename a folder or file by clicking on the *Rename* option. This renames the entry in the portal.

Clicking on *Delete* deletes the file/folder from the remote portal, and other users won't be able to view or download it. On Ice Cream Sandwich and above, you can select multiple entries for deletion.

Figure 5.19: More options are available by selecting the three dots button.

Some actions are not related to a specific folder or file. You can find these actions in the menu on the top action bar when no entry is selected (Gingerbread users need to click on the device menu button). Depending on the device screen width, some icons may overflow to the three dots button on the right. Click on this button to see all of the available actions.

The *Refresh* button fetches and updates the list of folders and files that have been changed in the portal.

The *Camera* button allows you to quickly take a picture and upload the image to the current folder. The image file name is automatically generated with a time stamp.

The *New Folder* button asks you for the name of the folder you want to create in the portal.

The *Upload* button displays the types of local files you can upload to the portal. Choosing *Image*, for example, shows all images that are stored locally on your device. Once you choose the files and confirm, these files are uploaded to the portal and are placed in the current folder. By default, you can upload images, videos, and audio files. If you have installed an app on your device that can open and browse any type of file, you will also see an option called *Other files*.

The *Favorites* menu option opens the favorites list. All files that have been marked as favorites show up in this list. You should mark your most important files as favorites because, as mentioned earlier, the *Favorites* feature gives you quick offline access to them. You can view the contents of items in the *Favorites* list, view their metadata and, of course, remove them from the list.

Next, let's look at the iOS Sync app.

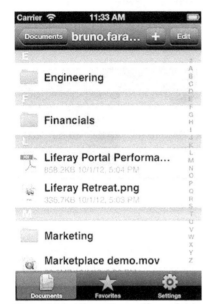

Figure 5.20: Liferay Sync offers a folder and files menu.

You can refresh the list by pushing it down. This updates all the files and folders that have been changed in the portal.

When you click on a file, this file is downloaded from the remote portal and, if a previewer for this file type is available, you can view the contents of the file. The next time you open a file, it won't download it again; instead, it opens the local copy.

There are 3 icons at the bottom of the screen when you open a file:

- Round icon with the letter "i" opens the details view, which displays the entry's metadata such as creation date, author, version, description, etc.

- Star icon at the center adds the selected file to the *Favorites* list. *Favorites* are special files that can be accessed and viewed even when you are offline (more details below). If a

iOS

After installing Liferay Sync for iOS, an empty screen appears asking you to set up the app. This screen appears whenever preferences are missing.

Click on *Settings* in the toolbar and enter your Liferay server credentials by filling in your *Login*, *Password*, and *Server* information. Your *Login* is either your user account's email address or screen name, whichever you use to log in to the portal in a browser. In the *Server* field, enter your portal's URL. In this example, the server URL is *http://www.liferay.com*. Click on *Test Connection* to check if your configuration is correct.

After you have successfully tested your connection, tap on the *Documents* toolbar section and you'll see a list of Liferay sites you have access to. You can browse the files of a site by tapping on its name or icon. This opens a list of the folders and files belonging to the site that you have permission to view.

From here, you can click on a folder to browse deeper into the folder hierarchy. You can also click on the *Back* button to navigate back to parent folders up to the initial *Sites* list.

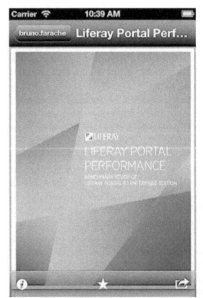

Figure 5.21: Local files are stored after they are downloaded.

file has already been marked as a favorite, clicking on the star icon removes the file from the *Favorites* list.

- Share icon displays sharing options. You can, for example, send the file as an email attachment, print the file, or copy it to your clipboard. Some external apps may also appear in this list. For example, you can share your file with social apps and messengers if they are available.

In the file list, there's an Edit button. Clicking on it switches the app to the edit mode as shown below:

Selecting one or more files or folders and clicking on the *Delete* button deletes the selected files or folders from the re-mote portal. Once you delete files or fold-ers from the remote portal, other users won't be able to view or download them.

Selecting only one file or folder enables the *Rename* button. Click on it to change the entry's name locally and remotely.

To quickly delete a file or folder from the portal, you can also swipe right and click on the *Delete* button in the file list view.

If you want to upload an image or video to the portal, click the *Plus* button at the top right corner. You should see three op-tions:

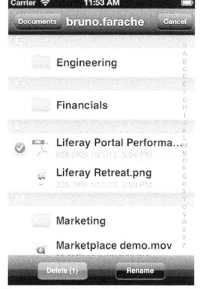

Figure 5.22: Edit mode is a key feature in Liferay Sync mobile.

- *Take a photo or video* opens your cam-era app and lets you take a photo or record a video and upload it.

- *Choose Existing* allows you to upload multiple photos or videos stored on your device.

- *Create New Folder* lets you type the name of the folder and creates it in the portal.

The *Favorites* toolbar section opens the favorites list. All files that have been marked as favorites show up in this list. You should mark your most important files as favorites because, as mentioned earlier, the *Favorites* feature gives you quick offline access to them. You can view the contents of items in the *Favorites* list, view their metadata and, of course, remove them from the list.

All downloaded files are stored on your device indefinitely. If you want to delete down-loaded files locally but don't want to remove them from the portal, go to *Settings* and click on the *Clear Cache* button.

5.8 Summary

In this chapter, we examined Liferay's Documents and Media Library, a powerful and customizable virtual shared drive. Liferay 6.1 introduced the ability to mount multiple external repositories to the Documents and Media library. The Documents and Media library can be used to store files of any kind. The Documents and Media Display portlet is meant to be configured to show chosen hierarchies of folders and files from the Documents and Media library. The Media Gallery is meant for presenting media files such as images or videos.

Document types and metadata sets provide a flexible way to distinguish between different types of files and to define custom metadata fields for them. Document previews are automatically generated by default, but Liferay supports integration with external tools that offer greater speed, higher quality, and additional functionality. Finally, we discussed Liferay Sync, an add-on product for Liferay 6.1 that allows your Liferay server to directly synchronize files on users' desktop and mobile environments.

## CHAPTER 6

DISPLAYING CONTENT DYNAMICALLY

Any type of content in Liferay is considered an asset. In chapters 2 and 3, we examined Liferay's most common type of asset: web content. Other types of assets include blog posts, wiki articles, message board posts, bookmarks, and documents. It's possible for developers to define custom asset types that utilize Liferay's asset framework. Originally, the asset framework was created to provide a mechanism for adding tags to blog entries, wiki articles, and web content without reimplementing the same functionality multiple times. The asset framework has been greatly extended since then and it now supports tags, categories, vocabularies, comments, ratings, and asset relationships.

This chapter covers the following topics:

- Tagging and categorizing content
- Using targeted, single value, and multi-value vocabularies
- Using faceted search
- Using the Asset Publisher
- Setting up display pages
- Adding relationships between assets

The Asset Publisher portlet is designed to display multiple assets. It has quite a few configuration options which we'll cover in this chapter. By default, abstracts (previews) of recently published assets are displayed by the Asset Publisher portlet and links to their full views are provided. You can configure the Asset Publisher portlet to display a table of assets, a list of asset titles, or the full content of assets. You can also configure the Asset Publisher to display only certain kinds of assets and you choose how many items to display in a list. The Asset Publisher portlet is very useful for displaying chosen types of content, for displaying recent content, and for allowing users to browse content by tags and categories. The Asset Publisher is designed to integrate with the Tags Navigation and Categories Navigation portlets to allow this.

6.1   Tagging and Categorizing Content

Tags and categories are two important tools you can use to help organize information on your portal. These tools help users to easily find the content they're looking for through search or navigation. Tagging and categorizing assets is easy. You can tag or categorize an asset at creation time or when editing an existing asset. If you click on the *Categorization* section of the form for creating or editing an asset, you'll find an interface for adding tags and categories. If no categories are available to be added to the asset (e.g., if no categories have been created), the Categories heading won't appear.

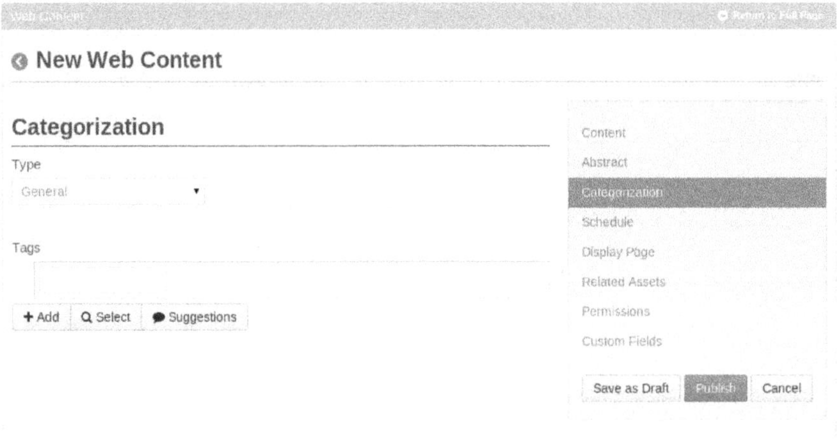

Figure 6.1: Here, the Web Content Display portlet's form for categorizing a new web content instance doesn't include a Categories heading since no categories have been created.

The Control Panel contains an interface for managing tags and categories for each site in the portal. This interface can be used to manage all your tags and categories in one place. It is important that you both tag and categorize your content when you enter it. Let's take a closer look at tags and categories.

Tags

Tags are an important tool that can help organize information on your portal and make it easier for users to find the content that they're interested in. Tags are words or phrases that you can attach to any content on the website. Tagging content makes your search results more accurate and enables you to use tools like the Asset Publisher to display content in an organized fashion on a web page. There are two ways to create tags: you can do it through the administrative console in the Control Panel or on the fly as content is created. By default, tags can be created by regular users and users can apply them to any assets which they have permission to create or edit.

While regular users can, by default, create new tags by applying them to any assets that they have permission to create or edit, only site administrators can access the *Tags* portlet in the Content section of the Site Administration area of the Control Panel. Here, site administrators can create new tags and edit any existing site tags. To create tags in the Control Panel, visit the site for which you want to create tags and then click on *Admin* →*Content*. Then click on *Tags* in the Content section on the left. From this screen, you can view existing tags and create new ones. To create a new tag, click *Add Tag* and enter a name for the tag.

You can also customize a tag's permissions and properties. This configuration, however, must be done by a server administrator. To implement this configuration, add a portal-ext.properties file to your Liferay Home directory with the following contents and then restart the server:

```
asset.tag.permissions.enabled=true
```

```
asset.tag.properties.enabled=true
```

Once this is done, you can change the permissions on a tag to make it viewable by guests, site members, or owner. You can also assign other permissions for managing tags, including permission to delete the tag, edit the tag, or edit the tag's permissions. You can also add properties to a tag. Properties are a way to add information to specific tags. You can think of tag properties as tags for your tags. Structurally, tag properties are key-value pairs associated with specific tags that provide information about the tags.

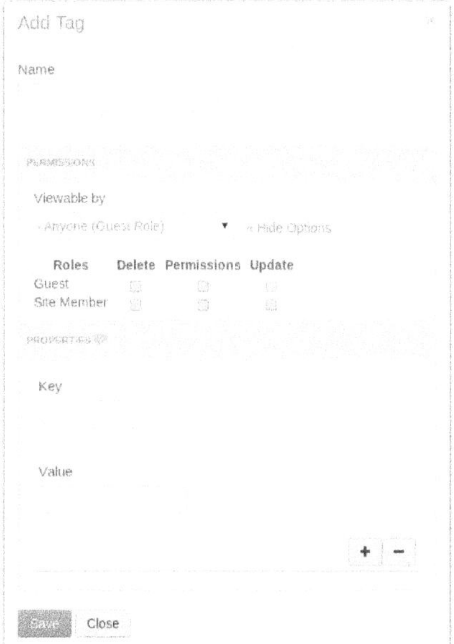

Figure 6.2: The Add Tag interface with editing of tag properties and permissions enabled. When managing a site's content, click on *Tags* and then *Add Tag* to create a new tag. The Add Tag interface allows you to enter a name for the tag, define permissions for the tag, and add properties to the tag.

Tags are not the only portal-wide mechanism for describing content: you can also use categories.

Categories

Categories are similar in concept to tags, but are designed for use by administrators, not regular users. Hierarchies of categories can be created, and categories can be grouped together in *vocabularies*. While tags represent an ad hoc method for users to group content together, categories exist to allow administrators to organize content in a more official, hierarchical structure. You can think of tags like the index of a book and categories like its table of contents. Both serve the same purpose: to help users find the information they seek.

Adding vocabularies and categories is similar to adding tags. Visit the site for which you want to create categories and then click on *Admin* →*Content*. Then click on *Categories* in the Content section on the left to view the categories administration portlet.

Clicking on a vocabulary on the left displays any categories that have been created under that vocabulary. To create a new vocabulary, click on the *Add Vocabulary* button. Enter a name and, optionally, a description. By default, the *Allow Multiple Categories* box is checked. This allows multiple categories from the vocabulary to be applied to an asset. If the box is unchecked, only one category from the vocabulary can be applied to add asset. The *Associated Asset Types* lets you choose which asset types the categories of the vocabulary can be applied to and which asset types are *required* to have an associated asset from the vocabulary. Lastly, you can configure the permissions of the vocabulary. Should the vocabulary be viewable by guests? Only site members? Only owners? Which of these roles should be able to delete the vocabulary, update it, or edit its permissions? By default, guests can view the vocabulary but only the owner can delete it, update it, or configure its permissions.

Creating new categories is similar to creating new tags except that categories must be added to an existing vocabulary and they can only be create by site administrators. However, once created, regular users can apply categories to any assets they have permission to create or edit. To create a new category, click the *Add Category* button in the categories administration portlet. Enter a name for the new category and, optionally, a description. Use the *To Vocabulary* dropdown list to select a vocabulary to which to add the category. Just as with tags, you can configure the permissions of the category, choosing which roles (guest, site member, owner) can view the category, apply it to an asset, delete it, update it, or configure its permissions. By default, categories are viewable by guests and site members can apply categories to assets. Also, you can add properties to categories, just as with tags. Category properties are a way to add information to specific categories. You can think of category properties as tags for your categories. Structurally, category properties are just like tag properties: they are key-value pairs associated with specific categories that provide information about the categories.

Once you have created some vocabularies and categories, you can take advantage of the full capabilities of categories by creating a nested hierarchy of categories. To nest categories, select the category that you'd like to be the parent category. Then drag any category that should be a child category onto it. You will see a plus sign appear next to the name of the category you are dragging if you can add it to the selected parent category; if you see a red *x* that means that you cannot add that category as a subcategory of parent category that you have selected.

After you have created a hierarchy of categories, your content creators will have them available to apply to content that they create. Click on *Web Content* in the Content section of the Site Administration area the Control Panel and click *Add* &rrar; *Basic Web Content*. Click on *Categorization* from the right-side menu and click *Select* on the vocabulary you'd like to apply. A dialog box appears with your categories. Select any relevant categories by checking the box next to them, and they'll be applied to the content.

Liferay 6.1 added several new features to vocabularies and categories. We mentioned a few of these already when we were discussing the *Allow Multiple Categories* and *Required* checkboxes for vocabularies and categories. The three new features are targeted vocabularies, single/multi-valued vocabularies, and separated widgets for every vocabulary.

Figure 6.3: When managing a site's content, click on *Categories* and then on *Add Vocabulary* to create a new vocabulary. By default, a vocabulary called *Topic* already exists. When adding new categories, make sure you're adding them to the correct vocabulary.

Targeted Vocabularies

Targeted Vocabularies allow you to decide which vocabularies can be applied to an asset type and which vocabularies are required for an asset type. To configure these settings, go to the categories administration portlet in the Control Panel and mouse over the vocabulary in the list until you see the edit icon to the right. Select the icon to reveal a dialog box like the one below.

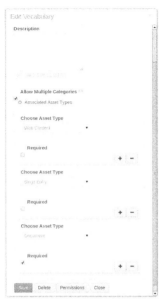

Figure 6.4: You can target vocabularies by checking the *Allow Multiple Categories* checkbox and then selecting the Asset Types.

The default value for *Associated Asset Types* is *All Asset Types*. You can fine tune your choices by using the + and - buttons, which narrows the scope of the vocabulary to specific assets. In the screenshot above, notice that the vocabulary is configured to be available for Web Content instances and Blog entries, but it is not required. It is mandatory, however, for Documents and Media files.

Single and Multi-valued Vocabularies

You can also decide if users can choose one or more categories from the same vocabulary to apply to an asset. If a vocabulary is single-valued you can only choose one. If it allows more, you can choose several categories from the vocabulary to apply to an asset.

You can configure the single-valued or multi-valued status of a vocabulary through the categories administration portlet. Edit a vocabulary and deselect the *Allow Multiple Categories* checkbox to create a single-valued vocabulary. Use the default option to create a multi-valued vocabulary.

Separated Widgets

A third feature of vocabularies and categories is that every vocabulary has its own separated widget. These widgets appear in the Categorization section of the form for editing an asset and they allow users to easily select appropriate categories for that asset.

It's important to use tags and categories with all your content, so that content is easier for users to find. Let's look at one of the ways users will make use of tags and categories: searching for content.

6.2 Searching for Content in Liferay

To stay organized, I (RS) used to use a paper-based planner. It had different sections for various areas of my life. Its initial incarnation came from a commercial company, but over the years I tweaked it into something that worked for me. This final

Figure 6.5: Multi-valued vocabularies allow multiple categories from the vocabulary to be applied to an asset. Single-valued vocabularies only allow one category from the vocabulary to be applied. Here, the *Cinema* and *Music* categories are selected to be applied but the *Sports* category is not.

version (before I went digital) had different tabs for different areas of my life that I wanted to keep track of: daily items like tasks, notes, a spiritual section, and agenda pages that kept track of things I needed to go over with specific people. A planning section had tabs for projects, family, future items, and reference.

Of course, since this was paper-based, it had its limitations. It was kind of hard to find stuff. Did I put the note I'd written about that new toy my daughter wanted in the notes section or in the family section? Or maybe it was on my *While Out* list, so I would remember to buy it before her birthday?

Liferay content can be like this. That important information you remember seeing—was it in a wiki article, a message boards post, or web content? Did you remember to tag it? If you don't have this kind of information, browsing to the content you're looking for could be difficult. Thankfully, Liferay includes a powerful, faceted search function. You can access this function through the Search portlet, which lets you drill down through the different types of content, tags, and categories to refine your search. Let's look at the search features Liferay provides for specific kinds of content and then examine how to use Liferay's faceted search.

Categorization

Type

Famous Noses

Cinema   Music

Q Select

Membership

Premium

Q Select

Tags

cool   fun   web content

＋Add   Q Select   ● Suggestions

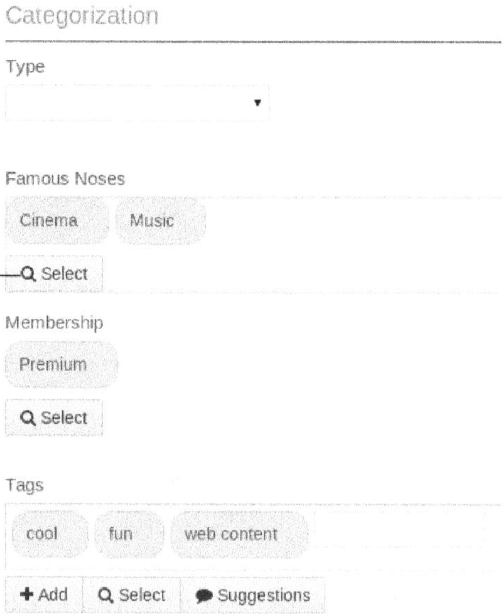

Figure 6.6: Vocabularies have their own widgets, making it easy to select available categories.

Searching for Specific Types of Content

Liferay provides several applications that allow users and administrators to search for content. First, there's the Search portlet. The Search portlet can be placed on a page to allow users to search for assets of any type. We'll learn how to use the Search portlet when we discuss Liferay's faceted search feature in the next section. There's also a Web Content Search portlet. This portlet can be placed on a page to allow users to search for web content instances. Users can't use the Web Content Search portlet to search for other kinds of content. However, the Blogs, Wiki, Message Boards, Documents and Media, and Web Content portlets all provide search bars that allow users to search among the specific types of assets with which these portlets allow users to interact. Note that all of these portlets are accessible from the Control Panel. They can also, except for the Web Content portlet, be placed on portal pages for end-users to use. The Web Content portlet is not designed for end users; it's intended for administrative use only.

Note: The Web Content Search portlet is deprecated in Liferay 6.2 and will be removed in Liferay 7.0. The Web Content Search portlet will be migrated to the Search portlet, which will be configured to only search for web content.

In order for content to be searchable, it must first be indexed. Liferay uses Lucene for indexing and searching for content. Please refer to the Lucene section of the portal properties file if you'd like to customize Liferay's indexing and search behavior. By default, Liferay indexes blog posts, wiki articles, and message board posts, Documents and Media files' descriptions, and web content instances. If a Documents and Media file is a text file, the file's content is indexed as well. Comments on blog posts, wiki articles, and Documents and Media files and text file attachments to wiki articles and message board posts are also indexed. Liferay automatically indexes content as it's added to the portal.

If you'd like to search among assets of a specific type and you'd like to include comments and attachments in your search, use the search bar of the appropriate portlet. For example, if you'd like to search for the term *Liferay* among wiki articles, enter the term *Liferay* into the Wiki portlet's search bar.

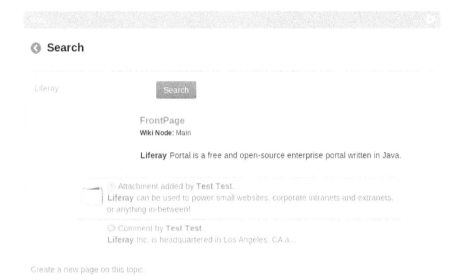

Figure 6.7: When using the Wiki portlet's search bar to search for *Liferay*, wiki articles, comments, and attachments containing the word *Liferay* are returned.

Wiki articles, comments, and text file attachments containing the word *Liferay* are returned as search results. The search results clearly show whether an individual search result is a wiki article, a comment, or an attachment. In the next section, we'll see how the Search portlet can be used to search through multiple types of content on Liferay. Its faceted search feature is a powerful tool that allows users to include or not include specific types of assets in a search. However, the Search portlet does not return comments or attachments as search results.

Searching for Portal Content Using Facets

To get started using faceted search, drop the Search portlet on a page and search for something. You'll see a page with results on the right and a collection of *facets* on the left.

Facets allow users of the Search portlet to select criteria with which to filter search results. A facet is a combination of the information about a specific indexed field, its terms, and their frequency. Facets are typically named by the field in question. From the Search

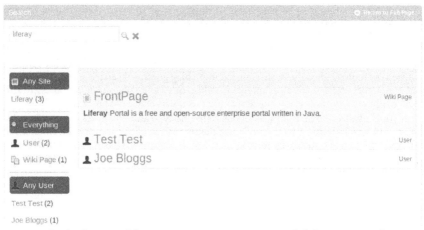

Figure 6.8: The first set of facets is content types. You can drill down to specific types of content that contain the search terms you entered.

portlet's Configuration window, administrators can configure the facets available to users for filtering search results. The default facets include the following:

- Site
- Asset type
- Asset tag
- Asset category
- Folder
- User
- Modified time range

For example, after searching for a certain term in the Search portlet, clicking on a specific site filters the search results to only display assets within the specified site. Clicking on a specific user filters the search results to only display assets added by the specified user. The frequency with which the term was found for each facet is listed in parentheses after the facet. It may jog your memory to see that the term you searched for appears in a blog entry, and that may be all you need to find what you were looking for. If, however, your memory is more foggy than that, or you're searching for something you're not sure is actually there, then the asset tags or asset categories facets may be more helpful to you.

For example, if you searched for a wireless phone, you might be more interested in content that has your search terms in it *and* has also been tagged by users. One or more tags might help you to find what you're looking for. Note that the number of tags that appear is configurable: by default it's 10, but there could be many more as a result of a particular search. We'll look at the configuration options later in the chapter. For now, let's learn how to drill down to narrow search results.

To drill down into the search, click on a facet to add it to the filter list. The results to the right are refined by the selected facets.

Here, we've refined the search to only show documents. We've also selected one of the tags, *cool*, to refine the search. The facets we've selected, *Document* and *cool*, appear in a list at the top, and there's a red "X" next to it that lets us remove it from our filter as we work to refile our search. Suppose that the two facets we selected weren't enough to filter our search into a small enough list to sort through. In this case, we could further refine the search by selecting another facet, as below.

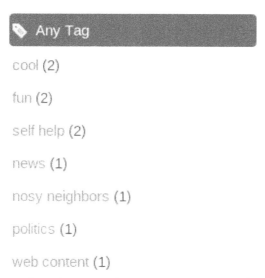

Figure 6.9: Asset tag facets let you see how many assets contain the terms for which you searched *and* contain certain tags. Click on a specific tag to narrow down the list of search results to those to which the tag has been applied.

Now we've also selected the *Music* category, which reduces the list of search hits on the right. In this way, you can interactively tweak the search results to narrow them down, making it easier to find that proverbial needle within the haystack.

Asset Types

Searching can only be done on assets. As has already been described in this chapter, just about any entity in the portal is an asset and can be indexed and searched. Under the hood, this means that these entities use Liferay's Asset API and have an Indexer class defined.

Developers can create custom searchable assets within the portal. This is described in the Asset Framework. section of the Liferay Developer Network. For this reason, you can have additional asset types defined in your portal beyond the ones that Liferay ships with by default. If this is the case, you might want to tweak the frequencyThreshold and the maxTerms settings to increase the number of asset types displayed past the default of 10. This is covered in the section below on search options.

Asset Tags

If tags have been applied to any asset that appears in the result set, it may be displayed in the Asset Tag facet. Tags are handled in a similar way to how asset types are handled: not all tags may appear. There may be many more than the 10 tags listed, but the default configuration for this facet is to show the top 10 most frequent terms. As with asset types, this can be modified by setting the max terms property.

Asset Categories

If categories have been applied to any asset that appears in the result set, they may be displayed in the Asset Categories facet. Asset categories work just like asset tags. As with

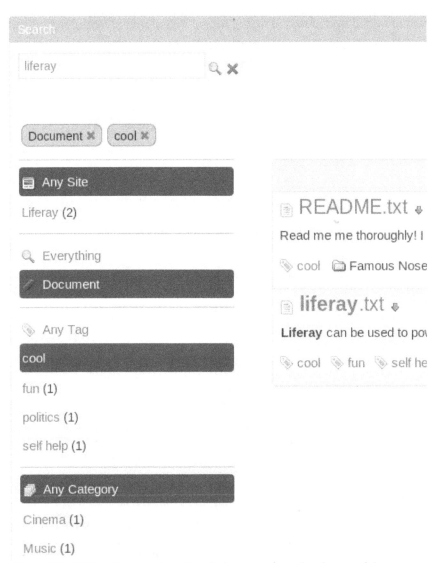

Figure 6.10: Drilling down creates a list of what you selected at the top of the screen.

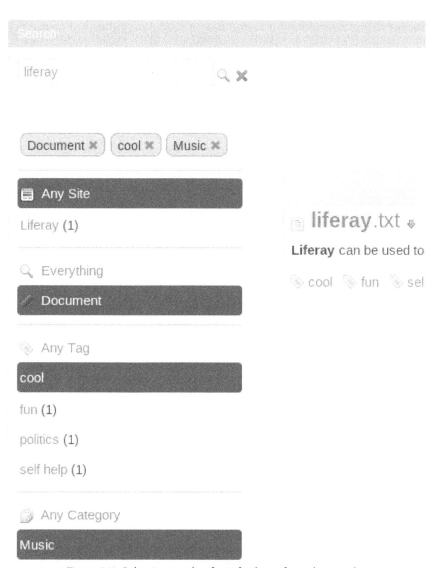

Figure 6.11: Selecting another facet further refines the search.

asset tags, you can modify the number of categories listed in the search by setting the max terms property.

Let's move on to advanced searching.

Advanced Searching

The Search portlet's search box is deceptively simple. Though you have only a single field for search, there's a search syntax inherited from Lucene that lets you create very powerful search queries. Let's look at some ways you can use search queries.

Searching for specific fields: By default, searches are performed against a long list of fields. Sometimes you want results for a term within a particular field. This can be achieved using the field search syntax [field] : [term]. For example, to search in the *Title* field for *Liferay*, use the following syntax:

```
title:liferay
```

If you search for a phrase within a field, surround the term with double quotation marks:

```
title:"Liferay Portal"
```

Wildcards: You can use wildcards in exactly the way you use them with your operating system: for a single character wildcard, use ?; for the multiple character wildcard, use *.

Boolean operators: You can use logic operators, such as AND, OR, NOT, +, and – in your searches. The AND operator matches assets in which the terms between the AND operator exist. For example, to search for both Liferay and Kaleo Workflow, use this query:

```
"liferay" AND "kaleo workflow"
```

The OR operator is the default; if there's no operator between two terms, the OR operator takes effect. OR finds matches if any term exists in an asset.

The + operator requires that the term exists somewhere in some field in the asset. If you wanted to search for something that *must* contain *liferay* and *may* contain *portal*, use this query:

```
+liferay portal
```

The NOT operator excludes assets that contain the term after the NOT operator. It requires that at least two terms be present:

```
"Liferay Portal" NOT "Liferay Social Office"
```

The – operator is similar: it excludes assets that contain the term after the – symbol:

```
"Liferay Portal" - "Liferay Social Office"
```

Grouping: You can use parentheses within your queries to form sub-queries, in a similar fashion to an SQL statement. For example, to search for *liferay* or *social office* and *website*, use this query:

```
(liferay OR "social office") AND website
```

As you can see, the search syntax is very powerful. There's more you can do with it than what is listed here; to view the full syntax, visit the Lucene URL above.

Next, we'll look at how the Search portlet can be configured.

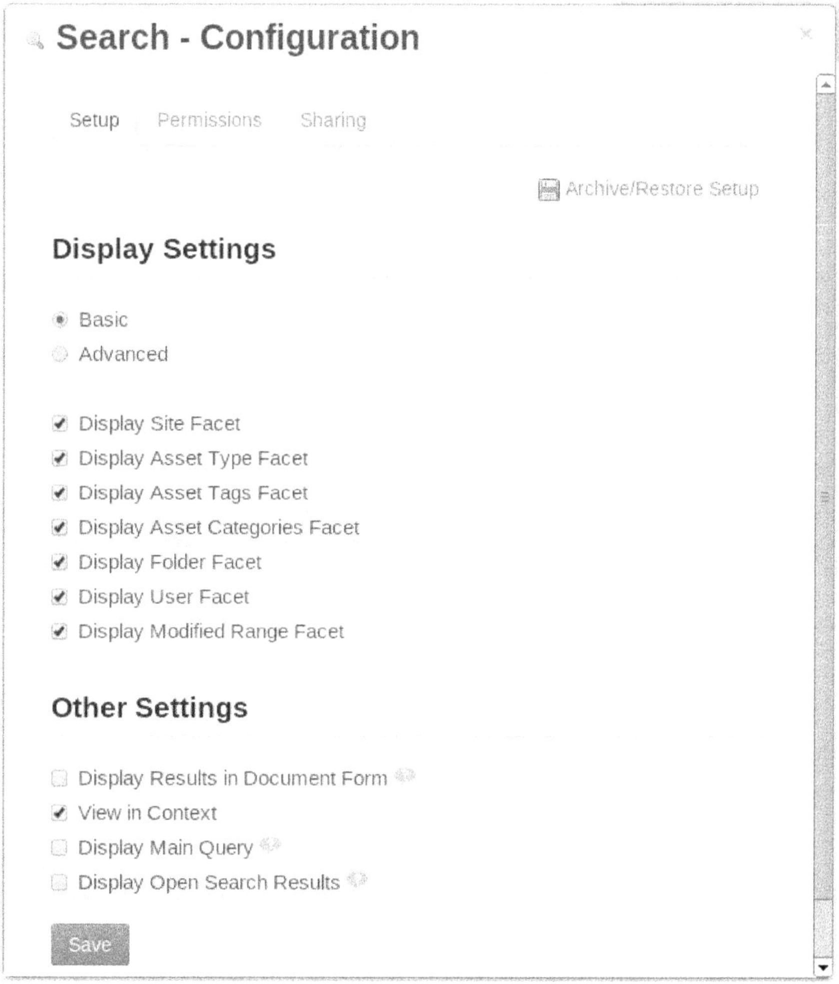

Search - Configuration

Setup   Permissions   Sharing

Archive/Restore Setup

Display Settings

- Basic
- Advanced

- ☑ Display Site Facet
- ☑ Display Asset Type Facet
- ☑ Display Asset Tags Facet
- ☑ Display Asset Categories Facet
- ☑ Display Folder Facet
- ☑ Display User Facet
- ☑ Display Modified Range Facet

Other Settings

- ☐ Display Results in Document Form
- ☑ View in Context
- ☐ Display Main Query
- ☐ Display Open Search Results

Save

Figure 6.12: Basic search configuration is pretty straightforward.

Setting Search Options

As with Liferay's other portlets, you can configure the Search portlet via the configuration screen, which looks like the below illustration.

Display Asset Type Facet: Toggles whether the Asset Type facet appears.

Display Asset Tags Facet: Toggles whether the Asset Tags facet appears.

Display Asset Categories Facet: Toggles whether the Asset Categories facet appears.

Display Modified Range Facet: Toggles whether the date modified range facet appears.

Display Results in Document Form: Never use this in production. Developers use this feature to view search responses in their generic, Document-based format. Part of a developer's job when writing search indexers is to convert Documents (the objects that get indexed) to the actual object and back again. This option allows developers to see how their objects are being indexed.

View in Context: When an asset is clicked, show it in the portlet to which it belongs.

Display Main Query: Show the exact search query that the portlet generated to the search engine. Again, never use this in production; this is for development purposes only.

Display Open Search Results: Shows results from third party Open Search plugins, if they are installed. This is for backward compatibility only: developers are encouraged to re-design their search code as described in *Liferay in Action*, and then custom assets are aggregated with native portal assets seamlessly.

These are the basic options. But you didn't miss the fact that there are also advanced options, did you?

Configuring advanced search requires a bit more technical acumen than you might expect, because there are so many properties to tweak. Thankfully, in most instances, you shouldn't need to change a thing. If you do, however, the configuration is done through a JSON object.

If you don't know what a JSON object is, don't worry: it's not a difficult concept. JSON stands for Java**S**cript **O**bject **N**otation. An Object is a software development term for anything that can be represented in code. Objects have *attributes*, or sometimes these are called *fields*, and they are very similar to fields you'd find on a form that you're filling out. Software developers use the word *object* to refer generically to anything like this that they can describe in the software; for all intents and purposes, objects could just as easily have been called Things. For example, one type of object used in Liferay is a User. A User can be represented in code, and it has many *fields*, such as a name, an email address, and more. JSON is one way of describing objects like this.

The object we're concerned with is called `facets`. Here's what it looks like, in all its glory, in JSON. Explanation of the settings follows the object below.

```
{"facets": [
    {
    "displayStyle": "asset_entries",
    "weight": 1.5,
    "static": false,
    "order": "OrderHitsDesc",
    "data": {
        "values": [
        "com.liferay.portlet.bookmarks.model.BookmarksEntry",
        "com.liferay.portlet.blogs.model.BlogsEntry",
        "com.liferay.portlet.calendar.model.CalEvent",
        "com.liferay.portlet.documentlibrary.model.DLFileEntry",
        "com.liferay.portlet.journal.model.JournalArticle",
        "com.liferay.portlet.messageboards.model.MBMessage",
        "com.liferay.portlet.wiki.model.WikiPage",
        "com.liferay.portal.model.User"
        ],
        "frequencyThreshold": 1
    },
    "label": "asset-type",
    "className": "com.liferay.portal.kernel.search.facet.AssetEntriesFacet",
    "fieldName": "entryClassName"
    },
    {
```

```
        "displayStyle": "asset_tags",
        "weight": 1.4,
        "static": false,
        "order": "OrderHitsDesc",
        "data": [
            "maxTerms": 10,
            "displayStyle": "list",
            "frequencyThreshold": 1,
            "showAssetCount": true
        },
        "label": "tag",
        "className": "com.liferay.portal.kernel.search.facet.MultiValueFacet",
        "fieldName": "assetTagNames"
        },
        {
        "displayStyle": "asset_tags",
        "weight": 1.3,
        "static": false,
        "order": "OrderHitsDesc",
        "data": {
            "maxTerms": 10,
            "displayStyle": "list",
            "frequencyThreshold": 1,
            "showAssetCount": true
        },
        "label": "category",
        "className": "com.liferay.portal.kernel.search.facet.MultiValueFacet",
        "fieldName": "assetCategoryTitles"
        },
        {
        "displayStyle": "modified",
        "weight": 1.1,
        "static": false,
        "order": "OrderHitsDesc",
        "data": {
            "ranges": [
                {
                    "range": "[past-hour TO *]",
                    "label": "past-hour"
                },
                {
                    "range": "[past-24-hours TO *]",
                    "label": "past-24-hours"
                },
                {
                    "range": "[past-week TO *]",
                    "label": "past-week"
                },
                {
                    "range": "[past-month TO *]",
                    "label": "past-month"
                },
                {
                    "range": "[past-year TO *]",
                    "label": "past-year"
                }
            ],
            "frequencyThreshold": 0
        },
        "label": "modified",
        "className": "com.liferay.portal.kernel.search.facet.ModifiedFacet",
        "fieldName": "modified"
        }
]}
```

Now that you've seen the object, don't be daunted by it. Here are all the settings within the object that you can tweak.

"className": This field must contain a string value which is the FQCN (fully qualified class name) of a java implementation class implementing the Facet interface. Liferay provides the following implementations by default:

```
com.liferay.portal.kernel.search.facet.AssetEntriesFacet
com.liferay.portal.kernel.search.facet.ModifiedFacet
com.liferay.portal.kernel.search.facet.MultiValueFacet
```

```
com.liferay.portal.kernel.search.facet.RangeFacet
com.liferay.portal.kernel.search.facet.ScopeFacet
com.liferay.portal.kernel.search.facet.SimpleFacet
```

"data": This field takes an arbitrary JSON object (a.k.a. {}) for use by a specific facet implementation. As such, there is no fixed definition of the data field. Each implementation is free to structure it as needed. The value defined here matches the implementation that's selected in the className attribute above.

"displayStyle": This field takes a string value and represents a particular template implementation which is used to render the facet. These templates are normally JSP pages (but can also be implemented as Velocity or Freemarker templates provided by a theme if the portal property theme.jsp.override.enabled is set to true). The method of matching the string to a JSP is simply done by prefixing the string with /html/portlet/search/facets/ and appending the .jsp extension.

For example, "displayStyle": "asset_tags" maps to the JSP

```
/html/portlet/search/facets/asset_tags.jsp
```

Armed with this knowledge a crafty developer could create custom display styles by deploying custom (new or overriding) JSPs using a JSP hook. See the *Liferay Developer Network* or *Liferay in Action* for more information on hook plugins.

"fieldName": This field takes a string value and defines the indexed field on which the facet operates.

For example, "fieldName": "entryClassName" indicates that the specified facet implementation operates on the entryClassName indexed field.

Note: You can identify available indexed fields by enabling the Search portlet's *Display Results in Document Form* configuration setting and then expanding individual results by clicking the + symbol to the left of their titles.

"label": This field takes a string value and represents the language key that is used for localizing the title of the facet when it's rendered.

"order": This field takes a string value. There are two possible values:

OrderValueAsc: This tells the facet to sort it's results by the term values, in ascending order.

OrderHitsDesc: This tells the facet to sort it's results by the term frequency, in descending order.

"static": This field takes a boolean value (true or false). The default value is false. A value of true means that the facet should not actually be rendered in the UI. It also means that it should use pre-set values (stored in its data field) rather than inputs dynamically applied by the end user. This allows for the creation of pre-configured search results.

Imagine you would like to create a pre-configured search that returns only images (i.e. the asset type is com.liferay.portlet.documentlibrary.model.DLFileEntry and the indexed field extension should contain the values bmp, gif, jpeg, jpg, odg, png, or svg). We would need two static facets, one with "fieldName": "entryClassName" and another with "fieldName": "extension". This could be represented using the following facet configuration:

```
{
    "displayStyle": "asset_entries",
    "static": true,
    "weight": 1.5,
    "order": "OrderHitsDesc",
    "data": {
    "values": [
        "com.liferay.portlet.documentlibrary.model.DLFileEntry"
    ],
    "frequencyThreshold": 0
    },
    "className": "com.liferay.portal.kernel.search.facet.AssetEntriesFacet",
    "label": "asset-type",
    "fieldName": "entryClassName"
```

```
},
{
    "displayStyle": "asset_entries",
    "static": true,
    "weight": 1.5,
    "order": "OrderHitsDesc",
    "data": {
    "values": ["bmp", "gif", "jpeg", "jpg", "odg", "png", "svg"],
    "frequencyThreshold": 0
    },
    "className": "com.liferay.portal.kernel.search.facet.MultiValueFacet",
    "label": "images",
    "fieldName": "extension"
}
```

"weight": This field takes a floating point (or double) value and is used to determine the ordering of the facets in the facet column of the search portlet. Facets are positioned with the largest values at the top. (yes, the current implementation is counter-intuitive and perhaps could be reversed in future versions).

Configuring search using a JSON object is a bit unusual, but as you can see, it's not as hard as it looks initially.

Summary

Search is a powerful component of Liferay Portal's asset framework. The proclivity of assets means that there is an extensible, robust, and configurable search mechanism throughout the portal that allows administrators to optimize the search experience of their users. Users also get an easy to use search interface that makes use of the tags and categories that they themselves apply to various pieces of content, regardless of the type of content. This makes Liferay's search truly "for the people."

There is an extended search syntax that lets you craft very specific searches. These searches can be used on large installations with lots of data to find the proverbial needle in the proverbial haystack. Administrators can tune the configuration of search portlets so that they are optimized for the contents of their communities.

Next, we'll look at how the Asset Publisher portlet makes even more extensive use of Liferay's asset framework to bring relevant content to users.

6.3   Using the Asset Publisher

As we create web content, it's important to keep in mind that to Liferay, the pieces of content are assets, just like message board entries and blog posts. This allows you to publish different kinds of content using Liferay's Asset Publisher. You can use the Asset Publisher to publish a mixed group of various kinds of assets such as images, documents, blogs, and of course, web content. This helps in creating a more dynamic web site: you can place user-created wiki entries, blog posts, or message board messages in context with your content. Let's examine some of its features.

Querying for Content

The Asset Publisher portlet is a highly configurable application that lets you query for mixed types of content on the fly. By giving you the ability to control what and how content is displayed from one location, the Asset Publisher helps you to "bubble up" the most relevant content to your users.

To get to all the portlet's options, click the *Options* button in the portlet's menu (the gear icon). On the Setup tab, you can configure the Asset Publisher's settings from the following three areas:

- Asset Selection

- Display Settings
- Subscriptions

Asset Selection allows you to configure which assets are displayed. You can set asset selection to either *dynamic* or *manual*. With dynamic asset selection, assets are automatically displayed based on certain rules or filters. For example, you can set the Asset Publisher to display only assets of a certain type or assets to which certain tags or categories have been applied. With manual asset selection, the Asset Publisher only displays assets that have been explicitly selected by an administrator.

The Asset Publisher supports a scope that restricts both manual and dynamic asset selection. The Asset Publisher can only display assets from its configured scope. By default, the Asset Publisher portlet is scoped to the site of the page to which it was added. However, you can customize the scope from the Asset Selection section of the Asset Publisher configuration window. To extend your Asset Publisher's scope, click *Select* under Scope and choose either *Global* to add the global scope or *Other Site...* to add the scope of anther site.

The Display Settings section of the Asset Publisher configuration window lets administrators customize many details that determine how content is displayed. The Subscription section allows administrators to enable, disable, or configure email subscriptions and RSS subscriptions. In the following sections, we'll explore the available configurations for the Asset Selection, Display Settings, and Subscriptions sections of the Asset Publisher's configuration window. Let's start by learning how select content manually. You'll see that it's very similar to using the Web Content Display portlet except that you can select assets of any type, not just web content instances.

Selecting Assets Manually

By selecting *Manual* from the select box beneath *Asset Selection*, you tell the Asset Publisher that you want to select content manually. You can configure multiple scopes, including the global scope, from which to select assets.

When selecting assets manually, you'll see a list of configured scopes under the Scope heading. Click the red "X" button at the right to remove a scope from the list. Click the *Select* button to add additional scopes to the Asset Publisher's configuration. After you've added a scope, a new Select button appears under the Asset Entries heading. A list of assets selected for display appears in the Asset Entries section. You can select assets to be displayed by clicking on the appropriate *Select* button. One button appears for each configured scope. By default, the available asset types include the following:

- Documents Folder
- Bookmarks Folder
- Blogs Entry
- Message Boards Message
- Web Content Instance
- Bookmarks Entry
- Wiki Page
- Document
- Web Content Folder

You can select any number of assets to be displayed. Note, however, that there's a display setting called *Number of Items to Display* that determines the maximum number of items to display (or, if pagination is enabled, the maximum number of items to display per page). The Asset Publisher enables you to mix and match different asset types in the same interface. When you're done selecting items to display, click *Save*. Any selected assets are added to the list of assets that are displayed by the portlet. Once you have your content

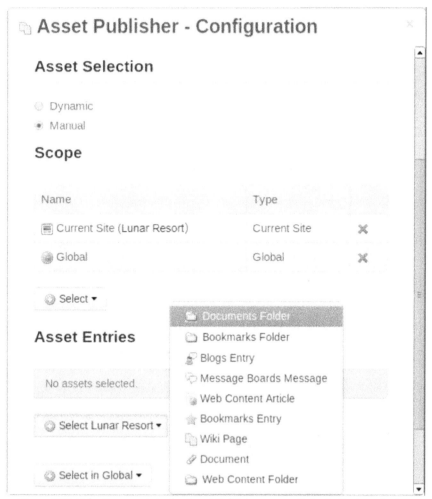

Figure 6.13: Selecting assets in the Asset Publisher manually is similar to selecting assets in the Web Content Display portlet except that you can select assets of any type, not just web content. You can also add scopes to expand the list of assets that available to be displayed in the Asset Publisher.

selected, you can configure the display types to configure how the content appears. We'll discuss the display settings in more detail after we finish discussing how to select assets for display.

While manual Asset selection allows you to select assets of various types from different scopes, it can be time-consuming to periodically update the assets that should be displayed. It's often more convenient to use the Asset Publisher to select content dynamically.

Selecting Assets Dynamically

The Asset Publisher's default behavior is to select assets dynamically according a set of customizable rules. These rules can be stacked on top of each other so that they compliment each other to create a nice, refined query for your content. You can define complicated rules for selecting assets for display and Liferay automatically takes permissions into account. Liferay's Asset Publisher performs well in these situations since it queries by search index instead of querying the database directly. You have the following options for creating rules for selecting content:

Scope: Choose the sites from which the content should be selected. This works the same way as with manual asset selection: assets can only be displayed if they belong to a configured scope.

Asset Type: Choose whether you'll display any assets or only assets of a specific type, such as only web content, only wiki entries, or any combination of multiple types.

Filter Rules: Add as many filters on tags or categories as you like. You can choose whether the content must contain or must not contain any or all of the tags or categories that you enter.

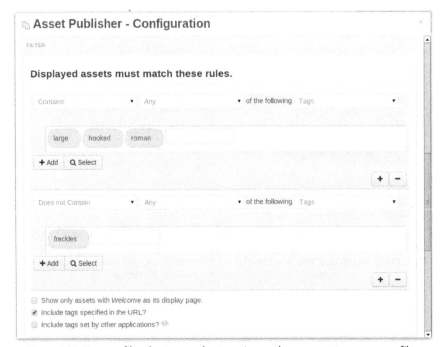

Figure 6.14: You can filter by tags and categories, and you can set up as many filter rules as you need.

Once you've set up your filter rules for dynamically selecting content, you can decide how the content will be displayed.

You can order the content returned by the filters by title, create date, modified date, publication date, etc. in ascending or descending order. For instance, suppose you have a series of "How To" articles that you want displayed in descending order based on whether the article was tagged with the *hammer* tag. Or, suppose you want a series of video captures to display in ascending order based on a category called *birds*. For these use cases, you can configure the ordering and grouping settings. You can also group by *Asset, Type* or *Vocabularies*. Vocabularies are groups of categories defined by administrators in the *Categories* section of the Control Panel.

The *Ordering and Grouping* section of the Asset Publisher allows you to precisely control how content is ordered and grouped when displayed. You can order the assets displayed by Asset Publisher in ascending or descending order by the following attributes:

- Title
- Create Date
- Modified Date
- Publish Date
- Expiration Date
- Priority

You can also configure a second ordering. The second ordering would be applied to any assets for which the first ordering wasn't sufficient. For example, suppose you chose to order assets by title and there are multiple assets with the same title. Then the second ordering would take effect. For example, you could order all the assets that had the same title by their publication dates.

You can establish grouping rules as well as ordering rules. You can group assets by type or by vocabulary. For example, suppose there's a vocabulary called *Membership Type* that belongs to your site. Suppose this vocabulary has two categories: *Premium* and *Regular*. If you group assets by Membership Type, all assets with the Premium category will be displayed in one group and all assets with the Regular category will be displayed in another group. Grouping rules are applied before any ordering rules: they're a way to divide up the displayed assets into separate lists. The ordering rules are applied separately to each group of assets.

Note that grouping and ordering rules are only one mechanism to control how your content will be displayed. You can refine the display through many other display settings which we'll examine next.

Configuring Display Settings

Open the *Display Settings* subtab of the Setup tab of the Asset Publisher's Configuration window. Here, you can configure many more settings that control the Asset Publisher's behavior and that determine how the Asset Publisher displays content. The Display Settings section gives you precise control over the display of your assets. There are many options available to configure how you want your content to appear. Many of these, such as printing, flags, ratings, comments, comment ratings, and social bookmarks work the same way they do in the Web Content Display portlet.

Show Add Content Button: When checked, this checkbox adds an *Add New* button that allows users to add new assets directly from the Asset Publisher portlet. This is checked by default.

Display Template: This selector lets you choose an application display template to customize how the Asset Publisher displays assets. Liferay creates the following display templates for each newly created site, including the default site:

- Abstracts: This display template shows the first 200-500 characters of the content, defined by the **Abstract Length** field. This is the default display template of the Asset Publisher.

- Table: This display template displays the content in an HTML table which can be styled by a theme developer.

- Title List: This display template displays the content's title as defined by the user who entered it.

- Full Content: This display template displays the entire content of the entry.

    There's also a Rich Summary display template that belongs to the global scope. This template provides a summary view of each asset along with a *Read More* link to the article's full content.

Abstract Length: Here, you can select the number of characters to display for abstracts. The default is 200.

Asset Link Behavior: The default value is *Show Full Content*. With this value selected, when the link to an asset is clicked, the full asset is displayed in the current Asset Publisher. (There's also a *View in Context* link that shows the article in the Wiki page's Wiki portlet.) If the value *View in a Context* is selected, clicking on an asset causes that asset to be displayed in the portlet to which the asset belongs. For example, a blog entry would be displayed in the Blogs portlet where it was created. Likewise, a forum post would be displayed in the Message Boards portlet where it was created. Similarly, a generic web content instance would be displayed in the Asset Publisher of its configured display page. See the section below on display pages for more information.

 Tip: When the Asset Publisher displays web content instances that have an associated small image, the small image becomes a link to the full instance. To use this feature, add or edit a web content instance that the Asset Publisher should display. Before clicking *Publish*, click on *Abstracts*, flag *Small Image*, and upload an image. Then click *Publish*. Once your web content instance appears in the Asset Publisher's list, clicking the small image takes you to the full instance.

Number of Items to Display: Here, you can select the maximum number of assets that can be displayed by the Asset Publisher. However, if pagination is enabled, there's no limit to the number of of assets that the Asset Publisher can display. So with pagination enabled, this number represents the maximum number of assets that can be displayed per page.

Pagination Type: This can be set to *None*, *Simple*, or *Regular*. With pagination set to *None*, the Asset Publisher displays at most the number of assets specified in the **Number of Items to Display** property. Setting the pagination type to *Simple* adds *Previous* and *Next* buttons that enable the user to browse through "pages" of assets in the Asset Publisher. Setting the pagination type to *Regular* adds more options and information including *First* and *Last* buttons, a dropdown selector for pages, the number of items per page, and the total number of results (assets being displayed).

Show Available Locales: Since content can be localized, you can have different versions of it based on locale. Enabling this option shows the locales available, enabling users to view the content in their language of choice.

Set as the Default Asset Publisher for This Page: The Asset Publisher portlet is an instanceable portlet; multiple Asset Publishers can be added to a page and each has an independent configuration. The default Asset Publisher for a page is the one used to display any web content associated with the page.

Enable Conversion To: If you have enabled Liferay Portal's OpenOffice/LibreOffice integration, you can allow your users to convert the content to one of several formats:

- DOC

- ODT

- PDF

- RTF

- SXW

- TXT

    Please refer to this guide's section on Liferay Server Administration for information on setting up Liferay's OpenOffice/LibreOffice document conversion functionality.

Enable ...: The Asset Publisher's Display Settings allow you to enable/disable the following options for displayed assets:

- Print

- Flags

- Related assets

- Ratings

- Comments

- Comment ratings

- Social bookmarks

    Enabling the Print option adds a *Print* link to the full view of an asset displayed in the Asset Publisher. Clicking *Print* opens a new browser window with a print view of the asset. Enabling flags, related assets, ratings, comments, comment ratings, or social bookmarks add links to the corresponding social features to the view full of the asset in the Asset Publisher.

 Tip: An alternate way to add comments and ratings to a page is through the *Page Comments* and *Page Ratings* portlets. Just add the portlets in the appropriate location near the asset you'd like to have feedback for. Note that starting in Liferay 6.2, these portlets can no longer be exported.

Show Metadata: Allows you to select various metadata types to be displayed (see below). For example, you can select tags and categories for display. Upon saving your configuration, the Asset Publisher displays tags and categories for each displayed asset. Then users can click on the tags and categories to manually filter the displayed assets.

The Display Settings section of the Asset Publisher has numerous options to help you configure how your content selections are displayed to your users. Even though there are many choices, it's easy to go through the options and quickly adjust the ones that apply to your situation. You'll want to use the Asset Publisher to query for different kinds of assets in the portal that contain relevant information for your users.

Show Metadata

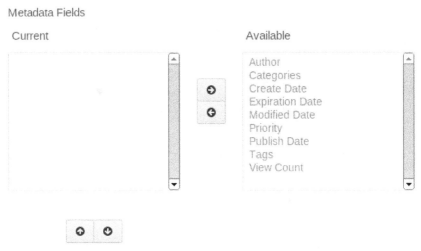

Figure 6.15: You can configure the Asset Publisher to display various kinds of metadata about the displayed assets.

Configuring Asset Publisher Subscriptions

The Asset Publisher portlet supports two kinds of subscriptions: RSS subscriptions and email subscriptions. To enable subscriptions, open the Asset Publisher's configuration window (click on the gear icon and select *Configuration*). In the configuration window, open the Subscriptions tab of the Setup tab. There are two options:

Enable RSS Subscription
Enable Email Subscription

Enabling RSS subscription creates an RSS feed containing links to all of the assets that the Asset Publisher is configured to display. A link to this RSS feed appears in at the bottom of the Asset Publisher portlet.

Enabling email subscription adds a *Subscribe* link to the Asset Publisher. Users wishing to be notified of newly published assets can click on this link to be added to the subscription list. Liferay periodically checks for new assets and sends emails to subscribed users informing them about the new assets. By default, Liferay performs this check every twenty-four hours but this can be customized by adding the following property to your portal-ext.properties file and changing the number:

```
asset.publisher.check.interval=24
```

Also by default, Liferay limits the number of assets that are retrieved from the database during this check to twenty. If you're interested in optimizing Liferay's performance, you can lower this limit. If you're not concerned about performance, you can remove this limit entirely. To customize the number of assets about which Liferay notifies subscribed users, add the following property to your portal-ext.properties file and change the number:

```
asset.publisher.dynamic.subscription.limit=20
```

+ Add ▾

The Asset Publisher offers two subscription options

The Asset Publisher offers two subscription options: RSS subscriptions and email subscriptions.

These options must be enabled by via the Asset Publisher's configuration window: navigate to Setup...
Read More »

RE: The Asset Publisher offers two subscription options

Flags, Ratings, Comments, and Comment Ratings can also be enabled for the Asset Publisher.

To access these options and more, open the Asset Publisher's configuration window, and navigate to Setup...
Read More »

Figure 6.16: When RSS subscriptions have been enabled for an Asset Publisher portlet, a link to the Asset Publisher's RSS feed appears. Users can subscribe to the Asset Publisher's RSS feed using their preferred RSS reader.

Next, we'll look at Display Pages, an addition to the asset framework introduced by Liferay 6.1.

Content Display Pages

If you've been using Liferay for a while, you might have noticed something about how Liferay handles web content—content is never tied directly to a page. While this can be useful (because it means that you don't have to recreate content if you want to display the same thing on multiple pages), it also means that you don't have a static URL for any web content, which is bad for search engine optimization.

As an improvement, Liferay introduced the concept of *display pages* and *canonical URLs*. Each web content entry on the portal has a canonical URL, which is the official location of the content that is referenced any time the content is displayed. A display page can be any page with an asset publisher configured to display any content associated with the page. When adding or editing web content, you can select a display page, but only pages with a configured asset publisher are available for selection.

To create a display page, you can create a page yourself, add an Asset Publisher portlet and configure it yourself. Alternatively, you can use the *Content Display Page* page template included with Liferay. If you're creating a Display Page manually, once you've added an Asset Publisher portlet to the page, open its configuration window. Then check the *Set as the Default Asset Publisher for This Page* box. Also, for its display settings, set the Display Style to *Abstracts* and the Asset Link Behavior to *View in Context*.

 Note: Web content linked in the Asset Publisher can be viewed by clicking their asset links. With the *View in Context* behavior checked, the link displays the Web Content in its configured display page. If the web content does not have a configured display page, it is displayed in the web content display portlet to which the asset belongs.

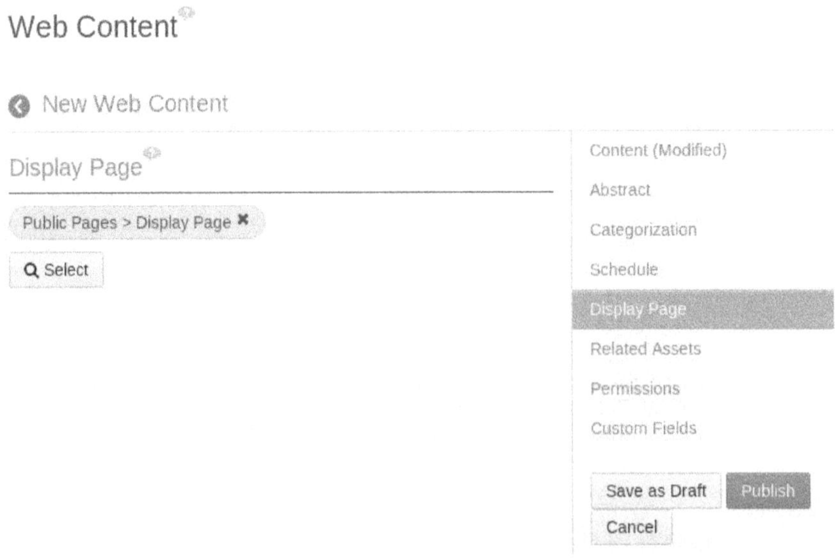

Web Content

New Web Content

Display Page

Public Pages > Display Page ✖

Q Select

Content (Modified)

Abstract

Categorization

Schedule

Display Page

Related Assets

Permissions

Custom Fields

Save as Draft   Publish

Cancel

Figure 6.17: You can select a display page for a web content instance when creating or editing one.

You may now be thinking, "Wait, you just told me that each Web Content item has its own URL, and that this is somehow related to pages where we display a whole bunch of content on the same page?" That's right. Just watch—create a display page called *My Web Content Display Page* somewhere on your portal, using the *Content Display Page* template. Now, on a different page, add a Web Content Display portlet. Click the *Add Web Content* button, enter a title and some content, click on *Display Page* at the right, and select the Display Page you just created. Then click *Publish*.

In the Asset Publisher of the *My Web Content Display Page*, click the *Read More* link to display the full content. Notice that the canonical URL for content appears in your browser's address bar. If you create your own custom display page, any additional portlets that you place on the page are displayed along with the content when you access it via the canonical URL. If you used the *Content Display Page* page template for your display page, it not only features a configured Asset Publisher portlet but also a Tags Navigation, a Categories Navigation, and a Search portlet. These tools help users to quickly identify relevant content.

localhost:8080/web/guest/~/lunar-resort-information

Figure 6.18: The Canonical URL

Next, let's learn about another new feature introduced by Liferay 6.1.

6.4 Defining Content Relationships

Related Assets was a feature introduced in Liferay 6.1 that enables you to connect an asset to other assets within the same site or to global assets, even if they don't share any tags and aren't in the same category. We've already seen that you can show related assets within the display for a specific asset, and with the Related Assets portlet you can show links to any assets which are related to content displayed on that page.

The Related Assets portlet is based on the Asset Publisher and possesses essentially the same interface with one key difference. The Asset publisher displays any content that meets the criteria selected in the portlet configuration. The Related Assets portlet only displays content that meets the criteria, and also is listed as a related asset for a piece of content that is currently published on the page where it is placed. Let's take a look at the Related Assets portlet.

As a prerequisite for the Related Assets portlet to display related assets, you have to configure it to show the content you want displayed. To do this, go to the Asset Publisher portlet and select the *gear* icon in the upper right corner of the portlet. Under the *Setup* tab, set type of asset(s) to display using the *Asset Type* menu. The default value is set to *Any*. You can narrow the scope of the portlet to display any single category of asset type or select multiple assets from the menu.

Filter options let you set minimum requirements for displaying assets by their categories, tags, and custom fields. Ordering and Grouping allows you to organize assets using the same criteria. Display settings allow you to customize how assets are shown in the portlet. They can be listed by title, in a table, by abstract or full content. You can convert assets to different document types like ODT, PDF, and RTF. You can choose to show various metadata fields such as author, modification date, tags, and view count. You can even enable RSS subscriptions and customize their display settings.

When you are finished setting the Source and Filter options, click *Save*. But hold on a minute. You saw the message that says, You have successfully updated the setup, but there still aren't any assets displayed in the related assets portlet. Why? You cannot see any related assets until you select an asset in the Asset Publisher.

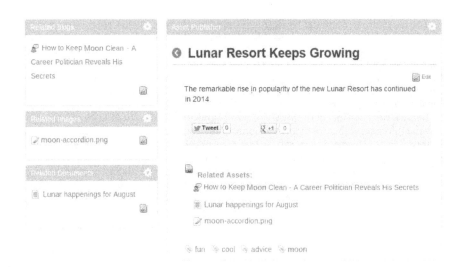

Figure 6.19: Select an asset in the Asset Publisher to see its related assets displayed in the Related Assets portlet. In the screenshot, we renamed the three Related Assets portlets on the left and updated their configurations.

Once you select an asset, its related assets are displayed in the Related Assets portlet, as in the image above.

6.5   Summary

In this chapter, we explored Liferay's asset framework. Any type of content in Liferay is considered an asset and can utilize the features provided by the asset framework: tags, categories, comments, ratings, and relationships. We examined the Asset Publisher portlet and looked at the many configuration options for choosing what kinds of assets to display and how to display them. We saw that the Asset Publisher portlet is designed to integrate with the Tags Navigation and Categories navigation portlets to allow users to browse content more easily. We also learned about the Display Page attribute of web content, the Content Display Page page template, and canonical URLs for assets. Assets can have display page associated with them so that the full view of the asset is displayed on the display page. The display page of an asset is used in the asset's canonical URL.

## CHAPTER 7

TARGETING CONTENT TO YOUR AUDIENCE

Liferay's Audience Targeting app allows you to divide your audience into user segments, target specific content to different user segments, and create campaigns for different user segments. It also allows you to quickly measure the effectiveness of your campaigns. User segments allow you to configure your website to display different assets to different users. Campaigns allow you to display specific content to different user segments for fixed periods of time. They also allow you to measure the interaction of the targeted user segments with the chosen content.

Suppose you'd like to display advertisements to users of your website. You'd like to display one set of advertisements to one user segment and another set of advertisements to another user segment. Maybe this should dynamically change every week based on your marketing goals. Or maybe you have created several sets of news articles for your website that would be interesting to different user segments. You'd like to display news articles to users based on all the user segments to which they belong.

Liferay's Audience Targeting app, available from Liferay Marketplace, allows you to create multiple user segments which are defined by multiple rules based on session attributes, profile attributes, behavior, and information from social networks. Developers can easily create additional rules and rule types with minimal coding efforts. The Audience Targeting App also allows you to create campaigns that target a specific user segment. Campaigns last for fixed periods of time and each campaign has a priority. If you are running several campaigns on your website at the same time, the priority field determines which campaign takes precedence. Campaigns allow you to configure different assets to be displayed at different periods of time to the targeted user segment.

The Audience Targeting App adds an *Audience Targeting* section to the Configuration section of the Site Administration area of the Control Panel and an Audience Targeting Simulator to the Dockbar. The following three applications are also included with the Audience Targeting app:

- User Segment Content Display
- User Segment Content List
- Campaign Content Display

You can add these applications to any portal page. In the next sections, we'll explain how to use the *Audience Targeting* section of the Configuration section of the Site Administration area of the Control Panel to manage user segments and campaigns. Then we'll explain how to use each of Audience Targeting applications and the Audience Targeting Simulator.

7.1   Installation and Uninstallation

The easiest way to install the Audience Targeting app is via Liferay Marketplace. Make sure to install the correct version of the app. Choose CE if you're running Liferay CE and EE if you're running Liferay EE.

If you're running Liferay on JBoss, make sure to have your `jboss-deployment-struc-ture.xml` file configured correctly. See the Installing Liferay on JBoss instructions for details.

If you're running Liferay on Weblogic, note that the Audience Targeting app is only supported on Liferay 6.2 EE SP10 and above.

If you can't uninstall the Audience Targeting app via Marketplace or you want to manually uninstall it, follow these steps:

1. Delete your `[Liferay Home]/data/osgi` folder.

2. Delete your app server's work and temp directories. E.g.., if you're running Liferay on Tomcat, delete your `[Liferay Home]/tomcat-[version]/work` and `[Liferay Home]/tomcat-[version]/temp` folders.

3. Restart your app server.

7.2   Managing User Segments

The *Audience Targeting* section of the Configuration section of the Site Administration area of the Control Panel allows you to manage user segments and campaigns.

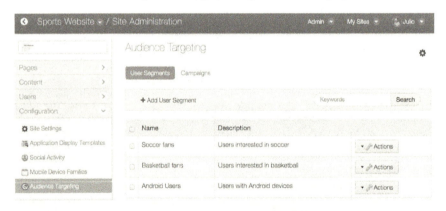

Figure 7.1: Click on *Site Administration · Configuration →Audience Targeting* to manage user segments and campaigns for a site.

A user segment represents a subset of the total group of portal users (logged in or not). A user segment is defined by one or more rules that users have to match in order to belong to that user segment. Click on *Site Administration →Configuration →Audience Targeting →New User Segment* to add a new user segment. All the rules that have been deployed appear under the Rules heading. Drag a rule to the right to apply the rule to the user segment. Once a rule has been applied, you can adjust the rule's parameters. E.g., once the

Gender rule has been applied, you can select *Male* or *Female*. Once the Age rule has been applied, you can select an *Older than* value and a *Younger than* value. For example, you could define a *Women over 30* user segment by applying the Gender rule and selecting *Female* and applying the Age rule and setting the *Older than* attribute to 30. Once you've customized the rules for the new user segment, entered a name and, optionally, a description, click *Save* to actually create the user segment.

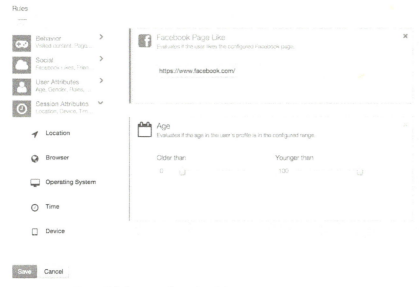

Figure 7.2: Drag a rule to the right to create a user segment.

To configure permissions for creating, editing, and deleting user segments, visit the Roles section of the Control Panel and search for *Audience Targeting Resources*.

Both user segments and campaigns are inherited in your site hierarchy. Therefore, user segments and campaigns defined in the Global scope will be available to any site. User segments and campaigns created in a site will be available to all of its child sites.

User Segment Rules

Custom rules can be created by developers and deployed as OSGi plugins. See the Extending the Audience Targeting Application tutorial for details.

These are some of the rules that are included with the app by default:

- User Attributes
    - Age (from the user profile)
    - Gender (from the user profile)
    - Role (regular role, organization role or site role)
    - Membership (site member, organization member, user group member)
- Social
    - Like of a specific Facebook page
    - Number of Facebook friends
    - City, Age, Gender, Education, etc. from your Facebook profile

- Session Attributes

    - Location (obtained from the IP address)
    - Browser, Device, Operating system
    - Time

- Behavior

    - Viewed page or content
    - Score Points rule.

The Score Points rule assigns 1 point to a user each time the user views a page or content that's been categorized under the user segment to which the rule has been applied. Once a user exceeds the configured threshold, the user matches this rule. For example, suppose that your website is about sports and you have pages and content about basketball, tennis, and soccer. You would like to divide your audience into three user segments (Basketball fans, Tennis fans, and Soccer fans) in order to display the most relevant content to them on your site's front page. After creating these three user segments using the Score Points rule with a threshold of, say, 20, you should appropriately categorize the content which would be most relevant to each user segment. E.g., apply the *Basketball fans* user segment to content about basketball, apply the *Tennis fans* user segment to content about tennis, etc. Now, every time a user (even a guest user) visits a page or views a piece of content categorized for a user segment to which the Score Points rule has been applied, the user will start accumulating points. Once the user has accumulated enough points, the user will belong to the user segment. After a user has visited more than 20 pages or pieces of content related to basketball, the user will belong to the Basketball fans user segment. Once the user belongs to a user segment, you can use that information to direct more relevant information to the user in your website using the User Segment Content Display application.

Categorizing Pages and Content for User Segments

Each new user segment that's created can be used to categorize pages or content.

Note: Page categorization is a feature added by the Audience Targeting app. In a regular Liferay Portal 6.2 instance without the Audience Targeting app installed, pages cannot be categorized.

The Audience Targeting app adds two select buttons to the Categorization section of pages and assets: *User Segment* and *User Segment (Global)*. These buttons allow you to assign one or more site-scoped or global user segments to the content. This categorization has mainly two purposes:

- Assigning points to users using the Score Points rule
- Showing dynamic lists of content in the User Segment Content List application

You don't have to create categories for each of your user segments. User segments are distinct from regular vocabularies. The Categorization section of pages and assets contains distinct select buttons for user segments and regular vocabularies.

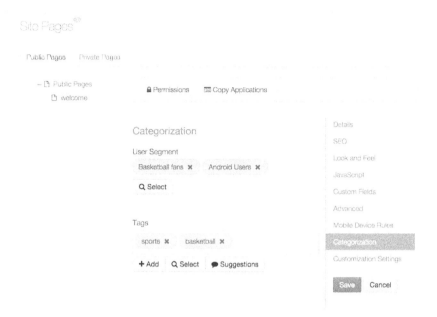

Figure 7.3: Pages and content can be categorized for user segments.

Managing User Segment Reports

When managing user segments, you can click *Actions   Reports* next to a user segment to see the list of reports available for each user segment. Click *Actions →View Report* to view the report or *Actions →Update Report* to generate a new report. Reports display a summary of interesting information related to each user segment. For example, the Content Views report shows the asset that's been most viewed by users that belong to the user segment.

Additional reports can be created by developers and deployed as OSGI plugins. See the Extending the Audience Targeting Application tutorial for details. Reports are generated daily by default. However, you can generate a report at any time. To generate a new report when currently viewing a report, click on the *Update Report* button in the top right corner.

7.3 Managing Campaigns

A campaign represents an effort to expose a certain user segment to a certain set of assets within a specific period of time. To manage campaigns for a site, navigate to *Site Administration   Configuration →Audience Targeting →Campaigns*. To create a new campaign, you need to select a user segment to target, a start date and an end date, and a priority, as well as a name and, optionally, a description. You also have to indicate whether or not the campaign you create should be active or inactive. When you've entered the required information, click *Save*. The user segment you select when creating a campaign represents the portal users targeted by the campaign. The start and end dates together specify the duration of the campaign. There can be multiple campaigns active at the same time that target the same user segment. In these situations, the priority attribute of the campaigns determines which campaign takes precedence. Finally, you can activate or deactivate a campaign via the active attribute of a campaign. Deactivating a campaign disables the effect of the campaign within the portal. Deactivating a campaign is like deleting the campaign

Figure 7.4: the Content Views report shows the asset that's been most viewed by users that belong to a user segment.

except that a deactivated campaign can be reactivated later. It can be useful to deactivate a campaign if a problem is found with the way content is being displayed. Once the problem has been corrected, the campaign can be reactivated.

For example, suppose you wanted the ability to display certain content (for example, advertisements about your new Android app) to female baseball fans during the months leading up to the World Series. To achieve this, you could use the Gender rule (configured to female), the Device Rule (configured for Android devices) and the Score Points rule to define a user segment called *Female Baseball Fans*. The Score points rule assigns 1 point to a user each time the user visits a page or views an asset categorized under the user segment *Female Baseball Fans*. When a user accumulates a certain number of points (specified by the value of the Score Points rule's *Score Points Threshold* attribute), the user matches this rule. After creating this user segment, you would create a new campaign targeting this segment, select start and end dates, choose a priority, choose *Active*, and then click *Save*. To actually present content to the users belonging to the *Female Baseball Fans* user segment, you need to use the Campaign Content Display application.

To configure permissions for creating, editing, and deleting campaigns, visit the Roles section of the Control Panel and search for *Audience Targeting Resources*.

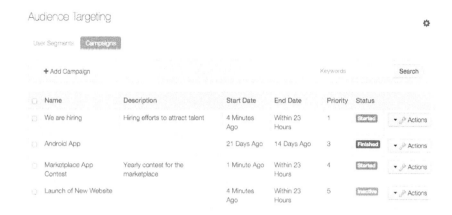

Figure 7.5: Click on *Site Administration · Configuration →Audience Targeting →Campaigns* to manage campaigns for a site.

Managing Campaign Priorities

The priority of your campaigns becomes important when multiple campaigns are running at the same time on your website. The Campaign Content Display application can be configured to display content based on the campaign your users match. When a user matches multiple campaigns, the one with the highest priority takes precedence.

If you have several Campaign Content Display applications around your website configured to display different content per campaign, changing the priority of one campaign automatically affects all the Campaign Content Display applications. Similarly, if a campaign is deactivated or if a campaign's date range is exceeded, all of the Campaign Content Display applications on your website are affected.

Defining Tracking Actions

One of the most interesting features of campaigns is that they allow you to measure the effectiveness of a campaign. This provides your marketing team with real feedback from users. When creating a campaign, you can define the user actions that you want to track. The Audience Targeting app can display reports of how often those actions are triggered. For example, suppose you want to run a campaign for an event that your company is hosting next month. For this event, imagine that you have created a main page for the event which contains a Youtube video and a banner which says "Register Now". Imagine also that you have a blog entry about the event displayed on several different pages of your website and a Register page which contains the form to pay for the event. In this campaign, your goal is to get as many people to register as possible. However, you will probably be interested in tracking the following information to see if there is something not working as your team expected:

- Visits to the main page of the event
- Clicks to view the video
- Number of users who watched the video until the end
- Clicks on the Register Now banner
- Views of the blog entry about the event
- Views of the Register form
- Number of users who started to fill out the Register form

• Number of users who completed the registration

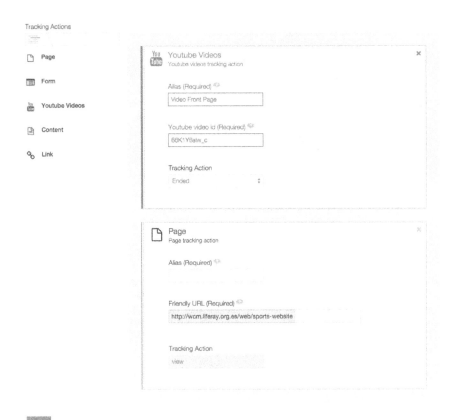

Save

Figure 7.6: Drag and drop tracking actions to the right to configure a campaign.

You could drag and drop *tracking actions* from the palette to track all the actions mentioned above. More types of tracking actions can be created by developers and deployed as OSGI plugins. See the Extending the Audience Targeting Application tutorial for details.

The tracking actions use an analytics engine called *Audience Targeting Analytics* that can be configured per site or per portal instance. To configure the analytics engine per site, go to *Site Administration →Site Settings*. To configure it per portal instance, go to *Control Panel →Portal Configuration*. Tracking all the actions of all your users (even guest users) can be a very heavy load for your server. Therefore, it's best to disable the tracking of any actions about which you don't need information.

Campaign Reports

Reports are available for campaigns. You can click *Actions Reports* next to a campaign to see the list of reports available. More reports can be created by developers and deployed as OSGI plugins. See the Extending the Audience Targeting Application tutorial for details.

The Content Views report shows the number of times that different assets have been viewed via the Campaign Content Display application by users in the context of the current campaign. For example, if you configured five Campaign Content Display applications around your website to display content for a campaign, the Content View report for the campaign would show how many times was that content displayed to different users.

The Tracking Actions report shows the number of times that the actions tracked by the campaign have been triggered by users. Consider the example that we introduced earlier in the section on tracking actions: you've created a campaign for an event that your company will host soon. For this event, you have created a main page for the event which contains a Youtube video and a banner which says "Register Now". You also have created a blog post about the event which is displayed on several different pages of your website. Lastly, you have a Register page which contains the form to pay for the event. For this example, the Tracking Actions report would show you how many users visited the event page, how many watched the video, how many clicked on the banner, how many viewed the blog post about the event, how many started filling the registration form, etc. This information helps you measure the effectiveness of your campaign. You can use this information to evaluate whether or not the users are following the engagement path you had prepared.

7.4 Using the Audience Targeting Applications

The Audience Targeting app not only adds the Audience Targeting application to the Site Administration area of the Control Panel, it also includes the following instanceable applications which can be added to any portal page:

- User Segment Content Display
- User Segment Content List
- Campaign Content Display

All of these applications support Application Display Templates (ADTs) so that site administrators can customize the look and feel of the application. Any of Liferay Portal's out-of-the-box Asset Publisher ADTs can actually be re-used for these Audience Targeting applications.

User Segment Content Display

The User Segment Content Display application allows administrators to specify exactly which content to display to a user based on the user segments that the user belongs to. You can specify multiple rules according to the following format:

- If the user [belongs|does not belong] to [any|all] of the following user segments [specify a list of user segments], then display this content: [specify a specific asset].

You can specify any number of *if* clauses when configuring the User Segment Content Display application's rules. However, an *otherwise* clause always follows the last *if* clause so that the application knows what to display if the user doesn't match any user segments. *Don't display anything* is an option for the *otherwise* clause.

For example, you can add a User Segment Content Display application to a page and configure the following rules for it:

- If the user *belongs* to *any* of the following user segments: *Tennis fans*, then display this content: *tennis_picture.jpg*.
- If the user *belongs* to *any* of the following user segments: *Basketball fans*, then display this content: *basketball_picture.jpg*.
- If the user *belongs* to *any* of the following user segments: *Soccer*, then display this content: *soccer_picture.jpg*.
- Otherwise, *Don't display anything*.

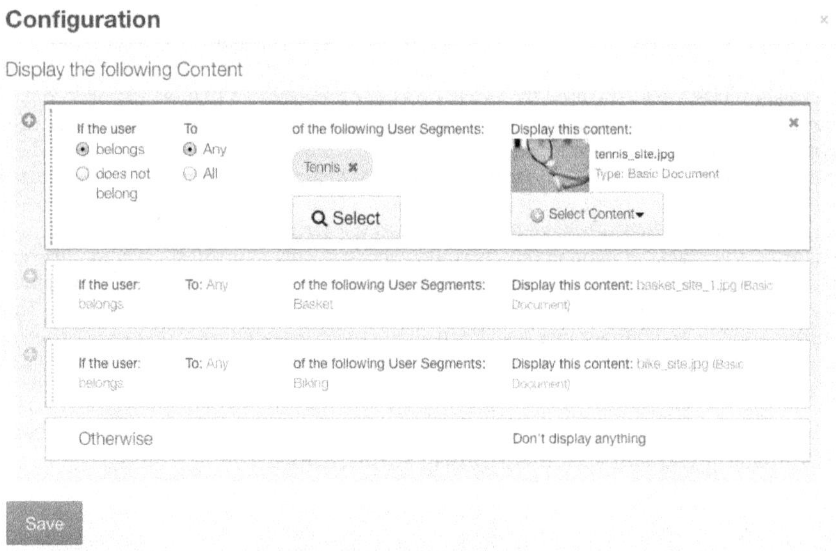

Configuration ×

Display the following Content

Figure 7.7: You can configure the User Segment Content Display application to display content according to rules that you define in the application's configuration window.

Once a User Segment Content Display application has been added to a page and been configured this way, users (even guest users) will see a different image based on the user segment to which they belong. The application won't even be visible to a user if the user doesn't belong to any of the configured user segments.

The User Segment Content Display application allows site administrators to preview the various assets that have been configured to be displayed to different user segments.

User Segment Content List

The User Segment Content List application displays content that has been categorized for the user segments that match the user segments to which the current user belongs. For example, suppose that your website has several assets categorized under the following user segments: *Tennis fans, Soccer fans,* and *Basketball fans.* When a user that belongs to the Tennis fans user segment views this application, the application displays a list of assets categorized for the Tennis fans user segment. If the user belongs to multiple user segments, then a list of articles that have been categorized for any of the matching user segments will be shown.

By default, the User Segment Content List application is configured to display assets of any type that have been categorized for any user segment that matches the current user. However, you can configure the User Segment Content List application to display only assets of specific types. For example, you can configure the User Segment Content List application to only display web content articles and documents.

Campaign Content Display

The Campaign Content Display application is similar to the User Segment Content Display application except that instead of displaying an asset based on the user segments to which a user belongs, it displays an asset based on the campaigns that a user matches. However, the Campaign Content Display application's display rules are simpler than those

Figure 7.8: In the User Segment Content Display application, site administrators can preview the various assets that have been configured to be displayed to different user segments.

Figure 7.9: The User Segment Content List application displays content that matches the user segments which fit the current user. You can configure the User Segment Content List application to display assets of any kind or only specific kinds of assets.

of the User Segment Content Display application. You can specify multiple rules for the
Campaign Content Display application according to the following format:

- If the user belongs to this campaign: [select a campaign], then display this content:
  [specify a specific asset].

As with the User Segment Content Display application, you can specify any number
of *if* clauses when configuring the Campaign Content Display application. An *otherwise*
clause always follows the last *if* clause so the Campaign Content Display application knows
what to display if the user doesn't match any campaigns. These rules cannot be ordered
manually as they can with the User Segment Content Display application. The order of
the rules is based on the priority of the campaigns.

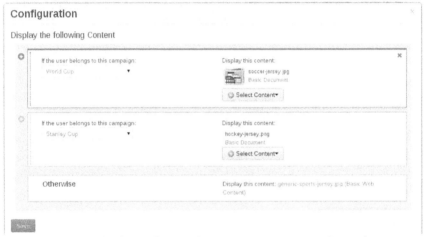

Figure 7.10: The rules for configuring the Campaign Content Display application to
display content are similar to the rules of the User Segment Content Display
application, but simpler.

For example, suppose that you've created two campaigns called *World Cup* and *Stanley
Cup*, designed to target users who are interested in the World Cup of soccer and the Stanley Cup of hockey. You could add a Campaign Content Display application to a page and
configure it with the following rules:

- If the user belongs to this campaign: *World Cup*, then display this content: *soccer-
  jersey.jpg*.
- If the user belongs to this campaign: *Stanley Cup*, then display this content: *hockey-
  jersey.jpg*.
- Otherwise, display this content: *generic-sports-jersey.jpg*

Once a Campaign Content Display application has been added to a page and been configured this way, portal users who match the World Cup campaign will see a certain image
in the application. Users who match the Stanley cup campaign will see a different image
in the application. Users who don't match either campaign will see the default image. Of
course, once a campaign has ended, no users will match that campaign. Once all campaigns have ended, all users will see the default image.

The Campaign Content Display application, like the User Segment Content Display
application, allows site administrators to preview the different assets that will be displayed
for different campaigns.

7.5 Simulating User Segments and Campaigns

The Audience Targeting app includes a simulator feature. The Audience Targeting Simulator allows administrators to preview the way portal pages appear to different users. It does so by allowing site administrators to modify the matched user segments or campaigns. The Audience Targeting Simulator is accessible via the Dockbar. The Simulator icon appears below the Add, Preview, and Edit icons but above the Edit Controls icon on the left side of the Dockbar. Clicking on the Simulator icon opens a panel which has two tabs: *User Segments* and *Campaigns*. By default, the Audience Targeting Simulator is only visible to site administrators and users with the View permission for the Audience Targeting Simulator.

 Note: Permissions pertaining to the Audience Targeting Simulator and other features of the Audience Targeting app can be granted via the Roles section of the Control Panel. When defining permissions for a role, go to *Site Administration Configuration* to find the *Audience Targeting, Audience Targeting Resources*, and *Audience Targeting Simulator* sections.

The User Segments tab of the Audience Targeting simulator displays a list of all the user segments matched by the current user as well as all the user segments not matched by the current user. Any matched user segment can be unselected and any unmatched user segment can be selected. This allows site administrators to simulate how the website would appear to different users. Clicking on the *Simulate* button makes your website appear to you the way it would appear to the selected user segments. The simulation continues until you click the *Stop Simulation* button. This allows site administrators to navigate around their site as if they were a user that matched the selected user segments.

The Campaigns tab of the Content Targeting Simulator displays all matched campaigns and all unmatched campaigns. It does not offer a *Simulate* option yet. However, since campaigns target specific user segments, it's easy to simulate how your site would look if certain campaigns were matched.

7.6 Liferay Audience Targeting Rules

Rules enable Audience Targeting administrators to define how users are classified into the user segments they create.

Basically, a rule evaluates if the current user matches or not one or several conditions. Rules can be configured and combined differently for each user segment to create a very specific classification algorithm. A user must match all rules in a user segment to be classified into it.

Behavior Rules

These rules allow to classify users based on their navigation behavior.

These rules will not work properly if content tracking or page tracking are not enabled. They can be enabled in Control Panel > Portal Settings > Audience Targeting Analytics (for portal level configuration) or in Control Panel > Site Settings > Audience Targeting Analytics (for site level configuration).

Content Visited

Evaluates if the user has visited the selected content.

Figure 7.11: Audience Targeting Simulator

Page Visited

Evaluates if the user has visited the selected page.

Score Points

Evaluates if the user has visited any page or content categorized under this user segment a number of times equals or higher than the configured threshold.

Social Rules

These rules allow you to classify users based on their profiles in social networks (e.g.Facebook).

These rules will not work properly if login through the specific social network (Single Sign On) is not enabled and properly configured. Follow these steps to enable Facebook Sigle Sign on in Liferay:

1. Sign in to the Facebook Developers site and add a new App. For more information, read the Facebook app developer guide[1]. After going through all the steps, you will finally have a new App with an Application ID and an Application Secret.

---

[1]https://developers.facebook.com/docs/guides/appcenter

2. Log in as a Portal administrator in your Liferay Portal and go to Control Panel →Portal Settings →Authentication →Facebook. Check Enable and copy your Application ID and Application Secret to their respective fields. Finally click Save.

3. To verify that the Facebook Single Sign On works properly, sign out and then click the Facebook option in the Sign In box. Enter your Facebook username and password in the prompted pop-up and click Login. You should be automatically signed in to your Liferay Portal with your Facebook user.

Read the Liferay User Guide[2] for more information.

Facebook Age

Evaluates if the age in the user's Facebook profile is in the configured range.

Facebook City

Evaluates if the city in the user's Facebook profile matches the configured value.

Facebook Education

Evaluates if the education in the user's Facebook profile matches the configured values.

Facebook Friends

Evaluates if the user has more or less friends in Facebook than the selected value.

Facebook Gender

Evaluates if the gender in the user's Facebook profile matches the selected value.

Facebook Page Like

Evaluates if the user likes the configured Facebook page.

User Attributes Rules

These rules allow to classify users based on the attributes.
These rules will not work properly if the corresponding attributes are not available. Follow the given instructions for each rules in such cases.

Age

Evaluates if the age in the user's profile is in the configured range.

Gender

Evaluates if the gender in the user's profile matches the selected value.

Regular Role

Evaluates if the user has the selected regular role assigned.

---

[2]https://dev.liferay.com/discover/portal/-/knowledge_base/6-2/integrating-existing-users-into-liferay

Site Member

Evaluates if the user is member of the selected site.

Site Role

Evaluates if the user has the selected role assigned in the selected site.

Organization Member

Evaluates if the user is member of the selected organization.

Organization Role

Evaluates if the user has the selected role assigned in the selected organization.

User Group Member

Evaluates if the user is member of the selected user group.

User Signed In

Evaluates if the user is signed in in the portal.

Session Attributes Rules

These rules allow to classify users based on their session attributes. Session attributes usually refer to the context in which the user accesses.

These rules will not work properly if the corresponding session attributes are retrieved through any tools that are not currently available or properly configured. Follow the given instructions for each rules in such cases.

Browser

Evaluates if the user is accessing with the selected browser.

Device

Evaluates if the user is accessing with the selected device.

This rule is based on the existing Device Families. To manage Device Families go to Site Administration →Configuration →Mobile Device Families.

Location

Evaluates if the user is accessing from a country and region that match the configured values.

Operating System

Evaluates if the user is accessing with the selected Operating System.

Time

Evaluates if the user is accessing at a time that is within the configured range.

Notice that the reference time is that of the server.

7.7 Summary

In this chapter, we learned how to use Liferay' audience targeting app. This app allows you to define custom user segments, target specific content to different user segments, and create campaigns for different user segments. Liferay's audience targeting app allows you generate reports so that you can measure the effectiveness of your campaigns. Liferay's audience targeting app includes a simulator so that you can preview how your site would appear to users belonging to different user segments. You can create user segments by applying various rules that reference session attributes, profile attributes, behavior, and possibly other information, such as information from social networks. It's also easy for developers to create additional rules and rule types.

## CHAPTER 8

PERSONALIZATION AND CUSTOMIZATION

In this chapter, we discuss several ways Liferay users can customize pages, applications, and the way they use your portal. We'll cover the following topics:

- Personal Sites
- Customizable Pages and Applications
- Application Display Templates
- Using a Rules Engine

Personal sites allow each portal user to manage and customize a set of public and/or private pages and any associated content or applications. Public pages provide a means of making content publicly available. Private pages provide a means for users to create content and use applications that should be hidden from other users. Liferay 6.1 introduced the concepts of customizable pages and applications. Administrators can designate certain pages or applications as "customizable," which allows each user to make and save their own customizations. Portlet layouts can also be customized with the use of application display templates. Application display templates allow a portlet's look and feel to be completely customized. Liferay Enterprise Edition provides a rules engine which allows administrators to create custom portal rules and simplify complex blocks of code containing lots of if-else statements. Let's start by discussing personal sites.

8.1 User Personal Sites

By default, newly created users in Liferay are each granted a personal site. Each user functions as the site administrator of his or her personal site. Personal sites are fully customizable but cannot have more than one member. The public pages of personal sites provide a space for users to add content and applications that they'd like to make accessible to anyone, including guests. User blogs are often placed on public personal site pages. Content and applications that users would like to reserve for personal use are often placed on the private pages of personal sites. For example, each user can add a Documents and Media portlet to his or her private pages and use it as an online private file repository.

If you'd like to disable personal sites for your portal, just add the following properties to your portal-ext.properties file:

```
layout.user.public.layouts.enabled=false
layout.user.private.layouts.enabled=false
```

Note that the public and private page sets of personal sites are handled separately. You can leave one page set enabled while disabling the other.

What if you initially had user personal sites enabled for your portal but then disabled them? Each existing user's personal site remains on your portal until the next time they log in, at which point it's removed.

You can allow users to create personal sites but not have them automatically created for new users. To do this, first make sure that `layout.user.public.layouts.enabled` and `layout.user.private.layouts.enabled` are not set to `false`. You don't need to explicitly set them to `true`—true is the default. Then add the following properties to your `portal-ext.properties` file:

```
layout.user.public.layouts.auto.create=false
layout.user.private.layouts.auto.create=false
```

If the following properties are all set to `true`, which is the default, then users will have personal sites and public and private pages will be automatically created for new users.

```
layout.user.public.layouts.enabled
layout.user.private.layouts.enabled
layout.user.public.layouts.auto.create
layout.user.private.layouts.auto.create
```

There are number of portal properties you can use to customize the automatically created pages. You can customize the names of the default pages, the portlets that appear on the pages, the themes and layout templates of the default pages, and more. Please refer to the Default User Public Layouts and Default User Private Layouts sections of the `portal.properties` file for details. You can find an HTML version of the this file here: `http://docs.liferay.com/portal/6.2/propertiesdoc/portal.properties.html`.

Prior to Liferay 6.1, administrators could disallow users from being able to modify the pages and portlets of their personal sites by setting the following properties:

```
layout.user.public.layouts.modifiable=true
layout.user.private.layouts.modifiable=true
```

As of Liferay 6.1, this property is obsolete. However, you can customize the modifiable portions of personal sites through Liferay's permissions system by removing permissions from roles. To disallow all portal users from modifying something, remove the relevant permission from the User role.

Historically (prior to Liferay 5.1), only power users received personal sites. Back then, they were called personal communities. If you'd like only power users to receive personal sites, add the following properties to your `portal-ext.properties` file:

```
layout.user.public.layouts.power.user.required=true
layout.user.private.layouts.power.user.required=true
```

Personal sites are a dynamic feature of Liferay Portal. They allow users to manage and customize their own pages and content on your portal. Next, let's look at how users can customize applications.

8.2   Page Customizations

Liferay 6.1 introduced the concept of page customizations. Administrators can designate public pages or sections of public pages to be customizable. When a user visits such a page, a notification appears stating that the user can customize the page. Users can make customizations only in the sections of pages designated by administrators. Customizations are based on the rows and columns of a page layout. Page customizations are only visible to the user who made the customizations. By default, site members can make page customizations but non-site members and guests can't.

To enable page customizations as an administrator, first navigate to the page you'd like to let site members modify. Then click on the *Edit* button at the left side of the page, expand the *Customization Settings* area, and click on the *Show Customizable Sections* button.

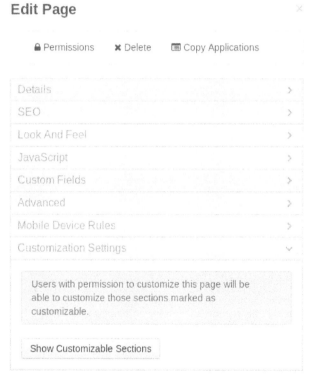

Figure 8.1: To enable page customizations, click on the *Edit* button at the left side of the page, expand the *Customization Settings* area, and click on the *Show Customizable Sections* button.

Once you've clicked the *Show Customizable Sections* button, you'll see one or more red regions, depending on the layout template of your page. Check one or more of the *Customizable* boxes to allow site members to customize certain sections of the page. Regions that you've designated as customizable are colored green.

When site members visit your customizable page, they'll see a notification saying, "You can customize this page." Site members can toggle between viewing their customized page and viewing the default page by clicking the *View Default Page* or *View My Customized Page* links just below the Dockbar. There's also a *Reset My Customizations* link that restores a

Figure 8.2: Check one or more of the *Customizable* boxes to allow site members to customize certain sections of the page.

user's customized page to the match the default page. This allows users to discard one set of customizations and start a new set without having to manually undo each customization that they'd previously made.

Note that non-administrator site members can access the Add menu from the left side of the screen when viewing their customizable page even if they don't ordinarily have permission to view this menu. This allows them to add portlets to the sections of the page that they're allowed to customize. If they click *View Default Page*, the Add menu will disappear from the Dockbar since they're not allowed to modify the default page.

Figure 8.3: Non-administrator site members can customize their own versions of customizable pages but can't modify the default page.

Administrators of customizable pages have the same two views as site members: the *default page* view and the *customized page* view. Changes made to the *default page* affect all users, whereas changes made to the *customized page* affect only the administrator who made the changes. Changes made by administrators to non-customizable sections in the *default view* are immediately applied for all users. However, changes made by administrators to customizable sections do *not* overwrite users' customizations.

Users can make two kinds of customizations to customizable regions. First, they can configure portlet applications within the customizable regions. Second, they can add portlets to or remove portlets from the customizable regions.

The portal doesn't allow users to change a non-instanceable portlet's configuration inside a customizable region since those kinds of portlets are tied to the site to which they've been added. If this were allowed, the customization would affect all users, not just the one who customized the region. Therefore, changes to the portlet configuration in a customizable region are only possible for instanceable portlets, whose portlet configuration only affects that one user.

For example, suppose that you, as an administrator, selected the right column of the Welcome page of the Lunar Resort site to be customizable. A member of the Lunar Resort site could take the following steps to make a personal customization of the Welcome page:

1. Navigate to the Welcome homepage by clicking *Go To ▸ Lunar Resort* from the Dockbar.
2. Remove the Hello World portlet from the right column of the page.
3. Add the Language portlet to the right column of the page by clicking *Add*, clicking on *Applications*, searching for *Language*, and clicking *Add* next to its name.
4. Configure the Language portlet by clicking on the gear icon and selecting *Configuration* and then opening the *Display Style* dropdown menu and choosing *Select Box*.

The Language portlet is useful to have on your portal's homepage if you expect users who speak different languages to access your portal. Users can select their language in the Language portlet to view a translation of the portal into their native language. After closing the Configuration dialog box of the Language portlet, the customized Welcome page looks like this:

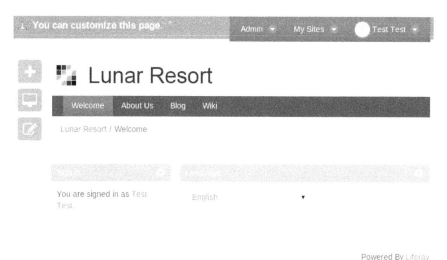

Figure 8.4: In this example, the user removed the Hello World portlet, added the Language portlet, and changed the display style from icons to a select box.

To allow users to customize a page, administrators must grant users permission to *Customize* pages under the Site section. This can be achieved by assigning permission to a role, then assigning this role to the appropriate users. For example, if we want any logged user to be able to customize our customizable pages, we could assign the *Customize* permission to the role *User*. If we want site members to be able to customize the customizable pages of their sites, we would accept the default setting. By default, the *Customize* permission is assigned to the role *Site Member*.

In addition to granting the ability to customize portlet configurations, the *Customize* permission allows users to customize the look and feel of portlets and to import or export portlet settings. Next, let's look at how to use application display templates.

8.3 Using Application Display Templates

The application display template (ADT) framework allows portal administrators to override the default display templates, removing limitations to the way your site's content is displayed. With ADTs, you can define custom display templates used to render asset-centric applications. For example, you may want to show blog entries horizontally instead of vertically, or list your assets in the asset publisher portlet in different sizes.

Let's go through a simple use case to illustrate how creating a custom ADT can improve your site. Suppose you're customizing the Lunar Resort site and want to allow users to communicate with other interested travelers. Specifically, you want to configure the Wiki portlet for collaboration with Facebook or Twitter. With ADTs, you can launch a template editor, create a custom template, and configure your portlet host that template. Custom templates let you re-skin your portlet and give you ultimate control over its appearance and functionality in your portal.

Before attempting to change the ADT for your application, you'll need to select a site for your custom template to reside in. Choosing the *Global* context makes your template available across all sites. To choose a site to house your ADT, navigate to the Control Panel *Sites* and click on a site from the list. If you select the Global context, the *Application Display Templates* page of the Control Panel's Configuration Menu shows you a list of sample templates available for your portlets. These sample templates differ from the default templates already configured in the portlets. If you choose a site to host your template, you must create a custom template for that site's portlets.

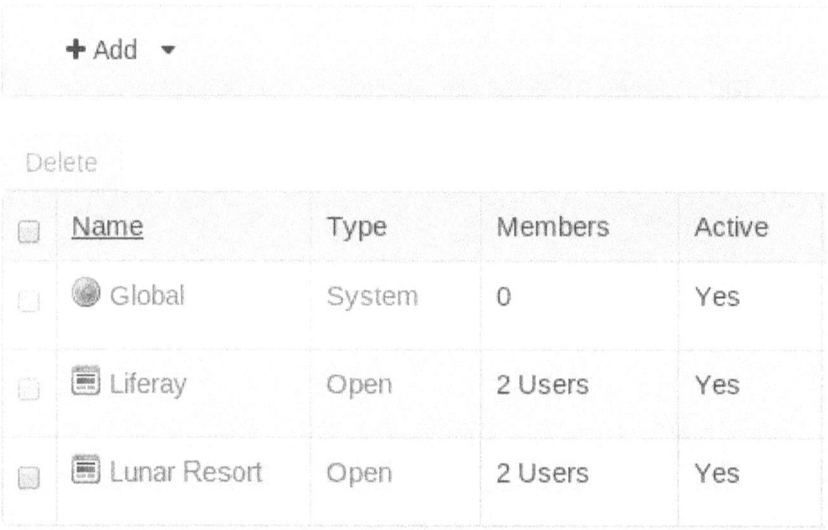

	Name	Type	Members	Active
	Global	System	0	Yes
	Liferay	Open	2 Users	Yes
	Lunar Resort	Open	2 Users	Yes

Figure 8.5: In the Control Panel, you can choose the context in which your application display template resides.

If you'd like to add an ADT, select the portlet you'd like to customize. The list below specifies the portlets that can be customized using ADTs. It also provides sample template descriptions:

- *Asset Publisher*: displays abstracts, icons, related assets, and print/edit actions for assets. Optionally includes asset bookmarks and ratings.
- *Blogs*: displays titles, authors, and abstracts compactly for blog entries.
- *Categories Navigation*: displays a column for each vocabulary. Each column includes the name of a vocabulary with the vocabulary's top level categories listed underneath.
- *Media Gallery*: displays images in a carousel.
- *Site Map*: displays a column for each top level page. Each column includes the name of a top level page with the page's immediate children listed underneath.

- *Tags Navigation*: displays asset tags colored by popularity: red (high), yellow (medium), and green (low).
- *Wiki*: displays social bookmarks and ratings for wiki pages and their child pages.

To create a new ADT, click *Add* and select the template you'd like to create, based on portlet type. Then enter the name and, optionally, a description and a small image to use. You can select the language type for your template (FTL or VM). Lastly, the *Script* option lets you browse your file system for a template on your file system, or you can launch the editor and create one directly. On the left side of the template editor, you'll notice a palette of common variables used for making templates. This is a great reference when creating your template. To place one of the variables into the template editor, simply position your cursor where you want it placed, and click the variable name.

Think it can't get any better? Guess again! If the variable name doesn't give you enough information on the variable's functionality, you can hover your pointer over it for a more detailed description. Because there are multiple kinds of ADTs, there are also different variables for each ADT. Thus, each template has a different set of variables only applicable for that specific template.

▼ Script

Figure 8.6: Liferay offers a versatile script editor to customize your ADT.

You can also use the autocomplete feature to add variables to your template. It can be invoked by typing $\{$ which opens a drop-down menu of available variables. By clicking one of the variables, the editor inserts the variable into the editor.

You also have the ability to embed same-type templates into other templates. For example, suppose you have an existing Wiki ADT and would like to create another similar Wiki ADT. Instead of starting from scratch, you can import the existing Wiki ADT into your new one and build off of it. In other words, you can utilize ADTs as generic templates which allow for reusable code to be imported by Velocity or FreeMarker templates in the system. For more information on how to create a custom template, visit the Liferay Developer Network.[1]

Another cool feature is the *Export/Import* functionality. You can take advantage of this feature by clicking the gear icon at the top right of the screen and selecting *Export/Import*. For more information on using this feature, visit the Export/Import section of this guide.

After you've completed the initial set up and saved your ADT, you can manage your ADT through its *Actions* button. This provides several options:

- *Edit*: lets you modify the ADT's setup properties.
- *Permissions*: lets you manage the permissions *Delete*, *Permissions*, *Update*, and *View* for the ADT.
- *Copy*: creates a copy of the ADT.
- *Delete*: deletes the ADT.

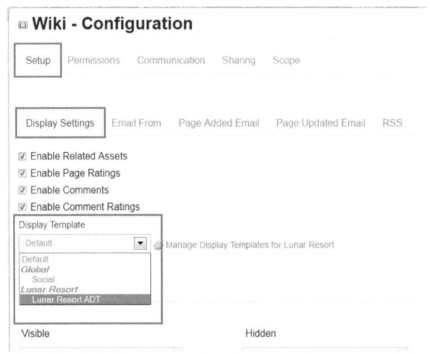

Figure 8.7: In the *Configuration* menu of a portlet, you can edit and manage available ADTs.

Additionally, your ADT generates a static URL and a WebDAV URL. These values access the XML source of your template. You can find these URLs by clicking the ADT from the menu and expanding the *Details* section. With the WebDAV URL, site administrators are capable of adding, browsing, editing, and deleting ADTs on a remote server. If you'd like to learn more about what the WebDAV URL can do, visit the *Document Management* chapter's *WebDAV access* chapter.

---

[1]https://dev.liferay.com/develop/tutorials/-/knowledge_base/6-2/application-display-templates

To enable your ADT for a portlet, navigate to the portlet you want to modify and open its *Configuration* menu. In the *Display Settings* sub-tab located within the *Setup* tab, select your ADT from the *Display Template* drop-down menu. You'll notice they're separated by context type. Also, you can manage site-specific display templates for your portlet. do this by clicking the *Manage Display Templates for [SPECIFIC_SITE]* link next to the *Display Template* drop-down menu. A window will display with a list of your configured templates only available for your site with options to add new templates or edit existing templates.

Now that you know the general functions of ADTs, let's create our own. This brief demonstration will show you just how easy, yet powerful, ADTs can be for your portal.

1. Add the Media Gallery portlet to a page by navigating to *Add Content and Applications* →*Applications* →*Content Management* →*Media Gallery*.

2. Select the *Options* gear from the top right corner, then click *Configuration*.

3. Enable the *Show Actions* and *Show Folder Menu* display settings. Then click *Save* and close the popup.

4. Click the *Multiple Media* link and select two custom photos to display. Then click *Save*, and navigate back to the main portlet screen.

5. Notice the default format of the pictures. To change the display template for this portlet, navigate back to the *Options* gear and click *Configuration*.

6. From the *Display Template* drop-down menu, select *Carousel*. Then click *Save*.

Figure 8.8: After applying the Carousel ADT, your pictures are displayed as a carousel slideshow.

The Media Gallery portlet is transformed into a carousel slideshow. At this time, it's perfectly natural to be experiencing "I can conquer the world" feelings, just as Liferay's mascot, Ray, exudes in the image above. ADTs have that kind of power to transform your site into an enjoyable and convenient home for users.

Customizing the user interface of Liferay's bundled portlets provides the ultimate customization experience for Liferay users. Next, let's look at how to use Liferay's rules engine.

8.4   Using Liferay's rules engine

Liferay Portal Enterprise Edition provides an implementation of a JSR-94 compliant rules engine. This rules engine is provided as a Web Plugin and is based on the popular open source Drools project.

Why use a rules engine?

If you are not familiar with rules engines, you may be wondering why you would want to use one. In most applications, complex rule processing often takes the form of nested if-else blocks of code which can be very difficult to decipher and to maintain. If rules change, a developer must work with a business user to define the new rules. The developer must then read through the existing logic to understand what is happening and make the necessary modifications. The changes must then be recompiled, tested, and redeployed. A rules engine provides a means to separate the rules or logic of an application from the remaining code. Separating these rules provides several distinct advantages.

- A rules engine allows for a more declarative style of programming where the rules define what is happening, without describing how it is happening. This makes it much easier to read than nested 'if-else' blocks of code. It's also easier to make changes without introducing bugs in your code.

- The rules are written in a language that is easier for non-developers to understand. This makes it easier for business users to validate and even modify the rules without having to involve developers.

- A rules engine allows for changes to be made to the rules without requiring that you recompile your application. If your code must pass through a strict deployment workflow, this can be a huge time saver and can also save a significant amount of money.

After all this, you may be interested in using Liferay's rules engine, so let's get started with it.

Installation

The Drools web plugin is available to Liferay Enterprise Edition customers through Liferay Marketplace. It's called the Drools EE app and you'll find it categorized as a Utility app.

The Drools web plugin provides a rules engine implementation. By itself, it doesn't provide any observable changes to the portal user interface or any additional functionality. To see the rules engine in action, you can download and install the Sample Drools portlet that contains two rule definitions that illustrate how to leverage the rules engine in your custom code. The Sample Drools portlet is available through the Customer Portal.

Let's examine the sample portlet to see how it works.

Configuring the Sample Drools Portlet

Begin by downloading and installing the Sample Drools portlet. The Sample Drools portlet is available to Liferay Enterprise Edition customers through the customer portal. The name is sample-drools-portlet, and you'll find it in the list of web plugins.

After installation is complete, log in as an administrator and add the portlet to a page. Initially, the portlet indicates the name of the currently logged in user and a message stating that there are no results. To see results in the portlet, we need to create and tag assets in the site to which you added the portlet.

From the Dockbar, click *Admin* →*Content* and create a new web content instance in your site. Before publishing the web content instance, tag the article with *americas*. Then, navigate to *My Account* from the Dockbar and click on the *Addresses* link on the right side of the screen. Enter a Brazilian, Canadian, Mexican, or US based address and click *Save*. Navigate back to the page with the Sample Drools portlet. The Sample Drools portlet should now be displaying the web content instance that you created.

The default rule that's being evaluated displays a list of assets based on the current user's address. For example, if the current user's country is set to Brazil, Canada, Mexico, or the United States, the Sample Drools portlet displays a list of assets that have been tagged with the *americas* tag.

Welcome Test Test!

O beautiful for halcyon skies,
For amber waves of grain,
For purple mountain majesties
Above the enameled plain!

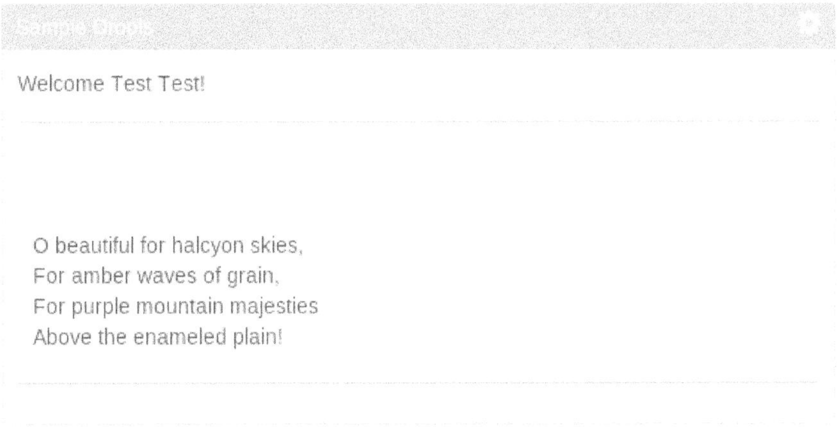

Figure 8.9: By default, the Sample Drools portlet returns personalized content based on the addresses set on the form for editing a user account. This form is accessible from the Dockbar via *[User Name]* →*My Account*. Users with addresses in Brazil, Canada, Mexico, or the United States will see a list of assets tagged with the "americas" tag in the Sample Drools portlet.

Now that you've seen how the Sample Drools portlet works, let's take a look closer at the rules themselves.

Rules Definitions

Rule definitions can be written using Drools' declarative language. Rule files are text files that often have a .drl extension. A rule file can contain multiple rules. In addition to the standard Drools' declarative language, a domain specific language (DSL) can be created for your specific problem domain. Creating a DSL can make your rules even easier for business users to create and maintain your applications rules but does require some additional work up front. For additional information on creating a DSL for your problem domain please refer to the Domain Specific Languages section of the official Drools Documentation.[2]

To see examples of a rules definition file, access the following directory in the Sample Drools portlet:

```
sample-drools-portlet/WEB-INF/src/com/liferay/sampledrools/dependencies
```

---

[2]http://docs.jboss.org/drools/release/5.2.0.Final/drools-expert-docs/html/ch05.html#d0e6217

To see how rules work in action, look at the rule defined in `rules_user_address_content.drl`.

At first glance, this `.drl` file looks a lot like a Java class file. This example starts with a comment describing the rule. Single line comments can begin with either a `*##` or `*//*` and multi-line comments begin with `_/*_` and end with `_*/_`.

```
##
## Rules
##
## This sample program will return personalized content based on the user's
## addresses set in the My Account section of the Control Panel.
##
## For example, suppose the current user has an address in the United States and
## is a member of the Liferay site. All assets within the Liferay site
## that are tagged with "West Coast Symposium" will be returned.
##
```

Following the comments is a package declaration. The package declaration is optional in a Drools, but if it appears, it must be at the beginning of the file. The package denotes a collection of rules. Unlike Java, the package name does not represent a folder structure; it's only a unique namespace. The `;` at the end of the package declaration and all other statements is optional.

```
package com.liferay.sampledrools.dependencies;
```

After the package declaration are a series of `import` statements. Import statements in the rule file are used just like the import statements in Java classes. Classes that are imported can be used in the rules.

```
import com.liferay.portal.kernel.search.BooleanClause;
import com.liferay.portal.kernel.search.BooleanClauseOccur;
import com.liferay.portal.kernel.search.BooleanClauseFactoryUtil;
import com.liferay.portal.kernel.search.BooleanQuery;
import com.liferay.portal.kernel.search.BooleanQueryFactoryUtil;
import com.liferay.portal.kernel.search.Document;
import com.liferay.portal.kernel.search.FacetedSearcher;
import com.liferay.portal.kernel.search.Field;
import com.liferay.portal.kernel.search.Hits;
import com.liferay.portal.kernel.search.Indexer;
import com.liferay.portal.kernel.search.SearchContext;
import com.liferay.portal.kernel.search.facet.AssetEntriesFacet;
import com.liferay.portal.kernel.search.facet.Facet;
import com.liferay.portal.kernel.search.facet.ScopeFacet;
import com.liferay.portal.kernel.util.GetterUtil;
import com.liferay.portal.kernel.util.KeyValuePair;
import com.liferay.portal.kernel.util.LocaleUtil;
import com.liferay.portal.kernel.util.StringUtil;
import com.liferay.portal.kernel.util.Validator;
import com.liferay.portal.model.Address;
import com.liferay.portal.model.Group;
import com.liferay.portal.model.Contact;
import com.liferay.portal.model.User;
import com.liferay.portal.service.AddressLocalServiceUtil;
import com.liferay.portal.util.PortalUtil;
import com.liferay.portlet.asset.model.AssetEntry;
import com.liferay.portlet.asset.service.AssetEntryLocalServiceUtil;

import java.util.ArrayList;
import java.util.Collections;
import java.util.List;
```

The next line declares the `dialect` for the package. In this case, we will be using Java for any of the code expressions that we'll encounter. The other possible value for the dialect is `MVEL`, which is a powerful expression language for Java-based applications. See `http://mvel.codehaus.org/` for details. If necessary, the dialect can also be specified at the rule level to override the package level dialect.

```
dialect "java"
```

In this rule file, we have only a single function, which is listed next. Functions allow you to insert Java code that can be evaluated at run time into your rule file. Functions are commonly used as a as part of the consequence clause of the rule statement. Functions are similar to Java methods but you use the *function* keyword to define a function. The function's parameters and the return type are declared as they would be in a Java method. In this example, the getAssetEntries function returns a java.util.List object that contains AssetEntry objects based on the user, classNameIds, and assetTagName provided in the function call.

```
function List getAssetEntries(
    User user, long[] classNameIds, String assetTagName) {

    List<Group> groups = user.getMySites();

    long[] groupIds = new long[groups.size()];

    for (int i = 0; i < groups.size(); i++) {
        Group group = groups.get(i);

        groupIds[i] = group.getGroupId();
    }

    if ((classNameIds == null) || (classNameIds.length == 0) ||
        (groupIds.length == 0) || Validator.isNull(assetTagName)) {

        return Collections.emptyList();
    }

    SearchContext searchContext = new SearchContext();

    Facet assetEntriesFacet = new AssetEntriesFacet(searchContext);

    assetEntriesFacet.setStatic(true);

    searchContext.addFacet(assetEntriesFacet);

    Facet scopeFacet = new ScopeFacet(searchContext);
\index{Scope}

    scopeFacet.setStatic(true);

    searchContext.addFacet(scopeFacet);

    searchContext.setAttribute("paginationType", "regular");
    searchContext.setCompanyId(user.getCompanyId());
    searchContext.setGroupIds(groupIds);
    searchContext.setIncludeStagingGroups(false);
    searchContext.setScopeStrict(false);
    searchContext.setUserId(user.getUserId());

    BooleanQuery booleanQuery = BooleanQueryFactoryUtil.create(searchContext);

    booleanQuery.addExactTerm(Field.ASSET_TAG_NAMES, assetTagName);

    BooleanClause booleanClause = BooleanClauseFactoryUtil.create(
        searchContext, booleanQuery, BooleanClauseOccur.MUST.getName());

    searchContext.setBooleanClauses(new BooleanClause[] {booleanClause});

    List<AssetEntry> assetEntries = new ArrayList<AssetEntry>();

    Indexer indexer = FacetedSearcher.getInstance();

    Hits hits = indexer.search(searchContext);

    for (int i = 0; i < hits.getDocs().length; i++) {
        Document document = hits.doc(i);

        String entryClassName = document.get(Field.ENTRY_CLASS_NAME);

        long entryClassPK = GetterUtil.getLong(
            document.get(Field.ENTRY_CLASS_PK));
        long rootEntryClassPK = GetterUtil.getLong(
            document.get(Field.ROOT_ENTRY_CLASS_PK));
```

```
    if (rootEntryClassPK > 0) {
        entryClassPK = rootEntryClassPK;
    }

    AssetEntry assetEntry = AssetEntryLocalServiceUtil.fetchEntry(
        entryClassName, entryClassPK);

    if (assetEntry != null) {
        assetEntries.add(assetEntry);
    }
}

return assetEntries;
}
```

Alternatively, this function could've been written in a helper class and then imported using a *function import*. So if we had created a helper class called AddressContentHelper the import would look like this:

```
import function
com.liferay.sampledrools.dependencies.AddressContentHelper.getAsetEntries;
```

The last section of the rules file contains the actual rules. The syntax of a rule is very straightforward.

```
rule "name" attribute when condition then consequence end
```

The rule name is required and it must be unique within the package as declared above. Names with spaces must be enclosed in double quotes. It is considered a best practice to always enclose your rule names in double quotes.

```
rule "Initialize Rules"
```

The attributes section is optional. In our first rule, we have a single attribute called salience. The salience attribute is an integer value that acts as a priority weighting. The number can be positive or negative and defaults to the value of 0. Rules with a higher salience value are given a higher priority. It is considered a best practice to write attributes one to a line. In our example, the first rule is one that should be evaluated before any other so it is given a high salience value of 1000. None of our other rules have a salience attribute set, so they all default to a value of 0.

```
salience 1000
```

The when keyword marks the conditional section of the rule. It is also referred to as the Left Hand Side (LHS). The when keyword is followed by zero or more condition elements that must be met before the consequence will be called. If there are no condition elements, then the condition is always evaluated as true.

The most common type of conditional element is a *pattern*. Patterns match against *facts*. Facts are statements that are known to be true. Facts can be inserted by the Java code that invokes the rules engine or they can be declared in the rule file itself.

In the first rule of our rule file (Initialize Rules), the only condition is that the rule must operate on a User object.

```
when user : User();
```

In more complex rules, the pattern may include constraints or may evaluate the properties of Java objects. For example, the second rule of this rule file is called *Get European Content*. This rule includes the following pattern which ensures that a user's address contains the country name France, Germany, or Spain.

```
userAddress : Address(country.getName(Locale.US) in ("France", "Germany", "Spain"));
```

The consequence section of the rule follows the conditional section. It's also known as the Right Hand Side (RHS) or action part of the rule. The consequence section begins with the keyword then and it is intended to modify the working memory data. Drools provides some convenience methods that make it easier to modify the working memory. In this rule, we use the insertLogical method which places a new object into the working memory and retracts it when there are no more facts supporting the truth of the current rule. After the consequence section of the rule, the rule is terminated with the keyword end.

```
then List<Address> userAddresses = AddressLocalServiceUtil.getAddresses(
      user.getCompanyId(), Contact.class.getName(), user.getContactId());

   for (Address userAddress : userAddresses) {
      insertLogical(userAddress); } end
```

Following the initial rule in our example, there are three additional rules that will be evaluated. Each of these rules evaluates the userAddress that was inserted into the working memory to determine what type of content should be displayed to the end user.

For additional documentation on the Drools rules language, please see the official Drools documentation.[3]

8.5 Summary

In this chapter, we discussed personal sites for portal users. We showed how to enable or disable them, how to set whether or not pages should be automatically created, and how to customize automatically created pages. We also examined general customizable pages that don't belong to personal sites. Administrators can designate certain pages or portions of pages to be customizable and site members can configure these portions of the pages, add or remove portlet applications, and save their configurations.

We also discussed how you can use Liferay's rules engine with Liferay EE. As you can see from the Sample Rules portlet, using a rules engine can be a powerful way to decouple the rules of your application from the front-end and back-end code. These rules are written in a declarative language that business users can read and verify. Additionally, rule definitions can be modified without modifying the underlying Java code, re-compiling, or redeploying your applications.

---

[3]http://docs.jboss.org/drools/release/5.2.0.Final/drools-expert-docs/html/

## CHAPTER 9

COLLABORATION SUITE

Liferay Portal ships with a robust suite of collaboration applications which you can use to build communities of users for your site. These applications provide all the features that you would expect of standalone versions outside of a portal setting. The difference with Liferay's collaboration suite, however, is that all of the applications share a common look and feel, security model, and architecture. They inherit the strengths of being part of Liferay's development platform so you can use them in combination with Liferay's user management and content management features to build a well-integrated, feature-rich web site.

This chapter focuses on how to use Liferay's collaboration suite. We explain how to set up and administer:

- Blogs
- Calendars
- Message Boards
- Wikis
- Polls
- Announcements
- Chat
- Mail

Let's jump right in and begin by exploring Blogs.

9.1 Expressing Yourself Using Blogs

The word *Blog* is an apostrophe-less contraction of the two words *web* and *log*. Blogs were first popularized by web sites such as Slashdot (http://slashdot.org) which have the format of a running list of entries to which users could attach comments. Over time, more and more sites such as Digg, del.icio.us, and Newsvine adopted the format, empowering users to share their opinions and generating lively discussions.

Over the course of time, blogging sites and applications began to appear, such as blogger.com, blogspot.com. TypePad, WordPress, and Web Roller. These applications allow *individuals* to run their own web sites in the same format: a running list of short articles to which readers who are registered with the site can attach threaded comments. People who run a blog are called *bloggers*, and sometimes they build a whole community of readers who are interested in their blog posts. Anyone can have a blog, in fact, there are several famous people who run their own blogs. It gives people an outlet for self-expression that they would not otherwise have, and the ubiquity and wide reach of the Internet ensures that if you have something important and interesting to say, somebody will read it.

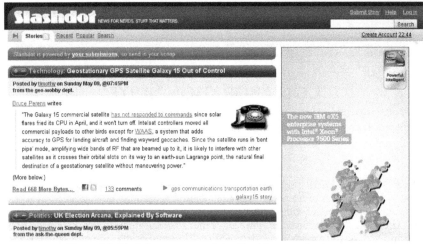

Figure 9.1: Slashdot was one of the first blogs on the Internet.

Liferay Portal has a Blogs portlet which allows you to provide a blogging service to users of your web site. In fact, Liferay extensively uses the Blogs portlet on http://www.liferay.com/community/blogs to provide community members and employees with blogs of their own. In addition to the Blogs portlet, there's also a Blogs Aggregator portlet which can take entries from multiple users' blogs and put them all in one larger list. We will go over how to use both of these portlets to create a blogging site for your users.

The Blogs Portlet

The Blogs portlet is available from the *Collaboration* section of the *Add →Applications* menu. Notice that it is an instanceable portlet, meaning that it supports scopes. This allows you to use the Blogs portlet to create a shared blog to build a site like Slashdot or to create multiple personal blogs to build a site like http://blogger.com. What's the difference? Adding the Blogs portlet to a site page creates a shared blog for members of the site that the page belongs to. Adding the Blogs portlet to a user's personal site creates a blog just for that user. The Blogs portlet works the same way in both cases. And of course, you can change the Blog portlet's scope to have different blogs on different pages in the same site.

By default, the Blogs portlet displays the latest entry in its entirety. When you first add the portlet to a page, it has no entries, so the portlet is empty. There are several display options to let you configure it to look the way you want it to look. Before we start adding entries, let's configure the portlet so that it displays entries the way you want them.

Configuring the Blogs Portlet

The Blogs portlet is easy to configure. Click on the *Options* icon in the portlet's title bar and select *Configuration*. Beneath the Setup tab, there is another row of options.

Figure 9.2: The initial view of the Blogs portlet.

Display Settings: changes various display options for the Blogs portlet. To choose the right settings, you should think about the best way to display your entries as well as how you want users to interact with bloggers.

- *Maximum Items to Display:* choose the total number of blog entries to display on the initial page. You can select up to one hundred to be displayed.

- *Display Template:* choose between *Full Content, Abstract,* or *Title.* Setting this to Abstract shows the abstract, or if there isn't one, only the first 30 words of your blog entries, with a Read More link at the bottom of each that expands to the whole entry. To learn how to customize your own display templates visit the *Using application display templates* section of the *Personalization and Customization* chapter.

- *Enable Flags:* flag content as inappropriate and send an email to the administrators.

- *Enable Related Assets:* select related content from other portlets to pull into their blog entry for readers to view.

- *Enable Ratings:* lets readers rate your blog entries from one to five stars.

- *Enable Comments:* lets readers comment on your blog entries.

- *Enable Comment Ratings:* lets readers rate the comments which are posted to your blog entries.

- *Enable Social Bookmarks:* lets users tweet, Facebook like, or +1 (Google Plus) about blog posts. You can edit which social bookmarks are available in the *Social Bookmarks* section of the Configuration menu.

- *Display Style:* select a simple, vertical, or horizontal display style for your blog posts.

- *Display Position:* choose a top or bottom position for your blog posts.

- *Social Bookmarks:* choose social bookmarks to enable for blog posts, which includes Twitter, Facebook, and plusone (Google Plus).

Email From: defines the *From* field in the email messages that users receive from the Blogs portlet.

Entry Added Email: defines a subject and body for the emails sent out when a new Blog entry has been added.

Entry Updated Email: defines a subject and body for the emails sent out when a new Blog entry has been updated.

RSS: choose how blogs are displayed to RSS readers. Here, you can choose how you want your blog entries to be published as feeds to readers and outside web sites.

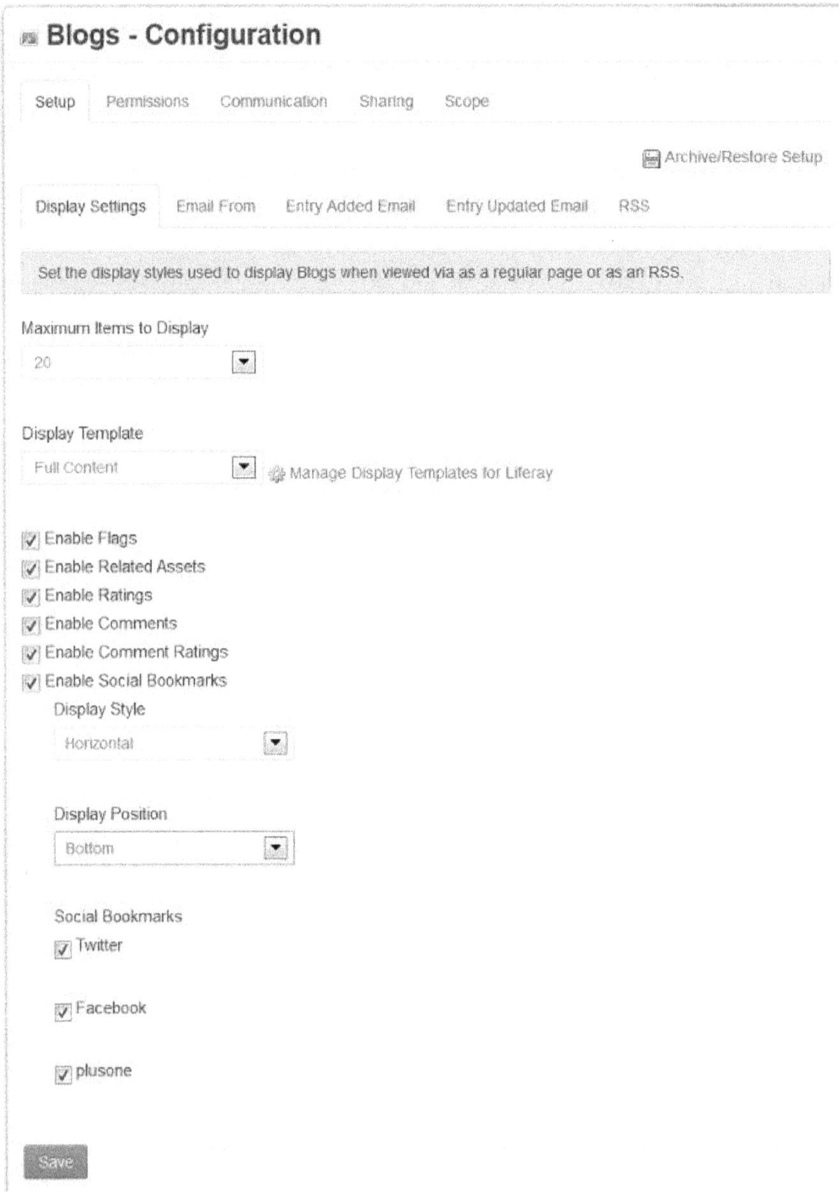

Blogs - Configuration

Setup   Permissions   Communication   Sharing   Scope

Archive/Restore Setup

Display Settings   Email From   Entry Added Email   Entry Updated Email   RSS

Set the display styles used to display Blogs when viewed via as a regular page or as an RSS.

Maximum Items to Display

20

Display Template

Full Content   Manage Display Templates for Liferay

☑ Enable Flags
☑ Enable Related Assets
☑ Enable Ratings
☑ Enable Comments
☑ Enable Comment Ratings
☑ Enable Social Bookmarks
   Display Style

   Horizontal

   Display Position

   Bottom

   Social Bookmarks
   ☑ Twitter

   ☑ Facebook

   ☑ plusone

Save

Figure 9.3: The Blogs portlet's *Configuration* menu offers a plethora of display settings.

- *Maximum Items to Display:* choose the total number of RSS feeds to display on the initial page. You can choose up to one hundred to be displayed.

- *Display Style:* choose between *Full Content, Abstract,* and *Title.* These options work just like the ones above for blog entries.

- *Format:* choose which format you want to deliver your blogs: Atom 1.0, RSS 1.0, or RSS 2.0.

Now that you have the Blogs portlet looking the way you want it, you'll want to review permissions for it—especially if you're working on a shared blog.

Permissions

If you have a personal blog, the default permissions should work well for you. If you have a shared blog, you may want to modify the permissions on the blog. The default settings make it so only the owner of the site to which the portlet has been added is able to add entries. This, of course, is great if the Blogs portlet has been added to a user's personal pages, but doesn't work so well for a shared blog. But don't worry: it's easy to share a blog with multiple users.

First, create a role for your bloggers and add them to the role (roles are covered in chapter 13). Next, click the *Permissions* button on the Blogs portlet. A list of both portal and site roles is displayed, and currently only the owner is checked. Check off any other role or team that should have the ability to add blog entries, and then click *Save.* Once this is done, users in the roles or teams that you selected are able to post to the shared blog.

Now that everyone's able to post, let's look at how posts work.

Adding Blog Entries

Now you're ready to begin adding blog entries. Click the *Add Blog Entry* button. The following data entry screen appears:

There isn't much difference between this screen and any other data entry screen within Liferay Portal. You get a title, a way of scheduling when the entry is to appear, and a rich editor that allows you to format your entry the way you want, complete with embedded images, videos, and the like. Note also that as you type, the entry is automatically saved as a draft at periodic intervals. This gives you peace of mind in using the portlet from within your browser, since you won't lose your entry in the event of a browser crash or network interruption. You can also tag your entries using the same tagging mechanism found everywhere else in the portal.

The Blogs portlet also supports trackbacks and pingbacks. Trackbacks are special links that let you notify another site that you explicitly linked to them in the *Content* field. For example, if you wanted to write an entry in your blog and reference some other site's entry, you might put the URL to the other entry in the *Content* field and the trackback URL in the *Trackbacks Sent* field. If you have multiple URLs you want to send trackbacks to, separate them with spaces.

If you want others who link to your blog to let you know about the link via trackbacks, leave the *Allow Trackbacks* box checked. This generates a URL that is displayed with your blog entry. Others who want to link to your entry can use this URL for the link, to send trackbacks to your blog.

Note that trackbacks only work when the protocol is supported by both the linker and the linkee. A newer way to support similar link notification functionality is *pingbacks.* Pingbacks are XML-RPC requests that are similar to trackbacks except they're automatically sent when you link to another site. They're easier to use because you don't have to do anything extra: if you link to another site in your blog entry, Liferay sends a pingback to the other site to notify that site that you linked to it. Similarly, if someone links to your blog entry, Liferay can receive a pingback from that person's site and record the link.

You can enter a description of your post beneath the Abstract heading, and this can be used by the Abstract display style. Below this is the Categorization heading, where you can attach tags and/or categories to your blog entry. You should definitely consider doing this: it improves search results for blog entries, and it gives you more navigation options that you can pass on to your users. For example, you can add the Tags Navigation portlet to another column on your blogs page, allowing users to browse blog entries by tag.

Below this is the Related Assets heading. If there's some other content in the portal that's related to your blog, you can choose it here. For example, you might want to write a blog entry talking about a particular discussion that happened on the forums. To link those two assets together, select the forum thread under Related Assets.

Once you've finished your blog entry, click *Publish*. You'll go back to the list of entries, and now your entry is displayed. Here is what it looks like when the display template is set to *Full Content* and the maximum items to display is set to ten:

You can see that in the summary view, you don't see the trackback/pingback link, and you only see the number of comments that have been added. If you were to click the *Read More* link, you would see the entirety of the article, all the comments in a

Figure 9.4: After clicking *Add Blog Entry*, a new window appears with configuration options for your new blog entry.

threaded view, and the trackback/pingback link which others can use to link back to your blog entry.

The full view of the blog entry also contains links to share blog entries on social networks, such as Twitter, Facebook, and Google Plus. This gives your readers an easy way to share blog entries with friends, potentially driving further traffic to your site. As you can see, the Blogs portlet is a full-featured blogging application that gives you and your users the ability to enter the blogosphere with an application that supports anything a blogger needs.

Of course, Liferay is a portal, and as a portal, it excels at aggregating information from multiple places. For that reason, it also includes the Blogs Aggregator portlet so that you can "bubble up" blog entries from multiple users and highlight them on your site. Let's look next at how that works.

Aggregating Blog Entries

You can set up a whole web site devoted just to blogging if you wish. The Blogs Aggregator portlet allows you to publish entries from multiple bloggers on one page, giving further visibility to blog entries. This portlet is also very straightforward to set up. You can add it to a page from the *Collaboration* category in the *Add →Applications* menu.

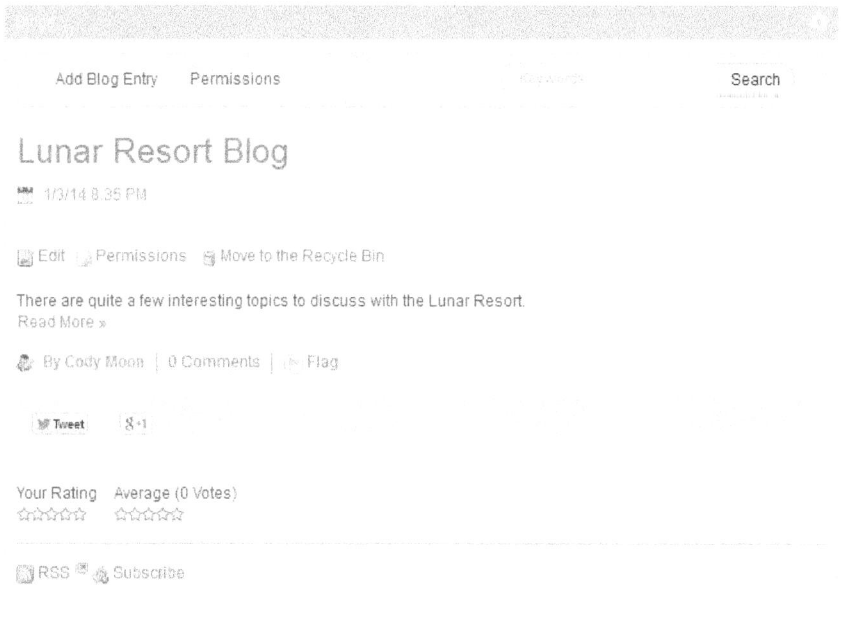

Add Blog Entry   Permissions   Search

Lunar Resort Blog

1/3/14 8:35 PM

Edit   Permissions   Move to the Recycle Bin

There are quite a few interesting topics to discuss with the Lunar Resort.
Read More »

By Cody Moon | 0 Comments | Flag

Tweet   8 +1

Your Rating   Average (0 Votes)
☆☆☆☆☆   ☆☆☆☆☆

RSS   Subscribe

Figure 9.5: This sample blog entry gives you an idea of what new content and features are displayed on your page.

If you click *Configuration* from the options button in the title bar of the portlet, the Blogs Aggregator's configuration page appears. From here, you can set several configuration options.

Selection Method: select Users or Scope here. If you select Users, the Blogs Aggregator aggregates the entries of every blogger on your system. If you want to refine the aggregation, you can select an organization by which to filter the users. If you select Scope, the Blogs Aggregator contains only entries of users who are in the current scope. This limits the entries to members of the site where the Blogs Aggregator portlet resides.

Organization: select which organization's blogs you want to aggregate.

Display Style: select from several different styles for displaying blog entries: *Body and Image, Body, Abstract, Abstract without Title, Quote, Quote without Title*, and *Title*.

Maximum Items to Display: select maximum number of entries the portlet displays.

Enable RSS Subscription: creates an RSS feed out of the aggregated entries. This lets users subscribe to an aggregate feed of all your bloggers. Below this checkbox, you can configure how you want the RSS Feed displayed:

- **Maximum Items to Display:** select maximum number of RSS items to display.
- **Display Style:** select from several different styles for displaying RSS feeds: *Abstract, Full Content*, and *Title*.
- **Format:** select which web feed language to use for your feed, which includes *Atom 1.0, RSS 1.0*, or *RSS 2.0*.

Show Tags: for each entry, displays all the tags associated with the blogs.

When you've finished setting the options in the portlet, click *Save*. Then close the dialog box. You'll notice the Blogs Aggregator looks very much like the Blogs portlet, except that

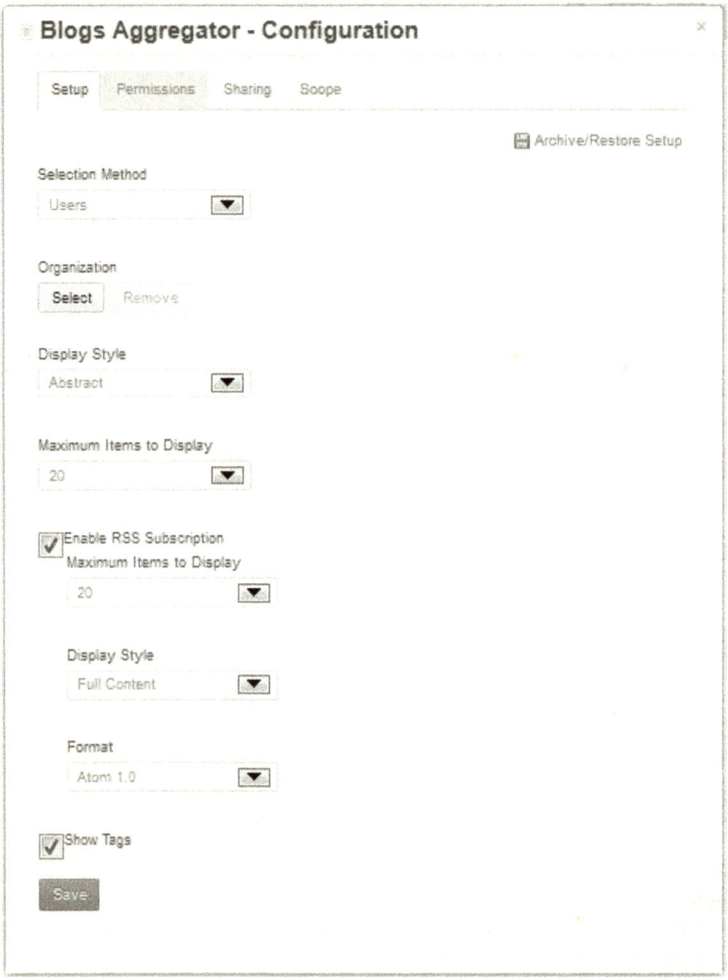

Blogs Aggregator - Configuration   ×

Setup   Permissions   Sharing   Scope

                                      Archive/Restore Setup

Selection Method

| Users ▼ |

Organization

Select   Remove

Display Style

| Abstract ▼ |

Maximum Items to Display

| 20 ▼ |

☑ Enable RSS Subscription
Maximum Items to Display

| 20 ▼ |

Display Style

| Full Content ▼ |

Format

| Atom 1.0 ▼ |

☑ Show Tags

Save

Figure 9.6: You can navigate to the Blogs Aggregator Configuration menu by selecting the *Options* gear from the portlet's title bar and selecting *Configuration*.

the entries come from more than one author. This makes it nice and familiar for your users to navigate.

The Blogs Administrator Portlet

In the Control Panel there's a portlet for managing your site's blog entries. Most of the time, the Blogs portlet is the only tool you'll need to manage your blog entries. If, however, you need to massively delete blog entries, the blogs administrator portlet is the perfect tool for you.

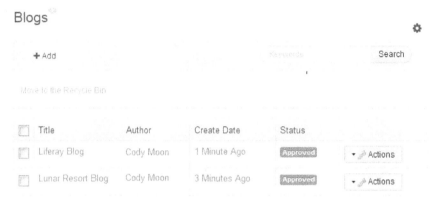

Figure 9.7: The Blogs Administrator portlet lets you delete large sets of blog entries.

Note that it's only for batch processing of blog entries; for the full set of tools for managing blog entries, your best bet is to use the Blogs portlet. Next, let's look at Liferay's improved Calendar portlet available from Liferay Marketplace.

9.2 Managing Events and Resources with Liferay's Calendar Portlet

As of Liferay 6.2, Liferay no longer includes the core Calendar portlet that was included in Liferay 6.1 and previous versions. Instead, Liferay provides a new Calendar portlet on Liferay Marketplace. The new Calendar portlet upgrades several features of the old Calendar portlet and adds additional features. The features you're used to from the old Calendar portlet are still available. You can add events and configure email notifications. You can use the Calendar portlet as a shared calendar for an entire site or as a personal calendar. All content created through the old Calendar is imported automatically by the new Calendar. Some of the new features include an improved look and feel, more configuration options, the ability to assign multiple calendars to a site or user, the concept of calendar resources, and event invitations.

Configuring the Calendar Portlet

Once you've added the new Calendar portlet to a page, open its configuration dialog box by clicking on the gear icon in the portlet's title bar and selecting *Configuration*. The Setup tab provides two sub-tabs of configurable settings: *User Settings* and *RSS*.

User Settings: On this screen, you can customize your calendar's default view and settings. You can set the *Time Format* to *AM/PM* or to *24 Hour*. *AM/PM* is the default; with this time format, times such as 8AM or 11PM are displayed. With the *24 Hour* time format, these times are displayed as 08:00 and 21:00. *Default Duration* refers to event duration.

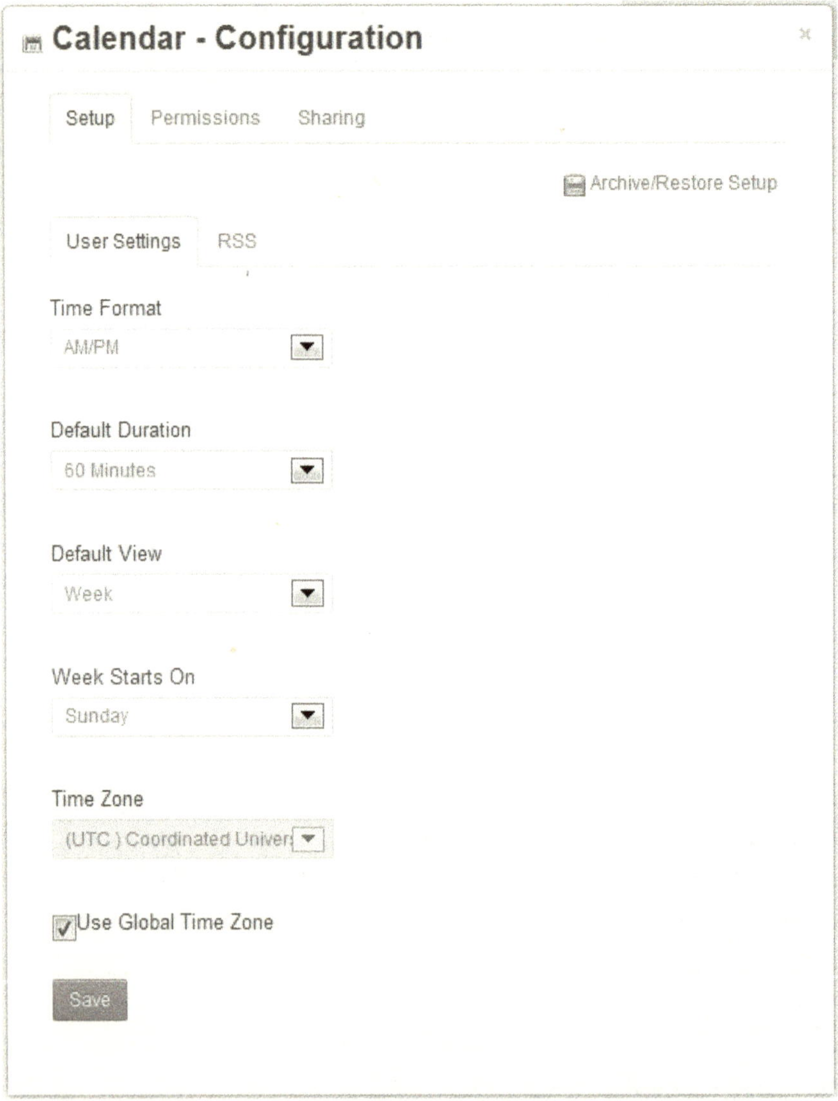

Calendar - Configuration

Setup   Permissions   Sharing

Archive/Restore Setup

User Settings   RSS

Time Format

AM/PM ▼

Default Duration

60 Minutes ▼

Default View

Week ▼

Week Starts On

Sunday ▼

Time Zone

(UTC) Coordinated Univer ▼

☑ Use Global Time Zone

Save

Figure 9.8: The Setup →User Settings tab provides several new configuration options that weren't available from the old Calendar portlet.

When you add a new event to the calendar, the time you set here specifies how long events last by default. You can set the *Default View* to *Day*, *Week*, or *Month*. You can set *Week Starts On* to *Sunday*, *Monday*, or *Saturday*. For *Time Zone*, you can either specify a particular time zone like *Pacific Standard Time* or *China Standard Time* or you can check the *Use Global Time Zone* box. If you check *Use Global Time Zone*, your calendar uses the portal-wide time zone that an administrator can set via *Control Panel →Portal Settings →Display Settings →Time Zone*.

RSS: You can enable and customize your RSS Subscriptions for your calendar from this screen. You have the following options: *Enable RSS Subscription*, *Maximum Items to Display*, *Display Style*, *Format*, and *Time Interval*. These options are explained in more detail in the Blogs section.

Next, let's look at how to use the new Calendar portlet.

Using the Calendar Portlet

The first thing you'll notice about Liferay's new Calendar portlet is its revamped look and feel. There's a monthly mini-calendar which provides you with an overview of upcoming events. There's also a larger, more detailed calendar area. You can set the large calendar area to display a *Day*, *Week*, or *Month* view. The *Day* view displays a day as a single column, divided into hours and half-hours. The *Week* view is similar but displays seven days as seven columns, divided into hours and half-hours. The month view displays a traditional calendar view with days represented as boxes. In the previous section, we saw how to configure the default display view of the calendar.

Adding New Calendars

You can add new personal or site calendars from the default view of the new Calendar portlet and choose which calendar's events to display. To add a new personal or site calendar, mouse over *My Calendars* or *Current Site Calendars*, click on the arrow icon, and select *Add Calendar*. To manage your personal or site calendars, navigate to the same drop-down menu and select *Manage Calendars*. All users can manage their personal calendars. By default, only site administrators can manage site calendars.

On the Manage Calendars screen, you can click *Add Calendar* to create a new calendar. As usual, you can enter a name and description for the calendar and configure its permissions. Flag the *Default Calendar* checkbox if you'd like the new calendar to be the default calendar. All sites, including personal sites, have a default calendar. When a calendar is first visited, the events from the default calendar are displayed. You can customize the events that appear in the main area of the calendar portlet by clicking on the colored boxes corresponding to the calendars. When you click on a colored box, its color disappears and the events of that calendar are no longer displayed. Click on an uncolored box to view the events of the corresponding calendar.

When adding a calendar, you can also specify whether or not to enable comments and ratings for your calendar's events. Comments and ratings can be enabled/disabled on a per calendar basis. They are disabled by default. Additionally, you can specify a color for your calendar. Events created in the new calendar will default to the color you choose.

You can edit a calendar to change its name, description, or color. You can also change the calendar's default calendar status and flag or unflag the *Enable Comments* and *Enable Ratings* checkboxes to enable or disable comments and ratings for a calendar's events.

Adding Events to a Calendar

It's very easy to add events to a calendar: just click on any day of the calendar and you'll see an event creation popup appear. If you've selected the *Day* or *Month* view, you can click on the specific time when your event begins.

Figure 9.9: You have options to add or manage calendars. Also, you can toggle the colored boxes beside your calendars to show/hide your planned events.

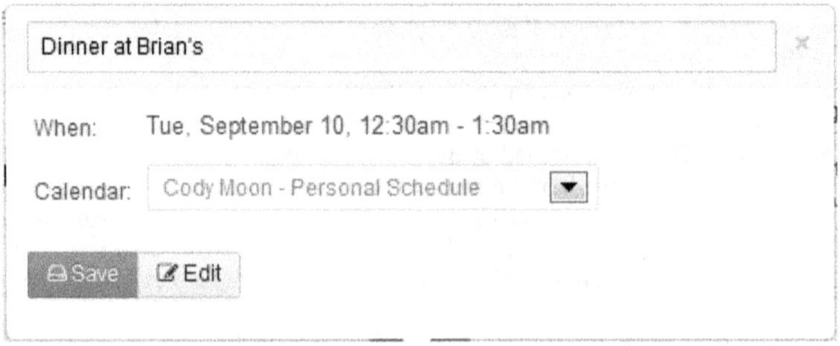

| Dinner at Brian's | ✕ |

When: Tue, September 10, 12:30am - 1:30am

Calendar: Cody Moon - Personal Schedule   ▼

🖫 Save   ✐ Edit

Figure 9.10: When you click anywhere on the calendar, you'll see the event creation popup appear. Click *Edit* to specify details for your event.

In the new event popup, you can select the calendar in which you'd like to create the new event. This is useful since sites and users can have multiple calendars. You can click *Save* to create the event right away or you can click *Edit* to specify more event information.

The *Title* you enter determines the name of the event as it's displayed on the calendar. The *Start Date* and *End Date* times determine when your event takes place. You can click on the date text box to change the day and you can specify times by selecting a particular hour and minute of the day. Note: Even though the *Day* and *Week* views of the calendar break days into hours and half-hours and display events in these time-slots, that's just for convenience. You're free to specify whatever start times and end times you like, such as 11:37am and 12:08pm. Check the *All Day* box if your event lasts for an entire day. Check the *Repeat* box if your event takes place over multiple days. Checking this box opens another popup.

In the Details collapsible section, you can specify four pieces of information. Under *Calendar*, you can select the calendar to which you'd like to add your event. Remember that sites and users can have multiple calendars. Under *Description*, you can explain the purpose of your event and add any details that you think might be useful. Use the *Location* field to specify where your event takes place. Lastly, the *Viewable by* field lets you set the permissions for your calendar.

Figure 9.11: You can specify event details such as the event title, start date, end date, description, location, and more.

Figure 9.12: The *Repeat* box allows you to specify whether an events repeats daily, weekly, monthly, or yearly, how often it repeats, and when (or if) it ends.

For more advanced permissions options, select the *More Options* link. A list of roles for which you can permission appears in the left column. The other columns represent permissions which can be configured for the event:

- Add Discussion
- Delete Discussion
- Permissions
- Update Discussion

Discussions refers to comments on the event. So the Add Discussion, Delete Discussion, and Update Discussion permissions determine whether a role can add, delete, or update a comment on an event. The Permissions permission determines whether a role can update an event's permissions.

In the Invitations collapsible section, you can invite users, organizations, or other calendar resources to an event. To invite a user, group, or resource, start typing the name of the entity you'd like to invite and a list of matches will appear. Select the one you want or hit *Enter* if the entity you'd like to invite is at the top of the list. All the entities you've invited to your event appear as a list under the *Pending* heading, which shows how many pending invitations there are. If you accidentally invited the wrong entity, mouse over its name in the *Pending* list, click on the arrow icon that appears, and click *Remove*. If you'd just like to check the status of a resource, click on *Check Availability* instead. When you click on *Check Availability* for a calendar resource, its schedule is displayed in this calendar view. If you like to overview the availability of all the invited entities, just click on *Resources Availability*.

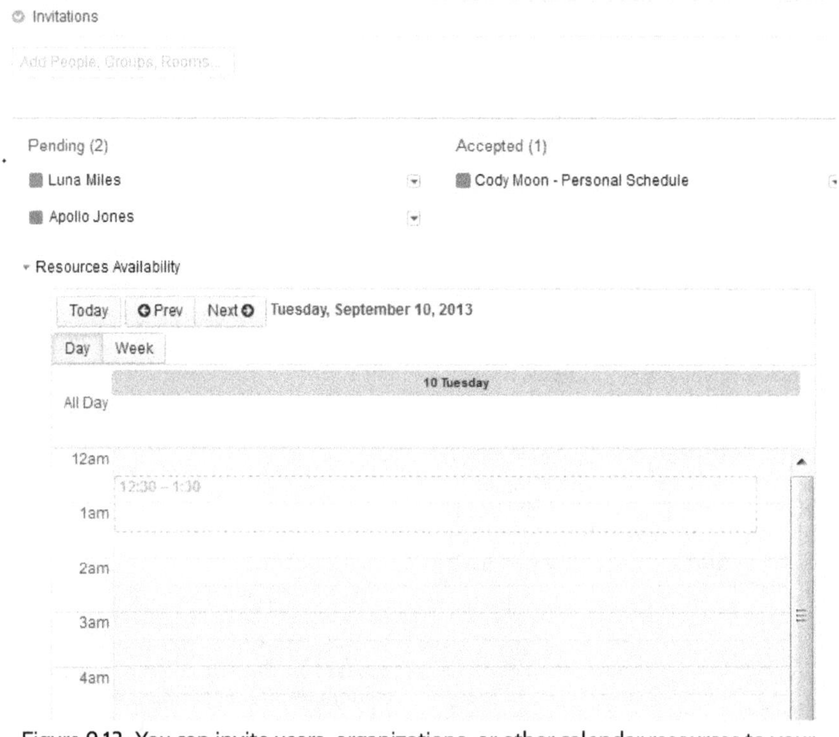

Figure 9.13: You can invite users, organizations, or other calendar resources to your event and can check their availability in a calendar view.

The Reminders collapsible section lets you specify up to two times when event reminder notifications will be sent via email. For example, you might like event notifications to be send one day and one hour before your event. Email is currently the only supported event notification type. To avoid confusion, the event time in notification emails is shown in the user's time zone, and the time zone is also displayed. Of course, Liferay can only calculate this properly if both the portal's and the user's time zones are set correctly. Users should set this for themselves when they create accounts. To set the portal's time zone, see the section *Configuring Additional Portal Settings* in chapter 17.

The Categorization and Related Assets collapsible sections let you tag the event and select related assets, respectively. By tagging your event, it will come up in searches related to that specified tag. In addition, related assets including blogs, message boards, web content, calendar, bookmarks, wikis, and documents can be selected to include with your calendar event. When you're done specifying event details, click *Save*.

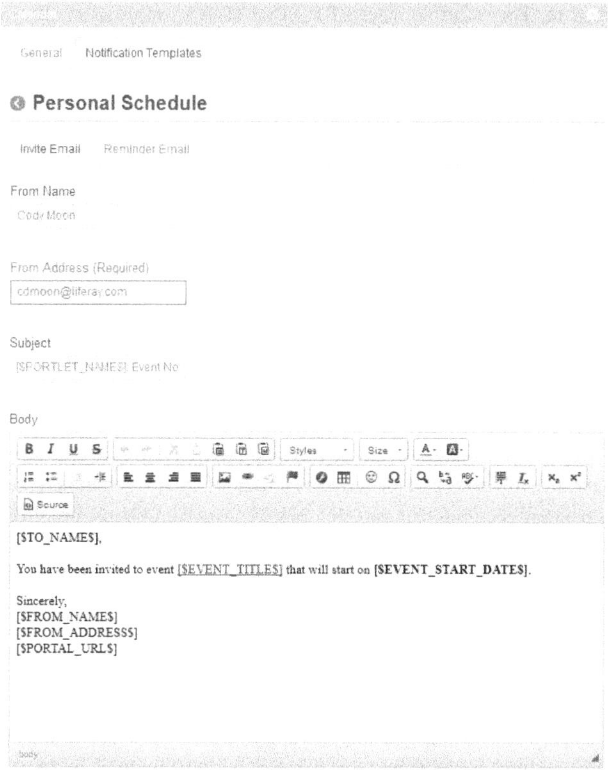

Figure 9.14: The *Calendar Settings →Notification Templates* tab lets you customize the email templates for emails that are automatically sent out to remind users of upcoming events or invite users to new events.

Liferay's Calendar portlet supports social activities. Whenever a calendar event is added or updated, a corresponding social activity notification is created. If the event was added or updated in a calendar that the current user has permission to view, the social activity will be viewable in the Activities portlet. If the Social Networking portlets have been installed (they're available as an app on Liferay Marketplace; search for *Social Networking CE* or *Social Networking EE*), the social networking notifications will also appear in all the appropriate portlets, such as the Friends' Activities or Members' Activities portlets.

Calendar administrators can customize the email notification templates for event invitation and event reminder emails. To customize a calendar's email templates, open the calendar's Calendar Settings window by clicking on the small arrow next to the calendar's name in the default view of the calendar portlet and selecting *Calendar Settings*. By default, the General tab of the Calendar Settings appears, where you can edit the calendar's name, description, color, default calendar status, and whether or not calendar events and ratings are enabled or disabled. Click on *Notification Templates* at the top of the screen to view a new tab. Then click on either *Invite Email* or *Reminder Email* to customize event invitation or event reminder emails. You can customize the name that appears on the sent emails, the address from which to send the email, the subject, and the body of the email. As with Liferay's other other email notification templates (e.g., the Message Boards' notification email templates), a definition of terms appears below the email body editor. This definition of terms list specifies variables that you can you can use when customizing the email template. For example, [$EVENT_LOCATION$] represents the event location, [$EVENT_START_DATE$] represents the event start date, and [$EVENT_TITLE$] specifies the event title.

To respond to an event invitation, you can click *Accept*, *Maybe*, or *Decline* when viewing the event in the Calendar portlet. The default event invitation notification emails contain links to their corresponding events. This allows users easy access to events in the Calendar portlet so they can respond to event invitations.

Adding and Using Calendar Resources

You might be wondering, "It makes sense to invite users and organizations to an event, but what about other calendar resources? What are they used for? How can you add them?" Good questions. Calendar resources can represent just about anything that you think might be important to an event. For example, your department might have a limited number of rooms and projectors to use for presentations. You can add the various rooms and projectors as calendar resources and add them to events. This way, when new events are added, the event organizer can check the availability of important resources against events that have already been planned. So, how can you add new calendar resources? You might have noticed that the new Calendar portlet has two tabs in the main portlet window: Calendar and Resources. Click on the *Resources* tab of the portlet to view, edit, add, or delete resources.

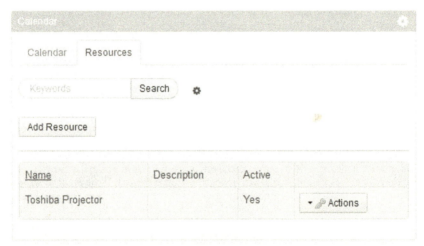

Figure 9.15: Click on the *Resources* tab of the portlet to view, edit, add, or delete resources.

Click on the *Add Resource* button to add a new calendar resource. You'll be able to enter a name and description for your resource, specify whether or not it should be active, apply tags and categories, and configure its permissions.

Once you've created a calendar resource, you can click on the *Actions* button next to it and select one of the following four options: *Edit*, *Permissions*, *Delete*, or *View Calendars*. The *View Calendars* option exists since calendar resources, like sites and users, can have more than one calendar associated with them. Click *Actions* → *View Calendars* and then click on *Add Calendar* to add a new calendar in which the selected calendar resource appears.

Liferay's new Calendar portlet provides an easy-to-use scheduling tool. Sites and users can have multiple calendars, calendar events can include calendar resources and calendar

General

◉ New Calendar for Toshiba Projector

Name

Description

Color

Default Calendar
Enable Comments
Enable Ratings
Permissions
Viewable by

Anyone (Guest Role)   ▼   More Options »

Save   Cancel

Figure 9.16: Click on *Add Calendar* to add a new calendar in which the selected calendar resource appears.

resources have their own schedules of availability. We hope this flexible system meets the needs of your organization.

Exporting and Importing Calendar Data

Liferay's Calendar portlet allows data to be exported or imported as LAR files. Both calendar events and resources can be exported or imported. As with all LAR files, data can only be imported into a version of Liferay that's the same as the one from which it was exported. To access the interface for exporting or importing calendar data, click on the *gear* icon in the portlet header and select *Export / Import*. By default, the Export tab appears which allows you to define a new export process or use an existing one to export calendar data. If you'd like to import data, click on *Import*. You'll be able to define a new import process by selecting an existing LAR file or by using an existing import process.

To define a new export process, you first have to choose a name for the LAR file to be generated. `Calendar-201308061558.portlet.lar` is an example of a typical Calendar portlet LAR filename. Notice that by default, a timestamp is included in the LAR filename. First you have the option of including the Configuration of your calendar in the LAR file. Next, you have to define a data range. You can select *All* to export calendar data regardless of when it was created or last modified. Alternatively, you can specify a data range. In this case, only calendar data which was created or modified at or after the start date and before the end date will be exported. Next, you can choose which kinds of calendar data to export: calendar events, resources, or both. For each selected kind of calendar data, you can choose to export associated comments, ratings, or both. Finally, you can choose whether or not to export the permissions defined for the specific Calendar portlet window from which you're exporting data. Click *Export* to export your data into a LAR file. You should see a message stating *Your request completed successfully* and you'll be able to click on the LAR file's name to download it.

To define a new import process, click on *Import* from the Export / Import window. Then either drop a LAR file into the box outlined by the dashed lines or click on the button to browse to and select the LAR file to import. Once selected, you'll be able to choose whether to import calendar events, resources, or both and whether to import the comments and ratings associated with these calendar events and resources. You'll also be able to choose whether or not to import the permissions for the Calendar portlet window from the LAR file. Once you've made these selections, click *Continue* and you'll be able to choose a strategy for updating data:

- The *Mirror* strategy means that all data and content inside the imported LAR will be created as new the first time while maintaining a reference to source. Subsequent imports from the same source will update the entries instead of creating new entries.
- The *Mirror with Overwriting* is the same as the Mirror strategy except that if an entry with the same name is found, it is overwritten.
- The *Copy as New* strategy means that all data and content inside the imported LAR will be created as new entries within the current site every time the LAR is imported.

You must also specify an option for assigning ownership of the imported data:

- *Use the Original Author* means that authorship of imported content will be preserved, if possible. If the original author of the imported content is not found, the current user will be assigned as the author.
- *Use the Current User as Author* means that the current user will be assigned as the author of the imported content regardless of the original author.

Upgrading the Calendar Portlet

In Liferay 6.1 and previous versions, an older version of the Calendar portlet was included as one of the core portlets. If you're upgrading from Liferay 6.1 or a previous version to Liferay 6.2 or a later version, all the calendar events that existed prior to 6.2 will still be available after your upgrade. After following these steps for upgrading Liferay, all you need to do to access previously added events is deploy the new Calendar portlet. You can browse through the new Calendar to confirm that the upgrade succeeded: you should be able to view and edit calendar events that were added via the old calendar portlet.

The old Calendar portlet included certain calendar event types such as appointments, birthdays, holidays, and meetings. The new Calendar portlet doesn't include this explicit notion of event types. However, by using categories, the upgrade process preserves the functionality provided by the old Calendar portlet's notion of event types. When upgrading, the old calendar event types are migrated to categories. The upgrade creates a vocabulary called *Calendar Event Types* and adds the old event types as categories in this vocabulary. Upon upgrading, any calendar events that had one of the old event types receive the corresponding category from the Calendar Event Types vocabulary instead.

Next, let's look at one of the most widely used applications provided by Liferay: its message boards.

9.3   Discuss, Ask, and Answer Using the Message Boards

Liferay's Message Boards portlet is a state of the art forum application similar to many forums in which you may have participated. The difference, of course, is that Liferay's message boards can inherit the abilities of the Liferay development platform to provide an integrated experience that others cannot match.

There are countless web sites out there where it is clearly evident that there is no link whatsoever between the main site and the message boards. In some cases, users are even required to register twice: once for the main site and once for the message boards. Sometimes it is three times: for the site, for the message boards, and for the shopping cart. By providing a message boards portlet along with all of the other applications, Liferay provides a unique, integrated approach to building web sites. You can concentrate on building your site while Liferay does the integration work for you.

The Message Boards portlet offers many configuration options. They are straightforward to use and are the reason why this portlet is a full-featured forum application for your web site. To get started, add a Message Boards portlet to your site. Once it is added, click the *Options* icon in the portlet's title bar and click *Configuration*. There are two rows of tabs. The first tab in the top row is titled *Setup*. This is where you can configure the application the way you want it to behave on your site.

General

The first tab beneath *Setup* is labeled *General*. Here, you can enable anonymous posting, subscribe by default, flags, ratings, and thread as question by default. You can also choose whether you want the message format to be BBcode or HTML and choose how long posts display on the message board. Anonymous posting, subscribe by default, flags, and ratings are selected by default and the default message format is BBcode.

Enabling *Allow Anonymous Posting* allows users without an account on the system to post messages to your message boards. Whether or not you you'll want to do this depends on the type of community you are building. Allowing anonymous posting opens your site to anyone who might want to spam your forums with unwanted or off topic advertising messages. For this reason, most of those who implement message boards turn anonymous posting off by unchecking this box.

Enabling the *Subscribe by Default* option automatically subscribes users to threads they participate in. Whenever a message in a thread is added or updated, Liferay sends a notification email to each user who is subscribed to the thread.

You can set the *Message Format* to either BBCode or HTML. This determines the markup language of users' actual message board posts. Different WYSIWYG editors are presented to users depending on which option is enabled. Both editors have a *Source* button which allows users to view the underlying BBCode or HTML of a message. Users can compose messages using either the WYSIWYG or Source view and can switch between views during message composition by clicking on the *Source* button.

Enabling *Enable Flags* allows your users to flag content which they consider to be objectionable. If you are allowing anonymous posting, you might use flags in combination with it if you have someone administering your message boards on a day-to-day basis. That way, any unwanted messages can be flagged by your community, and you can review those flagged messages and take whatever action is necessary. Using flags is also a good practice even if you're not allowing anonymous posting.

Enabling *Enable Ratings* enables your users to give certain posts a score. This score is used by Liferay Portal's social activity system to rank your site members by how helpful their contributions are. You can read more about social activity later in this chapter and in chapter 9.

Enabling the *Thread as Question by Default* option automatically checks the mark as question box in the new thread window. Threads marked as questions display the flag "waiting for an answer." Subsequent replies to the original message can be marked as an answer.

Lastly, you can set the amount of time a post is displayed until it is taken away. You have options of 24 hours, 7 days, 30 days, and 365 days. After the time has passed, the post is removed from the message board.

Email From

This tab allows you to configure the name and email address from which message board email notifications are sent. The default name and email address are those of the default administrator account: The name is Test Test and the email address is test@life-ray.com. Make sure to update this email address to a valid one that can be dedicated to notifications.

Message Added Email

This tab allows you to customize the email message that users receive when a message is added to a topic to which they are subscribed.

Enabled: allows you to turn on the automatic emails to subscribed users. Uncheck the box to disable the message added emails.

Subject: lets you choose a prefix to be prepended to the subject line of the email. This is usually done so that users can set up message filters to filter the notifications to a specific folder in their email clients.

Body: allows you to write some content that should appear in the body of the email.

Signature: lets you add some content to appear as the signature of the email.

Below the fields is a section called *Definition of Terms* which defines certain variables which you can use in the fields above to customize the email message. Some of these variables are for the message board category name, the site name, and more.

Message Updated Email

The Message Updated Email tab is identical to the Message Added Email tab, except it defines the email message that users receive whenever a topic is updated.

Thread Priorities

You can define custom priorities for message threads on this tab. These allow administrators to tag certain threads with certain priorities in order to highlight them for users. By default, three priorities are defined: Urgent, Sticky, and Announcement. To define a thread priority, enter its name, a URL to the image icon that represents it, and a priority number which denotes the order in which that priority should appear.

There is also a field on this form that allows you to select a localized language for your priorities. If you need to do this, you can select the language from the selection box.

User Ranks

On this tab, users can be ranked according to the number of messages they have posted. You can set up custom ranks here. Defaults have been provided for you, going from zero messages all the way up to one thousand.

In addition to ranks, you can also choose labels for certain users to have displayed in their profiles as shown by the Message Boards application. These labels correspond to memberships these users have in your portal. Below are examples of using the label *Moderator*. The Moderator label in this configuration is applied for anyone who is a part of any of the Message Boards Administrator groups: the site role, the organization, the organization role, the regular role, or the user group. Of course, you probably wouldn't want to create a role, organization, organization role, site role, and user group all with the same name in your portal, but you get the idea.

```
Moderator=organization:Message Boards Administrator

Moderator=organization-role:Message Boards Administrator

Moderator=regular-role:Message Boards Administrator

Moderator=site-role:Message Boards Administrator

Moderator=user-group:Message Boards Administrator
```

As you can see, all you need to do is set the rank, the collection type, and the name of the type. In the example above, anyone who has a site role, an organization role, a regular role, or is in a user group called *Message Boards Administrator*, or anyone who is the organization owner gets the moderator rank.

As with thread priorities, on this tab you can define whether your ranks are localized in a particular language.

RSS

Message board threads can be published as RSS feeds. This tab allows you to enable/disable RSS subscriptions and define how the feeds are generated.

Maximum Items to Display: lets you select the number of items to display in the feed.

Display Style: lets you select the style. You can publish the full content, an abstract, or just the title of a thread.

Format: allows you to choose the format: RSS 1.0, RSS 2.0, or Atom 1.0.

Permissions

The default page that the Message Boards portlet displays has three buttons on it. Click the one labeled *Permissions*. This allows you to define which roles have the ability to add a category of threads or to ban abusive users from the message boards. Select the roles and permissions you want to configure and then click *Save*.

Adding Categories

You are now ready to add categories to your message boards. Click the *Add Category* button. Enter a name for the category and a description of the category.

Categories can have different display styles. The available categories must be set in portal property message.boards.category.display.styles and the default category in message.boards.category.display.styles.default. When creating a new category, you can select the display style you like for that category. By default, Liferay provides two predefined display styles, although many more can be easily added:

Default: classic display style for general purpose and discussions.

Question: designed for discussions in a format of questions and answers.

You can add as many categories to your message boards as you wish. As we saw above, categories can have subcategories. You can add any number of top-level categories to a message board. You can also edit any category and add subcategories to an unlimited level. For usability reasons, you don't want to nest your categories too deep, or your users will have trouble finding them. You can always add more categories as your message boards grow. Finally, each category can have any number of threads.

At the bottom of the form for creating or editing a message board category is a check box for enabling the mailing list function. If don't want to add a mailing list to the category

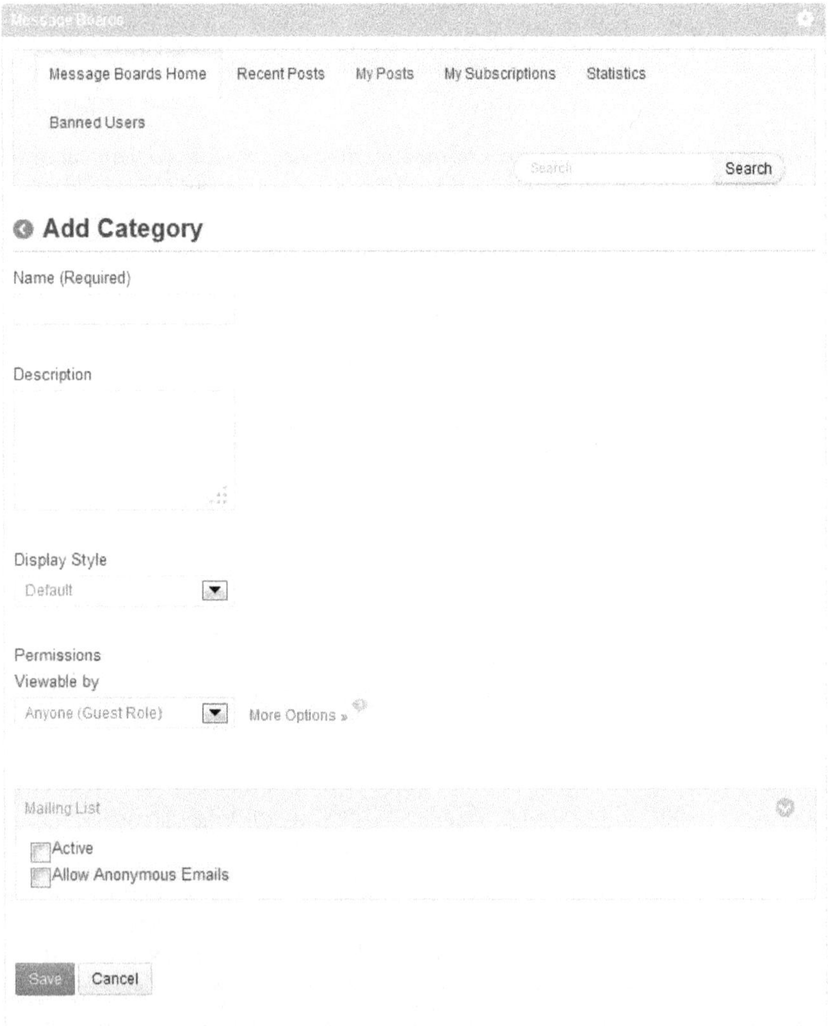

Figure 9.17: You have several options when creating a Message Boards Category.

you're creating, click *Save* now. You can always edit an existing category to add, edit, or remove a mailing list.

Also, you may merge with a Parent Category by navigating to a category's *Actions* →*Move* button. From this window, you can enable the *Merge with Parent Category* check box and click the *Select* button to choose the parent category.

Once one or more categories have been added to a message board, they appear in a list on the message board's home. The list displays the names of the categories and the numbers of subcategories, threads, and posts in each one. To add a subcategory to category, click on the category's name in the list and then click the *Add Subcategory* button. By default, when you click the *Add Subcategory* button, the form for adding a subcategory is populated with the properties of the parent category. This includes the parent category's display style (Default or Question) and mailing list configuration. Of course, you can change the display style or mailing list configuration of a subcategory just as with a new category.

Liferay's Message Boards portlet supports two different mechanisms for sending email notifications: user subscriptions and mailing lists. Let's discuss user subscriptions first and then mailing lists.

User Subscriptions and Mailing Lists

The first mechanism Liferay uses for sending email notifications is user subscriptions. Users can subscribe to particular categories and threads. Liferay uses the message board's configured *Email From* address to send email notifications to subscribed users whenever a new post is created or an existing post is updated. Liferay can import email replies to message board notifications directly into the message board. This is a very useful features since it allows users to interact on the message board via email without needing to log in to the portal and view the message board page directly. However, this feature is not enabled by default. To enable this feature, add the following line to your portal-ext.properties file:

```
pop.server.notifications.enabled=true
```

As this property suggests, Liferay's message boards user subscription mechanism uses the POP mail protocol. When an email reply to a message board notification is read by Liferay, the reply is posted to the message board and then deleted from the mail server. Deleting the message from the mail server is the POP protocol's default behavior and Liferay assumes that your POP mail server behaves this way. Most POP clients offer an option to leave mail on the mail server after it's been downloaded but you shouldn't exercise this option. If you configure mail to be left on the mail server, Liferay will repeatedly send copies of each retained message along with each new email notification that's sent to subscribed users.

When enabling message boards to import replies to email notifications, you should decide whether or not you want to you a mail server subdomain to handle notifications. By default the following line is set in your portal properties:

```
pop.server.subdomain=events
```

This property creates a special MX (mail exchange) subdomain to receive all portal-related email (e.g., events.liferay.com). If you don't want to use the subdomain approach, you can unset this value to tell Liferay to use the *Email From* address specified in the portlet preferences to receive message board notification email replies. For example, the *Email From* address could be set to *replies@liferay.com*.

If you don't want to use a mail server subdomain, add the following line to your portal-ext.properties file:

```
pop.server.subdomain=
```

If you're not using a mail subdomain, Liferay parses the message headers of emails from the *Email From* address to determine the message board category and message ID. If you keep the pop.server.subdomain=events default, the email notification address takes the following form: *mb.[category_id][message_id]@events.liferay.com*. In this case, Liferay parses the email address to find the category and message ID. Parsing the email address is safer than parsing message headers since different email clients treat message headers differently. This is why the events subdomain is enabled by default.

Additionally, you can configure the interval on which the POPNotificationListener runs. The value is set in one minute increments. The default setting is to check for new mail every minute, but you can set it to whatever you like:

```
pop.server.notifications.interval=1
```

The second mechanism Liferay uses for sending email notifications is mailing lists. Any category in a Liferay message board can have its own mailing list. Liferay's mailing list mechanism, unlike its user subscription mechanism, supports both the POP and the IMAP protocols. POP is the default protocol but each message board's mailing list is configured independently. If you choose the IMAP protocol for a category's mailing list, make sure to configure the IMAP inbox to delete messages as they are pulled by the email client that sends messages to the users on the mailing list. Otherwise, each email message that's retained on the server will be sent to the mailing list each time there's a new post or an update in the category.

When a mailing list is enabled for a message board category, Liferay listens to the specific email inbox that's configured for the mailing list. Enabling the mailing list function allows users on the mailing list to simply reply to the notification messages in their email clients. Liferay pulls the messages from the email inbox it's configured to listen to and automatically copies those replies to the appropriate message board thread.

With both user subscriptions and mailing lists, users can reply to message board notification emails and Liferay imports their replies to the message board. However, with mailing lists, users reply to the mailing list and Liferay listens to the specific inbox configured for the mailing list and copies messages to the appropriate message board category. With user subscriptions, by default, email replies to message board notifications are not imported to the message boards. This feature has to be enabled in your portal-ext.properties file. Once this feature has been enabled, users can reply to a specific address and have their replies copied to the message board.

Note: Since any number of sites can use a globally scoped message board, globally scoped message boards do not support user subscriptions or mailing lists. Make sure to use a site-scoped or page-scoped message board if you need user subscriptions or a mailing list with your message board.

To enable the mailing list functionality for a category, you need a dedicated email address for the category. Once you click the *Active* check box, a number of other options appear. When a mailing list is activated, Liferay imports messages it receives from the mailing list to the message board. Liferay looks for a Liferay user with the sender's email address. If the sender isn't a Liferay user and the *Allow Anonymous Emails* box is unchecked, the message is thrown away and not posted to the message board. If the *Allow Anonymous Emails* box is checked, anyone can send email to the message board category's dedicated email account and Liferay copies the messages to the message board.

Email Address: lets you enter the email address of the account that will receive the messages.

Next, there are two sections: *Incoming* and *Outgoing*. These define the mail settings for receiving mail and for sending mail. The Incoming tab has the following options:

Protocol: lets you select POP or IMAP.

Server Name: lets you enter the host name of the mail server you are using.

Server Port: allows you to specify the port on which your mail service is running.

Use a Secure Network Connection: lets you use an encrypted connection if your server supports it.

User Name: lets you enter the login name on the mail server.

Password: lets you enter the password for the account on the server.

Read Interval (Minutes): allows you to specify how often Liferay will poll the server looking for new messages to post to the message board.

The Outgoing section has the following options:

Email Address: lets you enter the email address that messages from this category should come from. If you want your users to be able to reply to the categories using email, this should be the same address configured on the *Incoming* tab.

Use Custom Outgoing Server: allows you to use a different mail server than the one that is configured for the portal. If you check this box, more options appear.

Server Name: lets you enter the host name of the SMTP mail server you are using.

Server Port: allows you to specify the port on which your mail service is running.

Use a Secure Network Connection: allows you to use an encrypted connection if your server supports it.

User Name: lets you enter the login name on the mail server.

Password: lets you enter the password for the account on the mail server.

When you're finished configuring the mailing list for your category, click *Save*.

Managing User Subscriptions with the Message Boards Subscription Manager

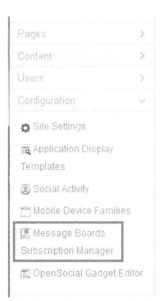

Figure 9.18: To make sure that the Message Boards Subscription Manager was successfully installed, look for the *Message Boards Subscription Manager* entry in the Configuration section of Site Administration.

The Message Boards Subscription Manager is available as an app from Liferay Marketplace. It allows site administrators to manage the subscriptions of their site's message board. Without the Message Boards Subscription Manager, users must manage their own message board subscriptions. The Message Boards Subscription Manager is available for both Liferay CE and EE—make sure to select the correct version when downloading and installing the app. Once installed, the Message Boards Subscription Manager appears in the Configuration section of Site Administration.

The subscription manager allows managing the subscriptions of both the site-scoped message board and the subscriptions of any page-scoped message boards that may exist within the site. To access the Message Boards Subscription Manager, navigate to your site's Site Administration page, select *Configuration*, and click on *Message Boards Subscription Manager*. You'll see a list of the categories that have been created within your site's site-scoped message board. Click *Actions* →*View* next to a category to view the category's threads in a new browser tab. Click *Actions* →*Manage Subscriptions* to view a list of users which can be subscribed or unsubscribed from the message board category.

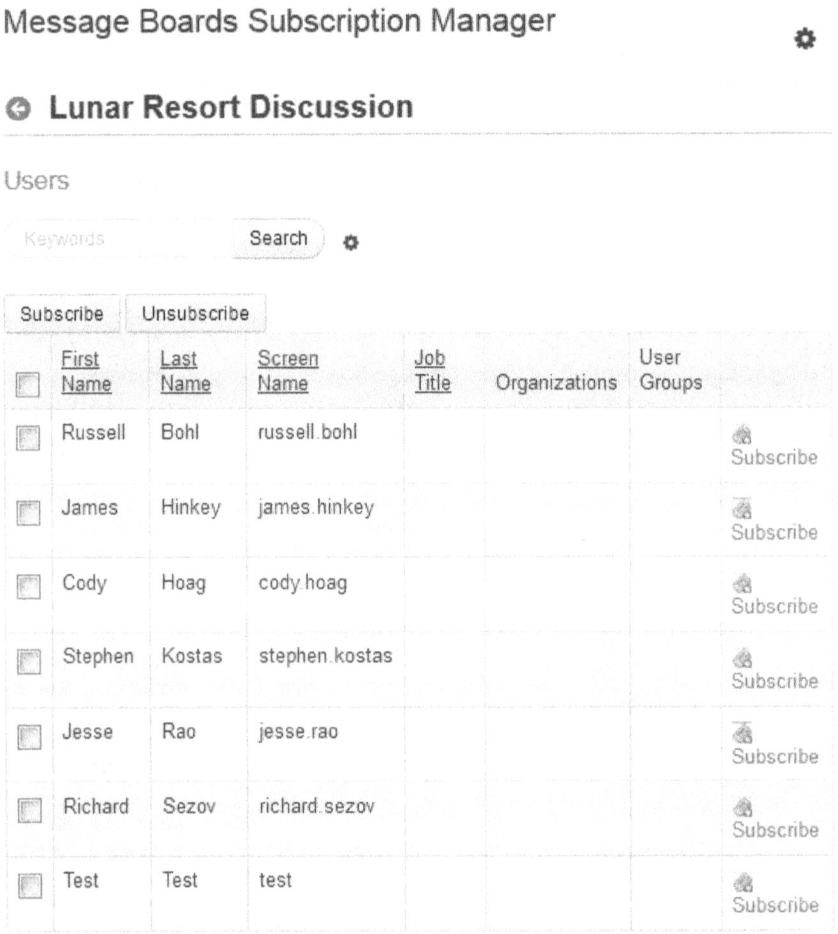

Message Boards Subscription Manager   ⚙

⊙ Lunar Resort Discussion

Users

| Keywords | Search ⚙ |

| Subscribe | Unsubscribe |

☐	First Name	Last Name	Screen Name	Job Title	Organizations	User Groups	
☐	Russell	Bohl	russell.bohl				🐜 Subscribe
☐	James	Hinkey	james.hinkey				🐜 Subscribe
☐	Cody	Hoag	cody.hoag				🐜 Subscribe
☐	Stephen	Kostas	stephen.kostas				🐜 Subscribe
☐	Jesse	Rao	jesse.rao				🐜 Subscribe
☐	Richard	Sezov	richard.sezov				🐜 Subscribe
☐	Test	Test	test				🐜 Subscribe

Figure 9.19: The Message Board Subscription Manager allows site administrators to subscribe or unsubscribe selected users from any category within their site's message board.

Click on the *Subscribe* or *Unsubscribe* links next to a user's name to subscribe or unsubscribe the user from the selected message board category. Alternatively, you can use the checkboxes to select a group of users and use the *Subscribe* or *Unsubscribe* buttons above the list of users to subscribe or unsubscribe a number of users at once. The Message Boards Subscription Manager is easy to use but it's a great tool for site administrators who need to make sure that certain users receive emails from important message board categories.

Using the Message Boards

Upon seeing Liferay's Message Boards portlet, your users will immediately recognize that the interface is similar to many other implementations they've seen before. Message boards are nothing new to the Internet, and many people have been using them for quite a long time. For that reason, Liferay's message boards will seem very familiar to your users.

Threads can be viewed in many ways. At the top of the portlet is a set of tabs: *Recent posts*, *My Posts*, *My Subscriptions*, and for administrative users, *Statistics* and *Banned Users*. The Recent Posts tab shows all posts from all categories by date, so you can keep up on all the most recent discussions in the message boards. The My Posts tab shows all of the posts for the user that is currently logged in. This is a convenient way to get back to a previous conversation in order to retrieve some pertinent information. The My Subscriptions tab allows a user to manage thread subscriptions. If you lose interest in a particular topic, you may want to visit this tab and unsubscribe from a thread.

For administrators, the Statistics tab shows the number of categories, the number of posts, and the number of participants in your message boards. It also has a list of who the top posters to your message boards are. The Banned Users tab shows all of the users who have been banned from posting on the message boards.

Posting New Threads

To post a new thread simply select the *Post New Thread* button. You will see a message editing form. The body field on this form is different from that of the other portlets in Liferay. The reason for this is to support *BBCode*, which is a standard form of markup used in many message board products. Before BBCode was invented, many message board products would allow users to enter HTML to format their messages. This, however, enabled attackers to insert malicious code into the message board. BBCode was invented to provide users a way of formatting their messages without allowing them to enter HTML. Similarly, Liferay supports BBCode in the message boards portlet because the other editor—which is used for the Content Management System, the Blogs portlet, and other portlets—produces HTML. This is appropriate for those other portlets, as they are only used by privileged users, but it is not appropriate for the message boards. Besides this, many users of message boards are familiar with BBCode and are used to it, and the editor that is provided for Liferay's Message Boards portlet makes it very easy to use.

The message boards editor is quite rich. It supports bold, italicized, underlined, and crossed-out text, links, images, colors, lists, tables, alignments, quotation blocks, code blocks, different fonts and font sizes, and more. There are even a bunch of smiley faces that you can use.

Users who have Moderator access to the board can modify the priority of messages. You can also use the editor to quote from messages that you are replying to, to insert emoticons, to add preformatted text, and more. Messages that are posted to the message boards are shown by default in a threaded view so that replies are attached to the proper parent message. This makes it easy to follow along with conversations.

When viewing a message board thread, users are given several options. At the top right of the thread are three icons, allowing users to view threads in a combination view, flat view, or tree view. A combination view shows the threads at the top as subjects only, with the flat view underneath. A flat view shows all of the messages in the order in which they

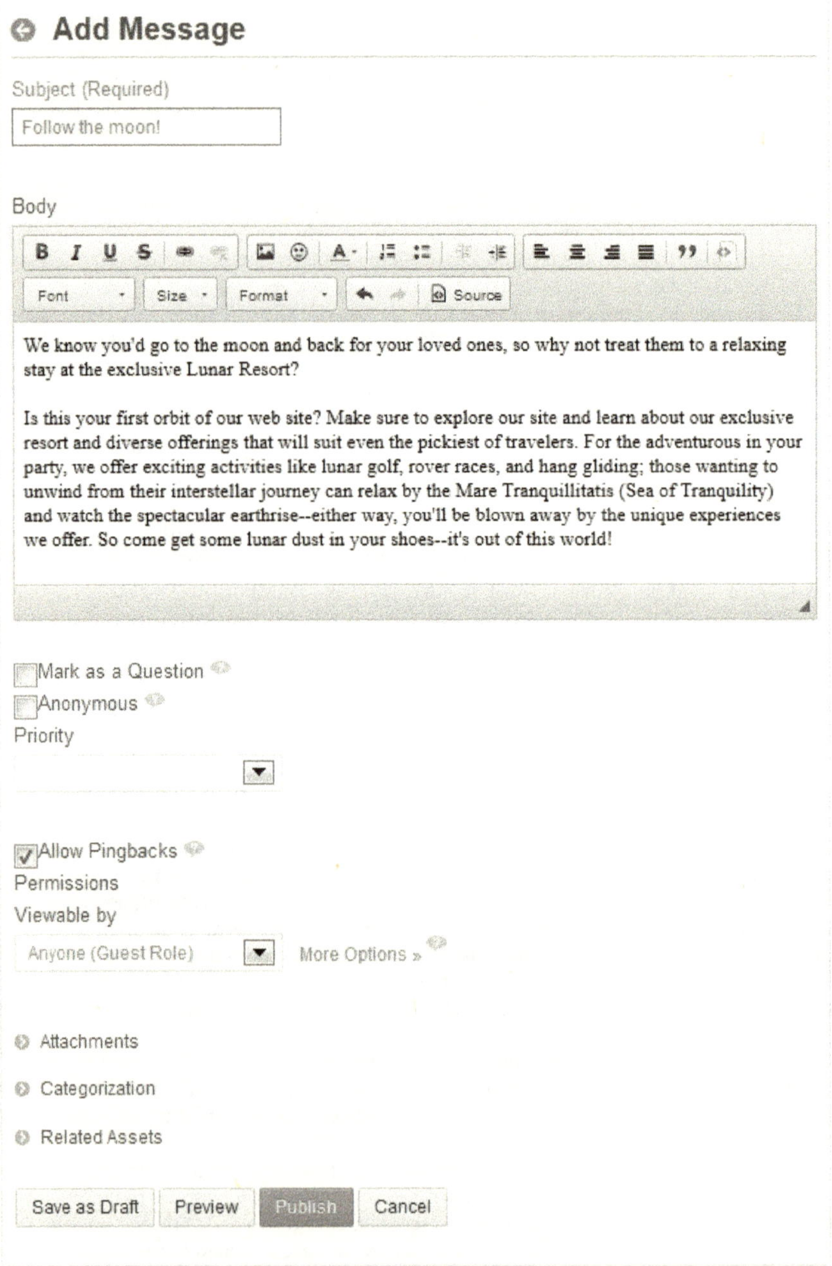

⊗ Add Message

Subject (Required)

Follow the moon!

Body

| B | I | U | S | ⊕ | | 🖼 | ☺ | A ▾ | ≔ | ≔ | | ⁂ | ⁂ | | | 🖹 | 🖹 | 🖹 | 🖹 | ” | ⟨⟩ |

| Font ▾ | Size ▾ | Format ▾ | ↩ | ↪ | ⊗ Source |

We know you'd go to the moon and back for your loved ones, so why not treat them to a relaxing stay at the exclusive Lunar Resort?

Is this your first orbit of our web site? Make sure to explore our site and learn about our exclusive resort and diverse offerings that will suit even the pickiest of travelers. For the adventurous in your party, we offer exciting activities like lunar golf, rover races, and hang gliding; those wanting to unwind from their interstellar journey can relax by the Mare Tranquillitatis (Sea of Tranquility) and watch the spectacular earthrise--either way, you'll be blown away by the unique experiences we offer. So come get some lunar dust in your shoes--it's out of this world!

▢ Mark as a Question ⊙
▢ Anonymous ⊙
Priority

[▼]

☑ Allow Pingbacks ⊙
Permissions
Viewable by

[Anyone (Guest Role)   ▼]   More Options » ⊙

⊙ Attachments

⊙ Categorization

⊙ Related Assets

| Save as Draft | Preview | Publish | Cancel |

Figure 9.20: The *Follow the moon* message board post gives you an idea of what it takes to add a message board message.

Figure 9.21: Liferay's dynamic editor even includes a wide range of smiley faces!

are posted. A tree view shows all of the messages in a threaded view, so that replies are next to the messages they are replying to.

When viewing a thread, users can click links allowing them to post a new thread, subscribe to the thread they are viewing, or if they have administrative access, lock a thread or move a thread to another category. Subscribing to a thread causes Liferay to send the user an email whenever a new message is posted to the thread. If you have enabled the mailing list feature for the category in which the thread resides, users can simply reply to these messages in order to post back to the thread, without having to visit your site.

The Message Boards portlet is also highly integrated with Liferay's user management features. Posts on the message board show users' pictures if they have uploaded one for themselves, as well as the dates that users created an ID on your site.

Message Board Administrative Functions

The Message Boards portlet provides for the day to day administration of the message threads. You may wish to separate this function out by a role, and then delegate that role to one or more of your users. That would free you up to concentrate on other areas of your web site. To do this, you can create a role called Message Board Administrator. This role can be scoped by the portal, an organization, or a site. If you have a portal scoped role, members of this role will be able to administer any Message Boards portlet in the portal. If it is an organization or site scoped role, members of this role will be able to administer a Message Boards portlet in only the organization or site which assigned the role to them.

Go to the Control Panel and create this role. Once it is created, click *Actions* →*Define Permissions*. Click the *Content* drop-down list. Browse the list until you find the Message Boards portlet and then click on it. You will then see a screen which allows you to configure the various permissions on the portlet.

Select the permissions you would like message board administrators to have and then click *Save*. You can add users to this role and they will inherit the permissions. Message Board administrators can perform all of the functions we have already presented, including creating and deleting categories and posting threads. In addition to these, a number of other functions are available.

Moving Threads

Many times a user will post a thread in the wrong category. Administrators may in this case want to move a thread to the proper category. This is very easy to do. You can select the *Actions* menu to the right of the thread and choose *Move*. Or, if you are already viewing the thread and you have administrative access, there is a link at the top of the thread labeled

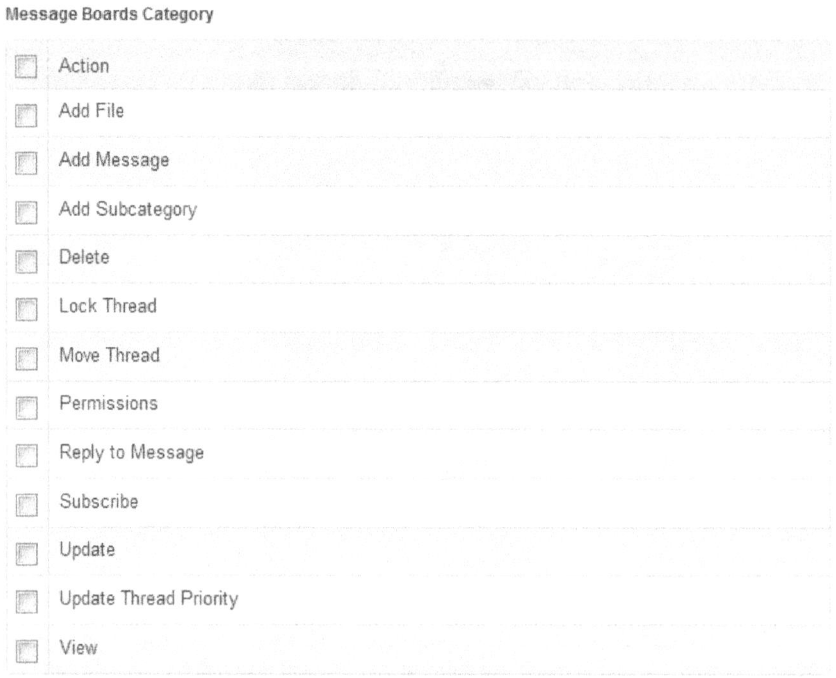

Message Boards Category

☐	Action
☐	Add File
☐	Add Message
☐	Add Subcategory
☐	Delete
☐	Lock Thread
☐	Move Thread
☐	Permissions
☐	Reply to Message
☐	Subscribe
☐	Update
☐	Update Thread Priority
☐	View

Figure 9.22: Defining Permissions for the Message Board Administrators can be done by navigating to *Actions →Define Permissions*.

Move Thread. Click this link. You will be presented with a simple form which allows you to select a category to which to move the thread and a check box which allows you to post a message explaining why the thread was moved. This message will be posted as a reply to the thread you are moving. When finished, click the *Move Thread* button and the thread will be moved.

Deleting Threads

Users with administrative access to the message boards can delete threads. Sometimes users begin discussing topics that are inappropriate or that reveal confidential information. In this case, you can simply delete the thread from the message boards. This is easy to do. First, view the list of threads. Next to every thread is an *Actions* button. Click *Actions →Move to the Recycle Bin* to delete the thread. This does not prevent users from re-posting the information, so you may need to be vigilant in deleting threads or consider the next option.

Banning Users

Unfortunately, sometimes certain users become abusive. If you wind up with a user like this, you can certainly make attempts to warn him or her that the behavior he or she is displaying is unacceptable. If this does not work, you can ban the user from posting on the message boards.

Again, this is very easy to do. Find any post which was written by the abusive user. Underneath the user's name/profile picture is a link called *Ban this User*. Click this link to ban the user from the message boards.

If after taking this action the user apologizes and agrees to stop his or her abusive behavior, you can choose to reinstate the user. To do this, click the *Banned Users* tab at the top of the Message Boards portlet. This will show a list of all banned users. Find the user in the list and select *Unban this User*.

Splitting Threads

Sometimes a thread will go on for a while and the discussion completely changes into something else. In this case, you can split the thread where the discussion diverges and create a whole new thread for the new topic. Administrative users will see a *Split Thread* link on each post. To split the thread, click the link. You will be brought to a form which allows you to add an explanation post to the split thread. Click *OK* to split the thread.

Editing Posts

Administrative users can edit anyone's posts, not just their own. Sometimes users will post links to copyrighted material or unsuitable pictures. You can edit these posts, which allows you to redact information that should not be posted or to censor profanity that is not allowed on your message boards.

Permissions

Permissions can be set not only on threads, but also on individual posts. You can choose to limit a particular conversation or a post to only a select group of people. To do this, click the *Permissions* link on the post and then select among the *Delete, Permissions, Subscribe, Update, and View* permissions for the particular role to which you want to grant particular access. This function can be used, for example, to allow some privileged users to post on a certain thread, while others are only allowed to view it. Other combinations of the above permissions are also possible. Next, let's discuss Liferay's Wiki portlet.

9.4 Working together with the Wiki

Liferay's Wiki portlet, like the Message Boards portlet, is a full-featured wiki application which has all of the features you would expect in a state of the art wiki. Again, though, it has the benefit of being able to take advantage of all of the features of the Liferay platform. As such, it is completely integrated with Liferay's user management, tagging, and security features.

So, what is a wiki? Basically, a wiki is an application which allows users to collaboratively build a repository of information. There are, of course, many implementations of this idea, the most famous of which is Wikipedia. Wikipedia is a full online encyclopedia developed collaboratively by users from all over the world, using a wiki. Another example would be Liferay's wiki, which is used for collaborative documentation of the Community Edition of Liferay Portal.

A wiki application allows users to create and edit documents and link them to each other. To accomplish this, a special form of markup is used which is sometimes called wikitext. Unfortunately, the proliferation of many different wiki applications resulted in slightly different syntax for wikitext in the various products, as each new wiki tried to focus on new features that other wikis did not have. For that reason, a project called WikiCreole was started. This project resulted in the release of WikiCreole 1.0 in 2007, which is an attempt to define a standard wiki markup that all wikis can support.

Rather than define another wikitext syntax, Liferay's Wiki portlet supports WikiCreole as its syntax. This syntax is a best-of-breed wiki syntax and should be familiar to users of other wikis. The portlet provides a handy cheat sheet for the syntax on the page editing form, with a link to the full documentation if you wish to use some of WikiCreole's advanced features.

Getting Started with the Liferay Wiki

The Wiki portlet works just like the other portlets developed by Liferay. Add the portlet to a page using the *Add →Applications* menu and then click *Configuration* in the portlet's *Options* menu in the Wiki portlet's title bar. You'll see some options are likely to be familiar to you by now such as sharing the application with websites, Facebook, Google Gadgets, etc. You will also notice that the communication tab has some additional options not seen in the other portlets.

The communication tab of the configuration window allows you to configure communication across portlets, using predefined public render parameters. From here you can modify six public render parameters: categoryId, nodeId, nodeName, resetCur, tag, and title. For each parameter you can:

- Ignore the values for this parameter that come from other portlets. For example, the wiki portlet can be used along with the tags navigation portlet. When a user clicks on a tag in the tags navigation portlet, the wiki shows a list of pages with that tag. In some cases an administrator may want the wiki portlet to always show the front page independently of any tag navigation done through other portlets. This can be achieved by checking the Ignore check box so that the values of the parameter coming from those other portlets are ignored.

- Read the value of a parameter from another portlet. This is an advanced but very powerful option that allows portlets to communicate without configuring it beforehand. For example, imagine that the wiki portlet is used to publish information about certain countries. Imagine further that a custom portlet that allows browsing countries for administrative reasons was written and placed on the same page. We could associate to this second portlet a public render parameter called *country* to designate the name of the country. Using this procedure, we can cause the wiki to show the information from the country being browsed through in the other portlet. You can do this here for the wiki by setting the value for the title parameter to be read from the country parameter of the other portlet.

Once you have set the options the way you want them, click *Save*.

Managing Wikis

The Wiki portlet can contain many wikis. By default, it contains only one, called *Main*. To manage Wikis, navigate to your site's *Site Administration →Content* page and select *Wiki*. This page allows you to add, modify, and delete wikis. The Main wiki has already been added for you.

At the top of this screen is a *Permissions* button. Clicking this allows you to define which roles have access to create wikis. If you have created a specific role for creating wikis, you can click the box in the *Add Node* column and then click *Submit*, and that role will have access to create new wikis in this portlet.

Clicking the *Add Wiki* button prompts you to enter a name and description for the new wiki. You can also set up some default permissions. When you create a new wiki, it appears in a list at the top of the main page of the Wiki portlet.

Next to each wiki in the list of wiki nodes is an *Actions* button. This button contains several options:

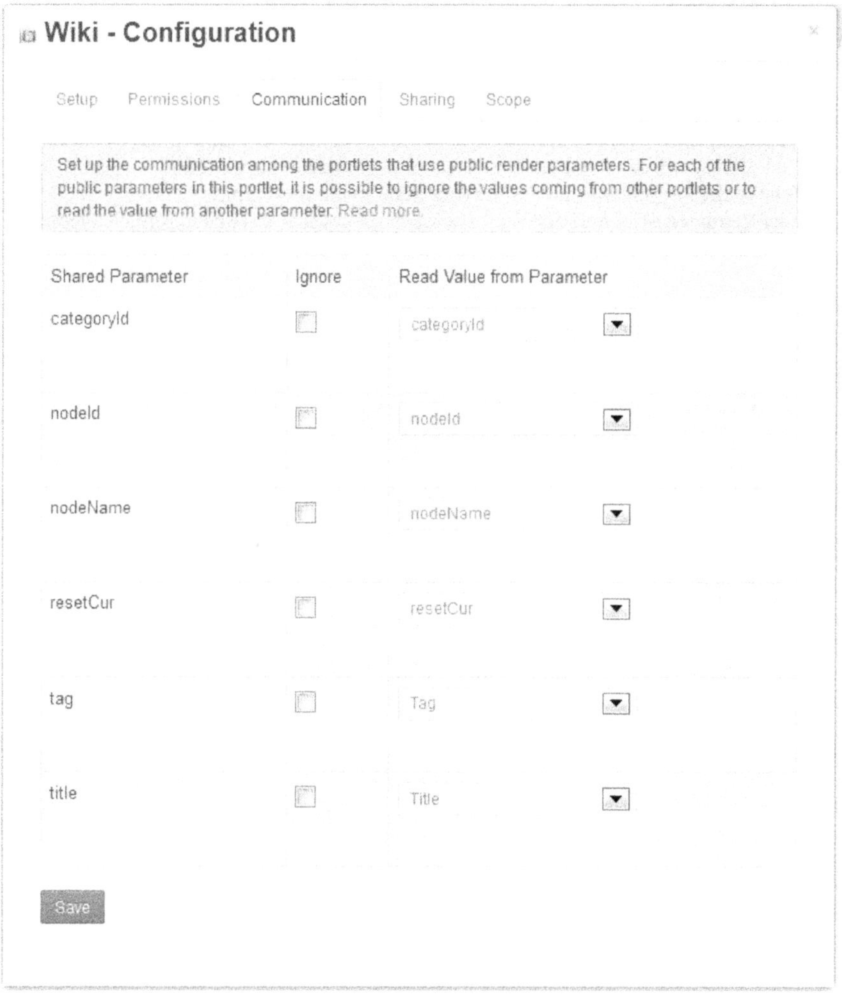

Wiki - Configuration

Setup   Permissions   Communication   Sharing   Scope

Set up the communication among the portlets that use public render parameters. For each of the public parameters in this portlet, it is possible to ignore the values coming from other portlets or to read the value from another parameter. Read more.

Shared Parameter	Ignore	Read Value from Parameter	
categoryId	☐	categoryId	▼
nodeId	☐	nodeId	▼
nodeName	☐	nodeName	▼
resetCur	☐	resetCur	▼
tag	☐	Tag	▼
title	☐	Title	▼

Save

Figure 9.23: For each of the public parameters in this portlet, it is possible to ignore the values coming from other portlets or to read the value from another parameter.

Edit: lets you edit the name and description of the wiki.

Permissions: lets you define what roles can add attachments to wiki pages, add pages to the wiki, delete pages, import pages to the wiki, set permissions on the wiki, subscribe to the wiki, update existing pages, and view the wiki.

Import Pages: allows you to import data from other wikis. This lets you migrate off of another wiki which you may be using and use the Liferay wiki instead. You might wish to do this if you are migrating your site from a set of disparate applications (i.e. a separate forum, a separate wiki, a separate content management system) to Liferay, which provides all of these features. Currently, MediaWiki is the only wiki that is supported, but others are likely to be supported in the future.

RSS: opens a new page where you can subscribe to an RSS feed using Live Bookmarks, Yahoo, or a chosen application from your machine.

Subscribe: allows you to subscribe to a wiki node, and any time a page is added or updated Liferay will send you an email informing you what happened.

Move to the Recycle Bin: moves the wiki node to the recycle bin.

View Removed Attachments: displays attachments that have been removed from the wiki node.

To go back to your wiki, navigate back to the Wiki portlet you added to your page. Then click the *Options →Configuration* button, which contains several other options which you may have seen on other portlets.

The *Display Settings* tab gives you several options for how the wiki should be displayed. *Enable Related Assets, Enable Page Ratings, Enable Comments*, and *Enable Comment Ratings* are similar to the same options in other portlets. They give you the ability to set how you want users to interact with wiki documents: a little, a lot, or not at all. The *Display Template* drop-down option lets you choose the application display template for your portlet. Below this, you can set which wikis are visible in the Wiki portlet by default and which are hidden. You might host two wikis on a given site, exposing one to the public and keeping the other private for site members.

The *Email From, Page Added Email*, and *Page Updated Email* tabs are similar to the ones for notification email settings for other portlets, allowing you to customize who wiki emails come from and the format and text of the email that is sent when a page is added or updated.

Finally, the Wiki portlet also supports RSS feeds as the other collaboration portlets do, and you can configure its options in the *RSS* tab.

Adding and Editing Wiki Pages

By default, there is one page added to your wiki, called *FrontPage*. To get started adding data to your wiki, click the *Edit* link. You will be brought to a blank editing page.

You can now begin to add content to the page. Notice that there is a very convenient *Show Syntax Help* link which can help with the wiki syntax. You can use this syntax to format your wiki pages. Consider, for example, the following wiki document:

```
== Welcome to Our Wiki! ==
\index{Wiki}
\index{Wiki}

This is our new wiki, which should allow us to collaborate on
documentation. Feel free to add pages showing people how to do stuff.
Below are links to some sections that have already been added.

[[Introduction]]

[[Getting Started]]

[[configuration]]

[[Development]]
```

[[Support]]

[[Community]]

Figure 9.24: By clicking *Edit*, you can create/modify your wiki content.

This produces the wiki article you see on the facing page.

This adds a simple heading, a paragraph of text, and several links to the page. Since the pages behind these links have not been created yet, clicking one of those links takes you to an editing screen to create the page. This editing screen looks just like the one you used previously when you wrote the front page. Liferay displays a notice at the top of the page stating that the page does not exist yet, and that you are creating it right now. As you can see, it is very easy to create wiki pages. All you have to do is create a link from an existing page. Note that at the top of the screen you can select from the Creole wiki format and the HTML editor that comes with Liferay. We recommend that you stick with the Creole format, as it allows for a much cleaner separation of content and code. If you want all of your users to use the Creole format, you can disable the HTML format using the portal-ext.properties file. See chapter 14 for details about how to configure this.

At the bottom of the page editing screen, you can select *Categorization* to add tags. The tags link your wiki to categories. You can create categories using the Site Administration page, in the *Content →Categories* section. Categories are hierarchical lists of headings under which you can create wiki pages. This allows you to organize your content in a more formal fashion.

Page Details

When viewing a page, you can view its details by clicking the *Details* link which appears in the top right of the page. This allows you to view many properties of the page. There are several tabs which organize all of the details into convenient categories.

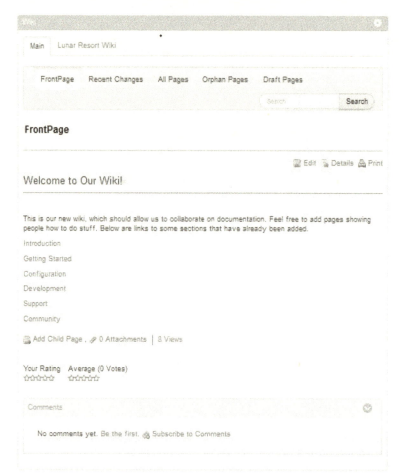

Figure 9.25: By using the syntax help guide, you can format your wiki headings and text.

Details

The Details tab shows various statistics about the page, and also allows you to perform some actions on the page.

Title: displays the title of the page.

Format: displays the format for the page—either Creole, HTML, or MediaWiki.

Latest Version: displays the latest version of the page. The wiki portlet automatically keeps track of page versions whenever a page has been edited.

Created By: displays the user who created the page.

Last Changed By: displays the user who last modified the page.

Attachments: displays the number of attachments to the page.

Convert To: offers different conversion formats for the wiki page: DOC, ODT, PDF, RTF, SXW, and TXT.

RSS Subscription: displays links which allow you to subscribe to the page as an RSS feed in three formats: RSS 1.0, RSS 2.0, and Atom 1.0.

Email Subscription: contains links allowing you to subscribe to the entire wiki or just to this page.

Advanced Actions: contains links allowing you to modify the permissions on the page, make a copy of the page, move (rename) the page, or move the page to the recycle bin.

History

This tab shows a list of all of the versions of the wiki page since it was created. You can revert a page back to a previous state and you can also compare the differences between versions by selecting the versions and then clicking the *Compare Versions* button.

Incoming/Outgoing Links

The next two tabs are for incoming and outgoing links. These are wiki links to and from the page. You can use this tab to examine how this page links to other pages and how other pages link back to this page.

Attachments

The last tab is for attachments. You can attach any file to the wiki. This is mostly used to attach images to wiki articles which can then be referenced in the text. Referencing them using the proper WikiCreole syntax renders the image inline, which is a nice way to include illustrations in your wiki documents.

Navigating in the Wiki Portlet

At the top of the portlet is a list of links which allow you to navigate around the wiki. Simply click on the wiki's name to begin browsing that wiki. After this is a set of navigation links:

Recent Changes: takes you to a page which shows all of the recently updated pages.

All Pages: takes you to a flat, alphabetical list of all pages currently stored in the wiki.

Orphan Pages: takes you to a list of pages that have no links to them. This can happen if you take a link out of a wiki page in an edit without realizing it's the only link to a certain page. This area allows you to review wiki pages that are orphaned in this way so that you can re-link to them or delete them from the wiki if they are no longer relevant.

Draft Pages: takes you to a list of pages which have not yet been published. Users can edit pages and save their changes as drafts. They can come back later to finish their page changes and publish them once they have been approved.

Search: allows you to a term here and click the *Search* button to search for items in the wiki. If the search term is not found, a link will be displayed which allows you to create a new wiki page on the topic for which you searched.

The Wiki portlet is another full-featured Liferay application with all of the features you expect from a state of the art wiki. Next, we'll look at how Liferay handles live chat.

9.5 Find out what others think or do using Polls

How well do you know your users? Do you ever wonder what they're thinking? Is using your site easy for them? How do they feel about the hot-button issues of the day? Do they prefer dogs over cats? What about the new policy that management wants to implement? What's their favorite ice cream flavor? When you use Liferay's Polls feature you can find out the answer to these and other questions that should help you better understand your users.

There are two portlets involved in making and displaying a poll: the *Polls* portlet, which is accessed through the Site Administration page, and the *Polls Display* portlet, which can be added to any page in the portal.

The Polls portlet helps you set up the poll question and the possible answers users can select. The Polls Display portlet is an instanceable portlet that lets you select which poll to display, and is the portlet you put on the page so users can vote.

The Polls portlet allows users and administrators to create multiple choice polls that keep track of the votes and display results on the page. Many separate polls can be managed; a separate portlet called Polls Display can be configured to display a specific poll's questions and results.

The Polls Display Portlet allows users to vote for a specific poll's questions and see the results. Questions must be created from the Polls portlet on the Site Administration page. You can display one question at a time or you can combine several questions inside a nested portlet to create a survey.

We'll begin by creating a poll.

Creating a Poll

On your site's Site Administration page, navigate to the *Polls* link under Content. Click the *Add Question* button. A form appears that allows you to fill out all the information for your poll.

Title: Enter the name of the poll question.

Polls Question: Enter the text of the poll question.

Expiration Date: Enter the date and time you want the poll to expire.

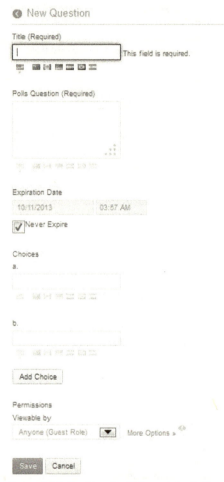

Figure 9.26: Besides the Title and the Polls Question, you must enter data for each of the Choices fields when creating a new poll.

Choices: Enter at least two answer options for the poll question.

Add Choice: Enter additional answer options for the poll question.

Permissions: Manage who can view and edit the poll.

When you have finished creating your poll, click *Save*, and it is added to the Polls portlet.

As more polls are created in the Control Panel, they become accessible through the Polls Display portlet until they are either deleted or they expire. You can set an expiration date for a poll by selecting the day and time in the Add Poll form or in the New Question form. The default is set to *Never Expire*.

When a poll expires, users can't enter votes any more, but if a Polls Display portlet is still publishing it, the poll results are displayed on the page. To remove an expired poll from a page, remove the Poll Display portlet or configure it to show another poll question. See the section below for more details about the Polls Display portlet.

Permissions can be set on individual polls as they are set elsewhere in Liferay Portal. Permissions can be used, for example, to allow some privileged users to vote on a certain poll question, while others can only view it. For further information about permissions, please see chapters 15 and 16.

As you can see, creating a poll is fairly straightforward. Next, let's complete the two-step process and put your poll on a page.

Adding a Poll to a Page

Now that you have created your poll question, it's time to present it to your users. Navigate to your site and add the Polls Display portlet to a page. It is available from the *Add* →*Applications Content Management* menu.

The Polls Display portlet may look strange when it first appears on your page. That's because it's not configured. Before visitors to your site can use the poll, they must be able to access it. Click on the link labeled *Please configure this portlet to make it visible to all users, and a dialog box like the one below appears.

Figure 9.27: In the initial configuration of the Polls Display portlet, the Question field will remain blank until you select the appropriate poll question.

Under the Setup tab is a menu option labeled *Question*. Selecting this option displays the name of the poll you created. Choose it, click *Save*, and it is displayed on the page. That, in a nutshell, is how you create a poll, but there is another way to add a question to the Polls Display portlet.

Start by navigating to your site and placing the Polls Display portlet on a page. Using the icons in the lower left of the portlet, choose the *Add Question* button. A new form appears that lets you create another question. When you are done filling out the form, click *Save* and you new poll appears on the page.

Once the poll question has been successfully placed on the page, you can perform other tasks by using the icons in the lower left corner of the portlet. Besides adding questions, you can also edit the currently selected question or select existing questions.

Edit Question: Displays a similar dialog box to the one used to create the poll.

Select Question: Displays the same dialog box as Configuration, allowing you to choose different questions from the drop-down menu.

Add Question: Allows you to create a new question.

You can also manage the Polls Display portlet by clicking the gear symbol in the upper right corner of the portlet's title bar. Now let's see the poll results.

Viewing the Poll Results

When you create a poll question, it appears in a list in the *Content* section of Site Administration. After users vote in the poll, the data is collected here. If you select it, the name and the question, as well as a breakdown of the poll results appears, including percentages and total number of votes per answer and the total number of votes cast.

Figure 9.28: These three buttons, highlighted in red, allow you to manage the configuration of the poll. Notice this poll has expired.

Below this is an item called *Charts*. This option shows the poll results represented in various graphs. The graphs are *Area, Horizontal Bar, Line, Pie,* and *Vertical Bar.*

There is also a listing of the users who voted in your poll, how they voted, and a time/date stamp of when their votes were cast. Registered users are represented by their screen name while Guest users are represented by a number.

With Liferay Polls you can do many things. You can ask users very specific questions or you can use Polls to create a little fun for your community. As with most things in Liferay, you are only limited by your imagination. Next, let's learn how to use Liferay's Announcements portlet.

9.6   Sending Alerts and Announcements in Your Portal

Suppose you're running a portal with lots of users. Maybe you have thousands or tens of thousands of users (or more!). Wouldn't it be nice to have an easy way to periodically communicate important information to them? And wouldn't it be even nicer to have easy ways to periodically send information to specific groups of users? For example, maybe you'd like to send a reminder about a new policy to all of the site administrators on your portal. Or maybe you'd like to send a reminder to all the members of a certain site to submit an answer to this week's poll question. Liferay provides two portlets that meet this need: the Alerts portlet and the Announcements portlet.

The Alerts and Announcements portlets let you broadcast important information to different groups of users. Each alert or announcement can be created in a specific scope so that you can manage which announcements are sent to which users. Furthermore, each portal user can configure how they'd like to receive announcements: click on *[User Name]* →*My Account* from the Dockbar and then on *Announcements* in the Miscellaneous category. There's a menu for customizing the delivery options for alerts and announcements. You can select a different configuration for each type of alert or announcement: General, News, or Test. Each kind of announcement that's broadcast to a user is viewable from the Alerts or Announcements portlet, of course. But alerts and announcements can also be sent via email or SMS (Short Message Service, i.e., text).

You can also create roles in Liferay to assign to users that should have access to announcing general announcements. For instance, if you'd like an employee in your site to have strict control over what is announced, you can assign them to an Announcements role. To create a simple Announcement role, you'll need to navigate to the *Control Panel Roles* →*Add* →*Regular Role.* Specify the name of your role as *Announcements,* click *Save,* and then select the *Define Permissions* tab. For this particular role, you'll need to grant two permissions:

Polls

Lunar Resort Poll

Which word best describes the Lunar Resort?

%	Votes			
36%	4		a.	Fun
9%	1		b.	Wacky
27%	3		c.	Inspiring
27%	3		d.	Stunning

Total Votes: 11

Charts: Area, Horizontal Bar, Line, Pie, Vertical Bar

Actual Votes

Page 1 of 1 ▼	20 Items per Page ▼	Showing 11 results.

← First Previous Next Last →

User	Choice	Vote Date
Test Test	a. Fun	4 Hours Ago
Ashton Allen	b. Stunning	16 Minutes Ago
Buster Banks	c. Wacky	14 Minutes Ago
Casey Collins	d. Stunning	14 Minutes Ago
Dean Davis	a. Inspiring	14 Minutes Ago

Figure 9.29: Selecting a poll in the Polls portlet allows you to see all the information related to the poll results.

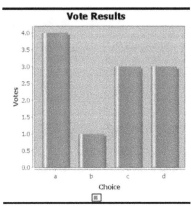

Figure 9.30: This is what the vertical bar graph for the Lunar Resort poll results looks like.

- *Control Panel →General Permissions →Add General Announcements*
- *Site Administration →Applications →Announcements →Add Entry*

You'll need to click *Save* after selecting each permission. Now you have a simple Announcements role that can add an entry to the Announcements portlet and add general announcements to your site! Of course, you can add additional permissions to give the Announcements role more access, if you prefer.

Let's look at how to create announcements in the Announcements portlet. When you view the Announcements portlet as an administrator, you'll see two tabs: Entries and Manage Entries. Non-administrators only see the Entries tab which displays a list of announcements. To add a new announcement, click on *Manage Entries* and then select a *Distribution Scope*. The distribution scope determines the group of users to which your announcement is sent. Announcements created in the General distribution scope are sent to everyone. If the distribution scope is set a particular site or role, only members of that site or role receive the announcements.

Once you've selected a distribution scope, you'll see a list of all the announcements that have already been created in that scope. You can click the *Actions* button next to an announcement to edit or delete it. Click *Add* to create a new announcement. In addition to the Distribution scope, you can provide the following information:

Title: The title of the announcement. When the announcement is displayed in the portlet, the full title always appears in bold. If a URL was entered, the title serves as a link to the site specified in the URL field.

URL: The URL is optional. If entered, it must be a valid URL, starting with *http://*. For example, an announcement about a news story could include a link to the news article.

Content: The body of the announcement. You can use the familiar CK editor to write the body of your announcement. Use the *Source* button to switch between the editor view and the HTML view.

Type: Can be *General*, *News*, or *Test*. Each user can specify a different delivery mechanism for each type of announcement. For example, a user can specify that she'd like to receive general announcements via email and text, news announcement via email only, and no special delivery mechanism for test announcements. Each user can customize their delivery options by navigating to *[User Name] →My Account* from the Dockbar and then clicking on *Announcements* in the Miscellaneous category.

Priority: Can be either *Normal* or *Important*.

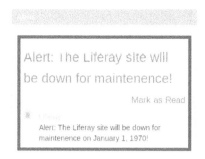

Figure 9.31: The Alerts portlet provides administrators with an easy way to communicate important information to appropriate groups of users.

Display Date: This determines when the announcement will be sent to users and will appear in the Announcements portlet. By default, the *Display Immediately* box is flagged. This sets the display date to be equal to the creation date. Unflag this box if you'd like to enter a custom display date. For example, administrators can create announcements that won't be displayed until a specified future date. This date can be days, weeks, months, or years in the future. Once the *Display Immediately* box is unflagged, clicking on the Display Date field opens the date-picker widget.

Expiration Date: This determines when the announcement expires. Once an announcement expires, it's no longer displayed by the Announcements portlet to any users. Clicking on the Expiration Date field opens the date-picker widget.

Title	Type	Modified Date	Display Date	Expiration Date	
Radio Liferay	General	1 Hour Ago	1 Hour Ago	Within 1 Month	Actions
Remember to answer today's Liferay poll	General	0 Seconds Ago	0 Seconds Ago	Within 1 Month	Actions

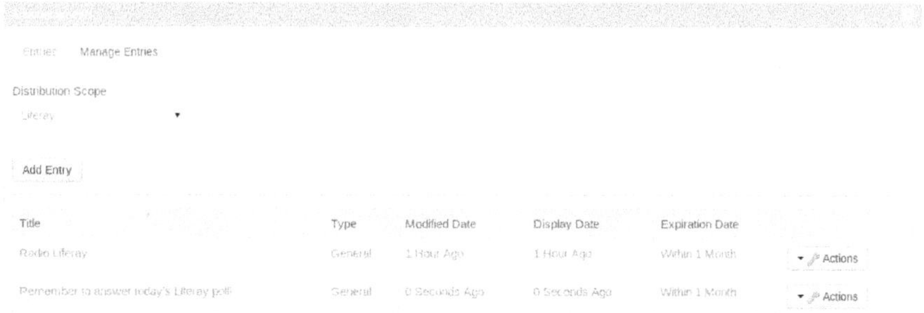

Figure 9.32: The Annoucements portlet displays a list of annoucements to regular users. It also provides administrators with an interface for managing and adding entries.

The Alerts portlet works the same way as the announcements portlet. It's a different portlet because it's designed to be be used only for important messages or message that may require users to take some action. The Alerts portlet only displays alerts and the Announcements portlet only displays alerts. The Alerts portlet displays alerts with a bold red box around each alert message to draw attention to the displayed entries. Site administrators can place the Alerts and Announcement portlets on different pages if they'd like to separate important alerts from more mundane announcements.

Next, let's see what you can do with Liferay's Chat feature.

9.7   Staying in touch with the Chat

Liferay's Chat portlet provides a convenient way of allowing users to send each other instant messages when they are logged into your web site. It appears as a bar at the bottom of every page, showing who is logged on, their statuses, and any chats the logged-in user has open.

Figure 9.33: Liferay's Chat Portlet offers ways to update your status and notifications through the *Settings* menu.

The Chat portlet is distributed with the Liferay bundles, but is not included as part of the .war distribution, as it is a separate plugin. If you installed the Liferay .war manually on your application server, you can install the Chat portlet by accessing Liferay Marketplace. You can go to Marketplace by navigating the Control Panel and clicking *Store* under the *Apps* heading. You can learn more about Marketplace and how to purchase/download an app in the *Liferay Marketplace* chapter.

The Chat portlet is very simple to use. To change the settings, click *Settings* (found near the lower right corner next to *Online Friends*). Here you can set your status, choose whether or not to show that you are online, whether or not to play a sound if someone sends you a message while you have the window or tab in the background, and whether to enable desktop notifications for new messages. The Chat portlet displays the number of your friends who are online. Click the *Online Friends* link and then click on a friend's name to open a chat window. You can have multiple chats open at a time, and can have one or more of them minimized.

Filtering Available Users

By default, all online portal users appear in the Chat portlet. If you want to filter who appears in your contact list you can, but the configuration must be done by someone who has administrative access to the server. The configuration change must be made at the time the chat portlet is deployed.

To filter users, create a portlet-ext.properties file to override some properties of your Chat portlet's portlet.properties file. You could modify your chat portlet's portlet.properties file directly, but it's a best practice to override it instead.

Before you deploy your Chat portlet, extract it to your file system. You can create the portlet-ext.properties file in the chat-portlet/WEB-INF/src directory. It gets copied over to your chat-portlet/WEB-INF/classes directory upon deployment. When you're finished making changes to your portlet-ext.properties file, you'll zip the directory structure back into a .war file for deployment. Note that the Chat portlet must be redeployed for settings in properties files to take effect.

The property that refines the list of users that show up in the Chat portlet is buddy.list.strategy. Some common values are listed here:

```
buddy.list.strategy=all
buddy.list.strategy=sites
buddy.list.strategy=social
buddy.list.strategy=sites,social
```

The default value is all. To show only other users of the sites a user belongs to, set buddy.list.strategy to sites. Setting buddy.list.strategy to social makes only a user's social connections available in the Chat portlet. Note that you can also combine values by separating them with a comma. Combined values behave like a logical AND statement. Thus, sites,social shows other users of the sites a user belongs to, and the user's social connections.

You can also further refine the sites setting by using the property buddy.list-.site.excludes. This property allows you to exclude specific sites in your portal from the buddy.list.strategy=sites setting. This is especially useful if you have a default site that all portal users belong to, but you still want to filter the users that appear in the Chat portlet by site. If this default site isn't excluded, then all portal users show up in the chat portlet when buddy.list.strategy is set to sites. The site name to give for buddy.list.site.excludes is the value of the name column for the Group table in your portal's database. It must be entered in the same case as it is in the database. For example, if you want to exclude a site called Default, enter buddy.list.site.excludes=Default. That site is then ignored when determining the users to show in the Chat portlet.

The social setting for buddy.list.strategy has further filtering options as well. You can set the allowed types of social relationships through the property buddy.list-.allowed.social.relation.types. By default this property is set to 2,12. Those values correspond, respectively, to the *Friend* and *Connection* social relationship types. The values for some additional social relationship types are listed here along with those of *Friend* and *Connection*:

```
TYPE_BI_CONNECTION = 12
TYPE_BI_COWORKER = 1
TYPE_BI_FRIEND = 2
TYPE_BI_ROMANTIC_PARTNER = 3
TYPE_BI_SIBLING = 4
```

These are bidirectional social relationship types as defined in Liferay's social API. It's important to note that these aren't available out-of-the-box. You must install apps that make use of them before you can leverage them in your portal. For example, Liferay's Social Networking app from the Marketplace makes use of the "Friend" social relationship type. Similarly, Liferay Social Office uses the "Connection" social relationship type. Developers can make use of any of the social relationship types available in the API.

Jabber Server Integration

Liferay 6.1 introduced Jabber server integration to Liferay's Chat portlet. Jabber is the original name of the XMPP (Extensible Messaging and Presence Protocol) protocol, an open-standard communications protocol based on XML. Using a chat server helps Liferay's chat scale to very large installations and allows for communication between different chat clients. For example, Jabber server integration allows users using the chat portlet in their browser windows to chat with other users using desktop clients like Empathy, Pidgin, or Kopete.

Jabber server integration is not enabled by default since it requires a running Jabber server. Once you have installed and started a Jabber server, you can enable Jabber server integration by creating a portlet-ext.properties file to override some properties of your Chat portlet's portlet.properties file. You could modify your Chat portlet's portlet.properties file directly, but it's a best practice to override it instead.

Installation Steps

You can use any chat server that supports Jabber. The Chat portlet's Jabber server integration feature was tested with versions 3.7.0 and 3.7.1 of Openfire, a real time collaboration server distributed under the Open Source Apache License. You can download Openfire from http://www.igniterealtime.org/projects/openfire/. To enable Jabber chat integration, follow these steps:

1. Start your chat server. If you are using Openfire on a Linux/Mac system, you can start/stop the chat server by executing the openfire shell script in the openfire-/bin directory. Usage: ./openfire start or ./openfire stop

2. Override the portlet.properties file in your /chat-portlet/WEB-INF/src/ directory with a portlet-ext.properties file in the same directory. When you deploy the portlet, the properties files should be copied to your /chat-portlet/WEB-INF/classes/ directory. If you have already deployed the Chat portlet, create the portlet-ext.properties file in your /chat-portlet/WEB-INF/classes/ directory. The contents of your portlet-ext.properties file should like this:

```
jabber.enabled=true
jabber.import.user.enabled=true
jabber.host=localhost
jabber.port=5222
jabber.service.name=<Host Name>
jabber.resource=Liferay
jabber.sock5.proxy.enabled=false
jabber.sock5.proxy.port=-1
```

Note that you must change jabber.service.name to the "Host Name". If you are using Openfire, you can find the Host Name by using the Openfire administration web tool. If you did not set up administrative credentials when you started Openfire, the default credentials are username: admin, password: admin.

Additionally, make sure that you set jabber.enabled to true and have added the correct values to jabber.host and jabber.port. If you installed your chat server on a remote machine or chose to not use the default port, change jabber.host and jabber.port accordingly.

3. Deploy your Chat portlet. Remember that this portlet must be of version 6.1 or higher.

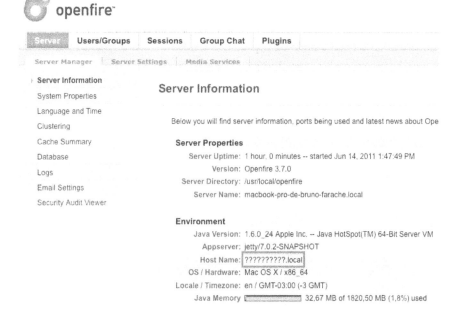

Figure 9.34: View your server information using the Openfire Administration Web Tool.

Single Sign On

If the property jabber.import.user.enabled is set to true, the Chat portlet will import the user automatically to Jabber after he logs in to the portal. Once the user is imported, he can use any Jabber client using the same screen name and password he uses to log in to the portal. His buddies will be also imported as they become online in the Chat portlet.

Note that it's a "lazy import". Users are imported only after they log in to the portal and their buddies will be added to his list only if they see each other within the Chat portlet. They won't be able to use other Jabber chat clients until they log in to the portal.

If jabber.import.user.enabled is set to false, users need to create their Jabber account and add buddies manually. They have to create their accounts using the same screen name and password they use in the portal. If they don't, the Chat portlet won't be able to connect to their Jabber account.

Alternatively, since Openfire integrates with LDAP, if you are using Openfire and your portal is also using LDAP for authentication, you can disable the jabber.import.user.enabled property.

Next, let's look at how you can integrate your email addresses with Liferay's Mail portlet.

9.8 Integrating your email with Liferay Mail

Liferay's Mail portlet enables your users to interact with their email using an easy to use, ubiquitous web interface. If your mail system supports the IMAP protocol, you can use the Mail portlet to integrate your users' mail with the rest of your web site. You can also connect the Mail portlet to a mail account provided by Google.

The Mail portlet is distributed with the Liferay bundles, but is not included as part of the .war distribution, as it is a separate plugin. If you installed the Liferay .war manually on your application server, you can install the Mail portlet by accessing Liferay Marketplace. You can go to Marketplace by navigating the the Control Panel and clicking *Store* under the *Apps* heading. You can learn more about Marketplace and how to purchase/download an app in the *Liferay Marketplace* chapter.

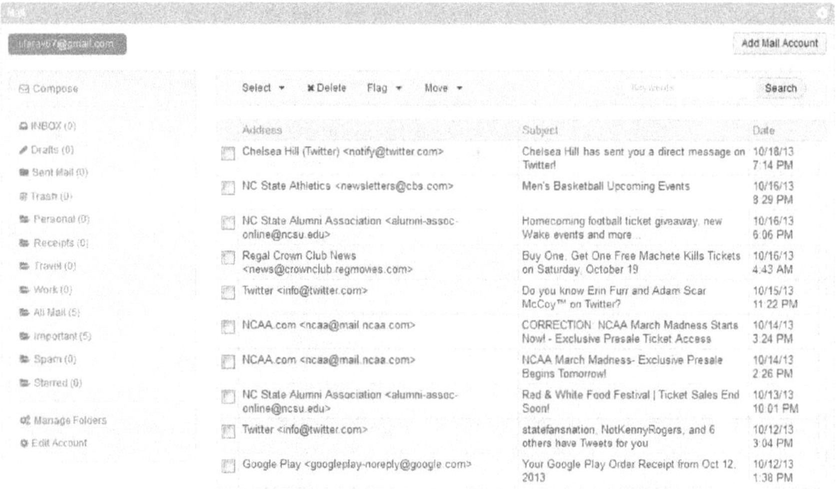

Figure 9.35: Read, reply, and create messages using Liferay's Mail Portlet.

To connect the Mail portlet with an email account, click the *Add Mail Account* link. From there, you are given a choice between a Custom email Account or a Gmail Account. Choose the option that you wish, and fill out the form that appears.

For a Gmail account, all you need to do is provide your email address and your password, and the portlet will take care of the rest.

For a Custom Mail Account, the following fields are necessary:

Address: lets you enter the email address which receives mail for this account.

Login: lets you choose a user name for logging into the account.

Password: lets you choose a password for logging into the account.

Save Password: allows Liferay to save your password so you won't have to enter it next time you access your mail account.

Incoming Host Name: allows you to specify the host name for your IMAP (Internet Mail Access Protocol) or POP server.

Incoming Port: allows you to specify the port upon which the IMAP or POP service is running.

Use Secure Incoming Connection: allows you to use an encrypted connection to the server provided that your server supports it.

Outgoing SMTP Server: lets you enter the host name of your SMTP (Simple Mail Transfer Protocol) server.

Outgoing Port: allows you to specify the port upon which the SMTP service is running.

Use Secure Outgoing Connection: allows you to use an encrypted connection to the server provided that your server supports it.

When finished, click *Save*. Your new email account now appears as a tab at the top of the page along with the button for adding a mail account. In this way, you can add as many mail accounts as you want in order to view them in the portlet.

Click the tab for the mail account you just configured to be brought to an interface which allows you to read your mail and compose new messages. To read a message, click on it. To compose a new message, click the *Compose* link on the left side of the portlet. A form appears which allows you to compose an email message using the same rich text editor that appears everywhere else in Liferay. You can read, reply, and create messages, as well as manage all of your folders in Liferay's Mail portlet.

The Mail portlet is a great way to integrate a familiar service with other the collaboration features that Liferay provides.

9.9 Summary

We have explored many of the portlets in Liferay's collaboration suite. The Blogs and Blogs Aggregation portlets can be used to manage shared blogs or blogs belonging to a group of people at once. These portlets have all the features you would want in a blog, including rich text editing, links to news aggregators, tags, RSS feeds, and more.

The Calendar portlet, likewise, can be used to manage a shared calendar or a group calendar. It includes features for events, event notification, repeatable events, and import and export to and from the standard iCalendar format.

Discussion becomes easy with Liferay's Message Boards portlet. This portlet can be used to manage heavily trafficked discussion forums with ease. It inherits all of the security features of the Liferay platform and includes administrative functions for thread priorities, moving threads, nested discussion categories, banning users, and more.

Liferay's Wiki portlet is a state of the art wiki application that users can make use of to collaborate on web pages. Again, it inherits the strengths of the Liferay platform in the form of security, interface, and search. You can use the wiki portlet to manage several wiki nodes or use many wiki portlets to manage one node each.

The Polls portlet is a fun way to interact with users of your site to get an understanding of what they're thinking at any given time. It allows you to create multiple choice polls that keep track of the votes and display results on the page. You can view these results in a number of ways, including charts.

The Announcements portlet allows administrators to create and manage announcements and allows users to view the announcements. The announcements can be sent via email or text or they can simply be displayed on the portal. The Announcements portlet provides a good way for administrators to communicate to different groups of users since each announcement can be scoped to a specific site or role.

Liferay provides a chat solution for your portal that's very easy to use. It allows logged-in users to see who else is logged in to the portal and view their status. Users can go invisible if they don't want others to know that they're online. Users can chat with each other via instant messages. You can also set up a Jabber chat server and configure Liferay to use it; this allows users who have logged in to your portal via their browsers to chat with users using traditional desktop clients.

Integrating mail with your portal is easy with the Mail portlet. You can add as many custom or Gmail mail accounts as you wish, and this portlet can keep them all organized in one place, together with the rest of the things Liferay is aggregating for you.

Liferay's collaboration platform is a full suite of integrated applications that empower users to work together. You can use them to great effect to enhance your portal and to build a vibrant, active community.

## CHAPTER 10

SOCIAL NETWORKING

Since the first social networks rose to popularity, concepts such as *Friend* and later *Like*— previously reserved for direct human interaction—have taken on new meaning in an always-online, information driven culture. It could be argued that social networks have transformed the way people interact with their friends, relatives and colleagues. Friends, connections, followers, circles and lists have enabled people to connect and stay connected in ways they'd never been able to before. Initially, these concepts proved to be highly successful for casual web sites but they didn't take to the business world as quickly. But many organizations are now realizing the importance of leveraging social interactions for more than just recreation. Liferay's robust social features make it a great platform for business web sites, casual web sites and everything in between.

Social applications have many differences when compared to Standard applications that are vital to a social networking site. Standard applications have general and user specific data, whereas social applications can share data within a defined network. This variation is a huge advantage when trying to communicate important information to a large group of people. This difference in communication settings is illustrated below:

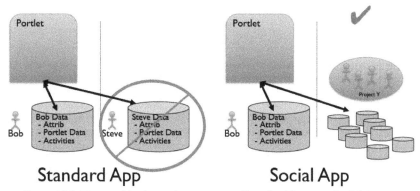

Figure 10.1: The graphic above demonstrates Standard Apps vs. Social Apps.

Liferay has a constantly improving set of social features which enable you to encourage social interactions on your own portal and to leverage the power and popularity of other social networks. In this chapter, we'll discuss:

- General use social portlets
- Social portlets for personal pages
- Configuring personal pages for social networking
- How to connect users using Liferay social relations
- Social equity
- Integrating Liferay with other social sites

When we're finished, you'll be well equipped to use Liferay to power your social network.

10.1   Leveraging Social Portlets, Activities Tracking, and User Connections

Liferay has many portlets available for social interaction and collaboration. Some of these portlets are designed to help you work together as a team, while others are designed to foster social interactions between team members at your organization.

Some of the social networking portlets should be used on the public pages of your portal, while others should be used as part of a user's personal site. As you might expect, the portlets intended for personal page use are more focused on simple social interactions while the ones which can be placed on any site help teams interact and improve productivity.

Unless otherwise noted, these portlets are provided with minimal configuration options. Most of them have at least two configuration options—the option to change permissions for the portlet view and sharing options for connecting the portlet to other web sites. Some of the social networking portlets provide additional options for customizing feed lengths or display styles. Additional styling changes can be made through custom CSS.

Using the Core Liferay Social Portlets

Out-of-the box, Liferay provides four social portlets:

- Activities
- User Statistics
- Group Statistics
- Requests

The Activities portlet displays information about user activity in the site to which the portlet was added. User activities tracked by the Activities portlet include updates to the Documents and Media library, blog posts, message boards posts, wiki pages, and bookmarks. The Activities portlet also tracks information about web content but only displays this information if the logged-in user is a site administrator. The Activities portlet functions similarly to Facebook's news feed: it provides a summary of recent site activity. The Activities portlet could be used on a site's public or private pages to show what site members have been up to or it could be used on the public or private pages of a user's personal site. When added to a personal site, the Activities portlet just shows the activities of a single user.

Note that the Activities portlet provides links to the assets described in its activities feed. However, the links to the assets won't work unless there's a way to display the assets on the page. For example, suppose that the user Joe Bloggs uploaded a document called *Lunar Resort happenings for August* to a site. If the Activities portlet has been placed on a page

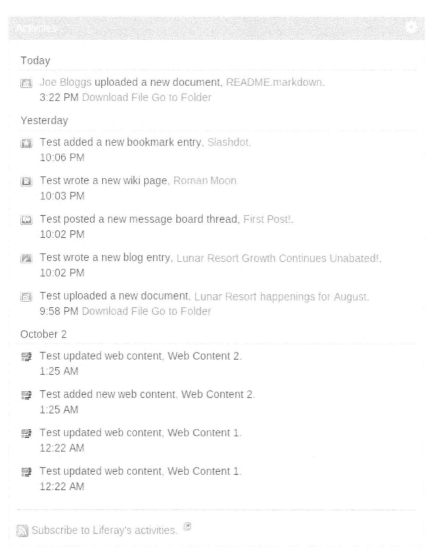

Figure 10.2: The Activities portlet displays information about asset-related user activity
in the current site. It only displays information about web content if the current user is
a site administrator.

of that site, it will display a feed entry with a link to the *Lunar Resort happenings for August* document. However, the link won't work unless there's a Documents and Media portlet or a Documents and Media Display portlet for the document to be displayed in. Remember add the appropriate portlets to the page of the Activities portlet if you want the Activities portlet's links to work.

The User Statistics and Group Statistics portlets integrate with Liferay's social activity system which tracks user activity and assigns points for various actions. They're useful for displaying various kinds of statistical information such as the most active users, the average number of activities per day and the highest periods of activity. The exact information that's displayed is configurable and you can add counters to track many different kinds of information such as the number of comments on users' assets, number of subscriptions to users' assets, number of blog entries by the user, number of blog entry updates by the user, number of message board posts, etc. Although these are core Liferay portlets, they're only useful if Liferay's social activity system has been enabled for your site. We'll discuss the User Statistics and Group Statistics in more detail once after we've discussed Liferay's social activity system.

Lastly, the Requests portlet can be added to pages of users' personal sites to allow users to respond to social requests such as friend requests. The Requests portlet is usually added to the private page set of a personal site since only one user, the owner of the personal site, is allowed to use it. The Requests portlet is a core Liferay portlet but is only useful if there's some way to send social requests, such as friend requests. This functionality can be added by installing the Social Networking app from Liferay Marketplace. It's also possible to develop and deploy custom portlets that implement Liferay's social API to enable social requests. Please refer to the Liferay Developer Network or the Javadocs for information about Liferay's social API.

Installing the Social Networking Portlets

Social Activity can be enabled on a per-site basis in Liferay Portal. The Activities, User Statistics, and Group Statistics portlet can be used out-of-the box. Liferay provides additional social networking functionality in the form of the Social Networking app that's available from Liferay Marketplace. The Social Networking app provides a number of social portlets that allow you do anything from building an intranet to improve your team's ability to collaborate to building a public social networking site to rival Facebook or LinkedIn!

The Social Networking app provides the following portlets:

- Friends
- Friends' Activities
- Wall
- Map
- Members
- Members' Activities
- Meetups
- Summary

If these social networking portlets aren't enough to satisfy your needs, make sure to check out Liferay Social Office which is also available as an app on Liferay Marketplace. Social Office provides additional portlets and functionality including contacts, microblogs, events, tasks, private messaging, site templates, and a custom theme.

You can manage the plugins in your portal from the Control Panel. If you're logged in as an administrator, go to the Control Panel and click on *App Manager* in the *Apps* section. From here, you can administer all your plugins. For now, we'll deal with the *Social*

Networking app. Under the Apps heading, click *Store* to navigate to Liferay Marketplace.
Install and download the *Social Networking* portlet to your portal instance.

Now that we have our social plugins ready to go, let's learn how to use them!

Using Social Networking on Public Pages

There are several social portlets that are designed for use on public portal pages. The goal
of these is to use social connections to help a group work together more closely. These
include the **Members**, **Meetups**, **Summary**, and **Activities** portlets.

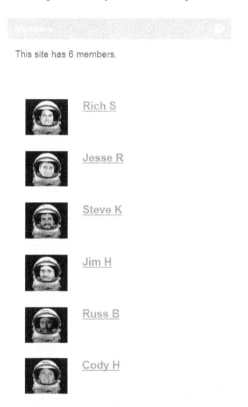

Figure 10.3: The *Members* portlet displays all the members of a particular site.

The Members portlet is a simple list of all the current site's members. The only configuration options you have are permissions, which are the same for every portlet. For
example, you might change the permissions so only members of the current site can view
the portlet.

The Meetups portlet is a tool for creating casual meetings for users of your portal. Anyone can create a "meetup" and give it a title, description, date/time, maximum number of
attendees, price and provide an image. Any meetups that are created are displayed in the
portlet for anyone to view. Users can register for the meetup, which lets the organizer
keep track of who's coming.

The options for creating a meetup are essentially the same as those for creating a calendar event and the Meetups portlet shares some functionality with the Calendar. For more
information on the Calendar portlet and configuring events, see chapter 8.

Figure 10.4: Meetups are organized in the two tabs *All Meetups* and *My Meetups*.

The Activities portlet comes in two varieties: the standard Activities portlet and the Members' Activities portlet. The basic function of the portlets are the same—they both display a feed of what users are doing on the portal. The difference is that Activities displays what's going on across the entire portal, while Members' Activities displays only what members of the current site have been doing. There's also a Friend's Actvities portlet that's intended for use on users' personal pages. In the Configuration dialog box of any variety of the Activities portlet, you can use the *Maximum Activities to Display* dropdown menu to set a limit on how many activities can be displayed at once in the portlet window.

The Map portlet allows you to view the locations of site members, both locally and

Figure 10.5: All of your site members' activities are listed with brief descriptions and time stamps.

internationally. Only members of the site to which the Map portlet has been added are displayed. In order to configure the Map portlet, you need to install the IP Geocoder portlet (available from Liferay Marketplace) and configure it to access MaxMind GeoIP or GeoLite on your server. For more information on configuring geolocation services, visit the MaxMind support page at http://www.maxmind.com/app/installation?city=1. Once you've installed the Geocoder portlet and configured it to access MaxMind GeoIP or GeoLite, you'll need a key from Google to access Google's Maps API so your Map portlet will work. Visit https://developers.google.com/maps/documentation/javascript/tutorial#api_key to learn how to obtain a valid Google API key. To configure the Map portlet using the GeoLite City database, use the following steps:

1. Install the Social Networking plugin, if you haven't already done so.

View Larger Map »

Figure 10.6: The Map portlet can be placed on a single user's page to display one
location or on the main site page to display all users' location.

2. Install the IP Geocoder portlet. (Both the Social Networking and IP Geocoder apps
   can be installed from Martketplace.)

3. Shut down your application server.

4. Download the Geo Lite City database from http://www.maxmind.com/download/
   geoip/database/GeoLiteCity.dat.gz.

5. Unzip the .dat file to your desired storage location.

6. Create a portlet-ext.properties file in the /[ROOT]/webapps/ip-geocoder-
   -portlet/WEB-INF/classes/ directory of your Liferay installation.

7. Add the property maxmind.database.file=[database file] to this file.

   Note: Make sure your the file's directory path is separated by \\. For example:
   E:\\ce\\bundles\\GeoLiteCity.dat.

8. Create a portlet-ext.properties file in the /[ROOT]/webapps/social-net-
   working-portlet/WEB-INF/classes/ directory of your Liferay installation.

9. Add the property map.google.maps.api.key={Your API Key} to this file. If
   you haven't done so already, you'll need to generate a Google Maps API Key.[1]

10. Restart your application server.

11. Enjoy the Maps portlet!

Next, let's look at the social networking portlets designed for use on personal pages.

Using Social Networking on Personal Pages

In addition to the portlets available for general use, there are a handful that can only be
used on personal pages. These include the Summary, Wall, Friends, and Friends' Activities portlets. These portlets can be used to create profile pages similar to Facebook's or
Google+'s.

---

[1]https://developers.google.com/maps/documentation/javascript/tutorial#api_key

Figure 10.7: You can get creative with Social Networking portlets and make a custom designed profile page.

The Summary portlet provides a quick overview of a user's profile. When posted in a user's personal site, it displays the user's name, profile picture and job title. Users can add additional personal information by clicking on *Edit* in the portlet and filling in information in the *About Me* section. This portlet is essential to any social implementation on Liferay, because it has the *Friend Request* button. This enables users to initiate social relationships. Note that this portlet simplifies a much more powerful underlying social networking API that defines many different kinds of relationships, including friends. Your developers can take advantage of this API to create powerful social applications. For more information on this, see *Liferay in Action* (Manning Publications)[2] or the Liferay Developer's Network.[3]

The Wall portlet provides a place for users to leave messages on other users' profiles. The messages can only be plain text as no formatting or HTML is supported. Once a post is added to their wall, users have the ability delete it or respond to it with a quick link to post on the original poster's wall.

The Friends portlet shows a list of all the user's friends with links to their profiles. The Friends' Activities portlet displays information about a user's friends' activities on the portal.

Now that we've discussed the functions of the suite of social networking portlets that ships with Liferay, let's put them all together and make a social web site.

---

[2]http://manning.com/sezov
[3]https://dev.liferay.com

Liferay's Social Tools in Action

To get started with Liferay's social features, let's set up the public pages of our users' personal sites to include social apps. Because of Liferay's flexible page layout options, we have a large number of options for how to set the pages up. For simplicity's sake, we'll make something that's fairly similar to the original Facebook layout.

Setting up Users' Personal Pages

Before we start adding portlets to pages, we should configure Liferay so that everyone (or some subset of everyone) has the same social features. We have two ways to do this with advantages and disadvantages to each.

User Groups: Placing users into a group enables you to create a user group site for them. The pages and portlets defined by the user group site are copied to members' personal sites. With the user group site, you can control whether users can modify pages and you can push changes out to users in the future. Once the site template is assigned to a user group, you can set the *Default User Associations* to have all users be the member of a particular group in *Portal Settings* in the Control Panel. The advantage of this is that it can be managed entirely through the GUI and it's easy to configure. If you base your user group's site on a template, you can use the *Enable propagation of changes from the site template* option to manage all user pages simply by changing the template. This is the recommended way to manage personal pages across the portal. For more information on user group sites, see chapter 15.

Portal Properties Configuration: The legacy way to do this is with the configuration file. You can specify a default layout and portlets for personal pages in your `portal-ext-.properties` file. Note that this method applies changes to all users' personal sites. However, it does not provide as much maintainability or as many customization options as does using user group sites. User group sites allow you to choose what's modifiable by the user. For more information on the `portal-ext.properties` method, see *Default User Private Layouts* and *Default User Public Layouts* in chapter 20.

Because it's the recommended method, we'll use the user group method to create the layouts. As an administrator, go to the Control Panel and select *Site Templates* from under the *Sites* section. Click *Add* and fill out the form. We'll call our new site template *Social Layout*. Click *Save*.

Tip: Unchecking *Allow Site Administrators to Modify the Pages Associated with this Site Template* only prevents users from modifying the specific pages contained in the template but does not disable a user's ability to add or modify additional pages.

Once you've created the template, choose *Actions →View Pages*. Let's change the name of the page from the default to *My Profile* and add some portlets to the page. Back in the Control Panel, select *User Groups* from the *Users* section. Once there, click *Add* and name the group *Social Users*. When creating a user group, you have the option to set a user group site; use this option and select the Social Layout template for your Public Pages.

Now go to *Portal Settings* and select *Users* from the submenu. From the Users page, go to the *Default User Associations* tab and enter *Social Users* in the User Groups section. Now all users on the portal get a Social Profile page. Now the question is, how do we encourage users to visit each others fancy new profile pages?

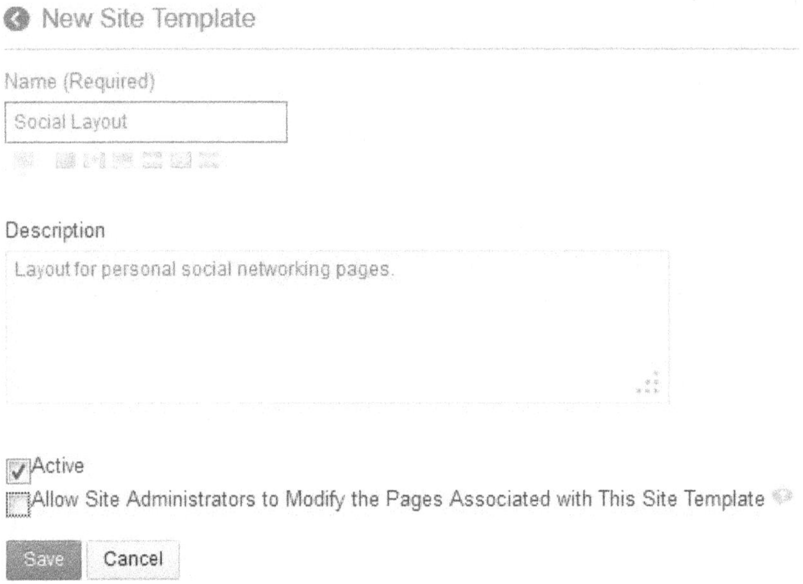

⬅ New Site Template

Name (Required)

Social Layout

Description

Layout for personal social networking pages.

☑ Active
☐ Allow Site Administrators to Modify the Pages Associated with This Site Template

Save   Cancel

Figure 10.8: You can give your site template a custom name and description and also specify several configuration settings..

Connecting Users Through Collaboration

There are many ways that social networks connect users. These generally involve some kind of mutual interest or experience. On a site like Facebook, you can connect with people from school, from work or from other personal connections. On a music based networking site like Last.fm, you can connect with people who have similar tastes to yours. With Liferay's social networking collaboration is the key to connection.

Using our example site of lunar-resort.com, we can take a closer look at ways users can be connected through hierarchies and ways they can connect to each other. We'll look at a handful of portlets, both those designed specifically for connecting users and those that can create connections as a side-effect of just getting work done.

The Site Members Directory portlet can provide a simple way for users to connect. If we have a site dedicated to Lunar Resort astronauts, we can place a Site Members Directory portlet on that site, listing all the users that have joined that site. Users can connect by sending requests to other users on that list. This isn't the worst way to get users connected but it probably won't be very effective. Why not? Well, other than sharing some very basic common interests, we haven't really had any interactions.

The Activities portlet provides a similar but more effective means of connection. Because it shows a list of what other users are doing, this portlet helps users discover who is among the most active across the site or the portal, and thus who might be a good connection.

Probably the most effective way users can connect is by interacting with other users. Every portlet in the Collaboration category provides information on who is contributing, regardless of how. You can see who is creating a thread in a message board, editing a wiki article, blogging or creating a calendar event. Users can use these to connect based on content—if I find your blog interesting, or if you answer my question on the message board, we can use that as a point to connect as friends to further our interactions. This way, instead of our connection being forced or arbitrary, we've connected based on the fact that we've directly interacted and share a common interest—just like people did before they had the internet.

"Friend" is only the default social relationship as implemented by Liferay's social portlets. You can design things so that users are automatically connected through Site and Organization membership. And there are many other relationship types beyond Friend: your developers can take advantage of these by using Liferay's social API. This is covered in *Liferay in Action* and the *Liferay Developer Network*. Now that you've got all these social applications running on your system, you might wonder: how can I measure social interaction? How do I identify the best contributors to my site? Liferay has an answer: social activity measurements.

10.2 Measuring Social Activity

When you have a lot of user interaction on your web site, it can be helpful to try to separate the signal from the noise. Liferay contains a lot of applications which end users can use to communicate with each other and provide information. Some of this information is good and helpful and some of it can be rather unhelpful. Using Liferay's Social Activity feature will help show which users are making real, valuable contributions.

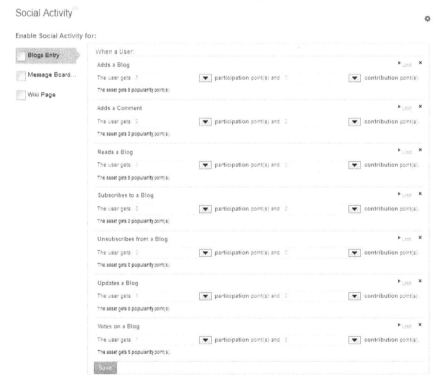

Figure 10.9: The Social Activity page of the Control Panel allows you to enable social activity for assets and specify points for participation and contributions.

To activate Social Activity, you'll first need to determine which collaboration applications you want to use Social Activity. There are currently three types of content you can use with Social Activity - Blogs Entries, Message Board Messages, and Wiki Pages. Activation is a la carte - so you can use it on one, two, or all three applications. Social Activity tracks three metrics from within each of these applications two are for the user - *Participation* and *Contribution* - and the other, *Popularity*, is for the asset involved.

Let's activate Social Activity for Blogs Entries. Check the box next to *Blog Entry*. You now have options to set point values and limits on several different actions for blogs. You'll notice each item on the list has dropdowns you can use to set the number of participation and contribution points; popularity points are tied directly to contribution points. In addition to that, you can expand the box by clicking *Limits* in the top right of each list item. You can use this to set a limit on how many times a user can perform this activity with a specific asset and receive the requisite points. For some activities, you can set limits on both participation and contribution points, but on new content creation, you can only set limits on participation points.

It might not be immediately obvious, but for all actions that do not involve the creation of a new asset, all of the contribution points go to the original asset creator and all popularity points go to the original asset. That means if *Votes on a Blog* is set to have 1 *Participation* point and 5 *Contribution* points (and therefore 5 *Popularity* points), the user who votes on the asset will receive 1 participation point, the user who created the asset will receive 5 contribution points, and the asset will receive 5 popularity points.

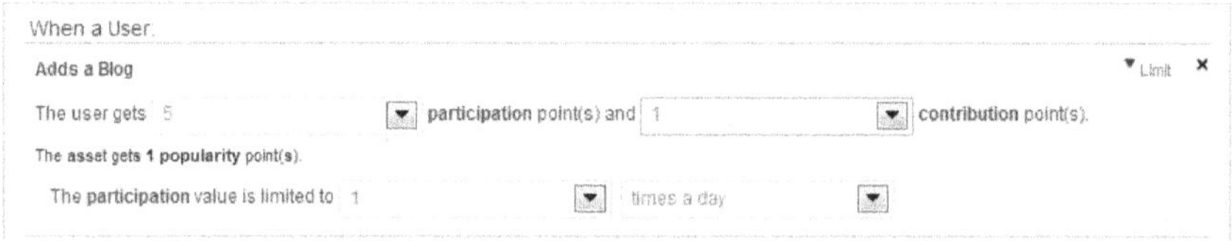

Figure 10.10: You can set limits for your site's social activity.

It's easy to assign points—you can arbitrarily assign points for just about anything—the challenge is making the points significant in some way. As mentioned before, the primary purpose of social activity tracking is to make sure that users who regularly contribute to the portal and participate in discussions are recognized as such. So the central piece of the social equity display is the *User Statistics* portlet.

The User Statistics portlet displays a list of users ranked by an amalgamation of their participation and contribution scores. By clicking on the Configuration icon for the portlet, you can change some of the specifics of the rankings. There are five check boxes that you can enable or disable:

Rank by Contribution: If this is checked, a user's contribution score will be used as a factor in calculating their rank.

Rank by Participation: If this is checked, a user's participation score will be used as a factor in calculating their rank.

Show Header Text: Determines whether the title shows or only the rankings.

Show Totals: Toggles the display of the users activity score next to their name.

Display Additional Activity Counters: You can toggle the display of any number of other pieces of information next to the users name in the statistics, ranging from the number of comments on assets a user has created to the number of wiki articles that the user has created. If you want to display multiple data points, you can click the *plus* button to add one and the *minus* button to remove one. You can have as many data points displayed as you want, but displaying too many might make your portlet a little unwieldy.

The *Group Statistics* portlet provides some more advanced data analytics. If you add it to a page, and click on the configuration icon, you can select the assets to track. You can click the *plus* button to add additional slots, and choose from the various metrics available for each slot, covering virtually any action that a user can perform on content in the portal.

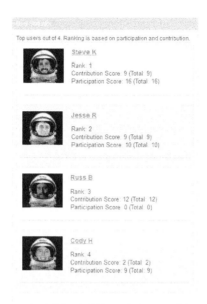

Figure 10.11: The User Statistics portlet gives rankings to promote user contributions and participation.

If you decide that you're displaying too many metrics, you can click the *minus* button for a particular slot on the configuration view to remove it.

There are a wide-ranging number of actions that you can provide social credit for. Users can receive credit for everything from subscribing to a blog to writing wiki articles. You can easily tweak the numbers in the Control Panel if it becomes clear that certain activities are weighted too high or too low.

Social Activity can be an invaluable tool for portals that are heavily driven by community-created content. It allows you to easily recognize users who are major contributors and it indicates to new users whose advice will be most trustworthy. Social Activity is easy to set up and can be configured differently for each site, increasing the flexibility of your portal.

Beyond Liferay's social API, there is also support for the OpenSocial standard.

10.3 Exporting Portal Apps as Widgets and OpenSocial Gadgets

OpenSocial is a framework designed for the creation of socially themed application programming interfaces (APIs). OpenSocial applications, called *gadgets*, can be used in any web-based application that supports them. They are characterized as simple, widely available, and easy to deploy. Gadgets are especially popular on social networking sites. They can, however, be used in many different ways throughout your site.

Liferay allows any OpenSocial gadget to be used on a page. An OpenSocial gadget is specified in an XML document and consists of embedded HTML and JavaScript. Liferay allows gadgets to communicate with each other and with portlets. This allows your gadgets to run seamlessly without your having to constantly check or update their content. They automatically update based on their connections with other applications. OpenSocial gadgets support numerous open web technologies such as *OAuth*, which we'll discuss in more detail later in the chapter.

Gadgets are socially aware and can share data across a community of users. You can define your own groups and create gadgets to communicate information based on pages (community/team pages), applications (gadgets/widgets/portlets), data, users, roles and authorization, and policies. In short, you can develop gadgets to allow individuals to access and share data within their social networks.

Adding OpenSocial Gadgets

The OpenSocial plugin can be installed through Liferay Marketplace for both Liferay CE and EE. Installing the OpenSocial plugin enables you to add OpenSocial gadgets to pages, just like you'd add portlets. There are two types of gadgets:

- "Adhoc" gadgets that users can add to a page via URL
- Gadgets published by the Control Panel that are available portal-wide

First, we'll go through steps to add an Adhoc gadget to a page.

Adding Adhoc Gadgets

This method is a quick way to add a gadget to a single page. To do this, go to the *Add →More* menu and add *OpenSocial Gadget* to the page. The portlet displays a link to pick a gadget for display:

Figure 10.12: Configure a gadget to display in your portlet.

Click the configure link and a configuration window opens. Next, you need to insert a URL to an OpenSocial gadget. We'll insert the URL for a colorful calculator which is:

```
http://www.labpixies.com/campaigns/calc/calc.xml
```

After pasting the URL into the text field, click *Save* and your new gadget is visible on your page.

This particular gadget allows you to change its "skins" to fit your needs. Likewise, there are many other user-friendly interactive gadgets that give you flexibility to fit them into your themed sites. As you find gadgets that would work nicely throughout your portal, you can publish them for portal-wide use. You'll learn that next.

Adding Gadgets for Portal-wide Use

You can easily make gadgets available for adding to pages as you would any other application. We'll demonstrate this by adding a *To-Do List* gadget for portal-wide use.

1. Go to the Control Panel and select *OpenSocial Gadget Publisher* under the *Apps* heading

2. Click *Publish Gadget*

3. Insert the URL for the *To-Do List* gadget.[4]

---

[4]http://www.labpixies.com/campaigns/todo/todo.xml

Figure 10.13: The calculator gadget displays seemlessly on your page.

4. Select an appropriate category for your gadget

5. Click *Save*

Figure 10.14: Configure new gadgets with ease.

Your *OpenSocial Gadget Publisher* should now look like this:

Clicking *Actions* next to the gadget enables you to edit, refresh, change permissions on, or delete the gadget. Here is a brief listing of what these four buttons do:

Edit: allows you to change the URL or category.

Figure 10.15: Publish gadgets for portal-wide use via the OpenSocial Gadget Publisher.

Refresh: manually refreshes the gadget cache to reflect changes that have been made to the gadget that may not currently be displayed in the portlet.

Permissions: gives you the basic *View, Update, Delete,* and *Permissions* options for each role on your site.

Delete: removes the listing for the gadget.

If you navigate to *Add →Applications →Gadgets,* you should see the *To-Do List* gadget.

Figure 10.16: You can conveniently list your gadgets within the *Gadgets* category.

In the next section, we'll demonstrate how to share OpenSocial gadgets with other sites.

Sharing OpenSocial Gadgets

OpenSocial consists of a set of APIs for social networking. Liferay implements the OpenSocial standard, so you can be assured that your gadgets run on Liferay. That also means gadgets hosted by a Liferay Portal instance can be deployed and run in any standard OpenSocial container. It may be beneficial for you to share gadgets from your Liferay server with other sites, such as iGoogle. Google's iGoogle lets users customize their own page and add gadgets to their page. Your Liferay Portal users can share their portlets and other OpenSocial gadgets on iGoogle or any other OpenSocial-compatible site. Let's try this now.

Warning: The iGoogle site was removed from Google on November 1, 2013: https://support.google.com/websearch/answer/2664197. Sharing your Liferay OpenSocial gadgets to iGoogle is longer possible. A third-party replacement can be found at http://www.igoogleportal.com.

For our example, we'll share Liferay's *Loan Calculator* on iGoogle.

1. Add the *Loan Calculator* portlet onto your Liferay page

2. Click the gear icon in the upper right corner of the portlet and select *Configuration*

3. Select the *Sharing* tab and the *OpenSocial Gadget* sub-tab

4. Check the box labeled *Allow users to add Loan Calculator to iGoogle*. Also, replace "localhost:8080" with the name of your public domain and port.

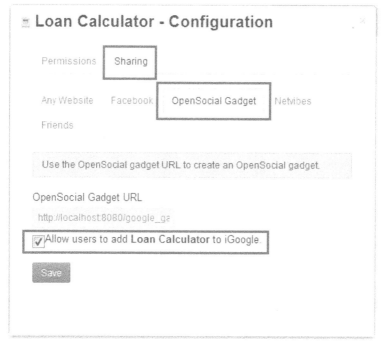

Figure 10.17: Allow users to add your portlet as an OpenSocial Gadget in iGoogle.

5. Click Save

6. Close out the window and navigate back to the wrench icon in the upper right corner of your portlet. There is a new option named *Add to iGoogle* available. Click on this button to add your portlet to your iGoogle page.

Your portlet is now available on your iGoogle page!

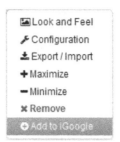

Figure 10.18: Users simply click the *Add to iGoogle* button to add your portlet to their iGoogle page.

By going through this process, Liferay shared the URL of your portlet to iGoogle. The URL you provided is unique to your specific instance of the portlet. This allows you to share multiple instances of the same portlet as different Google Gadgets.

You could use this sharing capability to let users view what's happening on your portal at a glance. As you can imagine, you can share all kinds of information from your portal gadgets and portlets with your various circles of friends, colleagues, and fellow community members.

Gadget Personalization

Liferay allows gadgets on your site to be personalized with data from third-party applications. Some of the third-party sites that authorize users to access application data include Evernote, Facebook, Google, Netflix, Photobucket, and Yahoo. Of course, many users feel uncomfortable giving away their private credentials to access these applications. Fortunately, Liferay allows you to use *OAuth* to protect your credentials while you access resources on these sites.

OAuth is an open standard that authorizes third-party applications to interact with a user's resources. Users can share their private resources from one site with another site without supplying typical credentials, such as their user name and password. OAuth uses request and access tokens as well as a token secret to authenticate the users of your gadget. For more information on OAuth and how it can be incorporated into your portal, visit the OAuth section of this guide.

Let's see how to implement OAuth in a custom OpenSocial gadget!

OAuth Admin Configuration

OpenSocial defines a specification that allows gadgets to incorporate OAuth to access protected resources from service providers. A brief example is provided to demonstrate how easy it is to leverage OAuth within gadgets on your site.

For this example, we'll set up a demo Twitter account gadget using OAuth. First we must configure your gadget. Follow the steps below to acquire the consumer key and secret given by the service provider.

1. Similar to previous examples, add the Twitter Demo gadget to your page. Go to the Control Panel and click on *OpenSocial Gadget Publisher* under the *Apps* heading. Click *Publish Gadget* and insert the Twitter Demo URL:

   ```
   https://raw.github.com/dejuknow/opensocial-gadgets/master/Twitter/Twitter.xml
   ```

2. Click *Save*

3. For OAuth-enabled gadgets, you can select the *Manage OAuth* button from the *Actions* tab. Select *Manage OAuth* for your Twitter gadget. As shown below, you have several options under "twitter" that you must fill in to configure your gadget. You must also register your gadget with Twitter to access the Consumer Key and Consumer Secret.

Figure 10.19: Twitter allows you to manage OAuth for your Twitter gadget.

4. Go to https://dev.twitter.com and click *Get started with the platform* to begin registering your gadget.

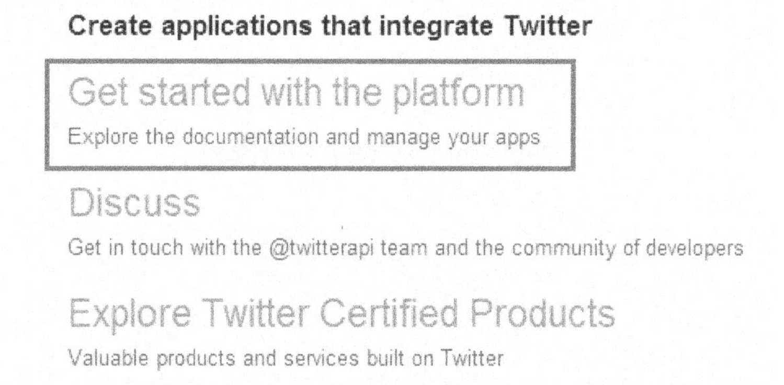

Create applications that integrate Twitter

Get started with the platform
Explore the documentation and manage your apps

Discuss
Get in touch with the @twitterapi team and the community of developers

Explore Twitter Certified Products
Valuable products and services built on Twitter

Figure 10.20: Select *Get started with the platform* from within the *Developers* page.

5. Navigate to the *REST API* heading and click *Manage & create your applications*. Then click *Create New App*.

6. Fill in the *Name*, *Description*, and *Website* fields with what you prefer.

   a. For the *Callback URL* field, enter Liferay's default callback URL[5]. Replace "myLiferayServer" with an appropriate value—for this demonstration, use your machine's local loopback address: 127.0.0.1:8080.

   b. Finally, select the *Create your Twitter application* tab at the bottom of the page.

---

[5]http://myLiferayServer/opensocial-portlet/gadgets/oauthcallback

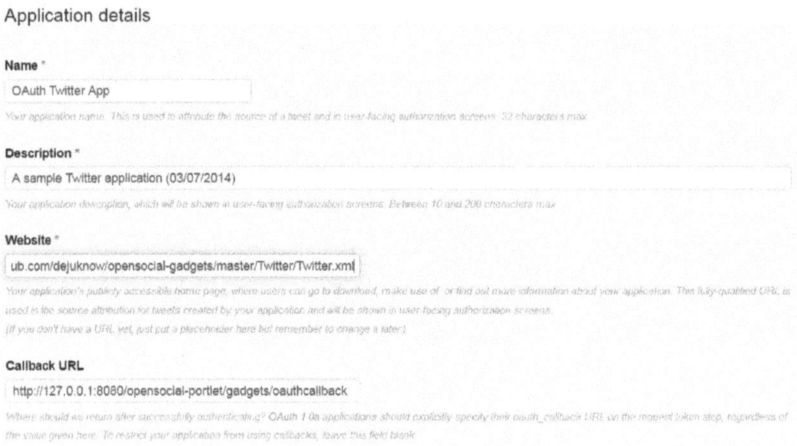

Application details

Name *

OAuth Twitter App

Your application name. This is used to attribute the source of a tweet and in user-facing authorization screens. 32 characters max.

Description *

A sample Twitter application (03/07/2014)

Your application description, which will be shown in user-facing authorization screens. Between 10 and 200 characters max.

Website *

ub.com/dejuknow/opensocial-gadgets/master/Twitter/Twitter.xml

Your application's publicly accessible home page, where users can go to download, make use of, or find out more information about your application. This fully-qualified URL is used in the source attribution for tweets created by your application and will be shown in user-facing authorization screens.
(If you don't have a URL yet, just put a placeholder here but remember to change it later.)

Callback URL

http://127.0.0.1:8080/opensocial-portlet/gadgets/oauthcallback

Where should we return after successfully authenticating? OAuth 1.0a applications should explicitly specify their oauth_callback URL on the request token step, regardless of the value given here. To restrict your application from using callbacks, leave this field blank.

Figure 10.21: Fill in *Application Details* to setup connectivity between your Twitter gadget and your portal.

7. You are given the OAuth setting that you need to configure your gadget on Liferay. Copy the Consumer Key and Consumer Secret to your clipboard.

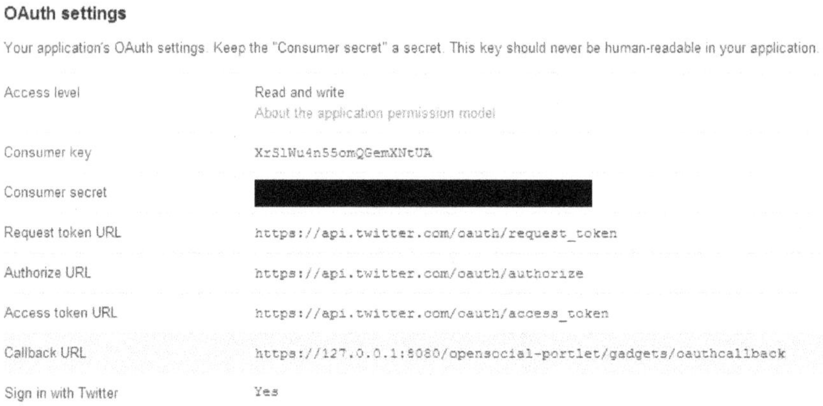

OAuth settings

Your application's OAuth settings. Keep the "Consumer secret" a secret. This key should never be human-readable in your application.

Access level	Read and write
	About the application permission model
Consumer key	XrSlWu4n55omQGemXNtUA
Consumer secret	████████████████████
Request token URL	https://api.twitter.com/oauth/request_token
Authorize URL	https://api.twitter.com/oauth/authorize
Access token URL	https://api.twitter.com/oauth/access_token
Callback URL	https://127.0.0.1:8080/opensocial-portlet/gadgets/oauthcallback
Sign in with Twitter	Yes

Figure 10.22: Here are the *Consumer Key* and *Consumer Secret* (value is blacked out for security reasons).

8. Enter your Consumer Key and Consumer Secret under the *Manage OAuth* that you navigated to earlier. Also, select HMAC_SYMMETRIC for the *Key Type* and then click *Save*.

   Note: Liferay offers PLAINTEXT and RSA_PRIVATE as alternative key types. HMAC symmetric and RSA private are commonly used production key types, whereas plain text should never be used in real-world settings.

9. Navigate to the *Settings* tab and under *Application Type*, select *Read and Write*. Also, select the *Allow this application to be used to Sign in with Twitter* checkbox. Then click *Update this Twitter application's settings* at the bottom of the page.

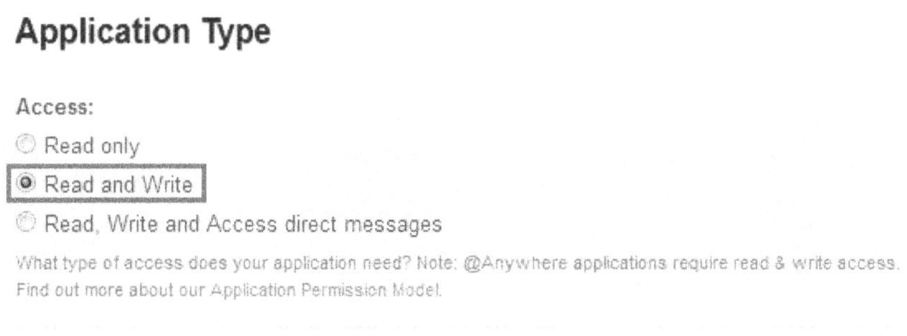

Application Type

Access:

○ Read only

◉ Read and Write

○ Read, Write and Access direct messages

What type of access does your application need? Note: @Anywhere applications require read & write access. Find out more about our Application Permission Model.

Figure 10.23: Select the *Read and Write* option to enable two way communication.

10. Navigate back to the *Details* tab and, at the bottom of the page, click *Create my access token*.

Congratulations! Your Twitter gadget is now configured with OAuth.
Next, we'll configure the gadget within Liferay Portal.

Incorporating OAuth Within Your Site

Now that your gadget is registered with Twitter and is configured with OAuth, you can add it to your Liferay Portal. The OAuth client you configured in the previous section allows users to protect their credentials while accessing resources on your site. For this section, we'll demonstrate how to add the OAuth-configured gadget to your page.

1. Navigate to *My Private Pages* and click *Add More... →Twitter Gadget*. If your gadget is configured correctly, it should appear like this:

Personalize this gadget

Figure 10.24: Your OAuth configured Twitter gadget awaits personalization with your Twitter account.

2. Click on *Personalize this gadget* to be redirected to the service provider.

3. Fill in your Twitter user name and password and select *Authorize app*

4. Your Twitter Gadget should now show your last 20 tweets from your timeline. Your gadget should look similar to the snapshot below:

5. Using this gadget, you can tweet your current status and have it display on your Liferay site and Twitter page. To change the amount of tweets displayed, click on the wrench icon in the upper right corner and select *Configuration*. Under the *Setup* tab, you can type the number of tweets to display.

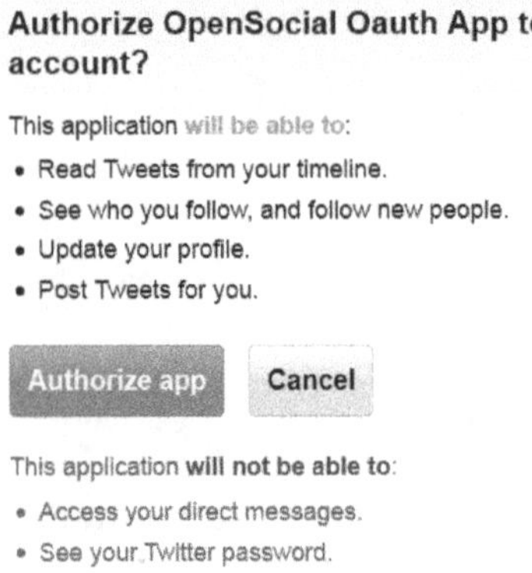

**Authorize OpenSocial Oauth App to use your
account?**

This application will be able to:

- Read Tweets from your timeline.
- See who you follow, and follow new people.
- Update your profile.
- Post Tweets for you.

This application **will not be able to**:

- Access your direct messages.
- See your Twitter password.

Figure 10.25: Authorizing your OpenSocial application to use your account is
straightforward.

6. Lastly, you can tweet and view your Twitter timeline. The snapshot below displays
   what the Twitter Gadget looks like when tweeting.

   As you can see, OAuth is easy to configure and offers users the freedom to securely
   add valuable data from third-party sites.

Creating and Editing OpenSocial Gadgets

Figure 10.26: Check out your Twitter gadget timeline!

OpenSocial gadgets are XML documents, so as part of Liferay's OpenSocial integration, a gadget editor is included. The gadget editor is a complete development environment for gadgets providing syntax highlighting, a preview function, undo/redo
options, and built in tabs for working on multiple gadgets at once. You can also organize and manage gadgets through a simple file manager embedded into the portlet. To access the gadget editor, go to *Site Administration Configuration →Content* and
click *OpenSocial Gadget Editor*.

Once you have created and saved a gadget using the editor, click on the wrench next
to the file to rename, delete, publish or get the URL for your gadget. If you want to
display your gadget somewhere, click *Publish* to choose a category and display your

gadget in the application menu or click *Show URL* to get a URL to display your gadget on any site that supports OpenSocial.

In addition to the social interactions that you can create on your portal, Liferay can integrate with some other popular social networks. This enables you to leverage their power and popularity for your portal's content.

10.4   Integrating with Facebook

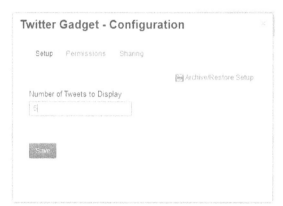

Figure 10.27: Configure the number of Tweets to display.

Facebook is currently the number one social network in the world with somewhere over 1 billion active users. If you're trying to build acommunity on your portal, you don't want to neglect a bridge to that many possible users. With that in mind, Liferay provides a few easy ways for you to integrate your portal with Facebook.

Facebook Sign On

Like many web sites you may visit, any portal running on Liferay can be set up to use Facebook for sign in. This makes it easier for users to sign in to your site, since they won't need to remember another user name and password, For more information on setting up Facebook sign on, see chapter 15.

Using your Portlets as Facebook Applications

You can add any Liferay portlet as an application on Facebook. To do this, you must first get a developer key. A link for doing this is provided to you in the Facebook tab in any portlet's Configuration screen. You will have to create the application on Facebook and get the key and canvas page URL from Facebook. Once you've done this you can copy and paste their values into the Facebook tab. Your portlet is now available on Facebook.

This integration enables you to make things like Message Boards, Calendars, Wikis, and other content on your portal available to a much larger audience (unless you already have a billion users on your site, in which case, kudos to you).

10.5   Integrating with Twitter

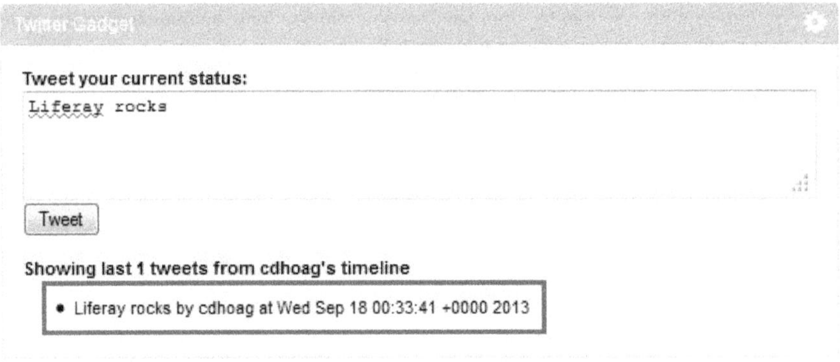

Figure 10.28: Here is your Twitter gadget just the way you like it!

Liferay Portal also provides integration with Twitter via the Twitter app on Liferay Marketplace. Once you register your Twitter username with the app, your tweets are shown in your Activities portlet along with your activity feed. Make sure that you get the appropriate version of the app for your Liferay instance. The Twitter CE app is intended for Liferay Portal CE, while the Twitter EE app is intended for Liferay Portal EE.

There are two ways to register your Twitter username with the app after you install it. The first is through the Twitter portlet after you add it to a page. Click the link in the portlet and then enter your Twitter username in the Twitter field. Alternatively, from the Dockbar select *User →My Account →Social Network* and then enter your Twitter username in the Twitter field.

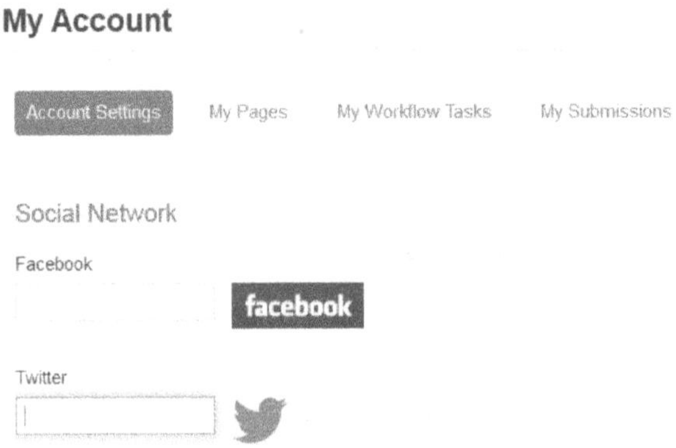

Figure 10.29: Register your Twitter account.

It's important to note that your tweets are displayed *only* in an Activities portlet. If you want your tweets to show up on a page, there must be an Activities portlet on it. Also, you need to wait a few minutes after registering your Twitter username for your tweets to show up. Keep in mind that the Activities portlet shows your tweets in order according to the date and time that you originally made them. Therefore, if you haven't tweeted in a while, then your tweets might be pushed off the Activities feed by more recent activity. You can change the number of items shown in the Activities feed in the portlet's Configuration.

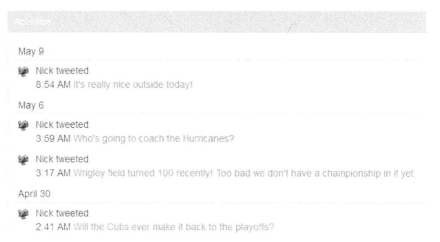

Activities

May 9

🐦 Nick tweeted
   8:54 AM It's really nice outside today!

May 6

🐦 Nick tweeted
   3:59 AM Who's going to coach the Hurricanes?

🐦 Nick tweeted
   3:17 AM Wrigley field turned 100 recently! Too bad we don't have a championship in it yet.

April 30

🐦 Nick tweeted
   2:41 AM Will the Cubs ever make it back to the playoffs?

Figure 10.30: Your tweets are displayed in an Activities portlet.

10.6 Summary

Websites like Facebook and Twitter have attracted hundreds of millions of users by simply giving users a way to connect and communicate with each other. With Liferay, you have the power to either build a portal around social features or enhance a portal built around content and collaboration by providing users with the tools to connect and interact.

To get started, you can use a selection of portlets designed to make users' personal public pages a place where they can interact with each other by learning about other users and communicate using a simple messaging system. Using the now ubiquitous concept of "friends," users can also form a long term connection with other users they frequently work with or with whom they share similar interests.

Outside of users' personal pages, you have a variety of portlets, like the activity portlets, which are designed to help users identify other users that might be working on similar projects, and keep track of what's going on around the portal. You can even use the Social Activity feature to give credit where credit is due and recognize the users who contribute the most.

Reaching even further out, Liferay provides integration with other sites and services that enable you to connect with users outside of your portal, either by pulling content from other websites using OpenSocial integration, or by pushing content on your portal out to a broader audience using Facebook integration. We've outlined the tools you have available, now it's up to you to leverage Liferay's Social Networking features in the way that best fits your portal.

## CHAPTER 11

USING WEB FORMS AND DYNAMIC DATA LISTS

As needs change in business and organizations, the technology used to fulfill those needs must adapt as well. People use electronic means to do things that years ago were done using manual processes. For example, you may want your team to sign up on your web site for a holiday party. Or maybe every fall, you need to put up a job posting board, only allowing administrators to create new job posts. Maybe you want to allow users to manage a notebook or To-Do list on their private pages. In all of these cases, you want to enter in custom sets of data, allow your users to add their information, and be able to access the set of data.

In the past, you'd need to be a developer to accomplish any of this. Today, you can do it without writing a single line of code. Enter Liferay's *Dynamic Data Lists*. This is an easy way to create, aggregate, and display new data types. Data Lists are flexible enough to handle all types of data, and you don't have to write any code. Simply put, Liferay gives you the power to perform the following actions:

- Define your own data definitions

- Create new lists from those definitions

- Customize the input forms for ease of use

- Customize the output format

- Integrate lists into Workflow

All of this capability can be easily distilled into two concepts: data defining and data displaying. These data lists are dynamic for a reason: they are flexible and powerful. Whether you want to collect simple input from the user or develop an entire data entry system for real estate listings, Dynamic Data Lists have your use case covered. Combined with the flexibility provided through templates and the power of languages like Velocity, entire applications can be built in a short time.

11.1 Building a List Platform in Liferay and Defining Data Types

To expand and extend the social capabilities of our site, we want to build a new, radical platform on Liferay: custom-built lists that users can share and collaborate on with their friends (or enemies, depending on their Social Relation type). Marketing has come up with a great name for our new service: list.it. Our beautiful list.it dashboard will give users the power to generate their own lists, see the lists of their friends and tally the results of certain types of lists (surveys, anyone?). Liferay makes this as simple as throwing some Dynamic Data List Display and Form portlets on the public and private pages of users' personal sites.

When new users log in to list.it, they are going to want to build a few lists for themselves. Chances are, many of the lists they would want to create—to do lists, shopping lists and memos come to mind—are already defined in the portal. All the user has to do is create a new list, choose that pre-defined data type, and have at it! A number of data definitions ship with the portal's default site to help you get started. These include *To Do, Issues Tracking, Meeting Minutes*, and *Contacts*. Use these on their own to generate new data lists or tweak them to fit your use case.

If none of the built-in data definitions suits your needs, you can define your own. Perhaps we want to allow our list.it users (who would probably call themselves "list-ers" or "list-ies") to create their own data types for lists they create. In this case, they would need to have unfettered access to the content of their private user site where they can create a new data type.

Using data lists to outline a new data model is as simple as point and click. You now have a list.it account and have been dying to bug your friends and family to sign up for "volunteer" work: helping you move into a new apartment. Using an intuitive visual editor, you can quickly draw up the skeleton for that volunteer list in minutes. Since data lists exemplify a unique type of content for your site, you can find them in the Content section Site Administration area of the Control Panel. To manage the dynamic data lists of your site, click *Admin* from the Dockbar and select *Content*. Then click on *Dynamic Data Lists*.

From the Dynamic Data Lists portlet in the Control Panel, you can either click *Add* to create a new dynamic data list from an existing data type or you can click *Manage Data Definitions* to add or edit data definitions. Liferay 6.2 introduced the *Copy* action which copies the DDM templates associated with an existing data definition. You can access the Copy button by navigating to *Manage Data Definitions* and clicking *Actions →Copy* next to a data definition. The Copy menu includes options for copying the form and displaying templates associated with the data definition. We'll discuss how to manage and create form and display templates later in the chapter. When you're finished, the copied data definition can be accessed in the *Manage Data Definitions* menu. The Copy feature lets you create new data definitions based on existing ones. You can use the copied version as a checkpoint and work off of it.

If you want to use a new data type, you need to create a definition for it. From the Dynamic Data Lists portlet in the Control Panel, click *Manage Data Definitions* and click the *Add* button. The first thing you

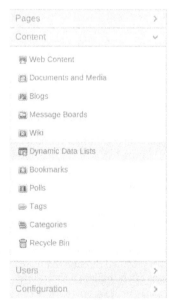

Figure 11.1: You can manage dynamic data lists from the Content section of the Site Administration area of the Control Panel.

should enter is a name for the definition and a description. Create a new data definition called *Volunteer Sign-Up*. When creating a new data definition, you have a palette of fields to lay out, as well as a blank canvas to construct the definition. The interface looks similar to creating and editing web content structures covered previously. Let's explore the different data types at our disposal:

Boolean: presents a checkbox to the user and stores either a true (checked) or false (unchecked) based on state.

Date: a preformatted text field that displays a convenient date picker to assist in selecting the desired date. The format for the date is governed by the current locale.

Decimal: similar to *Number*, except that it requires a decimal point (.) be present.

Documents and Media: select an existing uploaded document to attach to the data record. Also has the ability to upload documents into the Document Library.

HTML: An area that uses a WYSIWYG editor to enhance the content.

Integer: similar to *Number*, except that it constrains user input to non-fractional numbers.

Link to Page: Inserts a link to another page in the same site.

Number: a text box that only accepts numbers as inputs, but puts no constraints on the kind of number entered.

Radio: presents the user with a list of options to choose from using radio button inputs. Values are stored as strings. Similar to *Select*.

Select: a selection of options for the user to choose from using a combo box. Can be configured to allow multiple selections, unlike *Radio*.

Text: a simple text field for any string input.

Text Box: a large text box for long text input.

Figure 11.2: You can combine many different kinds of fields to form a list definition and you can configure various settings and properties for each field.

Using that reference as a nice cheat-sheet, you can now create the data type you need for "Volunteer Work Sign-Up." Use a *Text* type for the name. For all the tasks your friends and family can volunteer to do for you, use *Select* to allow users to choose from a list of tasks. Finally, don't forget a *Documents and Media* field users can upload images of themselves. After all, how much more official-feeling and fun is it if you can print out some nifty badges? To add these fields, drag them from the palette on the left to the work area on the right.

When creating data definitions, you can also customize the appearance of the input fields and provide helpful tips and hints for those entering data. Some data types have specific configuration options but all have some in common. The following properties can be edited in three ways: 1) by double-clicking on any field, 2) by clicking the wrench icon in the upper-right corner of the field or 3) by clicking the *Settings* tab when the field is selected. Let's take a look at the properties you can edit for each of these field types:

Type: Lists the type of field placed in the definition. This is not editable but is available to reference from a display template.

Field Label: Sets the text that can be displayed with the field. This is the human-readable text that the user sees.

Show Label: When set to *Yes*, the label is shown with the form field.

Required: When set to *Yes*, this field must have data in it for a new entry to be submitted (not available for Boolean).

Name: The name of the field internally, automatically generated. Since this is the variable name that you can read the data from in a display template, you should give a more memorable name here.

Predefined Value: If you would like example data or a default value for the user to start with, enter it here. The field's value defaults to this when adding a new entry.

Tip: Each field can have a small help icon, with a tooltip attached that displays helpful information. If you would like to provide text for the tooltip you may enter it here.

Indexable: When set to *Yes*, Liferay is able to index your field for search.

Repeatable: When set to *Yes*, the field is repeatable. Your users can then add as many copies of this field as they like.

Width: Sets the visual width of the form on the page. It does not affect the values that are stored. Possible values are *Small*, *Medium* and *Large* (not available for Boolean, Documents and Media, Radio, and Select).

Multiple: When set to *Yes*, allows the user to select more than one option. This defaults to no (only available for Select).

Options: Changes the options available for selection. You're able to add and remove options as well as edit each individual option's display name and VALUE (ONLY AVAILABLE FOR RADIO AND SELECT).

In addition to dragging the fields around to create your desired forms, you can stack inputs within inputs by dragging a field within another field. You can organize your data into unlimited levels of hierarchy, creating the clearest, most logical data model. There is also a duplicate button on each field (the middle button), allowing you to easily clone any field as many times as you need.

Another method to edit your data definition is switching to *Source* mode and manually customizing your structure by editing its XML file. You'll notice by default the *View* mode is selected. Click the *Source* tab to switch to Source mode. This method is for the more experienced developers.

Data definitions also have the capability of inheriting characteristics from other definitions. When a parent data definition is configured, the child definition inherits the parent's fields and settings. Using this feature is helpful when you want to make a similar data definition to one you've already created. For instance, if you'd like to create an advanced sign-up sheet in addition to a regular sign-up sheet, you can simply inherit the characteristics of the regular sheet and only add the additional fields necessary for the advanced sheet. When the advanced sheet is configured, it will display its parent's fields in addition to its own fields.

After you've saved your data definition, Liferay provides a WebDAV URL and a static URL. These values access the XML source of your data definition. To obtain these values, return to your data definition after it has been saved. To learn more about WebDAV or if you'd like to see WebDAV in action, visit the *Document Management* chapter's *WebDAV access* chapter.

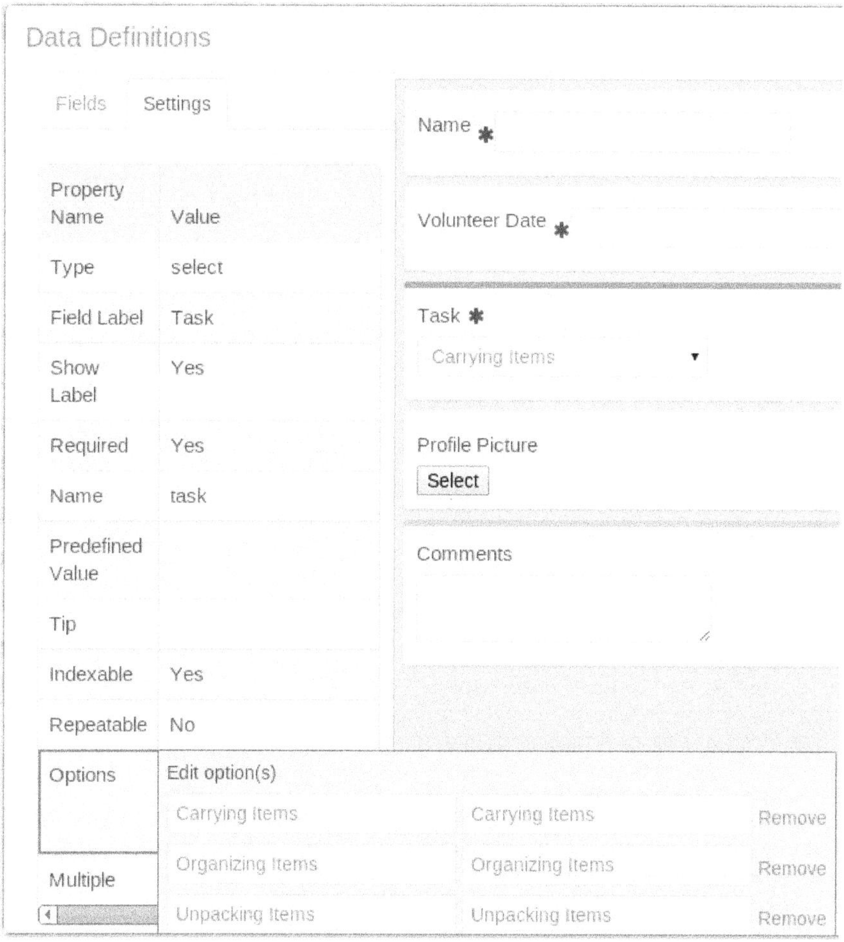

Data Definitions

Fields	Settings		Name ✱
Property Name	**Value**		Volunteer Date ✱
Type	select		
Field Label	Task		Task ✱
Show Label	Yes		Carrying Items ▼
Required	Yes		Profile Picture
Name	task		Select
Predefined Value			Comments
Tip			
Indexable	Yes		
Repeatable	No		

Options	Edit option(s)		
	Carrying Items	Carrying Items	Remove
Multiple	Organizing Items	Organizing Items	Remove
◄	Unpacking Items	Unpacking Items	Remove

Figure 11.3: You can edit the properties of data fields. This allows you to, for example, add and edit selectable options for the *Task* drop-down menu on the Spring Move-In Sign Up form.

That really covers the basic tools that users of list.it need to get rolling with an unlimited array of custom types. Plus, you can always come back and change your form. If you find you needed to add some more information, simply come back to the data definition and fix it. All your data lists that use it are then instantly updated with the new or changed fields.

All that's left to do is build a new data list and let your users play with it.

11.2   Creating Data Lists

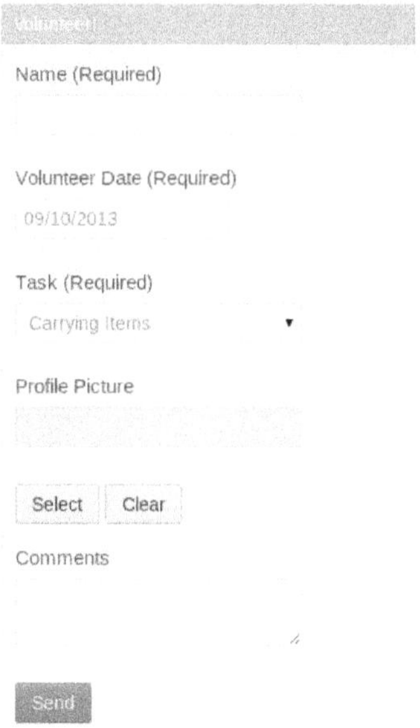

Figure 11.4: You can enter a new data record by clicking on *Admin →Content* from the Dockbar, clicking on *Dynamic Data Lists*, clicking on an existing list, and then clicking on the *Add* button next to the list's name. Alternatively, you can install the Dynamic Data List Form portlet, add it to a page, and configure it to allow users to submit new data records for a lists.

Building out new lists really isn't all that different from creating new pieces of web content. Just as you can create new Web Content Structures to control the input of a particular type of web content, you can use Data List Definitions to control the input of new list types. Similarly, just as you create a new piece of web content, selecting the Structure you would like to use with it, list.it users (we'll call them *Listies*) choose the Definition they want to use when creating a new list. Now that a data definition is in place, all that remains is to create a new data list to capture the information we're going after. This is the easiest step in creating the list, with only a few clicks between a data definition and robust data entry and delivery.

To create a new volunteer list with the "Volunteer Sign-Up" definition:

1. From the Dockbar, click on *Admin* &rrar; *Content* and then on *Dynamic Data Lists*.

2. Click on *Add* to create a new list based on a data definition, which in our case is the volunteer sign-up.

3. Give the data list a name, like *Spring Move-In Sign Up* and a description to assist administrative users in the future.

4. Last and most importantly, click *Select* under the *Data Definition* section—this is where you set the data model that drives this list.

5. Choose the *Volunteer Sign-Up* data definition you created, then click *Save*.

Now that you've created your brand new volunteer list, you can pester everyone you know to sign up. But what would it look like for them to add an entry to this list? The data definition you've previously created (or selected) defines the layout as well, which means the form looks just the way you laid it out.

But how will this data appear? How will my awesome, new Volunteer Sign-Up sheet or that boring Jobs Listing look? The answers to these pressing, burning questions bring us to the mecca that is the display side of this equation.

Using Data List Forms

A nice way to enable people to use your forms is the Dynamic Data List Form portlet. This portlet is tailored to entering new records. When you deploy that data list for your users to sign up for a retreat, or your family members to volunteer to help you move, using the data list form allows you to simplify the sign-up process and hide the contents of the list.

The Dynamic Data List Form portlet is not a core Liferay portlet like the Web Content Display portlet. However, it's freely available on Liferay Marketplace. Just search for and install the Dynamic Data List Form (or Dynamic Data List Form EE) portlet. Using the Dynamic Data List Form is similar to using the Web Content Display portlet: just set it up, point it to a list (either existing or new) and let it go. This is very easy to do.

To display a list inside the portlet, add the Dynamic Data List Form portlet to a page: Click the *Add* button on the left side of the screen, click on *Applications*, search for *Dynamic Data List Form*, then click *Add* next to its name. With the portlet on the page, click on the *Select List* gear icon. This opens a configuration popup, where you can select a list to use for the form entries. When configuring the portlet, make sure to check the *Allow Multiple Submissions* box if you'd like users to be able to add multiple records for a list. If this box is not checked, once a user fills out an entry, the portlet displays a message stating that a record has already been submitted. If the *Allow Multiple Submissions* box is checked, each time a user visits your page with the Sign-Up form, the Dynamic Data List Form portlet presents them with a form to fill out.

> **Note:** If you want to allow guests to submit DDL forms, you'll need to enable the *Allow Multiple Submissions* feature. Liferay treats the Guest user as one user. Therefore, if a guest submits a DDL form, Liferay assumes the Guest user filled out their one form and it won't allow any other guests to submit a form. Thus, allowing the Guest user to submit multiple submissions allows all your guests to submit DDL forms.

Once records have been submitted for lists, you can publish the lists anywhere in your portal. Read on to find out more about that.

Using Default Displays

Lists are published in the portal through the Dynamic Data List Display portlet. If Listies don't customize the display, their lists look something like this:

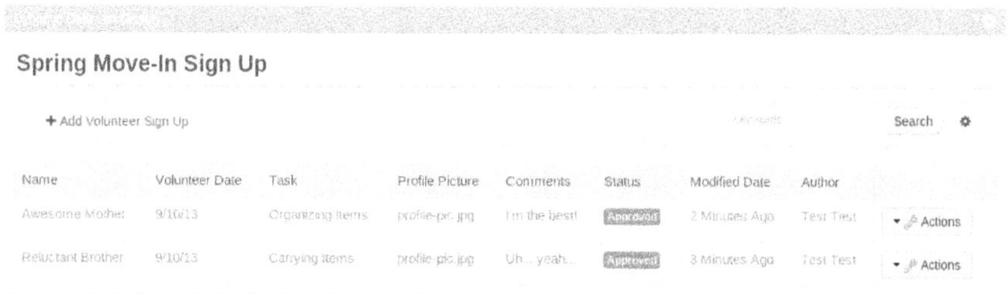

Spring Move-In Sign Up

Name	Volunteer Date	Task	Profile Picture	Comments	Status	Modified Date	Author	
Awesome Mother	9/10/13	Organizing Items	profile-pic.jpg	I'm the best!	Approved	2 Minutes Ago	Test Test	▾ Actions
Reluctant Brother	9/10/13	Carrying Items	profile-pic.jpg	Uh... yeah...	Approved	3 Minutes Ago	Test Test	▾ Actions

+ Add Volunteer Sign Up   Search ⚙

Figure 11.5: The default data list display in the Control Panel shows the list's records and allows record to added, edited, or removed.

This isn't all that exciting, but it allows users to see the list's contents, and if they have permission, to add and/or edit list items. Within a site like list.it, this type of interaction is used for display-only lists that the user chooses to expose to others, or for the user's own private lists. But you can improve the display. You can show the data in a spreadsheet, so you can view the responses to your Volunteer Sign-Up in a comfortable, easy-to-read format. The Dynamic Data List Display portlet provides an easy way for a user (such as a member of a site) to interact with whatever list is active and available.

While it's possible to ask everyone to contribute to the data list within the control panel, it's much better to give them a simple way to access the list. Liferay provides the Dynamic Data List Display portlet to ease the integration of your new list onto your site. With your list in hand, head over to the page you want and add the portlet. It works much like the Dynamic Data List Form portlet and the Web Content Display portlet: use the gear icon to select a list for display or use the pen/paper icon to add a new list. The Dynamic Data List Display portlet is a Liferay core portlet, unlike the Dynamic Data List Form portlet. The default display spills out the contents of the list, but can be configured to use a different display template, which is explored later in this chapter. The two important configuration options to consider are:

Editable: allows users that have permission to add new entries to the list. By default, this is disabled and when enabled, administrators are the only ones with add permission. To easily grant access to other users, edit the permissions on the list you'd like to grant access to, and grant the Add Record permission.

Spreadsheet View: displays the list in a dynamic spreadsheet view. This allows users with permission to interact with the list in the same way as in a standard spreadsheet program.

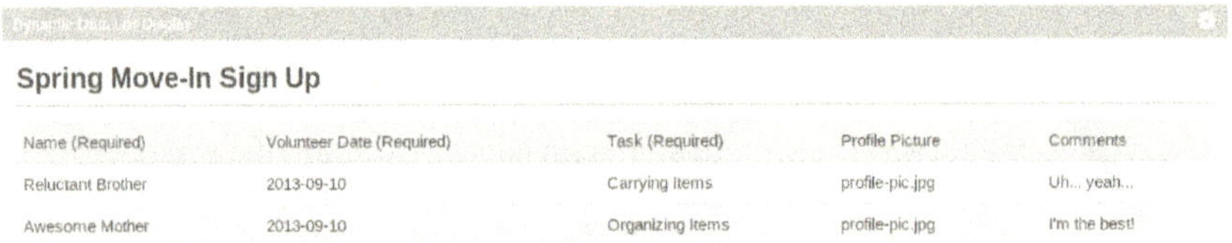

Spring Move-In Sign Up				
Name (Required)	Volunteer Date (Required)	Task (Required)	Profile Picture	Comments
Reluctant Brother	2013-09-10	Carrying Items	profile-pic.jpg	Uh...yeah...
Awesome Mother	2013-09-10	Organizing Items	profile-pic.jpg	I'm the best!

Figure 11.6: The Dynamic Data List Display portlet allows users to view the records belong to a list in either a standard or a spreadsheet view. This figure shows the spreadsheet view.

Now, as useful as this default display is, and it's certainly useful for my to do list and my memo notes, it can be an awkward way to ask my volunteers to sign up. In fact, any time I want other Listies to interact with my lists and contribute responses, I really just want a simple form to show them. They don't need to see the full range of responses. And in some cases, it can be hazardous to your health for everyone to see the responses. Then you don't have to explain why your sister-in-law won't work with your brother on the same task because of his B.O. problem. For reasons like that, you'll need to customize the data entry form or the display of the list. Liferay lets you do exactly that using a custom *form template* or *display template*.

11.3   Make it Pretty: Creating Custom Displays

When creating custom lists and data definitions, you can control not only how the input form appears to your users but also how the list itself displays. Eventually you may realize you need to create another sign-up sheet but you don't need the same level of detail provided by the Volunteer Sign-Up data definition you created. Liferay empowers you to customize both the input and output of your lists to unlimited levels. Dynamic data lists provide two areas to customize: form templates and display templates. This covers the forms of lists (*form templates*), as well as the display of the list contents (*display templates*).

Form Templates

The default data entry form is the entire data model you created in a data definition, including required and optional fields. Listies who create new lists using a data definition will see every item in that definition on the input form. What if, however, you want a quick sign-up form to find out who's coming to dinner tonight? Using a form template you can customize the form's display any way you want. You can limit the fields displayed for entry or change the order of elements. To access and create new templates, go to the Dockbar and click *Admin   Content*, click on Dynamic Data Lists, click on *Manage Data Definitions*, then click on the *Actions* button next to your data definition of choice and select *Manage Templates*. When you click on *Add Form Template*, you're presented with the same kind of graphical, drag-and-drop interface used for creating the data definition. Move items around, delete unwanted fields from view and save when ready.

Note: Form templates were called *detail templates* prior to Liferay 6.2.

Note that data definitions can have multiple templates. You can choose the template you want to use for display in either a dynamic data list display or a dynamic data list form portlet (see below). You should create as many templates as you might need, and you can prototype them in the portlets to see how each feels.

Now your friends and enemies alike will be impressed with your list.it skills. It may look to the untrained eye like you've single-handedly created three or four different data types for your lists but you know better. You used the power that form templates provide, using one data model that encompasses the maximum information you might need (like preferred activity, favorite color and ideal schedule). Then you quickly churned out four different form templates with a few mouse clicks. Now that you have such a vast amount of data collection options, how will you display them? However you want, as you're about to find out.

Display Templates

For every data definition, you have an unlimited number of displays you can create. If you created a special "Thanksgiving Dinner Sign-Up" list using your "Volunteer Sign-Up" definition, you wouldn't want to confuse fellow Listies by displaying data fields you never asked for. "Preferred task?" a friend might say, "I don't remember seeing *that* on the sign-up form!" To avoid such embarrassing situations, you should create a custom display to match that list. Taking it even further, you could provide a fancy, JavaScript-driven image carousel preview of all the attendees of the party. This would complement your other displays and be another bragging right on list.it. Display templates give you the power to do all this and more.

Note: Display templates were called *list templates* prior to Liferay 6.2.

Just like form templates, display templates are found in the Manage Templates section of a data definition. With display templates you can customize the display of a list in precisely the same way as you can customize web content. Display templates can be written in FreeMarker or Velocity, pulling data from the data definition in the same way that web content templates pull data from their structures. Also similar to web content templates, display templates can be embedded in other display templates. This allows for reusable code, JS library imports, or macros which will be imported by Velocity or FreeMarker templates in the system. Embedding display templates provides a more efficient process when you have a multitude of similar data definitions. Just import an embedded display template and work off of it for your new display template. We'll look at a simple example, but for more information on using template scripts to pull data from a backing structure, see web content templates in chapter 3.

The first thing we need to do is create a new display template for our "Volunteer Sign-Up" data definition. As with many other features in Liferay, there are multiple ways to do this, depending on your context.

From the Dynamic Data List Display portlet:

1. Navigate to the page with your DDL Display portlet and make sure your list is selected in the portlet's configuration.

2. Find the *Add Display Template* icon on the bottom-left corner of the portlet window and click it to create a new template. If you don't see the icon, sign in as a user with permission to create templates.

From the Dockbar/Control Panel:

1. Click on *Admin* →*Content*.

2. Navigate to *Dynamic Data Lists* →*Manage Data Definitions*.

3. Find your data definition in the list, then click *Actions   Manage Templates*.

4. Now you can click on *Add Display Template* to create a new template.

Fill out the form with a name and a description. Next, choose a templating language. Just like web content templates, you can choose between FreeMarker or Velocity. There is no functional difference between the two. Once you choose the script language, you can upload a template file or use the display template editor to type in a script manually. Inside the editor, you have access to a palette featuring common variables related to your selected template language. Additionally, you can hover your pointer over a variable in the palette for a more detailed description. To place a variable into the display template code, position your cursor where you want it placed, and click the variable name in the palette. Another useful tool in the display template editor is the autocomplete feature. In a FreeMarker template, it can be invoked by typing $\{$ which opens a drop-down menu of common variables. Upon selecting one of the variables, the editor inserts the variable into your display template code.

We want to write a FreeMarker template to give us a summary of who is helping on the tasks in our move. To do that, we need to access the records for the list and pull out the name and task for each volunteer. Within the template, we have access to a number of helper variables to find out what records we have access to:

```
reserved_ddm_structure_id
```

```
reserved_record_set_description
```

```
reserved_record_set_id
```

```
reserved_record_set_name
```

Inside a template, these variables give us the ID for the record set (that contains all of the volunteers in our list), as well as the name, description and data definition. We can easily retrieve all the records through a service call to DDLRecordLocalService. To gain access to this service, we need to use a helper utility called serviceLocator that retrieves an instance of the service for us. Once we have the service, we can retrieve the list of records (our list of volunteers). Accessing the service with the serviceLocator can be done with the following line of code:

```
<#assign DDLRecordLocalService =
    serviceLocator.findService(
    "com.liferay.portlet.dynamicdatalists.service.DDLRecordLocalService")>
```

We store a handle to our service in DDLRecordLocalService so we can use the service to retrieve our list of volunteers:

```
<#assign records = DDLRecordLocalService.getRecords(reserved_record_set_id)>
```

Now that we have our records, we can iterate through the list and display the data from each record that we want to show. To access a field from a record entry (such as the volunteer's name), we call the getFieldValue method and pass in the field's name. Each dynamic data list record has a number of other similar methods (see the com.liferay.portlet.dynamicdatalists.model.DDLRecord interface[1] but you'll probably use getFieldValue most often. This method returns the content of the field.

```
${cur_record.getFieldValue("name")}
```

Now all we have to do is set the results in some appealing way. In this example, we've made it very simple by using an unordered list for the results (<ul>). Here is the complete source for the template:

```
<h1>Task Summary</h1>

Here are the tasks that people have signed up for on "${reserved_record_set_name}".

<#assign DDLRecordLocalService =
    serviceLocator.findService(
    "com.liferay.portlet.dynamicdatalists.service.DDLRecordLocalService")>

<#assign records = DDLRecordLocalService.getRecords(reserved_record_set_id)>

<ul>
<#if records?has_content>
    <#list records as cur_record>
        <li>
        <em>${cur_record.getFieldValue("name")}</em>
            will help with ${cur_record.getFieldValue("task")}
        </li>
    </#list>
</#if>
</ul>
```

Once you've typed the template's source into the editor window, click *Save* to save the display template. With the display template selected, your list display can now be a summary of tasks as shown below.

All the knowledge you have accrued through building out your award-winning content can be brought to bear in display templates. With the full power of FreeMarker or Velocity templates at your fingertips, you have easy access to all the data in the list, as well as the full complement of helper methods and the Alloy UI JavaScript library to make easy work of dynamic displays.

---

[1]http://docs.liferay.com/portal/6.2/javadocs

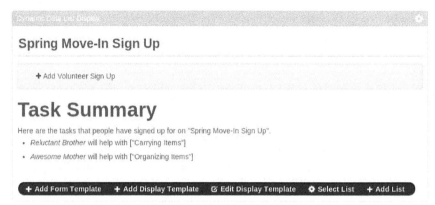

Figure 11.7: This display template provides a list of users who've volunteered along with the tasks for which they volunteered.

If you're not a Listie and you happen to be deploying custom lists in an environment that requires approval from other users, then it's not enough to just create the list and display a form. What you need is a real integration with workflow. Workflow integrates smoothly with Dynamic Data Lists.

Figure 11.8: Once the workflow plugin has been installed, you can choose a workflow when creating a new dynamic data list.

Using Workflow

Liferay integrates the powerful features of workflow and the data capabilities of dynamic data lists in *Kaleo Forms*. Workflow is not enabled in the dynamic data list portlets by default, so you can focus on the core task of building custom forms backed by a data list. After this is done, you can deploy custom workflows to the form and its data. Though Kaleo Forms is only available in Liferay EE, you can still apply a workflow to a list when creating it in Liferay CE.

If you don't have a workflow engine installed, you need install the Kaleo Web plugin. This plugin is included in the *Kaleo Workflow CE* and *Kaleo Workflow EE* apps which are available from Liferay Marketplace. To manually deploy the Kaleo workflow plugin, just copy the plugin .war file to the deploy folder of you application server. Once workflow is installed, you have a new option when creating a list:

Choose the workflow you'd like to use. This requires that every record must pass through the workflow process. Now if you need to preview or edit entries as they're coming in, it's easy to integrate it into your daily workflow.

Creating a Kaleo Form

Kaleo Forms EE is an app that provides you with greater control over the list creation and entry process. The Kaleo Forms EE
app is available from Liferay Marketplace. It includes both the
Kaleo Designer portlet and the Kaleo Forms portlet. The Kaleo
Designer portlet provides an easy-to-use UI that helps streamline the creation of workflow definitions. The Kaleo Forms portlet lets you create web forms and basic applications. The Kaleo
Forms EE app bundles these applications together, you can create workflows that govern the processing of web forms and applications.

For lists to appeal to companies all over the world (and make your new site not just a resounding success but attract profitable businesses), business users must be able to control the workflow of list entry and review those entries when made. There should also be a cool dashboard you make all of your changes. Using Kaleo Forms, users can create lists that follow a workflow, called a *process*, or create new *entries* in a process. Creating a new process is easy, straightforward, and effective.

Starting a New Process

Defining processes that must be followed in data collection and entry is a fundamental part of business. Historically, this hasn't been fun or easy but Kaleo forms makes it as easy as possible. A process is just another way to describe a workflow that's imposed on a list. When you place a Kaleo Forms portlet on a page, you are presented with a dashboard with two tabs: *Summary* and *Processes*. The summary view shows an inbox view which shows tasks that are assigned to you and tasks that are assigned to your roles. The sum- mary view also lets you view your pending requests and your completed requests. If any process definitions have been defined, you can submit records to a list from the summary view. The processes view allows you to add process definitions and manage ones that have already been created.

To build a list in Kaleo Forms with a workflow:

1. Add the Kaleo Forms portlet to a page.

2. Within the Kaleo Forms portlet, click on the *Processes* tab.

3. Click on *Add Process* and a form appears.

4. Enter a name and, optionally, a description. Entering a description helps your users understand the purpose of this process.

5. Select the appropriate list, workflow and forms you want to use in this process.

Figure 11.9: When using the Kaleo Forms portlet to create a new workflow process, you need to complete this form.

6. Click *Save* to save your process.

While the form looks complicated, it's easy to complete. There are a few pieces that make up a process and when you click on one, you can browse a list and select the appropriate piece to insert.

Selecting an Entry Definition   The first part of a new Kaleo process is also the simplest one: the entry definition. This is just another way to refer to a data definition. All of the available data definitions can be chosen, including our awesome "Volunteer Sign-Up List." Just as with normal data lists, you can always create a new entry definition from the list view by clicking *Add*.

Selecting an Initial Form   One of the advantages of using Kaleo forms to present your list as a process is that it grants you complete control over the form template. You can always use a default template, which displays all the fields from your entry definition. You can also, however, create multiple form templates for use in different stages of the process. When you create a form template, you can specify what *mode* to put it in:

Create: *Create* mode gives a display for creating the initial entry. The first stage of any workflow requires you to create a new entry, so the initial form template must be a create mode form. All fields marked required must be included on create mode forms.

Edit: *Edit* mode is used for any stage of the workflow process. For instance, you might want to separate information that need not be saved from information that must. Other stages in the workflow could be a great place to store additional, non-required, information. Required fields can be absent from an edit mode form.

Once you have chosen an initial display template (it must be a create mode template, not an edit template), all that's left to do is configure the workflow for your process.

Selecting a Workflow You can now select a workflow to apply to your new list-defined process. Any of the available workflows can be chosen. You can also create new ones from the selection screen. Simply choose *Add Workflow* and a Workflow Designer screen appears allowing you to define a new workflow by dragging elements in a flow chart.

Figure 11.10: You'll see this form when editing or creating a new workflow with Kaleo Designer

We'll keep ours simple; just choose *Single Approver Definition*. This gives us a starting point (entry creation) and a *review* task, which we can use to add additional information in a secondary form.

Assigning Workflow Task Forms Many workflows offer the option of having multiple editorial and review stages. During these stages, you might want to offer different forms that allow the user to add more information to the entry. Kaleo forms offers you the opportunity to fine-tune the stages of workflow to use different forms.

From the view to assign forms to tasks:

1. Choose the workflow task by clicking on it. This selects the task in the chart.

2. In the details pane on the left-hand side there is a property called Forms. Double click to edit the *value*.

3. Start typing the name of a form template and it appears.

4. Click *Save* to save the form assignment.

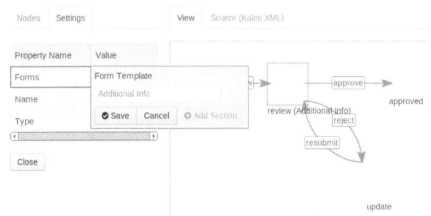

Figure 11.11: When creating or editing a Kaleo process, click *Assign* under Workflow Task Forms. Then click on a task, such as review, from the graphical view. Look for the *Forms* property in the Settings tab; you can use this property to assign a form template to a task.

You can assign forms to as many tasks as you need until you're satisfied with the workflow. After this stage, save the process and it's ready to be used in Kaleo Forms.

Using a Kaleo Form

Once you have a new Kaleo Form process, you can add new entries through the Summary tab in Kaleo Forms. Once the form is filled out and submitted, it enters the workflow you selected for the process.

After you have created an entry, (depending on the configured workflow) the next task in the workflow may have an additional form to complete. If so, there will be an option to enter it:

1. Next to the entry in progress, click the *Actions* button.

2. Click *Complete form*.

After the new entry has worked its way through the entire workflow, it is added to the data set collected. The owner of that data set (who created the Kaleo process) can view and edit the entries collected.

If you are a Listie, or a list.it developer, you're now prepared to show your lists to the world. That is, in fact, the reason you created list.it in the first place, right?

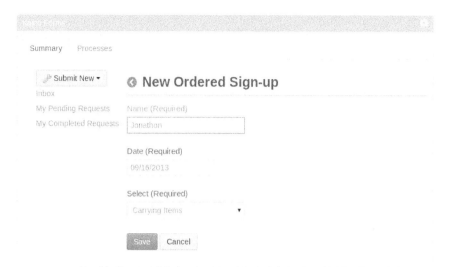

Figure 11.12: When adding a new entry to a process, you're presented with the process's configured form template for the initial display.

11.4 Summary

Our list.it experience is now much more enjoyable than when we first signed up. As new Listies, we had no idea how to define our own data types for our lists, let alone how to create a list. You can now be the envy of your co-workers as you breeze through list and data definition setup. Once you have your new lists set up, you can work through building new, custom input forms for the data. Your friends on list.it will thank you and wonder how you were able to accomplish it all. That's nothing next to the masterpiece of design that you can show off in your custom displays through display templates. Once the lists have the precise look and feel you envisioned, then living among the Listies will not only be easy, but fun and exciting.

With the ability to create dynamic sets of data and customize both the data display as well as the entry, the possible combinations are limitless. Dynamic Data Lists can be viewed as a way to deliver small-scale applications that display desired information quickly. Whether you're building a site like list.it or a real estate listing service, you'll find the limitless power of dynamic data lists enticing, easy to use, and above all, empowering.

CHAPTER 12

USING WORKFLOW

Liferay Portal includes a workflow engine called Kaleo. In Greek, Kaleo means "called ones," which is appropriate for a workflow engine that calls users to participate in a process designed for them. Kaleo workflow allows a user to define any number of simple to complex business processes/workflows, deploy them, and manage them through a portal interface. The processes have knowledge of users, groups and roles. You don't have to write a single line of code to accomplish this: all you have to do is create one XML document. And if you're a Liferay EE customer, you get a graphical workflow designer which gives you a point and click interface to create workflows.

To explain how to use Kaleo Workflow, this chapter covers:

- Enabling workflow

- Creating workflow definitions

- Configuring assets to use workflow process definitions

- Using workflow with other applications

Once we're done with this chapter, you should be familiar with how to use Liferay's Kaleo workflow to set up approval process for any kind of content before it is published to your portal.

12.1 Enabling workflow

Liferay's Kaleo workflow engine can be installed for both CE and EE versions of Liferay. The web plugin's name is kaleo-web and is bundled in the *Kaleo Forms EE* and *Kaleo Workflow CE* apps on Liferay marketplace, wich you can access through the Apps section of the Control Panel. Installing the plugin adds a *Workflow* option under the *Configuration* section of your Control Panel.

The kaleo-web plugin comes bundled with one worfklow called the Single Approver Workflow. This workflow requires one approval before an asset can be published. One of the conveniences of using Liferay's workflow engine is that any roles specified in the workflow definition are created automatically when the definition is deployed. This provides a level of integration with the portal that third party engines cannot match. The Single Approver Workflow contains three roles, each with different scopes. You can deduce the

297

scope of each role by its name: Site Content Reviewer, Organization Content Reviewer and Portal Content Reviewer.

Let's jump right in and create a workflow process definition.

12.2   Creating new workflow definitions

A Kaleo workflow, called a *process definition*, is defined in an XML file and is executed by users of the portal. You can create as many different workflow definitions as needed to manage the work done on your portal. Your workflows can define new user roles to manage the approval process or use roles that already exist in your portal.

The XML file has several parts which define the workflow. To get an idea of how this works, we'll examine the default single-approver-definition.xml file which is included in the Liferay Kaleo plugin.

The key parts of the workflow definition are the asset or workflow-enabled action that's running through the workflow, the nodes of the workflow, and the transitions between nodes. Assets are any kind of asset registered in Liferay: web content, wiki articles, message board threads, blogs entries, and even comments, are workflow-enabled. Workflow-enabled actions in the portal include Page Revision and User addition or editing. Developers can also create their own assets to use with workflows (see *Liferay in Action* or *Liferay Developer Network* for more information). Nodes represent stages of the workflow and there are several types. Transitions occur between nodes and indicate what the next node should be.

Think of workflow as a state machine made up of nodes. A node can be a state, a task, a condition, a fork, a join, or a timer. Transitions are used to move from one node to another. Each type of node has different properties. For example, states execute actions automatically and require no user input. Tasks block until user input completes a transition to another state. The transition then moves the workflow to the next task or state. This cycle continues until the end Approved state is reached. For example, you could create a workflow which goes through two approvers. Initiating the workflow puts it in the In Review state and then transitions to a task which requires user input. Users approve or reject the asset as part of the task. When the first user approves the asset in the workflow, a condition checks to see if there are two approvals. Since there is only one, workflow transitions back to the task. When the second user approves the asset, the condition finds there are two approvers and it triggers a different transition to the Approved state.

Let's learn about the Single Approver Workflow's components and look in detail at how you'd create a workflow using a single approver.

Starting a workflow definition

Below is a diagram of a single approver workflow definition. It has only two tasks (Update and Review) and two states (Initial State and Approved).

First you should define the schema. For Liferay workflows using Kaleo, liferay-workflow-definition-6_2_0.xsd should be your schema. You can find this schema in the definitions folder of the Liferay source or a good XML editor can cache it from Liferay's web site. Here's how you define it in your workflow definition's XML file:

```
<workflow-definition
    xmlns="urn:liferay.com:liferay-workflow_6.2.0"
    xmlns:xsi="http://www.w3.org/2001/XMLSchema-instance"
    xsi:schemaLocation="urn:liferay.com:liferay-workflow_6.2.0
        http://www.liferay.com/dtd/liferay-workflow-definition_6_2_0.xsd"
>
```

Next you define a name and description for the workflow. This appears in the control panel when users choose and configure workflows.

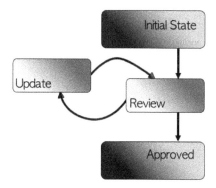

Figure 12.1: The default single approver workflow. Arrows represent transitions and boxes represent states and tasks.

```
<name>Single Approver</name>
<description>A single approver can approve a workflow content.</description>
<version>1</version>
```

After that, you define your initial state.

Creating an initial state

In this case, the state is simply that the asset has been created. States can contain actions and transitions. Actions can contain scripts. You can specify the language of the script with the `<script-language>` tag. Scripts can be written in Groovy, JavaScript, Ruby or Python (see chapter 18 for more information on leveraging scripts in workflow). For a state, the action is triggered automatically and then executes a transition. Transitions move you to a new state or task.

```
<state>
    <name>created</name>
    <metadata>
        <![CDATA[{"xy":[36,51]}]]>
    </metadata>
    <initial>true</initial>
```

From the initial state, you transition to a new task, where further processing is blocked so the asset can be reviewed.

```
    <transitions>
        <transition>
            <name>review</name>
            <target>review</target>
        </transition>
    </transitions>
</state>
```

The next step is to create a task.

Creating tasks

The task has several parts and is the most complex part of the definition. Tasks are linked with roles in order to choose who should complete the task. Roles are notified that there's new content in need of review. If you define a role that doesn't exist, it is created automatically.

The first task listed in the single-approver-definition.xml workflow definition is the *update* task. Though it appears first in the file, it's actually not the first task in the workflow. The *update* task is the task that's assigned by the workflow if the asset is rejected by an approver. It's listed first because it's the default task: when this task is triggered, the workflow process is reset back to the beginning. In this task, the asset is assigned back to the content creator, who receives an email notification and is required to resubmit the asset. Once the task is resubmitted, it goes back to the review stage.

You can also see the task is assigned to <user/>. This tag always assigns the task back to the user who created the asset.

```
<task>
    <name>update</name>
    <metadata>
        <![CDATA[{"transitions":{"resubmit":{"bendpoints":[[303,140]]}},"xy":[328,199]}]]>
    </metadata>
    <actions>
        <action>
            <name>reject</name>
            <script>
                <![CDATA[
                    Packages.com.liferay.portal.kernel.workflow.WorkflowStatusManagerUtil.
                        updateStatus(
                        Packages.com.liferay.portal.kernel.workflow.WorkflowConstants.
                        toStatus("denied"), workflowContext);
                    Packages.com.liferay.portal.kernel.workflow.WorkflowStatusManagerUtil.
                        updateStatus(
                        Packages.com.liferay.portal.kernel.workflow.WorkflowConstants.
                        toStatus("pending"), workflowContext);
                ]]>
            </script>
            <script-language>javascript</script-language>
            <execution-type>onAssignment</execution-type>
        </action>
        <notification>
            <name>Creator Modification Notification</name>
            <template>
                Your submission was rejected by ${userName}, please modify and resubmit.
            </template>
            <template-language>freemarker</template-language>
            <notification-type>email</notification-type>
            <notification-type>user-notification</notification-type>
            <execution-type>onAssignment</execution-type>
        </notification>
    </actions>
    <assignments>
        <user />
    </assignments>
    <transitions>
        <transition>
            <name>resubmit</name>
            <target>review</target>
        </transition>
    </transitions>
</task>
```

The *review* task is the first task in the workflow. This is where portal users with the proper role review the content and decide to reject it (move it back to the beginning) or accept it (transition it to the next step).

Once the transition has been made to this task, a notification is sent to those who are assigned to the task. You can edit the name or content of the notification in the XML file. Once the reviewer completes their review and exits the workflow task, another email is sent to the original submitter indicating that the review is completed.

```
<task>
    <name>review</name>
    <metadata>
        <![CDATA[{"xy":[168,36]}]]>
    </metadata>
    <actions>
        <notification>
```

```
        <name>Review Notification</name>
        <template>
            ${userName} sent you a ${entryType} for review in the workflow.
        </template>
        <template-language>freemarker</template-language>
        <notification-type>email</notification-type>
        <notification-type>user-notification</notification-type>
        <execution-type>onAssignment</execution-type>
    </notification>
    <notification>
        <name>Review Completion Notification</name>
        <template>
            Your submission has been reviewed and the reviewer has
            applied the following ${taskComments}.
        </template>
        <template-language>freemarker</template-language>
        <notification-type>email</notification-type>
        <recipients>
            <user />
        </recipients>
        <execution-type>onExit</execution-type>
    </notification>
</actions>
```

You must also assign the task to a specific role or roles. This role doesn't have to be the role you notified. For example, you might want to notify all the content creators any time a new item is submitted. Regardless of who you're notifying, you definitely want to send a notification to anyone who is responsible for approving content.

Sending notifications

Notifications need an execution-type which can be onAssignment, onEntry or on-Exit.

- onAssignment generates and sends the notification when the user is assigned the task in the workflow. **Note:** onAssignment notification will not work if you wish to notify a user that is not part of the workflow.

- onEntry generates and sends the notification when entering the workflow task or state.

- onExit generates and sends the notification when exiting the workflow task or state.

Notifications also need a notification-type which can be email, im or priv-ate-message. Note that both the private-message and im types are placeholders for now; that functionality is in Liferay's Social Office product but has not yet been integrated into Liferay Portal. Your notification type and execution type should complement each other. You wouldn't want to use an onExit execution type with a private message, because the user won't receive that message until he or she logs back in. Generally speaking, email notifications work best with onExit or onAssignment, while IM or private message work better with onEntry.

Email and private message notifications can also be created as plain text or you can create formatted content using FreeMarker or Velocity templating languages. When creating the notification, you need to specify the template-language as text, freemarker or velocity.

In this workflow, anyone who is capable of approving the content is notified onAssignment. This includes administrators and site and organization owners. The role--type tag helps the system sort out who should receive the notification based on the scope and can be set as *site*, *organization* or *portal*. When you specify a role-type to define the scope of the workflow notification, please note that the portal role is equvalent to the *regular* role-type declaration in our XML snippet below.

```
<assignments>
    <roles>
        <role>
            <role-type>organization</role-type>
            <name>Organization Administrator</name>
        </role>
        <role>
            <role-type>organization</role-type>
            <name>Organization Content Reviewer</name>
        </role>
        <role>
            <role-type>organization</role-type>
            <name>Organization Owner</name>
        </role>
        <role>
            <role-type>regular</role-type>
            <name>Administrator</name>
        </role>
        <role>
            <role-type>regular</role-type>
            <name>Portal Content Reviewer</name>
        </role>
        <role>
            <role-type>site</role-type>
            <name>Site Administrator</name>
        </role>
        <role>
            <role-type>site</role-type>
            <name>Site Content Reviewer</name>
        </role>
        <role>
            <role-type>site</role-type>
            <name>Site Owner</name>
        </role>
    </roles>
</assignments>
```

Once the content is approved you'll want to transition to a new state.

Using transitions

In this case, you only need a single approver, then the transition goes to the final approved state. In more complex workflows, you might transition to a second tier approver.

```
<transitions>
    <transition>
        <name>approve</name>
        <target>approved</target>
    </transition>
    <transition>
        <name>reject</name>
        <target>update</target>
        <default>false</default>
    </transition>
</transitions>
</task>
```

Finally, we define our end state. Remember states automatically run all actions that are assigned to them, so a script executes and sets the state of the content to *approved*. Workflow scripts are completely contained within XML workflow definitions.

You could also write a customized script if there were actions outside the standard one that you need to perform on your asset. The script below, written in JavaScript, sets the status of the asset to *approved*. Of course, there's much more you can do with scripts. You don't even have to use JavaScript: if you want, you can change the <script-language> to another supported language (Ruby, Groovy or Python) and rewrite the action with additional details to meet your needs.

```
<state>
    <name>approved</name>
    <metadata>
```

```
    <![CDATA[
        {"xy":[380,51]}
    ]]>
</metadata>
<actions>
    <action>
        <name>approve</name>
        <script>
            <![CDATA[
                import com.liferay.portal.kernel.workflow.WorkflowStatusManagerUtil;
                import com.liferay.portal.kernel.workflow.WorkflowConstants;

                WorkflowStatusManagerUtil.updateStatus(
                    WorkflowConstants.toStatus("approved"), workflowContext);
            ]]>
        </script>
        <script-language>groovy</script-language>
        <execution-type>onEntry</execution-type>
    </action>
</actions>
</state>
```

To create longer workflows, you'd create additional states, tasks and transitions according to your requirements. For instance, if you wanted to have a second level of review before an item is approved, you'd create a new task in between the *review* task and the *approved* state. The task itself might have similar content to *review* but you would assign it to a different role. The *review* task would transition to your new task and the new task would transition to the *approved* state.

You can also use *forks* and *joins* to create more complex workflows.

Using forks and joins

Forks and joins are used for parallel processing. For example, say you have a new offer you'd like to put up on your site but it needs to go through both the sales manager and the marketing manager first. You can set up a workflow that notifies both managers at the same time so they can approve them individually. This way, you're not waiting for one manager's approval before you can send the notification to the other manager. The below illustration shows how a workflow with a fork and a join might be designed.

You can transition to a fork from a task or state. From the fork, you can transition to multiple tasks or states which occur in parallel. In the previous example, when we have multiple transitions from one task, they're mutually exclusive: you either trigger one or the other. The transitions are also serial, meaning one must occur before the next one can occur. With a parallel workflow, you can have different approvals going through different users at the same time. For example, you could use this to separate two different departments' approval chains on a single asset. A fork should be formatted like this:

```
<fork>
    <name>review_fork</name>
    <transitions>
        <transition>
            <name>node_1</name>
            <target>review_one</target>
        </transition>
        <transition>
            <name>node_2</name>
            <target>review_two</target>
        </transition>
    </transitions>
</fork>
```

To bring a fork back together, transition both nodes of the fork back to a single join. A join is formatted similarly to a fork, except that any transitions are serial, not parallel, as in the example below.

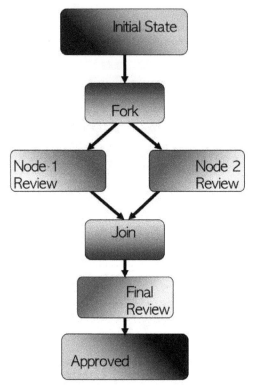

Figure 12.2: Parallel Approval Design

```
<join>
    <name>approved</name>
    <transitions>
        <transition>
            <name>result</name>
            <target>done</target>
            <default>true</default>
        </transition>
    </transitions>
</join>
```

Another important consideration when creating parallel approvals is each node needs its own "rejected" state for cases where content is approved in one node but rejected in another. Another feature you can use in custom workflows along with forks and joins is Timers. While using parallel workflow enables you to speed up your process by getting content in front more people at once, instead of making them wait in line, timers allow you to add some urgency to the process.

Timers

Timers help make sure important tasks in a workflow aren't forgotten or left undone because of an oversight or the absence of someone on the critical path. The basic concept of the timer is that after a period of time specified, a specific action occurs. There are two main elements for a Timer, the *Task Timer* and the *Timer Action*.

Timers occur within a Task element and are formatted like:

```
<task>
    ...
    <task-timers>
        <task-timer>
            <name></name>
            <delay>
                <duration></duration>
                <scale></scale>
            </delay>
            <timer-actions>
                ...
            </timer-actions>
        </task-timer>
    </task-timers>
    ...
</task>
```

The outer element is `<task-timers>` because you can have multiple timers with multiple actions. The specific `<task-timer>` then contains the element `<delay>` which has a `<duration>` and `<scale>`. The duration can be any number, whole or fractional, and it's significance is defined by the scale. The scale tells you what unit of time the duration is talking about - seconds, minutes, hours, days, weeks, months or years. Once you've determined the time, you'll want to pick an action - either a notification, reassignment or a custom script.

Notifications are pretty simple - if a certain amount of time passes and an action isn't completed yet, the user assigned to the task will receive a fresh notification. With the timer, you have all of the standard notification types available and you can choose a different notification type than was used for the original notification. For example, you could create a definition such that when a new item is submitted to the workflow, all members of the *Content Reviewer* role receive a notification. You could then use a timer to say if the content hasn't been reviewed within two hours each member of the *Content Reviewer* role will receive a second notification via instant messenger.

A Notification would be formatted like this:

```
<timer-actions>
    <timer-notification>
        <name></name>
        <template></template>
        <template-language>text</template-language>
        <notification-type>im</notification-type>
    </timer-notification>
</timer-actions>
```

Reassignments are designed to keep the workflow moving, even if a key person is out of the office. With a timer set to reassign, after the specified amount of time has passed, the task can be assigned to a new role. Building off of our example above, if the Content Reviewers all received the IM notification after two hours, but the content still wasn't approved after four hours, the workflow could be set to automatically reassign to the task to the *Administrator* role.

A Reassignment would be formatted like this:

```
<timer-actions>
    <reassignments>
        <assignments>
            <roles>
                <role>
                    <role-type></role-type>
                    <name></name>
                </role>
                ...
            </roles>
        </assignments>
    </reassignments>
</timer-actions>
```

Obviously we can't think of everything, so if you have an idea for using timers in your workflow that doesn't fit into our design, you could access Liferay's scripting engine to create a custom action to happen after a specified amount of time. For example, if you had means of sending electric shocks through employees chairs if they weren't doing their work, and had created a Liferay portlet to access the shock mechanism, you could use a custom script to zap any users who were at their desk that hadn't reviewed content assigned to them.

```
<timer-actions>
    <action>
            <name></name>
            <script>
                  <![CDATA[
                  ]]>
            </script>
            <script-language></script-language>
            <execution-type></execution-type>
    </action>
</timer-actions>
```

For more information on using scripting in Liferay, please refer to chapter 18.

Using workflows and approvals is necessary for virtually any organization and timers are an excellent way to help mitigate the potential headaches caused by having multiple bottlenecks through the process. Using timers in conjunction with other workflow features can help you create powerful workflows for your organization.

Putting it all together

The Kaleo workflow engine is deeply integrated with Liferay Portal. It can generate roles scoped for organizations, sites and for the whole portal based on workflow definitions. You can also customize workflow options for individual sites.

Users are the most important part of the workflow, since they're the ones who do all the work. To make a user a part of the workflow process, you assign them a role which you defined in your workflow. When you're creating your workflow definition, you can create new roles by defining them in the XML file or by using roles which you have already created in your portal. Roles created automatically are always portal scoped, so if you want to use site or organization scoped roles, create the roles before deploying your workflow to the portal.

A portal administrator can create a default workflow definition scheme for each application which applies for the entire portal; site and organization administrators can customize the settings for their sites and organizations. Now that we've seen how to create workflow definitions, let's discuss how to use them.

12.3   Configuring assets to use workflow process definitions

All your global workflow configuration can be done via the control panel. Everything you need to do in the portal can be done through simple GUI controls.

You can find the Workflow section under the Configuration heading in the control panel. There are three tabs under Workflow which are used to configure workflow in the portal: *Definitions*, *Default Configuration* and *Submissions*. These tabs let you upload definitions, enable workflow for your portal's resources, and The default workflow behavior you specify here will apply throughout your Liferay Portal.

From the *Definitions* tab you can see the currently available workflow definitions and add newly created workflow definitions you'd like to use in the portal. Clicking *Upload Definition* allows you to enter a title for a new workflow definition, browse to your local XML file, and upload it to your Liferay instance. Once you add a file here, it's added to the portal and is immediately available for use.

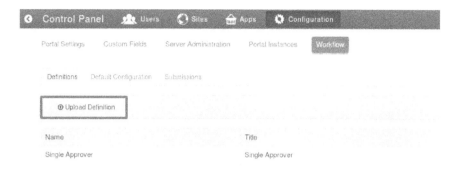

Figure 12.3: Adding a Workflow Definition

Under *Default Configuration*, you can set the workflow behavior for all workflow-enabled actions in the portal; available resources include Page Revision, User, Blogs Entries, Web Content Articles, Comments, Message Boards Messages, and Wiki Pages. You can also add a custom potlet to this list by using Liferay's API. You can choose from two default workflow options in Default Configuration: *No Workflow* or *Single Approver*, which we looked at in detail earlier in the chapter.

When you set the default workflow configuration of a resource, any new action on that resource defaults to that configuration, throughout the portal. An administrator can edit the workflow behavior for each site's resources individually through the *Workflow Configuration* section of a particular site's Site Administration section. The interface for making changes at the site level is similar to that of the Control Panel interface; the only difference is that you are in the Site Administration section and the changes you specify are only applicable to the scope you have selected here.

In the *Submissions* tab you can see any currently pending assets or any assets which were previously approved.

Let's learn more about configuring workflows for both the portal and individual sites next.

Configuring workflow

After you have uploaded workflow definitions and set the default workflow behavior you can go up to *Default Configuration* and enable workflow for specified actions in your portal.

By setting default workflow configuration behavior from the Control Panel, your specified settings are implemented at the global portal scope. If you need to set the workflow configuration for a specific site, you can do so from the *Site Administration* section. You can get there from the Control Panel by clicking *Sites*, clicking on a site from the list, and opening the *Configuration* menu. The *Workflow Configuration* option lets you modify workflow behavior for the sleected site's resources that can be workflow enabled.

My Workflow Tasks

My Workflow Tasks is a personalized version of the Workflow Tasks and it's found in the user's My Account section. Here you'll find specific tasks which were assigned to you or assigned to a role of which you are a member. You can also view your completed tasks by opening the Completed tab.

Workflow administrative users review and approve content from their My Worfklow Tasks section. By clicking the link to the asset, you can view it, and the Actions dropdown

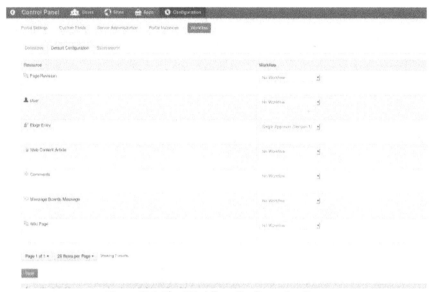

Figure 12.4: The Workflow Configuration Page

My Account

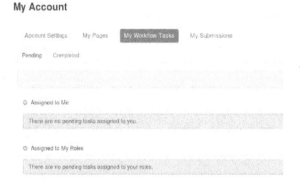

Figure 12.5: My Workflow Tasks Page

lets you approve, reject, or reassign assets assigned to you. For assets assigned to your roles, you can assign the listed assets to be reviewed by yourself or another user. Whether or not an asset is assigned to you or to your role, you can update the due date as well.

My Submissions

My Submissions is found in your user's My Account section of the portal. From this screen you can view any assets you have submitted for review. Those currently under review are listed under the *Pending* tab and those that have been reviewed are listed under the *Completed* tab.

Besides viewing your work, you can also withdraw a submission from the review process by clicking on *Withdraw Submission* from the *Pending* tab.

Using Kaleo Workflow Processes in Liferay Portal

Figure 12.6: The My Submissions Page

Before workflow can be used, you must define which types of assets on the portal are workflow-enabled. If you have created additional definitions, you must also choose the workflow definition to use for each asset that is workflow-enabled.

To demonstrate how this works, we'll create a press release. Press releases should be posted in the *Newsroom* section of the web site, so before setting specific workflow configuration options or creating content, create the Newsroom site. When you click Save, you'll be redirected to the Site Administration section of the portal where you can work on the Newsroom site further. Under Configration, in Workflow Configuration, set Web Content to use the Single Approver workflow.

Next, create two users, a Content Creator and a Content Reviewer. The Content Creator logs in and creates a new press release for the Lunar Resort and clicks *Submit for Publication*. This triggers the workflow process and notifies the Content Reviewer. When the Content Reviewer logs in, he or she can assign the workflow task to him- or herself and approve the content.

Once the content is approved, it can be posted on the Press Releases page in a Web Content Display portlet.

There's more. EE customers get extra features that enable them to create workflows without having to deal with XML.

12.4   Using workflow with other applications

Above we saw an example of using workflow with Liferay web content. The process is the same for all resources that are workflow-enabled. However, while configuring your resources to use workflow in the Default Configuration tab of the Workflow section, you may have noticed a note that "The workflows for the following resources can be configured within their respective portlets". resources listed are *Documents* and *Dynamic Data Lists Records*. Workflow configuration is more specifically enabled for Documents and Media folders and Dynamic Data Lists (i.e., each individaul list).

To see how this works for a Documents and Media folder, create a new page in the default site called *Documents and Media* and add the Documents and Media portlet to this

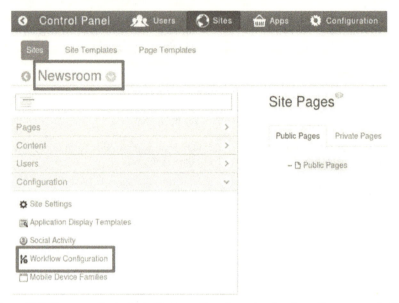

Figure 12.7: You can select which site to work on by using the drop-down menu in the Site Administration section of the portal.

Figure 12.8: Before a Content Reviewer can approve content, he must assign it to himself or have an administrator assign it to him.

page. Then click *Add → Folder*, enter the name *My Documents*, and click *Save*. Mouse over your new My Documents folder, click on the black arrow that appears at the top right corner of the folder, and select *Edit*.

By default, the *Use document type restrictions and workflow of the parent folder* button is selected. To enable workflow for this folder, select the *Define specific document type restrictions and workflow for this folder* button. After you've selected this button, a *Default Workflow for all Document Types* drop-down menu appears. By default, you can select *No workflow* or *Single Approver*. Any custom workflows that you added also appear in this drop-down menu. You can add custom workflows through the Workflow page in the Portal section of the Control Panel.

After you've selected the *Single Approver* workflow and clicked *Save*, workflow takes effect for the My Documents folder. Try adding a new document to your My Documents folder—notice that the *Publish* button now says *Submit for Publication* since workflow is enabled. Any users assigned to the (Portal, Organization, or Site) Content Reviewer roles can

Figure 12.9: Workflow for Documents and Media must be enabled at the folder level. Edit a folder to select a workflow.

see that your document has been submitted for publication by navigating to My Account and clicking on *My Workflow Tasks*. Ordinarily, the same user who submitted a document for publication wouldn't also approve it but we'll do this to demonstrate how the process works.

Figure 12.10: You can use the document type restrictions and workflow of the parent folder or you can define specific document type restrictions and workflow for this folder.

Like with Documents and Media folders, workflow is configured for a Dynamic Data List at the list level. That is, when you add a New List for users, you can enable workflow for that particular list. No Workflow is the default setting, but you can select the Single Approver definition or any definition you uploaded to use in the portal. When a user submits an item to a list that was configured to use a workflow, they'll see the item's status as Pending. Once the list item has been approved by an administrative user, the status changes to Approved.

Navigate to the My Account and click on *My Workflow Tasks*. Documents and Data Lists that you submitted for publication appear under *Assigned to My Roles* since you're an administrator. Click *Actions →Assign to Me* next to your document. Then click *Actions →Approve* next to the document or list when it appears in the

Assigned to Me category. That's it—your resources have passed through the workflow!

12.5   Summary

In this chapter, we explained how to install the Kaleo workflow plugin for Liferay EE. Liferay's Kaleo workflow engine is included with Liferay CE. We discussed how to create new workflow definitions and examined the XML schema for them. We looked at how to choose different workflow processes for different asset types. We also explained how end-users can interact with the approval process. Finally, we discussed how to use workflow with different types of applications such as Documents and Media and Dynamic Data Lists. In the next chapter, we'll look at Kaleo forms and the Kaleo workflow designer.

KALEO FORMS: DEFINING BUSINESS PROCESSES

In the last chapter, you saw the elements that comprise a workflow definition and learned how to create a workflow definition.
In this chapter, you'll learn about the Kaleo Forms Admin application for Liferay EE. This application lets you create workflow
definitions using an intuitive UI. Using the workflow designer
saves you the time and trouble of having to deal directly with the
XML.

Developers who are used to working with XML can create
workflow definitions with little struggle. Other users may not be so comfortable with it. In
fact, even skilled developers can make mistakes that break a definition and require time to
troubleshoot. To help streamline the creation of workflow definitions and empower more
users to create custom workflows, Liferay provides the Kaleo Forms Admin application in
Liferay 6.2 EE.

There are two pieces to the workflow designer: *Kaleo Forms Admin* and *Kaleo Forms Display*. These two portlets are included in the Kaleo Forms app and can be downloaded from
Liferay Marketplace. Kaleo Forms Admin contains a wizard that guides you through each
step in the creation of a workflow process. This includes a drag and drop interface for creating new workflow definitions without having to write XML. Kaleo Forms Display allows
you to work with a process in its associated workflow. In other words, Kaleo Forms Admin
is for *creating* workflow processes, while Kaleo Forms Display is for *using* them.

Let's look at Kaleo Forms Admin first.

13.1 Kaleo Forms Admin

You can access Kaleo Forms Admin from the Dockbar by clicking *Admin →Site Administration →Content* and then clicking *Kaleo Forms Admin*. The portlet then appears with a listing
of the processes that you've defined. If you're coming here for the first time, however,
there won't be any, so create one. Click *Add*. You'll see the screen below. This is the first
step in the *New Process Wizard*. For this example, give your process the name *Lunar Resort
News Content*, add a description, and then click *Next*.

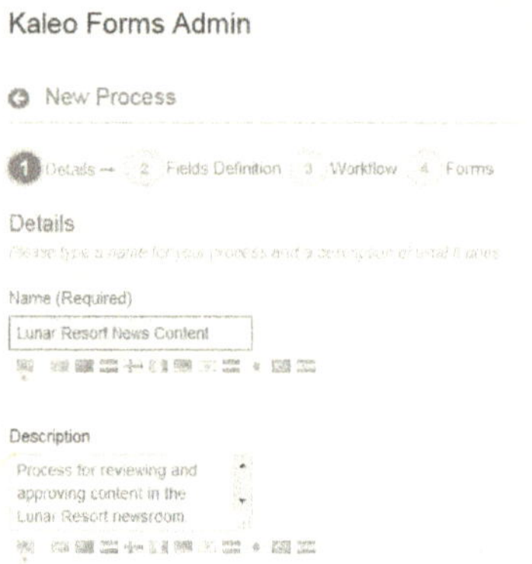

Kaleo Forms Admin

○ New Process

① Details →   2 Fields Definition   3 Workflow   4 Forms

Details

Name (Required)

Lunar Resort News Content

Description

Process for reviewing and
approving content in the
Lunar Resort newsroom

Figure 13.1: The first step of the New Process Wizard.

The second step in the New Process Wizard lets you define the fields that can appear in your forms. To the right of the To Do field, click the *Actions* button and select *Choose*. Now that you've chosen a field definition for your forms, you can move on to the next step in the wizard to add or define a workflow for those forms. Click *Next*.

The third step in the New Process Wizard is really where the meat and potatoes of Kaleo Forms Admin is. This is where you choose or define a workflow to use for your forms. The Single Approver workflow is included by default. To get a look at how it's defined, click *Actions* and then *Edit*. The graphical interface for editing or defining a workflow appears below the Details section of the Single Approver edit screen.

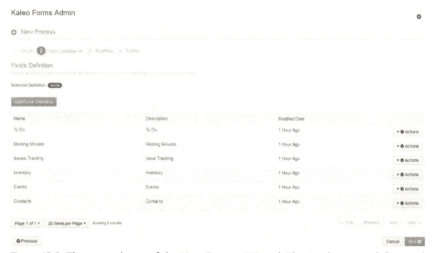

Figure 13.2: The second step of the New Process Wizard. This is where you define and choose the fields for your forms.

This graphical view is where Kaleo Forms Admin can help you build a workflow without having to write any XML. There are eight types of nodes you can add to a definition. The node types are **Condition**, **End**, **Fork**, **Join**, **Join XOR**, **Start**, **State** and **Task**. Notice that Start and End aren't node types we've previously discussed; that's because they're actually just State nodes, with certain fields pre-filled to help streamline the creation process. Since every workflow has a start and end state, you'd have to do this anyway.

Each node you add has a pop-up menu letting you edit or delete the node. As you hover your mouse over the edges of a node, notice your mouse pointer changes to a cross. The cross indicates you can connect the current node to another node. Hold down your mouse button and drag the mouse to start drawing your transition to another node. If you stop before reaching the edge of the next node, a pop-up displays node types you can create and connect to on-the-fly. To connect with an existing node, continue dragging the connector

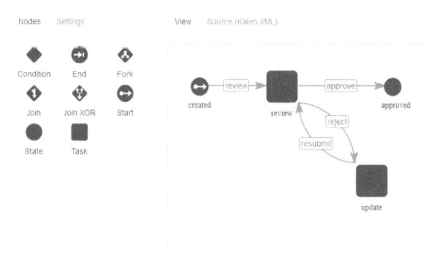

Figure 13.3: The graphical view for editing or defining a workflow.

to that node.

To get a feel for how the designer works, go ahead and use the workflow designer to duplicate the default workflow definition. Go back to the previous step and click *Add Workflow*. When you choose this option, it creates a blank workflow definition with start and end nodes. To make this work, you'll add two tasks, fill in the relevant information, assign the tasks properly, and create the transitions.

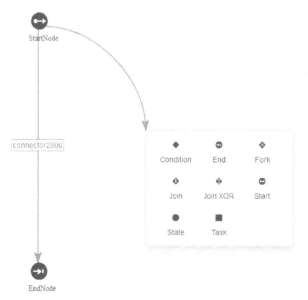

Figure 13.4: Create transitions to existing or new nodes. The connector pop-up let's you create and connect to new nodes on-the-fly.

First add two tasks, then use the edit icon to name them *Review* and *Update*.

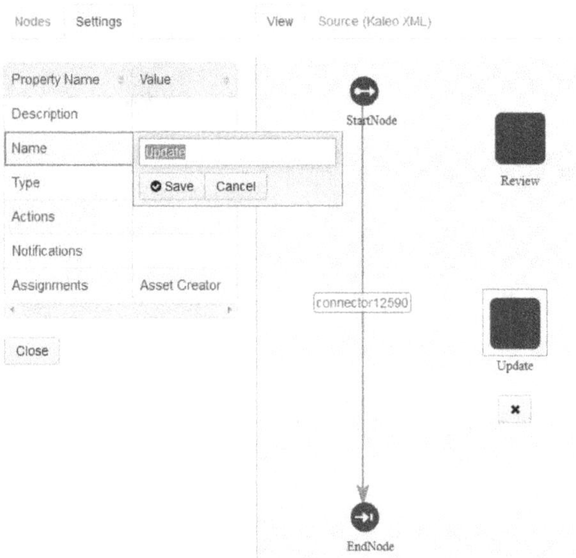

Figure 13.5: Edit a node by clicking on its node icon and modifying its settings.

Next, connect the nodes so Review has four nodes, as follows: one receiving the transition from **StartNode**, one sending a transition to **Update**, one receiving a transition from **Update**, and one sending a transition to **EndNode**.

Next, you want to add the correct assignments and notifications. Click on *Review*. The box on the left shows all the properties of the Review node. In the *Assignments* category, set the *Assignment Type* to *Role Type*, the *Role Type* to *Regular*, and the *Role Name* to *Portal Content Reviewer*

Now set the notifications. Double-click on *Notifications* and create a notification with the Notification Type set to *User Notification* and the Execution Type set to *On Assignment*.

Together, the assignment and notification settings specify that a user receives a notification in their Dockbar when assigned a form in this workflow. Now move to the Update node and assign it to the *Content Creator* role with its own user notification.

Next, go through all the transitions and make sure they're named correctly. What are the transitions? Workflow transitions connect one node to another. On exiting the first node, processing continues to the node pointed to by the transition. Every time you created an arrow from one node to another, Kaleo Designer created a transition. By default, these transitions get system generated names, so we'll rename them all to something more human-readable. First, click on the arrow going from the Start node to the Review node and set the name to *Submit* and set *Default* to true—you'll leave all the others as false. Set the name of the Review to Update transition to *Reject* and the Update to Review transition to *Resubmit*. Lastly, set the name of the Review to Endnode transition to *Approve*.

Now look at the generated XML. It should look a lot like the default workflow, only a tiny bit messier, as the nodes are written in the order they were created, not in the logical order that happens when a human writes the code. Once you're finished, click *Publish*. Your workflow is now ready to use!

Back on the third step of the New Process wizard, click *Actions Choose* next to the workflow you just created. Then click *Next*.

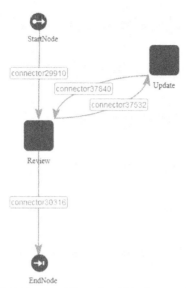

Figure 13.6: Your workflow should look something like this.

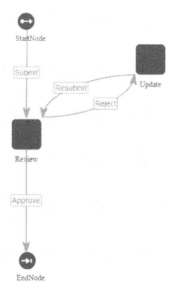

Figure 13.7: Your completed workflow should look like this.

The fourth and final step of the New Process wizard is for creating or assigning a form to each task you've defined in the workflow. Each task appears in a row with its form (if it has been assigned one) and a button that lets you assign a form. Therefore, you have *create*, *update*, and *review* listed as your tasks.

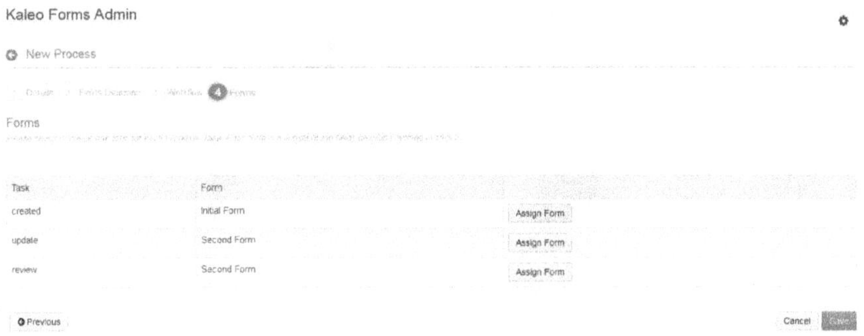

Figure 13.8: The fourth step in the New Process wizard lets you assign a form to each task.

Go ahead and click on the *Assign Form* button next to the created task. On the next page, click the *Add Form* button. The screen that appears lets you create a new form. First, give the form the name *Initial Form*, since it's the first form in the process. Next, take a look at the available fields. This is a simple review task so you won't need all the fields that are in the form by default. To delete a field, mouse over it and click the *Trash* icon that appears. Go ahead and delete all but the *Assigned To*, *Severity*, *Start Date*, *Status*, and *Title* fields. Your form should now look like the one in the screenshot here.

Figure 13.9: Basic form creation.

If you delete a field by accident or simply want to add another field to your form, you can do so by dragging and dropping its icon from the *Fields* tab on the left to the form itself on the right. Fields already on the form that can appear on it only once are grayed out. You can also edit the settings of a field in the form by mousing over it and clicking the wrench icon. For example, the settings for the Assigned To field are shown in this screenshot.

Since you don't need to change any of the field settings in this form, go ahead and click *Save*. On the next screen, choose your new form from the *Actions* button next to it. Now that you're familiar with the basics of form creation and assignment, create a form titled *Second Form* to use for the update and review tasks. Give it the following fields:

- Assigned To
- Attachment
- Comments
- Description
- End Date
- % Complete
- Severity
- Start Date
- Status
- Title

Make sure you choose the new form for your update and review tasks. When you're done assigning forms to tasks, click *Save*. Your new process is complete, and is listed in the Kaleo Forms Admin portlet. Congratulations!

Figure 13.10: Once created, your process is listed in Kaleo Forms Admin.

Now it's time to look at how to use workflow processes in the Kaleo Forms Display portlet.

13.2   Kaleo Forms Display

The Kaleo Forms Display portlet makes use of the workflow processes that you create in the Kaleo Forms Admin portlet. Add the Kaleo Forms Display portlet to a page if you haven't done so yet. Any forms available for processing through the workflow can be initiated through the *Submit New* button, as the below image indicates.

Figure 13.11: The Kaleo Forms Display portlet.

To initiate a process in the workflow, click *Submit New ▸ Lunar Resort News Content*. The portlet now displays the form you assigned to the first task in your workflow. Fill out the form and click *Save*.

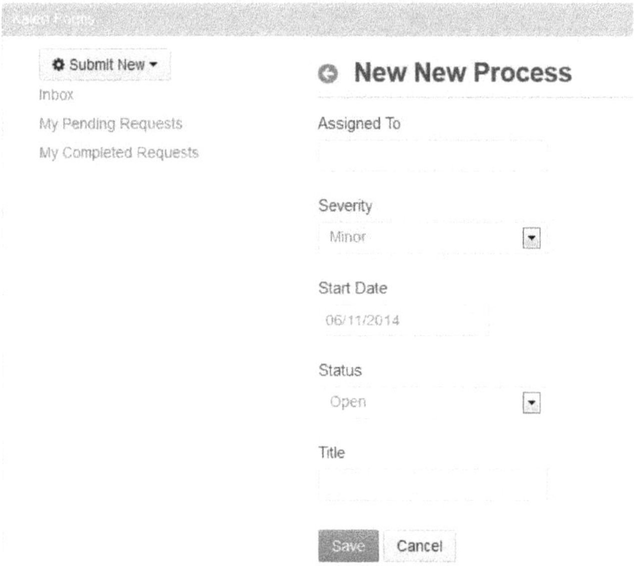

Kaleo Forms

⚙ Submit New ▾

Inbox

My Pending Requests

My Completed Requests

◉ **New New Process**

Assigned To

Severity

Minor ▾

Start Date

06/11/2014

Status

Open ▾

Title

Save Cancel

Figure 13.12: Submitting a new process.

The workflow now automatically guides the form on to the next step. For example, if you submit a new process using the Single Approver process created in the section above, it is assigned automatically to the Portal Content Reviewer role. If you are a Portal Content Reviewer, the task then appears in the *Assigned to My Roles* section of the Kaleo Forms Display portlet, and you receive a notification in your Dockbar. You can then assign it to yourself using the portlet and complete the task.

Figure 13.13: The workflow automatically assigns the task to a specific role.

13.3   Summary

As you can see, Liferay Portal and the Kaleo Workflow engine combine to create a robust environment for web content management. The Kaleo Forms portlets allow you to manage all available workflows in the portal. You can create your portal's workflows by using Kaleo Forms Admin's drag and drop interface. Simple workflows can be managed using the default configuration and GUI tools, while more complex workflows can be created to meet the workflow management needs of almost any portal. Through this chapter and the previous one, you've taken a look at the various elements of a workflow and been shown how to use those elements to create your own custom workflows. You've also seen how properly to use the various elements of a workflow like Assignments and Notifications, as well as newer and more advanced features like Parallel Workflows, Timers, and Custom Scripts.

It's not enough to understand each individual step of the workflow process: one of the keys to using Kaleo workflow is to understand how each step interacts with the other elements. If you understand these relationships, you can figure out which features will work best for your organization. We hope you'll use the information we've covered on workflows to craft suitable processes for your portal.

## CHAPTER 14

LIFERAY UTILITY APPLICATIONS

In this chapter we'll look at some Liferay utility applications that might be useful for you. The Software Catalog has been replaced by Liferay Marketplace but can still be installed as a plugin. Please see chapter 13 for information about Liferay Marketplace and managing Liferay plugins. The Reports, JasperReports, and Knowledge Base applications are only available to EE customers. In this chapter we'll discuss following applications:

- Bookmarks
- Software Catalog
- Shopping
- Reports and JasperReports
- Knowledge Base
- Akismet
- Weather
- OAuth

Liferay's Bookmarks application is a simple way for users to keep track of URLs in the portal that can also be used by an administrator to publish relevant links to groups of users. The Software Catalog allows you to define a set of software items to display to visitors. The Knowledge Base application allows you to create articles and organize them into full books or guides that be published on your portal.

14.1 Capturing Web Sites with the Bookmarks Portlet

Many of us enjoy collecting things we value. They may be stamps, comic books, sea shells, or fabulous shoes. The list goes on and on. But have you considered URLs collectible? Having a thorough collection of links can be a great way to add value to your portal's usability.

With Liferay's Bookmarks application, users collect and manage URLs in the portal. They can add, edit, delete, export and import bookmarks. Users can use links to access regularly visited web sites. Administrators can publish links tailored to specific groups of users. Both internal pages as well as external sites can be bookmarked.

Adding and Using Bookmarks

Navigate to your portal and add the Bookmarks application to your page by selecting *Add* →*Applications*. The portlet looks like this by default:

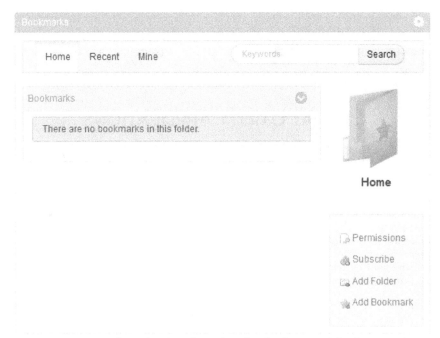

Figure 14.1: Initially, no bookmarks are listed in this form until they're created.

Across the top of the portlet are links labeled Home, Recent, and Mine. There is also a Search field and button.

Home: returns you to the top level of the portlet.

Recent: displays a list of the latest bookmarks that have been added.

Mine: displays a list of the bookmarks you added to the portlet.

Search: lets you search for bookmarks by name, category, or tags.

When you select the *Permissions* button on the right, a list of Roles and their associated permissions appears. The options are Add Entry, Add Folder, Permissions, and View. When you are finished selecting the permissions, click *Save*.

Clicking the *Add Folder* button in the Bookmarks application reveals the *New Folder* form. Here you can choose the folder's name, a description of its contents, and who can view it. Under More Options, you can set portlet permissions for various Roles to the folder. Click *Save* when you are finished.

To create a bookmark, click the *Add Bookmark* button. This form is similar to the New Folder form but has a few more options.

Click *Select* to choose the folder for the new bookmark. Click *Remove* to delete a bookmark from the selected folder. As stated above, a removed link goes into the list of general bookmarks that aren't associated with a folder. These are listed in the bookmarks section, below the folders, in the portlet.

Below the Permissions there are additional options for Categorization and Related Assets, just like in other Liferay applications. Please see chapter 6 on the Asset Framework for further information about this.

Figure 14.2: When you use the Add Bookmark form, you must enter a valid URL in the required field.

Once you have added a new bookmark, it appears in the portlet. From here, you can manage your bookmark using familiar Liferay editing features. Collecting and organizing your links is a snap when you use Liferay's Bookmarks application.

Organizing Bookmarks by Folder

You can store all your important links in one place and you can manage this data easily using folders. You can create, edit, and delete bookmark folders. You get to decide how many bookmarks or folders are displayed on a page. Bookmark folders can have any number of subfolders.

Here's an example of what one bookmarks portlet might look like. Bookmark Folders are displayed above individual bookmarks.

In this example, there are six bookmark folders, three of which have subfolders. The columns showing the number of folders and the number of entries show the subfolders and the entries contained within each top level folder. Note that total number of bookmarks includes those in the subfolders.

Using the Actions button on the right, you can edit the folder, manage folder permissions, delete the folder, add a subfolder, or add a bookmark to the folder.

As your collection of links grows, you may need to add more subfolders to keep things in order. Should you decide a link needs to move from one folder to another, you can manage this using the Edit option for that link.

Moving a Link

Just for fun, let's move a link from the main bookmarks folder into a subfolder one level down. We'll move the Liferay link into the Trivia subfolder in the Sports & Games folder. The Trivia subfolder is a child of the Sports & Games folder. We'll move the link to the Sports & Games folder first before moving it into the Trivia subfolder.

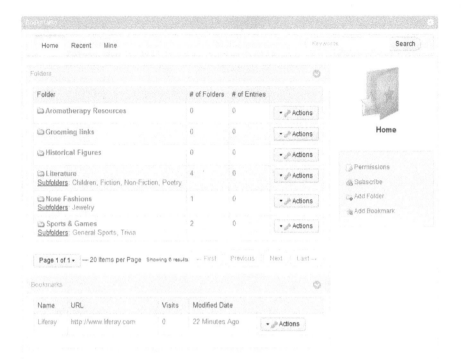

Figure 14.3: Individual bookmarks, not associated with a folder, are listed separately.

To achieve this, we select *Edit* from the Actions button for the link. In the Edit view, find the section called *Folder*. When applicable, this section contains breadcrumb links to allow you to navigate freely among the other folder levels. Currently, there are two buttons here labeled Select and Remove. Click the *Select* button and a new window appears, like the one below. Clicking the *Remove* button here doesn't affect the link. It is used solely for moving links out of folders and subfolders back into the main Bookmarks view.

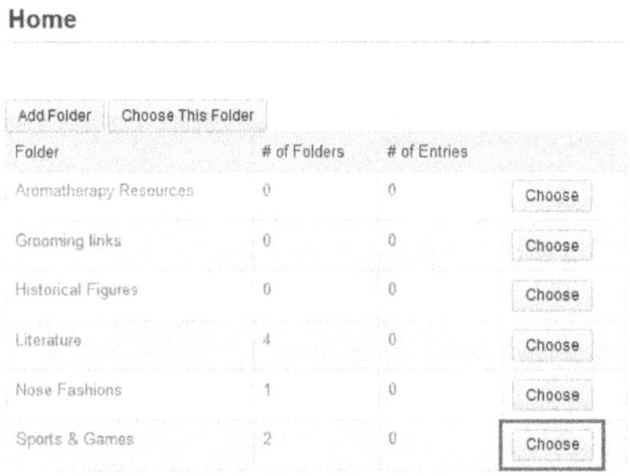

Home

Add Folder	Choose This Folder		
Folder	# of Folders	# of Entries	
Aromatherapy Resources	0	0	Choose
Grooming links	0	0	Choose
Historical Figures	0	0	Choose
Literature	4	0	Choose
Nose Fashions	1	0	Choose
Sports & Games	2	0	Choose

Figure 14.4: Select the Choose button next to the desired folder.

Now choose the *Sports & Games* folder. When you do this, notice how the link's Folder section changes to reflect the new location of the link. When you choose *Save*, you return to the Bookmarks portlet. Notice that the Liferay link is no longer under the Bookmarks section. Select *Sports & Games* to reveal its contents. In the example below, you can see the Liferay link is now in the bookmarks section of the Sports & Games folder.

Figure 14.5: When you move a link to a folder, it remains in the bookmarks section until it's moved into a subfolder.

Select *Edit* from the Actions button next to the Liferay link, then click *Select*. Navigate to the *# of Folders* number next to the Sports & Games folder and choose the *Trivia* subfolder. Again, notice the change in the folder-level breadcrumbs. Click *Save* and the Sports & Games folder view appears. change in the link's folder section, which now displays *Trivia*. Click *Save* and the Sports & Games folder view appears. Select *Trivia* to see your link in the subfolder's bookmarks list. Piece of cake, right?

To move a link out of a subfolder and into a higher-level folder, edit the link in the subfolder and choose *Select*. In the resulting window, select the appropriate folder from the breadcrumbs at the top. In this example, we selected *Sports & Games* for consistency. This opens a new window, like the one below, showing the other folder options.

Figure 14.6: In this view, you can move the link into several different locations.

You can choose one of the other subfolders from the list, or you can choose *Home* from the breadcrumbs at the top. When you verify that the desired folder is the one currently displayed in the breadcrumbs, click *Choose This Folder*. Then click *Save* and you're done. If you don't like any of the subfolders listed, you can place the link into a new subfolder by using the *Add Subfolder* button.

If you choose *Remove* instead of Select in the above example, you take the link out of both subfolders and return it to the main bookmarks view.

Now that you have an understanding of how bookmark folders are used, let's create our own plugin repository.

14.2   Creating Your Own Plugin Repository

As your enterprise builds its own library of portlets for internal use, you can create your own plugin repository to make it easy to install and upgrade portlets. This will allow different departments who may be running different instances of Liferay to share portlets and install them as needed. If you are a software development house, you may wish to create a plugin repository for your own products. Liferay makes it easy for you to create your own plugin repository and make it available to others.

You can create your plugin repository in two ways:

1. Use the Software Catalog in the Control Panel to create the repository by using its graphical interface and an HTTP server.

2. Create an XML file using the Liferay Plugin Repository DTD [1] and an HTTP server.

Both methods have their benefits. The first method allows users to upload their plugins to an HTTP server to which they have access. They can then register their plugins with the repository by adding a link to it via the Control Panel's graphical user interface. Liferay will then generate the XML necessary to connect the repository to a Control Panel running on another instance of Liferay. This XML file can then be placed on an HTTP server and its URL can be added to the Plugin Installer, making the portlets in this repository available to the server running Liferay.

The second method does not require an instance of Liferay to be running. You can upload plugins to an HTTP server of your choice, then create an XML file called `liferay-plugin-repository.xml` manually. If you make this file available on an HTTP server (it can be the same one which is storing the plugins or a different one), you can connect the repository to a Plugin Installer in the Control Panel running on an instance of Liferay.

We will first look at creating a plugin repository using the Software Catalog in the Control Panel.

Software Catalog

You will want to use the Software Catalog if you will have multiple users submitting portlets into the repository and if you don't want to worry about creating the `liferay-plugin-repository.xml` file yourself.

 Tip: The Software Catalog plugin was deprecated in Liferay 6.2 and is disabled by default. To activate it, navigate to the Control Panel →*Plugins Configuration* and scroll through the list of portlets until you find *Software Catalog*. Select *Software Catalog* and click the *Active* checkbox. Then click *Save*.

You can add the Software Catalog portlet to your page by navigating to *Add → Applications* and selecting it from the *Tools* category.

Each site in your portal can have an instance of the Software Catalog. The Software Catalog can be managed from your site's Site Administration page. This means different sites can have different software repositories, so you can host several software repositories on the same instance of Liferay if you wish, they just have to be in different sites. Choose the site that will host the plugin repository and go to the Site Administration page. You can change the site that you're on by navigating to the Dockbar's *My Sites* drop-down menu and selecting your desired site.

---

[1]http://www.liferay.com/dtd/liferay-plugin-repository_6_2_0.dtd

Figure 14.7: The Software Catalog portlet can be added to any of your site pages.

The Software Catalog has several tabs. The first tab is labeled Products. The default view of the portlet, when populated with software, displays what plugins are available for install or download. This can be seen in the version on Liferay's home page.

We will use an example site in order to better illustrate how to use the Software Catalog portlet. Assume you, as the portal administrator, have created a site called *Old Computers*. This site will be for users to collaborate on setting up and using old computers with obsolete hardware and operating systems. Users who participate in the site will eventually get upgraded to a more privileged status and get their own blog page. To implement this, you have created a My Summary portlet which displays the user's name, picture, and description from his or her user profile. Because this portlet is generic enough that it could be useful to anyone using Liferay, you have decided to make it available in your own software catalog.

The first step in adding a plugin to your software repository is to add a license for your product. A license communicates to users the terms upon which you are allowing them to download and use your software. Click the *Licenses* tab and then click the *Add License* button that appears. You will then see a form which allows you to enter the title of your license, a URL pointing to the actual license document and check boxes denoting whether the license is open source, active or recommended.

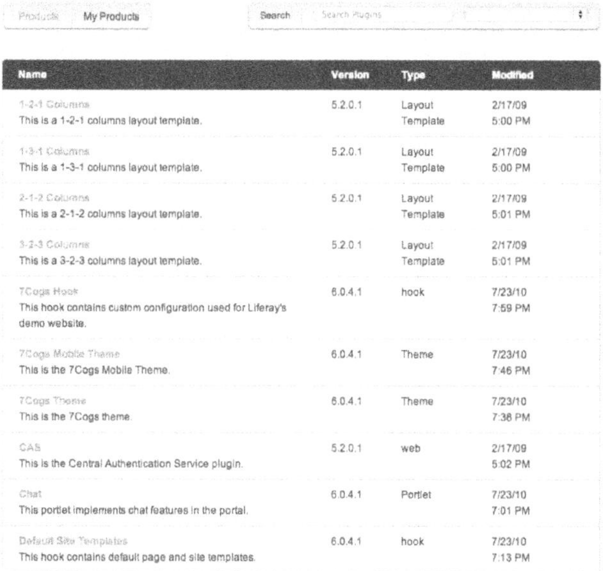

Name	Version	Type	Modified
1-2-1 Columns	5.2.0.1	Layout	2/17/09
This is a 1-2-1 columns layout template.		Template	5:00 PM
1-3-1 Columns	5.2.0.1	Layout	2/17/09
This is a 1-3-1 columns layout template.		Template	5:00 PM
2-1-2 Columns	5.2.0.1	Layout	2/17/09
This is a 2-1-2 columns layout template.		Template	5:01 PM
3-2-3 Columns	5.2.0.1	Layout	2/17/09
This is a 3-2-3 columns layout template.		Template	5:01 PM
7Cogs Hook	6.0.4.1	hook	7/23/10
This hook contains custom configuration used for Liferay's demo website.			7:59 PM
7Cogs Mobile Theme	6.0.4.1	Theme	7/23/10
This is the 7Cogs Mobile Theme.			7:46 PM
7Cogs Theme	6.0.4.1	Theme	7/23/10
This is the 7Cogs theme.			7:38 PM
CAS	5.2.0.1	web	2/17/09
This is the Central Authentication Service plugin.			5:02 PM
Chat	6.0.4.1	Portlet	7/23/10
This portlet implements chat features in the portal.			7:01 PM
Default Site Templates	6.0.4.1	hook	7/23/10
This hook contains default page and site templates.			7:13 PM

Figure 14.8: This is an example of a populated Software Catalog from liferay.com

When you have finished filling out the form, click the *Save* button. Your license will be saved. Once you have at least one license in the system, you can begin adding software products to your software catalog. Click the *Products* tab, then click the *Add Product* button.

Your next step will be to create the product record in the software catalog. This will register the product in the software catalog and allow you to start adding versions of your software for users to download and/or install directly from their instances of Liferay. You will first need to put the .war file containing your software on a web server that is accessible without authentication to the users who will be installing your software. In the example above, the *Old Computers* site is on the Internet so you would place the file on a web server that is accessible to anyone on the Internet. If you are creating a software catalog for an internal Intranet, you would place the file on a web server that is available to anyone inside of your organization's firewall.

To create the product record in the Software Catalog portlet, click the *Products* tab, then click the *Add Product* button. Fill out the form with information about your product.

Name: The name of your software product.

Type: Select whether this is a portlet, theme, layout template, hook or web plugin.

Licenses: Select the license(s) under which you are releasing this software. You must first add a license using the *License* tab before you can select it in the *New Product* form.

Author: Enter the name of the author of the software.

Page URL: If the software has a home page, enter its URL here.

Tags: Enter any tags you would like added to this software.

Short Description: Enter a short description. This will be displayed in the summary table of your software catalog.

Long Description: Enter a longer description. This will be displayed on the details page for this software product.

Permissions: Click the *Configure* link to set permissions for this software product.

Site ID: Enter a site ID. A site ID is a name space which identifies the site that released the software. For our example, we will use *old-computers*.

Figure 14.9: The *New Product* screen provides a recommended licenses setting for your product.

Artifact ID: Enter an Artifact ID. The artifact ID is a unique name within the name space for your product. For our example, we will use *my-summary-portlet*.

Screenshot: Click the *Add Screenshot* button to add a screen shot of your product for users to view.

When you have finished filling out the form, click the *Save* button. You will be brought back to the product summary page and you will see your product has been added to the repository.

Notice in the version column, *N/A* is being displayed. This is because there are not yet any released *versions* of your product. To make your product downloadable, you need to create a version of your product and point it to the file you uploaded to your HTTP server earlier.

Before you do that, however, you need to add a *Framework Version* to your software cata-log. A Framework version denotes what version of Liferay your plugin is designed for and works on. You cannot add a version of your product without linking it to a version of the framework for which it is designed.

Why is this so important? Because as Liferay gains more and more features, you may wish to take advantage of those features in future versions of your product, while still keeping older versions of your product available for those who are using older versions of Liferay. This is perfectly illustrated in the example My Summary portlet we are using. Liferay had a My Summary portlet of its own, which does exactly what we have described here. This portlet was added to the suite of portlets which Liferay provides in the Social Networking plugin. This plugin makes use of the many social networking features which have been added to Liferay. So rather than just displaying a summary of your informa-tion, the Social Networking portlet adds features such as status updates, a *wall* for each user in his or her profile that other users can *write* on, the ability to become *friends* with other users—thereby granting them access to their profiles—and more.

None of this would work in older versions of Liferay, because the core engine that en-ables developers to create features like this is not there. So in this case, you would want to keep the older My Summary portlet available for users who have not yet upgraded and make the newer social portlets available to those using latest version of Liferay. This is what *Framework Versions* does for you. If you connect to Liferay's software repositories with an old version of Liferay Portal, you will see the My Summary portlet. If you con-nect to Liferay's software repositories with new version of Liferay, you will see the social portlets.

So click the *Framework Versions* tab and then click the *Add Framework Version* button.

Give the framework a name, a URL and leave the *Active* check box checked. For our example, we have entered 6.2.0 for the name, because our portlet should work on that version and higher, and http://www.liferay.com for the URL. Click *Save*.

Now go back to the *Products* tab and click on your product. You will notice a message is displayed stating the product does not have any released versions. Click the *Add Product Version* button.

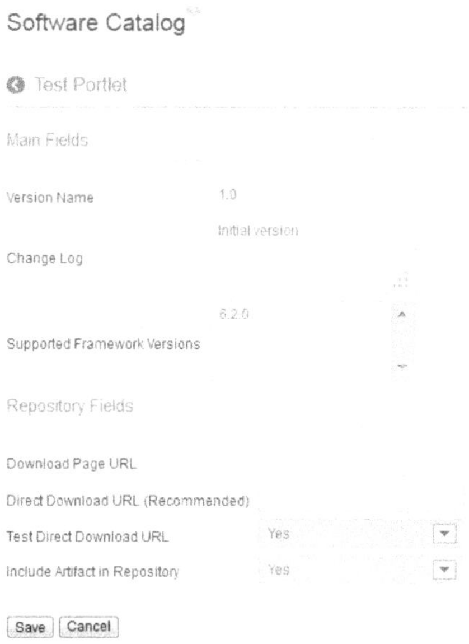

Figure 14.10: Versions usually increment by *.1* for every new release.

Version Name: Enter the version of your product.

Change Log: Enter some comments regarding what changed between this version and any previous versions.

Supported Framework Versions: Select the framework version for which your software product is intended. Enter a + at the end of the version number if you want to specify a version plus any future versions.

Download Page URL: If your product has a descriptive web page, enter its URL here.

Direct Download URL (Recommended): Enter a direct download link to your software product here. The Plugin Installer portlet will follow this link in order to download your software product.

Test Direct Download URL: Select *Yes* if you'd like Liferay to test the download URL for its validity.

Include Artifact in Repository: To enable others to use the Plugin Installer portlet to connect to your repository and download your plugin, select *Yes* here.

When you are finished filling out the form, click the *Save* button. Your product version will be saved and your product will now be available in the software repository.

Generating the Software Catalog

The Software Catalog works by generating an XML document which the Plugin Installer reads. Using the data from this XML document, the Plugin Installer knows where it can download the plugins from, what version of Liferay the plugins are designed for, and all other data about the plugins that have been entered into the Software Catalog portlet.

In order to get your Software Catalog to generate this XML data, you will need to access a particular URL. If you have created a friendly URL for your site (for example, the default site, which is called *guest*, has a friendly URL of /guest already configured for it), you can use the friendly URL. If not, you will first need to know the Group ID of the site in which your Software Catalog portlet resides. Obviously, it is much easier if you are using Friendly URLs, which we highly recommend.

Next, go to your browser and go to the following URL:

```
http://<server name\>:<port number\>/software_catalog?<Friendly URL name or Group ID\>
```

For example, if you are on the same machine as your Liferay instance, and that instance is running on port 8080, and your group ID from the database is 10148, you would use the following URL:

```
http://localhost:8080/software_catalog?10148
```

If you have also created a friendly URL called *old-computers* for this site, you would use the following URL:

```
http://localhost:8080/software_catalog?old-computers
```

If you have configured everything properly, an XML document should be returned:

```
<?xml version="1.0" encoding="UTF-8"?>

<plugin-repository\>
    <settings/>
    <plugin-package>
        <name>My Summary</name>
        <module-id>old-computers/my-summary-portlet/1.0/war</module-id>
        <modified-date>Thu, 20 Sep 2013 18:28:14 +0000</modified-date>
        <types>
            <type>portlet</type>
        </types>
        <tags>
            <tag>social</tag>
            <tag>profile</tag>
        </tags>
        <short-description>My Summary</short-description>
        <long-description>My Summary</long-description>
        <change-log>Initial Version</change-log>
        <download-url>
```

```
        http://www.liferay.com/portlets/my-summary-portlet-6.2.0.war
    </download-url>
    <author>Cody Hoag</author>
    <screenshots/>
    <licenses>
        <license osi-approved="true">LGPL</license>
    </licenses>
    <liferay-versions/>
  </plugin-package>
</plugin-repository>
```

You can now give the URL to your software repository out on your web site and other administrators of Liferay can enter it into the Plugins Installation module of their Liferay Control Panels to connect to your repository.

If you want to serve your repository off of a static web server, you can save this document to a file called liferay-plugin-package.xml and put this file on your HTTP server. You can then give out the URL to the directory which holds this file on your web site and anyone with an instance of Liferay will be able to point their Plugin Installer portlets to it.

Benefits of the Software Catalog

As you can see, the Software Catalog makes it easy for you to create a repository of your software. Users of Liferay can configure their Plugin Installers to attach to your repository and the proper versions of your software will be automatically made available to them by a single click. This is by far the easiest way for you to keep track of your software and for your users to obtain your software.

Another benefit of the Software Catalog is that you can make available to your users a standard interface for manually downloading your software. For those who prefer to manually download plugins, your Software Catalog gives them an interface to go in, find your software either by browsing or by searching, preview screen shots and download your software—and you don't have to build any of those pages yourself. Simply configure your software in the portlet and all of that is done for you.

How can you do this? The Software Catalog is also available as a portlet. You can add it to any page on your web site through the *Add →Applications* menu. You can find the portlet in the *Tools* category.

Manually Creating A Software Catalog

If you do not wish to use the Control Panel to create your software catalog, you can create it manually by manually typing out the XML file that the Software Catalog section of the Control Panel would normally generate. Note that if you do this, you will not be able to use the Software Catalog portlet as a graphical user interface to your software that end users can use to download your software manually: you will have to build this yourself. Keep in mind many instances of Liferay Portal sit behind a firewall without access to the Internet. Because of this, if you are making your software available to Internet users, some of them will have to download it manually anyway, because their installations are firewalled. In this case, the Software Catalog portlet is the easiest way to provide a user interface for downloading your software.

If you still wish to use a text editor to create your software catalog, you can. To manually create a software catalog, obtain the DTD for the XML file from Liferay's source code. You will find this DTD in the *definitions* folder in the Liferay source. It is a file called liferay-plugin-package_6_2_0.dtd. Use this DTD with a validating XML editor (a good, free choice is jEdit with all the XML plugins) to create your software catalog manually.

Connecting to a Software Catalog

If there is a software catalog of plugins you would like to point your instance of Liferay to, all you need is the URL to the catalog. Once you have the URL, go to the App Manager in the Control Panel and click the *Install* tab. You will see there is a field in which you can enter a URL to a plugin repository.

Enter the URL to the repository to which you wish to connect and click *Save*. The portlet will connect to the repository and items from this repository will be shown in the list.

If all this talk of catalogs has put you in the mood to do some shopping, then it's probably a good time to get acquainted with Liferay's Shopping application. Let's go down that aisle next.

14.3   Shopping

Would your organization like to make some money selling promotional items? Are you an artist looking to share your work with the world? Perhaps your company produces a publication that customers want to purchase? If you have something of value the visitors of your site want or need, then Liferay's Shopping application can help you get these items to your customers with a secure transaction.

The Shopping portlet uses PayPal and allows you to choose the credit cards your store accepts. You can organize your inventory with categories and subcategories. A search function helps users find items quickly. Users place items in a shopping cart, allowing them to purchase multiple items at once. There is also an email notification system to alert customers when their transactions are processed.

Before we start printing money, let's first create an online store.

Setting up shop

To begin setting up a store, place the Shopping application on a page in your site. Like the Message Boards portlet, the Shopping portlet takes up a lot of space. It's best, therefore, to dedicate an entire page to the application. The Shopping portlet is available from the *Add Applications* menu on the left side panel under Shopping.

Figure 14.11: Start setting up the store by entering items and categories in the shopping portlet.

The shopping portlet has four tabs across the top:

Categories: shows the categories of items in your store. For example, if you're selling music, you might have categories for various genres, such as pop, rock, metal, hip hop, and the like. The portlet defaults to this view.

Cart: shows the items the user has selected to purchase from your store. It displays the order subtotal, the shipping cost, and a field for entering a coupon code. There are buttons for updating the cart, emptying the cart, and checking out.

Orders: displays a list of all previous orders placed, containing options to search for orders by the order number, status, first name, last name and/or email address.

Coupons: lets you define coupon codes to offer discounts to your customers. You can enter the coupon code, discount type, and whether it is active or not. Search looks for a particular coupon offer while Add Coupon opens a new form to key in the coupon data. Delete removes a coupon.

Below the tabs are breadcrumbs for navigating between the categories and subcategories you create. In fact, this would be a good time to start creating some categories.

Creating Categories

It's not difficult to create categories. Simply click the *Add Category* button to display the Category form. In this form enter the *Name*, *Description*, and set the *Permissions* for the category. That's all there is to it.

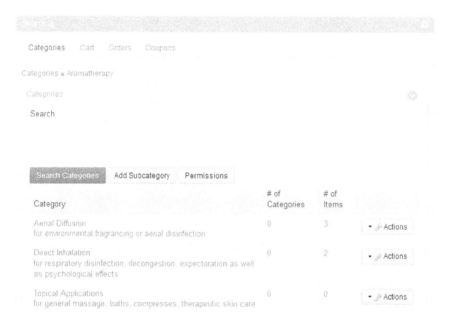

Figure 14.12: In this figure there are three subcategories for the Aromatherapy category. The first subcategory has three items, the second has two, and the third is empty.

When you click *Save*, your new category is listed in the portlet, along with the number of subcategories and the number of items that are in the category. You can edit the category, set permissions for it or delete it using the *Actions* button.

Each category can have unlimited subcategories and you can add subcategories to any category. Notice as you add categories and subcategories, navigational breadcrumbs appear in the portlet. Use these to move through the store inventory.

Creating Items

When you select a category, you'll see its items appear. You create items the same way you create categories. Use the *Add Item* button to open the new item form. Enter data for the SKU number, name, description, and item properties. You can select checkboxes to spec-

Shopping

Categories   Cart   Orders   Coupons

Categories » Aromatherapy » Aerial Diffusion

Categories

Figure 14.13: Breadcrumbs are an important navigational tool in the shopping portlet.

ify whether the item requires shipping and whether it is a featured item. Enter the stock quantity to record how many items are available and set the appropriate permissions.

The Fields area is where you add additional fields to set specific characteristics for the item. These can include things like sizes and colors. The additional fields appear in the item form as pull-down menus.

The Prices area is for all data pertaining to the item's cost, minimum, and maximum quantities, quantity discounts, taxes, and shipping costs.

The Images area lets you add photos to the item form. You can add a link to the photo or upload the file locally. Choose from three sizes of images. You must select the appropriate check box for the image you want to display. When you're finished creating a new item, click *Save*.

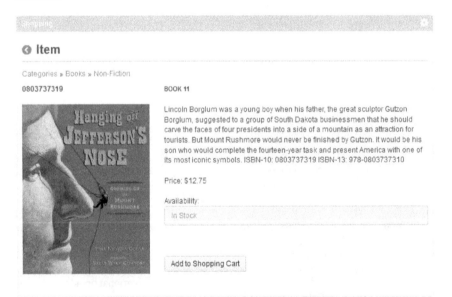

Figure 14.14: The image in this figure is the medium sized option.

As products are added, they are listed in the Items section of the portlet. If the item you just created needs to go into one of your new categories or subcategories, you can assign it to the category by editing the item. Choose the *Select* button (next to the *Remove* button), and this displays a dialog box listing all the shop categories. Choose the desired category from the list to relocate the item to its new location. Notice how the breadcrumbs reflect this change in the item form. For a tutorial on categories, breadcrumbs, and item relocation, visit the *Moving a Link* section in this chapter.

You can make changes to any item through *Actions* →*Edit*. Finding an item is easy, using the *Search* function.

That's how you create an item for the store. Now let's examine some of the shopping portlet's configuration options.

Configuration

By selecting the *gear* icon in the top right of the portlet, you can manage the configuration options of the shopping application. In the Setup view, there are tabs for Payment Settings, Shipping Calculation, Insurance Calculation, and Emails.

Payment Settings

The payment settings section is where you configure all the functions related to transactions for your store.

PayPal Email Address: is the address of your store's PayPal account which is used for payment processing.

Note that PayPal can be disabled by entering a blank PayPal address in the field. Credit cards can likewise be disabled. Payments to the store are not required when these settings are disabled. The credit card function does not process payments; it instead stores the card information with the order so you can process the transaction separately.

Credit Cards: sets the type of credit cards your store accepts.

The Current column holds the cards your store takes. The Available column holds cards not accepted by your shop. These can be moved easily from one column to another by selecting a card and clicking one of the arrow buttons. The arrows below the Current window allow you to choose the order credit cards are displayed on the form.

Currency: sets the appropriate currency your shop accepts.

Tax State: sets the applicable state where your business is responsible for paying taxes.

Tax Rate: sets the percentage of taxes your store is responsible for paying. This rate is added as a sales tax charge to orders.

Minimum Order: sets the minimum amount required for a sale.

Shipping and Insurance Calculation

Both the Shipping and Insurance forms have identical options.

Formula: sets the equation for determining shipping and insurance costs. They're calculated on either a flat rate based on the total purchase amount or on a percentage of the total amount spent.

Values: sets the shipping and insurance fees based on a range of figures that the total order amount falls under.

Emails

This form sets the addresses for customer email notifications. Use the list of term definitions below to customize the correspondence with your customers.

Emails From: sets the email address from which order and shipping notifications are sent.

Confirmation Email: Use this form to customize the email message customers receive when an order is received.

Shipping Email: Use this form to customize the email message customers receive when an order has been shipped.

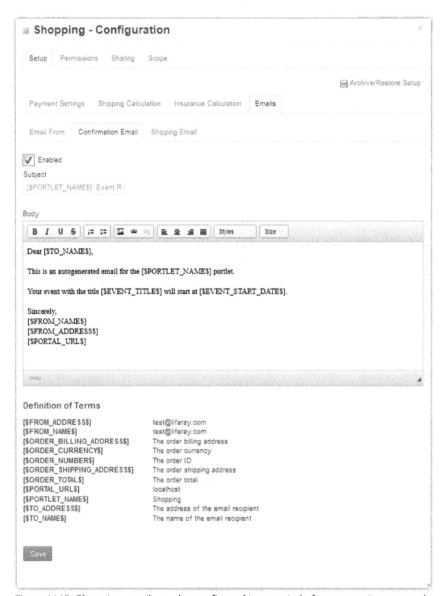

Figure 14.15: Shopping emails can be configured in a myriad of ways to suit your needs.

So far we have added the shopping portlet to your site, created categories and items for your store, set up payment options, and configured customer communication options. These are the basics required to get your store up and running. Now let's review the buying process.

Using the shopping cart

Logged in users are given a shopping cart to store the items they wish to buy. Customers can manage items and their quantities directly from the cart, allowing them to purchase a single product or multiple products at once. Customers can also key in coupon codes to take advantage of any discounts your store has to offer. Products can be placed in the cart from any category or subcategory. The cart's appearance can be customized to reflect the overall design of your store.

When buyers select an item, they see the item's description displaying all of its relevant information. The figure below is typical of what an item's description might look like.

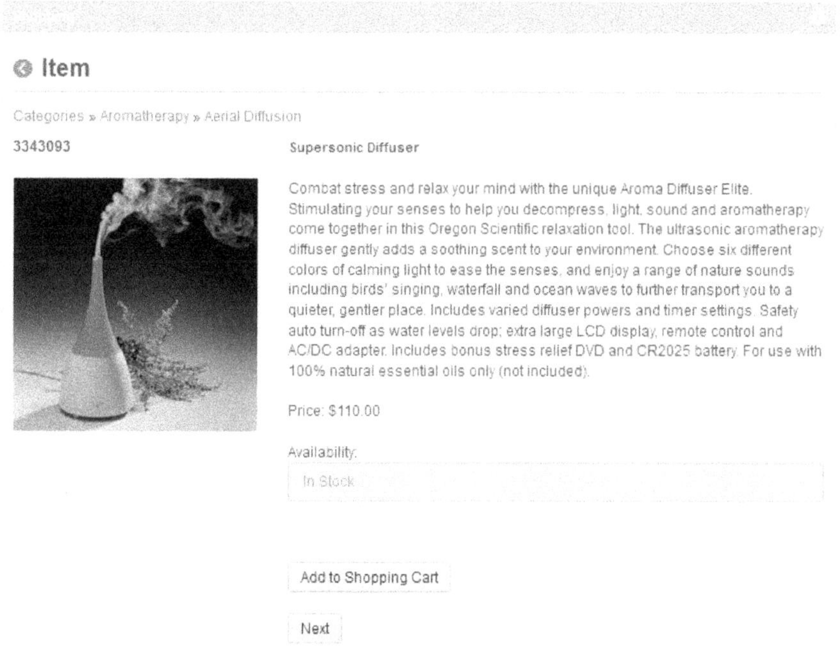

Item

Categories » Aromatherapy » Aerial Diffusion

3343093   Supersonic Diffuser

Combat stress and relax your mind with the unique Aroma Diffuser Elite. Stimulating your senses to help you decompress, light, sound and aromatherapy come together in this Oregon Scientific relaxation tool. The ultrasonic aromatherapy diffuser gently adds a soothing scent to your environment. Choose six different colors of calming light to ease the senses, and enjoy a range of nature sounds including birds' singing, waterfall and ocean waves to further transport you to a quieter, gentler place. Includes varied diffuser powers and timer settings. Safety auto turn-off as water levels drop; extra large LCD display, remote control and AC/DC adapter. Includes bonus stress relief DVD and CR2025 battery. For use with 100% natural essential oils only (not included).

Price: $110.00

Availability:

In Stock

Add to Shopping Cart

Next

Figure 14.16: Your product's SKU number is listed above the image.

Below the product description is the Availability field indicating whether the item is in stock. There are also two buttons for managing the shopping experience:

Add to Shopping Cart: places the item in your cart for checkout.

Next: lets you to scroll through all the items in the category, giving you the option to add to the cart as you go.

After adding an item to the cart, click Back (blue arrow) to return to the product description and continue shopping by navigating the category breadcrumbs at the top of the form. You can also continue shopping by scrolling through a category, item by item, using the *Previous* and *Next* buttons at the bottom of the product description.

Each time you add an item to the cart, a running tally of the cart's contents is kept. Quantities for each item are controlled using drop-down menus. The order subtotal and shipping costs appear above a field where coupon codes can be entered. When you have finished adding products to the cart, you have three options:

Update Cart: lets you change the quantity of an item being purchased. If a minimum number of items has been set in the item description, the field under the Quantity column shows that number by default. You can adjust the exact number of items you want with the drop-down menus in the cart.

Empty Cart: lets you clear the contents of the cart to either start shopping again or to stop shopping.

Checkout: sends you to a new form to verify the billing address, shipping address, and the credit card information. You can also add comments about the order if necessary.

Figure 14.17: The shopping cart gives a preview of the items you'd like to buy.

When you're ready to checkout, click the *Checkout* button at the bottom of the screen. When all the data has been entered correctly, click *Continue* to see the order summary. After reviewing the summary, click *Finished* and you are given confirmation the order has been placed, along with the order number. Use this number to search for the order history and keep track of its status.

Customizing the shopping cart with a hook

If you think the shopping cart looks a little basic for your purposes, you can customize it by using a hook. To learn more about changing the appearance of the shopping cart, consult the *Liferay Developer Network* or see section 8.3 in *Liferay in Action*.

Now your online store is set up, you have inventory, you have a payment system, and you have sales rolling in. All is good. Some day there will be customers with questions about their orders. Let's go over the orders next.

Managing Orders

On the Orders tab, there are fields for finding specific orders. Search for orders using the order number, order status, first or last name on the order, or by the email address associated with the account. For more information on searching in Liferay Portal, see the Faceted Search section in chapter 6 of this guide.

Below the search fields is the orders list. Orders can be deleted or edited using the *Actions* button. When you select an order from the Orders tab, or if you edit an order, you see a summary of the order details along with some options across the bottom.

Invoice: creates a printer-friendly copy of the order that can be sent to a customer.

Resend Confirmation Email: lets you notify the customer that the order has been received and is being processed.

Send Shipping Email: notifies the customer that the order is *en route*. You can also include a tracking number with this email to allow the customer to follow the delivery process.

Delete: removes the order from the system.

Cancel: closes the Edit view and returns the user to the main orders view.

You can also add comments about the order and subscribe to the comments to get any updates on the order.

Managing Coupons

The Coupons view of the Shopping application lets you provide coupon codes for special sale events or other discounts. You can determine the type of discount to apply and whether it is currently active. You can search for coupons and create new coupons from this form.

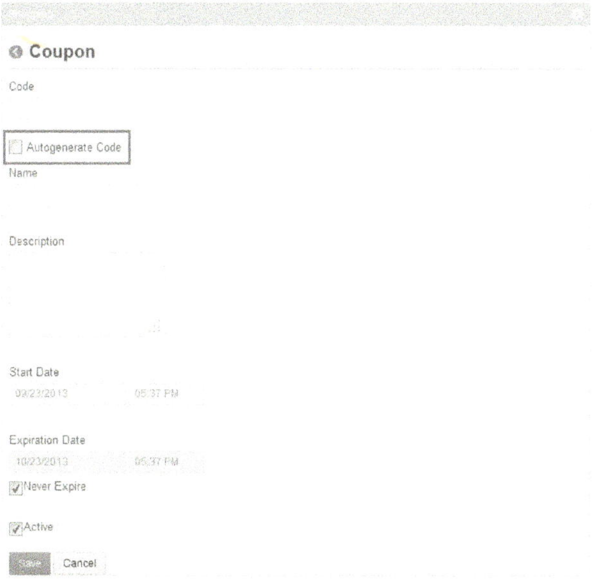

Figure 14.18: Create a coupon code automatically when you select the Autogenerate Code box.

To add a coupon, enter the coupon code in the Code field. If no code is specified, you can create one automatically by selecting the *Autogenerate Code* checkbox. After entering the coupon's name and description, you can set the coupon's start and expiration dates. Additional options let you activate the coupon and set it to never expire.

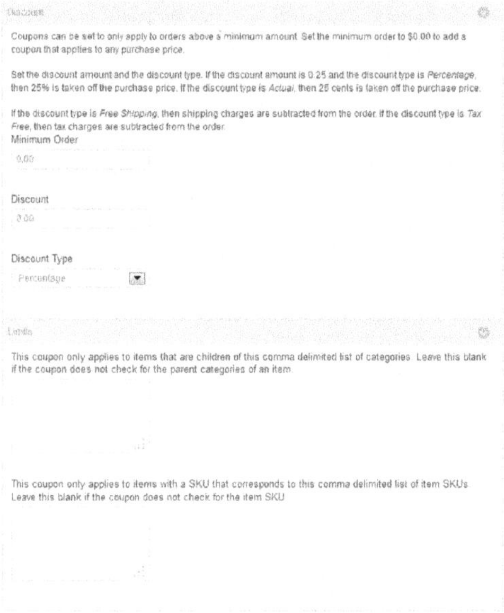

Figure 14.19: Customize your coupon parameters under Discounts and Limits.

Under the Discount section, you can set the minimum order amount required for the discount, the discount amount, and the discount type. Types can be based on a percentage, a fixed amount, free shipping, or a tax free sale. The Limits section lets you set coupon restrictions based on a list of categories and/or SKU numbers.

Integrating the Amazon Rankings portlet

If your store sells books, you can use Liferay's Amazon Rankings application to display them alongside the main shopping portlet. Both of these are found in the Shopping category under *Add Applications* in the left menu. The Amazon Rankings application lets you highlight the books in your store's inventory outside of the typical category structure. Books are arranged in ascending order according to Amazon's Best Sellers Rank. Book cover images displayed in the portlet come from the images in the product's description.

Setting up your Amazon Web Services account   To use Amazon rankings, you must first setup an Amazon Associates Program account. This gives you the *associate ID tag* you need to enter in your portal-ext.properties file. Then you need to join the Amazon Product Advertising API group. This yields the *access key id* and the *secret access key* that also must go into your portal-ext.properties file.

Amazon License Keys are available.[2]

Add the following lines to your portal-ext.properties file and populate the values for the associate ID tag, access key ID, and secret access key. Ensure there are no spaces between the = sign and the property values.

---

[2]https://aws-portal.amazon.com/gp/aws/developer/registration/index.html/

```
amazon.access.key.id=
amazon.associate.tag=
amazon.secret.access.key=
```

Note that these keys are provided by Amazon for personal use only. Please consult Amazon at http://www.amazon.com for more information.

To obtain the amazon.associate.tag, visit the Amazon Associate program[3] and apply, if necessary. Your associate tag is the *Tracking ID* listed in the upper left corner of the Associates Central[4] page.

 Tip: Make sure to create your affiliate program before generating an access key; otherwise, the access key will not be linked to your affiliate program.

If your Amazon Web Services key is set improperly, you can't add books to your Shopping portlet.

Setting up the Amazon Rankings portlet After setting up your Amazon Web Services account, choose the books to display in your store. Select *Configuration* from the Amazon Rankings portlet in the upper right corner. Go to the *Setup* tab and enter the International Standard Book Numbers (ISBNs) in the textbox, separated by spaces. The portlet accepts 10-digit ISBNs rejecting ISBNs that letters.

When you are finished setting up the rankings, books appear in the portlet similar to the example below. Clicking on the book's cover image opens the book's Amazon page.

Figure 14.20: Using the Amazon Rankings application can be a nice addition to your store.

Now that you have a good grasp on Liferay's Shopping and Amazon Rankings applications, let's learn how to generate reports in Liferay.

---

[3]https://affiliate-program.amazon.com/gp/associates/apply/main.html
[4]https://affiliate-program.amazon.com/gp/associates/network/main.html

14.4   Generating Reports in Liferay

Liferay's Reports portlet allows administrators to create reports
and schedule report generation runs. In order to work, the Reports portlet needs to be combined with an appropriate implementation such as the JasperReports web plugin. You can use
Liferay's Reports portlet to create professional reports containing charts, images, subreports, etc. When a report is generated,
data is dynamically pulled from Liferay's database into a template. Data can be pulled into Jasper reports via JDBC and Jasper

reports can be exported to many different file formats including PDF, HTML, XLS, RTF,
CSV, or XML. The Reports and JasperReports plugins are available as apps on Liferay
Marketplace. You can purchase, download, and install the Reports and JasperReports
apps directly from your Liferay instance's Control Panel interface or you can navigate
to http://www.liferay.com/marketplace in your browser, purchase and download
the apps, and copy the .lpkg files to your Liferay instance's /deploy folder.

Using the Reports Portlet

Once you've installed the Reports and Jasper Reports EE applications, log in to your portal
as an administrator and navigate to *Site Administration*. If your applications have been
successfully deployed, you'll find a *Reports Admin* entry in the *Configuration* section on the
left menu.

The Reports Admin portlet has three
tabs:

* *Reports*
* *Definitions*
* *Sources*

The Reports tab shows a list of all generated reports. The Definitions tab shows
a list of report definitions. The most important features of a report definition are
the data source, which determines where
to find the data to be displayed in a report, and the template, which determines
which information to display and how to
display it. The Sources tab allows you to
add new data sources which can be selected by report definitions. Note: your

Figure 14.22: To check that the Reports EE
and Jasper Reports EE applications have
been successfully deployed to your Liferay
server, look for the *Reports Admin* entry in
the Configuration section of your Site
Administration page.

portal's database is automatically set up as a default data source called *Portal*. The *Portal* data source does not appear on the Sources tab but is selectable on the form for
adding/editing a report definition.

In order to generate a report, you need to a have one or more report definitions configured. To create a report definition, you need a data source and a report template. If you'd
like to use your portal's database as your report definition's data source, use the default
data source called *Portal*. If you'd like to use a different data source, navigate to the *Sources*
tab of the Reports Admin portlet and click on the *Add Source* button. Enter a name for the
new data source and enter the JDBC connection information:

* Driver Class Name
* URL
* User Name

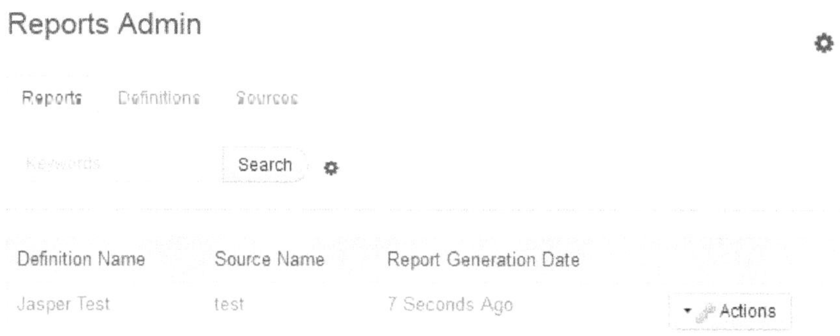

Reports Admin

Reports   Definitions   Sources

Keywords   [Search] ⚙

Definition Name	Source Name	Report Generation Date	
Jasper Test	test	7 Seconds Ago	▾ Actions

Figure 14.23: Use the *Sources* tab of the Reports Admin portlet to define data sources for report definitions. Use the *Definitions* tab to define report definitions, generate reports, and schedule reports for generation. Use the *Reports* tab to browse through and download generated reports.

- Password

For example, to connect to a MySQL database called *data_source* installed on the Liferay server, you could use the following credentials:

- Driver Class Name: *com.mysql.jdbc.Driver*
- URL: jdbc:mysql://localhost/data_source?useUnicode=true&characterEncoding=UTF-8&useFastDateParsing=false
- User Name: *[MySQL User Name]*
- Password: *[MySQL Password]*

Click on the *Test Database Connection* button to make sure that you've entered the connection information correctly. Liferay will respond with a success or error message depending on whether or not it was able to connect to the data source. From the Reports Admin portlet's Sources tab, you can see a list of all the data sources that have been added. You can configure data sources' permissions to customize who can edit them and you can delete data sources that should no longer be used.

Once your data source has been saved, make sure that your report template is ready for use. If you're using Jasper and need to create a Jasper template, consider using a tool like iReport Designer or Jaspersoft Studio to create your template. iReport is built on top of Netbeans IDE while Jaspersoft Studio is Eclipse-based.

Once you've created a Jasper template (.jrxml file), you're ready to create a report definition. Liferay handles compiling the template, populating the template with data, and exporting the report. For more information on using iReport Designer and on the Jasper Report lifecycle, please refer to Jaspersoft's wiki[5] and documentation.[6]

To add a report definition, navigate to the *Definitions* tab of the Reports Admin portlet and click *Add Report Definition*. Enter a definition name and, optionally, a description. Select a data source for your report definition. Remember that you can use your portal's database as your database by selecting the default *Portal* data source. Then select a Jasper template (.jrxml file) for your report template. Optionally, you can add report parameters and values to your report definition and they'll be injected into the template at runtime when the report is generated. Lastly, you can configure the permissions of your new

[5]http://community.jaspersoft.com/wiki/ireport-designer-getting-started
[6]http://community.jaspersoft.com/documentation?version=7114

report definition. By default, new reports, report definitions, and data sources are site-scoped. For this reason, new report definitions are set to be viewable by site members. When you've completed your new report definition, click *Save*.

Now you're ready to use your report definition to generate reports manually or schedule them to be generated. From the Report Admin portlet's Definitions tab, click *Actions* →*Add Report* next to your report definition. You can choose any of the following reports formats:

- CSV
- HTML
- PDF
- RTF
- TXT
- XLS
- XML

You can configure email notifications or specific email recipients. Email notifications just inform users that a report has been generated and provide a link to the report's location in the portal. Email recipients actually receive copies of the report as email attachments. You can customize the account from which report notifications and deliveries are sent as well as the messages themselves from the configuration window of the Reports Admin portlet. When generating a report, you can also configure the permissions of the report to be generated. By default, generated reports are site-scoped and are viewable by site members.

To configure reports to be generated on a schedule, click *Actions* →*Add Schedule* next to your report definition from the Report Admin portlet's Definitions tab. You can select a start date and, optionally, an end date. You can also select how often to repeat the report generation event:

- *Never*
- *Daily*
- *Weekly*
- *Monthly*
- *Yearly*

As on the *Add Report* form, you can select a report format, configure email notifications and email recipients, and configure the permissions of the reports to be generated. When you're done setting up your report generation schedule, click *Save*. Great! Now your reports will automatically be generated on the dates you've configured. You can create multiple reports from a single report definition. You can also edit a report definition, configure a report definition's permissions, or delete a report definition from the Report Admin portlet's Definitions tab.

Once one or more reports have been generated, they'll appear in the Reports Admin portlet's Reports tab. To edit a report's permissions or to delete a report, use the *Actions* button next to the report's name. To view details about a report, click on its name. From the details view of a report, you can download the report by clicking *Actions* →*Download* next to the report file. You can also deliver the report by clicking *Actions* →*Deliver Report*, choosing an email recipient, and clicking *Deliver*. To delete the report file, click *Actions* →*Delete*.

Configuring the Reports Admin Portlet

To configure the Reports Admin portlet, navigate to the Reports Admin portlet in the Control Panel, click on the *wrench* icon at the top right corner of the portlet, and select *Configuration*. There are three tabs:

- *Email From*
- *Delivery Email*
- *Notifications Email*

The Email From tab allows you to customize the name and email address of the account that sends report notifications within your portal. For example, you could set the name to *Reports Admin* and the email address to *reports@liferay.com*. The Delivery Email tab allows you to customize the email message that's sent when a report is delivered to a portal user. When a report is delivered to a portal user, it's included as an attachment to this email message. Finally, the Notifications Email tab allows you to customize the message that's sent when a report notification is sent to a portal user. In this case, the report is not included as an attachment; the email message just provides a link to the report's location in the portal.

Using the Reports Display Portlet

Installing the Reports EE and JasperReports EE apps not only adds the Reports Admin portlet to the Control Panel but also makes the Reports Display portlet available. The Reports Display portlet provides the same functionality as the Reports tab of the Reports Admin portlet. The Reports Display portlet allows users to download or deliver reports but not to add, edit, or delete report definitions or data sources.

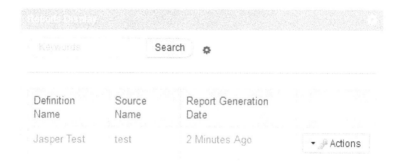

Figure 14.24: Here, the Reports Display portlet shows only a single report.

The Reports Display portlet is intended to be placed within a site's private pages to allow site members to access site-scoped reports. It can also be placed within a site's public pages. In this case, reports will only be displayed to users that have permission to view the reports. For example, if a guest views a site's public page to which the Reports Display portlet has been added, site-scoped reports will not be visible; only reports for which the View permission has been added to the Guest role will appear in the Reports Display portlet.

Creating a Sample Jasper Report in Liferay

To create a sample Jasper report in Liferay, follow this section's instructions. We'll use your portal's database as our report definition's data source and we'll use a simple Jasper template that was created using iReport Designer.

1. Save the following Jasper template to a file named `sample-report.jrxml` somewhere on your machine's file system.

```xml
<?xml version="1.0" encoding="UTF-8"?>
<jasperReport xmlns="http://jasperreports.sourceforge.net/jasperreports"
    xmlns:xsi="http://www.w3.org/2001/XMLSchema-instance"
    xsi:schemaLocation="http://jasperreports.sourceforge.net/jasperreports
    http://jasperreports.sourceforge.net/xsd/jasperreport.xsd"
    name="sample-report2"
    language="groovy"
    pageWidth="595"
    pageHeight="842"
    columnWidth="555"
    leftMargin="20"
    rightMargin="20"
    topMargin="20"
    bottomMargin="20"
>
        <property name="ireport.zoom" value="1.0"/>
        <property name="ireport.x" value="0"/>
        <property name="ireport.y" value="0"/>
        <queryString language="SQL">
                <![CDATA[select * from User_]]>
        </queryString>
        <field name="userId" class="java.lang.Long">
                <fieldDescription><![CDATA[]]></fieldDescription>
        </field>
        <field name="screenName" class="java.lang.String">
                <fieldDescription><![CDATA[]]></fieldDescription>
        </field>
        <field name="emailAddress" class="java.lang.String">
                <fieldDescription><![CDATA[]]></fieldDescription>
        </field>
        <field name="createDate" class="java.sql.Timestamp">
                <fieldDescription><![CDATA[]]></fieldDescription>
        </field>
        <field name="modifiedDate" class="java.sql.Timestamp">
                <fieldDescription><![CDATA[]]></fieldDescription>
        </field>
        <group name="userId">
                <groupExpression><![CDATA[$F{userId}]]></groupExpression>
        </group>
        <group name="screenName">
                <groupExpression><![CDATA[$F{screenName}]]></groupExpression>
        </group>
        <group name="emailAddress">
                <groupExpression><![CDATA[$F{emailAddress}]]></groupExpression>
        </group>
        <group name="createDate">
            <groupExpression><![CDATA[$F{createDate}]]></groupExpression>
        </group>
        <background>
            <band splitType="Stretch"/>
        </background>
        <title>
            <band height="79" splitType="Stretch">
                <staticText>
                    <reportElement x="0" y="0" width="555" height="51"/>
                        <textElement>
                            <font size="24" isBold="true"/>
                        </textElement>
                        <text><![CDATA[Sample Report: Users]]></text>
                </staticText>
            </band>
        </title>
        <pageHeader>
            <band height="35" splitType="Stretch"/>
        </pageHeader>
        <columnHeader>
            <band height="61" splitType="Stretch">
                <staticText>
                    <reportElement x="0" y="0" width="63" height="20"/>
                    <textElement>
                        <font size="14" isItalic="true"/>
                    </textElement>
                    <text><![CDATA[userId]]></text>
                </staticText>
                <staticText>
                    <reportElement x="63" y="0" width="90" height="20"/>
                      <textElement>
```

```
                              <font size="14" isItalic="true"/>
                        </textElement>
                        <text><![CDATA[screenName]]></text>
                  </staticText>
                  <staticText>
                        <reportElement x="153" y="0" width="128" height="20"/>
                        <textElement>
                              <font size="14" isItalic="true"/>
                        </textElement>
                        <text><![CDATA[emailAddress]]></text>
                  </staticText>
                  <staticText>
                        <reportElement x="281" y="0" width="141" height="20"/>
                              <textElement>
                                    <font size="14" isItalic="true"/>
                              </textElement>
                              <text><![CDATA[createDate]]></text>
                  </staticText>
                  <staticText>
                        <reportElement x="422" y="0" width="133" height="20"/>
                        <textElement>
                              <font size="14" isItalic="true"/>
                        </textElement>
                        <text><![CDATA[modifiedDate]]></text>
                  </staticText>
                  </band>
            </columnHeader>
            <detail>
                  <band height="125" splitType="Stretch">
                        <textField>
                              <reportElement x="0" y="0" width="63" height="20"/>
                              <textElement/>
                              <textFieldExpression><![CDATA[$F{userId}]]></textFieldExpression>
                        </textField>
                        <textField>
                              <reportElement x="63" y="0" width="90" height="20"/>
                              <textElement/>
                              <textFieldExpression><![CDATA[$F{screenName}]]></textFieldExpression>
                        </textField>
                        <textField>
                              <reportElement x="153" y="0" width="128" height="20"/>
                              <textElement/>
                              <textFieldExpression><![CDATA[$F{emailAddress}]]></textFieldExpression>
                        </textField>
                        <textField>
                              <reportElement x="281" y="0" width="141" height="20"/>
                              <textElement/>
                              <textFieldExpression><![CDATA[$F{createDate}]]></textFieldExpression>
                        </textField>
                        <textField>
                              <reportElement x="422" y="0" width="133" height="20"/>
                              <textElement/>
                              <textFieldExpression><![CDATA[$F{modifiedDate}]]></textFieldExpression>
                        </textField>
                  </band>
            </detail>
            <columnFooter>
                  <band height="45" splitType="Stretch"/>
            </columnFooter>
            <pageFooter>
                  <band height="54" splitType="Stretch"/>
            </pageFooter>
            <summary>
                  <band height="42" splitType="Stretch"/>
            </summary>
      </jasperReport>
```

2. Log in to your portal as an administrator, navigate to Site Administration, and navigate to the Reports Admin portlet.

3. Navigate to the Definitions tab and click *Add Report Definition*.

4. For the definition name, enter *Jasper Test*.

5. Leave the data source selection as the default: *Portal*.

6. Browse to and select the sample-report.jrxml template that you created in step 1, then click *Save* to create your report definition.

7. Click *Actions →Add Report* next to your Jasper Test report definition, choose the PDF report format, and click *Generate*.

8. Navigate to the Reports Admin portlet's Reports tab and click on the report you generated.

9. Click *Actions &rrar; Download* next to the sample-report.pdf file.

This report should list all of your portal's users, displaying the userId, screenName, emailAddress, createDate, and modifiedDate of each user.

Sample Report: Users

userId	screenName	emailAddress	createDate	modifiedDate
10157	10157	default@liferay.com	2013-05-02 21:39:32.0	2013-05-02 21:39:32.0
10195	test	test@liferay.com	2013-05-02 21:39:35.0	2013-05-02 21:39:50.0
10504	joe.bloggs	joe.bloggs@liferay.com	2013-05-03 20:20:03.0	2013-05-07 14:43:34.0

Figure 14.25: This reports lists all portal users by userId, screenName, emailAddress, createDate, and modifiedDate.

Now that we understand how to generate Jasper reports in Liferay, let's see what the Knowledge base application has to offer.

14.5 Knowledgebase

Liferay's Knowledge Base portlet provides a means for creating and organizing articles within a site. The knowledge base is perfect for creating and organizing information more formally than in a wiki. For example, it can be used to organize and display professional product documentation. It's easy to set up the knowledge base with a workflow that requires articles to be approved before they are published. Additionally, it allows administrators to create article templates. Templates can be used to insure certain kinds of articles possess a common structure and include certain kinds of information. Knowledge base articles can be categorized to make them easy to find. They can also be organized hierarchically to form complete books or guides. The Knowledge Base portlet is available as an app from Liferay Marketplace. You can purchase, download, and install the Knowledge Base EE app directly from your Liferay instance's Control Panel interface or you can navigate to http://www.liferay.com/marketplace in your browser, purchase and download the app, and copy the .lpkg file to your Liferay instance's /deploy folder.

Knowledge Base Display Portlet

The Knowledge Base app actually consists of four portlets that can be placed on site pages as well as one that adds a page to Site Administration. The four portlets that can be placed on a page are Knowledge Base (Display), Knowledge Base Article, Knowledge Base Search, and Knowledge Base Section. When placed on a page, the Knowledge Base display portlet presents many of the same options to an administrator that are available from the Knowledge Base page of Site Administration.

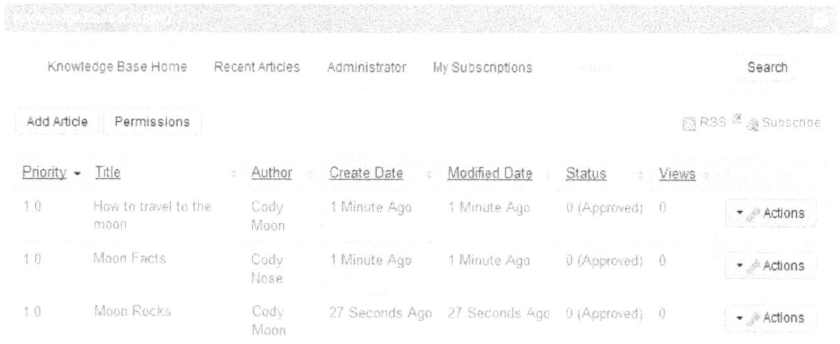

Priority ▾	Title	Author	Create Date	Modified Date	Status	Views	
1.0	How to travel to the moon	Cody Moon	1 Minute Ago	1 Minute Ago	0 (Approved)	0	▾ Actions
1.0	Moon Facts	Cody Nose	1 Minute Ago	1 Minute Ago	0 (Approved)	0	▾ Actions
1.0	Moon Rocks	Cody Moon	27 Seconds Ago	27 Seconds Ago	0 (Approved)	0	▾ Actions

Knowledge Base Home   Recent Articles   Administrator   My Subscriptions   Search

Add Article   Permissions   RSS Subscribe

Figure 14.26: The Knowledge Base Display portlet displays your recently added articles in a list.

You can use the four links at the top of the Knowledge Base Display portlet to control what it displays.

Knowledge Base Home: shows you a list of all top level articles.

Recent Articles: shows you a list of articles in order from most recent activity to least recent activity.

Administrator: shows you a list of all articles, regardless of which ones are parents or children of the others.

My Subscriptions: shows you a list of articles you are subscribed to.

The *Add Article* button is available from the Knowledge Base Home or Administrator view of the Knowledge Base Display portlet or from the Articles tab of the Knowledge Base page of Site Administration. Use this button to create an article for the knowledge base. When creating an article, you can use the same WYSIWYG editor you used to create wiki pages. Articles, however, are not the same as wiki pages; they must be created in HTML, not MediaWiki or Creole. Click the *Source* button in the editor to view the HTML source of what you've written or write some HTML yourself.

Figure 14.27: You can create a new Knowledge Base Article using the WYSIWYG editor.

In addition to entering a title and creating content for your article, you can use the editor to add attachments, add tags, and set permissions. By default, view permission is granted to the guest role, meaning anyone can view your article. After you're done using the editor, you can save it as draft and continue working on it later or you can submit it for publication. Your article may need to be approved before being published, depending on the workflow defined for your portal.

You can find the *Permissions* button next to the Add Article button in the Knowledge Base display portlet or on the Knowledge Base page of Site Administration. Click this button to define permissions that apply to the Knowledge Base Display portlet generally, not to particular articles. Here, you can define which roles can add articles and templates, which are granted knowledge base administrator privileges, which can change permissions on articles, which can subscribe to articles, and which can view templates.

Users may need to be granted access to the knowledge base page of Site Administration in order to exercise some of the above permissions. For example, suppose the user role has been granted the *Add Article* and the *View Templates* permissions. A user will be able to add

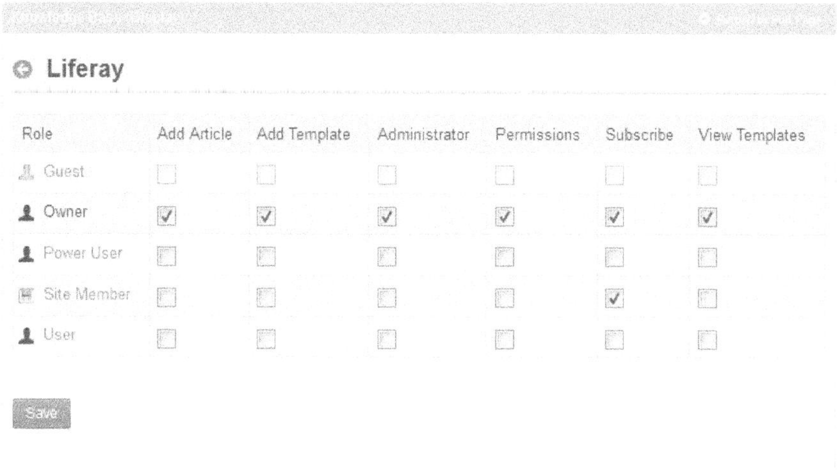

Figure 14.28: Set various permissions for each of your portal's roles in the Knowledge Base Permissions interface.

articles from the Knowledge Base Display portlet but will need access to the knowledge base page of Site Administration in order to view templates. Note that the Knowledge Base Display permissions are distinct from the Knowledge Base Admin portlet. The display permissions define what a user can do with the Knowledge Base Display portlet on a page while the admin permissions define what a user can do on the Knowledge Base page of Site Administration.

Knowledge Base Page of Site Administration

The Knowledge Base page of the Site Administration interface has two tabs: one for articles and one for templates. The *Articles* tab shows all the articles in the knowledge base and lets you perform actions on them. The *Templates* tab shows all the templates defined in the knowledge base and lets you perform actions on them.

Administrators can perform the following actions on an article:

View: displays an article. From here, you can add a child article, edit the article, change its permissions, move it or delete it.

Edit: allows you to change the title and content of an article as well as add attachments, select topics and add tags.

Permissions: lets you configure the permissions on a specific article.

Subscribe: lets you to choose to be notified of any updates to a particular article.

Move: lets you change an article's position in the hierarchy by choosing a new parent article for it.

Delete: lets you remove an article from the knowledge base.

These actions are similar to the ones that can be performed from the Administrator view of the Knowledge Base Display portlet. However, the Knowledge Base Display portlet is intended to be placed on a page for the end user so an additional action is available: *RSS* is a link to an RSS feed of an article. Also, the *View* action is only available from the Site Administration page since the Knowledge Base Article portlet can be used to display an article on a page.

The Templates tab of the Knowledge Base page of Site Administration allows administrators to create templates to facilitate the creation of articles. A template basically functions like a starting point for the creation of certain types of articles. Click the *Add Template*

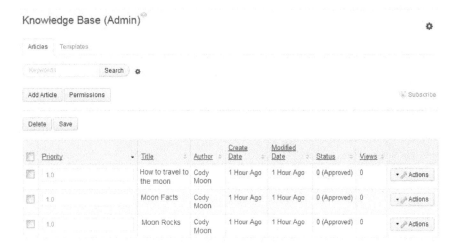

Figure 14.29: Administrators can control knowledge base articles and templates from the *Site Administration · Content* page.

button on the Templates tab of the Knowledge Base page of Site Administration to create a new template.

Navigate back to the Templates tab of the Knowledge Base page of Site Administration. You can perform the following actions on a template:

View: displays a template. From here, you can use the template to create an article, edit the template, modify the permissions on the template or delete it.

Edit: allows you to change the title and content of a template.

Permissions: allows you to configure the permissions on a template. You can choose roles to have permission to update, view, delete or change the permissions on templates.

Delete: lets you remove a template from the knowledge base.

To use a template to create a new article, you have to view the template and then click *Use this Template*. This brings you to the New Article editor with the contents of the template copied for you.

Knowledge Base Article Portlet

The Knowledge Base Article portlet can be placed on a page to display an entire article. When you first place this portlet on a page, it displays the message *Please configure this portlet to make it visible to all users*. This message is a link to the configuration dialog box for the portlet. Click *Select Article* to choose an article to display. Pick an article and then click *Save*. When your page refreshes it will display the article in the portlet.

The Knowledge Base Article portlet allows users to rate and comment on the article it displays. There are also links at the top of the portlet users can use to subscribe to an RSS feed of the knowledge base, subscribe to the article, view the history of the article, or print the article.

Knowledge Base Section Portlet

The Knowledge Base Section portlet allows administrators to selectively show articles associated with a specific section. For example, a news site might have a *World* section, a *Politics* section, a *Business* section and an *Entertainment* section. In order to use sections, you need to set the `admin.kb.article.sections` property in your knowledge base

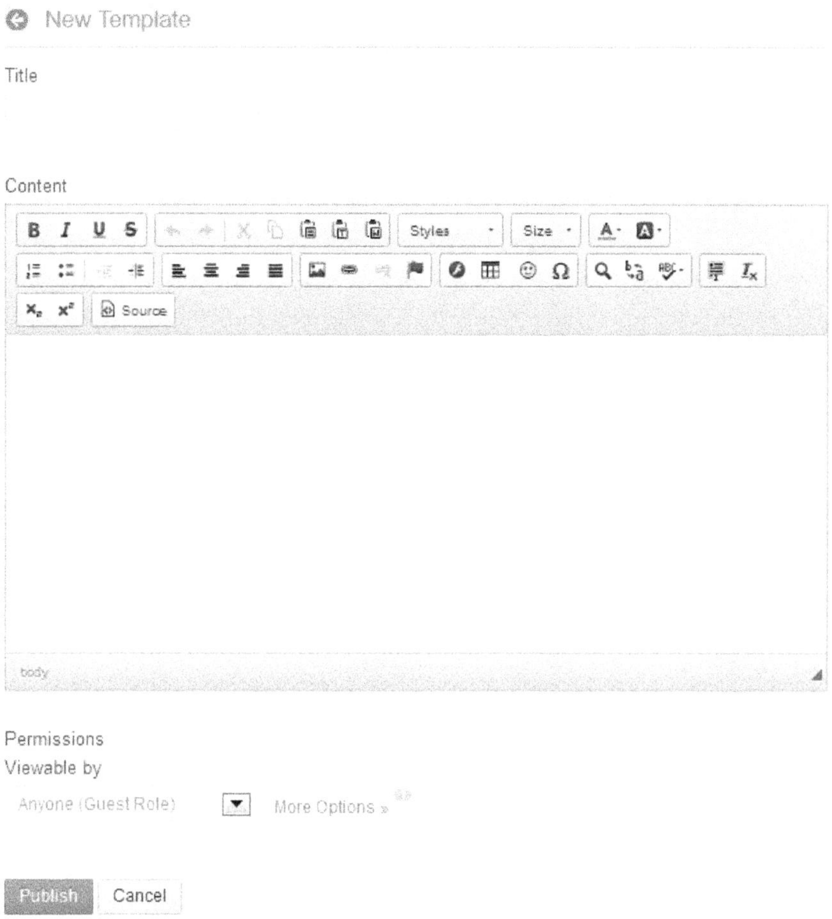

Figure 14.30: As an administrator, you can add a new template to your knowledge base by navigating to *Site Administration · Content →Knowledge Base (Admin)*.

portlet's `portlet.properties` file and redeploy the portlet. You can find the `portlet.properties` file in the knowledge base portlet's source directory. Updating the one in your server's directory won't work. Use comma delimited section names to set the property, like `admin.kb.article.sections=World,Politics,Business,Entertainment`, for example.

Once you have defined some sections in your knowledge base's `portlet.properties` file, your users will see a multi-select box in the Add Article and Edit Article screens that allows them to select which section an article belongs to. You can add any number of Knowledge Base section portlets to a page and you can configure each portlet to display articles from any number of sections.

The Knowledge Base section portlet has some additional configurations that allow an administrator to select a display style (title or abstract), an article window state (maximized or normal), how to order the articles, how many articles to display per page, and whether or not to show pagination.

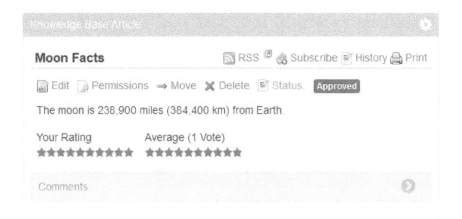

Figure 14.31: Display articles using the Knowledge Base Article portlet.

Figure 14.32: Here's an image of Knowledge Base Section portlets being displayed on a page.

Knowledge Base Navigation

Wikis often have deeply nested articles that can be hard to find by browsing. Liferay's knowledge base's ability to selectively display articles makes it easier to browse than a Wiki. The knowledge base also features some other aids to navigation. The Knowledge Base Search portlet allows you to search for articles in the knowledge base. This portlet presents the search results to you in order from most relevant to least relevant.

You can also use the Categories Navigation portlet in conjunction with the Knowledge Base Display portlet. When both of these portlets are placed on a page you can select a topic in the Categories Navigation portlet and the Knowledge Base Display portlet will show all of the articles that match the topic. You can create topics from the Categories page of *Site Administration →Content*.

You can select topics for articles when you are creating or editing them.

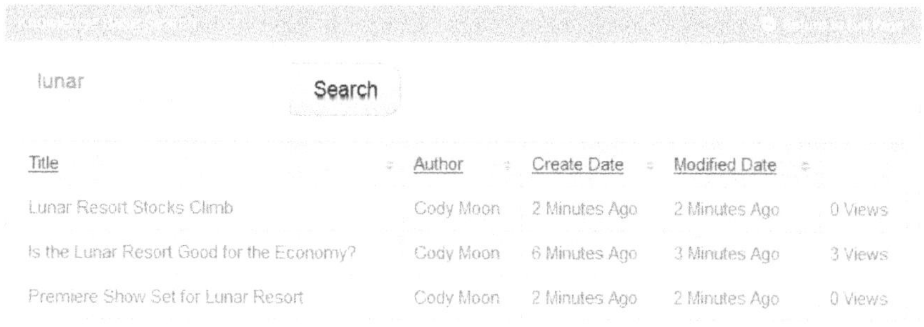

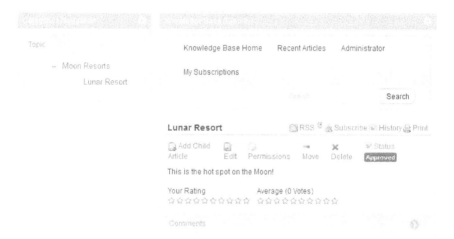

Figure 14.33: The Knowledge Base Search portlet helps you search the knowledge base for keywords.

Figure 14.34: Use the Categories Navigation portlet to search articles that match a specific topic.

14.6 Akismet

Akismet is a web-based spam detection service. The Akismet app, available from Liferay Marketplace, integrates Liferay with Akismet to provide spam detection for Liferay's message boards, blogs, wikis, and comments. When you install the Akismet app from Liferay Marketplace, two portlets are added to the Control Panel: the *Akismet* portlet is added to the Configuration section and the *Spam Moderation* portlet is added to the Content section of Site Administration.

In order to enable Liferay to use Akismet, you need to visit http://akismet.com, create an account, and generate an API key. Once you've generated an API key, navigate to the Configuration section of the Control Panel and click on *Akismet*. Enter your API key into the provided field and check the *Enabled for Message Boards* and *Enabled for Discussion* boxes. The term "discussions" is another way to refer to comment threads in Liferay. Optionally, you can customize the *Reportable Time* and the *Check Threshold*. The Reportable Time indicates the time in days after a post is created or updated that it can be marked as spam or not spam. The Check Threshold indicates the number of posts after which Akismet will no longer check posts. After you've finished configuring Akismet, click *Save*.

To see Akismet in action, add some message board posts or comment on some existing Liferay assets. See if you can get Akismet to mark one as spam. If Akismet doesn't mark a post as spam, you can always manually do as an administrator. Once one or more posts have been marked as spam, navigate to the Content section of the Site Administration section of the Control Panel, then click on *Spam Moderation*. Here, you can find all the message board posts, discussions (comments), and wiki pages that have been marked as spam. You can select all the posts that you agree are spam and delete them. You can also select any posts that you don't agree are spam and mark them as *Not Spam*. If you're not sure about a post, click the *Actions* button and select *View in Context* to view the post in its original setting.

14.7   Weather

Liferay's Weather portlet displays basic weather-related information (temperature, conditions) for multiple configurable locations. It's available as an app from Liferay Marketplace. For each configured location, a link to Open Weather Map is provided that points to more detailed information. The Weather portlet also provides a search bar that allows users to find information about locations that aren't listed by the portlet. Searching via the search bar forwards the user to Open Weather Map, where the search is executed.

Figure 14.35: Liferay's Weather portlet displays basic weather-related information (temperature, conditions) for multiple configurable locations.

To configure the displayed locations, open the Weather portlet's configuration window. In the first text area, enter the names of the cities about which you'd like weather information to be displayed. Alternatively, you can use zip codes. Enter one city or zip code per line. For the temperature format, you can choose between Celsius and Fahrenheit.

14.8 OAuth

Liferay's OAuth utility authorizes third-party applications to interact with a user's resources. It's available as an app from Liferay Marketplace. Let's say you're hosting Liferay Portal and have
users and customers coming to your web site. You want them
to have access to a third party resource, like Twitter, and be able
to access their accounts from your site. In the past, they would
have to provide their Twitter user names and passwords, but not
if you use OAuth. For this reason, a popular characterization for
the OAuth client is the "valet key for your web services."

OAuth is a handshake mechanism where, instead of asking for personal information,
Liferay redirects users to a service provider like Twitter, where they can tell Twitter to allow
Liferay limited access to their accounts. This example is similar to our earlier "valet key"
characterization. You wouldn't want a valet driver opening your glove box, storage spaces,
hood, and other personal compartments in your vehicle. You would only want the valet to
access what is necessary to park your car. OAuth is based on this same idea: it gives a site
just enough information to do what it needs and nothing more. This assures users that
their personal information is safe, but gives them freedom to take advantage of valuable
resources they typically use from the service provider's site.

Registering OAuth Applications

The first thing you'll need to do is register an application for OAuth's services. To access
the OAuth Admin page, navigate to the Control Panel and, under the *Users* heading, select
OAuth Admin. Then select *Add* to create a new OAuth application in the OAuth registry.
You'll be given the following options:

Application Name: the display name for your application

Description: the short description that is attached to your application

Website URL: your application's URL

Callback URI: the URI where users are redirected after authentication is complete

Access Level: select the *Read* or *Write* access level. For the *Read* access level, the user
can only view the application's contents, but not modify them. The *Write* access level gives
the user permission to access and modify the application's contents.

After you're finished registering the OAuth app, click *Actions View*. You'll notice Liferay generated two Application Credentials: the *Consumer Key* and *Consumer Secret*. The
consumer key is a value used by the application to identify itself to the service provider.
Likewise, the consumer secret is a value the application uses to establish ownership of the
consumer key.

Take note of your application credentials; you'll need them when configuring your application with OAuth. To learn how to configure an application with OAuth, visit the Authorizing Access to Services with OAuth. tutorial. Once you have your application configured to use OAuth, visit the next section to begin authorizing requests via OAuth.

Authorizing Requests via OAuth

Once you have your application configured to use OAuth, you can place your application
on a page and test out the process. Here is a basic synopsis of what's happening during
the authorization process.

The app you registered in the previous section and configured with the consumer key
and secret on the Developer Network[7] is characterized as a service provider. The service

---

[7]https://dev.liferay.com/develop/tutorials/-/knowledge_base/6-2/
authorizing-access-to-services-with-oauth

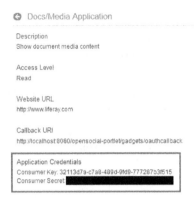

Figure 14.36: You'll need the application credentials to implement OAuth in your application.

provider uses OAuth to allow users access to its protected resources. These protected resources are data controlled by the service provider, which can only be accessed by the application through authentication. By configuring an application in Liferay to use OAuth, you're keeping all private information you have between a third-party service provider and the portal separate. Essentially, OAuth bridges the connection between the portal and third-party services without the user sharing any protected resources between them.

Once your OAuth application is placed on a portal page, you'll be asked to grant or deny the third-party service provider limited access to your portal.

Figure 14.37: You can grant or deny the service provider access to your.

Congratulations! You've successfully installed your OAuth app and authorized access between a service provider and Liferay Portal!

14.9 Summary

In this chapter, we examined several Liferay utility applications: the Bookmarks portlet, the Shopping portlet, the Software Catalog, the Reports and JasperReports applications, the Knowledge Base, the Akismet application, the Weather portlet, and the OAuth application.

The Bookmarks portlet allows users and administrators to collect and share useful link to pages either within or outside of the portal. The Shopping portlet allows you to use PayPal to set up your portal for E-commerce activity. The Software Catalog allows you to define a set of software items to make available to visitors to your portal. Remember that the Software Catalog has been replaced by Liferay Marketplace. If you want to use it, you'll have to manually install it as a plugin. The Reports application is an EE-only application that provides a Reports Admin portlet in the Control Panel for creating reports and scheduling report generation. When combined with a suitable implementation, such as the JasperReports application (also EE-only), you can upload report definitions in the Reports Admin portlet, generate reports, and export reports to a wide variety of formats.

The Knowledge Base application is an EE-only application that allows you to create articles and organize them into full books or guides that be published on your portal. The Akismet application offers a web-based spam detection service for your portal's message boards, blogs, wikis, and comments. The Weather portlet provides users with a summary of weather-related information for multiple locations and provides a links to Open Weather Map for more detailed information for each location. Lastly, the EE-only OAuth application manages third-party applications' access to your portal's resources and vice versa. Next, let's take a tour of the Liferay Marketplace and learn how to manage Liferay plugins.

## CHAPTER 15

LEVERAGING THE LIFERAY MARKETPLACE

Liferay Marketplace is an exciting hub for sharing, browsing, and downloading Liferay-compatible applications. As enterprises look for ways to build and enhance their existing platforms, developers and software vendors are searching for new avenues to reach this market. Marketplace leverages the entire Liferay ecosystem to release and share apps in a user-friendly, one-stop site.

This chapter covers the following topics:

- Users, Companies, and Apps

- Accessing Liferay Marketplace

- Finding, Downloading, and Installing Apps

- Managing Apps

- Plugins and Plugin Management

- Plugin Types: Portlets, Themes, Layout Templates, Hooks, Web Plugins, and OSGi Bundles

- Installing Plugins from Repositories

- Installing Plugins Manually

- Plugin Troubleshooting and Configuration Issues

In a nutshell, the Liferay Marketplace is a repository for applications built on the Liferay Platform. You can find and download applications directly from the Marketplace on the web or use an existing Liferay installation to access and install applications onto the running Liferay web site. Once installed, you can manage the applications through Liferay's Control Panel.

15.1 Marketplace Concepts: Users, Companies, and Apps

Anyone can browse the apps available on Liferay Marketplace at http://liferay.com/marketplace, but a liferay.com user account is required for purchasing and downloading apps. You can browse, purchase, and download apps from the Marketplace website or from a running Liferay portal. Accessing Liferay Marketplace from a running Liferay portal makes it very easy to download and install apps. Once an app has been purchased, it takes just one click to download the app and one click to install it. Updating or uninstalling the app are also one-click processes. A liferay.com user account is required regardless of whether you access Liferay Marketplace via the browser or via an existing Liferay installation.

Many official Liferay apps, as well as some third party apps, are available free of charge. Other apps require you to pay a fee in order to access them. When you purchase an app, you can do so on your own behalf or on behalf of a company. Apps purchased on your own behalf are associated with your personal liferay.com user account. Apps purchased on behalf of a company are associated with the company's account and can be accessed by any users who belong to the company. Once you've purchased an app, you're free to download and install any available version of the app whenever you like. We'll explain how to set up a company account, manage company apps and join companies after we discuss how to access Liferay Marketplace.

15.2 Accessing the Liferay Marketplace

There are two ways to access the Marketplace.

1. Via the website: Using your favorite browser, you can navigate to the marketplace at http://liferay.com/marketplace.

2. Via Liferay: If you have a Liferay portal up and running, you can use the Apps section of the Control Panel to access Marketplace content.

The Basics

No matter which method you choose, you will see the same content and apps.

If you are new to the Marketplace, the easiest way to access it is by using your browser. Navigate to http://liferay.com/marketplace to access the Marketplace home page.

In the center of the page, you will see a number of icons. Each icon represents an individual app, and apps are organized by category:

- New and Interesting: The latest apps added to the marketplace

- Featured apps: Liferay features a different set of apps each month

- Most Viewed: The top 10 most viewed apps

If you click on the title of an app, you can access details about the app, including a description, the author's name, screenshots, price, latest version, number of downloads, a link to the developer's website, a link to the license agreement for the app, a link to report abuse, and a Purchase button. You'll also be able to view version history, read reviews left by other users, or write your own review.

If you click on the Purchase button, you'll be prompted to choose a purchase type. You can purchase an app for your personal account or for your company. If your company has already been registered, select it in the drop-down list. If your company hasn't been registered, click the *Register Your Company* link to register your company with Liferay Marketplace. Please see the *Creating a Company* section below for details.

The left side of each page in the http://liferay.com/marketplace site contains a Marketplace navigation menu. This menu contains links to various categories of apps available from Marketplace. Clicking on the individual categories allows you to browse the apps in that category. To view all the apps on Marketplace at once, click the *Apps* link and then the *See All* link in the Apps portlet.

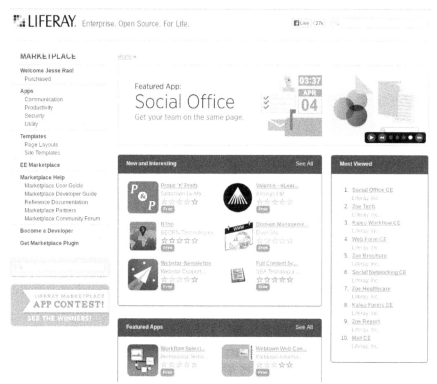

Figure 15.1: You can access and browse the Marketplace home page without a liferay.com account but you need an account in order to purchase and download apps.

Below the navigation menu is the search bar. This search checks the titles and descriptions of apps against your search terms.

Logging In

You do not need a liferay.com account in order to browse the Marketplace. However, if you wish to purchase and download an app, you need to establish a liferay.com account and agree to the Marketplace Terms of Use. To get a new liferay.com account, visit http://www.liferay.com, click *Sign In*, then *Create Account*, and sign up! Once you are signed in, you can fully utilize the Marketplace to find and use Marketplace apps.

If you are a developer and wish to create and upload new apps, you must also register as a developer in Marketplace. Just go to http://liferay.com/marketplace and click *Become a Developer* from the *Marketplace* menu.

Once you register as a developer, your *liferay.com* homepage will have links for adding your apps to Marketplace, and managing them after they're uploaded.

Marketplace Profile

Once you register a developer account with your liferay.com account, your existing liferay.com Home page will contain a new section in the left navigation menu entitled *Development*. You now have two *Apps* links: one under the main navigation menu and one

Home » Apps » Productivity » Web Form CE   Back

Web Form CE

Liferay, Inc.

Latest Version: 2.0.1

Total Downloads: 8024

♠ Developer Website

☼ Support

▤ License Agreement

⚠ Report Abuse

Current Requirements
Liferay Portal 6.2 CE GA1+

Past Versions Work With
Liferay Portal 6.1 CE GA2
Liferay Portal 6.1 CE GA2+

🔒 **Security Disabled:** This app has Liferay's PACL Security Manager disabled.

The web forms portlet is a tool that allows a web administrator to define a form to be published in the website. Users visiting the website can then fill the form which is then sent to a configured email address or saved (to file or to database). The title, introductory description of the form, email address, and many other options shown to the users are configurable through the portlet's configuration screen. It is possible to have multiple forms on the same page or spread across multiple pages. Saving options also include the ability to save as an external CSV (Comma-Separated Values) file, or save the values to a custom Database table for further processing.

Figure 15.2: Click on a Marketplace app to view details, ratings, and reviews of the app.

in the *Development* section. The *Apps* link under your name is where you go when you want to vies and download yuor purchased apps from the Marketplace. The *Apps* link under the *Development* menu will let you manage existing apps and add new apps to the Marketplace. To see information on your app's performance, use the *Metrics* link in the Development menu. If you submit an app, it will be reviewed before appearing on the liferay.com Marketplace.

Your liferay.com Home page is a private page. It's distinct from your public liferay.com Profile page.

Managing Apps

The *Develoment* menu in your liferay.com home page is where you'll go to manage and monitor your own marketplace apps, and the *Apps* link in your main navigation menu lets

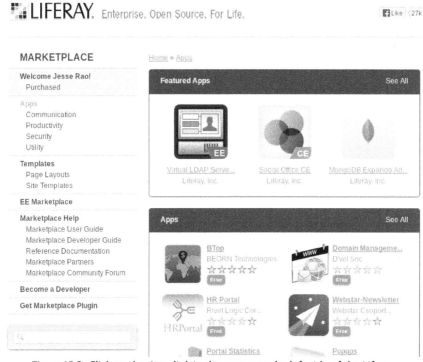

Figure 15.3: Click on the *Apps* link in the menu on the left side of the Liferay Marketplace homepage and then on the *See All* link in the Apps portlet to browse all the Marketplace apps at once.

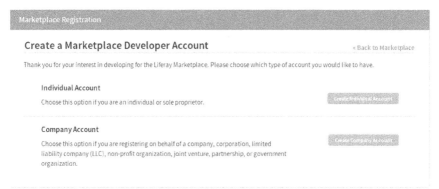

Figure 15.4: Click on the *Become a Developer* link in the menu on the left side of the Liferay Marketplace homepage to register a developer's account, either as an individual or a company.

you view and download apps you purchased from the Marketplace.

The Apps link in the menu under your name lists your purchased apps. From this screen, you can find information about the authors of the apps you have purchased and download or re-download the app (for example, if you lost your copy or have re-installed Liferay and wish to re-deploy the app). This option is also useful for downloading apps and deploying them to offline instances of Liferay that do not have direct access to liferay.com.

Purchased Apps

We recommend that you log into your portal instance and install purchased apps through the Control Panel. This will provide your portal instance with automatic update notices should they become available. Apps that are downloaded can be hot deployed by following instructions found in the FAQ.

Russell Bohl's Apps

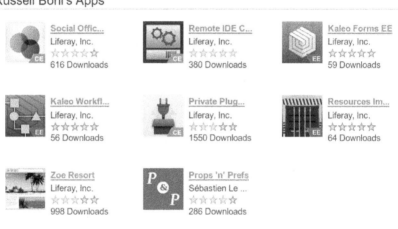

Showing 8 results.   Items 20 ⬦   Page 1 ⬦ of 1   ⏮ First ◀ Previous Next ▶ Last ⏭

Figure 15.5: On your liferay.com home page, the *Apps* link in the left navigation menu lets you view and download your purchased apps.

If possible, it's best to log into your portal instance and install purchased applications through the *Store* link in the Control Panel's *Apps* section. This will provide your portal instance with automatic update notices should they become available. If you download applications this way, they can be hot-deployed.

The *Development* menu is where developers go to manage their Marketplace apps. The Apps link lists apps you have authored and uploaded, and gives you an *Add New App* link that let's you submit an app to be added to the Marketplace. The Metrics link will show you details such as the number of downloads, the current price and other relevant information. Please see the Marketplace chapter of the Developer Guide for details on this topic.

Clicking on *Add an App* allows you to upload a new app and make it available in the marketplace. Please see the Marketplace chapter of the Developer Guide for more detail on authoring your own app.

Creating a Company

To create and register a company with Liferay Marketplace, click the *Become a Developer* link in the left-hand navigation menu of the Marketplace home page. You can create an indi-

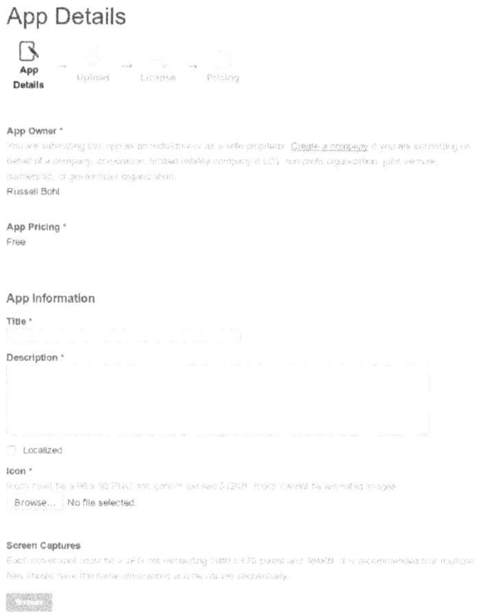

Figure 15.6: This is part of the form you need to submit when submitting an app to Liferay Marketplace.

vidual or a company developer account. If you'd like to create an account on behalf of your company, your first step is to see if your company already exists on Liferay Marketplace. Enter your company name into the search box and check if it's already been registered. If someone else from your company has already created a company account on Liferay Marketplace, you can click the *Request to Join this Company* button. This will send an email notification to your company's Marketplace admin (the one who created your company's Marketplace account). Your company's Marketplace admin will then be able to add you to the company. If the company name you'd like to use is available, click the *Register Your Company* button to move on to the next step.

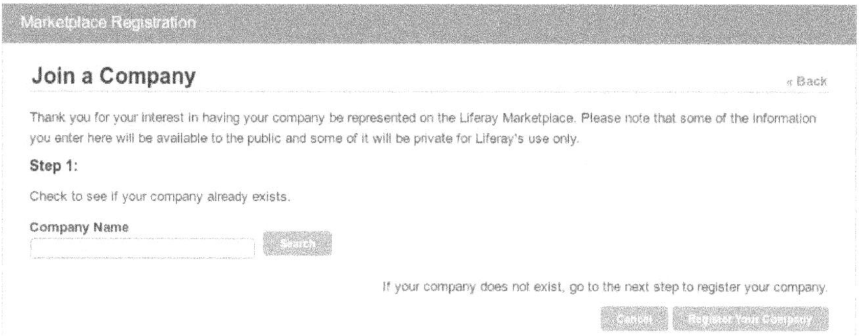

Figure 15.7: You can upload apps as an individual or on behalf of your company.

Your second step is to fill out your company's information. The public information you must provide includes a company logo, the company name, a company description, a company email address and a homepage URL. The private information you must provide includes a company address, your company's country, region, city, postal code and phone number. Additional private information required for validation includes a company email address and a legal tax document. Once your company's Marketplace registration has been approved, you will be your company's Marketplace admin! This means you'll be responsible for handling Marketplace users' requests to join your company. Don't worry, you don't have to be stuck with this responsibility. Once you've added other users to your company, you can promote some of them to be company Marketplace admins too.

15.3   Finding Apps

There are several ways to search for and find apps you are interested in.

1. Browsing Categories: Click on a category (for example, *Communication* or *Productivity*) to see a list of interesting apps in that category. Upon clicking a category, you are presented with a list of featured apps for that category, as well as a canonical listing of all apps. Also, on the right, are lists of the Most Viewed apps within that category.

Figure 15.8: When searching for apps for your portal, you can browse through the complete list of Marketplace apps or browse by category.

2. Searching: To search for an app, type in search criteria in the search box under the navigation menu on the left and click *Search*. Apps matching the specified search criteria are displayed.

Next, let's talk about app versioning.

Versions

Figure 15.9: You can search for apps using the search box in the navigation menu. Results are returned if your search terms match an app's title or description.

Apps are often updated to include new features or fix bugs. Each time an app is updated, its version number is changed. The version number is specified by the app developer and often follows established norms, such as 1.0 →1.1 →2.0 or 1.0.1 →1.0.2 →1.2.0 and so on. Generally, the higher the numbers, the newer the version.

When viewing an app's details, click on the *Version History* tab to see a list of versions of the app. In some cases, not all historical versions of apps are available, depending on the app. Usually, you will want to download and install the latest available app for the version of Liferay you are using (See Compatibility below).

Compatibility

Some apps are written to work across a wide range of Liferay Platform releases. Others are dependent on a specific Liferay Platform release (or a handful of such releases). When viewing individual apps, each version of the app that is available also describes the range of Liferay Platform versions the app is compatible with. Make sure to choose a version of the app that is compatible with your Liferay Platform release.

Reviews	Version History	Access Control

Version History

Version	Change Log	Supported Framework Versions	Date Added
1.0.0		Liferay Portal 6.1 CE GA2	August 30, 2012
1.0.1	► Change Log	Liferay Portal 6.1 CE GA2	December 28, 2012
1.0.2	► Change Log	Liferay Portal 6.1 CE GA2+	August 22, 2013
2.0.0	► Change Log	Liferay Portal 6.2 CE GA1+	November 2, 2013
2.0.1	► Change Log	Liferay Portal 6.2 CE GA1+	January 23, 2014

Figure 15.10: Look at an app's supported framework versions to check if it's compatible with your version of Liferay.

To check if an app is compatible with your version of Liferay, click on the App and then click on the *Version History* tab. The Version History tab displays not only the list of versions of the app but also the app's supported framework versions and the dates of each version of the app. The supported framework version of the app tells you whether or not the app is compatible with your version of Liferay.

15.4   Downloading and Installing Apps

Once you've found an app you wish to download and install, click on the name of the app
to display its detailed information screen.

Figure 15.11: Click on an app to read a description and view additional details.

This screen offers a number of items to help you learn more about the app. You can
find the primary information about the app on the left side of the screen, below the app's
icon. In the center display, you see a set of screenshots along with a description of the app.
Beneath the screenshots, you can find a description of the app. Below that, you can read
reviews and view the version history of the app. Each app provides at least the following
information:

- Author: The creator of the app. This can be either an individual or a company.

- Rating: The average rating of the app on a scale from zero to five stars. The number
  of ratings is also shown.

- Latest Version: The latest released version of this app

- Total Downloads: The number of times the app has been downloaded

- Supported By: Who to contact if you need support for this app

- Developer Website: A link to the developer's own website

- Purchase/Free: The button to click on to purchase the app. You must purchase an
  app before you can download it.

In the lower section, you will find Reviews and Version History tabs for this app. Check
this area to find out what other people are saying about this app. In addition, on a separate tab, you will find the history of versions for this app, where you can download other
versions (for example, if you are using an older version of the Liferay Platform, you may
need to download a specific version of this app that is compatible with the version of the
Liferay Platform you are using).

Downloading and Installing

You've chosen an app, read the reviews and want to download and use the app! There are two ways to install the app. Ultimately, both methods result in the same outcome: the app you've chosen is installed onto your local running Liferay instance.

Liferay Hot Deploy

Apps on the Liferay Marketplace consist of individual Liferay Plugins (for example: a portlet, a hook, or a collection of multiple plugins). Ultimately, these apps must be installed on a running Liferay instance before they can be used. Deploying an app to a running Liferay instance is automatically done through the process of *hot deploy*. When using your Liferay portal's *Control Panel* to install apps from the Marketplace, when you click *Purchase* or *Install* to download and use a given app, it will be downloaded and hot deployed to your local running Liferay instance.

For some Liferay installations, the hot deploy mechanism is disabled, in order for the site administrator to manage (or prevent) the deployment of plugins. In this case, the app will still be downloaded and stored in the hot deploy directory (with a .1pkg extension in its filename), but must be manually deployed using the custom process used for deploying other plugins.

Please see the later section *Installing Plugins Manually* to learn more about hot deploy, its behavior on various app servers, and how to manually deploy Marketplace apps in situations where hot deploy cannot be used.

Installing through the Control Panel

The easiest way to install an app is to do so from your Liferay Control Panel. This requires that you have already installed Liferay on your local machine and that you can log in as an administrator. Once you are logged in as an administrator, click the *Admin* menu from the Dockbar and choose *Control Panel*.

Figure 15.12: As an administrator, you can access the Marketplace interface from the Control Panel of a running Liferay portal.

Click on either the *Store* or the *Purchased* links beneath the Apps heading. Before you can access Marketplace via the Control Panel, you need to associate your liferay.com login credentials with your local administrator account. Enter your liferay.com email address and password so your Liferay installation can connect to the liferay.com Marketplace.

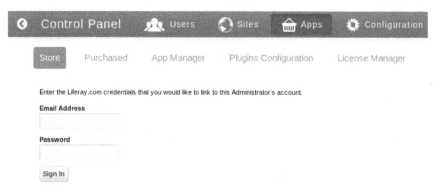

Figure 15.13: Before you can access Marketplace via the Control Panel you need to link your liferay.com credentials with your Liferay instance's administrator account.

 Tip: Any local user with administrative privileges can use the Marketplace to browse and install apps from the Marketplace, by entering their liferay.com credentials in the above login screen. This allows multiple administrators to manage the apps installed on the local Liferay instance. Once a link is established between a local administrator account and a liferay.com account, there is no way to undo this, short of re-installing Liferay.

Once you've successfully linked the accounts, you will be presented with the same Marketplace screens that you'd see if you were accessing the Marketplace webpage via your browser. You will be able to browse, search, and install apps directly from the Marketplace. Click on the *Store* link under the Apps heading in the Control Panel to browse the apps available from the liferay.com Marketplace. Browse to the app you wish to install, click on the *Purchase* or *Free* button, and then click on the appropriate button to confirm your purchase on the next screen. The app will be downloaded and deployed to your local Liferay installation.

You can view and manage all the apps you've purchased by clicking on the *Purchased* link under the Apps heading in the Control Panel. Clicking on the *Purchased* link shows you a list of those apps which you've downloaded in the past, including apps you may have purchased/downloaded while using other Liferay installations.

The apps which you downloaded and installed on the currently running instance of Liferay are listed as Installed. Apps which you have previously downloaded or purchased on other Liferay instances that are incompatible with the current one are listed as Not Compatible. You need to re-download/re-install the appropriate version of these apps if you wish to use them on your running instance of Liferay.

Downloading through liferay.com

The second way to install an app is to download it first, then in a separate step, deploy it to your running Liferay instance. This is especially useful in situations where you do not wish to deploy the app directly to your production environment, or in cases where the target Liferay instance that is to receive the app is behind a corporate firewall or otherwise does not have direct access to the Marketplace.

In this case, using your browser, you will find the app on the Liferay Marketplace. Once found, click on the *Purchase* or *Free* button when viewing the individual app. This will cause

Purchased Products

Figure 15.14: Purchased Apps

the app to be placed in your *Purchased* list on your personal Home page. Navigate to your Home page and click on *Apps*. Each app is listed; click on the one you just purchased, or whatever app you want to download. You'll find a list of app versions and Liferay versions. Choose the version of the app you want, making sure the Liferay version corresponds to the version of the Liferay installation where you'll install the app. Click *App* and the app is downloaded to your local machine in the same way any other file would be downloaded. This file can then be hot-deployed to Liferay by copying it to Liferay's hot deploy directory.

15.5 Creating and Uploading Apps

Creating apps for the Liferay Marketplace is very easy and intuitive. To find out more information about creating your own Liferay apps, visit the Liferay Marketplace Developer Guide and get started creating apps today!

Next, we'll discuss general Liferay plugin management. We'll explain the differences between the various types of Liferay plugins and show how to manually deploy plugins to Liferay.

15.6 Plugin Management

One of the primary ways of extending the functionality of Liferay Portal is by the use of plugins. *Plugin* is an umbrella term for installable portlet, theme, layout template, hook, Ext and web module Java EE .war files. Though Liferay comes bundled with a number of functional portlets, themes, layout templates, hooks and web modules, plugins provide a means of extending Liferay to be able to do almost anything.

Portlets

Portlets are small web applications that run in a portion of a web page. The heart of any portal implementation is its portlets, because all of the functionality of a portal resides in its portlets. Liferay's core is a portlet container. The container's job is to manage the portal's pages and to aggregate the set of portlets that are to appear on any particular page. This means the core doesn't contain application code. Instead, all of the features and functionality of your portal application must reside in its portlets.

Tip: Liferay 4.4.2 and below support the Portlet 1.0 standard: JSR-168. Liferay 5.0 and above support the Portlet 2.0 standard: JSR-286. You cannot run Portlet 2.0 portlets in Liferay 4.4.2, but because the Portlet 2.0 standard is backwards-compatible, portlets written to the 1.0 standard still run in Liferay 5.x and above.

Portlet applications, like servlet applications, have become a Java standard which various portal server vendors have implemented. The JSR-168 standard defines the portlet 1.0 specification and the JSR-286 standard defines the portlet 2.0 specification. A Java standard portlet should be deployable on any portlet container which supports the standard. Portlets are placed on the page in a certain order by the end user and are served up dynamically by the portal server. This means certain *givens* that apply to servlet-based projects, such as control over URLs or access to the HttpServletRequest object, don't apply in portlet projects, because the portal server generates these objects dynamically.

Portal applications come generally in two flavors: 1) portlets can be written to provide small amounts of functionality and then aggregated by the portal server into a larger application or 2) whole applications can be written to reside in only one or a few portlet windows. The choice is up to those designing the application. The developer only has to worry about what happens inside of the portlet itself; the portal server handles building out the page as it is presented to the user.

Most developers nowadays like to use certain frameworks to develop their applications, because those frameworks provide both functionality and structure to a project. For example, Struts enforces the Model-View-Controller design pattern and provides lots of functionality, such as custom tags and form validation, that make it easier for a developer to implement certain standard features. With Liferay, developers are free to use all of the leading frameworks in the Java EE space, including Struts, Spring MVC and Java Server Faces. This allows developers familiar with those frameworks to more easily implement portlets and also facilitates the quick porting of an application using those frameworks over to a portlet implementation.

Additionally, Liferay allows for the consuming of PHP and Ruby applications as portlets so you do not need to be a Java developer in order to take advantage of Liferay's built-in features (such as user management, sites, organizations, page building and content management). You can also use scripting languages such as Groovy if you wish. You can use the Plugins SDK to deploy your PHP or Ruby application as a portlet and it will run seamlessly inside of Liferay. We have plenty of examples of this; to see them, check out the Plugins SDK from Liferay's public code repository.

Does your organization make use of any Enterprise Planning (ERP) software that exposes its data via web services? You could write a portlet plugin for Liferay that can consume that data and display it as part of a dashboard page for your users. Do you subscribe to a stock service? You could pull stock quotes from that service and display them on your page, instead of using Liferay's built-in Stocks portlet. Do you have a need to combine the functionality of two or more servlet-based applications on one page? You could make them into portlet plugins and have Liferay display them in whatever layout you want. Do you have existing Struts, Spring MVC or JSF applications you want to integrate with your portal? It is a straightforward task to migrate these applications into Liferay, then they can take advantage of the layout, security and administration infrastructure that Liferay provides.

Themes

Figure 15.15: Envision Theme from Liferay's Theme Repository

Themes are hot deployable plugins which can completely transform the look and feel of the portal. Most organizations have their own look and feel standards which go across all of the web sites and web applications in the infrastructure. Liferay makes it possible for a site designer to create a theme plugin which can be installed, allowing for the complete transformation of the portal to whatever look and feel is needed. There are lots of available theme plugins on Liferay's web site and more are being added every day. This makes it easier for those who wish to develop themes for Liferay, as you can now choose a theme which most closely resembles what you want to do and then customize it. This is much easier than starting a theme from scratch. You can learn more about theme development in *Liferay in Action* or the Liferay Developer Network.

Figure 15.16: Murali Theme from Liferay's Theme Repository

Layout Templates

Layout Templates are ways of choosing how your portlets will be arranged on a page. They make up the body of your page, the large area into which you can drag and drop portlets. Liferay Portal comes with several built-in layout templates. If you have a complex page layout (especially for your home page), you may wish to create a custom layout template of your own. This is covered in *Liferay in Action* or the Liferay Developer Network.

Hook Plugins

Hook plugins were introduced with Liferay 5.2. As the name implies, they allow "hooking" into Liferay's core functionality. This means they enable developers to override or replace functionality that is in the core of the system. You can hook into the eventing system, model listeners and portal properties. You can also override Liferay's core JSPs with your own. Hooks are very powerful and have been designed to replace most of the reasons for using the extension environment with something that is easier to use and hot deployable.

Web Plugins

Web plugins are regular Java EE web modules designed to work with Liferay. Liferay supports integration with various Enterprise Service Bus (ESB) implementations, as well as Single Sign-On implementations, workflow engines, and so on. These are implemented as web modules used by Liferay portlets to provide functionality.

OSGi Bundles

OSGi (Open Services Gateway initiative) is a framework for developing modular Java applications. Liferay 6.2 introduced support for the OSGi module framework. It hosts an OSGi runtime and allows administrators to deploy OSGi bundles to Liferay. OSGi web application bundles are very similar to standard web application archives except that they must include additional metadata so that they can operate in an OSGi framework. The OSGi specification does not require a specific file extension for web application bundles but they typically have a .jar file extension. Sometimes a .war file extension is used instead.

 Note: Liferay 6.2's OSGi runtime is experimental and unsupported. It should be considered a technology preview at this time.

Deploying an OSGi bundle to Liferay is easy: just copy the bundle to your [Liferay Home]/data/osgi/modules directory. Undeploying is just as easy: just remove the bundle from the [Liferay Home]/data/osgi/modules directory. Note: If you copy an OSGi bundle to your [Liferay Home]/deploy directory, Liferay automatically copies it to your [Liferay Home]/data/osgi/modules directory.

To test Liferay's OSGi module framework and deploy mechanism, you can use the test--module-framework-shared bundle from Liferay's plugin repository on Github.[1] In order to deploy the module framework test plugin from a clone of the liferay-plugins repository, you should first add the following lines to your build.[username].properties file in your liferay-plugins directory. If this file doesn't exist yet, create it.

```
liferay.home=[path-to-your-liferay-installation]
auto.deploy.dir=${liferay.home}/deploy
```

Then navigate to the

```
liferay-plugins/shared/test-module-framework-shared
```

directory in a terminal and run ant deploy. Of course, Apache Ant must be installed on your system for this to work. When the test-module-framework-shared bundle has been deployed, the following message appears in the console:

```
Activate Test Component
```

When you remove the test-module-framework-shared bundle from the ${LIFE-RAY_HOME}/data/osgi/deploy directory, another message appears:

```
Deactivate Test Component
```

If you'd like to customize your Liferay Portal instance's module framework behavior, please refer to the Module Framework section of the portal.properties file. For example, you can set a comma-delimited list of directories to scan for modules to deploy, specify how to often to scan the directories for changes, etc. Remember not to make customizations to the portal.properties file itself but to instead add customized properties to a portal-ext.properties file in your Liferay Home directory.

---

[1]https://github.com/liferay/liferay-plugins/tree/master/shared/
test-module-framework-shared

Configuring Plugins

Liferay Portal has a section of the Control Panel called Plugins Configuration, which you can find under the Apps heading of the Control Panel. The Plugins Configuration section not only allows you to see what plugins are installed on your portal, but also enables you to configure which portal roles can access certain plugins. It also allows you to activate or deactivate portlet plugins. From the Control Panel, click on *Plugins Configuration* to find an interface which allows you to view and manage installed portlet, theme, and layout template plugins.

The default view of the Plugins Configuration section shows which plugins are already installed on the system. For portlet plugins, you can click on the plugin's name to view whether or not it's active and to view or configure the portlet's permissions. You don't have to uninstall a plugin to prevent users from accessing the plugin's functionality; instead, you can deactivate the plugin. To deactivate a plugin, click on the plugin's name in the Plugins Configuration section of the Control Panel and remove the flag from the *Active* checkbox. Then click *Save*. To reactive the plugin later, just flag the *Active* checkbox again and click *Save*.

On the Portlet Plugins tab, you have to click on a specific portlet in order to view the plugin's active/inactive status and to configure the portlet's permissions. The active/inactive status doesn't apply to themes or layout templates: if a theme or layout template has been installed, then it's available for use. The Theme and Layout Template Plugins tabs of the Plugins Configuration section directly display which portal roles can access them.

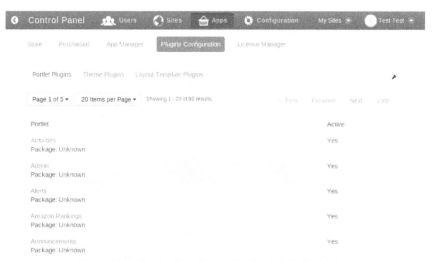

Figure 15.17: Plugins Installation Portlet Tab Default View

It's easy to browse through the lists of installed plugins since the plugins are listed alphabetically. You can also change the number of items per page and navigate to a specific page if you know where a particular plugin appears in the list. This is a standard feature of Liferay and you will see it in most of Liferay's portlets.

Note that the Plugins Configuration section of the Control Panel is for basic configuration: it allows you to active or deactivate portlet plugins, view the existing permissions configuration for various plugins and/or modify the configurations for existing roles. If you need to add permissions to new roles for certain portlets, use the Roles section of the Control Panel and the *Actions* →*Define Permissions* button. Next, let's learn how to install plugins manually.

Installing Plugins Manually

Installing plugins manually is not quite as easy as installing plugins via the Marketplace interface but it's still quite simple. There are several scenarios in which you would need to install plugins manually rather than from Liferay's repositories:

- Your server is firewalled without access to the Internet. This makes it impossible for your instance of Liferay to connect to the plugin repositories.

- You are installing portlets which you have either purchased from a vendor, down-loaded separately or developed yourself.

- For security reasons, you do not want to allow portal administrators to install plug-ins from the Internet before they are evaluated.

You can still use the Control Panel to install plugins that are not available from the online repositories. This is by far the easiest way to install plugins.

If your server is firewalled, you will not be able to install plugins directly from the Life-ray Marketplace. Instead, you will need to download the .lpkg file (in the case of a Mar-ketplace app) or .war file (in the case of an individual plugin). Then navigate to the Con-trol Panel and click on *App Manager* under the Apps heading. Then click on *Install*. This gives you a simple interface for installing an .lpkg or .war file containing an app or plu-gin to your Liferay Portal. Use the *File Upload* option to browse to and install from a local .lpkg or .war file. Use the *URL* option to install from a remote .lpkg or .war file.

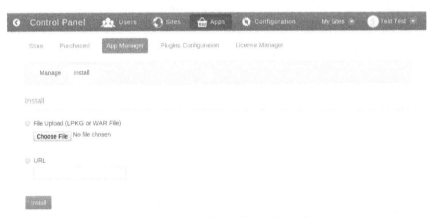

Figure 15.18: Installing a Plugin Manually

That's all the information the App Manager needs in order to deploy your portlet, theme, layout template, hook, or web plugin. Click the *Install* button and your plugin will be up-loaded to the server and deployed. If it is a portlet, theme, or layout template you should see it in the appropriate tab of the Plugins Configuration interface.

If you do not wish to use the App Manager to deploy plugins, you can also deploy them at the operating system level. The first time Liferay starts, it creates a *hot deploy* folder which is, by default, created inside the Liferay Home folder. This folder generally resides one directory up from where your application server is installed, though it may be else-where depending on which application server you are running. To find out where the Liferay Home folder is for your application server, please see the section on your server in this guide's Installation and Setup chapter. The first time Liferay is launched, it creates a folder structure in Liferay Home to house various configuration and administrative data. One of the folders it creates is called *deploy*. If you copy a portlet or theme plugin into this folder, Liferay hot deploys it and makes it available for use just as though you'd installed it via App Manager in the Control Panel. In fact, this is what the App Manager does behind the scenes.

You can change the defaults for this directory structure so it is stored anywhere you like by modifying the appropriate properties in your portal-ext.properties file. Please see the above section on the portal-ext.properties file for more information.

To have Liferay hot deploy a plugin, copy the plugin into your hot deploy folder, which by default is in [Liferay Home]/deploy. If you are watching the Liferay console, you should see messages like the following ones:

```
16:11:47,616 INFO [PortletAutoDeployListener:71] Copying portlets for
/Users/stephenkostas/java/liferay/bundles/liferay-portal-6.0.4/deploy/weather-portlet-6.0.4.1.war

Expanding:
/Users/stephenkostas/java/liferay/bundles/liferay-portal-6.0.4/deploy/weather-portlet-6.0.4.1.war
into
/Users/stephenkostas/java/liferay/bundles/liferay-portal-6.0.4/tomcat-6.0.26/temp/20100729161147694

16:11:48,072 INFO [PortletAutoDeployListener:81] Portlets for
/Users/stephenkostas/java/liferay/bundles/liferay-portal-6.0.4/deploy/weather-portlet-6.0.4.1.war
copied successfully. Deployment will start in a few seconds.

Jul 29, 2010 4:11:50 PM org.apache.catalina.startup.HostConfig
deployDirectory

INFO: Deploying web application directory weather-portlet

16:11:50,585 INFO [PortletHotDeployListener:222] Registering portlets
for weather-portlet
\index{portlet}

16:11:50,784 INFO [PortletHotDeployListener:371] 1 portlet for
weather-portlet is available for use
```

The *available for use* message means your plugin was installed correctly and is available for use in the portal.

Plugin Troubleshooting

Sometimes plugins fail to install. There can be different reasons for installation failure based on several factors, including

- Liferay configuration

- The container upon which Liferay is running

- Changing the configuration options in multiple places

- How Liferay is being launched

You can often tell whether or not you have a plugin deployment problem by looking at the Liferay server console. If the hot deploy listener recognizes the plugin, you'll see a *plugin copied successfully* message. If this message is not followed up by an *available for use* message then you have an issue with your plugin deployment configuration, probably due to one of the factors listed above.

Let's take a look at each of these factors.

Liferay Configuration Issues

Tip: This applies to Liferay versions prior to version 4.3.5. Liferay versions above 4.3.5 are able to auto detect the type of server it is running on, which makes things a lot easier. If you are running a newer version of Liferay, you can skip this section. If you are upgrading from one of these versions, continue reading.

Liferay by default comes as a bundle or as a .war file. Though every effort has been made to make the .war file as generic as possible, sometimes the default settings are inappropriate for the container upon which Liferay is running. Most of these problems were resolved in Liferay 4.3.5 with the addition of code that allows Liferay to determine which application server it is running on and adjust the way it deploys plugins as a result. If you have upgraded from one of these older versions, you may still have settings in your portal.ext.properties file that are no longer needed. One of these settings is the manual override of the default value of auto.deploy.dest.dir.

In versions of Liferay prior to 4.3.5, there is a property called auto.deploy.dest.dir that defines the folder where plugins are deployed after the hot deploy utilities have finished preparing them. This folder maps to a folder the container defines as an auto-deploy or a hot deploy folder. By default in older versions of Liferay, this property is set to ../web-apps. This default value works for Tomcat containers (if Tomcat has been launched from its bin folder) but will not work for other containers that define their hot deploy folders in a different place. In newer versions of Liferay, this value is automatically set to the default for the application server upon which Liferay is running.

For example, Glassfish defines the hot deploy folder as a folder called autodeploy inside the domain folder where your server is running. By default, this is in [Glassfish Home]/domains/domain1/autodeploy. JBoss defines the hot deploy folder as a root folder inside the server configuration you are using. By default, this is in [JBoss Home]-/server/default/deploy. WebLogic defines this folder inside the domain directory. By default, this is in [Bea Home]/user_projects/domains/[domain name]/auto-deploy.

The best thing to do when upgrading to newer versions of Liferay Portal is to remove this property altogether. It is not needed, as the autodetection of the container handles the hot deploy location. If, for whatever reason, you need to customize the location of the hot deploy folder, follow the instructions below.

You will first need to determine where the hot deploy folder is for the container you are running. Consult your product documentation for this. Once you have this value, there are two places in which you can set it: in the portal-ext.properties file and in the Plugin Installer portlet.

To change this setting in the portal-ext.properties file, browse to where Liferay was deployed in your application server. Inside of this folder should be a WEB-INF/classes folder. Here you will find the portal-ext.properties file. Open this file in a text editor and look for the property auto.deploy.dest.dir. If it does not appear in the file, you can add it. The safest way to set this property, as we will see later, is to define the property using an absolute path from the root of your file system to your application server's hot deploy folder. For example, if you are using Glassfish, and you have the server installed in /java/glassfish, your auto.deploy.dest.dir property would look like the following:

```
auto.deploy.dest.dir=/java/glassfish/domains/domain1/autodeploy
```

Remember, if you are on a Windows system, use forward slashes instead of back slashes, like so:

```
auto.deploy.dest.dir=C:/java/glassfish/domains/domain1/autodeploy
```

Save the file and then restart your container. Now plugins should install correctly.

If you are having hot deploy trouble in Liferay versions 4.3.5 and greater, it is possible the administrator of your application server has changed the default folder for auto deploy in your application server. In this case, you would want to set auto.deploy.dest.dir to the customized folder location as you would with older versions of Liferay. In Liferay 4.3.5 and greater, this setting still exists but is blank. Add the property to your portal-ext.properties file and set its value to the fully qualified path to the auto deploy folder configured in your application server.

Deploy Issues for Specific Containers

Some containers, such as WebSphere®, don't have a hot deploy feature. Unfortunately, these containers do not work with Liferay's hot deploy system. But this does not mean you cannot install plugins on these containers. You can deploy plugins manually using the application server's deployment tools. Liferay is able to pick up the portlet plugins once they get deployed to the container manually, especially if you add it to the same Enterprise Application project that was created for Liferay.

When Liferay hot deploys portlet and theme .war files, it sometimes makes modifications to those files right before deployment. In order to successfully deploy plugins using an application server vendor's tools, you will want to run your plugins through this process before you attempt to deploy them.

Navigate back to the *Configuration* tab of the Plugin Installer. Enter the location you would like plugin .war files to be copied to after they are processed by Liferay's plugin installer process into the *Destination Directory* field. You will use this as a staging directory for your plugins before you install them manually with your server's deployment tools. When you are finished, click *Save*.

Now you can deploy plugins using the Plugin Installer portlet or by dropping .war files into your auto deploy directory. Liferay will pick up the files, modify them and then copy the result into the destination directory you have configured. You may then deploy them from here to your application server.

Example: WebSphere ® Application Server

1. If you don't have one already, create a portal-ext.properties file in the Liferay Home folder of your Liferay installation. Add the following directive to it:

   auto.deploy.dest.dir=${liferay.home}/websphere-deploy

2. Create a folder called websphere-deploy inside your $LIFERAY_HOME folder. This is the folder where the Lucene index, Jackrabbit config and deploy folders are.

3. Make sure the web.xml file inside the plugin you want to install has the following context parameter in it:

   com.ibm.websphere.portletcontainer.PortletDeploymentEnabled

   false

Liferay versions 5.2.2 and higher will automatically inject this into the web.xml file on WebSphere containers.

4. The WebSphere deploy occurs in two steps. You will first use Liferay's tools to "pre-deploy" the file and then use WebSphere's tools to do the actual deployment. This is because Liferay makes deployment-time modifications to the plugins right before they are actually deployed to the application server. For other application servers, this can usually be done in one step, because Liferay can make the modifications and then copy the resulting .war file into an autodeploy folder to have it actually

deployed. Because WebSphere does not have an autodeploy feature, we need to separate these two steps.

5. Deploy your .war file using Liferay's Plugin Installer or by copying it into $LIFE-RAY_HOME/deploy. Liferay will make its modifications, and because we changed the auto.deploy.dest.dir in the first step, it will copy the resulting .war file into $LIFERAY_HOME/websphere-deploy. You will see a *copied successfully* message in the log.

6. Use WebSphere's tools to deploy the .war file. Make the context root for the .war file equal to the file name (i.e., /my-first-portlet). Once the .war file is deployed, save it to the master configuration.

7. Go back to the *Applications →Enterprise Applications* screen in the WebSphere Admin Console. You will see your portlet is deployed but not yet started. Start it.

8. Liferay will immediately recognize the portlet has been deployed and register it. The portlet will be automatically started and registered upon subsequent restarts of WebSphere.

Experienced WebSphere system administrators can further automate this by writing a script which watches the websphere-deploy directory and uses wsadmin commands to then deploy plugins automatically.

Changing the Configuration Options in Multiple Places

Sometimes, especially during development when several people have administrative access to the server at the same time, the auto deploy folder location may inadvertently be customized in both the portal-ext.properties file and in the Control Panel. If this happens, the value in the Control Panel takes precedence over the value in the properties file. If you go into the Control Panel and change the value to the correct setting, plugin deployment will start working again.

15.7 Summary

In this chapter, we introduced Liferay Marketplace, your one-stop shop for browsing and downloading Liferay-compatible applications. We looked at how to browse, purchase, download, and install apps. You can do this either through liferay.com/marketplace or through Liferay Portal's Control Panel. When you purchase apps, you can do so via your personal account or on your company's behalf. For information about developing and uploading apps to Liferay Marketplace, please see the Marketplace chapter of the Liferay Developer guide at http://www.liferay.com/marketplace/developer-guide.

After discussing Liferay Marketplace, we discussed general plugin management. We covered Liferay portlet plugins as well as layout, theme, hook, Ext, and web plugins. Finally, we looked at how to manually deploy plugins to Liferay and discussed some configuration issues.

## CHAPTER 16

USER MANAGEMENT

You know how all these retailers advertise themselves as a "one stop shop" for anything you want? The idea is they have so much stuff that chances are whatever you're looking for is there. Liferay's Control Panel is something like this. If you want to create users, organizations, sites, configure permissions and plugins and pretty much anything else, you can do it from the Control Panel. When signed in to Liferay as an administrator, you can access the Control Panel from the Dockbar by clicking *Admin* →*Control Panel*.

The Control Panel is organized into four main areas: Users, Sites, Apps, and Configuration. The Users section lets you create and manage users, organizations, user groups, roles, and password policies. If monitoring has been enabled for your portal, you can also view all of the live portal sessions of your users from this area of the Control Panel. If the Audit plugins have been installed from Liferay Marketplace, the Audit section also appears.

In this chapter, you'll learn everything having to do with managing users, and you'll see examples of some of the user management concepts discussed earlier:

- Users
- Organizations
- User Groups
- Roles
- Password Policies
- Monitoring
- Audit Trails

Let's begin examining Liferay's Control Panel by looking at how to manage users in Liferay Portal.

16.1 The Users Section of the Control Panel

The Users section of the Control Panel is used for most administrative tasks involving user management. There, you'll find an interface for the creation and maintenance of the following portal entities: users, organizations, user groups, and roles.

Figure 16.1: The Users section of the Control Panel allows portal administrators to manage users, organizations, user groups, and roles. It also allows administrators to monitor users' live portal sessions if monitoring has been enabled for the portal.

Since we explained how to manage sites, teams, site templates, and page templates in chapters 2 and 3, we won't discuss them in detail here. Nevertheless, remember that it's possible and sometimes simpler to use sites, site memberships, and teams to organize users and manage permissions than it is to use organizations, user groups, and custom roles.

As a portal administrator, you'll use the Users section of the Control Panel to create users, organizations, and user groups, implement security via roles and permissions, and administer your users. Note that only users with the administrator role, which is a portal scoped role, have permission to view the Control Panel. You can, of course, grant permissions to view one or more sections, such as the Users section, to custom roles.

Adding and Editing Users

Are you using Liferay's default administrative user, Test Test (test@liferay.com)? If so, let's add a user account for yourself and configure your new account so it has the same administrative access as the default administrator account. From the Dockbar, click *Admin* and select *Control Panel*. Then click on *Users and Organizations*. Click the *Add* button and select *User*. Fill out the Add User form using your name and email address. When you are finished, click *Save*.

After you submit the form, the page reloads with a success message. An expanded form appears that allows you to fill out a lot more information about the user. You don't have to fill anything else out right now. Just note that when the user account was created, a password was automatically generated. If Liferay was correctly installed and a mail server was set up (see chapter 14), an email message with the user's new password was sent to the user's email address. This, of course, requires that Liferay can properly communicate with your SMTP mail server.

If you haven't yet set up your mail server, you'll need to use this page to change the default password for your user account to something you can remember. You can do this by clicking on the *Password* link in the box on the right, entering the new password in the two fields and clicking *Save*. Next, you should give your user account the same administrative rights as the default administrator's account. This allows you to perform administrative tasks with your own account instead of having to use the default administrator account. In production, you should always delete or disable the default administrator account to secure your portal.

On the form for editing a user, click the *Roles* link in the menu on the right side of the screen. This page shows the roles to which your account is currently assigned. You should have one role: Power User. By default, all users are assigned the Power User role. The Power User role doesn't grant any special permissions. It can safely be ignored. Alternatively, it can be used to extend the User role. If there are certain custom permissions that you'd like all of your portal users to have, you can grant these custom permissions to the Power User role. You can also customize the default roles a new user receives via *Default User Associations*. We'll learn to do this when we look at Portal Settings in the next chapter.

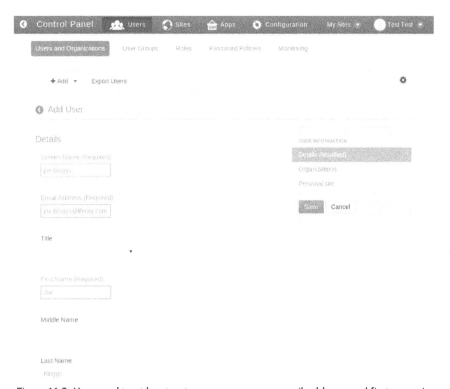

Figure 16.2: You need to at least enter a screen name, email address, and first name in order to create a new user account.

We want to assign the Administrator role to our user account. On the form for editing a user, after having clicked on *Roles* at the right side of the screen, click the *Select* link under Regular Roles. A dialog box pops up with a list of all the regular (portal-scoped) roles in the portal. Select the Administrator role from the list. The dialog box disappears and the role is added to the list of roles associated with your account. Don't forget to click the *Save* button which is at the bottom of the blue bar of links on the right side of the screen. You are now a portal administrator. Log out of the portal and then log back in with your own user account. Next, let's look at some other aspects of user management.

User Management

If you click on *Users and Organizations* in the Control Panel, you should now see your user account in the list of users. If you want to change something about a particular user, you can click the *Actions* button next to that user.

Edit: takes you back to the Edit User page where you can modify any aspect of the user account including the screen name, email address, first name, last name, site and organization memberships, roles, etc.

Permissions: allows you to define which roles have permissions to edit the user.

Manage Pages: allows you to edit the personal pages of a user.

Impersonate User: opens another browser window which allows you to browse the site as if you were the user.

Deactivate: deactivates the user's account.

◀ Edit User *Joe Bloggs*

Details

Screen Name (Required)

joe.bloggs

Email Address (Required)

joe.bloggs@liferay.com

Title

▼

First Name (Required)

Joe

Middle Name

Last Name

Bloggs

Suffix

▼

🖼 Change   ✖ Delete

Joe Bloggs

USER INFORMATION

Details

Password

Organizations

Sites

User Groups

Roles

Personal site

Categorization

IDENTIFICATION

Addresses

Phone Numbers

Additional Email Addresses

Websites

Instant Messenger

Social Network

SMS

OpenID

MISCELLANEOUS

Announcements

Display Settings

Comments

Custom Fields

Save   Cancel

Figure 16.3: Once you've completed the basic form for creating a new user account, you'll see a much more detailed form for editing the user and adding additional information.

Note that most users can't perform most of the above actions. In fact, most users won't even have access to the Control Panel. You can perform all of the above functions because you have administrative access.

Next, let's look at how to manage organizations.

Organizations

Organizations are used to represent hierarchical structures of users such as those of companies, businesses, non-profit organizations, churches, schools, and clubs. They are designed to allow distributed user administration. Organizations can be used, for example, to represent a sports league. The league itself could be modeled as a top-level organization and the various sports (soccer, baseball, basketball, etc.) could be modeled as suborganizations. The teams belonging to the various sports could be modeled as sub-organizations of the sports organizations. So, for example, you could have an organization hierarchy that looks like this:

- Atlantic Sports League
    - Atlantic Soccer Association
        * Midway Soccer Club
        * Fairview Soccer Club
        * Oak Grove Soccer Club
    - Atlantic Baseball Association
        * Five Points Baseball Club
        * Riverside Baseball Club
        * Pleasant Hill Baseball Club
    - Atlantic Basketball Association
        * Bethel Basketball Club
        * Centerville Basketball Club
        * New Hope Basketball Club

Whenever you have a collection of users that fit into a hierarchical structure, you can use organizations to model those users. In Liferay, organization administrators can manage all the users in their organization *and* in any suborganization. Referring to the hierarchy above, for example, an organization administrator of the Atlantic Sports League could manage any users belonging to the league itself, to any of the associations, or to any of the associations' clubs. An organization administrator of the Atlantic Soccer Association could manage any users belonging to the Atlantic Soccer Association itself, or to the Midway Soccer Club, Fairview Soccer Club, or Oak Grove Soccer Club. However, an administrator of the Atlantic Soccer Association would not be able to manage users belonging to the Atlantic Baseball Association or to the Bethel Basketball Club.

Organizations and suborganization hierarchies can be created to unlimited levels. Users can be members of one or many organizations. The rights of an organization administrator apply both to his/her organization and to any child organizations. By default, members of child organizations are implicit members of their parent organizations. This means, for example, that members of child organizations can access the private pages of their parent organizations. This behavior can be customized in your portal's por-tal-ext.properties configuration file.

Since organizations are designed for distributed user administration, organization administrators have an entirely different set of privileges than site administrators. Site administrators are responsible for the pages, portlets, and content of their site. They are also responsible for managing the membership of their site. To this end, they can set the membership type to Open, Restricted, or Private. They can also add users to or remove users from their site but cannot manage the users themselves. Organization administrators, on the other hand, can edit users belonging to their organization or any suborganization. They cannot add existing users to their organization but they can create new users within their organization. Only portal administrators can add existing users to an organization.

Many simple portal designs don't use organizations at all; they only use sites (see chapters 2 and 3 for more information on sites). Remember that the main purpose of organizations is to allow for distributed user management. They allow portal administrators to delegate some of their user management responsibilities to organization administrators. If you don't anticipate needing to delegate user management responsibilities, your portal design need not include organizations. In order to decide whether or not your portal design should include organization, think about your portal's function. A simple photo-sharing web site, for example, could be powered by sites only. On the other hand, organizations are useful for corporations or educational institutions since their users can easily be placed into a hierarchical structure. In fact, organizations in Liferay are designed to model any group hierarchy, from those of government agencies all the way down to those of small clubs. Of course, users can belong both to organizations and to independent sites. For example, a corporation or educational institution could create a social networking site open to all portal users, even ones from separate organizations.

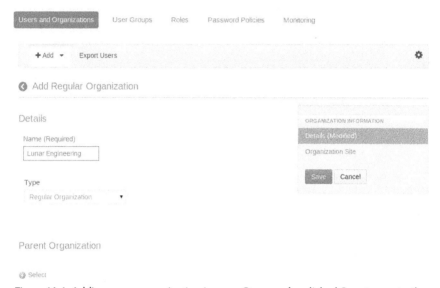

Figure 16.4: Adding a new organization is easy. Once you've clicked *Save* to create the organization, you can specify additional details about the organization.

Additionally, organization administrators can assign organization-scoped roles to members of their organization. For example, consider an IT Security group in a corporate setting. You could have a suborganizaton of your IT organization that handles security for all of the applications company-wide. If you grant the IT Security organization the portal administrator role, all the members of the organization would have administrative access to the entire portal. Suppose further that a user in this organization was later hired by the Human Resources department. The simple act of removing the user from the IT Security organization also removes the user's administrative privileges, since the privilege came from the IT Security organization's role. By adding the user to the HR organization, any roles the HR organization has (such as access to a benefits system in the portal) are transferred to the user. In this manner, you can design your portal to correspond with your existing organization chart and users' permissions are granted according to their positions in the chart.

Of course, this is only one way to design it. If you have more complex requirements for permissions within an organization, you can create custom organization-scoped roles to assemble the permissions you wish to grant to particular users. Alternatively, you could consider attaching a site to your organization and using site teams to assemble the sets of permissions (see below). We'll discuss roles and permissions in more detail later in this chapter.

Does your organization need to have its own site? Many organizations don't, but since some do, Liferay allows sites to be attached to organizations. If an organization has an attached site, the organization's administrators are treated as the site administrators of the attached site. This means that they can manage the pages, portlets, and content of the site as well as the users of the organization. Members of an organization with an attached site are treated as members of the organization's site. This means that they can access the private pages of the organization's site, along with any portlets or content there. The capability of attaching sites to organizations allows portal administrators to use organizations to facilitate distributed portal administration, not just distributed user administration. Next, let's learn how to create and manage organizations.

To add an organization, click the *Users and Organizations* link in the Control Panel. Then click the *Add* button and choose *Regular Organization*. To attach a site when you create an organization, click on *Organization Site* at the right and check the *Create Site* box. If you don't know right now if your organization needs a site, that's fine. You can always add one later if the need arises.

Name: Enter a name for the organization.

Type: Choose whether this is a regular organization or a location. A location cannot have any suborganizations.

Parent Organization: Select an organization in the system to be the direct parent of the organization you are creating. Click the *Remove* button to remove the currently configured parent.

> **Tip:** By creating an organization, you automatically become both a member and receive the Organization Owner role, which gives you full administrative rights within the organization. This means that you can, for example, appoint other users to be organization administrators or organization owners. Organization owners are equivalent to organization administrators except that they can assign the Organization Owner and Organization Administrator roles to other users; they can also remove the memberships of other Organization Administrators or Owners. Organization administrators can't make these role assignments and can't manage the memberships of other Organization Administrators or Owners.

Fill out the information for your organization and click *Save*. As when creating a new user, after you click *Save* to submit the form, a success message appears along with a new form which lets you enter additional information about the organization. Organizations can have multiple email addresses, postal addresses, web sites, and phone numbers associated with them. The Services link can be used to indicate the operating hours of the organization, if any.

For now, click on the *Back* icon. This takes you back to the list of organizations. Click the *Actions* button next to the new organization you created. This shows a list of actions you can perform on this organization.

Edit: lets you specify details about the organization, including addresses, phone numbers, email addresses and websites.

Manage Site: lets you create and manage the public and private pages of the organization's site. This only appears for organizations that have attached sites.

Assign Organization Roles: lets you assign organization-scoped roles to users. By default, Organizations are created with three roles: Organization Administrator, Organization User and Organization Owner. You can assign one or more of these roles to users in the organization. All members of the organization automatically get the Organization User role so this role is hidden when you click Assign Organization Roles.

Assign Users: lets you search and select users in the portal to be assigned to this organization as members.

Add User: adds a new user in the portal and assigns the user as a member of this organization.

Add Regular Organization: lets you add a child organization to this organization. This is how you create hierarchies of organizations with parent-child relationships.

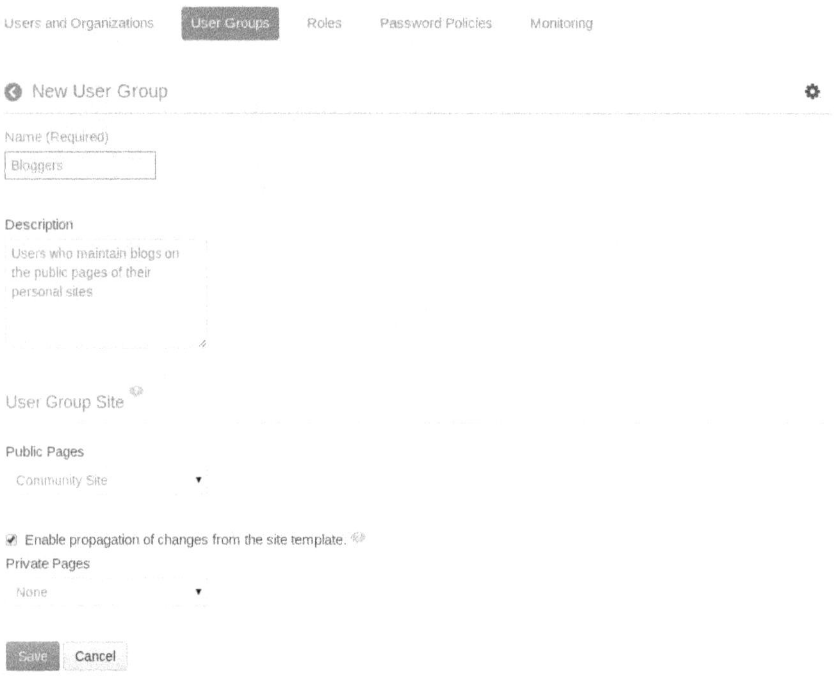

Users and Organizations   **User Groups**   Roles   Password Policies   Monitoring

◀ New User Group   ⚙

Name (Required)

| Bloggers |

Description

| Users who maintain blogs on the public pages of their personal sites |

User Group Site

Public Pages

| Community Site ▼ |

☑ Enable propagation of changes from the site template.
Private Pages

| None ▼ |

Save Cancel

Figure 16.5: When creating a new user group, you can select a site template for the public or private pages of the user group site. If you don't select a site template at creation time, you can edit the user group later to add one.

Add Location: lets you add a child Location, which is a special type of organization that cannot have any children added to it.

Delete: removes this organization from the portal. Make sure the organization has no users in it first.

If you click the *View* button at the top of the Users and Organizations page and select *View Hierarchy* you can view both a list of users who are members of this organization and a list of all the suborganizations of this organization.

Users can join or be assigned to sites when they share a common interest. Users can be assigned to organizations when they fit into a hierarchical structure. Users groups provide a more ad hoc way to group users than sites and organizations. Let's look at them next.

16.2   User Groups

User Groups are designed to allow portal administrators to create groups of users that traverse the organizations hierarchy. They can be used to create arbitrary groupings of users who don't necessarily share an obvious hierarchical attribute. Users can be assigned to multiple user groups. For example, consider a software company with many offices and departments within each office. The company's office/department structure could be modeled through organizations. In this situation, it might make sense to create user groups for developers, office managers, accountant, etc. User Groups are most often used to achieve one of the following goals:

- To simplify the assignment of several roles to a group of users. For example, in a University portal, a user group could be created to group all teachers independently of their organizations to make it easier to assign one or several roles at once to all the teachers.

- To simplify membership to one or more sites by specifying a group of users. Using the previous example, all teachers could be members of the sites *University Employees* and *Students and Teachers Collaboration Site* by adding the *Teachers* user group as a member.

- To provide predefined public or private pages to the users who belong to the user group. For example, the *Teachers* user group could be created to ensure the home page on all teachers' personal sites has the same layout and applications.

Creating a user group is easy. Navigate to the Control Panel, click on the *Users Groups* link and then click on the *Add* button. There's only one required field: Name. It's usually best to enter a description as well. Click *Save* and you will be redirected back to the *User Groups* page of the Control Panel.

Note in the figure above that a user group can have a site, with public and private pages. A user group site is a special type of site that determines the base pages of the personal sites of all the user group members. User group sites work similarly to site templates, except that user group site pages are not copied for each user. Instead, they are shown dynamically along with any custom pages that the user may have on his/her personal site. For this reason, users are not allowed to make any modifications to the pages that are *inherited* from the user group. Optionally, the administrators of the user group can define certain areas as customizable, just like they can for regular sites. This allows users to decide which applications they want to place in certain areas of each page, as well as customize the configurations of the applications.

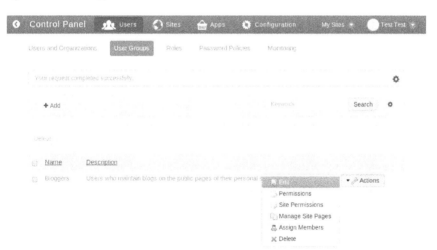

Figure 16.6: To edit the pages of a user group site, click *Actions →Manage Site Pages* next to the user group you'd like to edit.

As with the other resources in the portal, you can click the *Actions* button next to a user group to perform various operations on that group.

Edit: allows you to modify the name or description of the user group.

Permissions: lets you define which roles have permissions to view, edit, delete, assign members to the user group, etc.

Site Permissions: lets you define which roles have permissions to manage the user group site, to specify who can administer its pages, export and import pages and portlet content, manage archived setups and configure its applications.

Manage Site Pages: allows you to add pages to the user group site, import or export pages, organize the page hierarchy, modify the look and feel of the pages, add a logo or access other options from the Manage Site interface.

Assign Members: lets you search for and select users in the portal to be assigned to this user group as well as view the users currently belonging to the user group .

Delete: removes the user group.

If your user group has a site, two options named *Go to the Site's Public Pages* and *Go to the Site's Private Pages* also appear as links in your user group's Actions menu. Clicking one of these links opens the user group's site in a new browser window. Any changes you make to the site are saved automatically. You can safely close the browser window when you're done.

Creating and Editing a User Group

A user group's site can be administered from the Control Panel. Click on *User Groups* from the Control Panel to see a list of existing user groups. To edit a user group, click on its name or description. You can also click on the *Actions* button to see the full list of actions that can be performed on a user group. When editing a user group, you can view its site, if it exists, by clicking the *Open Pages* link under Public Pages or Private Pages (read below for details on user group sites).

As an example of how user group sites can be used, let's create a user group called *Bloggers* along with a simple site template. We'll call the site template *Bloggers* too. It should contain a single *Blog* page with the Blogs and Recents Bloggers portlets on it. First, navigate to the User Groups page of the Control Panel. Then click *Add* and enter the name *Bloggers* for your user group, and optionally, a description. Click *Save* to create your user group.

Our next step is to assign an existing user to the *Bloggers* group.

Assigning Members to a User Group

Navigate to *Users and Organizations* and create a new user called *Joe Bloggs*. Then navigate to the User Groups page of the Control Panel and click *Actions* →*Assign Members* next to the Bloggers group. Click the *Available* tab to see a list of users that can be assigned to the group.

From this list, one or more users can be assigned as members of the user group. After the user group has been created and several users have been added to it, you can add all those users at once as members of a site in one step from the *Site Memberships* UI of the site. You can also use the user group when assigning a role to users from the roles management UI. The next section explains how to use user group sites.

User Group Sites

Liferay allows users to each have a personal site consisting of public and private pages. Permissions can be granted to allow users to customize their personal sites at will. Originally, the default configuration of those pages could only be determined by the portal administrator through the portal-ext.properties file and, optionally, by providing the configuration in a LAR file. You can still configure it like this but it isn't very flexible or easy to use.

By using User Group Sites, portal administrators can add pages to the personal sites of all the users who belong to the site in an easy and centralized way. All the user group site's public pages are shown as part of the user's public personal site. All the user group

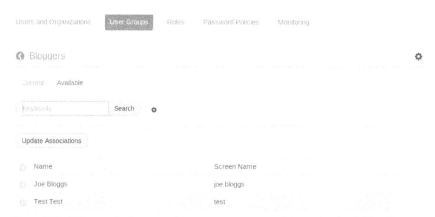

Figure 16.7: When assigning members to a user group, click on the *Available* tab to see a list of users able to be added to the user group.

site's private pages are shown as part of the user's private site. If a user belongs to several user groups, all of its pages are made part of his public and private site. In an educational institution's portal, for example, teachers, staff and students could get different default pages and applications on their personal sites.

The pages a user's personal site *inherits* from a User Group still belong to the User Group and thus cannot be changed in any way by the user. What the user group administrators can do is define certain areas of the pages as customizable to allow the users to choose which applications and what configuration should be shown in those areas. If a user has permission to add custom pages to his/her personal site, besides those *inherited* from a user group, the custom pages are always shown last.

Since the *inheritance* of pages is done dynamically, this system, which was introduced in Liferay 6.1, can scale to hundreds of thousands of users or even millions of them without an exponential impact in performance. Previous versions of Liferay used a different technique that required user group pages be copied to each user's personal site. For portals upgrading from previous versions of Liferay, you can keep the old behavior but it has been left disabled by default. You can enable it by adding the following line to your portal-ext.properties file:

```
user.groups.copy.layouts.to.user.personal.site=true
```

When this property is set to true, once the template pages have been copied to a user's personal site, the copies may be modified by the user. Changes done to the originals in the User Group will only affect new users added to the user group. Users with administrative privileges over their personal sites can modify the pages and their content if the *Allow Site Administrators to Modify the Pages Associated with This Site Template* box has been checked for the template. When a user is removed from a user group, the associated pages are removed from the user's personal site. Moreover, if a user is removed from a group and is subsequently added back, the group's template pages are copied to the user's site a second time. Note that if a user group's site is based on a site template and an administrator modifies the user group's site template after users have already been added to the group, those changes only take effect if the *Enable propagation of changes from the site template* box for the user group was checked.

Tip: Prior to Liferay 6.1, pages from different user groups could be combined on users' personal sites by using a naming convention. Liferay 6.1 simplifies the way user groups' sites work by disallowing page combination. Set the property *user.groups.copy.layouts.to.user.personal.site* to true if you want to preserve the page combination functionality.

You can create a user group's site manually or base it on a site template. To create a user group's site manually, use the *Actions* menu mentioned above and choose *Manage Site Pages*. You can add a new public or private page by selecting the appropriate tab and then clicking the *Add Page* button. Once the user group has at least one public or private page in place, you can go back to the *Actions* menu and click on the *Go to the Site's Public Pages* or *Go to the Site's Private Pages* link to open the user group's site in a new browser window. In the new window, you can add more pages and portlets and configure site settings.

You can also base a user group's site on a template. When editing a user group, use the Public Pages and Private Pages drop down lists to select a site template. Leave the *Enable propagation of changes from the site template* box checked to automatically update users' personal sites if the associated site template changes. If you uncheck this box but recheck it later, the template pages are copied to the users' sites, overwriting any changes they may have made. You can allow users to make changes to the pages they receive from the user group by enabling the customization options on each page.

This flexibility lets you achieve almost any desired configuration for a user's personal site without having to modify it directly. When a user is assigned to a user group, the configured site pages are copied directly to the user's personal site.

Continuing with the example above, we will create a site for our sample user group. Edit the *Bloggers* user group. Choose an existing Site Template from the drop down menu for the user group's public pages and click *Save*. After the page reloads you can click to see the pages and make any changes desired, add additional pages, etc.

Also, try visiting the public site of one of the users who belongs to the user group. You'll see that all of the pages in the user group appear as part of the user site, including ones copied from the site template and ones added afterwards.

16.3 Roles and Permissions

Roles are used to collect permissions that define a particular function within the portal, according to a particular scope. Roles can be granted permissions to various functions within portlet applications. A roles is basically just a collection of permissions that defines a function, such as Message Board Administrator. A role with that name is likely to have permissions relevant to the specific Message Board portlets delegated to it. Users who are placed in this role will inherit these permissions.

If you navigate to the Control Panel and click on *Roles*, you'll find a single interface which lets you create roles, assign permissions to them, and assign users to the roles. Roles can be scoped by portal, site, or organization. To create a role, click the *Roles* link and then click the *Add* button. You can choose a Regular, Site or Organization role. A regular role is a portal-scoped role. Make a selection and then type a name for your role, a title and a description. The name field is required but the title and description are optional. If you enter a name and a title, the title will be displayed in the list of roles on the Roles page of the Control Panel. If you do not enter a title, the name will be displayed. When you have finished, click *Save*.

In addition to regular roles, site roles, and organization roles, there are also teams. Teams can be created by site administrators within a specific site. The permissions granted to a team are defined and applied only within the team's site. The permissions defined by regular, site, and organization roles, by contrast, are defined at the portal level, although

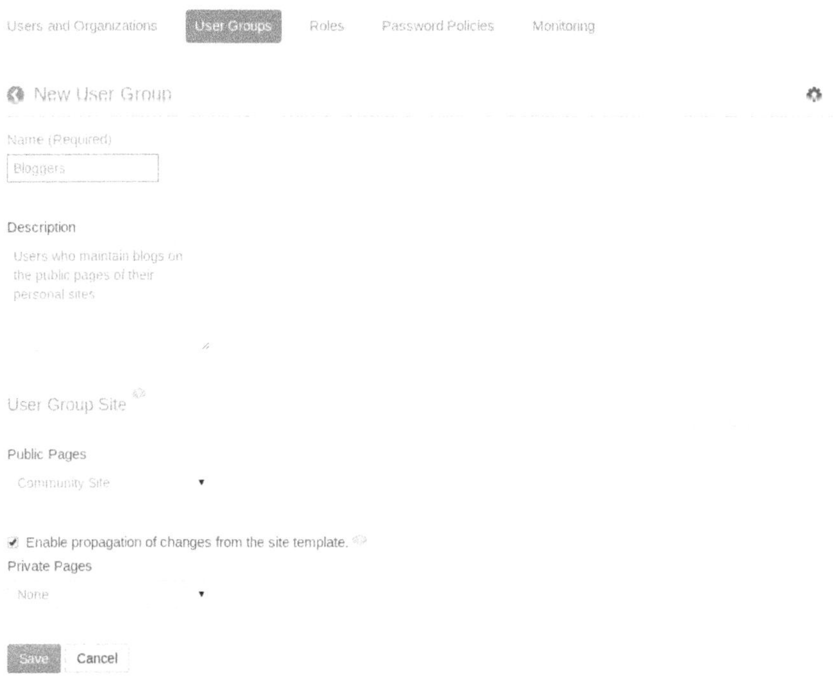

Users and Organizations   User Groups   Roles   Password Policies   Monitoring

New User Group

Name (Required)

Bloggers

Description

Users who maintain blogs on
the public pages of their
personal sites

User Group Site

Public Pages

Community Site ▼

☑ Enable propagation of changes from the site template.
Private Pages

None ▼

Save   Cancel

Figure 16.8: You can select a site template to apply to a user group's public or private
pages if the public or private page set is empty. If pages have already been added to
the page set, you'll have to remove them before you can apply a site template the
page.

they are applied to different scopes. The differences between the four types of roles can
be described as follows:

- Regular role: Permissions are defined at the *portal* level and are applied at the *portal*
  level.

- Site role: Permissions are defined at the *portal* level and are applied to one *specific
  site*.

- Organization role: Permissions are defined at the *portal* level and are applied to one
  specific organization.

- Team: Permissions are defined within a *specific site* and are assigned within that
  specific site.

For more information about teams, please refer to chapter 3.

After you save, Liferay redirects you to the list of roles. To see what functions you can
perform on your new role, click the *Actions* button.

Edit: lets you change the name, title or description of the role.

Permissions: allows you to define which users, user groups or roles have permissions
to edit the role.

Define Permissions: defines what permissions this role grants. This is outlined in the
next section.

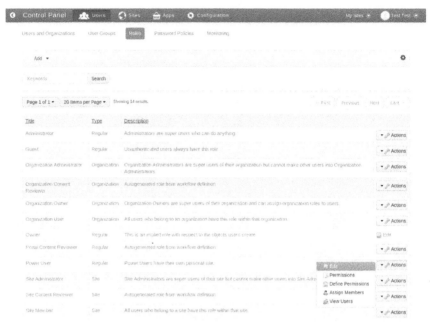

Figure 16.9: To examine all the roles defined for your portal, navigate to the Control Panel and click on *Roles*.

Assign Members: lets you search and select users in the portal to be assigned to this role. These users will inherit any permissions that have been assigned to this role.

View Users: allows you to view the users who have been assigned to this role.

Delete: permanently removes a role from the portal.

Next, let's learn about the difference between the (portal/site/organization) administrator and owner roles that Liferay provides out-of-the-box.

Out-of-the-box Liferay Roles

If you navigate to the Control Panel and click on *Roles*, you'll see a list of all the roles that have been created in your portal. This list includes roles that Liferay provides out-of-the-box and any additional custom roles. These are some of Liferay's out-of-the-box roles:

- Guest: The Guest role is assigned to unauthenticated users and grants the lowest-level permissions within the portal.
- User: The User role is assigned to authenticated users and grants basic basic permissions within the portal.
- Power User: By default, the Power User role grants the same permissions as the User role. It's designed to be an extension point for distinguishing regular users from more privileged users. For example, you can set up your portal so that only Power Users have personal sites.
- Site Member: The Site Member role grants basic privileges within a site, such as the ability to visit the site's private pages.
- Site Administrator: The Site Administrator role grants the ability to manage *almost* all aspects of a site including site content, site memberships, and site settings. Site Administrators cannot delete the membership of or remove roles from other Site

Administrators or Site Owners. They also *cannot* assign other users as Site Administrators or Site Owners.

- Site Owner: The Site Owner role is the same as the Site Administrator role except that it grants the ability to manage *all* aspects of a site, including the ability to delete the membership of or remove roles from Site Administrators or other Site Owners. They *can* assign other users as Site Administrators or Site Owners.
- Organization User: The Organization User role grants basic privileges within an organization. If the organization has an attached site, the Organization User role implicitly grants the Site member role within the attached site.
- Organization Administrator: The Organization Administrator role grants the ability to manage *almost* all aspects of an organization including the organization's users and the organization's site (if it exists). Organization Administrators cannot delete the membership of or remove roles from other Organization Administrators or Organization Owners. They also *cannot* assign other users as Organization Administrators or Organization Owners.
- Organization Owner: The Organization Owner role is the same as the Organization Administrator role except that it grants the ability to manage *all* aspects of an organization, including the ability to delete the membership of or remove roles from Organization Administrators or other Organization Owners. They *can* assign other users as Organization Administrators or Organization Owners.
- Administrator: The administrator role grants the ability to manage the entire portal, including global portal settings and individual sites, organizations, and users.

Tip: It's easy to overlook the differences between site and organization owners and site and organization administrators. Remember that site and organization administrators *cannot* delete the membership of or remove the administrator or owner role from any other administrator or owner. They also *cannot* appoint other users as site or organization administrators or owners. Site and organization owners *can* delete the membership of or remove the administrator or owner roles from other site or organization administrators. They *can* appoint other users as site or organization administrators or owners.

Next, let's examine how to configure the permissions granted by different roles.

Defining Permissions on a Role

Roles serve as repositories of permissions. When a roles is assigned to a user, the user receives all the permissions defined by the role. So, to use a role, you need to assign members to it and define the permissions you want to grant to members of the role.

When you click on the *Actions* button for a portal-scoped role and select *Define Permissions*, you'll see a list of all the permissions that have been defined for that role. To add permissions to a role, drill down through the categories of permissions on the left side of the screen and click on a specific category (such as *Site Administration →Pages →Site Pages*. In the center of the screen, you'll see the permissions that belong to that category. Flag the checkboxes next to the permissions that you'd like to add the role, then click *Save*. For non-portal scoped roles, you need to click on the *Options* link on individual portlets, then *Configuration*, then *Permissions* to assign permissions within the site that owns the portlet.

Portal permissions cover portal-wide activities that comprise several categories, such as site, organization, location, password policy, etc. This allows you to create a role that, for example, can create new sites within the portal. This would allow you to grant users that particular permission without making them overall portal administrators.

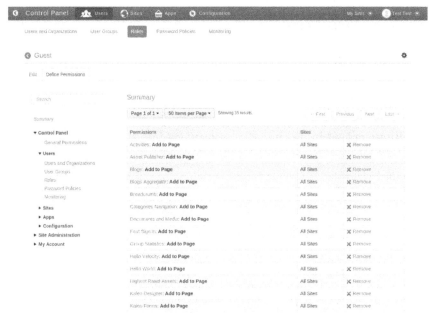

Figure 16.10: When defining permissions on a role, the Summary view provides a list of permissions that have already been defined for the role. The area on the left side of the screen lets you drill down through various categories of portal permissions.

For Liferay 6.2, the permissions fall into the following hierarchy of categories:

- Control Panel
  - General Permissions
  - Users
    * Users and Organizations
    * User Groups
    * Roles
    * Password Policies
    * Monitoring
  - Sites
    * Sites
    * Site Templates
    * Page Templates
  - Apps
    * Store
    * Purchased
    * App Manager
    * Plugins Configuration
    * License Manager
  - Configuration
    * Portal Settings
    * Custom Fields

* Server Administration
* Portal Instances
- Site Administration
  - Pages
    * Site Pages
  - Content
    * Recent Content
    * Web Content
    * Documents and Media
    * Blogs
    * Message Boards
    * Wiki
    * Dynamic Data Lists
    * Bookmarks
    * Polls
    * Software Catalog
    * Tags
    * Categories
    * Recycle Bin
  - Users
    * Site Memberships
    * Site Teams
  - Configuration
    * Site Settings
    * Site Template Settings
    * Application Display Templates
    * Social Activity
    * Mobile Device Families
  - Applications
    * [too many to list]
- My Account
  - Account Settings
  - My Pages

The three basic categories of permissions are Control Panel, Site Administration, and My Account. By default, any portal user can manage their user account via the permissions belonging to the My Account category. Site administrators can access the site administration tools belonging to the Site Administration category. And portal administrators can access the entire Control Panel. For custom roles, you can mix and match permissions from as many categories as you like.

The permissions in the Site Administration &rrar; Applications categories govern the content that can be created by core portlets such as the Wiki and Message Boards. If you pick one of the portlets from this list, you'll get options for defining permissions on its content. For example, if you pick Message Boards, you'll see permissions for creating categories and threads or deleting and moving topics.

Site application permissions affect the application as a whole. So, using the Message Boards as an example, an application permission might define who can add the Message Boards portlet to a page.

The Control Panel permissions affect how the Control Panel appears to the user in the Control Panel. The Control Panel appears differently to different users, depending on their permissions. Some Control Panel portlets have a Configuration button and you can define who gets to see that. You can also fine-tune who gets to see various applications in the Control Panel.

Message Boards

Application Permissions

	Action	Sites
☐	Add to Page	All Sites ⚙ Change
☐	Configuration	All Sites ⚙ Change
☐	Permissions	All Sites ⚙ Change
☐	View	All Sites ⚙ Change

Resource Permissions

Messages

	Action	Sites
☐	Add Category	All Sites ⚙ Change
☐	Add File	All Sites ⚙ Change
☐	Add Message	All Sites ⚙ Change
☐	Ban User	All Sites ⚙ Change
☐	Lock Thread	All Sites ⚙ Change
☐	Move Thread	All Sites ⚙ Change
☐	Permissions	All Sites ⚙ Change
☐	Reply to Message	All Sites ⚙ Change
☐	Subscribe	All Sites ⚙ Change
☐	Update Thread Priority	All Sites ⚙ Change
☐	View	All Sites ⚙ Change

Message Boards Category

	Action	Sites
☐	Add File	All Sites ⚙ Change

Figure 16.11: You can fine-tune which actions are defined for a role within a specific application like the Message Boards.

Each possible action to which permissions can be granted is listed. To grant a permission, flag the checkbox next to it. If you want to change the scope of a permission, click the *Change* link next to the gear icon next to the permission and then choose a new scope. After you finish defining permissions for a role, click *Save*. For a portal-scoped Message Boards Administrator role, you might want to grant content permissions for every Message Boards action listed. After you click *Save*, you'll see a list of all permissions currently granted to the role. From the Summary view, you can add more permissions or go back by clicking on the *Back* icon.

The list of permissions that you can define for a role may seem overwhelming. However, these permissions ensure that you can customize exactly which areas of your portal you'd like different collections of users to be able to access. Sometimes you might find that a certain permission grants more or less access than what you expected—always test your permissions configurations!

For example, suppose that you need to create a role called User Group Manager. You'd like to define the permissions for the User Group Manager role so that users assigned to this role can add users to or remove users from any user group. To do this, you can take the following steps:

1. Click on *Admin* →*Control Panel* from the Dockbar and then click on *Roles*.
2. On the Roles screen, click *Add* →*Regular Role*.
3. After naming your role and entering a title, click *Save*.
4. Click on *Define Permissions* and drill down in the menu on the left to *Control Panel* →*Users* →*Users and Organizations*.
5. Under the *General Permissions* heading, flag *Access in Control Panel* and *View*. This lets user group managers access the User Groups Control Panel portlet and view existing user groups.
6. Since you'd like user group managers to be able to view user groups and assign members to them, you'd also check the *Assign Members* and *View* permissions under the *Resource Permissions   User Group* heading.
7. Click *Save*.

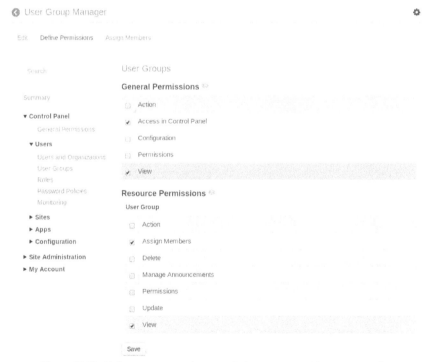

Figure 16.12: Make sure to test the permissions you grant to custom roles.

You might expect that these permissions would be enough to allow users assigned to the User Group Manager role to add or remove any users to or from any user group. After all, we've granted user group managers permissions to view user groups and assign members and we've granted them access to User Groups in the Control Panel. However,

we're forgetting an important permission. Can you guess what it is? That's right: we
haven't granted the User Group Manager role permission to view users! Although user
group managers can assign members to user groups, they don't have permission to view
users at the portal level. This means that if they click *Assign Members* for a user group and
click on the *Available* tab, they'll see an empty list.

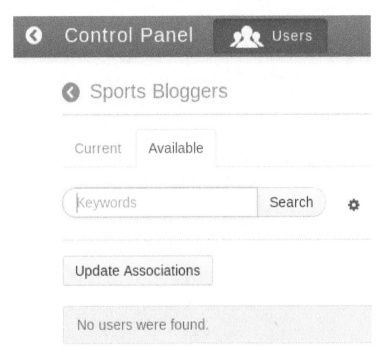

Figure 16.13: Users assigned to the User Group Manager role can't find any users to add!

To fix this, log in as an administrator and click *Admin   Control Panel* from the Dockbar.
Then click on *Roles* and then on *Actions →Define Permissions* next to the *User Group Manager*
role. Then, drill down to the *Control Panel →Users →Users and Organizations* category and
flag the *View* permission under the *Resource Permissions &rrar; User* heading. *View*. Click
Save. Once you've saved your permissions configuration, users who've been assigned to
the User Group Manager role will be able to browse the portal's entire list of users when
assigning users to a user group.

Roles are very powerful and allow portal administrators to define various permissions
in whatever combinations they like. This gives you as much flexibility as possible to build
the site you have designed.

Permission for Delegating Social Activities Configuration

As of Liferay 6.2, there's a permission that allows site administrators to delegate responsibility for configuring social activities to other users. To assign this permission to a role,
first navigate to the Control Panel and click on *Roles*. If you'd like to add a new role, do
so. Then click *Actions* next to the role to which you'd like to add social activities configuration permissions and select *Define Permissions*. Next, drill down to the *Site Administration
→Configuration →Social Activity* permissions category. Flag all of the permissions and then
click *Save*:

- Access in Site Administration
- Configuration
- Permissions
- View

Once these permissions have been assigned to the chosen role, any users assigned to the role will be able to manage your site's Social Activities configuration.

Note About Permissions for Deleting Containers

Liferay Portal contains many types of portal resources upon which permissions can be defined. These include both assets and asset containers. The term *asset* refers to any kind of content in Liferay such as a web content article, blog entry, wiki article, message board post, or Documents and Media document. Asset containers are portal resources used for grouping specific kinds of assets. For example, web content folders, wiki nodes, message board categories, and Documents and Media folders are asset containers.

When configuring permissions for assets and asset containers, it's important to note that the permission to delete an asset container includes the permission to indirectly delete any assets in the container. This means that if a user has permission to delete an asset container, the user can delete all of the assets in that container even the user lacks permission to delete any of the assets in the container individually. Granting permission to delete a folder but not any of the contained assets is *not* a common use case. Nevertheless, it's important to note that assets in a container can be indirectly deleted if their asset container is deleted.

Note About the Power Users Role

Prior to Liferay 6.0, the default configurations of many Liferay portlets allowed power users, but not regular users, to access them. Liferay 6.0 and subsequent versions grant the same default permissions to both power users and regular users. This way, portal administrators are not forced to use the power users role. However, Liferay encourages those who do to create their own custom permissions for the role.

 Note: Prior to Liferay version 6.0, Power Users and Users did *not* have the same default permissions. So if are using Liferay 5.2 or a previous version, it's dangerous to remove the Power Users role from the default user associations: this could remove certain permissions you expect to apply to all users. If you decide to remove the Power Users role from the default user associations anyway, you will probably want to modify the permissions on certain portlets to make them accessible to all users. To do this, see the section on Plugins Configuration below.

Now that we've seen how to use organizations and user groups to manage users and how to use roles to define permissions, let's learn how to configure portal password policies.

Password Policies

Password policies can enhance the security of your portal. You can set requirements on password strength, frequency of password expiration, user lockout, and more. Additionally, you can apply different password policies to different sets of portal users. You define custom password policies or delegate user authentication to an LDAP server.

If you are viewing a page other than the Control Panel, click on *Admin →Control Panel* from the Dockbar. Next, click on the *Password Policies* link under the *Users* heading. You'll see that there's already a default password policy in the system. You can edit this in the same manner as you edit other resources in the portal: click *Actions* and then click *Edit*.

The Password Policy settings form contains the following fields. Enabling specific settings via the check boxes prompts setting-specific options to appear.

Name: requires you to enter a name for the password policy.

Description: lets you describe the password policy so other administrators will know what it's for.

Changeable: determines whether or not a user can change his or her password.

Change Required: determines whether or not a user must change his or her password after logging into the portal for the first time.

Minimum Age: lets you choose how long a password must remain in effect before it can be changed.

Reset Ticket Max Age: determines how long a password reset link remains valid.

Password Syntax Checking: allows you to set a minimum password length and to choose whether or not dictionary words can be in passwords. You can also specify detailed requirements such as minimum numbers of alpha numeric characters, lower case letters, upper case letters, numbers or symbols.

Password History: lets you keep a history (with a defined length) of passwords and prevents users from changing their passwords to one that was previously used.

Password Expiration: lets you choose how long passwords can remain active before they expire. You can select the age, the warning time and a grace limit.

Lockout: allows you to set a number of failed log-in attempts that triggers a user's account to lock. You can choose whether an administrator needs to unlock the account or if it becomes unlocked after a specific duration.

From the list of password policies, you can perform several other actions.

Edit: brings you to the form above and allows you to modify the password policy.

Permissions: allows you to define which users, user groups or roles have permission to edit the password policy.

Assign Members: takes you to a screen where you can search and select users in the portal to be assigned to this password policy. The password policy will be enforced for any users who are added here.

Delete: shows up for any password policies you add beyond the default policy. You cannot delete the default policy.

16.4   Monitoring

The last link in the Users section of the Control Panel is for monitoring. You can use the Monitoring page to view all of the live sessions in the portal. For performance reasons, this setting is usually turned off in production.

Another way of seeing what users are doing is to install the Audit plugin from Liferay Marketplace. You'll learn how to use that next.

16.5 Audit Trails

You've just finished lunch and are ready to get back to work. You
have a site in Liferay you use to manage your project, and before
you left, you were about to create a folder in your Documents
and Media library for sharing some requirements documentation. Sitting down at your desk, you navigate to the repository
and attempt to create the folder.

You do not have permission to perform this action, Liferay helpfully
tells you.

"*What?*" you blurt accidentally in surprise. "This is *my* project!"

"Ah, you too?" asks a co-worker helpfully from over the cube wall. "I lost access to a wiki
I was updating just a few minutes ago. I was about to enter a support ticket for it."

"Forget the ticket. Let's go see the portal admin now," you say.

And off you go, two floors down, to the far end of the building where, as you approach,
you can already hear stress in the portal admin's voice as he tries to reassure someone on
the phone.

"Yes, Mr. Jones. Yes, I'll fix it." (*Jones? The president of the company?* goes through your
mind.) "I'll get on it right away, Mr. Jones. It was just a mistake; I'll fix it. Thank you,
Mr. Jones," and he hangs up the phone.

"Problems?" you ask the portal admin, whose name is Harry. He does look rather har-
ried.

"Yeah, Tom," he says. "Somebody changed a bunch of permissions in the portal—it
wasn't me. I'm assuming you and Dick are here because of the same problem?"

"Yup," you say. "I lost access to a document repository folder."

"And I lost access to a wiki," Dick says helpfully.

"It was probably due to some site membership change. Let's take a look at the audit
portlet in the control panel and see what happened."

When in the course of human events it becomes necessary to see what users are doing
on your portal, you'll find Liferay makes this easy. If you're a Liferay Enterprise Edition
customer, you have access to two plugins—a hook and a portlet—that, in combination
with some settings in portal-ext.properties, enable you to see all the activity that
occurs in your portal. Using this, you can quickly find out what changes were made and by
whom. If you've delegated permission granting to any group of people, this is an essential
feature you're likely to use.

We'll come back to Tom, Dick and Harry's story later in the chapter. For now, let's look
at how to install Liferay's audit plugins so you can do the same thing Harry's about to do.

Installing and Configuring the Audit Plugins

Liferay's audit functionality is composed of two parts: a back-end piece that hooks into
Liferay events and a front-end piece that gives you an interface to see what's happening.
Both of these plugins are included in the Audit EE app which is available on Liferay Marketplace. Please refer to this guide's chapter on Leveraging the Liferay Marketplace for
information on installing plugins.

Once installed, you can set two properties in your portal-ext.properties file to
tweak the default settings.

com.liferay.portal.servlet.filters.audit.AuditFilter: By default, this is set to false, because the audit plugins aren't installed by default. When you set it to true, the audit hook
is able to capture more information about events, such as the client host and the client's
IP address.

audit.message.com.liferay.portal.model.Layout.VIEW: In Liferay's code, pages are referred to as *layouts*. Setting this to true, therefore, records audit events for page views.
It's turned off by default because this may be too fine-grained for most installations.

Once you've decided if you're going to use one or both of the two settings above, place them in your portal-ext.properties file and restart your Liferay server. Once it comes up, audit events are captured by Liferay, and you'll be able to use them to see what's happening in your portal.

Using Audit Events

Now that you're capturing audit events, it's easy to use them to view activities in your portal. Navigate to the Control Panel and you'll find a new entry in the Configuration section called *Audit Reports* (see the figure below).

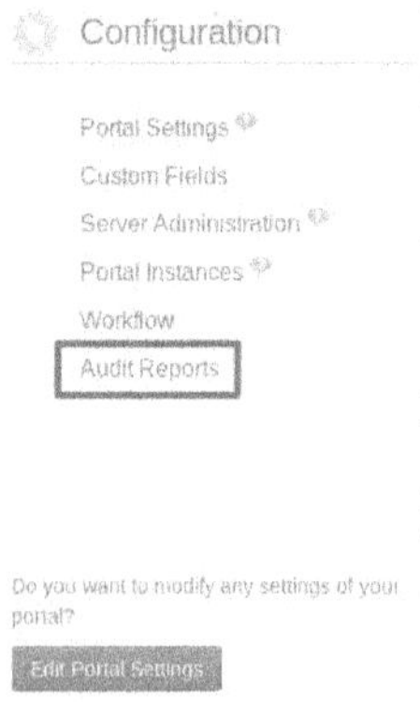

Clicking on *Audit Reports* shows you a list of the events Liferay has already captured (see the figure beblow), along with an interface for searching for events. You can browse the list but you'll likely need to use the search to find what you're looking for.

The figure above shows that Joe Bloggs logged in and performed some actions on the site. To view details about any of these events, all you need to do is click on an entry. You'll then see something like the figure below.

As you can see, depending on how many users you have in your portal, this list can get populated very quickly. For this reason, it's a good idea to keep the audit.message.com.liferay.portal.model.Layout.VIEW property set to false. This way, you don't clutter up your audit events with multiple page view events, which will definitely be the most often triggered event in your portal.

Now that you know how to browse and view audit events, let's learn how to search for specific events.

Figure 16.14: Once the Audit EE app has been installed, an Audit Reports entry appears in the Control Panel.

Viewing Audit Reports

Finding what you want in a big list of events is, to use the expression, like searching for a needle in a haystack. This is why the audit portlet provides a robust searching mechanism. By default, it looks pretty simple: there's only a single field for searching. Clicking the *gear* icon next to the search bar, however, reveals an advanced search dialog broken out by various fields you can use in your search.

Let's look at the options we have for search.

Match: You can search for matches to *all* the fields you've specified or *any* single field.

User ID: Specify the user ID you'd like to search for. This would be the user who performed some action in the portal you'd like to audit.

User Name: Specify the user name you'd like to search for. This is often easier than searching for a user ID, especially if you don't have access to the Liferay database to find the user ID.

Resource ID: Specify the ID of the resource that was modified or viewed in this audit record.

Resource Name: Specify the name of the resource that was modified or viewed in this audit record. For example, you could search for User resources to see if someone modified a user's account.

Resource Action: Specify an action that was performed on the resource. This could be any one of the following: add, assign, delete, impersonate, login, login_failure, logout, unassign, or update.

Session ID: Specify the session ID to search for. You'd use this if you were correlating a session ID from your web server logs with activity in Liferay.

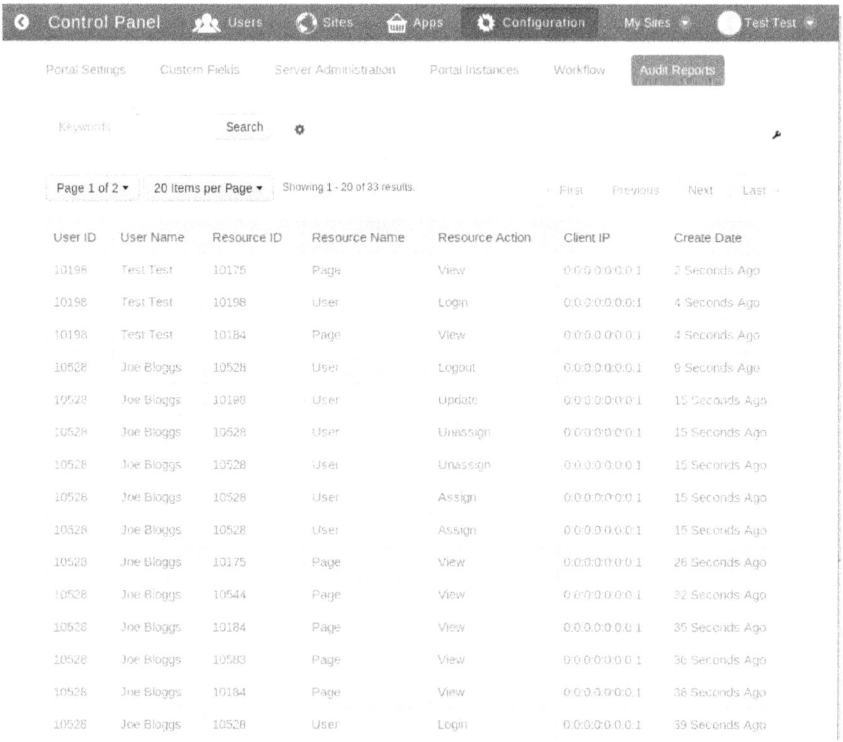

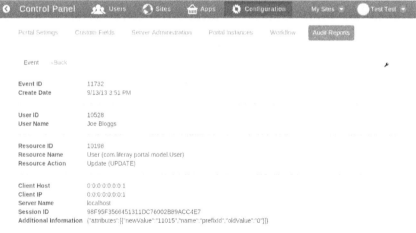

Figure 16.15: Liferay captures and stores events as soon as the Audit EE app has been installed.

Figure 16.16: Clicking an event in the list shows the details of that event. This event shows that Joe Bloggs updated his user account. Specifically, it shows that he updated his prefixId from 0 to 11015. The prefixId value represents a prefix for a real name like "Dr.", "Mr.", "Mrs.", or "Ms."

Client IP: Specify the IP address of the client that performed the activity you wish to audit.

Client Host: Specify the host name of the client that performed the activity you wish to audit.

Server Name: Specify the server name upon which the activity occurred. If you're using a cluster, each member of the cluster can be individually queried.

Server Port: Specify the server port upon which the activity occurred. You'd need this if you run a "vertical" cluster of multiple VMs on the same machine.

Start Date: Specify the low end of the date range you wish to search.

End Date: Specify the high end of the date range you wish to search.

Using this form, if you wanted to check to see if someone in the portal unassigned a user from a particular role, you might search for a resource name of *user* and a resource action of *unassign*. The results of such a search might look something like the figure below.

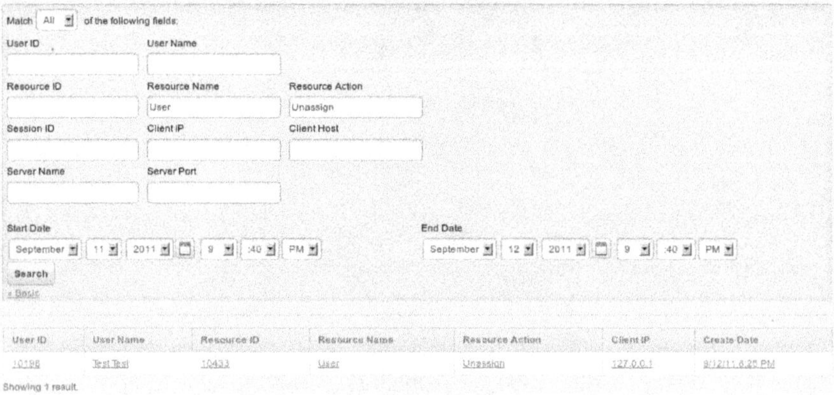

Figure 16.17: Searching for audit events is easy with the advanced search form provided by the audit portlet. You can specify various search criteria to find the types of events you're looking for.

Once you have the results of your search, you can click on any of the records returned to see the detail page for that record. The figure below shows, in this case, that the default administrative user removed the Power User role from Joe Bloggs.

As you can see, Liferay's audit portlets give you a lot of power to see what's happening in your portal. You can use this information to troubleshoot problems, determine ownership of particular actions, or, as Harry is about to do, find out who made permission changes they weren't supposed to make.

Conclusion of the Story

"Okay," says Harry, "let's fire up Liferay's audit system and see if we can figure out what happened."

You and Dick stand behind Harry's chair and watch as he enters a query into a form on the audit portlet. Clicking *search*, the screen fills up with audit events.

"Wow, that's a lot of unassign events." Harry says. "And look who the culprit is," he adds sarcastically.

"Who's Melvin Dooitrong?" Dick asks.

"That's my new intern," Harry says. "I'm gonna kill him." Harry pushes out his chair and walks down the row of cubes to the end, where a kid no more than 20 years old with disheveled hair sits, earbuds in his ears.

Event ID	11751
Create Date	9/13/13 4:51 PM
User ID	10198
User Name	Test Test
Resource ID	10528
Resource Name	User (com.liferay.portal.model.User)
Resource Action	Unassign (UNASSIGN)
Client Host	0:0:0:0:0:0:0:1
Client IP	0:0:0:0:0:0:0:1
Server Name	localhost
Session ID	BC1A4A24C8AB578B1389E9E8FAB8DE94
Additional Information	{"roleName":"Power User","roleId":10164}

Figure 16.18: If you've delegated portal administration to multiple users, you can use the audit plugins to determine who made what change. And, of course, you'll never leave the default administrative user enabled on a production system, right?

"Hey Melvin," Harry says as Melvin turns around to face him. "Didn't I ask you to move that set of users from site membership to organization membership?"

"Yeah," Melvin says, "I did that already."

"How'd you do it?"

"It was going to take a while to do it manually, so I wrote a script and executed it in the scripting host," Melvin replies, matter-of-factly.

"You did, did you? Well, guess what? Your script removed *everybody* from *all* sites."

"What?"

"Yeah, and now you're going to start adding them back, one by one, manually, starting with Mr. Jones...."

Tom and Dick back away slowly from Melvin's cube as Harry and Melvin continue to have their—let's call it a discussion. One thing is clear: they're having a better day than Melvin is.

16.6 Summary

In this chapter, we learned how to manage users, organizations, user groups, and roles via Liferay's Control Panel. Site memberships and teams aren't the only way for portal administrators to group and manage users: organizations can be used to arrange users into hierarchical structures and user groups are a flexible way to collect groups of users that transcend organizational hierarchies. You can create roles to define permissions and scope them for the entire portal or for a particular site or organization. User groups can be assigned to roles; in this case, each member of the user group is assigned to the role. We also looked at how to configure password policies for users and how to view audit trails of what your users are doing in the portal. We'll continue our coverage of Liferay's Control Panel next, where we'll examine configurable portal and server settings.

## CHAPTER 17

USING THE CONTROL PANEL

In the previous chapter, we learned how to use the Control Panel for user management. We learned how to manage users, organizations, user group, roles, and password policies. We also learned about user monitoring. In this chapter, we'll look at portal and server configuration options for Liferay. Now that you have been navigating in the Control Panel, you should be pretty familiar with how it works. The Control Panel is organized in four main areas: Users, Sites, Apps, and Configuration. The options in the *Configuration* section of the Control Panel category include configuration options which control how the portal operates and integrates with other systems you may have. In this chapter, we'll cover the following topics:

- Portal settings, such as user authentication options, mail host names, email notifications, identification settings, and display settings

- Custom fields

- Server administration options, including options for resources, log levels, properties, CAPTCHA, data migration, file uploads, mail, external services, scripts, and shutdown settings

- Portal instances

After you have created users, user groups, organizations, roles, sites, and teams your portal will be ready to host content and applications. You can configure Liferay's portal settings to fit your environment and your particular portal project. It's easy to adjust configuration settings using the portlet-driven user interface of Liferay' Control Panel. Let's start by examining Liferay's Portal Settings.

17.1   Configuring Portal Settings

Most global portal settings can be configured from the Portal Settings section of the Control Panel. The Configuration heading contains the following links:

General: lets you configure global settings, such as the company name, domain, the virtual host, a global portal logo, and more.

Authentication: allows you to configure user authentication methods and connections to LDAP and Single Sign-On servers.

413

Users: has three tabs labeled Fields, Reserved Credentials and Default User Associations. The Fields tab enables or disables some user fields, such as birthday or terms of use. The Reserved Credentials tab lets you reserve screen names and email addresses so users cannot register using them. You might use this to prevent users from registering on the portal with user names that contain profanity or that sound official, such as *admin* or *president*. The Default User Associations tab lets you configure default membership to roles, user groups, sites for new users and provides a check box which allows you to retroactively apply these to existing users.

Mail Host Names: lets you add a list of other mail host names to be associated with your organization. For example, your main domain might be mycompany.com but you might use mycompany-marketing.com for your email newsletters. Any domain names associated with your organization can go here.

Email Notifications: allows you to configure Liferay to send email notifications for certain events, such as user registrations, password changes, etc. You can customize those messages here.

Content Sharing: contains options for enabling site administrators to display content in one site from other sites they administer. You can also configure rules for whether subsites should be able to display content from their parent sites.

Let's discuss these settings in more detail.

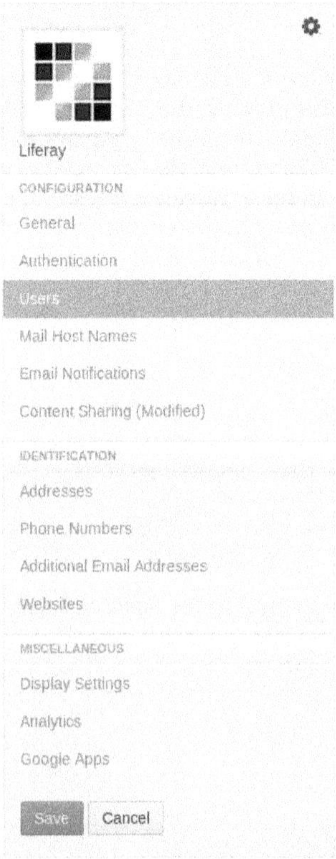

General

The General link takes you to a screen with three headings: Main Configuration, Navigation, and Additional Information. Under the Main Configuration heading, you can set the name of the company or organization that's responsible for running the portal. This name also defines the name of your portal's default site. Its default name is liferay.com so you will definitely want to change this to reflect the name of your company or organization. You can also set the mail domain, virtual host and content delivery network address here.

Under the Navigation heading, you can set a home page for your portal here as well as default landing and logout pages. For setting these pages, just use the part of the page's address that follows your domain. For example, if you want the default landing page to be http://localhost:8080/web/-guest/login, use /web/guest/login. You can also use the variables ${liferay:screenName} and ${liferay:userId} as part of the address. This comes in handy if you want to redirect users to their personal pages upon login. Alternatively, you can set the default login or logout page in a portal-ext.properties file with the properties de-

Figure 17.1: After clicking on *Portal Settings* in Liferay's Control Panel, you can configure any of the areas shown in this figure.

`fault.landing.page.path` and `default.logout.page.path`, respectively. For more information, see the `portal.properties` documentation entries for the Default Landing Page and Default Logout Page.

Under the Additional Information heading, you can specify a Legal name, ID, company type, SIC code, ticker symbol, industry and industry type.

Authentication

The Authentication page has several tabs: General, LDAP, CAS, Facebook, NTLM, OpenID, Open SSO and SiteMinder. You can use any of these authentication methods to configure how users will authenticate to Liferay. Since Liferay supports quite a few authentication methods, there are different settings for each.

The settings on the General tab of the Authentication page affect only Liferay functionality and don't have anything to do with the integration options on the other tabs. The General tab allows you to customize Liferay's standard authentication behavior. Specifically, the General tab allows you to select from several global authentication settings:

- Authenticate via email address (default), screen name, or user ID (a numerical ID auto-generated in the database—not recommended).

- Enable/Disable automatic log in. If enabled, Liferay allows a user to check a box which will cause the site to "remember" the user's log in by placing a cookie on his or her browser. If disabled, users will always have to log in manually.

- Enable/Disable forgotten password functionality.

- Enable/Disable request password reset links.

- Enable/Disable account creation by strangers. If you are running an Internet site, you will probably want to leave this on so visitors can create accounts on your site.

- Enable/Disable account creation by those using an email address in the domain of the company running the site (which you just set on the General page of Portal Settings). This is handy if you are using Liferay to host both internal and external web sites. You can make sure all internal IDs have to be created by administrators but external users can register for IDs themselves.

- Enable / Disable email address verification. If you enable this, Liferay will send users a verification email with a link back to the portal to verify the email address they entered is a valid one they can access.

By default, all settings except for the last are enabled. User authentication by email address is an important default for the following reasons:

1. An email address is, by definition, unique to the user who owns it.

2. People can generally remember their email addresses. If you have users who haven't logged into the portal for a while, it is possible they will forget their screen names, especially if they weren't allowed to use their screen names of choice (because they were already taken).

3. If a user changes his or her email address, it is more likely the user will forget to update his or her email address in his or her profile, if the email address is not used to authenticate. If the user's email address is not updated, all notifications sent by the portal will fail to reach the user. So it is important to keep the email address at the forefront of a user's mind when he or she logs in to help the user keep it up to date.

Next, we'll examine how to integrate existing users from other environments, such as LDAP servers, into Liferay.

17.2   Integrating Existing Users into Liferay

Liferay provides a number of user authentication options. You can configure Liferay to
connect to LDAP or NTLM servers so users from those environments can log in to your
Liferay server. You can also configure Liferay to allow users to log in via Facebook or
OpenId accounts. Liferay's Control Panel provides interfaces for setting up user authentication using the following services:

- LDAP
- CAS
- Facebook
- NTLM
- OpenId
- Open SSO
- SiteMinder

Let's start by learning how to connect Liferay to an LDAP server.

LDAP

You can use the LDAP tab of the Authentication page to connect Liferay to an LDAP directory. There are two places for you to configure the LDAP settings: here in the Control Panel or in your Liferay server's portal-ext.properties file. You can browse an
HTML version of Liferay's portal.properties file online at http://docs.liferay.
com/portal/6.2/propertiesdoc/portal.properties.html. We recommend you
use the Control Panel to configure LDAP server connection settings since your settings
will be stored in the database. Note that if you use both, the settings in the database will
be merged with the settings in portal-ext.properties. If there's a conflict or over-
lapping data, the LDAP server settings in the database take precedence over the servers
set in the portal-ext.properties file. Configuring the LDAP settings from the Control Panel is easier and does not require a restart of Liferay. The only compelling reason to
use the portal-ext.properties file is if you have many Liferay nodes which need be
configured to run against the same LDAP directory. In that case, for your initial deployment, it may be easier to copy the portal-ext.properties file to all of the nodes so the
first time they start up, the settings are correct. Regardless of which method you use, the
available settings are the same.

You configure the global values from the LDAP tab of the Authentication page.

Enabled: Check this box to enable LDAP Authentication.

Required: Check this box if LDAP authentication is required. Liferay will then not
allow a user to log in unless he or she can successfully bind to the LDAP directory first.
Uncheck this box if you want to allow users with Liferay accounts but no LDAP accounts
to log in to the portal.

LDAP Servers: Liferay supports connections to multiple LDAP servers. You can you
the Add button beneath this heading to add LDAP servers. We explain how to configure
new LDAP servers below.

Import/Export: You can import and export user data from LDAP directories using the
following options:

- *Import Enabled:* Check this box to cause Liferay to do a mass import from your LDAP
  directories. If you want Liferay to only synchronize users when they log in, leave
  this box unchecked. Definitely leave this unchecked if you are working in a clustered
  environment. Otherwise, all of your nodes would try to do a mass import when each
  of them starts up.

- *Import on Startup Enabled:* Check this box to have Liferay run the import when it starts up. Note: This box only appears if you check the *Import Enabled* box above.

- Export Enabled: Check this box to enable Liferay to export user accounts from the database to LDAP. Liferay uses a listener to track any changes made to the User object and will push these changes out to the LDAP server whenever the User object is updated. Note that by default on every login, fields such as LastLoginDate are updated. When export is enabled, this has the effect of causing a user export every time the user logs in. You can disable this by setting the following property in your portal-ext.properties file:

```
users.update.last.login=false
```

Use LDAP Password Policy: Liferay uses its own password policy by default. This can be configured on the Password Policies page of the Control Panel. Check the *Use LDAP Password Policy* box if you want to use the password policies defined by your LDAP directory. Once this is enabled, the Password Policies tab will display a message stating you are not using a local password policy. You will now have to use your LDAP directory's mechanism for setting password policies. Liferay does this by parsing the messages in the LDAP controls returned by your LDAP server. By default, the messages in the LDAP controls that Liferay is looking for are the messages returned by the Fedora Directory Server. If you are using a different LDAP server, you will need to customize the messages in Liferay's portal-ext.properties file, as there is not yet a GUI for setting this. See below for instructions describing how to do this.

Once you've finished configuring LDAP, click the *Save* button. Next, let's look at how to add LDAP servers.

Adding LDAP Servers

The Add button beneath the LDAP servers heading allows you to add LDAP servers. If you have more than one, you can arrange the servers by order of preference using the up/down arrows. When you add an LDAP Server, you will need to provide several pieces of data so Liferay can bind to that LDAP server and search it for user records. Regardless of how many LDAP servers you add, each server has the same configuration options.

Server Name: Enter a name for your LDAP server.

Default Values: Several leading directory servers are listed here. If you are using one of these, select it and click the *Reset Values* button. The rest of the form will be populated with the proper default values for that directory.

Connection: These settings cover the basic connection to LDAP.

- *Base Provider URL:* This tells the portal where the LDAP server is located. Make sure the machine on which Liferay is installed can communicate with the LDAP server. If there is a firewall between the two systems, check to make sure the appropriate ports are opened.

- *Base DN:* This is the Base Distinguished Name for your LDAP directory. It is usually modeled after your organization. For a commercial organization, it may look similar to this: dc=companynamehere,dc=com.

- *Principal:* By default, the administrator ID is populated here. If you have removed the default LDAP administrator, you will need to use the fully qualified name of the administrative credential you use instead. You need an administrative credential because Liferay will be using this ID to synchronize user accounts to and from LDAP

- *Credentials:* This is the password for the administrative user.

This is all you need to make a regular connection to an LDAP directory. The rest of the configuration is optional. Generally, the default attribute mappings provide enough data to synchronize back to the Liferay database when a user attempts to log in. To test the connection to your LDAP server, click the *Test LDAP Connection* button.

If you are running your LDAP directory in SSL mode to prevent credential information from passing through the network unencrypted, you will have to perform extra steps to share the encryption key and certificate between the two systems.

For example, assuming your LDAP directory happens to be Microsoft Active Directory on Windows Server 2003, you would take the following steps to share the certificate:

Click *Start →Administrative Tools →Certificate Authority*. Highlight the machine that is the certificate authority, right-click on it, and click *Properties*. From the General menu, click *View Certificate*. Select the Details view, and click *Copy To File*. Use the resulting wizard to save the certificate as a file. As with the CAS install (see the below section entitled *Single Sign-On*), you will need to import the certificate into the *cacerts keystore*. The import is handled by a command like the following:

```
keytool -import -trustcacerts -keystore [path-to-jdk]/jre/lib/security/cacerts -storepass \
changeit -noprompt -alias MyRootCA -file /some/path/MyRootCA.cer
```

The *keytool* utility ships as part of the Java SDK.

Once this is done, go back to the LDAP page in the Control Panel. Modify the LDAP URL in the Base DN field to the secure version by changing the protocol to https and the port to 636 like the following:

```
ldaps://myLdapServerHostname:636
```

Save the changes. Your Liferay Portal will now use LDAP in secure mode for authentication.

Users: This section contains settings for finding users in your LDAP directory.

- *Authentication Search Filter:* The search filter box can be used to determine the search criteria for user logins. By default, Liferay uses users' email addresses for their login names. If you have changed this setting, you will need to modify the search filter here, which has been configured to use the email address attribute from LDAP as a search criterion. For example, if you changed Liferay's authentication method to use screen names instead of the email addresses, you would modify the search filter so it can match the entered log in name:

```
(cn=@screen_name@)
```

- *Import Search Filter:* Depending on the LDAP server, there are different ways to identify the user. The default setting is usually fine:

```
(objectClass=inetOrgPerson)
```

If you want to search for only a subset of users or users that have different LDAP object classes, you can change this.

- *User Mapping:* The next series of fields allows you to define mappings from LDAP attributes to Liferay fields. Though your LDAP user attributes may be different from LDAP server to LDAP server, there are five fields Liferay requires to be mapped for the user to be recognized. You must define a mapping to the corresponding attributes in LDAP for the following Liferay fields:

  - *Screen Name* (e.g., *uid*)
  - *Password* (e.g., *userPassword*)

- *Email Address* (e.g., *mail* or *email*)
- *First Name* (e.g., *name* or *givenName*)
- *Last Name* (e.g., *sn*)

If you'd like to import LDAP groups as Liferay user groups, make sure to define a mapping for the Liferay group field so that membership information is preserved:

- *Group* (e.g., *member*)

The other LDAP user mapping fields are optional.

The Control Panel provides default mappings for commonly used LDAP attributes. You can also add your own mappings if you wish.

- *Test LDAP Users:* Once you have your attribute mappings set up (see above), click the *Test LDAP Users* button and Liferay will attempt to pull LDAP users and match them with their mappings as a preview.

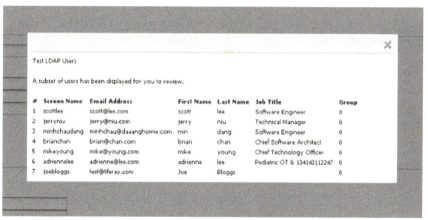

Figure 17.2: Testing LDAP Users

Groups: This section contains settings for mapping LDAP groups to Liferay user groups.

- *Import Search Filter:* This is the filter for finding the LDAP groups that you want to map to Liferay user groups. E.g.,

```
(objectClass=groupOfNames)
```

Enter the LDAP group attributes you want retrieved for this mapping. The following attributes can be mapped. The *Group Name* and *User* fields are required, the *Description* is optional.

- *Group Name* (e.g., *cn* or *o*)
- *Description* (e.g., *description*)
- *User* (e.g., *member*)

- *Test LDAP Groups:* Click the *Test LDAP Groups* button to display a list of the groups returned by your search filter.

Export: This section contains settings for exporting user data from LDAP.

- *Users DN:* Enter the location in your LDAP tree where the users will be stored. When Liferay does an export, it will export the users to this location.

- *User Default Object Classes:* When a user is exported, the user is created with the listed default object classes. To find out what your default object classes are, use an LDAP browser tool such as JXplorer to locate a user and view the Object Class attributes stored in LDAP for that user.

- *Groups DN:* Enter the location in your LDAP tree where the groups will be stored. When Liferay does an export, it will export the groups to this location.

- *Group Default Object Classes:* When a group is exported, the group is created with the listed default object classes. To find out what your default object classes are, use an LDAP browser tool such as *Jxplorer* to locate a group and view the Object Class attributes stored in LDAP for that group.

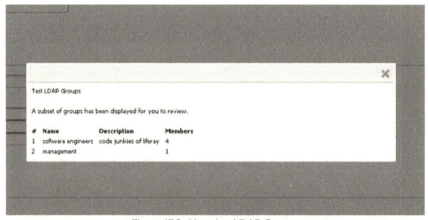

Figure 17.3: Mapping LDAP Groups

Once you've set all your options and tested your connection, click *Save*. From here, you can add another LDAP server or set just a few more options that apply to all of your LDAP server connections.

LDAP Options Not Available in the GUI

Although most of the LDAP configuration can be done from the Control Panel, there are several configuration parameters that are only available by adding to your Liferay server's portal-ext.properties file. These options may be available in the GUI in future versions of Liferay Portal but for now they can only be configured by editing the properties file.

If you need to change any of these options, copy the LDAP section from Liferay's portal.properties file into your portal-ext.properties file. Note that since you have already configured LDAP from the GUI, any settings from the properties file that match settings already configured in the GUI will be ignored. The GUI, which stores the settings in the database, always takes precedence over the properties file.

```
ldap.auth.method=bind
#ldap.auth.method=password-compare
```

Set either bind or password-compare for the LDAP authentication method. Bind is preferred by most vendors so you don't have to worry about encryption strategies. Password compare does exactly what it sounds like: it reads the user's password out of LDAP, decrypts it and compares it with the user's password in Liferay, syncing the two.

```
ldap.auth.password.encryption.algorithm=
ldap.auth.password.encryption.algorithm.types=MD5,SHA
```

Set the password encryption to used to compare passwords if the property ldap.auth-.method is set to password-compare.

```
ldap.import.method=[user,group]
```

If you set this to user, Liferay will import all users from the specified portion of the LDAP tree. If you set this to group, Liferay will search all the groups and import the users in each group. If you have users who do not belong to any groups, they will not be imported.

```
ldap.error.password.age=age
ldap.error.password.expired=expired
ldap.error.password.history=history
ldap.error.password.not.changeable=not allowed to change
ldap.error.password.syntax=syntax
ldap.error.password.trivial=trivial
ldap.error.user.lockout=retry limit
```

These properties are a list of phrases from error messages which can possibly be returned by the LDAP server. When a user binds to LDAP, the server can return *controls* with its response of success or failure. These controls contain a message describing the error or the information that is coming back with the response. Though the controls are the same across LDAP servers, the messages can be different. The properties described here contain snippets of words from those messages and will work with Red Hat's Fedora Directory Server. If you are not using that server, the word snippets may not work with your LDAP server. If they don't, you can replace the values of these properties with phrases from your server's error messages. This will enable Liferay to recognize them. Next, let's look at the Single Sign-On solutions Liferay supports.

SSO

Single Sign-On solutions allow you to provide a single login credential for multiple systems. This allows you to have people authenticate to the Single Sign-On product and they will be automatically logged in to Liferay and to other products as well.

Liferay supports several single sign-on solutions. Of course, if your product is not yet supported, you may choose to implement support for it yourself by use of the extension environment. Alternatively, your organization can choose to sponsor support for it. Please contact sales@liferay.com for more information about this.

Authentication: Central Authentication Service (CAS)

CAS is an authentication system originally created at Yale University. It is a widely-used open source single sign-on solution and was the first SSO product to be supported by Liferay.

Please follow the documentation for CAS to install it on your application server of choice.

Your first step will be to copy the CAS client .jar file to Liferay's library folder. On Tomcat, this is in [Tomcat Home]/webapps/ROOT/WEB-INF/lib. Once you've done this, the CAS client will be available to Liferay the next time you start it.

The CAS Server application requires a properly configured Secure Socket Layer certificate on your server to work. If you wish to generate one yourself, you will need to use the keytool utility that comes with the JDK. Your first step is to generate the key. Next, you export the key into a file. Finally, you import the key into your local Java key store. For public, Internet-based production environments, you will need to either purchase a signed key from a recognized certificate authority (such as Thawte or Verisign) or have your key signed by a recognized certificate authority. For Intranets, you should have your IT department pre-configure users' browsers to accept the certificate so they don't get warning messages about the certificate.

To generate a key, use the following command:

```
keytool -genkey -alias tomcat -keypass changeit -keyalg RSA
```

Instead of the password in the example (changeit), use a password you will remember. If you are not using Tomcat, you may want to use a different alias as well. For First and Last names, enter localhost or the host name of your server. It cannot be an IP address.

To export the key to a file, use the following command:

```
keytool -export -alias tomcat -keypass changeit -file server.cert
```

Finally, to import the key into your Java key store, use the following command:

```
keytool -import -alias tomcat -file %FILE_NAME% -keypass changeit
-keystore $JAVA_HOME/jre/lib/security/cacerts
```

If you are on a Windows system, replace $JAVA_HOME above with %JAVA_HOME%. Of course, all of this needs to be done on the system on which CAS will be running.

Once your CAS server is up and running, you can configure Liferay to use it. This is a simple matter of navigating to the *Settings Authentication →CAS* tab in the Control Panel. Enable CAS authentication and then modify the URL properties to point to your CAS server.

Enabled: Check this box to enable CAS single sign-on.

Import from LDAP: A user may be authenticated from CAS and not yet exist in the portal. Select this to automatically import users from LDAP if they do not exist in the portal.

The rest of the settings are various URLs, with defaults included. Change *localhost* in the default values to point to your CAS server. When you are finished, click *Save*. After this, when users click the *Sign In* link, they will be directed to the CAS server to sign in to Liferay.

Authentication: Facebook

Liferay Portal also enables users to log in using their Facebook accounts. To enable this feature, you simply need to select the *Enable* box and enter the Application ID and Application Secret which should have been provided to you by Facebook. Facebook SSO works by taking the primary Facebook email address and searching for the same email address in Liferay's User_ table. If a match is found, the user is automatically signed on (provided the user clicked *allow* from the Facebook dialog). If there isn't a match, the user is prompted in Liferay to add a user from Facebook. Once selected, a new user is created by retrieving four fields from Facebook (first name, last name, email address and gender).

Authentication: NTLM

NTLM is a Microsoft protocol that can be used for authentication through Microsoft Internet Explorer. Though Microsoft has adopted Kerberos in modern versions of Windows server, NTLM is still used when authenticating to a workgroup. Liferay Portal now supports NTLM v2 authentication. NTLM v2 is more secure and has a stronger authentication process than NTLMv1.

Enabled: Check this box to enable NTLM authentication.

Domain Controller: Enter the IP address of your domain controller. This is the server that contains the user accounts you want to use with Liferay.

Domain: Enter the domain / workgroup name.

Service Account: You need to create a service account for NTLM. This account will be a computer account, not a user account.

Service Password: Enter the password for the service account.

Authentication: OpenID

OpenID is a new single sign-on standard which is implemented by multiple vendors. The idea is multiple vendors can implement the standard and then users can register for an ID with the vendor they trust. The credential issued by that vendor can be used by all the web sites that support OpenID. Some high profile OpenID vendors are AOL, LiveDoor, and LiveJournal.

Please see the OpenID site [1] for a more complete list.

A main benefit of OpenID for the user is he or she no longer has to register for a new account on every site in which he or she wants to participate. Users can register on *one* site (the OpenID provider's site) and then use those credentials to authenticate to many web sites which support OpenID. Many web site owners often struggle to build communities because end users are reluctant to register for so many different accounts. Supporting OpenID makes it easier for site owners to build their communities because the barriers to participating (i.e., the effort it takes to register for and keep track of many accounts) are removed. All of the account information is kept with the OpenID provider, making it much easier to manage this information and keep it up to date.

Liferay Portal can act as an OpenID consumer, allowing users to automatically register and sign in with their OpenID accounts. Internally, the product uses OpenID4Java http://code.google.com/p/openid4java/ to implement the feature.

OpenID is enabled by default in Liferay but can be disabled here.

Atlassian Crowd

Atlassian Crowd is a web-based Single Sign-On product similar to CAS. Crowd can be used to manage authentication to many different web applications and directory servers.

Because Atlassian Crowd implements an OpenID producer, Liferay works and has been tested with it. Simply use the OpenID authentication feature in Liferay to log in using Crowd.

Authentication: OpenSSO

OpenSSO is an open source single sign-on solution that comes from the code base of Sun's System Access Manager product. Liferay integrates with OpenSSO, allowing you to use OpenSSO to integrate Liferay into an infrastructure that contains a multitude of different authentication schemes against different repositories of identities.

You can set up OpenSSO on the same server as Liferay or a different box. Follow the instructions at the OpenSSO site http://opensso.dev.java.net to install OpenSSO. Once you

---

[1]http://www.openid.net

have it installed, create the Liferay administrative user in it. Users are mapped back and forth by screen names. By default, the Liferay administrative user has a screen name of *test*, so in OpenSSO, you would register the user with the ID of *test* and an email address of *test@liferay.com*. Once you have the user set up, log in to Open SSO using this user.

In the same browser window, go to the URL for your server running Liferay and log in as the same user, using the email address *test@liferay.com*. Go to the Control Panel and click *Settings →Authentication →OpenSSO*. Modify the three URL fields (Login URL, Logout URL and Service URL) so they point to your OpenSSO server (i.e., only modify the host name portion of the URLs), click the *Enabled* check box and then click *Save*. Liferay will then redirect users to OpenSSO when they click the *Sign In* link.

Authentication: SiteMinder

SiteMinder is a single sign-on implementation from Computer Associates. Liferay 5.2 introduced built-in integration with SiteMinder. SiteMinder uses a custom HTTP header to implement its single sign-on solution.

To enable SiteMinder authentication in Liferay, check the *Enabled* box on the *SiteMinder* tab. If you are also using LDAP with Liferay, you can check the *Import from LDAP* box. If this box is checked, users authenticated from SiteMinder who do not exist in the portal will be imported from LDAP.

The last field defines the header SiteMinder is using to keep track of the user. The default value is already populated. If you have customized the field for your installation, enter the custom value here.

When you are finished, click *Save*. Now that we've looked at various options for integrating existing users into Liferay, let's look at other Liferay portal settings.

Shibboleth

Shibboleth is a federated single sign-on and attribute exchange framework that implements SAML (Security Assertion Markup Language). The Shibboleth plugin available from Liferay Marketplace allows Liferay to integrate with Shibboleth to provide SSO support. The Liferay Shibboleth plugin contains an autologin hook that automatically logs users into Liferay when they are authenticated to a Shibboleth identity provider and the HTTP request has a specific header attribute. All of the Shibboleth service provider and identity provider configuration is done outside of Liferay. All that the Liferay Shibboleth plugin needs to do is accept the header attribute from Shibboleth and log the user in.

The Shibboleth plugin adds a Shibboleth tab to the Authentication page of the Portal Settings section of the Control Panel.

There are four configuration options:

- *Enabled*
- *Import from LDAP*
- *Logout URL*
- *User Header*

Check or uncheck the *Enabled* box to enable or disable Shibboleth authentication for Liferay. If the *Enabled* box is not checked, the Shibboleth auto login hook is disabled and the automated login process will not work even if the user header is in the HTTP request. If you check the *Import from LDAP* box, then any users authenticated from Shibboleth that do not exist in Liferay will be imported into Liferay from LDAP. LDAP must already be enabled for this to work. The path you enter into the *Logout URL* field sets the logout URL for Shibboleth. The link is triggered when the user logs out of the portal. If the logout URL is incorrect or is not set, the user will not be logged out of Shibboleth. The *User Header* is the attribute name of the user header that is passed in from the Shibboleth service provider.

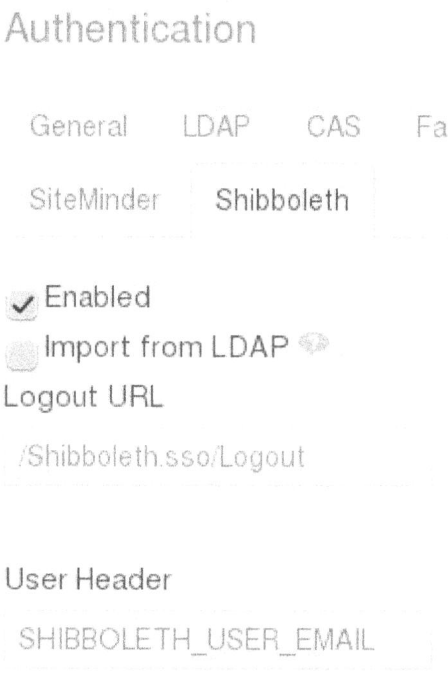

Authentication

General   LDAP   CAS   Facebook

SiteMinder   Shibboleth

✓ Enabled

Import from LDAP

Logout URL

/Shibboleth.sso/Logout

User Header

SHIBBOLETH_USER_EMAIL

Figure 17.4: You can enable/disable Shibboleth authentication for Liferay by navigating to the *Control Panel →Portal Settings &rrar; Authentication →Shibboleth.*

It should contain either the screen name or the email address of the user, which will be used to authenticate the user into the portal.

It's possible to configure the above four Shibboleth options via portal properties instead of via the Control Panel. To configure the Shibboleth plugin this way, add the following properties to your Liferay server's portal-ext.properties file and restart Liferay.

- shibboleth.auth.enabled=true: corresponds to the *Enable* box above
- shibboleth.import.from.ldap=false: corresponds to the *Import from LDAP* box above
- shibboleth.logout.url=/Shibboleth.soo/Logout: corresponds to the *Logout URL* box above
- shibboleth.auth.enabled=true: corresponds the *User Header* box above

Note that options selected via the Control Panel are saved to Liferay's database and take precedence over any options configured via portal properties.

SAML

 SAML is an XML-based open standard data format for exchanging authentication and authorization data between parties known as an identity provider and a service provider. An identity provider is a trusted provider that enables users to use single sign-on to access other websites. A service provider is a website that hosts applications and grants access only to identified users with proper credentials. SAML is maintained by the OASIS Security Services Technical Committee. See https://www.oasis-open.org/committees/security/ for more information. Liferay 6.1 EE and later versions support SAML 2.0 integration via the SAML 2.0 Provider EE plugin. This plugin is provided as an app from Liferay Marketplace that allows Liferay to act as a SAML 2.0 identity provider or as a service provider. First, we'll look at how to set Liferay up as an Identity Provider and then we'll look at how to set it up as a Service Provider.

Setting up Liferay as a SAML Identity Provider

In order to set Liferay up to act as a SAML Identity Provider, use the following steps:

1. Install the SAML 2.0 Provider EE app, either via the Control Panel's Marketplace interface or manually. To confirm that the plugin was successfully deployed, look for the *SAML Admin* entry in the Portal section of the Control Panel.

2. Next, you need to generate a keystore to use with SAML. You can generate a keystore using the Java keytool utility. Navigate to your [Liferay Home]/data directory in a command prompt or terminal and run the following command to generate a keystore there:

```
keytool -genkey -keyalg RSA -alias liferaysamlidp -keystore keystore.jks \
-storepass liferay -validity 360 -keysize 2048
```

   Upon running this command, you'll be prompted to enter the following information:

   - First and last name
   - Name of your organizational unit
   - Name of your organization
   - Name of your city or locality
   - Name of your state or province
   - Your country's two-letter country code

   This information will be included in the keystore. After you answer the questions, a keystore named keystore.jks is created with the alias (entity ID) liferaysamlidp and the password liferay. To keep this example simple, use the same password for liferaysamlidp as for the keystore itself: liferay.

3. Log in to your portal as an administrator and click on the *SAML Admin* entry in the Control Panel. For the SAML role, select *Identity Provider*, and for the Entity ID, enter the alias of the keystore you generated in your Liferay instance's data folder: liferaysamlidp. Then click *Save*.

4. After clicking *Save*, additional options appear in the SAML Admin Control Panel portlet. There are three tabs:

   - General

- Identity Provider
- Service Provider Connections

Leave the SAML role and Entity role as you configured them in step 3. In the Certificate and Private Key section, enter the same information that you entered when you generated your keystore, then click *Save*. After saving your certificate and private key information, you can view information about your certificate or download your certificate.

5. Finally, after you've saved your certificate and private key information, check the *Enabled* box at the top of the General tab and click *Save*. Great! You've successfully set Liferay up as a SAML Identity Provider!

To configure Liferay's SAML Identity Provider Settings, navigate to the Identity Provider tab of the SAML Admin Control Panel portlet. Of course, setting up Liferay as a SAML Identity Provider is only useful if you can connect to one or more SAML Service Providers. Navigate to the Service Provider Connections tab of the SAML Admin Control Panel portlet and click on the *Add Service Provider* button to add a SAML Service Provider. Right now, we don't have one to add but next, we'll learn how to set Liferay up as a SAML Service Provider.

After you've set up another Liferay instance as a Service Provider, you can come back to this Liferay instance's Control Panel and add the Service Provider: *Control Panel →SAML Admin &rrar; Service Provider Connections →Add Service Provider*.

Setting up Liferay as a SAML Service Provider

In order to set Liferay up to act as a SAML Service Provider, use the following steps. Many of the steps are similar to the ones for setting Liferay up to act as a SAML Identity Provider. A single Liferay instance can be configured as a SAML Identify Provider *or* a SAML Service Provider but not both! If you've already set up one Liferay instance as a SAML Identity Provider, use a *different* Liferay instance as a SAML Service Provider

1. Install the SAML 2.0 Provider EE app, either via the control panel's Marketplace interface or manually. To confirm that the plugin was successfully deployed, look for the *SAML Admin* entry in the Portal section of the Control Panel.

2. Next, you need to generate a keystore to use with SAML. You can generate a keystore using the Java keytool utility. Navigate to your [Liferay Home]/data directory in a command prompt or terminal and run the following command to generate a keystore there:

```
keytool -genkey -keyalg RSA -alias liferaysamlsp -keystore keystore.jks \
-storepass liferay -validity 360 -keysize 2048
```

Upon running this command, you'll be prompted to enter the following information:

- First and last name
- Name of your organizational unit
- Name of your organization
- Name of your city or locality
- Name of your state or province
- Your country's two-letter country code

This information will be included in the keystore. After you answer the questions, a keystore named keystore.jks is created with the alias (entity ID) liferay-samlsp and the password liferay. To keep this example simple, use the same password for liferaysamlsp as for the keystore itself: liferay.

3. Log in to your portal as an administrator and click on the *SAML Admin* entry in the Control Panel. For the SAML role, select *Service Provider*, and for the Entity ID, enter the alias of the keystore you generated in your Liferay instance's data folder: liferaysamlsp. Then click *Save*.

4. After clicking *Save*, additional options appear in the SAML Admin Control Panel portlet. Note that these options are different than if you were setting up Liferay as an Identity Provider. There are three tabs:

   - General
   - Service Provider (not Identity Provider!)
   - Identity Provider Connection (not Service Provider Connections!)

   Leave the SAML role and Entity role as you configured them in step 3. In the Certificate and Private Key section, enter the same information that you entered when you generated your keystore, then click *Save*. After saving your certificate and private key information, you can view information about your certificate or download your certificate.

5. Next, you need to configure an Identity Provider connection. Click on the *Identity Provider Connection* tab. Enter a name for the Identity Provider, enter its entity ID, and enter its metadata URL. If you already configured a separate Liferay instance as an Identify provider following the previous instructions, you'd enter the following information:

   - Name: *Liferay IdP*
   - Entity ID: *liferaysamlidp*
   - Metadata URL: *http://localhost:8080/c/portal/saml/metadata* (test this URL first)

6. Finally, after you've saved your certificate and private key information and configured an Identity Provider connection, check the *Enabled* box at the top of the General tab and click *Save*. Great! You've successfully set Liferay up as a SAML Service Provider!

If you'd like to configure Liferay's SAML Service Provider Settings, navigate to the Service Provider tab of the SAML Admin Control Panel portlet.

Note: The previous two sections explained how to use the SAML portlet's Control Panel interface to configure Liferay as an Identity Provider and as a Service Provider. It's possible to configure Liferay as an Identity Provider or as a Service Provider entirely through the portal-ext.properties file. However, we recommend using the Control Panel SAML interface because it specifies required fields and validates some fields.

Suppose that you have two Liferay instances running on ports 8080 and 9080 of your host. Suppose further that you've configured the Liferay running on port 8080 as a SAML Identity Provider and the Liferay running on port 9080 as a SAML Service Provider, following the instructions above. If your Identity Provider and Service Provider have been correctly configured, navigating to http://localhost:8080/c/portal/saml/sso-?entityId=liferaysamlsp initiates the SAML Identity Provider based login process. To initiate the SAML Service Provider based login process, just navigate to the Liferay running on port 9080 and click *Sign In*, navigate to http://localhost.9000/c/portal/login, or try to access a protected resource URL such as a Control Panel URL.

17.3 Configuring Additional Portal Settings

Go back to the Control Panel, and click on *Portal Settings* under the *Configuration* heading. We've already looked at the options available from the *General* and *Authentication* links. Now let's examine the other portal settings options.

Users

If you click on *Users* from the Portal Settings screen, you'll find three tabs: Fields, Reserved Credentials and Default User Associations.

The Fields tab allows you to enable/disable the following fields:

- Enable/disable requiring the Terms of Use

- Enable/disable user screen names autogeneration

- Enable/disable requiring the last names

- Enable/disable the birthday field

- Enable/disable the gender field

The next tab is Reserved Credentials. You can enter screen names and email addresses here that you don't want others to use. Liferay will then prevent users from registering with these screen names and email addresses. You might use this feature to prevent users from creating IDs that look like administrative IDs or that have reserved words in their names.

The Default User Associations tab has three fields allowing you to list (one per line) sites, roles, and user groups you want new users to become members of automatically. By default, Liferay assigns new users to both the Users role and the Power Users role.

If you have defined other user groups, sites or roles you want newly created users to be members of by default, enter them here. For example, you may have defined site templates in certain user groups to pre-populate end users' private pages. If there is a particular configuration you want everyone to have, you may want to enter those user groups here.

Mail Host Names

Mail Host Names appears after Authentication and Users on the Portal Settings screen of the Control Panel. You can enter other mail host names (one per line) besides the one you configured on the General tab. This lets the portal know which mail host names are owned by your organization.

Email Notifications

There are five tabs under the Email Notifications page of Portal Settings. The Sender tab allows you to set the portal's administrative name and email address. By default, these are Joe Bloggs and test@liferay.com. You can change them to whatever you want. This name and email address will appear in the From field in all email messages sent by the portal.

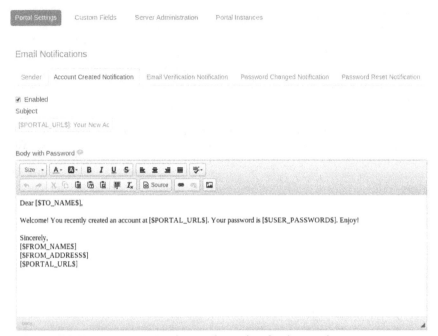

Figure 17.5: You can customize the email template for the email messages sent to users who have just created their accounts.

The other four tabs are Account Created Notification, Email Verification Notification, Password Changed Notification and Password Reset Notification. These tabs allow you to customize the email messages that are sent to users each time any of those four events occur.

A list of tokens, entitled "Definition of Terms," is provided so you can insert certain values (such as the portal URL or the user ID) when you are setting up the custom email messages.

Content Sharing

The Content Sharing section of the Portal Settings area of the Control Panel allows you to choose whether or or not site administrators can display content in sites from other sites they administer. For example, suppose that a certain user is a site administrator of two sites: *Engineering* and *Marketing*. The checkbox in the Content Sharing section of Portal Settings determines whether or not the site administrator can display content from the Marketing site in the Engineering site and vice versa.

The Content Sharing section of Portal Settings also allows you to choose a behavior for whether or not subsites can display content from parent sites and for configuring the defaults. There are three options:

Enabled by Default: This means that subsites can display content from parent sites by default but this can be disabled by a site administrator.

Disabled by Default: This means that subsites cannot display content from parent sites by default but this can be enabled by a site administrator.

Disabled: This means that subsites cannot display content from parent sites and this behavior cannot be changed by a site administrator.

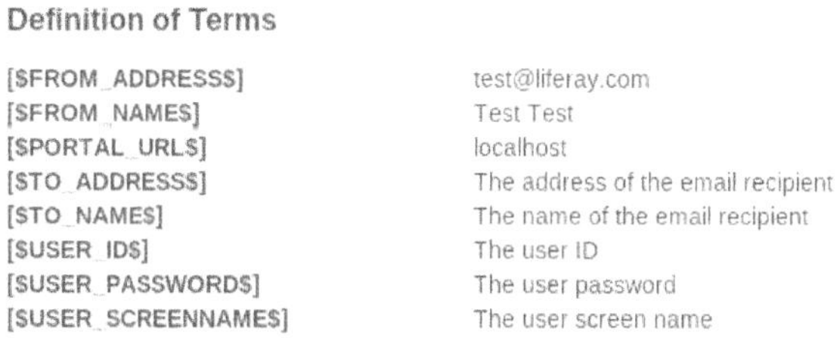

Definition of Terms

[$FROM_ADDRESS$]	test@liferay.com
[$FROM_NAMES$]	Test Test
[$PORTAL_URL$]	localhost
[$TO_ADDRESS$]	The address of the email recipient
[TO_NAMES]	The name of the email recipient
[$USER_ID$]	The user ID
[$USER_PASSWORD$]	The user password
[$USER_SCREENNAMES$]	The user screen name

Figure 17.6: You can refer to this list of variables that's available for use in email templates.

Identification

The identification section has several links for addresses, phone numbers and other information you can configure in your portal. This allows you to set up contact information for the organization that owns the portal. Developers can query for this information in their applications.

Miscellaneous: Display Settings

This section allows you to set the default portal language and the time zone. You can also set up a portal-wide logo which appears in the top left corners of portal pages.

Liferay's default theme is configured to display the portal logo. For custom themes, you can choose whether or not to display the logo. Be careful to choose an image file that fits the space. If you pick something too big, it might overlap with the navigation. Next, let's look at how to customize different types of portal assets using custom fields.

17.4 Custom Fields

Custom fields appear beneath Portal Settings under the Configuration heading of the Control Panel. Custom fields are a way to add attributes to many types of assets and resources in the portal. For example, if you're using Liferay Portal to create a site for rating books, you might create a custom field called *Favorite Books* for User resource. If you're using the Wiki for book reviews, you might add fields called *Book Title* and *Book Author*.

It's possible to add custom fields to following kinds of portal resources:

- Blogs Entry
- Bookmarks Entry
- Bookmarks Folder
- Calendar Booking
- Document
- Documents Folder
- Message Boards Category
- Message Boards Message
- Organization
- Page
- Role
- Site
- User
- User Group

Language and Time Zone

Default Language

English (United States)   ▼

Available Languages

Current   Available

Chinese (China)   Arabic (Saudi Arabia)
English (United States)   Basque (Spain)
French (Canada)   ⊙   Bulgarian (Bulgaria)
German (Germany)   ⊙   Catalan (Andorra)
Hungarian (Hungary)   Catalan (Spain)
Portuguese (Brazil)   Chinese (Taiwan)
Spanish (Spain)   Croatian (Croatia)
                                                     Czech (Czech Republic)
                                                     Danish (Denmark)
                                                     Dutch (Belgium)

                          ⊙ ⊙

Time Zone

(UTC.) Coordinated Universa ▼

Logo

☑ Allow site administrators to use their own logo?

                                      [logo]

                              🖾 Change   ✖ Delete

Look and Feel

Default Theme

Classic   ▼

Figure 17.7: You can specify various display settings for your portal including options for
the default language, other available language, time zone, portal logo, and default
themes for the portal and Control Panel.

- Web Content Article
- Wiki Page

The ability to add custom fields to any of these resources affords flexibility to portal
developers. For example, suppose you'd like to define a limitation on the number of users
that can be assigned to certain roles. A portal administrator can create a custom field
called *max-users* for the Role resource. Then a portal developer can create a hook plugin
that checks this field upon user assignment to roles to make sure that there aren't too many
users assigned to the role.

To add a custom field, click on the *Custom Fields* link in the Control Panel. Then choose
a resource, click on the *Edit* link next to it and select *Add Custom Field*.

From here you need to add the custom field key. The key appears as the label for the
field on the form. For some portal resources (like the User), custom fields are a separate
section of the form. For others, as can be seen above, custom fields are integrated with the

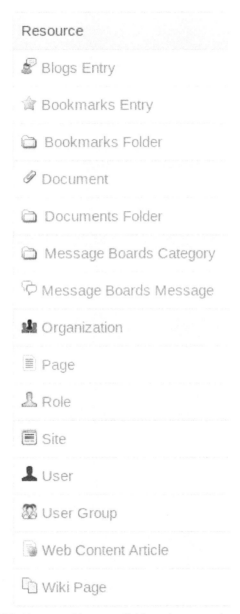

Figure 17.8: You can add custom fields to these portal resources.

default fields on the form. Additionally, developers can access custom fields programati-
cally through the ⟨liferay-ui:custom-attribute /⟩ tag.

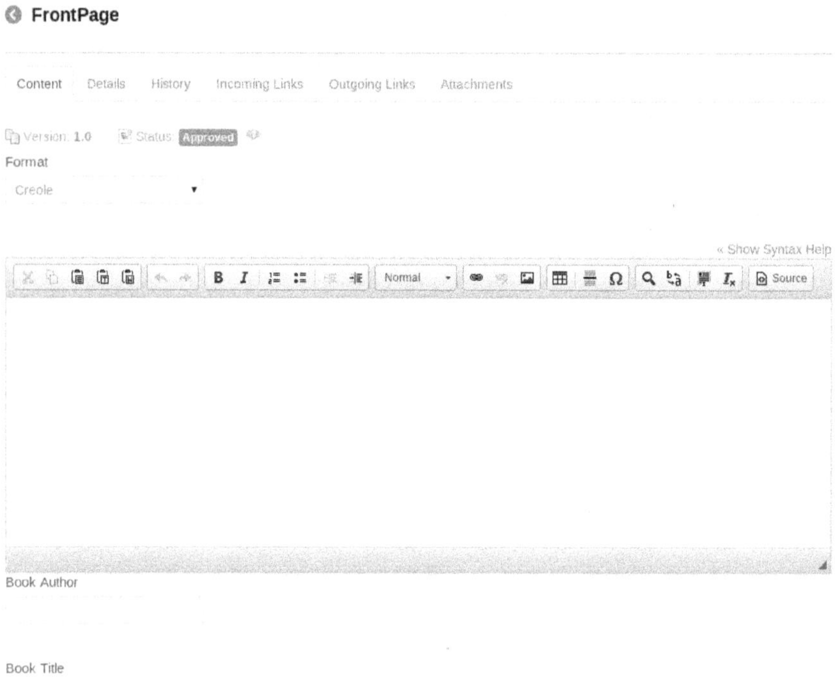

Figure 17.9: The book-author and book-title custom fields are integrated with the
rest of the form for editing a Wiki page.

You can create fields of many different types: text fields (indexed or secret), integers,
selection of multiple values and more. Once you've created a field, you cannot change its
type. However, you can delete custom fields and create new ones. Next, let's look at how
to apply server configurations.

17.5   Server Administration

The Server Administration page of the Control Panel lets you perform various tasks related to the portal server itself that aren't directly related to the resources in the portal.
Clicking the link makes this clear: you're immediately presented with a graph showing
the resources available in the JVM.

Resources

The first tab is called *Resources*. This tab contains the aforementioned graph plus several
server wide actions that an administrator can execute. These include the following:

   Run the garbage collector: You can send in a request to the JVM to begin the garbage
collection task.

Clear content cached by this VM: You can send in a request to the JVM to clear content stored in the local cache. Ehcache usage is split into two groups: local JVM scope and cluster scope. This action only clears the content of the local Ehcache.

Clear content cached across the cluster: You can send in a request to the JVM to clear content cached across the entire cluster. This action clears the content of the clustered Ehcache.

Clear the database cache: You can send in a request to the JVM to clear the database cache. Liferay uses Ehcache mainly, but not only, at the persistence layer for caching objects obtained from the database. This action only clears the database result cache.

Clear the direct servlet cache: You can send in a request to the JVM to clear the direct servlet cache. The direct servlet context is a feature that optimizes JSP serving performance by caching and accessing the generated servlets directly instead of accessing them over the application server's dispatcher chain. This is only suitable for cases where no filter is required for the JSPs. For production mode, this cache should be enabled to improve performance. In case emergency fixes need to be applied, this action allows an administrator to manually clear out the cache to force JSPs to reload. For development mode, the direct servlet context should be disabled to allow JSP servlets to be reloaded on the fly. See the Direct Servlet Context section of the `portal.properties` file for details.

Reindex all search indexes: You can send in a request to regenerate all search indexes. If you are not using a Solr search server this will impact portal performance so try to do this at non-peak times.

Reindex all spell check indexes: You can send in a request to regenerate all spell check indexes.

Reset preview and thumbnail files for the Documents and Media portlet: You can send in a request to reset the preview and thumbnail files for each item in your portal's Documents and Media libraries.

Generate Thread Dump: If you are performance testing, you can generate a thread dump which can be examined later to determine if there are any deadlocks and where they might be.

Verify database tables of all plugins: You can check all tables against their indexes for accuracy of data retrieval.

Verify Membership Policies: You can check that existing site membership policies have been correctly applied and automatically make updates if necessary. For example, suppose that someone manually changed the Liferay database or that the Liferay database was hacked, resulting in a user being assigned to a site in violation of a site membership policy. When the *Verify Membership Policies* button is clicked, the verify methods of all the site membership policies that have been implemented are triggered. These methods check that all site memberships are in accord with the site membership policies; if they are not, the necessary changes (such as removing users from forbidden sites) are made.

Clean up Permissions: This process removes the assignment of some permissions on the Guest, User, and Power User roles to simplify the management of "User Customizable Pages". Notably, the "Add To Page" permissions is removed from the Guest and User roles for all portlets. Likewise, the same permission is reduced in scope for Power Users from portal wide to scoped to "User Personal Site."

Log Levels

The Log Levels tab of the Server Administration page allows you to dynamically modify the log levels for any class hierarchy in the portal. If you have custom code you have deployed which isn't in the list, you can use the *Add Category* tab to add it. If you change the log level near the top of the class hierarchy (such as at com.liferay), all the classes under that hierarchy will have their log levels changed. If you are testing something specific, it is much better to be as specific as you can when you change log levels. Modifying them too high in the hierarchy generates a lot more log messages than you need.

Properties

Liferay and the JVM contain many settings which are defined as properties. There are two subtabs of the properties tab of the Server Administration page: one showing system properties and one showing portal properties.

The system properties tab shows an exhaustive list of system properties for the JVM, as well as many Liferay system properties. This information can be used for debugging purposes or to check the configuration of the currently running portal.

The portal properties tab shows an exhaustive list of the portal properties. These properties can be customized; you can peruse the full list of customizable properties online.[2] If you need to check the current value of a particular property, it can be viewed from this screen without having to shut down the portal or open any properties files.

CAPTCHA

By default, Liferay ships with its own simple CAPTCHA service which is designed to thwart bots from registering for accounts on sites powered by Liferay. If you want to instead use Google's reCAPTCHA service, you can enable this setting from the CAPTCHA tab of the Server Administration page.

Simply check the *Enable ReCAPTCHA* box and enter your public and private keys into the provided fields, then click *Save*. Liferay Portal will then use reCAPTCHA instead of simple CAPTCHA.

Data Migration

If you are upgrading from a previous release of Liferay Portal or if you need to migrate your data from one system to another, the Data Migration tab helps you to do that without your developers having to write custom scripts.

The first section lets you copy your entire Liferay database from the current database under which it is running to the database you specify in this set of fields. You'll need to enter the driver class name (and the driver will need to be on Liferay's classpath), the JDBC URL of the database to which you'll be copying your data and the credentials of a user with access to that database. Once you have all of this information entered, click *Execute* to copy the data.

The next section helps you migrate your documents. If you want to move off of the Jackrabbit JSR-170 repository to the file system, or to the Jackrabbit repository from the file system, or to any of the other repositories supported by the Documents and Media library, you can do so very easily. Make sure you have already set up your portal-ext.properties file so the hook is properly configured before running this migration. Select the Document Library hook that represents the location to which you want your documents to be migrated, then click *Execute*. Your documents will be migrated to the new repository. You can then shut down Liferay, make the new repository the default in the portal-ext.properties file, and then restart.

You can migrate images from the Image Gallery in the same manner. (In Liferay 6.0 and previous versions, the Document Library and Image Gallery were distinct repositories. In Liferay 6.1 and later versions, these have been combined into a single Documents and Media repository.)

File Uploads

Since Liferay allows users to upload files in various places, you may want to lock down the type of files and the size of files users are allowed to upload. The File Uploads tab of the Server Configuration tab lets you set the overall maximum file size and then override that

---

[2]http://docs.liferay.com/portal/6.2/propertiesdoc/portal.properties.html

size for specific applications within Liferay. You can limit the allowed file extensions generally or by application. You have a lot of flexibility as to how you want files to be managed within your portal.

Mail

Instead of using your Liferay server's portal-ext.properties file to configure a mail server, you can configure a mail server from the Mail tab of the Server Configuration section of the Control Panel. If your portal is to receive mail (see, for example, our coverage of the Message Boards portlet in chapter 8), you can connect a POP mail server. If your portal is to send mail, which is useful for sending notifications to users, you can connect to an SMTP server. We highly recommend setting up mail servers for your portal.

Note that if you configure mail server settings here in the Control Panel, these settings will override any mail server settings in your portal-ext.properties file.

External Services

Liferay Portal enables users to upload and share content via the Documents and Media library, a customizable and permissionable online repository. Users can upload files of any type to the Documents and Media library. Liferay ships with PDFBox and uses it to generate automatic previews for certain types of documents, by default. You can also install three additional tools that offer higher quality previews and document conversion functionality: OpenOffice or LibreOffice, ImageMagick and Xuggler. With Liferay configured to use these tools, you can generate automatic previews for many types of files including text files, office suite files, PDFs, images, audio files and videos. Users will also be able to use the conversion functionality to download documents in a variety of formats. Please see chapter 4 on Documents and Media for more information.

LibreOffice[3], ImageMagick[4], and Xuggler[5] are available from their respective websites. Make sure to choose the correct versions of these applications for your operating system. We recommend that you install the latest stable versions. LibreOffice 3.6, ImageMagick 6.7.7, and Xuggler 5.4 work with Liferay 6.2. You need to install LibreOffice and ImageMagick manually but you can install Xuggler from Liferay's Server Administration Control Panel interface.

 Tip: If you're running Liferay on a Linux server and experience a problem enabling Xuggler, check your server's glibc version. You might have to update glibc to version 2.6 or later in order for Xuggler to work.

Once you've installed these tools, you can use the External Services tab of the Control Panel to configure Liferay to use them.

OpenOffice/LibreOffice configuration

OpenOffice and LibreOffice are open source office suites which are usually run in graphical mode to create documents but they can also be run in "server" mode. When run in server mode, OpenOffice and LibreOffice can be used to convert documents to and from all of the file types it supports. Once configured, Liferay makes use of this feature to automatically convert content on the fly. You can install OpenOffice or LibreOffice on the same machine upon which Liferay is running or you can connect to a separate host.

---

[3]http://www.libreoffice.org
[4]http://www.imagemagick.org
[5]http://xuggle.com/xuggler/

If you've installed OpenOffice or LibreOffice on the same machine that's running Liferay, you can start it in server mode with the following command:

```
soffice --headless --accept="socket,host=127.0.0.1,port=8100;urp;"
--nofirststartwizard
```

Once OpenOffice or LibreOffice has been installed and is running in server mode, you can configure Liferay to use it either in your portal-ext.properties file or from the Control Panel. To enable OpenOffice/LibreOffice in your portal-ext.properties file, add the following line:

```
openoffice.server.enabled=true
```

If OpenOffice or LibreOffice is running on another server or on a non-default port, you must also specify these values. The default values are as follows:

```
openoffice.server.host=127.0.0.1
openoffice.server.port=8100
```

By default, when Liferay uses OpenOffice or LibreOffice to perform conversions, it uses a cache. The first time a document is converted, a copy is saved in the Liferay temp folder /liferay/document_conversion/. When Liferay receives a conversion request, it checks this folder to see if the converted document already exists. If the converted document is found, Liferay returns it to the user. Otherwise, it performs a fresh conversion and saves a copy in the temp folder. If the cache is turned off, Liferay will always regenerate the file regardless of whether a previously existing conversion already exists in the temp folder. You can turn the cache off by setting the following property:

```
openoffice.cache.enabled=false
```

To configure Liferay to use OpenOffice/LibreOffice from the Control Panel, navigate to the *Server Administration → External Services* page and check the *Enabled* box for OpenOffice. If OpenOffice/LibreOffice is running on a non-default port, you must also specify the port number. By default, OpenOffice runs on port 8100, which is the default port in the Control Panel. If you have something else running on this port, find an open port and specify it both in the command to start OpenOffice/LibreOffice in server mode and on the Control Panel's External Services configuration page. When you are finished, click *Save*. Now Liferay can perform many types of document conversions.

ImageMagick configuration

Once you've installed the correct version of *ImageMagick* for your operating system, which should include the installation of Ghostscript, you need to configure Liferay to use ImageMagick. You can do this either in your portal-ext.properties file or from the Control Panel. To enable ImageMagick in your portal-ext.properties file, add the following lines and make sure the search path points to the directories for the ImageMagick and Ghostscript executables. You may also need to configure the path for fonts used by Ghostscript when in Mac or Unix environments.

```
imagemagick.enabled=true
imagemagick.global.search.path[apple]=
  /opt/local/bin:/opt/local/share/ghostscript/fonts:/opt/local/share/fonts/urw-fonts
imagemagick.global.search.path[unix]=
  /usr/local/bin:/usr/local/share/ghostscript/fonts:/usr/local/share/fonts/urw-fonts
imagemagick.global.search.path[windows]=
  C:\\Program Files\\ImageMagick
```

To enable ImageMagick from the Control Panel, navigate to the *Server Administration* →*External Services* page, check the *Enabled* checkbox for ImageMagick and verify the paths to the ImageMagick and Ghostscript executables are correct.

Note that some older versions of ImageMagick are unable to properly run with Liferay. If this is the case, update to the latest version (ImageMagick 6.7.9-6 2012-09-25 Q16 or later). To check for the latest ImageMagick versions, visit http://www.imagemagick.org/script/binary-releases.php. See http://issues.liferay.com/browse/LPS-30291 for information on efforts to identify incompatible application versions with Liferay.

Xuggler configuration

Once you've installed the correct version of *Xuggler* for your operating system, you need to configure your environment variables. Depending on where you installed Xuggler, a configuration similar to the following should work on Unix-like systems:

```
export XUGGLE_HOME=/usr/local/xuggler
export LD_LIBRARY_PATH=$XUGGLE_HOME/lib:$LD_LIBRARY_PATH
export PATH=$XUGGLE_HOME/bin:$PATH
```

Once your environment variables are set up correctly, you can configure Liferay to use Xuggler either in your portal-properties file or from the Control Panel. If you'd like to use your portal-ext.properties file, just add the following line:

```
xuggler.enabled=true
```

To configure Liferay to use Xuggler in the Control Panel, navigate to the *Server Administration* →*External Services* page and check *Enabled*. That's it! You've successfully configured the Documents and Media library to use Xuggler for audio and video files.

Script

Liferay includes a scripting console which lets administrators execute migration or management code instantly. Several scripting languages are supported, including JavaScript, Groovy, Python, Ruby and Beanshell. This guide contains a chapter that explains how to use Liferay's scripting console and provides some examples. For further information about Liferay's APIs, please refer to the Liferay Developer Network, *Liferay in Action*, or Liferay's Javadocs.

Shutdown

If you ever need to shut down your Liferay Portal server while users are logged in, you can use the Shutdown tab to inform your logged-in users of the impending shutdown. You can define the number of minutes until the shutdown and a custom message that will be displayed.

Users will see your message at the top of their portal pages for the duration of time you specified. When the time expires, all portal pages will display a message saying the portal has been shut down. At this point, the server will need to be restarted to restore access. Next, let's examine how to manage multiple portal instances.

17.6 Portal Instances

Liferay Portal allows you to run more than one portal instance on a single server. The Portal Instances section of the Control Panel appears under the Configuration heading. This section lets you manage multiple portal instances from a single Liferay installation.

Each portal instance's data is kept separate from every other portal instance's data. All portal data, however, is kept in the same database.

Each portal instance requires its own domain name. Liferay directs users to the proper portal instance based on this domain name. So before you configure an instance, configure its domain name in your network first. When you're ready to add an instance, click the *Add* button here.

You'll be prompted for four fields and a check box:

Web ID: A general convention is to use the domain name for this. It's a user-generated ID for the instance.

Virtual Host: Put the domain name you configured in your network here. When **users** are directed to your Liferay server via this domain name, Liferay will then be able to send them to the proper portal instance.

Mail Domain: Enter the domain name for the mail host for this instance. Liferay will use this to send email notifications from the portal.

Max Users: Enter the maximum numbers of user accounts you would like your portal instance to support.

Active: Use this check box to choose whether to create an active or an inactive portal instance.

When you are finished filling out the form, click *Save*. Now navigate to the portal using your new domain name. You will see you are brought to what looks like a clean install of Liferay. This is your new portal instance which can now be configured any way you like.

17.7 Summary

In this chapter, we examined how to configure Liferay's portal settings. We looked at the different authentication options provided by Liferay. You can configure Liferay so that users can authenticate via LDAP, CAS, Facebook, NTLM, OpenID, OpenSSO, or Site-Minder. We also examined some general configuration options for the portal users, such as reserved credentials and default user associations.

Next, we learned how to configure mail host names, email notifications, content sharing, identification information, and portal display settings. We showed how to add custom fields to various portal entities such as users, pages, documents, wiki articles, message board posts, and more.

We also saw how to view and configure overall server settings. We saw how to view the memory currently being used by the server, as well as how to initiate garbage collection, a thread dump, search engine re-indexing and the clearing of various caches. We learned how to debug parts of the portal by changing log levels and by viewing the various properties defined in the portal. We learned how to properly notify users that the portal is about to shut down and how to set up external services like OpenOffice integration.

Lastly, we looked at how to create multiple portal instances on a single installation of Liferay and we showed how to view currently installed plugins. We hope this information helps you become an effective Liferay Portal Administrator.

Part II

Deploying Liferay Portal

## CHAPTER 18

INSTALLATION AND SETUP

Liferay Portal is one of the most flexible applications on the market today with regard to application server environments. It supports a wide variety of application servers, freeing you to use the Java application server you think is best. Liferay also scales very well: you can install Liferay Portal on everything from a shared hosting account to a multi-node cluster running a commercial application server and on everything in between. In fact, Liferay is used successfully in all of these scenarios every day.

You'll find that because Liferay is extremely flexible in its deployment options, it is also easy to install. If you already have an application server, you can use the tools for deployment that came with your application server. If you don't have an application server, Liferay provides several application server bundles from which to choose. These are pre-configured application servers with Liferay already installed in them. They're very easy to install and with a small amount of configuration can be made into production-ready systems.

The installation steps vary slightly according to your Liferay edition, so we'll be sure to let you know when they are different.

18.1 Editions of Liferay

Liferay ships in two editions: one for the community and one for enterprise subscribers. The community edition is the same Liferay Portal that has been available for years: frequently updated and bursting with the latest features, the Community Edition of Liferay Portal is offered for free under the Lesser GNU public license, a free software license with one important exception. This license gives you the flexibility to link Liferay with your own code in your portlet, theme, hook, layout, Ext or web plugins, no matter what license you use for your code. If, however, you modify Liferay directly, those modifications need to be released as free software under the terms of the license. The best way, of course, to do this is to contribute it back to the Liferay community. This is really the best of both worlds: you have the freedom use any license (or no license) if you use plugins, but if you modify Liferay directly, the community receives the benefits of any enhancements that you've made.

Liferay for enterprise subscribers is a supported version of Liferay Portal for the enterprise. The subscription and support package allows organizations to build their portals on a stable version of the product that is offered over an extended period of time. It's the best wayfor you to develop, deploy, and maintain your Liferay solution. It includes

- Liferay support
- Updates
- Fix Packs
- Cloud Services
- Liferay Portal Enterprise Edition

Now let's learn how to get a copy of Liferay Portal.

18.2   Obtaining Liferay Portal

The Liferay community can download Liferay Portal from our web site at http://www.liferay.com. Click the *Downloads* link at the top of the page, and you'll see multiple options for getting a copy of Liferay, including our convenient bundles or a .war package for installation on your application server of choice.

Liferay enterprise subscribers can download Liferay from the Customer Portal. You have a choice of the same open source app server bundles as community members, plus a few commercial alternatives, in addition to the .war package for manual installation.

So what is a bundle anyway? A bundle is an application server with Liferay preinstalled. This is the most convenient way to install Liferay. Liferay is bundled with a number of application servers; all you need to do is choose the one that best fits your needs. If you don't currently have an application server, you may want to start with the Tomcat bundle, as Tomcat is one of the smallest and most straightforward bundles to configure. If you have an open source application server preference, choose the server you prefer from the available Liferay Portal bundles. All the bundles ship with a Java Runtime Environment for Windows; if you are using a different operating system, you must have a JDK (Java Development Kit) installed prior to launching Liferay Portal.

Please note that Liferay is not able to provide application server bundles for proprietary application servers such as WebLogic or WebSphere, because the licenses for these servers don't allow for redistribution. Liferay Portal, however, runs just as well on these application servers as it does on the others. A .war file and dependency .jars are provided for proprietary application servers, and you'll need to follow a procedure to install Liferay on them.

Once you have Liferay, you can then plan out your installation. This is a two-step process: first, determine if you need Liferay Portal Security turned on, and second, install Liferay Portal, by using a bundle or by installing it manually on your existing app server. Next, we'll go over the steps it takes to install Liferay Portal.

18.3   Liferay installation overview

Before we begin, it's important to go over the various facets of the installation. They are:

1. Create your database.

2. Determine whether you want to use the Liferay managed data source or a data source managed by your application server. The Liferay managed data source is recommended.

3. Gather credentials for sending email notifications to users. Liferay supports a JNDI mail session as well as its built-in mail session.

4. Install a Liferay bundle or on an existing application server according to the instructions for your application server (see below).

5. Determine whether you'll use Marketplace or other third party applications. If you will, you should enable Liferay's Plugin Access Control List (PACL).

We'll go through the steps in order, so first we'll look at the Liferay database.

18.4 Liferay's database

The recommended way of setting up your Liferay database also happens to be the simplest. Liferay Portal takes care of just about everything. The only thing you need to do is create a blank database encoded for character set UTF-8. The reason for this is that Liferay is a multilingual application, and needs UTF-8 encoding to display all the character sets it supports.

Next, create an ID for accessing this database and grant it all rights—including the rights to create and drop tables—to the blank Liferay database. This is the ID you'll use to connect to the Liferay database, and you'll configure it later either in your application server or in Liferay's properties file so that Liferay can connect to it.

One of the first things Liferay Portal does when you bring it up for the first time is create the tables it needs in the database you just created. It does this automatically, complete with indexes.

If you create your database and grant a user ID full access to it, Liferay can use that user ID to create its indexes and tables automatically. This is the recommended way to set up Liferay, as it allows you to take advantage of Liferay's ability to maintain its database automatically during upgrades or through various plugin installs that create tables of their own. It is by far the best way to set up your Liferay installation.

If you'll be setting up Liferay's database with the recommended permissions, you can skip to the next section.

Note: The below instructions are not the recommended set up for Liferay installations, but the procedure is documented here so enterprises with more restrictive standards can install Liferay with more strict—but suboptimal—database settings. If it's at all possible, Liferay recommends that you use the automatic method as documented above instead of the procedure outlined below.

Even though Liferay can create its database automatically, some enterprises prefer *not* to allow the user ID configured in an application server to have the permissions over the database necessary for Liferay and its plugins to maintain their tables. For these organizations, Select, Insert, Update and Delete are the only permissions allowed so we will go over how to set up the database manually. If your organization *is* willing to grant the Liferay user ID permissions to create and drop tables in the database—and this is the recommended configuration—by all means, use the recommended configuration.

Creating the database is simple: grant the ID Liferay uses to access the database full rights to do anything to the database. Then install Liferay and have it create the database. Once the database is created, remove the permissions for creating tables and dropping tables from the user ID.

There are some caveats to running Liferay like this. Many Liferay plugins create new tables when they're deployed. In addition to this, Liferay has an automatic database upgrade function that runs when Liferay is upgraded. If the user ID that accesses the database doesn't have enough rights to create/modify/drop tables in the database, you must grant those rights to the ID before you deploy one of these plugins or start your upgraded Liferay for the first time. Once the tables are created or the upgrade is complete, you can remove those rights until the next deploy or upgrade. Additionally, your developers may create plugins that need to create their own tables. These are just like Liferay's plugins that do the same thing, and they cannot be installed if Liferay can't create these tables automatically. If you wish to install these plugins, you will need to grant rights to create tables in the database before you attempt to install them.

Once you have your database ready, you can install Liferay on your server.

18.5   Liferay Marketplace

The Liferay Marketplace is an integral part of the Liferay Portal experience. Starting with Liferay Portal 6.2, the Marketplace plugin is required to be installed alongside Liferay Portal. The Marketplace plugin enables a host of features that extend beyond just access to the online Liferay Marketplace. Some of the key features the Marketplace plugin enables are:

- Liferay Marketplace: direct access to our online Marketplace
- App Manager: ability to install, uninstall, and update apps
- Bundled Apps: easily manage apps that may come bundled with your Liferay Portal
- Developer Apps: ability to manage apps that you're developing
- License Manager: streamlined license management for your Liferay Portal and apps

The portal installation process attempts to deploy and register the Marketplace plugin automatically. If your environment supports/allows 1) hot deploy and 2) full database rights, the automatic deploy process takes care of itself. Many companies (especially in a production environment), however, limit automated processes and/or database access. Additionally, certain application servers (eg., WebSphere) do not support hot deploy, so you may need to deploy the Marketplace plugin manually. Depending on your environment's restrictions, you may need to follow one or more of the steps below to install the Marketplace plugin properly.

Server is Firewalled without Access to the Internet

Your server may be behind a firewall that prevents access to the Internet, or your security policy may not allow direct download and installation from the Internet. In these cases, you have 2 options:

1. From an Internet-enabled computer, download the Marketplace plugin.[1] Then allow Liferay to auto deploy it by dropping the downloaded .lpkg file into the Liferay deploy folder.

2. From an Internet-enabled computer, download the Marketplace plugin. Then use the Liferay App Manager to deploy the plugin.

Detailed instructions can be found under Installing Plugins Manually.

Application Server Does Not Support Hot Deploy

If your application server does not support hot deploy, you can't leverage Liferay's auto deploy feature. You can, however, manually deploy the plugin in two steps:

1. Use Liferay's tools to pre-deploy the file.

---

[1]https://www.liferay.com/marketplace/download

2. Then use your app server's tools to do the actual deployment.

This is because Liferay makes deployment-time modifications to the plugins right before they are actually deployed to the application server. Detailed instructions can be found under Deploy Issues for Specific Containers.

Limited Database Access

Some production environments do not have the necessary database permissions for Liferay and its plugins to maintain their tables. In these cases:

1. Grant the ID Liferay uses to access the database temporary full rights to the database.

2. Install Liferay and have it create the database.

3. Once the database is created, remove the permissions for creating tables and dropping tables from the user ID.

Detailed instructions are available.[2] It should be noted that most sophisticated Liferay apps—not just the Marketplace plugin—require new tables when deployed. If your environment restricts database access, you may need to repeat the above steps whenever you deploy a new app to the Liferay Portal.

18.6   Liferay Home

Liferay Portal uses a special folder defined as *Liferay Home*. This folder is usually one folder higher than the location of the application server itself. This is why the bundles place the application server one folder in from the bundle's root folder.

If Liferay is unable to create the resources it needs in this folder or if it finds itself running on certain application servers, it creates a folder called liferay in the home folder of the user ID that is running Liferay, and that becomes Liferay Home.

The home folder is important to the operation of Liferay. The aforementioned folders (data and deploy) are created there, and Liferay's properties configuration files are also stored there.

We recommend using the setup wizard to configure your database and mail sessions when you first configure Liferay. This creates a portal-setup-wizard.properties file where all the settings from the setup wizard are stored. When you begin customizing your portal's configuration, we recommend you create a separate properties file for that, called portal-ext.properties. This allows you to keep your server configuration properties separate from core properties like your database and mail server configurations. All the possible properties that can be placed in this file are documented in our reference documentation.

 Note: To avoid using the setup wizard so you can configure everything manually from a portal-ext.properties file, you must disable the Setup Wizard by specifying setup.wizard.enabled=false in the portal-ext.properties. Also, note that property values in portal-setup-wizard.properties (the file created in Liferay Home by the Setup Wizard) override property values in portal-ext.properties.

Let's move on and discuss Liferay Portal security.

---

[2]https://dev.liferay.com/discover/deployment/-/knowledge_base/6-2/
liferays-database

18.7   Configuring Liferay Portal Security

As you probably know, Liferay Marketplace is an online store for obtaining applications that run on the Liferay Portal platform. These applications are provided not only by Liferay, but also by partners and independent developers who want you to install and use their applications on your server. Many of these applications are excellent, and we recommend that you try them out for yourself.

Because many of the applications on Marketplace are *not* provided by Liferay, however, there's an issue of trust: how do you know these applications are doing what they're advertised to do? There is a vetting process that they go through before they're allowed on Marketplace, but if the source code is not provided, there's no way for even Liferay to know if an app has been properly represented. For this reason, Liferay Portal implements a security layer we call the Portal Access Control List, or PACL.

PACL forces an application to declare up front the functions from Liferay's APIs that it calls. Anything that's not declared is not allowed to run. It's similar to what you might see on your mobile phone when you install an app: you get to see the Liferay API functions the app uses, and then you can decide if you want to install that app based on the permissions it requires. This way, you see right away what portal data that app can access, and the app can do nothing else: you're protected—if you have PACL enabled. So if you plan to use apps downloaded from Marketplace, it's important to make sure PACL is enabled.

By default, Liferay's bundles have PACL turned off. The reason for this is that there is a small performance penalty for having PACL enabled. Since the only reason to have PACL enabled is to install untrusted third party apps from Marketplace (and not everybody does that), we decided to leave PACL turned off by default, so that your portal performs as fast as possible.

All of this is to say: if you intend to use Marketplace apps, please enable PACL. Later in this chapter, there are sections for all the app servers Liferay supports. Each of those sections has a subsection that explains how to enable Java security for that app server, which is a prerequisite for enabling PACL. Once you have Java security enabled, PACL can be enabled by adding one line to your portal-ext.properties or portal-setup-wizard.properties file:

```
portal.security.manager.strategy=liferay
```

Save the file and if Liferay is running, restart it. Your portal is now configured to check PACL-enabled Marketplace apps against their declared permissions.

Next, you'll make sure Liferay is configured properly for your network.

18.8   Choosing IPv4 or IPv6

Liferay Portal supports both the IPv4 and IPv6 address formats, though by default, Liferay uses IPv4 addresses. If you're on an IPv6 network, you'll need to change the configuration. If you'd like more information on the basics of these protocols, you can check out the reason[3] for using IPv6 addresses, and its technical details.[4]

To configure your portal to validate IPv6 addresses, you must complete a few simple steps. First, assuming you're using the Tomcat app server for your portal, navigate to the ${TOMCAT_HOME}/bin/setenv.bat file and set

```
-Djava.net.preferIPv4Stack=false
```

---

[3]http://www.google.com/intl/en/ipv6/
[4]http://en.wikipedia.org/wiki/IPv6

in CATALINA_OPTS. Then, create a `portal-ext.properties` file in your portal's home directory (if necessary) and set the `tunnel.servlet.hosts.allowed` property to the target hosts you want to allow (e.g., 0:0:0:0:0:0:0:1).

Now that you understand all the prerequisites for installing Liferay Portal, let's go ahead and get it done! First we'll go over installing Liferay from a bundle, and after this we'll provide instructions for installing Liferay manually on all the application servers it supports.

18.9 Installing a bundle

Liferay bundles contain the same directory structure regardless of application server. The top-level folder is named for the release of Liferay. This folder is called *Liferay Home*, and we refer to it thoughout this documentation.

Figure 18.1: Bundle directory structure

Inside this folder, there are folders for various purposes:

Data: This folder is used to store the embedded HSQL database the bundles use, as well as the configuration and data for the Jackrabbit JSR-170 content repository and the Lucene search index. It also contains the base directory where the OSGi framework can persist any of its operating files.

Deploy: Plugins that can be copied into this folder, and Liferay then deploys them. It is also used by Liferay Marketplace and Liferay's graphical plugin installer utility. This folder is created the first time Liferay Portal starts.

[Application Server]: The name of this folder is different depending on the bundle you've downloaded. This folder contains the application server in which Liferay has been installed.

In addition to Liferay Portal itself, bundles are shipped with a number of plugins already installed:

- kaleo-web: Liferay's workflow engine

- marketplace: Interface to Liferay Marketplace

- notifications: App that provides in-browser notifications for users

- opensocial: Allows deploying OpenSocial gadgets to Liferay Portal

- resources-importer-web: Imports theme resources with theme plugins

- sync-web: Allows Liferay Sync to connect to this installation to keep Documents and Media folders synchronized. You must have this plugin installed if you want to use Liferay Sync Mobile or Desktop.

- web-forms: App that allows users to create forms users can fill out. The results are then emailed to a specified email address.

- welcome-theme: A default website that gives new users a tour of what Liferay Portal has to offer.

- calendar: Liferay's calendar application. This used to be built-in, and is now a plugin, so it's included by default.

If you are an enterprise subscriber, the welcome theme is not included, and you receive a few more plugins:

- kaleo-designer-portlet: Subscriber plugin that offers a graphical interface for creating Kaleo workflows.

- kaleo-forms-portlet: Subscriber plugin that allows attaching forms to workflows.

Getting a Liferay bundle up and running is as easy as uncompressing the archive, copying a JDBC driver, and then starting the application server. Let's use the Tomcat bundle as an example:

1. Unzip the bundle to a location of your choice.

2. If you're setting up Liferay to be an actual server, copy your database's JDBC driver .jar to [Tomcat]/lib/ext (see the setup wizard section below). If you're setting up Liferay for demo purposes, you can skip this step.

3. Start Tomcat in the same way you would if you had downloaded it manually. Tomcat is launched by way of a script which is found in its bin folder. If you drop to a command prompt and go to this folder, you can launch Tomcat via the following command on Windows:

   startup

   or the following command on Linux/Mac/Unix:

```
./startup.sh
```

The Liferay/Tomcat bundle then launches. If you are on Windows, another command prompt window appears with Tomcat's console in it. If you are on Linux, you can see the Tomcat console by issuing the following command:

```
tail -f ../logs/catalina.out
```

Once Tomcat has started, it automatically launches a web browser that displays Liferay's setup wizard. If for some reason your browser doesn't load the wizard, launch your web browser and then go to http://localhost:8080.

Liferay CE ships with a sample web site that showcases Liferay's features. It contains many links describing the features of Liferay that we cover in detail throughout this book.

If you're installing Liferay on your own machine to explore its features, you likely want to leave the sample site there so you can examine it. If, however, you're installing Liferay on your server to run your own site, it's best to start with a clean system. Before running the setup wizard, you should remove the sample data from your Liferay installation. You must do this before running the setup wizard to get a clean database, and it's as simple as undeploying the application that installs the sample data.

There is one application included in the bundle that you need to remove:

- welcome-theme

To remove it, all you have to do is undeploy it. The method for doing this differs by application server and that, of course, depends on the bundle you have chosen. For example, on Tomcat you delete the application folder from the [Tomcat Home]/webapps folder. On GlassFish, you use the administrative console.

If you forget to undeploy the sample application before you run through the setup wizard and connect Liferay to your real database, the sample data is created in your database, and there isn't an easy way to clean it out. Make sure you get the sample data undeployed before setting up your server, or you'll have to drop your database and re-create it. That's not such a bad thing to have to do, since it's a brand new database. If you don't have a brand new database, you're working with an existing installation of Liferay, and you should follow the instructions on upgrading in chapter 18 instead of what's described here.

If you're a Liferay Portal Enterprise subscriber, you don't have the sample site, so you don't need to worry about this. The next step is to run through the setup wizard, which we'll cover below.

As you can see, bundles are the easiest way to get started with Liferay. They come preconfigured with a running Liferay instance that can be used immediately to explore all the things that Liferay can do. Bundles are the fastest way to create full production-ready Liferay installations. If you're using a bundle, skip to the section on the setup wizard below to continue your installation.

Of course, it's not always possible to use a bundle. You may already have an application server where Liferay should be installed. The bulk of this chapter describes how to install Liferay on all the application servers it supports, both open source and proprietary.

18.10 App Servers

When it comes time to install Liferay Portal on your server, you'll find it's easiest to do this by starting with a bundle. But many organizations can't do that. There may be an existing infrastructure into which you're installing Liferay, or you may have standardized on a particular application server. You'll be happy to know that Liferay Portal has been designed to work well with all the leading application servers and that it's easy and straightforward to install. But before we get started, we need to go over a few concepts; namely, data sources and mail sessions. These were touched on in the section on bundles above but we'll look at them in more detail now.

Using data sources

Liferay comes bundled with its own built-in data source. It's configured by a number of properties that are set in a properties file. By default, the setup wizard asks you for the necessary values and creates a configuration file that uses the built-in data source to connect to the database.

Liferay always recommends that you use the built-in data source. Sometimes, however, organizations prefer to use the data source provided by their application server of choice. In this instance, a JNDI lookup provides a handle to the data source and the application server manages the connection pools. Liferay supports using your application server's data source if you wish to do that.

To do this, you'll need to create your own configuration file and skip the setup wizard. Since you'd be creating this file *after* the wizard anyway, this isn't such a big deal. We show you how to do that after all the sections on application servers.

Since mail sessions are configured in a similar way to data sources, we'll look at them next.

Using mail sessions

Liferay's default configuration looks for a mail server on the same machine on which Liferay's running and it tries to send mail via SMTP to this server. If this is not your configuration, you'll need to modify Liferay's defaults. To do this, you'll use a portal-ext.properties file (see below).

In a similar fashion to databases, you have two ways to configure your mail server:

- Use your application server's mail session.

- Use the built-in mail session.

To use your application server's mail session, you must create it in your application server and it should point to your mail server. Once you've done that, you're ready to point Liferay to it. You can do this through the configuration file or through Liferay's control panel after it's been installed.

You now have all the background information you need. Next you need to make your decision: will you use Liferay's built-in data source, or the one provided by your application server? If you're planning to use the one provided by your server, you can't use Liferay's installation wizard, and you'll have to follow the instructions in the section below titled Manual Configuration.

In either case, your next step is to install Liferay onto your application server. What follows are sections for every application server that Liferay supports. Once you have Liferay Portal installed, the first thing you see is the setup wizard. To continue, follow the instructions for setting up Liferay on your application server, and then skip down to the section on the setup wizard.

Next, follow the instructions for installing Liferay on your particular application server in the section below.

18.11   Installing Liferay on an existing application server

This section contains detailed instructions for installing Liferay Portal using its .war file distribution. This allows system administrators to deploy Liferay in existing application server installations. It is recommended that you have a good understanding of how to deploy Java EE applications in your application server of choice.

Installing Liferay in five easy steps

There are five generic steps to installing Liferay on an existing application server:

1. Obtain the Liferay .war file and the dependencies archive.

2. Shut your application server down.

3. Extract the dependencies to a location on your server's global classpath. This allows both Liferay and plugins to access these dependencies.

4. Start your application server.

5. Deploy the Liferay .war file.

The instructions below are specific for each application server that Liferay supports. Liferay supports a wide combination of application servers and databases. Because of this, this section assumes MySQL as the database, that the database has already been created, and that you're using the setup wizard. If you're not using the setup wizard, see the sections above for information on how to set up Liferay manually.

We also assume your application server is already installed and running successfully. If you still need to install your application server, please follow your vendor's instructions first.

Since Liferay uses the UTF-8 character encoding, make sure that your application server has the Java -Dfile.encoding=UTF-8 parameter set before you proceed. Note that different application servers provide different means for setting this parameter. For example, in Tomcat this parameter goes in the setenv.sh or setenv.bat script. For other application servers, this parameter might go in a different script or might have to be set through an administration console.

The following instructions assume an installation on a local machine. When installing to a remote server, substitute localhost with the host name or IP of the server.

Tip: Note that Liferay *requires* JDK 6 or greater. Do not attempt to install Liferay 6.2 on an application server that runs under Java 5 or lower; it will not work. If you are running an application server that ships with a JDK and that JDK is version 5 or lower, you'll need to upgrade your application server to run current versions of Liferay Portal.

Without further ado, let's get to the application servers. The first one we'll cover is Mule Tcat. If you don't have an application server preference, and you want support all the way down to the application server from Liferay, then Mule Tcat is your solution. After we cover Mule Tcat, we'll look at all the supported application servers in alphabetical order.

18.12 Installing Liferay on Mulesoft Tcat

For this section, we will refer to your Tcat server's installation location as [TCAT_HOME]. If you don't already have an existing Tcat server, we recommend you download a Liferay/Tcat bundle[5]. If you have an existing Tcat server on which you'd like to deploy Liferay manually, please follow the steps below.

Your first step is to download the latest Liferay .war file and Liferay Portal dependencies[6]. The files are named according to the following conventions:

```
liferay-portal-6.2.x-[date].war
liferay-portal-dependencies-6.2.x-[date].zip
```

Next, let's get started by addressing Liferay's library dependencies.

Dependency Jars

To run Liferay Portal on your Tcat server, you first need to make some JAR files available on Tcat's global classpath. These include the Liferay Dependency JARs, a JDBC driver for your database, and some other dependencies that Liferay Portal requires.

1. Create the folder [TCAT_HOME]/lib/ext.

2. Extract the Liferay dependencies file and copy the .jars to [TCAT_HOME]/lib/ext.

3. Next, you need a few .jar files that are included as part of the Liferay Tcat bundle, but are not included with Tcat. You'll have to download them yourself, so let's get started. Place these .jar files into $TCAT_HOME/lib/ext:

---

[5]http://www.liferay.com/downloads/liferay-portal/available-releases
[6]http://www.liferay.com/downloads/liferay-portal/additional-files

- jta.jar: Support for Java transactions.[7]

- mail.jar: Support for the Java Mail API.[8]

- persistence.jar: Support for the Java Persistence API.[9]

- activation.jar: This is an implementation of the Java Activation Framework.[10]

- ccpp.jar: Enables Composite Capability/Preference Profiles.[11]

- jms.jar: The Java Messaging Service.[12]

- jutf7.jar: Provides UTF-7 and Modified UTF-7 charsets for Java.[13]

- junit.jar: Optional: lets you run unit tests.[14]

Although you can get each .jar listed above separately, it may be more convenient to get them by downloading the Liferay source code and copying them from there. Once you have downloaded the Liferay source, unzip the source into a temporary folder. You can find the .jar files in [LIFERAY_SOURCE]/lib/development.

4. Make sure the JDBC driver for your database is accessible by Tomcat. Obtain the JDBC driver for your version of the database server. In the case of MySQL, use mysql-connector-java-[version]-bin.jar. Download the latest MySQL JDBC driver.[15] Copy it to [TCAT_HOME]/lib/ext.

Now that you have the necessary libraries in place, we'll move on to configuring your domain.

Tcat Configuration

If you're installing Liferay Portal onto an existing Tcat server, you should be familiar with the Tcat Administration Console. The following instructions assume you have a Tcat server with the Administration Console and a separate, managed Tcat server instance where you'll deploy Liferay. To find information specific to Tcat server installation and management, see Mulesoft's Tcat Documentation[16] You have to do a few things to configure your managed Tcat server instance:

- Set environment variables

- Create a context for your web application

- Modify the list of classes/JARs to be loaded

- Specify URI encoding

Next, you'll configure your managed Tcat instance.

---

[7]http://www.oracle.com/technetwork/java/javaee/jta/index.html
[8]http://www.oracle.com/technetwork/java/index-138643.html
[9]http://www.oracle.com/technetwork/java/javaee/tech/persistence-jsp-140049.html
[10]http://www.oracle.com/technetwork/java/jaf11-139815.html
[11]http://mvnrepository.com/artifact/javax.ccpp/ccpp/1.0
[12]http://www.oracle.com/technetwork/java/docs-136352.html
[13]http://sourceforge.net/projects/jutf7/
[14]http://sourceforge.net/projects/junit/
[15]http://dev.mysql.com/downloads/connector/j/
[16]http://www.mulesoft.org/documentation/display/TCAT/Home

Figure 18.2: You can log in to the Tcat Administration Console to manage your Tcat servers.

1. To set the CATALINA_OPTS environment variable, you need to add a server profile. In the Tcat Administration Console, navigate to the *Administration* tab and click *Server Profiles*. Name the profile appropriately (*Liferay 6.2*, perhaps), provide a description if you wish, select the workspace where you'll keep your profile (/Profiles is a logical choice), and click the *Add Variable* button. Name it CATALINA_OPTS and give it the following value:

```
-Dfile.encoding=UTF8 \
-Dorg.apache.catalina.loader.WebappClassLoader.ENABLE_CLEAR_REFERENCES=false \
-Duser.timezone=GMT -Xmx1024m -XX:MaxPermSize=256m"
```

This sets the character encoding to UTF-8, sets the time zone to Greenwich Mean Time and allocates memory to the Java virtual machine.

Apply the profile to the Tcat server where you're deploying Liferay. To do so, go to the *Servers* tab, select the desired server, and select your profile from the *Set Profile* dropdown menu.

2. Create a file locally called ROOT.xml:

Click your server's name to edit its configuration. Using the *Files* tab, navigate to the directory [TCAT_HOME]/conf/Catalina/localhost and upload your ROOT.xml file. Setting crossContext="true" allows multiple web apps to use the same class loader. In the content above you will also find commented instructions and tags for configuring a JAAS realm, disabling persistent sessions and disabling sessions in general.

3. Still in your server's *Files* tab, open [TCAT_HOME]/conf/catalina.properties, click the *Edit catalina.properties* link, and replace the line:

```
common.loader=${catalina.base}/lib,${catalina.base}/lib/*.jar,${catalina.home}/lib, \
${catalina.home}/lib/*.jar
```

with:

```
common.loader=${catalina.base}/lib,${catalina.base}/lib/*.jar,${catalina.home}/lib, \
${catalina.home}/lib/*.jar,${catalina.home}/lib/ext,${catalina.home}/lib/ext/*.jar
```

This allows Catalina to access the dependency jars you extracted to [TCAT_HOME]/-lib/ext.

4. To ensure consistent use of UTF-8 URI Encoding, edit [TCAT_HOME]/conf/server.xml and add the attribute URIEncoding="UTF-8" where you see redirect-Port=8443, in the definition of your connectors (HTTP and AJP). For example:

Figure 18.3: You can edit your Tcat configuration files in the Administration Console.

Excellent work! Now it's time to configure your database.

Database Configuration

If you want Tcat to manage your data source, use the following procedure. If you want to use Liferay's built-in data source, you can skip this section.

1. Make sure your database server is installed and working. If it's installed on a different machine, make sure it's accessible from your Liferay machine.

2. Using the Tcat Administration Console, add your data source as a resource in the context of your web application specified in [TCAT_HOME]/conf/Catalina/localhost/ROOT.xml:

```
<Context...>
    <Resource
        name="jdbc/LiferayPool"
        auth="Container"
        type="javax.sql.DataSource"
        driverClassName="com.mysql.jdbc.Driver"
        url="jdbc:mysql://localhost/lportal?useUnicode=true&amp;characterEncoding=UTF-8"
        username="root"
        password="root"
        maxActive="100"
        maxIdle="30"
        maxWait="10000"
    />
</Context>
```

Note the above resource definition assumes your database name is *lportal* and your MySQL username and password are both *root*. You'll have to update these values with your own database name and credentials.

Your Tcat managed data source is now configured. Let's move on to your mail session.

Mail Configuration

If you want to manage your mail session within Tomcat, use the following instructions. If you want to use the built in Liferay mail session, you can skip this section.

Create a mail session bound to mail/MailSession. In the Tcat Administration Console, edit [TCAT_ HOME]/conf/Catalina/localhost/ROOT.xml and configure a mail session. Be sure to replace the mail session values with your own.

```
<Context...>
    <Resource
        name="mail/MailSession"
        auth="Container"
        type="javax.mail.Session"
        mail.pop3.host="pop.gmail.com"
        mail.pop3.port="110"
        mail.smtp.host="smtp.gmail.com"
        mail.smtp.port="465"
        mail.smtp.user="user"
        mail.smtp.password="password"
        mail.smtp.auth="true"
        mail.smtp.starttls.enable="true"
        mail.smtp.socketFactory.class="javax.net.ssl.SSLSocketFactory"
        mail.imap.host="imap.gmail.com"
        mail.imap.port="993"
        mail.transport.protocol="smtp"
        mail.store.protocol="imap"
    />
</Context>
```

Super! Your mail session is configured. Next, you need to connect Liferay to the mail session and database connections you just created.

Configuring your Database and Mail Session

In this section you'll specify appropriate properties for Liferay to use in connecting to your database and mail session.

1. If you are using Tcat to manage your data source, add the following line to the portal-ext.properties file in your *Liferay Home*. This points Liferay Portal to your data source:

   ```
   jdbc.default.jndi.name=jdbc/LiferayPool
   ```

   If you are using *Liferay Portal* to manage your data source, follow the instructions in the *Deploy Liferay* section for using the setup wizard.

2. If you want to use Liferay Portal to manage your mail session, you can configure the mail session in Liferay Portal. After starting your portal as described in the *Deploy Liferay* section, go to *Control Panel →Server Administration →Mail* and enter the settings for your mail session.
   If you are using Tcat to manage your mail session, add the following configuration to your portal-ext.properties file to reference that mail session:

   ```
   mail.session.jndi.name=mail/MailSession
   ```

Before you deploy Liferay Portal, let's look at configuring Portal Access Control Lists (PACL) with Liferay on Tomcat.

Enabling PACL

To enable PACL, you need to enable the security manager and add some required permissions to the server policy configuration file. This entails editing the CATALINA_OPTS variable and editing the catalina.policy file:

In the *Administration* tab of the Tcat Administration Console, click *Server Profiles* and click the profile applied to your Liferay Tcat server. Click the *Value* field of the CATALINA_-OPTS variable created earlier, and add the following parameter to it:

```
'-Djava.security.manager -Djava.security.policy==$CATALINA_BASE/conf/catalina.policy'
```

The double equals sign tells the app server to use this policy file on top of any existing security policies.

Edit $TCAT_HOME/conf/catalina.policy and add the required permissions:

```
grant {
    permission java.security.AllPermission;
};
```

Now you have PACL enabled and configured for your portal. Let's deploy Liferay!

Deploying Liferay

It's time to deploy Liferay as an exploded web archive in your $TCAT_HOME/webapps folder. The first step is to make sure your Tcat server is running; then follow these steps to deploy and start Liferay.

1. If you are manually installing Liferay on a clean Tcat server, delete the contents of the [TCAT_HOME]/webapps/ROOT directory. This removes the default home page.

2. In the Tcat Administration Console, click the *Deployments* tab and select *New Deployment*. Select the server where you're deploying Liferay and click *Upload New Webapp*. Browse to the liferay-portal-6.2.x-[date].war file you downloaded. Make sure you select *Advanced Options* while uploading Liferay, and under the *Name* field, type / to put the extracted Liferay into [TCAT_HOME]/webapps/ROOT.

3. Once you've entered all the deployment details, you can select *Deploy*. Once you see a *Successful* message in the Tcat Administration Console, you're ready to launch Liferay Portal on Tcat!

Now you can navigate to Liferay and follow the setup wizard. Congratulations on successfully installing and deploying Liferay on Mule Tcat!

18.13   Installing Liferay on GlassFish 4

Liferay Home is three folders above your GlassFish domain folder.

For example, if your domain location is /glassfish-4.0-web/glassfish4/glassfish/domains/domain1, Liferay Home is /glassfish-4.0-web/glassfish4/.

If you don't already have an existing GlassFish server, we recommend that you download a Liferay/GlassFish bundle.[17] If you have an existing GlassFish server or would like to install Liferay on GlassFish manually, please follow the steps below.

---

[17]http://www.liferay.com/downloads/liferay-portal/available-releases

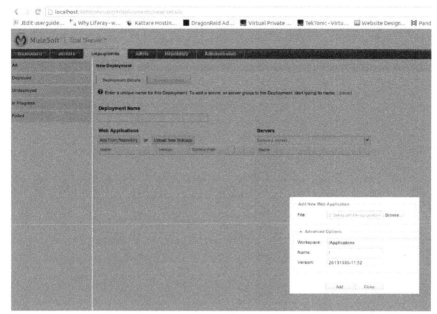

Figure 18.4: Upload your Liferay Portal WAR file using the Deployments tab of the Tcat Administration Console.

Before you begin, make sure you have downloaded the latest Liferay .war file and Liferay Portal dependencies.[18] The Liferay .war file should be called liferay-portal-6.-2.x-[date].war and the dependencies file should be called liferay-portal-dependencies-6.2.x-[date].zip.

These instructions assume that you are running the latest supported version of Glassfish (currently 4.0), have already configured a domain and server, and that you have access to the GlassFish administrative console.

Let's start out by installing the JAR files you will need.

Dependency Jars

Liferay depends on jar files found in the Liferay Dependencies Archive. You should also have installed your database driver.

1. Navigate to the folder that corresponds to the domain in which you'll be installing Liferay. Inside this folder is a sub-folder named lib (e.g. /glassfish-3.1-web-/glassfish3/glassfish/domains/domain1/lib).

   Unzip the Liferay dependencies archive so that its .jar files are extracted into this lib folder.

2. Make sure the JDBC driver for your database is accessible to GlassFish as well. Obtain the JDBC driver for your version of the database server. In the case of MySQL, use mysql-connector-java-{$version}-bin.jar. You can download the latest MySQL JDBC driver.[19] Extract the JAR file and copy it to lib.

---

[18]http://www.liferay.com/downloads/liferay-portal/additional-files
[19]http://www.mysql.com/products/connector/

Terrific, you have your JAR files just where you need them. Next, we'll configure your domain.

Domain Configuration

There are a couple of modifications you need to make in your domain to use Liferay Portal.

Before starting GlassFish, modify your domain's configuration to do the following:

- Set the file encoding
- Set the user time-zone
- Set the preferred protocol stack
- Prevent the application server from setting static fields (final or non-final) to null
- Increase the default amount of memory available.

Modify glassfish4/glassfish/domains/domain1/config/domain.xml, merging in the following JVM options into the current lists of JVM options within any <java-config> element in the file:

```
<jvm-options>-Dfile.encoding=UTF8</jvm-options>
<jvm-options>-Djava.net.preferIPv4Stack=true</jvm-options>
<jvm-options>-Dorg.apache.catalina.loader.WebappClassLoader.ENABLE_CLEAR_REFERENCES=false</jvm-options>
<jvm-options>-Duser.timezone=GMT</jvm-options>
<jvm-options>-Xmx1024m</jvm-options>
<jvm-options>-XX:MaxPermSize=512m</jvm-options>
```

There may be multiple lists of JVM options in your domain.xml file. For example, by default, GlassFish's glassfish4/glassfish/domains/domain1/config/domain.xml file contains two lists of JVM options. There's one list inside the <config name="server-config"> element's <java-config> element and another inside the <config name-="default-config"> element's <java-config> element. In both lists of JVM options, make sure that any existing options with values such as -Dfile.encoding, -Djava.net.preferIPv4Stack, -Dorg.apache.catalina.loader.WebappClassLoader.ENABLE_CLEAR_REFERENCES, -Duser.timezone, or -XX:MaxPermSize are replaced with the new values listed above.

For example, replace:

```
<jvm-options>-Xmx256m</jvm-options>
```

with this:

```
<jvm-options>-Xmx1024m</jvm-options>
```

Edit your domain1/config/config/server-policy.xml and append the following lines to the end of the file:

```
grant {
    permission java.security.AllPermission;
};
```

Delete, rename, or move the domain1/docroot/index.html file to another location to allow your Liferay Portal default page to be displayed.

Next, let's get your database configured.

Database Configuration

If you want to use GlassFish to manage your domain's data source, follow the instructions found in this section. If you want to use Liferay Portal to manage your data source, you can skip this section.

1. Start your domain's application server if it is not already running.

2. Go to the GlassFish console URL: http://localhost:4848

3. Under *Common Tasks,* navigate to *Resources →JDBC →JDBC Connection Pools*

Figure 18.5: In the GlassFish administration console, navigate to JDBC Connection Pools.

4. Click *New....*

5. On the first screen (Step 1 of 2), enter the name L i f e r a y P o o l for your connection pool, select the j a v a x . s q l . C o n n e c t i o n P o o l D a t a S o u r c e resource type, and se-lect your database driver vendor (e.g. MySQL). See figure 18.6.

6. Click *Next* to advance to the next step in creating your JDBC connection pool.

7. From the top of this screen (Step 2 of 2), scroll down to the *Additional Properties* sec-tion.

8. Replace or add the following properties ...

   Url: the URL of your connection pool.

   For example,

   ```
   jdbc:mysql://localhost:3306/lportal?useUnicode=true&amp;characterEncoding=UTF-8&amp; \
   emulateLocators=true
   ```

   Note, if you are using the above example, you should specify the name of your database in place of lportal. Likewise, if your database is not on the same host as GlassFish, specify your the database server's host name in place of localhost. Lastly, specify your database type in place of jdbc:mysql and use the correct port (3306 is for MySQL).

   User: the name of your database user.

   Password: your database user's password.

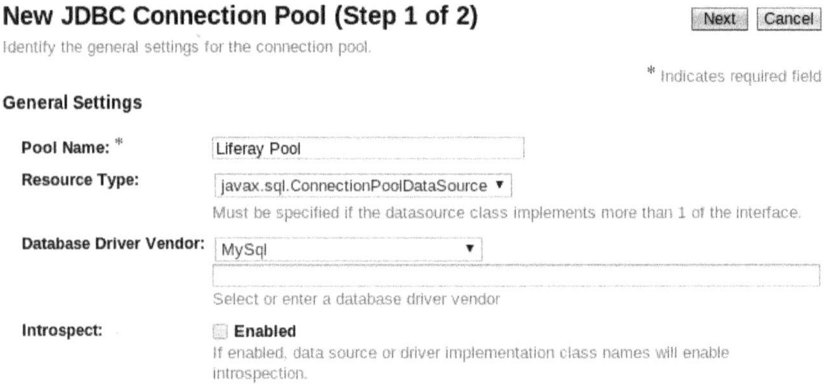

New JDBC Connection Pool (Step 1 of 2)   [Next] [Cancel]

Identify the general settings for the connection pool.

                                                            * Indicates required field

General Settings

Pool Name: *	Liferay Pool
Resource Type:	javax.sql.ConnectionPoolDataSource ▼
	Must be specified if the datasource class implements more than 1 of the interface.
Database Driver Vendor:	MySql ▼
	Select or enter a database driver vendor
Introspect:	☐ Enabled
	If enabled, data source or driver implementation class names will enable introspection.

Figure 18.6: It's easy to configure a new Glassfish JDBC Connection Pool. Just enter a pool name, select a resource type, and specify a database driver vendor.

9. Click *Finish*.

   You should now see your LiferayPool connection pool listed under *Resources → JDBC →JDBC Connection Pools*

10. Test your connection by selecting your LiferayPool connection pool and clicking *Ping*.

    If you get a message stating *Ping Succeeded*, you've succeeded in setting up a connection pool of your data source!

11. Now, you'll setup a JDBC resource to refer to the LiferayPool connection pool you just created.

12. Navigate to *Resources → JDBC → JDBC Resources* to show the current JDBC resources listed by their JNDI names.

13. Click *New....*

14. Set the JNDI name to jdbc/LiferayPool and select LiferayPool as the pool name.

15. Click *OK*.

Congratulations! You've now configured your domain's data source on GlassFish!

Mail Configuration

If you want to use GlassFish to manage your mail session, follow GlassFish's documentation on configuring a JavaMail session with a JNDI name of `mail/MailSession`. If you want to use Liferay Portal to manage your mail session, you can skip this step.

Domain Configuration - Continued

Let's tie up some loose ends with regards to Liferay being able to access your database and mail session.

1. Shutdown your domain's application server if it is currently running.

2. If you are using *Glassfish* to manage your data source, create a `portal-ext.properties` file in the *Liferay Home* folder mentioned at the beginning of this GlassFish installation section and add the following to your `portal-ext.properties` file in your *Liferay Home* to refer to your data source:

   ```
   jdbc.default.jndi.name=jdbc/LiferayPool
   ```

   Otherwise, if you are using *Liferay Portal* to manage your data source, follow the instructions in the *Deploy Liferay* section for using the setup wizard.

3. If want to use *Liferay Portal* to manage your mail session, you can configure the mail session within Liferay Portal. That is, after starting your portal as described in the *Deploy Liferay* section, go to *Control Panel →Server Administration →Mail* and enter the settings for your mail session.

   Otherwise, if you are using *GlassFish* to manage your mail session, add the following to your `portal-ext.properties` file to reference that mail session:

   ```
   mail.session.jndi.name=mail/MailSession
   ```

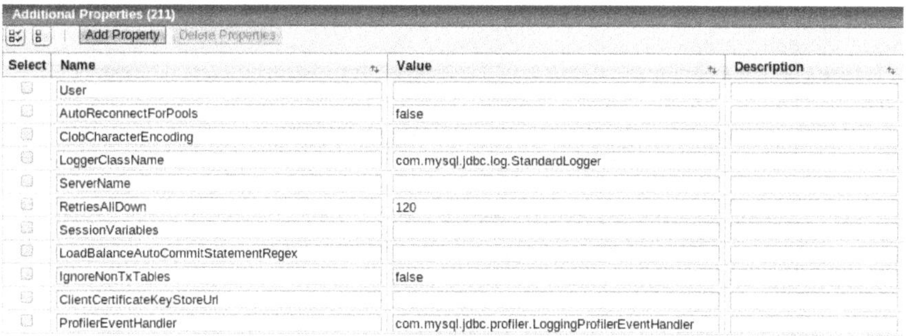
Additional Properties (211)
Add Property
Delete Properties
Select
Name
Value
Description
User
AutoReconnectForPools
false
ClobCharacterEncoding
LoggerClassName
com.mysql.jdbc.log.StandardLogger
ServerName
RetriesAllDown
120
SessionVariables
LoadBalanceAutoCommitStatementRegex
IgnoreNonTxTables
false
ClientCertificateKeyStoreUrl
ProfilerEventHandler
com.mysql.jdbc.profiler.LoggingProfilerEventHandler

Figure 18.7: GlassFish JDBC Connection Pool Properties

Liferay will now be able to communicate with your database and mail session.

PACL Configuration

To enable PACL on GlassFish, you need to make some security configurations. First, enable the security manager by editing `glassfish/domains/domain1/config/domain.xml` and make sure it contains the following configuration:

```
<java-config ...>
    ...
    <jvm-options>-Djava.security.manager</jvm-options>
    ...
</java-config>
```

Next, add the required permissions to the server policy configuration file.

```
glassfish/domains/domain1/config/server.policy
```

These include the following permissions:

```
grant {
    permission java.security.AllPermission;
};
```

Now let's go ahead and deploy Liferay.

Deploy Liferay

1. Start your domain's application server.

2. Go to the GlassFish console URL: http://localhost:4848

3. Click *Applications* in the tree on the left.

4. Click *Deploy.*

5. Under *Packaged File to Be Uploaded to the Server*, click *Choose File* and browse to the location of the Liferay Portal .war file. Enter *Context Root: /*

6. Enter *Application Name:* `liferay-portal`

7. Click *OK.*

Once you have deployed Liferay via GlassFish's administrative console, restart Glass-Fish.

Your installation of Liferay Portal on GlassFish is complete!

18.14   Installing Liferay on JBoss 7.1

Liferay Home is one folder above JBoss's install location.

1. Download and install JBoss AS 7.1.x into your preferred directory. This directory is referred to as $JBOSS_HOME throughout this section.

2. Download the latest version of the Liferay Portal .war file.

3. Download Liferay's Portal Dependencies.

Now that you have all of your installation files, you are ready to start installing and configuring Liferay on JBoss.

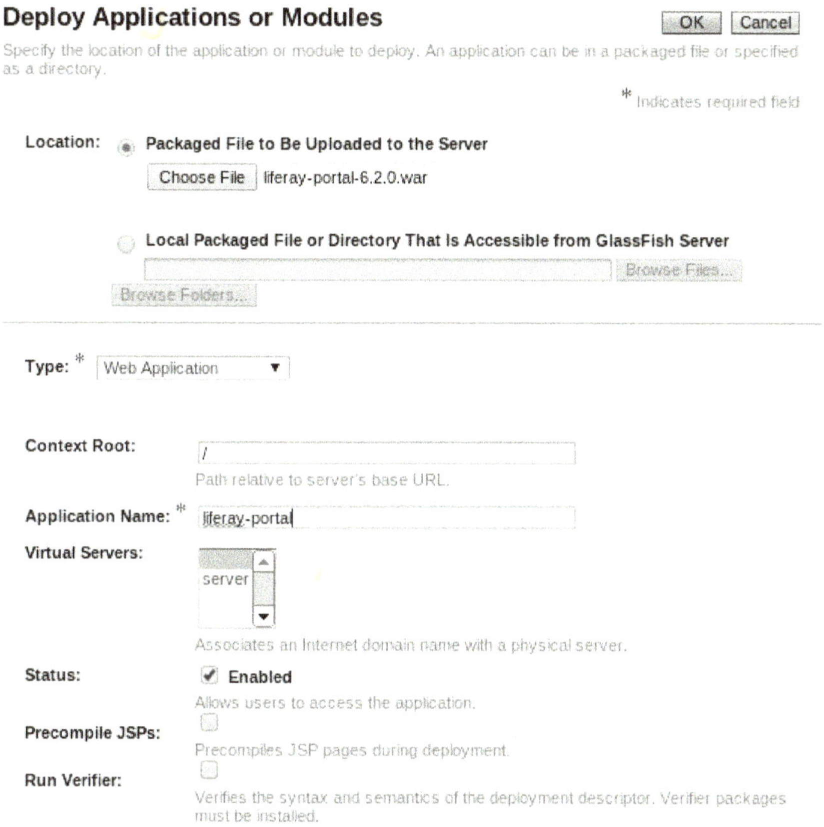

Deploy Applications or Modules   [OK] [Cancel]

Specify the location of the application or module to deploy. An application can be in a packaged file or specified as a directory.

* Indicates required field

Location: ● **Packaged File to Be Uploaded to the Server**

[Choose File] liferay-portal-6.2.0.war

○ **Local Packaged File or Directory That Is Accessible from GlassFish Server**

[   ] [Browse Files...]

[Browse Folders...]

Type: *   [Web Application   ▼]

Context Root: [/   ]
Path relative to server's base URL.

Application Name: * [liferay-portal   ]

Virtual Servers: [server   ▲]
[▼]
Associates an Internet domain name with a physical server.

Status: ☑ Enabled
Allows users to access the application.

Precompile JSPs: ☐
Precompiles JSP pages during deployment.

Run Verifier: ☐
Verifies the syntax and semantics of the deployment descriptor. Verifier packages must be installed.

Figure 18.8: GlassFish provides an administrative console which you can use to deploy Liferay.

Dependency Jars

Let's work with the dependency jar files first.

1. Create the folder $JBOSS_HOME/modules/com/liferay/portal/main. Unzip the the Liferay Portal Dependencies zip file and copy the .jar files to this folder.

2. Download your database driver .jar file and copy it into the same folder. For example, for MySQL, download the MySQL Connector/J driver[20] and put its .jar file into the $JBOSS_HOME/modules/com/liferay/portal/main folder.

3. Create the file module.xml in the $JBOSS_HOME/modules/com/liferay/portal/main folder and insert the following contents:

```
<?xml version="1.0"?>

<module xmlns="urn:jboss:module:1.0" name="com.liferay.portal">
    <resources>
        <resource-root path="mysql-connector-java-[version]-bin.jar" />
```

---

[20]http://dev.mysql.com/downloads/connector/j/

```
        <resource-root path="portal-service.jar" />
        <resource-root path="portlet.jar" />
    </resources>
    <dependencies>
        <module name="javax.api" />
        <module name="javax.mail.api" />
        <module name="javax.servlet.api" />
        <module name="javax.servlet.jsp.api" />
        <module name="javax.transaction.api" />
    </dependencies>
</module>
```

Make sure to replace [version] with the correct version of the MySQL JDBC driver. If you are using a different database, replace the MySQL jar with the driver jar for your database.

Great! You have your .jar files ready.

Running Liferay on JBoss 7.1 in Standalone Mode vs. Domain Mode

JBoss 7.1 can be launched in either *standalone* mode or *domain* mode. Domain mode allows multiple application server instances to be managed from a single control point. A collection of such application servers is known as a *domain*. For more information on standalone mode vs. domain mode, please refer to the section on this topic in the JBoss 7.1 Admin Guide. Liferay fully supports JBoss 7.1 when it runs in standalone mode but not when it runs in domain mode.

You can run Liferay on JBoss 7.1 in domain mode, but this method is not fully supported. In particular, Liferay's hot-deploy does not work, since JBoss 7.1 cannot deploy non-exploded .war files in domain mode. Instead, .war files are in the domain/data/-content directory. Deployments are only possible using the command line interface. This prevents many Liferay plugins from working as intended. For example, JSP hooks don't work on JBoss 7.1 running in domain mode, since Liferay's JSP override mechanism relies on the application server reloading customized JSP files from the exploded plugin .war file location. Other plugins, such as service or action hooks, should still work properly since they don't require JBoss to access anything (such as JSP files) from an exploded .war file on the file system.

 Note: This does not prevent Liferay from running in a clustered environment on multiple JBoss servers. You can set up a cluster of Liferay instances running on JBoss 7.1 servers running in standalone mode. Please refer to the chapter of this guide on Configuring Liferay for High Availability for information on setting up a Liferay cluster.

Configuring JBoss

Let's make some adjustments in your configuration to support using Liferay.

You can specify the JBoss server instance's configuration in the XML file $JBOSS_HOME/-standalone/configuration/standalone.xml. You must also make some modifications to your configuration and startup scripts found in the $JBOSS_HOME/bin/ folder. Lastly, you'll need to make some modifications in your $JBOSS_HOME/modules/. Let's start with the changes to standalone.xml.

Make the following modifications to standalone.xml:

1. Add the following system properties between the </extensions> and <management> tags:

```
<system-properties>
    <property name="org.apache.catalina.connector.URI_ENCODING" value="UTF-8" />
    <property name="org.apache.catalina.connector.USE_BODY_ENCODING_FOR_QUERY_STRING"
        value="true" />
</system-properties>
```

2. Add a timeout for the deployment scanner by setting `deployment-timeout="240"` as seen in the excerpt below.

```
<subsystem xmlns="urn:jboss:domain:deployment-scanner:1.1">
    <deployment-scanner deployment-timeout="240" path="deployments"
        relative-to="jboss.server.base.dir" scan-interval="5000"/>
</subsystem>
```

3. Add the following JAAS security domain to the security subsystem `<security-domains>` defined in element `<subsystem xmlns="urn:jboss:domain:security:1.1">`.

```
<security-domain name="PortalRealm">
    <authentication>
        <login-module code="com.liferay.portal.security.jaas.PortalLoginModule"
            flag="required" />
    </authentication>
</security-domain>
```

4. Disable the welcome root of the web subsystem's virtual server default host by specifying `enable-welcome-root="false"`.

```
<subsystem xmlns="urn:jboss:domain:web:1.1" default-virtual-server="default-host">
    <connector name="http" protocol="HTTP/1.1" scheme="http" socket-binding="http"/>
    <virtual-server name="default-host" enable-welcome-root="false">
        <alias name="localhost" />
        <alias name="example.com" />
    </virtual-server>
</subsystem>
```

5. Insert the following `<configuration>` element inside the web subsystem element `<subsystem xmlns="urn:jboss:domain:web:1.1" default-virtual-server="default-host" native="false">`.

```
<configuration>
    <jsp-configuration development="true" />
</configuration>
```

Now it's time for some changes to your configuration and startup scripts. Make the following modifications to your standalone domain's configuration script file `standalone.conf` (`standalone.conf.bat` on Windows) in your `$JBOSS_HOME/bin/` folder.

These modifications change the following options: - Set the file encoding - Set the user time-zone - Set the preferred protocol stack - Increase the default amount of memory available.

Make the following edits as applicable to your operating system:

On Windows, comment out the initial JAVA_OPTS assignment as demonstrated in the following line:

```
rem set "JAVA_OPTS=-Xms64M -Xmx512M -XX:MaxPermSize=256M"
```

Then add the following JAVA_OPTS assignment one line above the : JAVA_OPTS_SET line found at end of the file:

```
set "JAVA_OPTS=%JAVA_OPTS% -Dfile.encoding=UTF-8 -Djava.net.preferIPv4Stack=true
-Djava.security.manager -Djava.security.policy=$JBOSS_HOME/bin/server.policy
-Djboss.home.dir=$JBOSS_HOME -Duser.timezone=GMT -Xmx1024m -XX:MaxPermSize=256m"
```

On Unix, merge the following values into your settings for JAVA_OPTS, replacing any matching attributes with the ones found in the assignment below:

```
JAVA_OPTS="$JAVA_OPTS -Dfile.encoding=UTF-8 -Djava.net.preferIPv4Stack=true
-Djava.security.manager -Djava.security.policy=$JBOSS_HOME/bin/server.policy
-Djboss.home.dir=$JBOSS_HOME -Duser.timezone=GMT -Xmx1024m -XX:MaxPermSize=256m
```

Make sure you replace the $JBOSS_HOME references with the appropriate directory. You'll notice some Java security options. You'll finish configuring the Java security options in the *Security Configuration* section.

Lastly, navigate to the $JBOSS_HOME/modules/sun/jdk/main/module.xml file and insert the following path names inside the <paths>...</paths> element:

```
<path name="com/sun/crypto" />
<path name="com/sun/crypto/provider" />
<path name="com/sun/image/codec/jpeg" />
<path name="com/sun/org/apache/xml/internal/resolver" />
<path name="com/sun/org/apache/xml/internal/resolver/tools" />
```

The added paths resolve issues with portal deployment exceptions and image uploading problems on a Liferay Portal instance running on JBoss 7.1.x.

The prescribed script modifications are now complete for your Liferay installation on JBoss. Next you'll configure mail and the database.

Using the IBM JDK with JBoss

If you plan on using the IBM JDK with your JBoss application server, follow the instructions in this section. If you plan on using another type of JDK, you can skip this section.

Currently, there are bugs in the $JBOSS_HOME/modules/org/jboss/as/server-/main/jboss-as-<$JBOSS_VERSION>.Final.jar file regarding the IBM JVM (LPS-39705 and JBPAPP-9353), which requires additional steps to ensure a successful deployment with Liferay.

Open the $JBOSS_HOME/modules/com/liferay/portal/main/module.xml file and insert the following dependency within the <dependencies> element:

```
<module name="ibm.jdk" />
```

Next, you'll need to include a patch from Liferay's source code for one of JBoss' default .jar files. This can be done by downloading the liferay-portal repository's ZIP file by clicking *Download ZIP* on the repository's GitHub page. Once you've downloaded the Liferay source, unzip the source into a temporary folder. This location will be referred to as $LIFERAY_SOURCE.

In summary, you'll need to update the ServerDependenciesProcessor.class file in the jboss-as-[$JBOSS_VERSION].Final.jar file to specify the IBM JDK. The steps to insert the patch can be referenced below.

1. Copy the jboss-as-[$JBOSS_VERSION].Final.jar file from $JBOSS_HOME/-modules/org/jboss/as/server/main to the $LIFERAY_SOURCE/tools/ser-vers/jboss/patches/JBPAPP-9353/classes folder.

2. Navigate to the $LIFERAY_SOURCE/tools/servers/jboss/patches/JBPAPP--9353/classes directory in a command prompt and enter the following statement:

```
jar uf jboss-as-server-{[]\$JBOSS\_VERSION{]}.Final.jar \
org/jboss/as/server/deployment/module/ServerDependenciesProcessor.class
```

This command inserts the ServerDependenciesProcessor.class file into the jboss-as-[$JBOSS_VERSION].Final.jar file's org/jboss/as/server/deployment/module folder. You can reference the official documentation for updating a JAR file.[21]

3. Copy the jboss-as-[$JBOSS_VERSION].Final.jar file back to its original $JBOSS_HOME/modules/org/jboss/as/server/main folder.

Lastly, you'll need to make a few changes in your $JBOSS_HOME/modules directory.

1. Create the folder $JBOSS_HOME/modules/ibm/jdk/main. Create a new file called module.xml in that folder.

2. Insert this into the $JBOSS_HOME/modules/ibm/jdk/main/module.xml file:

```
<?xml version="1.0"?>

<module xmlns="urn:jboss:module:1.1" name="ibm.jdk">
    <dependencies>
        <system export="true">
            <paths>
                <path name="com/ibm" />
                <path name="com/ibm/crypto/provider" />
                <path name="com/ibm/jvm" />
                <path name="com/ibm/jvm/io" />
                <path name="com/ibm/jvm/util" />
                <path name="com/ibm/match" />
                <path name="com/ibm/misc" />
                <path name="com/ibm/net" />
                <path name="com/ibm/nio" />
                <path name="com/ibm/nio/ch" />
                <path name="com/ibm/security/auth" />
                <path name="com/ibm/security/bootstrap" />
                <path name="com/ibm/security/auth/module" />
                <path name="com/ibm/security/util" />
                <path name="META-INF/services" />
            </paths>
        </system>
    </dependencies>
</module>
```

Your JBoss application server is now configured to use the IBM JDK. Next, you'll learn about managing a data source with JBoss.

Database Configuration

If you want JBoss to manage your data source, follow the instructions in this section. If you want to use the built-in Liferay data source, you can skip this section.

Modify standalone.xml and add your data source and driver in the <datasources> element of your data sources subsystem.

1. First, add your data source inside the <datasources> element.

```
<datasource jndi-name="java:/jdbc/LiferayPool" pool-name="LiferayPool" enabled="true"
    jta="true" use-java-context="true" use-ccm="true">
    <connection-url>jdbc:mysql://localhost/lportal</connection-url>
    <driver>mysql</driver>
    <security>
        <user-name>root</user-name>
        <password>root</password>
    </security>
</datasource>
```

---

[21]http://docs.oracle.com/javase/tutorial/deployment/jar/update.html

Be sure to replace the database name (i.e. lportal), user, and password the appropriate values.

2. Add your driver to the `<drivers>` element also found within the `<datasources>` element.

```
<drivers>
    <driver name="mysql" module="com.liferay.portal"/>
</drivers>
```

Your final data sources subsystem should look like this:

```
<subsystem xmlns="urn:jboss:domain:datasources:1.0">
    <datasources>
        <datasource jndi-name="java:/jdbc/LiferayPool" pool-name="LiferayPool"
          enabled="true" jta="true" use-java-context="true" use-ccm="true">
            <connection-url>jdbc:mysql://localhost/lportal</connection-url>
            <driver>mysql</driver>
            <security>
                <user-name>root</user-name>
                <password>root</password>
            </security>
        </datasource>
        <drivers>
            <driver name="mysql" module="com.liferay.portal"/>
        </drivers>
    </datasources>
</subsystem>
```

Now that you've configured your data source, the mail session is next.

Mail Configuration

If you want JBoss to manage your mail session, use the following instructions. If you want to use the built-in Liferay mail session, you can skip this section.

Specify your mail subsystem in `standalone.xml` as in the following example:

```
<subsystem xmlns="urn:jboss:domain:mail:1.0">
    <mail-session jndi-name="java:/mail/MailSession" >
        <smtp-server ssl="true" outbound-socket-binding-ref="mail-smtp">
            <login name="username" password="password"/>
        </smtp-server>
        <pop3-server outbound-socket-binding-ref="mail-pop">
            <login name="username" password="password"/>
        </pop3-server>
    </mail-session>
</subsystem>
...
<socket-binding-group name="standard-sockets"
    default-interface="public"
    port-offset="${jboss.socket.binding.port-offset:0}">
...
<outbound-socket-binding name="mail-smtp">
    <remote-destination host="smtp.gmail.com" port="465"/>
</outbound-socket-binding>
    <outbound-socket-binding name="mail-pop">
        <remote-destination host="pop.gmail.com" port="110"/>
    </outbound-socket-binding>
</socket-binding-group>
```

You've got mail! Next, you'll make sure Liferay can connect using your new mail session and database.

Configuring data sources and mail sessions

Now that your data source and mail session are set up, you need to ensure Liferay Portal can access them.

1. First, navigate to the Liferay Home folder, which is one folder above JBoss's install location (i.e. $JBOSS_HOME/..).

2. If you're using *JBoss* to manage your data source, add the following configuration to your portal-ext.properties file in your *Liferay Home* to refer to your data source:

   ```
   jdbc.default.jndi.name=java:jdbc/LiferayPool
   ```

   If you're using *Liferay Portal* to manage your data source, follow the instructions for using the setup wizard.

3. If you're using *Liferay Portal* to manage your mail session, this configuration is done in Liferay Portal. That is, after starting your portal as described in the *Deploy Liferay* section, go to *Control Panel →Server Administration →Mail* and enter the settings for your mail session.

   If you're using *JBoss* to manage your mail session, add the following configuration to your portal-ext.properties file to reference that mail session:

   ```
   mail.session.jndi.name=java:mail/MailSession
   ```

Before you deploy Liferay Portal on your JBoss app server, you should enable and configure Java security so you can use Liferay's plugin security manager with your downloaded Liferay applications.

Security Configuration

When you're ready to begin using other people's apps from Marketplace, you'll want to protect your portal and your JBoss server from security threats. To do so, you can enable Java Security on your JBoss server and specify a security policy to grant your portal access to your server.

Remember, we set the -Djava.security.manager and -Djava.security.policy Java options in the standalone.conf.bat file earlier in the *Configuring JBoss* section. The -Djava.security.manager Java option enables security on JBoss. Likewise, the -Djava.security.policy Java option lists the permissions for your server's Java security policy. If you have not set these options, you'll need to do so before using Java security.

This configuration opens up all permissions. You can tune the permissions in your policy later. Create the $JBOSS_HOME/bin/server.policy file and add the following contents:

```
grant {
    permission java.security.AllPermission;
};
```

For extensive information on Java SE Security Architecture, see its specification documents.[22] Also, see section *Understanding Plugin Security Management*[23] on the Developer Network to learn how to configure Liferay plugin access to resources.

---

[22]http://docs.oracle.com/javase/7/docs/technotes/guides/security/spec/security-spec.doc.html

[23]https://dev.liferay.com/develop/tutorials/-/knowledge_base/6-2/plugin-security-and-pacl

JSF Configuration

If you plan on using JSF applications in your application server, follow the instructions below. In this section, you'll learn how to upgrade Mojarra and Weld so your app server's versions are identical to the versions used by Liferay Faces.

Upgrading Mojarra

Some versions of JBoss 7.1.x are not bundled with the correct Mojarra version necessary to use Liferay Faces. For example, JBoss AS 7.1.1 comes with Mojarra 2.1.7 in the global classpath. Since Liferay Faces uses Mojarra 2.1.21, you'll need to download a newer version of the jsf-api.jar and jsf-impl.jar artifacts.

1. Download jsf-api-2.1.21.jar and copy it to the following location:

   ```
   $JBOSS_HOME/modules/javax/faces/api/main/jsf-api-2.1.21.jar
   ```

2. Open the $JBOSS_HOME/modules/javax/faces/api/main/module.xml file and comment out the reference to the version of the JAR that comes with the server. For example:

   ```
   <!-- <resource-root path="jboss-jsf-api_2.1_spec-2.0.1.Final.jar"/> -->
   ```

3. Add a reference to the new JAR in the same module.xml file:

   ```
   <resource-root path="jsf-api-2.1.21.jar"/>
   ```

4. Add the following module to the <dependencies> section:

   ```
   <dependencies>
       ...
       <module name="com.sun.jsf-impl"/>
   </dependencies>
   ```

5. Download jsf-impl-2.1.21.jar and copy it to the following location:

   ```
   $JBOSS_HOME/modules/com/sun/jsf-impl/main/jsf-impl-2.1.21.jar
   ```

6. Open the $JBOSS_HOME/modules/com/sun/jsf-impl/main/module.xml file and comment out the reference to the version of the JAR that comes with the server. For example:

   ```
   <!-- <resource-root path="jsf-impl-2.1.7-jbossorg-2.jar"/> -->
   ```

7. Add a reference to the new JAR in the same module.xml file:

   ```
   <resource-root path="jsf-impl-2.1.21.jar"/>
   ```

Congratulations! You've officially upgraded Mojarra! If you'd like to verify that you're using the correct version of Mojarra at runtime, download the following demo portlet and add it to a portal page. You should see a bulleted list of version info at the bottom of the portlet.

Next you'll learn how to upgrade Weld.

Upgrading Weld

Some versions of JBoss 7.1.x are not bundled with the correct Weld version necessary to use Liferay Faces. For example, JBoss AS 7.1.1 comes with Weld 1.1.5 in the global class path. Since Liferay Faces uses Weld 1.1.10, you'll need to download a newer version of the weld-core.jar artifact.

1. Download weld-core-1.1.10.Final.jar and copy it to the following location:

   ```
   $JBOSS_HOME/modules/org/jboss/weld/core/main/weld-core-1.1.10.Final.jar
   ```

2. Open the $JBOSS_HOME/modules/org/jboss/weld/core/main/module.xml file and comment out the reference to the version of the JAR that comes with the server. For example:

   ```
   <!-- <resource-root path="weld-core-1.1.5.AS71.Final.jar"/> -->
   ```

3. Add a reference to the new JAR in the same module.xml file:

   ```
   <resource-root path="weld-core-1.1.10.Final.jar"/>
   ```

Now you're ready to deploy Liferay Portal.

Deploy Liferay

1. If the folder $JBOSS_HOME/standalone/deployments/ROOT.war already exists in your JBoss installation, delete all of its subfolders and files. Otherwise, create a new folder $JBOSS_HOME/standalone/deployments/ROOT.war.

2. Unzip the Liferay .war file into the ROOT.war folder.

3. In the ROOT.war file, open the WEB-INF/jboss-deployment-structure.xml file. In this file, replace the <module name="com.liferay.portal" /> dependency with the following configuration:

   ```
   <module meta-inf="export" name="com.liferay.portal">
       <imports>
           <include path="META-INF" />
       </imports>
   </module>
   ```

   This allows OSGi plugins like Audience Targeting to work properly, by exposing the Portal API through the OSGi container.

4. In the same jboss-deployment-structure.xml file, find the <jboss-deployment-structure> tag and update the 1.0 number within the xmlns attribute to 1.1.

5. To trigger deployment of ROOT.war, create an empty file named ROOT.war.dodeploy in your $JBOSS_HOME/standalone/deployments/ folder. On startup, JBoss detects the presence of this file and deploys it as a web application.

6. Remove eclipselink.jar from $JBOSS_HOME/standalone/deployments/ROOT.war/WEB-INF/lib to insure the Hibernate persistence provider is used instead of the one provided in the eclipselink.jar.

   Now it's time to start Liferay Portal on JBoss!

7. Start the JBoss application server. Now you are truly *the boss* when it comes to deploying Liferay Portal on JBoss!

18.15   Installing Liferay on Tomcat 7

Liferay Home is one folder above Tomcat's install location.

For this section, we will refer to your Tomcat server's installation location as $TOM-CAT_HOME. If you do not already have an existing Tomcat server, we recommend you download a Liferay/Tomcat bundle.[24] If you have an existing Tomcat server or would like to install Liferay on Tomcat manually, please follow the steps below.

Before you begin, make sure you have downloaded the latest Liferay .war file and Liferay Portal dependencies.[25] The Liferay files have the following naming conventions:

```
liferay-portal-6.2.x-[date].war
liferay-portal-dependencies-6.2.x-[date].zip
```

Next, let's get started by addressing Liferay's library dependencies.

Dependency Jars

Liferay Portal depends on several JAR files found in the Liferay Dependencies Archive. In addition to these, you need the proper driver for your database. You can get the necessary dependencies by following these steps:

1. Create a folder named ext in $TOMCAT_HOME/lib.

2. Unzip the Liferay Dependencies and copy the .jar files to $TOMCAT_HOME/lib/ext.

3. Download the support-tomcat.jar file.[26] Copy it into your $TOMCAT_HOME/-lib/ext directory. This JAR provides classes that extend some Tomcat-specific classes in order to support Liferay's runtime.

4. Next, you need to download a few third party .jar files that are included as part of the Liferay source distribution, but are not automatically included with Tomcat. Place these .jar files into $TOMCAT_HOME/lib/ext:

   - jta.jar: This .jar manages transactions.[27]
   - mail.jar: This .jar implements mail.[28]
   - persistence.jar: The Java Persistence API.[29]

5. Make sure your database's JDBC driver is accessible by Tomcat. In the case of My-SQL, use mysql-connector-java-{$version}-bin.jar. Download the latest MySQL JDBC driver.[30] Extract the JAR file and copy it to $TOMCAT_HOME/lib/ext.

6. There are a few other JARs that come with a typical Liferay bundle that you might want to download and place in your $TOMCAT_HOME/lib/ext folder. They include these:

   - activation.jar[31]
   - ccpp.jar[32]

---

[24]http://www.liferay.com/downloads/liferay-portal/available-releases
[25]http://www.liferay.com/downloads/liferay-portal/additional-files
[26]http://search.maven.org/#artifactdetails|com.liferay.portal|support-tomcat|6.2.1|jar
[27]http://www.oracle.com/technetwork/java/javaee/jta/index.html
[28]http://www.oracle.com/technetwork/java/index-138643.html
[29]http://www.oracle.com/technetwork/java/javaee/tech/persistence-jsp-140049.html
[30]http://dev.mysql.com/downloads/connector/j/
[31]http://www.oracle.com/technetwork/java/jaf11-139815.html
[32]http://mvnrepository.com/artifact/javax.ccpp/ccpp/1.0

- jms.jar[33]
- jutf7.jar[34]
- junit.jar[35]

You can download each third party .jar listed above from the provided websites, then place them into your $TOMCAT_HOME/lib/ext directory. However, they're also available in the Liferay source code, so if you have access to the Liferay source or would like to download it for this purpose, feel free to copy the .jar files from there. Assuming your local Liferay source directory is $LIFERAY_SOURCE, you can get all the third party .jar files listed above from $LIFERAY_SOURCE/lib/development, with the exception of ccpp.jar, which is found in $LIFERAY_SOURCE/-lib/portal.

Now that you have the necessary libraries in place, we'll move on to configuring your domain.

Tomcat Configuration

There are several configuration steps you need to complete before Tomcat can run Liferay. Let's get started.

1. First, you'll need to set the CATALINA_OPTS environment variable. Create a setenv.bat (Windows) or setenv.sh file (Unix, Linux, Mac OS) in the $TOMCAT_-HOME/bin directory. Populate it with following contents:

   - setenv.bat:

     ```
     if exist "%CATALINA_HOME%/jre@java.version@/win" (
         if not "%JAVA_HOME%" == "" (
             set JAVA_HOME=
         )

         set "JRE_HOME=%CATALINA_HOME%/jre@java.version@/win"
     )

     set "CATALINA_OPTS=%CATALINA_OPTS% -Dfile.encoding=UTF8
     -Djava.net.preferIPv4Stack=true
     -Dorg.apache.catalina.loader.WebappClassLoader.ENABLE_CLEAR_REFERENCES=false
     -Duser.timezone=GMT -Xmx1024m -XX:MaxPermSize=256m"
     ```

   - setenv.sh:

     ```
     CATALINA_OPTS="$CATALINA_OPTS -Dfile.encoding=UTF8
     -Dorg.apache.catalina.loader.WebappClassLoader.ENABLE_CLEAR_REFERENCES=false
     -Duser.timezone=GMT -Xmx1024m -XX:MaxPermSize=256m"
     ```

   This sets the character encoding to UTF-8, sets the time zone to Greenwich Mean Time, and allocates memory to the Java Virtual Machine.

2. Next, create a context for Liferay. Create a ROOT.xml file in $TOMCAT_HOME/-conf/Catalina/localhost. Populate it with the following contents to set up a portal web application:

   ```
   <Context path="" crossContext="true">

       <!-- JAAS -->
   \index{JAAS}

       <!--<Realm
   ```

---

[33]http://www.oracle.com/technetwork/java/docs-136352.html
[34]http://sourceforge.net/projects/jutf7/
[35]http://sourceforge.net/projects/junit/

```
        classNjame="org.apache.catalina.realm.JAASRealm"
        appName="PortalRealm"
        userClassNames="com.liferay.portal.kernel.security.jaas.PortalPrincipal"
        roleClassNames="com.liferay.portal.kernel.security.jaas.PortalRole"
/>-->

<!--
Uncomment the following to disable persistent sessions across reboots.
-->

<!--<Manager pathname="" />-->

<!--
Uncomment the following to not use sessions. See the property
"session.disabled" in portal.properties.
-->
\index{portal.properties}

    <!--<Manager className="com.liferay.support.tomcat.session.SessionLessManagerBase" />-->
</Context>
        Setting 'crossContext="true"' allows multiple web apps to use the same class
```

loader. In the configuration above you will also find commented instructions and
tags for configuring a JAAS realm, disabling persistent sessions and disabling sessions in general.

3. Next, make sure the libraries you added to $TOMCAT_HOME/lib/ext are loaded
when you start the server. Open $TOMCAT_HOME/conf/catalina.properties
and replace the line:

```
common.loader=${catalina.base}/lib,${catalina.base}/lib/*.jar,${catalina.home}/lib, \
${catalina.home}/lib/*.jar
```

with:

```
common.loader=${catalina.base}/lib,${catalina.base}/lib/*.jar,${catalina.home}/lib, \
${catalina.home}/lib/*.jar,${catalina.home}/lib/ext,${catalina.home}/lib/ext/*.jar
```

This allows Catalina to access the dependency jars you extracted to $TOMCAT_HOME/-
lib/ext.

4. We also need to ensure consistent use of UTF-8 URI Encoding. Edit $TOMCAT_-
HOME/conf/server.xml and add the attribute URIEncoding="UTF-8" where
you see redirectPort=8443, in the definition of your connectors (HTTP and AJP).
For example:

```
<Connector port="8080"
    protocol="HTTP/1.1"
    connectionTimeout="20000"
    redirectPort="8443"
    URIEncoding="UTF-8" />
```

5. Lastly, if you see a support-catalina.jar in your $TOMCAT_HOME/webapps di-
rectory, delete it.

Now Tomcat is configured to run Liferay! If you want to use Liferay to manage your
database and mail session (and we recommend you do), you can skip the next sections and
move to the section titled *Enabling PACL*. Next we'll look at configuring your database with
Tomcat.

Database Configuration

If you want Tomcat to manage your data source, use the following procedure. If you want to use Liferay's built-in data source, you can skip this section.

1. Make sure your database server is installed and working. If it's installed on a different machine, make sure it's accessible from the machine with Liferay.

2. Add your data source as a resource in the context of your web application specified in $TOMCAT_HOME/conf/Catalina/localhost/ROOT.xml:

```
<Context...>
    <Resource
        name="jdbc/LiferayPool"
        auth="Container"
        type="javax.sql.DataSource"
        driverClassName="com.mysql.jdbc.Driver"
        url="jdbc:mysql://localhost/lportal?useUnicode=true&amp;characterEncoding=UTF-8"
        username="root"
        password="root"
        maxActive="100"
        maxIdle="30"
        maxWait="10000"
    />
</Context>
```

Note: The above resource definition assumes your database name is *lportal* and your MySQL username and password are both *root*. You'll have to update these values with your own database name and credentials.

Your Tomcat managed data source is now configured. Next is your mail session.

Mail Configuration

If you want to manage your mail session with Tomcat, use the following instructions. If you want to use the built-in Liferay mail session, you can skip this section.

Create a mail session bound to mail/MailSession. Edit $TOMCAT_HOME/conf/-Catalina/localhost/ROOT.xml and configure a mail session. Be sure to replace the example mail session values with your own.

```
<Context...>
    <Resource
        name="mail/MailSession"
        auth="Container"
        type="javax.mail.Session"
        mail.pop3.host="pop.gmail.com"
        mail.pop3.port="110"
        mail.smtp.host="smtp.gmail.com"
        mail.smtp.port="465"
        mail.smtp.user="user"
        mail.smtp.password="password"
        mail.smtp.auth="true"
        mail.smtp.starttls.enable="true"
        mail.smtp.socketFactory.class="javax.net.ssl.SSLSocketFactory"
        mail.imap.host="imap.gmail.com"
        mail.imap.port="993"
        mail.transport.protocol="smtp"
        mail.store.protocol="imap"
    />
</Context>
```

Your mail session is configured. Next, you'll make sure Liferay can access your mail session and database.

Configuring your database and mail session

In this section you'll specify appropriate properties for connecting to your database and mail session.

1. If you are using *Tomcat* to manage your data source, add the following configuration to your portal-ext.properties file in your *Liferay Home* to refer to your data source:

```
jdbc.default.jndi.name=jdbc/LiferayPool
```

Otherwise, if you are using *Liferay Portal* to manage your data source, follow the instructions for using the setup wizard.

2. If want to use *Liferay Portal* to manage your mail session, you can configure the mail session in Liferay Portal. That is, after starting your portal as described in the *Deploy Liferay* section, go to *Control Panel →Server Administration →Mail* and enter the settings for your mail session.

Otherwise, if you are using *Tomcat* to manage your mail session, add the following configuration to your portal-ext.properties file to reference that mail session:

```
mail.session.jndi.name=mail/MailSession
```

It's just that easy! Before you deploy Liferay Portal, you should configure Portal Access Control Language (PACL) with Liferay on Tomcat.

Enabling PACL

To enable PACL, you need to enable the security manager and add some required permissions to the server policy configuration file. This entails editing two files in $TOMCAT_HOME you've already edited:

- In $TOMCAT_HOME/bin/setenv.sh (if on Linux, Unix, or Mac OS) or setenv.bat (if on Windows) enable the security manager by inserting the following code into the CATALINA_OPTS variable (inside the quotation marks):

```
-Djava.security.manager -Djava.security.policy=\$CATALINA\_BASE/conf/catalina.policy
```

- In $TOMCAT_HOME/conf/catalina.policy, add the required permissions:

```
grant {
    permission java.security.AllPermission;
};
```

To enable the security manager on Tomcat, the server must be started with the -security command line options. Shutdown your Tomcat instance and restart it with the following command:

```
./startup.sh -security
```

Tomcat reports the message Using Security Manager to your terminal. Now you have PACL enabled and configured for your portal.

Adding Mojarra

If you'd like to use JSF applications in your Tomcat application server, you'll need to add Mojarra. If you do not plan on using JSF applications in your application server, you can skip this section.

The typical binary ZIP version of Tomcat does not contain any JSF runtime JARs like Mojarra or MyFaces. This is because Tomcat is not a Java EE Application Server like Oracle GlassFish, Oracle WebLogic, JBoss AS, or IBM WebSphere. Also, Tomcat is not a Java EE Web Profile Server like Apache TomEE or Caucho Resin.

There are two ways to approach using Mojarra with Tomcat: upgrading Tomcat's context classpath or upgrading Tomcat's global classpath. Both methods require adding/editing two JARs, which can be downloaded below:

- jsf-api
- jsf-impl

The typical approach for using Mojarra with Tomcat is to include jsf-api.jar and jsf-impl.jar in the WEB-INF/lib folder in each JSF project. You can do this by specifying the jsf-api and jsf-impl artifacts without a scope, or with the scope set as compile (the default) in each JSF project:

```
<dependency>
    <groupId>com.sun.faces</groupId>
    <artifactId>jsf-api</artifactId>
    <version>2.1.21</version>
    <scope>compile</scope>
</dependency>
<dependency>
    <groupId>com.sun.faces</groupId>
    <artifactId>jsf-impl</artifactId>
    <version>2.1.21</version>
    <scope>compile</scope>
</dependency>
```

Although it is possible to install Mojarra in the Tomcat global classpath, it will not work properly without some small modifications to the jsf-impl.jar dependency. The problem stems from the fact that the Mojarra ConfigureListener class is automatically registered for all contexts under tomcat/webapps because it is specified as a <listener> in the META-INF/jsf-jsf_core.tld descriptor inside the jsf-impl.jar dependency. Additionally, the META-INF/services/javax.faces.ServletContainerInitializer will cause the FacesInitializer class to auto-register the ConfigureListener as well. Consequently, every request issued in all contexts invokes the Mojarra ConfigureListener. This can be a potential performance problem in a webapp environment and causes incompatibilities with a portlet environment. Therefore, it is necessary to disable automatic registration of the Mojarra ConfigureListener by modifying the contents of the jsf-impl.jar dependency.

To upgrade Tomcat's global classpath, follow the steps below:

1. Copy jsf-api.jar and jsf-impl.jar to the tomcat/lib folder.

2. Open a terminal window and navigate to the tomcat/lib folder:

   ```
   cd tomcat/lib
   ```

3. Create a temporary folder named jsf-impl and navigate into it:

   ```
   mkdir jsf-impl
   cd jsf-impl
   ```

4. Extract the Mojarra jsf-impl.jar dependency into the temporary folder:

```
jar xf ../jsf-impl-2.1.21.jar
```

5. Open the META-INF/jsf_core.tld file and remove the following lines:

```
<listener>
    <listener-class>com.sun.faces.config.ConfigureListener</listener-class>
</listener>
```

6. Remove the Mojarra servlet container initializer:

```
rm META-INF/services/javax.servlet.ServletContainerInitializer
```

7. Overwrite the Mojarra jsf-impl.jar dependency by creating a new archive:

```
jar cf ../jsf-impl-2.1.21.jar META-INF/ com/
```

8. Remove the temporary folder:

```
cd ../
rm -rf jsf-impl/
```

9. Follow only *one* of the following sub-steps below, depending on preference.

   9.1 Specify the liferay-faces-init.jar dependency in each JSF project in order for the Mojarra ConfigureListener to be automatically started by Tomcat:

```
<dependency>
    <groupId>com.liferay.faces</groupId>
    <artifactId>liferay-faces-init</artifactId>
    <version>3.1.3-ga4</version>
</dependency>
```

   9.2 Specify the Mojarra ConfigureListener as a listener in the WEB-INF/web.xml descriptor in each JSF project:

```
<listener>
    <listener-class>com.sun.faces.config.ConfigureListener</listener-class>
</listener>
```

10. Specify the jsf-api and jsf-impl dependencies as provided in each JSF project:

```
<dependency>
    <groupId>com.sun.faces</groupId>
    <artifactId>jsf-api</artifactId>
    <version>2.1.21</version>
    <scope>provided</scope>
</dependency>
<dependency>
    <groupId>com.sun.faces</groupId>
    <artifactId>jsf-impl</artifactId>
    <version>2.1.21</version>
    <scope>provided</scope>
</dependency>
```

You've officially added Mojarra to your application server. Now you can deploy Liferay.

Deploy Liferay

It's time to deploy Liferay as an exploded web archive within your $TOMCAT_HOME/web-apps folder.

1. If you are manually installing Liferay on a clean Tomcat server, delete the contents of the $TOMCAT_HOME/webapps/ROOT directory. This removes the default Tomcat home page. Extract the Liferay .war file to $TOMCAT_HOME/webapps/ROOT.

Now its time to launch Liferay Portal on Tomcat!

3. Start Tomcat by executing $TOMCAT_HOME/bin/startup.bat or $TOMCAT_HOME-/bin/startup.sh.

Congratulations on successfully installing and deploying Liferay on Tomcat!

18.16 Installing Liferay on Oracle WebLogic 12c (12.1.2 and higher)

In this section, you'll learn how to install Liferay on Oracle WebLogic 12c. Since you're using Oracle WebLogic, you may wonder if Liferay supports XA transactions. Liferay doesn't require XA transactions, but it supports XA. Let's get acquainted with how Liferay fits in with your current WebLogic domain.

Liferay by default defines *Liferay Home* as one folder above the domain to which you will be installing Liferay. For example, if your domain location is /Oracle/Middleware/user_projects/domains/base_domain, then your Liferay Home is /Oracle/Middleware/user_projects/domains.

For this section, the variable $WEBLOGIC_HOME refers to your WebLogic server's installation /Oracle/Middleware.

Before you begin, make sure you have downloaded the latest Liferay .war file and Liferay Portal dependencies.[36] The Liferay .war file is called liferay-portal-[version].war and the dependencies file is called liferay-portal-dependencies-[version].zip.

These instructions assume you have already configured a domain and server and that you have access to the WebLogic console.

If you still have the mainWebApp module installed, remove it first.

Let's get started by installing the .jar files Liferay needs.

Dependency Jars

Liferay needs the driver .jar file applicable for your database, as well as the .jar files contained in the Liferay Dependencies Archive. They should be on your domain's global classpath.

1. Navigate to the folder that corresponds to the domain where you'll install Liferay. Inside this folder is a lib folder. Unzip the Liferay Dependencies Archive and copy the dependency .jar files to the lib folder.

2. If WebLogic does not already have access to the JDBC driver for your database, copy the driver to your domain's lib folder as well.

So far so good. Your .jar files are in place and ready for Liferay.

Let's proceed with configuring WebLogic.

---

[36]http://www.liferay.com/downloads/liferay-portal/additional-files

Configuring WebLogic

You need to make the following adjustments in your configuration to support Liferay:

- Set WebLogic Server's memory arguments.
- Set the maximum size for Java's permanent generation space.
- Set the file encoding.
- Enable Lucene support.
- Enable AspectJ support.

You can set WebLogic Server's memory arguments in your setDomainEnv . [cmd|sh] environment script file found in your domain's bin folder. For the Sun JVM, set the WLS memory arguments for 64 bit and 32 bit architectures to -Xms256m -Xmx1024m at a minimum. For all other JVMs, set the 64 bit and 32 bit WLS memory arguments to -Xms512m -Xmx512m respectively.

Set the permanent generation space for 64 bit and 32 bit architectures to -XX:Perm-Size=256m.

Lastly, make sure to specify UTF-8 for Java's file encoding, by including -Dfile.en-coding=UTF8 as a Java property.

If you're on Windows, for example, you'd edit your setDomainEnv . cmd file and find the call to the commEnv . cmd script. After this call, you'd update your memory arguments and permanent generation space settings to be like the following code:

```
...
if "%JAVA_VENDOR"=="Sun" (
    set WLS_MEM_ARGS_64BIT=-Xms256m -Xmx1024m
    set WLS_MEM_ARGS_32BIT=-Xms256m -Xmx1024m
) else (
    set WLS_MEM_ARGS_64BIT=-Xms512m -Xmx512m
    set WLS_MEM_ARGS_32BIT=-Xms512m -Xmx512m
)
...
set MEM_PERM_SIZE_64BIT=-XX:PermSize=256m
set MEM_PERM_SIZE_32BIT=-XX:PermSize=256m
```

Later in the setDomainEnv . cmd file's clustering support section, you'd set the UTF-8 file encoding by appending -Dfile.encoding=UTF8 to the front of the list of Java property values, as done in the following line of code:

```
set JAVA_PROPERTIES=-Dfile.encoding=utf8 %JAVA_PROPERTIES% %CLUSTER_PROPERTIES%
```

Next, you need to specify some local environment settings to support Liferay's memory requirements, its use of the Apache Lucene search engine library, and its use of Aspect Oriented Programming (AOP) with AspectJ.

Open the startWebLogic . [cmd|sh] file from within your domain's folder—NOT the one in your server's bin folder. If you're on Windows, you'd add directives similar to those listed below, after the SETLOCAL command:

```
set "USER_MEM_ARGS=-Xmx1024m -XX:PermSize=512m"
set "MW_HOME=D:\Oracle\Middleware\wlserver_12.1"
set "JAVA_OPTIONS=%JAVA_OPTIONS% -da:org.apache.lucene... -da:org.aspectj..."
```

Make sure to set your MW_HOME value to your WebLogic server's location. On Linux, you'd make similar changes replacing %JAVA_OPTIONS% with $JAVA_OPTIONS.

Next, if you want to configure your database and/or mail session within WebLogic, start your WebLogic server.

Database Configuration

If you want WebLogic to manage your data source, use the following procedure. If you want to use Liferay's built-in data source, you can skip this section.

1. Select *Services →Data Sources*. Click *New →Generic Data Source*.

2. Give your data source a name, such as *Liferay Data Source*. The JNDI name should be jdbc/LiferayPool.

3. Choose the type of database and click *Next*.

4. Click *Next* three times. You should be on the *Connection Properties* screen. Enter the database name, the host name, the port, the database user name, and the password. WebLogic uses this information to construct the appropriate JDBC URL to connect to your database. Click *Next*.

5. WebLogic prompts you to confirm the information you've specified for your data source.

   Depending on the database you are using, you may need to specify additional parameters. If you need to access previous wizard pages to modify information, click *Back* to revisit those pages.

   When you're done specifying your configuration, click *Next*.

6. Click *Test Configuration* to make sure WebLogic can connect to your database successfully. When it does, click *Finish*.

7. You will be back to the list of data sources. Notice your new data source has no value in the *Target* column. Click on your data source to edit it.

8. Click the *Targets* tab and check off the server instance(s) to which you wish to deploy your data source. Then click *Save*.

Next, you'll configure a mail session in WebLogic.

Mail Configuration

If you want WebLogic to manage your mail sessions, use the following procedure. If you want to use Liferay's built-in mail sessions, you can skip this section.

1. Select *Mail Sessions* and create a new mail session which points to your mail server.

2. Give it the name *Liferay Mail* and give it the JNDI name of mail/MailSession and click *Next*.

3. Choose your server and then click *Finish*.

Now make sure Liferay can access this mail session.

Domain Configuration - Continued

Let's revisit domain configuration to make sure the app server can access your data source and mail session from Liferay Portal.

Create a portal-ext.properties file in your Liferay Home folder.

If you are using *WebLogic* to manage your data source, add the following configuration to your portal-ext.properties file to refer to your data source:

```
jdbc.default.jndi.name=jdbc/LiferayPool
```

If you are using *Liferay Portal* to manage your data source, follow the instructions in the *Deploy Liferay* section for using the setup wizard.

If want to use *Liferay Portal* to manage your mail session, you can configure the mail session in the Control Panel. After starting your portal as described in the *Deploy Liferay* section, go to *Control Panel →Server Administration →Mail* and enter the settings for your mail session.

If you are using *WebLogic* to manage your mail session, add the following configuration to your portal-ext.properties file to reference that mail session:

```
mail.session.jndi.name=mail/MailSession
```

Before we deploy Liferay, you should enable and configure Java Security so that you can use Liferay's plugin security manager with the Liferay apps you download and install.

Security Configuration

When you are ready to start using apps from Marketplace, you'll want to protect your portal and your WebLogic server from security threats. To do so, you must enable Java Security on your WebLogic server and specify a security policy to grant Liferay Portal access to your server.

First, you'll grant Liferay access to your server. This configuration opens all permissions— you can fine-tune your policy's permissions later. Create a policy file named weblogic.policy in your $WEBLOGIC_HOME/wlserver/server/lib folder and add the following contents:

```
grant {
    permission java.security.AllPermission;
};
```

To enable security on your WebLogic server and direct the server to your policy file, open the setDomainEnv.[cmd|sh] file in your domain's folder. Then set the -Djava.security.manager Java option and set the property -Djava.security.policy== to the location of your weblogic.policy file. You can specify both settings on the same line like this:

```
-Djava.security.manager -Djava.security.policy==$WEBLOGIC_HOME/wlserver/ser\
ver/lib
```

The double equals sign tells the app server to use this policy file on top of any existing security policies.

For extensive information on Java SE Security Architecture see its specification documents.[37] Also, see *Plugin Security and Pacl*[38] to learn how to configure Liferay plugin access to resources.

Next you'll learn how to configure your WebLogic application server for JSF applications.

JSF Configuration

If you'd like to deploy JSF applications on your WebLogic application server, you'll need to complete a few extra steps in your configuration process. If you do not plan on using JSF applications in your application server, you can skip this section. This section assumes you're using JSF 2.1 portlets.

Complete the first section to ensure JSF applications deploy successfully to your WebLogic application server.

---

[37]http://docs.oracle.com/javase/7/docs/technotes/guides/security/spec/security-spec.doc.html

[38]https://dev.liferay.com/develop/tutorials/-/knowledge_base/6-2/plugin-security-and-pacl

Configuration for Deploying JSF Portlets

1. To avoid a ViewExpiredException with Ajax, disable the Liferay Portal ETag-
   Filter by adding the following property in the portal-ext.properties file.

   ```
   com.liferay.portal.servlet.filters.etag.ETagFilter=false
   ```

   For more information on this exception, refer to FACES-1591.

2. You'll need to adjust your memory settings for your environment variables. For
   your memory settings to be permanently set, they need to be hard-coded in the
   startWebLogic.sh script. Just above the definition of your home domain, add
   the following lines:

   ```
   export MW_HOME=$HOME/Oracle/Middleware
   export USER_MEM_ARGS="-Xms512m -Xmx1024m -XX:CompileThreshold=8000 -XX:PermSize=128m \
   -XX:MaxPermSize=256m"
   ```

   Note that if you have many portlet WAR modules, you may need to increase memory. For example, the following lines reserves double the amount of memory:

   ```
   export MW_HOME=$HOME/Oracle/Middleware
   export USER_MEM_ARGS="-Xms1024m -Xmx2048m -XX:CompileThreshold=8000 -XX:PermSize=256m \
   -XX:MaxPermSize=512m"
   ```

3. If you're running the JSR 329 Portlet Bridge TCK, you'll need to include the trini-
   dad-api.jar dependency in the global classpath (in the lib folder).

4. In order for JSF 2.1 portlets to deploy correctly in WebLogic, the WEB-INF/weblo-
   gic.xml descriptor must be configured to fine-tune how class loading takes place.
   For a working example, please refer to the weblogic.xml descriptor from a demo JSF
   portlet.

5. Due to a deficiency in the XML parser that ships with WebLogic, it is necessary to
   include a custom Apache Xerces parser as a dependency. In order to include it in
   the proper position in the WebLogic classpath, the Xerces JARs are included in the
   Mojarra Shared Library. Therefore, it is necessary to add Xerces as a dependency in
   the portlet's WEB-INF/lib folder. For example:

   ```
   <dependencies>
       <dependency>
           <groupId>xerces</groupId>
           <artifactId>xercesImpl</artifactId>
           <version>2.11.0</version>
       </dependency>
   </dependencies>
   ```

6. If using ICEfaces, PrimeFaces, or RichFaces, all JARs related to these projects must
   exist in WEB-INF/lib.

Next, you'll need to upgrade Mojarra for your WebLogic application server.

Upgrading Mojarra

Liferay Faces requires JSF 2.1.21. However, the version of Mojarra that comes with WebLogic 12c is version 2.1.20. Therefore, it is necessary to upgrade Mojarra in WebLogic by
creating a new Shared Library WAR with the updated dependencies.

1. Make sure your MW_HOME environment variable is defined (completed in step 2 of
   the previous section).

2. Build the patched version of Mojarra:

   ```
   cd liferay-faces/support
   mvn -P weblogic clean install
   ```

3. Copy the patched version of Mojarra over the version that was shipped out-of-the-
   box:

   ```
   cp $HOME/.m2/repository/com/oracle/weblogic/glassfish.jsf_1.0.0.0_2-1-21/12.1.2-0-0/ \
   glassfish.jsf_1.0.0.0_2-1-21-12.1.2-0-0.jar $MW_HOME/wlserver/modules/ \
   glassfish.jsf_1.0.0.0_2-1-20.jar
   ```

   Since the Mojarra API and Implementation JARs are present in the global classpath,
   jsf-api.jar and jsf-impl.jar must not be included in WEB-INF/lib.

Now it's the moment you've been waiting for: Liferay deployment!

Deploy Liferay

1. Start your WebLogic server if it's not already started.

2. Go to *Deployments* and select the Liferay .war file from the file system, or click the
   Upload Your File(s) link to upload it and then click *Next*.

3. Select *Install this deployment as an application* and click *Next*.

4. If the default name is appropriate for your installation, keep it. Otherwise, give it a
   name of your choosing and click *Next*.

5. Click *Finish*. After the deployment finishes, click *Save*. Liferay precompiles all the
   JSPs, and Liferay launches.

Congratulations! You are now running Liferay on Oracle WebLogic 12c.

18.17   Installing Liferay on WebSphere 8.5

 Tip: Throughout this installation and configuration process, Web-
Sphere prompts you to Click Save to apply changes to Master Configuration. Do so intermittently to save your changes.

Liferay Home is in a folder called liferay in the home folder of the user ID that is run-
ning WebSphere.
   To work correctly on WebSphere 8.5, IBM's PM90932 patch must be installed.[39]
   Please also note that the WebSphere Application Liberty Profile is not supported by
Liferay.

---

[39]http://www-01.ibm.com/support/docview.wss?uid=swg1PM90932

Preparing WebSphere for Liferay

When the application server binaries have been installed, start the **Profile Management Tool** to create a profile appropriate for Liferay.

1. Click on *Create....* Choose *Application Server.* Click *Next.*

2. Click the Advanced profile creation option and then click *Next.* Why Advanced? You can specify your own values for settings such as the location of the profile and names of the profile, node and host. You can assign your own ports. You can optionally choose whether to deploy the administrative console and sample application and also add web-server definitions if you wish. Web server definitions are used with IBM HTTP Server. For more information about these options, please see the WebSphere documentation.

Optional Application Deployment

Select the applications to deploy to the WebSphere Application Server environment being created.

☑ Deploy the administrative console (recommended).
    Install a Web-based administrative console that manages the application server. Deploying the administrative console is recommended, but if you deselect this option, the information center contains detailed steps for deploying it after the profile exists.

☐ Deploy the default application.
    Install the default application that contains the Snoop, Hello, and HitCount servlets.

☐ Deploy the Installation Verification Tool application.
    Install the Installation Verification Tool (IVT) to verify that the creation of the application server is successful. IVT scans product log files for errors and verifies core product functionality by starting and monitoring the server process and querying servlets.

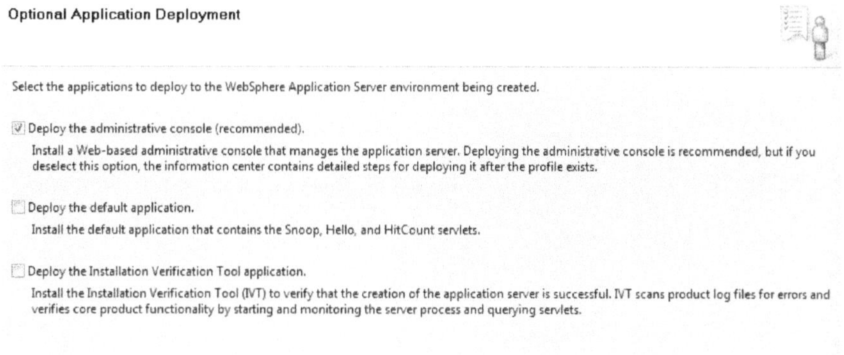

Figure 18.9: Choose the Advanced profile option to specify your own settings.

3. Check the box *Deploy the administrative console.* This gives you a web-based UI for working with your application server. Skip the default applications. You'd only install these on a development machine. Click *Next.*

4. Set profile name and location. Ensure you specify a performance tuning setting other than *Development,* since you're installing a server for production use. Please see the WebSphere documentation for further information about performance tuning settings. Click *Next.*

5. Choose node, server, and host names for your server. These will be specific to your environment. Click *Next.*

6. Administrative security in WebSphere is a way to restrict who has access to the administrative tools. You may want to have it enabled in your environment so that a user name and password are required to administer the WebSphere server. Please see WebSphere's documentation for further information. Click *Next.*

7. Each profile needs a security certificate, which comes next in the wizard. If you don't have certificates already, choose the option to generate a personal certificate and a signing certficate and click *Next.*

8. Once the certificates are generated, set a password for your keystore. Click *Next.*

9. Next, you can customize the ports this server profile uses. Be sure to choose ports that are open on your machine. When choosing ports, the wizard detects existing WebSphere installations and if it finds activity, it increments ports by one.

10. Choose whether you want this profile started when the machine starts. Click *Next*.

11. WebSphere ships with IBM HTTP Server, which is a rebranded version of Apache. Choose whether you want a web server definition, so that this JVM receives requests forwarded from the HTTP server. Please see WebSphere's documentation for details on this. When finished, click *Next*.

12. The wizard then shows you a summary of what you selected, enabling you to keep your choices or go back and change something. When you're satisfied, click *Next*.

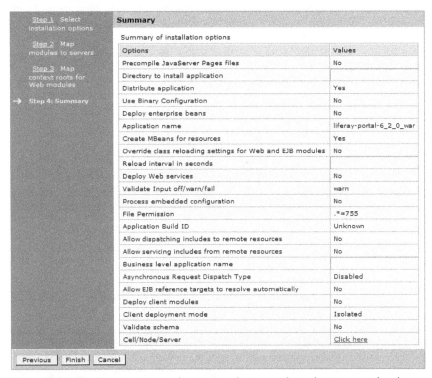

Figure 18.10: The Summary page shows you what you selected, giving you the chance to go back and change something if it's not exactly what you want.

WebSphere then creates your profile and finishes with a message telling you the profile was created successfully. You're now ready to install Liferay!

Copying portal dependencies

Liferay ships with dependency .jars it needs to have on the global classpath. These should be copied to WebSphere's global folder provided for this purpose:

```
[Install Location]/WebSphere/AppServer/lib/ext
```

If you have a JDBC database driver .jar, copy it to this location as well. Once you've copied the .jars, start the server profile you created for Liferay. Once it starts, you're ready to configure your database.

Database Configuration

If you want WebSphere to manage the database connections, follow the instructions below. Note this is not necessary if you're planning on using Liferay's standard database configuration; in that case, skip this section. You'll set your database information in Liferay's setup wizard after the install.

Figure 18.11: WebSphere JDBC providers

1. Start WebSphere.

2. Open the Administrative Console and log in.

3. Click *Resources →JDBC Providers*.

4. Click *New*.

5. For name, enter the name of JDBC provider (e.g. *MySQL JDBC Provider*).

6. For Implementation Class Name, enter:

```
com.mysql.jdbc.jdbc2.optional.MysqlConnectionPoolDataSource
```

7. Click *Next*.

8. Clear any text in classpath. You already copied the necessary `.jars` to a location on the server's class path.

9. Click *Next*.

10. Click *Finish*.

11. Click *Data Sources* under *Additional Properties*.

12. Click *New*.

13. Enter a name: *liferaydatabasesource*.

14. Enter JNDI: `jdbc/LiferayPool`.

15. Everything else should stay at the default values. Save the data source.

16. When finished, go back into the data source and click *Custom Properties* and then click the *Show Filter Function* button. This is the second from last of the small icons under the *New* and *Delete* buttons.

17. Type *user* into the search terms and click *Go.*

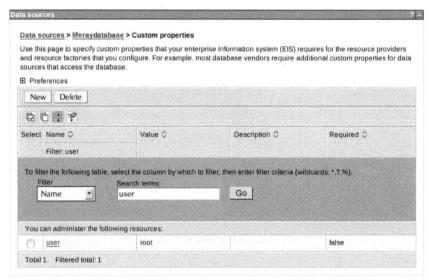

Figure 18.12: Modifying data source properties in WebSphere

18. Select the user property and give it the value of the user name to your database. Click *OK* and save to master configuration.

19. Do another filter search for the url property. Give it a value that Click *OK* and save to master configuration.

20. Do another filter search for the password property. Enter the password for the user ID you added earlier as the value for this property. Click *OK* and save to master configuration.

21. Go back to the data source page by clicking it in the breadcrumb trail. Click the *Test Connection* button. It should connect successfully.

Once you've set up your database, you can set up your mail session.

Mail Configuration

If you want WebSphere to manage your mail sessions, use the following procedure. If you want to use Liferay's built-in mail sessions, you can skip this section.

1. Click *Resources* →*Mail* →*Mail Providers.*

2. Click the Built-In Mail Provider for your node and server.

3. Click *Mail Sessions* and then click the *New* button.

4. Give it a name of *liferaymail* and a JNDI name of `mail/MailSession`. Click *OK* and save to master configuration.

5. Click *Security* →*Global Security* and de-select *Use Java 2 security to restrict application access to local resources* if it is selected. Click *Apply*.

Great! Now you're ready to deploy Liferay.

Deploy Liferay

1. Click *Applications* →*New Application* →*New Enterprise Application*.

2. Browse to the Liferay .war file and click *Next*.

3. Leave *Fast Path* selected and click *Next*. Ensure that *Distribute Application* has been checked, and click *Next* again.

4. Choose the WebSphere runtimes and/or clusters where you want Liferay deployed. Click *Next*.

5. Map Liferay to the root context (/) and click *Next*.

6. Ensure that you have made all the correct choices and click *Finish*. When Liferay has installed, click *Save to Master Configuration*.

You've now installed Liferay, but don't start it yet. If you wish to use PACL, you have one more thing to configure.

Enabling Security for Portal Access Control Lists

In the administrative console, go to *Security* $rarr; *Global Security*. Check the box to enable Java 2 security, and click *Apply*. Save to the master configuration.

Figure 18.13: Enabling security can be done by checking one box, but it still needs to be configured.

Next, you need to configure security for the Liferay profile you created. This requires editing a text file, which can be found nested several folders deep in WebSphere's pro-files directory. The exact path depends on how you've named your profile, but it will be something like this:

```
[profile_root]/config/cells/[cell_name]/nodes/[node_name]/app.policy
```

First, in each existing grant section, replace the content with java.security.All-Permission;. Then add the following lines to the bottom of the file:

```
grant codeBase "file:${was.install.root}/lib/-" {
  permission java.security.AllPermission;
};

grant codeBase "file:${was.install.root}/plugins/-" {
  permission java.security.AllPermission;
};

grant codeBase "file:${server.root}/-" {
  permission java.security.AllPermission;
};
```

Save the file. You should now stop the profile and restart it. Once it comes up, you're ready to start Liferay.

Start Liferay

1. If you plan to use Liferay's setup wizard, skip to the next step. If you wish to use WebSphere's data source and mail session, create a file called portal-ext.pro-perties in your Liferay Home folder. Place the following text in the file:

```
jdbc.default.jndi.name=jdbc/LiferayPool
mail.session.jndi.name=mail/MailSession
setup.wizard.enabled=false
```

2. Select the Liferay application and click *Start*.

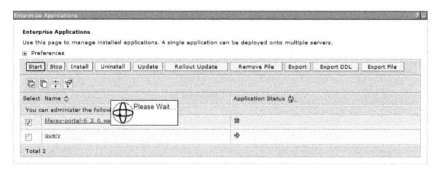

Figure 18.14: While Liferay is starting, WebSphere displays this spinny little graphic. Don't watch it too closely, or you might get hypnotized.

3. In the setup wizard, select and configure your database type. Click *Finish* when you're done.

   Liferay then creates the tables it needs in the database.

Congratulations! You've installed Liferay on WebSphere!

18.18   Using Liferay's setup wizard

To make it easy to configure Liferay optimally for your use, the first thing you see when browsing to your newly installed Liferay bundle is a setup wizard. This gives you a convenient way to configure Liferay for your purposes.

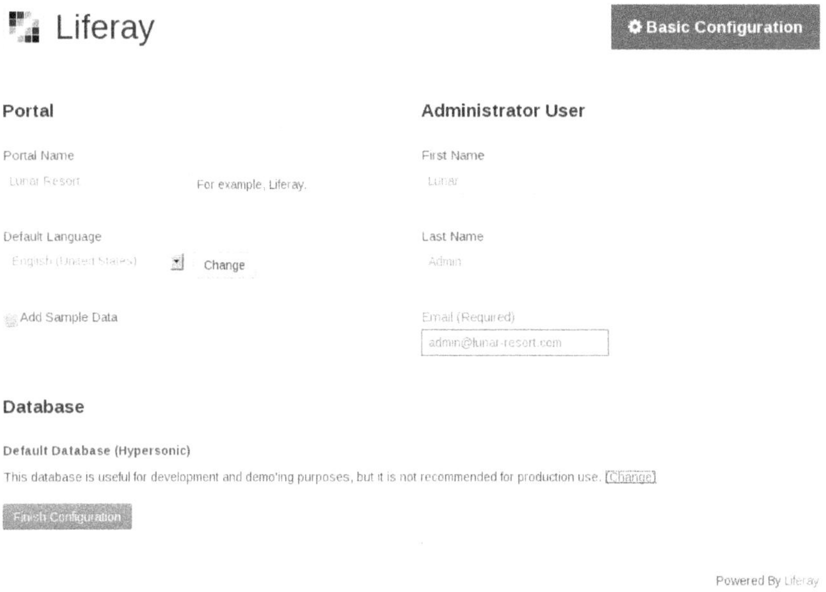

Figure 18.15: Supply the information for your site and your site's administrative account in the setup wizard.

There are three sections of the wizard: the portal, the administrator and the database. For the portal, you need to supply the following information:

Portal Name: the name of the web site you're powering with Liferay. In this book, we build a website for a lunar colony. This site is called Lunar Resort, so we've supplied Lunar Resort in the screenshot below.

Default Language: choose the default locale where your site resides.

For the administrator, you need to supply the following information:

First Name: the first name of the user that has the administrator account.

Last Name: the last name of the user that has the administrator account.

Email: the email address of the user that has the administrator account.

Liferay supports just about all the leading databases today:

- DB2

- MySQL

- Oracle

- PostgreSQL

- SQL Server

- Sybase

In addition to these, Liferay also supports a few embedded databases that are designed for development. We haven't listed these here because you're setting up a production Liferay server, and you shouldn't use an embedded database with a production box.

Before you fill out the database section of Liferay's setup wizard, you should already have created a database for Liferay to use. If you haven't, please see the section above entitled *Liferay's Database*.

Open the Database section of the wizard. From the select box, choose your database. You'll see a form which lets you specify the URL to the database, the driver class, and the user credentials (see below). Most of this is filled out already; all you should need to do is supply the name of your database and the server it's running on, as well as the user credentials.

Database

Use Default Database

Database Type

MySQL

JDBC URL (Required)

bc:mysql://localhost/lunar_resort

JDBC Driver Class Name (Required)

com.mysql.jdbc.Driver

User Name

root

Password

••••

Finish Configuration

Figure 18.16: Fill out the information for your database. We've chosen MySQL in this example and have created a database called *lunar_resort* to hold our Liferay data.

Once you've filled out the form, click *Finish Configuration*. You'll see a message stating that Liferay is being installed as it creates the tables and data it needs in its database. When it's finished, it tells you the location of the configuration file (portal-setup-wizard.properties) where it saved all your settings. From here, you can go to your home page.

Congratulations! You've just installed Liferay Portal! The next thing you need to do is set up your mail configuration, so Liferay can send email notifications to users. This is covered in the Manual Configuration section below.

Tip: The wizard is an extremely helpful tool, especially if you're setting up Liferay for the first time or creating a completely fresh portal instance. If you're a Liferay veteran and you already have your database information and various properties set up, you can skip the wizard by adding this line to your portal-ext.properties file:

```
setup.wizard.enabled=false
```

> **Tip:** In Liferay 6.2, the admin user test@liferay.com is created by the setup wizard even when a different user is specified. This means that two admin users are created: test@liferay.com and the specified user. Unless you're just installing Liferay for testing purposes, you should deactivate the test@liferay.com user after your database has been created.

18.19 Manual Configuration

You don't have to use the setup wizard to configure Liferay. The setup wizard behind the scenes creates a configuration file that you can create manually. Create a text file called portal-ext.properties in your Liferay Home folder. This file overrides default properties that come with Liferay. The first setting you'll override is the default configuration that points Liferay to the embedded HSQL database.

As stated above, there are two ways to set up the connection:

- Use the built-in connection pool.

- Use your application server's connection pool.

Use the setup wizard if you're using the built-in connection pool. If you want to use your application server's pool, continue with this procedure.

If you want to use your application server's connection pool, you will have to create one in your application server that points to your database. The connection pool should be called jdbc/LiferayPool. In the application server sections above, there are instructions for how to do this on each application server that Liferay supports. To tell Liferay to use your jdbc/LiferayPool connection pool, add the following directive to your portal-ext.properties file:

```
jdbc.default.jndi.name=jdbc/LiferayPool
```

Next, install Liferay according to the instructions for your application server. Once it's installed, you can set up the mail configuration.

For mail, you can use Liferay's control panel to create the configuration and this is the recommended way. Go to *Control Panel →Server Administration →Mail* and enter your settings for your mail session settings. If, however, you're setting up a lot of Liferay machines and they're all going to have similar mail configurations, it's easier to do the configuration once and then copy the configuration file to multiple machines. In this case, you'll want to use the portal-ext.properties file. To use the built-in mail session, use the following properties and customize their values for your environment:

```
mail.session.mail.pop3.host=localhost
mail.session.mail.pop3.password=
mail.session.mail.pop3.port=110
mail.session.mail.pop3.user=
mail.session.mail.smtp.auth=false
mail.session.mail.smtp.host=localhost
mail.session.mail.smtp.password=
mail.session.mail.smtp.port=25
mail.session.mail.smtp.user=
mail.session.mail.store.protocol=pop3
mail.session.mail.transport.protocol=smtp
```

To use your application server's mail session, create it first. Then specify it in the portal-ext.properties file:

```
mail.session.jndi.name=mail/MailSession
```

When you've finished, save the file.

All the instructions above assumed that you wanted to install Liferay Portal at the root context of your server. But what if that isn't the case? Next, you'll see how to use a different context for Liferay Portal.

18.20 Making Liferay Coexist with Other Java EE Applications

Liferay Portal by default is configured to sit at the root (i.e., /) of your application server. Dedicating your application server to running only Liferay Portal is a good practice, allowing for separation between your portal environment and your web application environment. This is generally a best practice for portals, which by definition are application development platforms in and of themselves. For that reason, your instance of Liferay is likely to be hosting many applications and even integrating several of them together on a single page. For this reason, you should design your system so your portal environment has all the resources it needs to do this. Configuring it so it is the sole consumer of any other .war files that get deployed to the application server helps to make sure your system performs optimally.

If, however, you want Liferay to share space on an application server with other applications, you can. In this instance, you may not want to make Liferay the default application in the root context of the server. If you want to install Liferay in a context other than the root context, follow the instructions from your app server vendor. No additional steps are necessary.

Now that you have Liferay installed in the context you wish, you'll want to understand Liferay's releases and the process for keeping your installation up to date. We'll spend a brief amount of time on that next.

18.21 Understanding Liferay's Releases

Which version of Liferay should you install? That's an easy question to answer: if this is a new installation, we recommend you install the latest version available. If you want to understand how Liferay releases work, read on. Otherwise, you can skip this section for now and read it later.

Liferay's release process follows a prescribed structure that is consistent from one release to the next. Each release has a specific number sequence attached to it, signifying the type of release it is: major, minor or maintenance release. Each release also has a term attached to it to indicate its intended level of quality.

EE subscribers have access to additional maintenance releases, along with specific *Fix Packs* and *Hot Fixes* that make applying updates to production environments safer and faster.

Let's start with an explanation of Liferay's version structure. Liferay versions are organized in a straightforward numerical system consisting of a three digit number. For example, 6.1.2. These numbers represent the type of the release: Major.Minor.Maintenance.

A change in the first or second digit of the version (e.g., 6.x to 7.x or 6.1 to 6.2) is a major or minor release. This means that there are changes in functionality or new functionality based on high demand. There are new features and bug fixes from prior releases. There are also architectural changes, changes to APIs (as part of the deprecation process), or changes to internal schema for frameworks such as Service Builder, because new features have been added. Customizations may be affected when installing. Customers should leverage the upgrade tools and documentation.

A change in the third digit of the version scheme (e.g, 6.2.1 to 6.2.2) is a maintenance release. This means that each maintenance release provides an improved level of security and reliability. Customizations are generally safe, but we recommend doing a review. No new features are included.

These rules are relaxed when a minor or major release is still in beta quality.

Now let's delve into the evolution of versions.

Release Process

Each release of Liferay has a surname that specifies its expected quality. This is needed because pre-releases of Liferay look very much like maintenance releases when viewed solely through their version numbers. The surname in general replaces the third digit in the version, but is visible through the logs and administration UIs. Here is a description of each surname and what it means:

- **Milestone** and **Beta:** (6.2 M1, 6.2 B1, 6.2 B2, ...) There can be zero or more of these types within each minor or major release. These releases are meant for testing and to provide Liferay feedback through the beta testing category in the forums. There will likely be major changes in milestone releases, but beta releases are considered "feature complete" and should have only bug fixes.

- **Release Candidates:** (6.2 RC1, 6.2 RC2) There can be zero, one, or more of these right after the beta releases. These releases appear near the end of the release process and are candidates for release. As such, they should have minimal to no bugs, but because they are very new, some minor bugs may have slipped by.

- **General Availability:** (6.2 GA1, 6.2 GA2, ...) There can be one or more of these re- leases. A General Availability release is a re-label of the last release candidate, based on internal testing and feedback from beta testers. These releases are stable and are made available via Liferay's Downloads page for CE and on the Customer Portal for EE.

Armed with this information, here's our advice for how to manage your Liferay instal- lation.

- When starting a new project, always use the latest stable version available; that is, the latest available GA. At the time of writing, the most recent version is Liferay CE 6.2 GA1 (6.2.0) or Liferay EE 6.1 GA2 (6.2.00).

- Always update to the latest maintenance release available for the functional version (major or minor) that you are using. For example, if you started your project with Liferay 6.2.0 GA1, it is recommended that you switch to GA2 if/when it becomes available to take advantage of bug fixes and improvements. If you have a subscrip- tion, you can benefit from the fixes faster by requesting fix packs and hot fixes from the support team.

- You are always welcome to use any preview, beta or release candidate. In fact, that's why they exist—so as many people as possible start using it and provide us their feedback. Please note, we do not recommend using pre-releases (milestones, betas, or release candidates) in production. You may not want to use these releases even during development if you have tight deadlines, since you may hit some unexpected bugs.

- Plugins that work in any GA or fix pack version will work in any later maintenance release. That is, a plugin developed for Liferay 6.2 GA1 will also work in Liferay 6.2 GA2 or a GA2 fix pack.

For more details on updating Liferay Portal, see Upgrading Liferay in chapter 19.

Liferay Portal is a very flexible application that runs well on several different server environments. It's simple to install and follows a systematic versioning system that makes it easy to keep current with the latest updates. The strength of the Liferay community helps detect potential issues early that are then reported through the forums and are later fixed in a series of maintenance releases.

18.22 Summary

This chapter is a guide to everything about installing Liferay. Whether you choose a Liferay bundle or an existing application server, Liferay Portal integrates seamlessly with your enterprise Java environment. It is supported on more application servers than any other portal platform, allowing you to preserve your investment in your application server of choice or giving you the freedom to move to a different application server platform. Liferay is committed to providing you this freedom: we have 500 test servers certifying our builds with roughly 10,000 tests per version of Liferay Portal. Each of those tests are run on all of our different supported combinations of application servers, databases and operating systems. Because of this, you can be sure we are committed to supporting you on your environment of choice. You can feel safe knowing you have the freedom to use the software platform that is best for your organization and that Liferay Portal runs and performs well on it.

## CHAPTER 19

ADVANCED PORTAL OPERATION

In this chapter, you'll find several advanced features of Liferay Portal, including portal maintenance, backup, and logging. You'll also learn how to access Liferay's web services remotely. It's generally not much more complicated to maintain a running Liferay instance than it is to maintain the application server upon which it's running. However, Liferay provides tools for logging, patching, and upgrading Liferay that you should know how to use. It's also important to follow secure backup procedures to protect your Liferay instance's source code, database, and properties files.

We'll discuss the following topics in this section:

- Backing Up a Liferay Installation
- Changing Logging Levels
- Patching Liferay
- Upgrading Liferay
- Sandboxing Portlets to Ensure Portal Resiliency
- Using Web Services for Remote Portlets (WSRP)
- Remotely Accessing Liferay Services

First, you'll learn how to back up a Liferay installation.

19.1 Backing up a Liferay Installation

Once you have an installation of Liferay Portal running, you'll want to have proper backup procedures in place in case of a catastrophic hardware failure of some kind. Liferay isn't very different from any other application that may be running on your application server. Nevertheless, there are some specific components you should include in your backup plan.

Backing up Source Code

If you have extended Liferay or have written any plugins, they should be stored in a source code repository such as Git, Subversion, or CVS, unless you're Linus Torvalds, and then tarballs are okay too (that's a joke). Your source code repository should be backed up on a regular basis to preserve your ongoing work. This probably goes without saying in your organization, as nobody wants to lose source code that's taken months to produce, but we thought we should mention it anyway.

If you're extending Liferay with an Ext plugin, you'll want to make sure you also store the version of the Liferay source on which your extension environment is based. This allows your developers convenient access to all the tools they need to build your extension and deploy it to a server.

Let's look at the items that need to be backed up in your Liferay installation.

Backing up Liferay's File System

Liferay's configuration file, portal-ext.properties, gets stored in the *Liferay Home* folder, which is generally one folder up from where your application server is installed (see the *Installation and Setup* chapter of this guide for specific details for your application server). At a minimum, this file should be backed up, but it is generally best to back up your whole application server.

If you've followed the non-plugin procedure (see chapter 19) to modify your Ehcache configuration, you'll have cache configuration files in the deploy location of Liferay. You'll need to back up this location. If you're using the plugin procedure (i.e., the recommended procedure), your cache configuration settings are stored in your source code repository, which is backed up separately.

Liferay stores configuration files, search indexes, and cache information in a folder called /data in Liferay Home. If you're using the File System store or the Advanced File System store, the media repository is stored here (by default) too. You should always back up the contents of your Liferay Home folder.

If you've modified the location where the Document Library stores files, you should also back up this location.

That covers the file system locations Liferay uses. Next, let's discuss how to back up Liferay's database.

Backing up Liferay's Database

Liferay's database is the central repository for all of the Portal's information and is the most important component that needs to be backed up. You can do this by backing up the database live (if your database allows this) or by exporting the database and then backing up the exported file. For example, MySQL ships with a mysqldump utility which allows you to export the entire database and data into a large SQL file. This file can then be backed up. In case of a database failure, this file can be used to recreate the state of the database at the time the dump was created.

If you're using Liferay's Documents and Media Library with the Jackrabbit JSR-170 repository to store documents in a database, the Jackrabbit database should be backed up also. If you've placed your search index into a database (not recommended; see chapter 19 for information on using Cluster Link or Solr), that database should be backed up as well.

Search indexes can be backed up as well, if you wish to avoid reindexing your entire portal after you do your restore. This is easiest to do if you have a separate Solr environment upon which your index is stored. If you're in a clustered configuration and you're replicating indexes, you'll need to back up each index replica.

Restoring your application server, your Liferay Home folder, the locations of any file system-based media repositories, and your database from a backup system should give you a functioning portal. Restoring search indexes should avoid the need to reindex when you bring your site back up after a catastrophic failure. Good, consistent backup procedures are key to successfully recovering from a hardware failure.

But what about maintenance while your server is running? Liferay lets you view a lot of what is going on through its logging system.

19.2 Liferay's Logging System

Liferay's logging system uses Log4j extensively to implement logging for nearly every class in the portal. If you need to debug something specific while the system is running, you can use the control panel to set logging levels by class dynamically.

To view the log levels, go to the control panel, click *Server Administration* in the Server section, and then click the *Log Levels* tab.

A paginated list of logging categories appears. These categories correspond to Liferay classes that have log messages in them. By default, all categories are set to display messages only if there is an error that occurs in the class. This is why you see ERROR displayed in all of the drop-down list boxes on the right side of the portlet.

Each category is filtered by its place in the class hierarchy. For example, if you wanted to see logging for a specific class that is registered in Liferay, you would browse to that specific class and change its log level to something that is more descriptive, such as DE-BUG. Once you click the *Save* button at the bottom of the list, you'll start seeing DEBUG messages from that class in your application server's log file.

If you're not sure which class you want to see log messages for, you can find a place higher up in the hierarchy and select the package name instead of an individual class name. If you do this, messages for every class lower in the hierarchy will be displayed in your application server's log file.

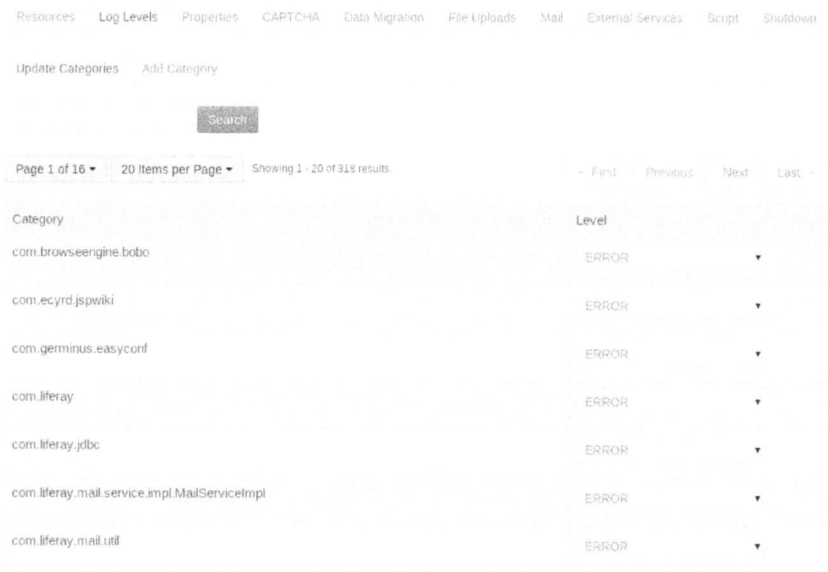

Figure 19.1: Log levels can be dynamically changed at runtime whenever you need to debug an issue.

Be careful when you do this. If you set the log level to DEBUG somewhere near the top of the hierarchy (such as com.liferay, for example), you may wind up with a lot of messages in your log file. This could make it difficult to find the one you were looking for, and causes the server to do more work writing messages to the log.

If you want to set the log level for one of your own classes in a deployed plugin, you can register that class with Liferay to control the log levels more easily, so long as your class uses Liferay's logging system to do its logging.

You will first need to import interfaces and implement logging in your class, with statements such as these (taken from Liferay's S3Store class):

```
import com.liferay.portal.kernel.log.Log;
import com.liferay.portal.kernel.log.LogFactoryUtil;
    ...

private static Log _log = LogFactory.getLog(S3Store.class);
```

You would then use this _log variable to create log messages in your code for the various logging levels:

```
_log.error(s3se.getMessage());
```

To enable your logging messages to appear in your server's log file via the control panel, click the *Add Category* tab on the same *Log Levels* page.

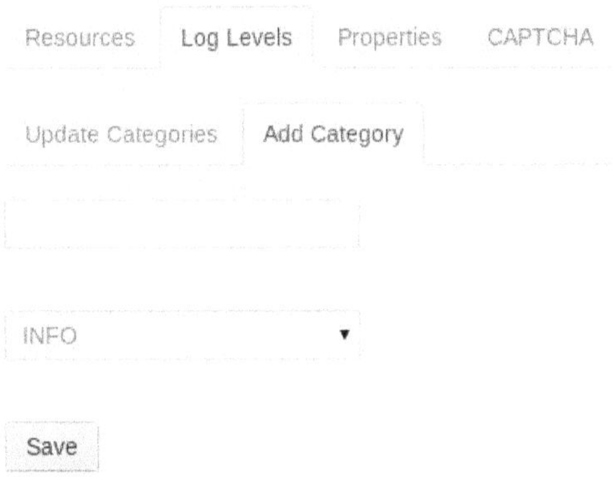

| Resources | Log Levels | Properties | CAPTCHA |

| Update Categories | Add Category |

INFO   ▼

Save

Figure 19.2: Adding your own logging classes is easy. To add a logging class, just specify it in this field.

You'll see you can add a logging category. Put in the fully qualified name of your class or of the package that contains the classes whose log messages you want to view, choose a log level, then click the *Save* button. You will now start to see log messages from your own class or classes in the server's log file.

Logs are great for figuring out issues in production. But what if Liferay contacts you via its support channel with a bug fix or a security enhancement? Read on to learn how to patch Liferay.

 Note: Logging changes within the control panel don't persist across restarts. If you want to make your changes persistent, you can create a META-INF/portal-log4j-ext.xml file and deploy it, using the portal-log4j.xml file from Liferay's source as a guide.

19.3 Patching Liferay

While we strive for perfection with every release of Liferay Portal, the reality of the human condition dictates that releases of the product may not be as perfect as originally intended. But we've planned for that. Included with every Liferay bundle is a patching tool that can handle the installation of two types of patches: hot fixes and fix packs.

A hot fix is provided to a customer when a customer contacts Liferay about an issue, and Liferay's support team—working with the customer—determines that the problem is indeed an issue with the product that needs to be fixed. Support fixes the bug and provides a hot fix to the customer immediately. This is a short-term fix that solves the issue for the customer as quickly as possible.

On a regular schedule, these hot fixes are bundled together into fix packs. Fix packs are provided to all of Liferay's customers and are component-based. This means any issues with the content management system will be bundled together separately from issues with another component, such as the message boards. This lets you determine which patches are critical and which are not, based on your usage. Of course, if Liferay issues a security advisory, that's something you're always going to want to patch.

Now that you know what patching is all about, let's check out the tool.

Installing the patching tool

If you're using a Liferay bundle, congratulations! The patching tool is already installed. Your job isn't done yet, however, because Liferay *might* have updated the patching tool. Always check the Customer Portal to see if the patching tool has been updated first. But even if you forget to check, the patching tool will tell you if it needs to be updated when you run it. A lot of planning and forethought has gone into the patching system to make it run as smoothly as possible.

You follow the same procedure whether you're installing or upgrading the patching tool. Once you've obtained it from the customer portal, unzip it to the Liferay Home folder. This is the folder where you've placed your portal-ext.properties file and where by default the data folder resides. This is generally one folder up from where your application server is installed, but some application servers are different. If you don't know where Liferay Home is on your system, check chapter 14 to see where this folder is for your specific application server.

If you're upgrading the patching tool, all you need to do is unzip the new version on top of the old version. Note that if you're doing this on LUM (Linux, Unix, Mac) machines, you'll need to make the patching-tool.sh script executable.

After the patching tool is installed, you need to let it auto-discover your Liferay installation. Then it will determine what your release level is and what your application server environment is. This is a simple command to run on LUM:

```
./patching-tool.sh auto-discovery
```

or on Windows:

```
patching-tool auto-discovery
```

From here on, for brevity we'll use the LUM version of the command. Why? Because Liferay is open source; there's no open source variant of Windows (ReactOS is still in alpha, so it doesn't count); and therefore my (RS) unscientific impression is that more people will run Liferay on open source technology than not. If I'm wrong, I'm wrong, but there are still many other examples of documentation that defaults to Windows, so we still get to be different.

If you've installed the patching tool in a non-standard location, you'll have to give this command another parameter to point it to your Liferay installation. For example, if you've installed a Liferay/Tomcat bundle in /opt/Liferay, you'd issue this command:

```
./patching-tool.sh auto-discovery /opt/Liferay/tomcat-7.0.21
```

In all, this is pretty simple. Now let's see how to use the patching tool to get your patches installed.

Installing patches

The absolute first thing you must do when installing one or more patches is to shut down your server. On Windows operating systems, files that are in use are locked by the OS, and won't be patched. On LUM systems, you can generally replace files that are running, but of course that still leaves the old ones loaded in memory. So your best bet is to shut down the application server that's running Liferay before you install a patch.

Liferay distributes patches as .zip files, whether they are hot fixes or fix packs. When you receive one, either via a LESA ticket (hot fix) or through downloading a fix pack from the customer portal, you'll need to place it in the patches folder, which is inside the patching tool's home folder. Once you've done that, it's a simple matter to install it. First, execute

```
./patching-tool.sh info
```

This shows you a list of patches you've already installed, along with a list of patches that *can* be installed, from what's in the patches folder. To install the available patches, issue the following command:

```
./patching-tool.sh install
```

Liferay copies files into the plugins in deployment time. If these files are patched in the portal, they need to be updated in the plugins as well. In these cases, the patching tool notifies you about the change. You can run the following command to update these files automatically:

```
./patching-tool.sh update-plugins
```

If you do not wish to have the patching tool update the plugins, it's enough to re-deploy them. If there are new indexes created by the patch, the patching tool notifies you to update them. To get the list, run this command:

```
./patching-tool.sh index-info
```

As there's no database connection at patching time, the patches needed to be created at portal startup. In order to get the indexes automatically created, add the following line to the portal-ext.properties file if the server has permissions to modify the indexes on the database:

```
database.indexes.update.on.startup=true
```

Otherwise, you have to create the indexes manually. Check the output of the ./patching-tool index-info command for more details.

Once your patches have been installed, you can verify them by using the ./patching-tool.sh info command, which now shows your patch in the list of installed patches. Next, you'll look at how to manage your patches.

Handling hot fixes and patches

As stated above, hot fixes are short term fixes provided as quickly as possible and fix packs are larger bundles of hot fixes provided to all customers at regular intervals. If you already have a hot fix installed, and the fix pack which contains that hot fix is released, you can rest assured the patching tool will manage this for you. Fix packs always supersede hot fixes, so when you install your fix pack, the hot fix that it already contains is uninstalled, and the fix pack version is installed in its place.

Sometimes there can be a fix to a fix pack. This is also handled automatically. If a new version of a fix pack is released, you can use the patching tool to install it. The patching tool uninstalls the old fix pack and installs the new version in its place.

Fix pack dependencies

Some fix packs require other fix packs to be installed first. If you attempt to install a fix pack that depends on another fix pack, the patching tool will notify you of this so you can go to the customer portal and obtain the fix pack dependency. Once all the necessary fix packs are available in the patches folder, the patching tool will install them.

The patching tool can also remove patches.

Removing or reverting patches

Have you noticed that the patching tool only seems to have an install command? This is because patches are managed not by the command, but by what appears in the patches folder. You manage the patches you have installed by adding or removing patches from this folder. If you currently have a patch installed and you don't want it installed, remove it from the patches folder. Then run the ./patching-tool.sh install command, and the patch is removed.

If you want to remove all patches you've installed, use the following command:

```
./patching-tool.sh revert
```

This removes all patches from your installation.

What we've described so far is the simplest way to use the patching tool, but you can also use the patching tool in the most complex, multi-VM, clustered environments. This is done by using profiles.

Using profiles with the patching tool

When you ran the auto-discovery task after installing the patching tool, it created a default profile that points to the application server it discovered. This is the easiest way to use the patching tool, and is great for smaller, single server installations. But we realize many Liferay installations are sized accordingly to serve millions of pages per day, and the patching tool has been designed for this as well. So if you're running a small, medium, or large cluster of Liferay machines, you can use the patching tool to manage all of them using profiles.

The auto-discovery task creates a properties file called default.properties. This file contains the detected configuration for your application server. But you're not limited to only one server which the tool can detect. You can have it auto-discover other runtimes, or you can manually create new profiles yourself.

To have the patching tool auto-discover other runtimes, you'll need to use a few more command line parameters:

```
./patching-tool.sh [name of profile] auto-discovery [path/to/runtime]
```

This will run the same discovery process, but on a path you choose, and the profile information will go into a [your profile name].properties file.

Alternatively, you can manually create your profiles. Using a text editor, create a [profile name].properties file in the same folder as the patching tool script. You can place the following properties in the file:

patching.mode: This can be binary (the default) or source, if you're patching the source tree you're working with. Liferay patches contain both binary and source patches. If your development team is extending Liferay, you'll want to provide the patches you install to your development team so they can patch their source tree.

patches.folder: Specify the location where you'll copy your patches. By default, this is ./patches.

war.path: No, no one's angry. This is a property for which you specify the location of the Liferay installation inside your application server. Alternatively, you can specify a .war file here, and you'll be able to patch a Liferay .war for installation to your application server.

global.lib.path: Specify the location where .jar files on the global classpath are stored. If you're not sure, search for your portal-service.jar file; it's on the global classpath. This property is only valid if your patching.mode is binary.

source.path: Specify the location of your Liferay source tree. This property is only valid if your patching.mode is source.

You can have as many profiles as you want, and use the same patching tool to patch all of them. This helps to keep all your installations in sync.

Now that you know how to patch an existing installation of Liferay, let's turn to how you'd upgrade Liferay from an older release to the current release.

19.4   Upgrading Liferay

Liferay upgrades are fairly straightforward. A consistent set of steps is all you need to follow to upgrade a standard Liferay installation. Things do get more complicated if your organization has used Ext plugins to customize Liferay. It's possible that API changes in the new version will break your existing code. This, however, is usually pretty easy for your developers to fix. Portlet plugins which use Liferay APIs should be reviewed and their services rebuilt against the new release. Theme plugins may require some modifications to take advantage of new features, and if they're using Liferay APIs, they should be reviewed. Much effort has been made to make upgrades as painless as possible; however, this is not a guarantee everything will work without modification. Ext plugins are the most complicating factor in an upgrade, so it is important to test as much as possible.

Prior to Liferay 6.1 SP2, you could upgrade only from one major release to the next major release. For example, you could upgrade directly from Liferay 5.2.x to 6.0.x, but not from 5.1.x to 6.0.x. If you needed to upgrade over several major releases, you needed to run the upgrade procedure for each major release until you reached the release you want. This doesn't mean you needed to run the procedure for every point release or service pack; you only needed to run the procedure for the major releases. A good practice was to use the latest version of each major release to upgrade your system.

Liferay introduced the *seamless upgrade* feature with Liferay 6.1. Seamless upgrades allow Liferay to be upgraded more easily. In most cases, pointing the latest version of Liferay to the database of the older version is enough. Of course, before upgrading, you should test the upgrade in a non-production environment. You should also always back up your database and other important information and make all the other appropriate preparations that we'll discuss in the section.

Now that we've discussed the general philosophy of upgrading, let's outline the procedure for upgrading to Liferay 6.2.

Preparing for an Upgrade

Before you begin upgrading Liferay to a new version, consider your current Liferay installation. If you're running Liferay EE, is it patched to the most recent Service Pack level? If
not, refer to the section on Patching Liferay before you upgrade; the upgrade process is
designed to occur on a fully patched Liferay. If you're running Liferay CE, make sure you
have the latest GA release.

Now that Liferay is updated to the latest release of its current version, the first upgrade
task is to size up your situation. Do this by asking yourself a few questions from the chart
below. First: What version of Liferay was the first version you installed? If it was 6.0 or
6.1, there are fewer steps, because you won't have to worry about migrating your permission algorithm. If, however, you never upgraded to permissions algorithm 6 or you're still
running a 5.x Liferay, you need to migrate to algorithm 6 before attempting to upgrade to
Liferay 6.2.

Next, if you're upgrading from a version of Liferay older than 6.1, you'll have to migrate
your image gallery over to Documents and Media. Finally, take note of all the plugins you
have installed. Every plugin must be updated to run on the current release. This is easy
to do with Marketplace: after you bring up Liferay 6.2, install from Marketplace any of the
plugins you had installed previously. For custom plugins, have your development team
update them to run on the new version of Liferay.

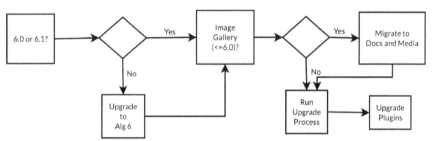

Figure 19.3: Use this flowchart to determine the steps to take for your upgrade.

The flowchart illustrates the procedure described above. Use it to determine your course
of action for the upgrade. Each step is described fully below so that you can perform your
upgrade as efficiently as possible. Be sure to test the upgrade in a non-production environment before upgrading your production Liferay instance.

 Note: In Liferay 6.2, the Global repository that was used to store Web
Content and Documents and Media is now its own site with the reserved
friendly URL /global; upgrading to Liferay 6.2 will fail if any sites are using the same URL. Before upgrading to Liferay 6.2, make sure no current
friendly URL violates the restriction.

Let's look at the preparatory tasks you should perform one by one.

Migrate to Algorithm 6

If your Liferay installation has existed for a while, you might be on a different permission
algorithm than the one that's available in Liferay Portal 6.1. Permission algorithms 1-5 were
deprecated in Liferay Portal 6.0 and were removed in 6.1, which means you must migrate
before you upgrade.

Important: Before upgrading a Liferay instance that's using one of permissions algorithms 1-5, you *must* migrate to permissions algorithm 6 before attempting to upgrade to Liferay 6.2. You can't use the seamless upgrade feature to upgrade directly to 6.2 because Liferay's permissions migration tool is not included with Liferay 6.2. Follow the instructions in this section to migrate to permissions algorithm 6 before continuing with your upgrade.

If you're on Liferay 5.2 or below, you must upgrade to the latest available release of Liferay 6.0 first. Please follow the instructions in the *Liferay Portal Administrator's Guide* to do this. We will assume for the rest of this section that you have upgraded to Liferay 6.0 but that's it's configured to use an older algorithm than algorithm 6.

The first thing you need to do, if this is not done already, is to upgrade your Liferay installation to algorithm 5. If you've already done that, great! You can skip the rest of this paragraph. If not, shut down your server, edit your portal-ext.properties file, and modify/add the following property so that it reads like this:

```
permissions.user.check.algorithm=5
```

Restart your server. As Liferay starts, it upgrades your permissions algorithm to algorithm 5. Review your system to make sure that your permissions configuration is working properly (it should be).

Next, log in as an administrator and navigate to the Control Panel. Go to *Server Administration* and select *Data Migration* from the menu along the top of the screen. A section entitled *Legacy Permissions Migration* appears at the bottom of the page.

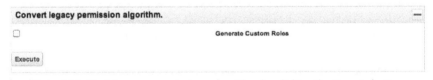

Figure 19.4: Update your permissions algorithm by clicking the *Execute* button.

Algorithms 5 and 6 do not support adding permissions at the user level. If you have permissions set for individual users, the converter can simulate this for you. To do this, it auto-generates roles for each individual permission, and then assigns those roles to the users who have individualized permissions. If you have a lot of these, you'll likely want to go through and clean them up after the conversion process. To generate these roles, check the *Generate Custom Roles* box. If you do not generate the roles, all custom permissions set for individual users are discarded.

Click *Execute* to convert all existing users and roles to algorithm 6. When the process completes, shut down your server. Edit your portal-ext.properties file and modify the algorithm property to show that you're now using algorithm 6:

```
permissions.user.check.algorithm=6
```

Restart your server. Congratulations! You've successfully migrated your installation to use the latest, highest performing permissions algorithm. Next, might need to explicitly set your Image Gallery storage option.

Migrate Your Image Gallery Images

Liferay 6.1 introduced a major change to how Liferay handles files. Liferay 6.0 and previous versions had a separate Document Library and Image Gallery. In Liferay 6.1 and 6.2, these are combined into the Documents and Media repository. If you were using Liferay's Image Gallery to store images, these can be migrated over during an upgrade, but you'll have to take some extra steps first.

In Liferay 6.0, you had three ways you could store images in the Image Gallery. You could use the DatabaseHook and store them as BLOBs in the database; you could use the DLHook to store them in the Document Library, or you could use the FileSystemHook to store them in a folder on your server's file system. Before you upgrade, you'll need to set whichever property you were using in your 6.0 portal-ext.properties file, because by default, none of them are enabled in 6.1. Setting one of the properties triggers the migration during the upgrade process. Below are the three properties; you'll need to set only *one* of them (the one you were using).

```
image.hook.impl=com.liferay.portal.image.DatabaseHook
image.hook.impl=com.liferay.portal.image.DLHook
image.hook.impl=com.liferay.portal.image.FileSystemHook
```

By default, Liferay 6.0 used the FileSystemHook. If you never customized this property for your installation, you'd use the FileSystemHook property above. If you customized the property, you should know which one you used, and it is likely already in your portal-ext.properties file.

The third thing you need to do to prepare for your upgrade is to review the new property defaults.

Review the Liferay 6.2 Properties Defaults

The next thing you'll need to look at are the defaults that have changed between your old Liferay instance's version and Liferay 6.2. These are preserved in a portal-legacy-[version].properties file in Liferay's /WEB-INF/classes folder and in the portal-impl/src folder of Liferay's source code. For example, here are some 6.1 legacy properties:

```
hibernate.cache.use_query_cache=true
hibernate.cache.use_second_level_cache=true
locale.prepend.friendly.url.style=1
passwords.encryption.algorithm.legacy=SHA
mobile.device.styling.wap.enabled=true
journal.articles.search.with.index=false
```

The passwords.encryption.algorithm.legacy and mobile.device.styling.wap.enabled properties do not exist in 6.1. In 6.2, the default values of some properties have changed and some new properties have been added:

```
hibernate.cache.use_query_cache=false
hibernate.cache.use_second_level_cache=false
locale.prepend.friendly.url.style=3
passwords.encryption.algorithm.legacy=
mobile.device.styling.wap.enabled=false
journal.articles.search.with.index=true
```

Please refer to the 6.1 and 6.2 versions of Liferay's portal.properties file for explanations of each of these properties. This file can be found in the your Liferay instance's /WEB-INF/lib/portal-impl.jar file. Online versions can also be found at http://docs.liferay.com/portal/6.1/propertiesdoc/portal.properties.html and http://docs.liferay.com/portal/6.2/propertiesdoc/portal.properties.html. Please also note the following changes in behavior:

1. By default, Liferay 6.1 used the DES encryption algorithm with a 56 bit key size for the company level encryption algorithm. company.encryption.algorithm=DES company.encryption.key.size=56 By default, Liferay 6.2 uses the much stronger AES encryption algorithm with a 128 bit key size for the company level encryption algorithm. AES-128 is believed to be secure, is fast, and is a standard for symmetric key encryption. company.encryption.algorithm=AES company.encryption.key.size=128 However, the upgrade for the company.encryption.algorithm property is only performed if the value for this properties was not customized, i.e., if it was still set to DES. The upgrade doesn't make any changes if a different algorithm was explicitly selected. (Note that this does not affect password encryption which a different property handles: passwords.encryption.algorithm.)

2. By default, Liferay 6.1 used the SHA algorithm for password encryption.

   ```
   passwords.encryption.algorithm=SHA
   ```

   By default, Liferay 6.2 uses a stronger algorithm, PBKDF2WithHmacSHA1/160/128000, for password encryption. PBKDF2 (Password-Based Key Derivation Function 2) is a key derivation function that's part of RSA's PKCS (Public-Key Cryptography Standards) series: PKCS #5, version 2.0. It's also described in the IETF's RFC 2898. The PBKDF2WithHmacSHA1/160/128000 algorithm uses a keyed-hash message authentication code using SHA-1 and generates 160-bit hashes using 128,000 rounds. One round is a single iteration of the key derivation function.

   ```
   passwords.encryption.algorithm=PBKDF2WithHmacSHA1/160/128000
   ```

   Performance is affected by password encryption during sign-in and password changes. In 2012, OWASP, the Open Web Application Security Project, recommended to use 64,000 rounds and to double the number of rounds each year. If using PBKDF2 with 128,000 rounds is too expensive for the hardware where you're running Liferay, you can downgrade your security algorithm to improve performance by choosing a smaller number. For example, you set the following property:

   ```
   passwords.encryption.algorithm=PBKDF2WithHmacSHA1/160/64000
   ```

   If you'd like your upgrade to migrate your password encryption algorithm, you need to specify the legacy password encryption algorithm from which you're migrating. For example, if you were using the 6.1 default before your upgrade, you'd set the following property:

   ```
   passwords.encryption.algorithm.legacy=SHA
   ```

   Set this property before performing an upgrade so that both existing users' and new users' passwords are re-encrypted with the new algorithm.

3. After upgrading from Liferay 6.1 to Liferay 6.2, users must sign back in to the portal even if they were using the *Remember Me* feature of the Sign In portlet. After the upgrade, the *Remember Me* feature works correctly: users can log in to the portal, close their browser, open a new browser window, navigate to the portal, and still be logged in.

If you don't like the 6.2 default properties, you can change them back in one shot by adding a system property to your JVM's startup. This differs by application servers. In Tomcat, you'd modify setenv.sh/setenv.bat and append the option -Dexternal-pro-perties=portal-legacy-[version].properties to the environment variable JA-VA_OPTS. The scripts setenv.sh or setenv.bat are not delivered with default Tomcat, but do exist in the bundles. If they're there, Tomcat uses them in the startup process, so it's a nice way to separate your own settings from Tomcat's default shell scripts. Alternatively, of course, you can override some or all of them in your portal-ext.properties along with your other overrides.

If you're not using Tomcat, check your application server's documentation to see how to modify runtime properties. Your final task is to catalog all the plugins you have installed, so you can install the new versions in your upgraded system.

Catalog All Installed Plugins

Finally, you need to take note of any plugins you have installed. Liferay's plugins are usually version-specific, so you'll need to obtain new versions of them for the new release of Liferay. If you have custom plugins created by your development team, they'll need to build, test, and optionally modify them to work with the new release of Liferay. Don't attempt an upgrade without collecting all the plugins you'll need first.

For Liferay 6.2, the Web Content List portlet is deprecated. During the deprecation period, the code will still be part of the product, but will be disabled by default. To enable Web Content List, you'll need to modify the liferay-portlet.xml file by setting the <include>false</include> tag to true. However, all the functionality of this portlet is provided by the Asset Publisher portlet. The Web Content List portlet is expected to be removed in the next release.

Once you've upgraded your permissions algorithm, reviewed your properties, and collected all the plugins you'll need, you're ready to follow the upgrade procedure. Remember to back up your system before you begin.

Upgrade Choices: Upgrade a Bundle or Upgrade Manually

There are two different procedures to upgrade Liferay. The first one, upgrading a Liferay bundle, is the most common. The second procedure is for manually upgrading a Liferay installation on an application server. We'll discuss both.

In both cases, Liferay auto-detects whether the database requires an upgrade the first time the new version is started. When Liferay does this, it upgrades the database to the format required by the new version. To perform this task, Liferay *must* be accessing the database with a database user account that can create, drop and modify tables. Make sure you have granted these permissions to the database user account before you attempt to upgrade Liferay. And, of course, we'll run the risk of overly repeating ourselves: back up your database.

Let's look at upgrading a bundle, which is the easiest upgrade path.

Upgrading a Bundle

If you're running a Liferay bundle, the best way to do the upgrade is to follow the steps below. The new Liferay is installed in a newer version of your bundle runtime. For example, the Liferay bundle for 6.1 uses a different version of Tomcat than the Liferay bundle for 6.2. We generally recommend you use the latest version of your runtime bundle, as it will be supported the longest.

1. Obtain the new bundle. Unzip the bundle to an appropriate location on your system.

2. Copy your portal-ext.properties file and your data folder to the new bundle.

3. Review your portal-ext.properties file as described above. Make sure you're using permissions algorithm 6. If you were using the Image Gallery, make the necessary modifications so your files are migrated to Documents and Media. Review the new defaults and decide whether you want to use them. Review any other modifications you've made.

4. Start your application server. Watch the console as Liferay starts: it upgrades the database automatically.

5. When the upgrade completes, install any plugins you were using in your old version of Liferay. Make sure you use the versions of those plugins that are designed for Liferay 6.2. If you have your own plugins, your development team will need to migrate the code in these ahead of time and provide .war files for you.

6. Browse around in your new installation and verify everything is working. Have your QA team test everything. If all looks good, you can delete the old application server with the old release of Liferay in it from the bundle directory. You have a backup of it anyway, right? As you can see, upgrading a bundle is generally pretty simple. But not everybody can use bundles: sometimes, specific application servers or application server versions are mandated by the environment you're in or by management. For this reason, Liferay also ships as an installable .war file that can be used on any supported application server.

Upgrading Manually

Running a manual upgrade is almost as easy as upgrading a bundle:

1. Verify your application server is supported by Liferay. You can do this by viewing the appropriate document on the Customer Portal (EE), in chapter 14 (because there are installation instructions for it), or on liferay.com (CE). If your application server isn't supported by Liferay 6.2, *do not continue!* You'll need to upgrade or switch to a supported application server first.

2. Obtain the Liferay Portal .war file and the dependency .jars archive.

3. Copy your customized portal-ext.properties file to a safe place and review it as described above, making all the appropriate changes.

4. Undeploy the old version of Liferay and shut down your application server.

5. Copy the new versions of Liferay's dependency .jars to a location on your server's class path, overwriting the ones you already have for the old version of Liferay. This location is documented for your application server in chapter 14.

6. Deploy the new Liferay .war file to your application server. Follow the deployment instructions in chapter 14.

7. Start (or, if your app server has a console from which you've installed the .war, restart) your application server. Watch the console as Liferay starts: it should upgrade the database automatically. Verify your portal is operating normally, and then install any plugins you were using in your old version of Liferay. Make sure you use the versions of those plugins designed for Liferay 6.2. If you have your own plugins, your development team will need to migrate the code in these ahead of time and provide .war files to you.

8. Browse around in your new installation and verify everything is working. Have your QA team test everything. If all looks good, you're finished.

That's all there is to it. Most everything is handled by Liferay's upgrade procedure. Note as stated above, if you have to upgrade over several Liferay versions, you will need to repeat these steps for each major release.

Post-Upgrade Tasks

After upgrading to Liferay 6.2, you should reindex your portal's search indexes. Liferay 6.2 indexes new information in many places, including Documents and Media, Web Content, and Bookmarks. To reindex all search indexes, navigate to the *Control Panel →Server Administration* and click on *Reindex all search indexes*. This invokes each of your portal's indexer classes, ensuring that your search indexes contain the updated data that 6.2 indexes.

Do you have some troublesome required portlets running in your portal? Wouldn't it be great if you could isolate them so they wouldn't affect the overall health of your portal? We'll show you how to use Liferay's Sandboxing feature to pen up those pesky portlets, next.

19.5   Sandboxing Portlets to Ensure Portal Resiliency

The performance, health, and stability of a portal deployment is heavily dependent upon the portlet modules deployed to it. If one portlet leaks memory or is extremely slow, your entire portal can crash due to a dreaded OutOfMemoryError or can slow to a crawl.

Liferay Portal 6.2 introduces a sandboxing feature that enables you to run troublesome portlets in their own container (or "sandbox"), reducing any adverse impact they may have on the health and stability of your portal. The feature is available in Liferay's Sandbox App. The app lets you create sandboxes to run portlets in separate JVMs, freeing your portal's JVM from the resource consumption of those portlets. We refer to the portal's JVM instance as the *Master Portal Instance (MPI)* and the sandbox JVMs as *Slave Portal Instances (SPIs)*. Since SPIs run on the same host as the MPI, communication between them is very fast. The fact that sandboxed portlets are running in SPIs is transparent to your users. Portal users continue to use these portlets as they normally do.

As a portal administrator, you'll be pleased to know that the app not only gives you the ability to section off plugins into SPIs, but also gives you the means to revive a SPI. The Liferay Sandbox App comes with a *SPI Administration* UI that lets you create, start, stop, and restart SPIs. In addition, it lets you configure options to restart SPIs that terminate unexpectedly, automatically.

The sandboxing feature has two limitations. First, only portlet and web plugins can be deployed on an SPI. Second, the portal ignores SPI portlet implementation classes that are not remote-safe. Implementation classes (such as asset renderers and pollers) that register with the portal fall into this category and are ignored by the portal. Therefore, the sooner you test and resolve any performance issues in such SPI portlets, the sooner you can deploy them back onto the Master Portal Instance to leverage such implementation classes in those portlets.

The Liferay Sandbox App is available on the Liferay Marketplace. You can purchase, install, and deploy the app as described in this guide's chapter on Leveraging the Liferay Marketplace.

Before creating and using sandboxes, we must enable the portal's resiliency functionality and optimize the database connection settings for your sandboxes.

Configuring the Portal for Sandboxing

The two types of portal properties you must modify for your portal to use sandboxing are the Portal Resiliency properties and Database Connection properties. You can set these in your portal-ext.properties file.

You must enable Portal Resiliency by setting the portal.resiliency.enabled property to true. In addition, you can optionally enable the portal to show special footers in sandboxed portlets. The footers display at the bottom of each sandboxed portlet, indicating the sandbox that is servicing the request. The footer helps you verify that a portlet is sandboxed and which sandbox it's in. To enable both of these resiliency properties, specify the following entries in your portal-ext.properties file:

```
portal.resiliency.enabled=true
portal.resiliency.portlet.show.footer=true
```

If you hadn't previously configured your database connection pools using your portal properties, you must do so in order to use the sandboxing feature. If you've been using JNDI to configure data sources on your app server, please convert to using Liferay's built-in data source by specifying it via JDBC properties in your portal-ext.properties file. Note, if you attempt to create or start a sandbox while having incorrect JDBC settings, the Sandbox Administration console displays a warning.

After you've configured your portal for sandboxing and restarted it, deploy the sandbox app. Then navigate to the Control Panel to see the *SPI Administration* link displayed in the *Configuration* section.

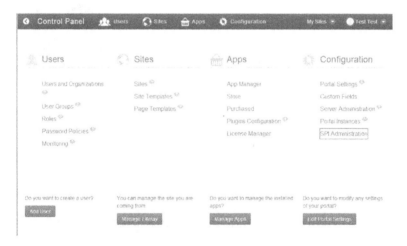

Figure 19.5: The Sandboxing App comes with an *SPI Administration* UI that's accessible from the portal's Control Panel.

Click the *SPI Administration* link to start creating SPIs for running new or troublesome portlets.

Creating an SPI

You can create and administer SPIs from the SPI Administration page accessible in the Configuration section of the Control Panel.

To add a new SPI, simply click on the *Add SPI* button.

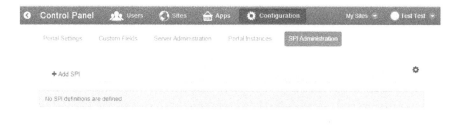

Figure 19.6: Click the *Add SPI* button to define a new "sandbox" (SPI).

The Add SPI panel divides the SPI's fields into General, SPI Configurations, and Advanced Configurations sections.

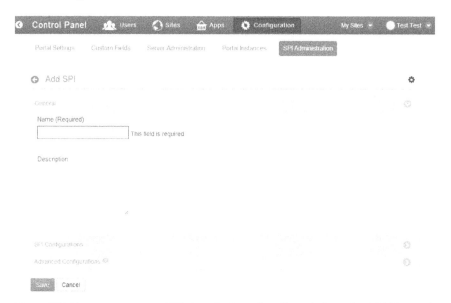

Figure 19.7: You can name your SPI, describe it, and configure it from the *Add SPI* panel.

In the General section, you must provide a unique name for the SPI and describe the SPI.

The SPI Configurations contains some of the most important settings for the SPI. It is broken into 4 sections: SPI Runtime, SPI Applications, Java Runtime, and Recovery Options.

Let's set the SPI's runtime options first.

Maximum Worker Threads: Enter the maximum number of worker threads that the SPI can use to process requests. By default, it is set to 100. You should tune this value, however, according to the number of threads allocated in the application server hosting your portal. This parameter functions similarly to the settings in most JEE application servers.

Figure 19.8: From the *SPI Runtime* section of your SPI, you can set its maximum number of working threads based the number of threads available to your portal that you'd like to designate for the SPI. You must also set a unique connector port for the SPI.

Connector Port: Enter the port number on which the SPI listens for requests from Liferay Portal. Each SPI runs on an embedded Apache Tomcat server instance. Each of the portal's SPIs must use a unique port and you must ensure that no other processes are using that port.

 Note: The SPIs and MPI serialize parameters and return values passed between them. The sandboxing feature uses an IPC framework called Intraband, to support communication between the MPI and SPIs.

Next, we'll pull those troublesome apps into the SPI.

The SPI Applications panel provides a way to select applications to be hosted in the SPI. All requests that call these applications are processed by the SPI.

Figure 19.9: All the portlets and web plugins that you've installed on your portal are available for moving into a SPI.

The panel lists non-core portlets and web plugins that have been installed on the portal. Since theme, layout template, hook, and Liferay EXT plugins are not supported in the sandbox, they're excluded from this list. In addition, the following applications are explicitly excluded:

- marketplace-portlet
- resource-importer-web
- spi-admin-portlet
- spi-provider-web
- wurfl-commercial-web
- wurfl-web

Next, we'll set the Java runtime resources for the SPI's JVM.

The **JVM Arguments** panel allows you to specify arguments to be passed to the Java Virtual Machine (JVM) running the SPI. These include memory settings, debugger options, etc. If you do not specify any values, the system automatically uses these values:

```
-Xmx512m -XX:PermSize=200m
```

Consider the JVM's performance tuning recommendations when setting these arguments. You can also consult the *Liferay Deployment Checklist* (available from the Customer Portal) for guidance on setting the JVM arguments.

In development, you may also choose to add debug settings to the JVM arguments.

Figure 19.10: You can specify Java runtime options optimal for your SPI's apps.

In the event that the SPI terminates unexpectedly, you may want to consider automatically restarting it and having the Sandboxing App send notifications to you and other stakeholders.

The Sandboxing App lets you configure email notifications for when an SPI crashes and lets you configure for the app to automatically restart the SPI.

Recovery Options

☑ Use Default Notification Options
Notification Recipients
michael.han@liferay.com

☑ Use Default Restart Options
Maximum Restart Attempts
3

Figure 19.11: You can have the SPI notify you and others if the SPI's apps crash it. And you can configure the maximum number of times to automatically revive the SPI, before requiring manual intervention.

Use Default Notification Options: Select this checkbox to use the globally defined notification options. Otherwise the notification options specified in this panel are used.

Notification Recipients: Enter a set of comma-delimited email addresses of people to be notified in the event that the SPI fails. This option is disabled if the *Use Default Notification Options* checkbox is selected.

Use Default Restart Options: Select this checkbox to use the globally defined restart options. Otherwise the restart options specified in this panel are used.

Maximum Restart Attempts: Enter the maximum number of times to attempt restarting the SPI in the event that the SPI fails. Once Liferay reaches the maximum number of restart attempts for the SPI, it refrains from restarting the SPI. At that point, manual operator intervention is required to restart it. This option is disabled if the *Use Default Restart Options* checkbox is selected.

Advanced Configurations

The Advanced Configurations section contains a series of optional parameters that should rarely be modified.

Java Executable: Enter the path to your JVM, specifically the path to your Java executable file (i.e., the java or java.exe file). You should generally not modify this value, assuming your Java executable is in your system's PATH.

SPI Ping Interval: Enter the number of milliseconds to wait between pings that the SPI sends to the portal to ensure the portal is alive. Pinging the portal prevents SPIs from becoming "zombie" processes, in the event that the portal terminates unexpectedly.

SPI Register Timeout: Enter the number of milliseconds allotted for the SPI to start. The default value is 300000 milliseconds (300 seconds). This should be ample time for a SPI to start. However, if you have a large number of applications in the sandbox, or the server has an insufficient CPU or insufficient memory resources, you may need to increase the amount of time.

SPI Shutdown Timeout: Enter the maximum amount of time (in milliseconds) that the SPI should need to gracefully shutdown. As with the SPI Register Timeout, this value may need to be increased on slower or overloaded machines.

You may also choose to allocate certain embedded Liferay functions (e.g., blogs, bookmarks, etc.) to an SPI. This is generally not recommended, but is made possible by the Sandboxing App. The SPI Core Applications panel lets you drag apps onto the SPI in the same way you can with the SPI Applications panel.

Now that you know how to add a SPI and configure it properly, let's learn how to operate the SPI.

Starting, Stopping, and Modifying an SPI

The Portal automatically starts SPIs on startup. However, when you first add a new SPI, you must start it manually.

Figure 19.12: When you first create a SPI, you'll need to start it manually. You can edit and delete SPIs that are not running.

Once successfully started, you can stop or restart a SPI. You can't, however, delete an SPI that is running. You must first stop the SPI.

You can edit an SPI's configuration too. Configuration changes made to a running SPI take effect after it's restarted.

Figure 19.13: SPI configuration modifications only take affect after the SPI has been restarted.

As you can see, operating SPIs is straightforward and easy to do.

If you have multiple SPIs, you may want to use global settings to configure the default options for them. Let's consider how to configure global settings for your SPIs next.

Configure Global Settings

The SPI Administration console allows you to configure a series of global settings. You can access them by clicking on the configuration gear icon as shown in the figure below.

Figure 19.14: Click on the global settings gear icon, in the upper right corner of the SPI Administration console, to set default configuration options for all of the portal's SPIs.

Once you've opened the configuration panel, the SPI Administration console enables you to configure global notification and set restart options for your SPIs.

Note that option values explicitly configured in an SPI take precedence over the global settings with respect to that SPI.

Let's look at the global notification options first.

Figure 19.15: You can set default notification and restart options for all of the portal's SPIs.

The notification options allow you to configure both the notfication email content and specify the recipients of the notification email. These values are used by all defined SPIs.

Notification Email From Address: Enter a default origin email address to use for notification emails sent from the SPIs.

Notification Email From Name: Enter a default name to use for the sender of the notification emails.

Notification Recipients: Enter a default comma-delimited list of email addresses to receive the notification emails.

Notification Email Subject: Enter a subject template for the notification emails.

Notification Email Body: Enter a body template for the notification emails.

That's simple enough. Let's take a look at the restart options too.

The restart options section allows you to configure how many times each SPI is restarted in the event that it terminates unexpectedly. In the example below, all SPIs are restarted 3 times before requiring administrator intervention to restart them.

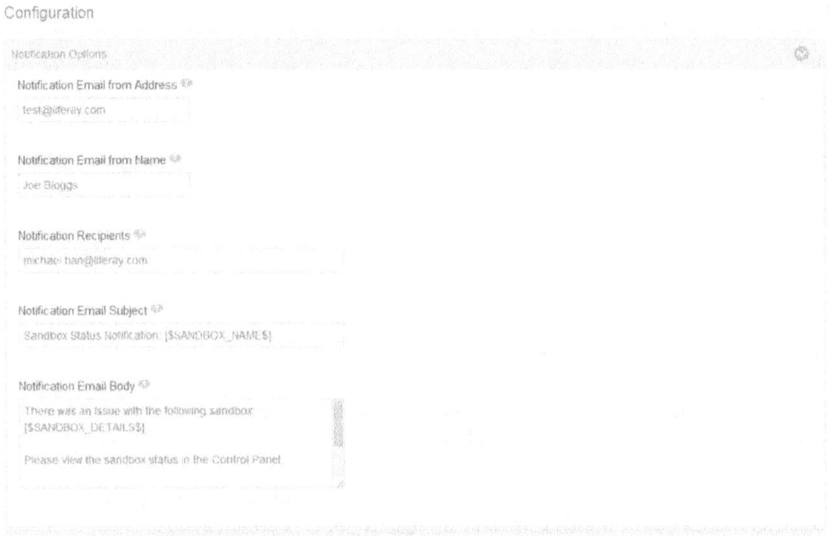

Figure 19.16: Via the SPI Administration's global configuration panel, you can set specific email notification options, including the sender's address, the sender's name, default recipients, a default email subject template, and a default email body template.

Let's recap what Liferay's Sandboxing App does for you. It lets you isolate portlets and web plugins that are known troublemakers or that you are simply just unsure about. You put them in their own sandbox JVM (or SPI), so they can still be used in your portal but are kept out of your portal's JVM. As an administrator, you can group plugins into SPIs and configure each SPI's runtime, notification, and recovery options. In addition, you can configure global default settings for your portal's SPIs. With the Sandboxing App, you can ensure your portal's resiliency while leveraging all the portlets (even leaky ones) that your users require.

Figure 19.17: You can set default restart options for your SPIs from the SPI Administration's global configuration panel.

Liferay Portal can serve portlets that are installed on the system, or it can serve portlets installed on another portal server. This is called Web Services for Remote Portlets. Have you ever wondered how to use WSRP in Liferay? We'll cover this next!

19.6 Using Web Services for Remote Portlets (WSRP)

The Web Services for Remote Portlets (WSRP) specification defines a web service interface for accessing and interacting with presentation-oriented web services in the form of portlets. What are presentation-oriented web services? These are web services that send user interfaces over the wire, rather than raw data like JSON objects or SOAP data envelopes. If an application is written as a portlet, this is an easy way to expose that application to end users on a completely different system, rather than sending just the data and having to craft an application to present that data. WSRP's presentation-oriented web services allow portals to display remote portlets inside their pages, as if locally deployed, without requiring any additional programming by developers.

Here are the two main components for WSRP:

Producer: A web service that exposes one or more portlets and is described using a Web Services Description Language (WSDL) document.

Consumer: A web service client that receives the data from the Producer and presents it to the user in a portlet window.

Below, you'll see how the components interact with each other. So without further ado, let's explore WSRP in Liferay!

WSRP with Liferay

Liferay provides a deployable WSRP portlet that supports the 1.0 and 2.0 specifications. The portlet is available from Liferay Marketplace as a CE or EE app. Once you've downloaded and installed the WSRP app, you have instant access to the portlet by navigating to the Control Panel and, under *Apps*, selecting *WSRP*.

Liferay Portal can be used as a WSRP producer or consumer. As a producer, it hosts portlets that are consumed by other portal servers (Liferay or non-Liferay) acting as WSRP consumers. The image below illustrates WSRP producers and consumers and how they interact.

As we mentioned in the previous chapter, there are two main components of the WSRP process: producers and consumers. Let's go through the basic process of how producers and consumers work together to bring the end user a remote portlet. First, the consumer

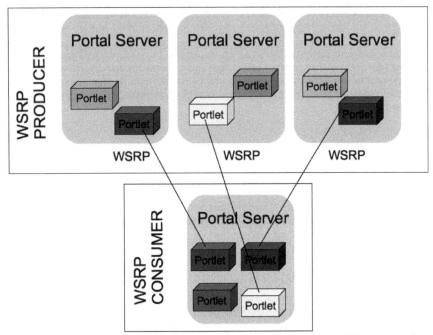

Figure 19.18: Portlets can interact with other portlets located on a different portal server using WSRP.

portal server establishes a connection with its producer portal server counterpart. This connection is made possible by giving the consumer the producer portlet's URL. The consumer then uses the URL to discover the producer's portlet and establish a connection. After the connection is made, the consumer acquires the producer's information and creates a consumer proxy portlet. The proxy portlet acts as an intermediary, relaying requests to and from the end user and the producer portlet.

For example, you can compare the proxy portlet to a TV satellite box. If you want to change the channel on your TV, you (end user) send the channel number you desire to the TV's satellite box (consumer's proxy portlet) via your TV's remote. When the satellite box receives the request to change the channel, it relays the request to a TV satellite (producer's portlet) which then sends the channel information back to the satellite box. Then, the satellite box displays the new channel to you on your TV. In this simple example, you're not directly requesting the TV satellite to change the channel, but rather, you're communicating with the satellite box, which acts as an intermediary between you and the satellite. This example directly relates to using WSRP with Liferay. Although the end users are sending requests to the consumer portlet, they're not receiving feedback from the consumer portlet itself, but rather its producer portlet located remotely.

Now that you know a little bit about the WSRP process, let's begin configuring WSRP on Liferay Portal. For this demonstration, we'll assume you have two portal servers.

Tip: If you're following along with this example and don't have an additional portal server, you can download another instance of Liferay Portal and have it running at the same time as your current Liferay instance to simulate an additional portal server. Remember, typical use cases have WSRP producers and consumers linked on differing portal servers. To run two portal instances locally at the same time, you'll need to change one of your portal's server configurations. Navigate to one of your portal's tomcat-[VERSION]\conf\server.xml and change the port= designations to different values (e.g., change 8080 to 18080). Also, you can specify the new port number for your browser launcher URL by adding browser.launcher.url=http://localhost:18080 to your portal's portal-ext.properties file.

To create a producer, go to the *Producers* tab and click *Add Producer*. Give your producer a name and choose the appropriate version of WSRP to use. Liferay displays a list of available portlets your producer can use. For demonstration purposes, select the Hello World portlet and click the *Save* button. The portal generates a WSDL document to define your producer. To view the WSDL document, click the URL link provided.

Figure 19.19: You can view the WSDL document for your producer by clicking the provided URL.

Now that we've created a producer, let's create a consumer on your second portal server.

On your consumer portal server, navigate to the Consumers tab and select the *Add Consumer* button. Give it a name and add the producer's WSDL URL in the *URL* field. There are also additional fields:

Forward Cookies: Allows the WSRP consumer to forward specific cookies from the user's browser session to the WSRP producer.

Forward Headers: Allows the WSRP consumer to forward specific HTTP headers from the user's browser session to the WSRP producer.

Markup Character Sets: Markup character encodings supported for the consumer are shown in a comma delimited list. UTF-8 is assumed and will be added automatically as a supported encoding.

Leave these additional fields blank for our demonstration. Lastly, we need to define the portlets that the end-user can use from this consumer. To do this, go to *Actions →Manage Portlets* for your consumer. Add the remote portlets that you've configured for your producer portal server. In this case, select the *Hello World* remote portlet and give the new portlet an arbitrary name. Now end users can "consume" or use the remote portlet just like any local portlet in the portal.

Next, you'll learn how to create custom remote portlets.

Creating Custom Remote Portlets

With the demand for dynamic portlets by end users, sometimes a finite, pre-selected list of remote portlets isn't enough. Because of this, Liferay allows you to make custom developed portlets remotely accessible for WSRP.

To enable your custom portlet for WSRP, you'll need to add the <remoteable> tag to your portlet's docroot/WEB-INF/liferay-portlet.xml file:

```
<liferay-portlet-app>
    <portlet>
        <portlet-name>RemoteSamplePortlet</portlet-name>
        <remoteable>true</remoteable>
...
    </portlet>
...
</liferay-portlet-app>
```

After editing your portlet's liferay-portlet.xml file, your custom portlet will appear in the list of portlets available when creating a WSRP producer. Congratulations! Now you can share all your portlets to end users using WSRP!

Next, we'll learn how to remotely access Liferay services.

19.7   Remotely Accessing Liferay Services

Liferay includes a utility called the *Service Builder* which is used to generate all of the low level code for accessing resources from the portal database. This utility is further explained in the *Liferay Developer Network* and in *Liferay in Action*, but it is mentioned here because of its feature which generates interfaces not only for Java code, but also for web services and JavaScript. This means that the method calls for storing and retrieving portal objects are all the same, and are generated in the same step.

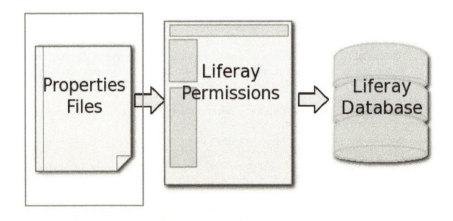

Figure 19.20: Liferay SOA's first layer of security is its properties files.

Because the actual method calls for retrieving data are the same regardless of how one gets access to those methods (i.e., locally or through web services), Liferay provides a consistent interface for accessing portal data that few other products can match. The actual interfaces for the various services are covered in the *Liferay Developer Network* and in *Liferay in Action*. Before these services can be used, administrators need to enable users to access these services remotely.

In the default portal.properties file, there is a section called **Main Servlet**. This section defines the security settings for all of the remote services provided by Liferay. Copy this section and paste it into your custom portal-ext.properties file. Then you can edit the default values to configure the security settings for the Axis Servlet, the Liferay

Tunnel Servlet, the Spring Remoting Servlet, the JSON Tunnel Servlet, and the WebDAV servlet.

By default, a user connecting from the same machine Liferay is running on can access remote services so long as that user has the permission to use those services in Liferay's permissions system. Of course, you are not really "remote" unless you are accessing services from a different machine. Liferay has two layers of security when it comes to accessing its services remotely. Without explicit rights to both layers, a remote exception will be thrown and access to those services will not be granted.

The first layer of security that a user needs to get through in order to call a method from the service layer is servlet security. The *Main Servlet* section of the portal-ext.properties file is used to enable or disable access to Liferay's remote services. In this section of the properties file, there are properties for each of Liferay's remote services.

You can set each service individually with the security settings that you require. For example, you may have a batch job which runs on another machine in your network. This job looks in a particular shared folder on your network and uploads documents to your site's Documents and Media portlet on a regular basis, using Liferay's web services. To enable this batch job to get through the first layer of security, you would modify the portal-ext.properties file and put the IP address of the machine on which the batch job is running in the list for that particular service. For example, if the batch job uses the Axis web services to upload the documents, you would enter the IP address of the machine on which the batch job is running to the axis.servlet.hosts.allowed property. A typical entry might look like this:

```
axis.servlet.hosts.allowed=192.168.100.100, 127.0.0.1, SERVER_IP
```

If the machine on which the batch job is running has the IP address 192.168.100.100, this configuration will allow that machine to connect to Liferay's web services and pass in user credentials to be used to upload the documents.

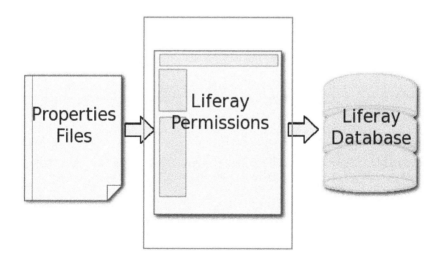

Figure 19.21: Liferay SOA's second layer of security is its permissions system.

The second layer of security is Liferay's security model that it uses for every object in the portal. The user account that accesses the services remotely must have the proper permissions to operate on the objects it attempts to access. Otherwise, a remote exception will be thrown. Portal administrators need to use Liferay's permissions system to grant access to these resources to the administrative user account that attempts to operate on them remotely. For example, say that a Documents and Media folder called *Documents* has been set up in a site. A role has been created called *Document Uploaders* which has the rights to add documents to this folder. Your batch job will be accessing Liferay's web services in order to upload documents into this folder. In order for this to work, you have to call the web service using a user account to which the *Document Uploaders* role has been assigned (or that has individual rights to add documents to the folder). Otherwise, you will be prevented from using the web service.

To call the web service using credentials, you would use the following URL syntax:

```
http://" + userIdAsString + ":" + password +
"@<server.com\>:<port\>/tunnel-web/secure/axis/" + serviceName
```

The user ID is the user's ID from Liferay's database. This can be obtained by logging in as the user and navigating to the *My Account* portlet in the Control Panel. The user ID appears on the Details page of the My Account portlet in the Control Panel.

For example, to get Organization data using a user that has the ID of 2 with a password of *test*, you would use the following URL:

```
http://2:test@localhost:8080/tunnel-web/secure/axis/Portal_OrganizationService
```

It is important to note here how *Password Policies* (covered in this guide's chapter on User Management can be used in combination with this feature. If you are enforcing password policies on your users (requiring passwords to take a certain form, requiring users to change their passwords on a periodic basis, etc.), any administrative user account which accesses Liferay's web services in a batch job will have its password expire too.

To prevent this from happening, you can add a new password policy which does not enforce the password expiration and add your administrative user ID to it. Then your batch job can run as many times as you need it to and the administrative user account's password will never expire.

In summary, accessing Liferay remotely requires the successful passing of two security checks:

1. The IP address must be pre-configured in the server's `portal-ext.properties` file.

2. The user ID being used must have permission to access the resources it attempts to access.

Accessing Liferay's JSON Web Services

To see which Liferay service methods are registered and available for use via JSON web services, open your browser to the following address:

```
http://localhost:8080/api/jsonws
```

The page lists the portal's registered and exposed service methods. Get each method's details by clicking the method name. You can view the full signature of each method, all its arguments, the exceptions that can be thrown, and its Javadoc! Using a simple form from within your browser, you can even invoke the service method for testing purposes.

To list registered services on a plugin (e.g. a custom portlet), don't forget to use its context path in your URL:

```
http://localhost:8080/[plugin-context]/api/jsonws
```

This lists the JSON Web Service API for the plugin.

Accessing Liferay's WSDL

After configuring the security settings properly, your first step in obtaining access to Liferay's remote SOAP web services is to access the WSDL. If you are on a browser on the same machine Liferay is running on, you can do this by accessing the following URL:

```
http://localhost:<port number\>/tunnel-web/axis
```

If, for example, you are running on Tomcat on port 8080, you would specify this URL:

```
http://localhost:8080/tunnel-web/axis
```

If you are accessing a web service that was created as part of a portlet plugin, the URL is similar, but uses the context of your application rather than the tunnel-web servlet. You can get a list of your Service Builder-generated WSDL documents by using the URL pattern below:

```
http://localhost:8080/your-portlet/axis
```

If you are on a different machine from the Liferay server, you will need to pass in your user credentials on the URL to access the WSDL:

```
http://<user ID\>:<password\>@<server name\>:<port number\>/tunnel-web/axis
```

In any case, once you successfully browse to this URL, you will see the list of web services. You can access the WSDL for each service by clicking on the *WSDL* link next to the name of the service. There are many services; one for each of the services available from the Liferay API.

Once you click on one of the *WSDL* links, the Web Service Definition Language document will be displayed. This document can be used to generate client code in any language that supports it. You can either save the document to your local machine and then generate the client code that way, or use your tool to trigger Liferay to generate the document dynamically by using one of the URLs above. For further information about developing applications that take advantage of Liferay's remote services, please see the *Liferay Developer Network* or *Liferay in Action*.

19.8 Summary

Liferay Portal is an easy environment to maintain. Backup procedures are simple and straightforward. Administrators have all the options they need to view and diagnose a running Liferay Portal server through its tunable logs. Patching Liferay is easy to do with Liferay's patching tool. It handles for you all the management of available patches, and makes it easy to install and uninstall them. Upgrading Liferay is also a snap, because Liferay does most of the work automatically. With easy migration tools and automated database upgrade scripts, you'll have your new version of Liferay Portal up and running in no time. It's also easy and secure for Liferay administrators to remotely access both built-in Liferay web services and custom services created using Service Builder.

## CHAPTER 20

USING SCRIPTING FOR ADVANCED FLEXIBILITY

Liferay provides a robust script engine that can be used to interpret scripts in Beanshell, Javascript, Groovy, Python, and Ruby. The script engine came out of Liferay's involvement with the Romulus project. It was originally developed to support non Java-based portlets, but has now been extended to handle a lot more. For example, when Liferay's workflow framework was introduced, the script engine was leveraged to support the execution of scripts from within a workflow module. A script console is now included in the Server Administration portlet in the control panel. It allows system administrators an easy way to execute scripts to perform repetitive user maintenance operations, bulk manipulations using the Liferay API to ensure consistency, or even system level operations.

This chapter helps you to understand Liferay's script engine and covers the following topics:

- Accessing Liferay's service layer from a script

- Running scripts from the script console

- Using the script engine with workflow

- Leveraging custom Java tools in the script engine

The most common thing you'll want to do is access Liferay's services. If you have any familiarity with Liferay's developer tools and API, this will be a snap for you. To access Liferay's scripting console, navigate to the Control Panel, click on *Server Administration* under the Configuration heading, then open the *Script* tab.

20.1 Accessing Liferay Services

In many cases, you'll want to interact with one of Liferay's many services. This is possible from all of the scripting languages supported, but the syntax is a little different for each language.

To illustrate the correct syntax for interacting with Liferay services, let's look at a simple example that uses the UserLocalService to retrieve a list of users and then prints their names to the log file. We'll initially implement the example in Java pseudo-code.

```
import com.liferay.portal.model.User;
import com.liferay.portal.service.UserLocalServiceUtil;
import java.util.List;
            .
            .
            .
                int userCount = UserLocalServiceUtil.getUsersCount();
List<User> users = UserLocalServiceUtil.getUsers(0, userCount);
     for (User user:users) {
        System.out.println("User Name: " + user.getFullName());
}
            .
            .
            .
```

Let's see first how this would work in Beanshell, which is very similar to Java.

Beanshell

Beanshell is a Java scripting language that's designed to run Java code with little or no changes. In this example, we only have one small change to make because Beanshell doesn't support the use of Java Generics.

```
import com.liferay.portal.model.User;
import com.liferay.portal.service.UserLocalServiceUtil;
import java.util.List;

int userCount = UserLocalServiceUtil.getUsersCount();
List users = UserLocalServiceUtil.getUsers(0, userCount);
     for (User user:users) {
        System.out.println("User Name: " + user.getFullName());
}
```

Next, we'll show the same thing in Groovy, another scripting language designed to be similar to Java.

Groovy

Groovy is also based on Java and is perhaps a little easier than Beanshell because literally any code written in Java also runs in Groovy. This means we can execute the exact same code from our Java example without any changes.

```
import com.liferay.portal.model.User;
import com.liferay.portal.service.UserLocalServiceUtil;
import java.util.List;

int userCount = UserLocalServiceUtil.getUsersCount();
List<User> users = UserLocalServiceUtil.getUsers(0, userCount);
     for (User user:users) {
        System.out.println("User Name: " + user.getFullName());
}
```

Of course, we could make this somewhat Groovier by simplifying the program as follows:

```
import com.liferay.portal.service.UserLocalServiceUtil

userCount = UserLocalServiceUtil.getUsersCount()
users = UserLocalServiceUtil.getUsers(0, userCount)
for (user in users){
    System.out.println("User Name: " + user.getFullName())
}
```

The script engine supports more than just Java-like languages. Despite the name, you should be aware that Javascript bears little resemblance to Java, but you can still use it in Liferay's script engine.

JavaScript

Liferay uses the Rhino JavaScript Engine to provide JavaScript support in the script engine. The following code provides a JavaScript version of our original Java program.

```
userCount = Packages.com.liferay.portal.service.UserLocalServiceUtil.getUsersCount();
users = new Packages.java.util.ArrayList;
users = Packages.com.liferay.portal.service.UserLocalServiceUtil.getUsers(0, userCount);
user = Packages.com.liferay.portal.service.UserLocalServiceUtil.createUser(0);

for (i=0;i<users.size();i++) {
    Packages.java.lang.System.out.println(users.get(i).getFullName());
}
```

You can see the JavaScript example is compact. Ruby is even more compact.

Ruby

Ruby is supported through the use of JRuby and our previous example could be implemented in Ruby as follows:

```
userCount = com.liferay.portal.service.UserLocalServiceUtil.getUsersCount();
users = com.liferay.portal.service.UserLocalServiceUtil.getUsers(0, userCount);
users.each{ |user| print user.getFullName() + "\n"}
```

Python users aren't left out either.

Python

Lastly, Liferay provides Python support based on Jython and the previous example could be implemented with the following code.

```
from com.liferay.portal.service import UserLocalServiceUtil
from com.liferay.portal.model import User

userCount = UserLocalServiceUtil().getUsersCount()
users = UserLocalServiceUtil().getUsers(0,userCount)

for user in users:
    print user.getFullName()
```

As you can see, Liferay's services can be accessed from any of these languages. Let's look at some practical examples of how you'd use this.

20.2   Running Scripts from the Control Panel

To see a very simple example of the script console in action, log into the portal as an administrator and navigate to the *Control Panel →Server Administration →Script*. Change the script type to Groovy and replace the code in the scripting console with the following:

```
number = com.liferay.portal.service.UserLocalServiceUtil.getUsersCount();
out.println(number);
```

Click the *Execute* button and check the scripting console or the log for the output.

Now let's implement a more realistic example. We'll retrieve some user information from the database, make some changes and then update the database with our changes. Our company has updated the terms of use and requires that everyone be presented with the updated terms of use on the next log in. When users agree to the terms of use, a boolean attribute called agreedToTermsOfUse is set in their user records. As long as the boolean is true, Liferay will not present the user with the terms of use. However, if we set this flag to false for everyone, all users will have to agree to it again to use the site.

We'll again use Groovy, so ensure that the script type is set to Groovy and execute the following code to check the status of the agreedToTermsOfUse user attribute:

```
import com.liferay.portal.service.UserLocalServiceUtil

userCount = UserLocalServiceUtil.getUsersCount()
users = UserLocalServiceUtil.getUsers(0, userCount)

for (user in users) {
    println("User Name: " + user.getFullName() + " -- " + user.getAgreedToTermsOfUse())
}
```

The code above just prints the value of the agreedToTermsOfUse attribute for each user. Next, we'll actually update each user in the system to set his or her agreedToTerms-OfUse attribute to false. We'll be sure to skip the default user as the default user is not required to agree to the Terms of Use. We'll also skip the admin user that's currently logged in and running the script. If you're logged in as someone other than test@liferay.com, be sure to update the following script before running it.

```
import com.liferay.portal.service.UserLocalServiceUtil
userCount = UserLocalServiceUtil.getUsersCount()
users = UserLocalServiceUtil.getUsers(0, userCount)

for (user in users){
        if(!user.isDefaultUser() &&
        !user.getEmailAddress().equalsIgnoreCase("test@liferay.com")) {
                        user.setAgreedToTermsOfUse(false)
            UserLocalServiceUtil.updateUser(user)
            }
        }
```

To verify the script has updated the records, run the first script again and you should see that all users (except the default user and your user) have been updated.

That's all that's needed to run scripts and to access the Liferay service layer. There are, however, some things to keep in mind when working with the script console:

- There is no undo

- There is no preview

- When using Local Services, no permissions checking is enforced

- Scripts are executed synchronously, so be careful with scripts that might take a long time to execute.

For these reasons, you should use the script console with care. It's best to test run your scripts on non-production systems before running them on production. Of course, Liferay's script engine has uses beyond the script console. Let's learn how to leverage Liferay's script engine for designing workflows.

20.3 Leveraging the Script Engine in Workflow

Liferay's Kaleo workflow engine provides a robust system for reviewing and approving content in an enterprise environment. Even if you don't leverage custom scripts, it's a powerful and robust workflow solution. Adding custom scripts takes it to the next level.

Examine the default Single Approver workflow definition included with Kaleo for an overview of how the feature works. The final step in the workflow runs a script that makes content available for use. As you can see in the snippet below, it uses JavaScript to access the Java class associated with the workflow to set the status of the content to *approved*.

```
<script>
<![CDATA[Packages.com.liferay.portal.kernel.workflow.WorkflowStatusManagerUtil.updateStatus
    (Packages.com.liferay.portal.kernel.workflow.WorkflowConstants.toStatus("approved"),
    workflowContext);]]>
</script>
<script-language>javascript</script-language>
```

At virtually any point in a workflow, you can use Liferay's scripting engine to access workflow APIs or other APIs outside of workflow. There are a lot of different ways you could use this. Here are a few practical ones:

- Getting a list of users with a specific workflow-related role
- Sending an email to the designated content approver with a list of people to contact if he is unable to review the content
- Creating an alert to be displayed in the Alerts portlet for any user assigned to approve content

Of course, before you try any of this, you need to know the appropriate syntax for inserting a script into a workflow. In an XML workflow definition, a script can be used in any XML type that can contain an *actions* tag: those types are <state>, <task>, <fork> and <join>. Inside of one of those types, format your script like this:

```
<actions>
    <action>
        <script>
            <![CDATA[*the contents of your script*]]>
        </script>
        <script-language>*your scripting language of choice*</script-language>
    </action>
    ...
</actions>
```

Here's an example of a workflow script created in Groovy. This one is designed to be used with a Condition statement in Kaleo. It accesses Liferay's asset framework to determine the category of an asset in the workflow. The script uses the category to automatically determine the correct approval process. If the category legal has been applied to the asset, the asset is sent to the Legal Review task upon submission. Otherwise, the asset is sent to the Default Review task.

```
<script>
    <![CDATA[
        import com.liferay.portal.kernel.util.GetterUtil;
        import com.liferay.portal.kernel.workflow.WorkflowConstants;
        import com.liferay.portal.kernel.workflow.WorkflowHandler;
        import com.liferay.portal.kernel.workflow.WorkflowHandlerRegistryUtil;
        import com.liferay.portlet.asset.model.AssetCategory;
        import com.liferay.portlet.asset.model.AssetEntry;
        import com.liferay.portlet.asset.model.AssetRenderer;
        import com.liferay.portlet.asset.model.AssetRendererFactory;
        import com.liferay.portlet.asset.service.AssetEntryLocalServiceUtil;

        import java.util.List;

        String className = (String)workflowContext.get(
            WorkflowConstants.CONTEXT_ENTRY_CLASS_NAME);

        WorkflowHandler workflowHandler =
            WorkflowHandlerRegistryUtil.getWorkflowHandler(className);
\index{workflow}

        AssetRendererFactory assetRendererFactory =
            workflowHandler.getAssetRendererFactory();
\index{workflow}

        long classPK =
            GetterUtil.getLong((String)workflowContext.get
            (WorkflowConstants.CONTEXT_ENTRY_CLASS_PK));

        AssetRenderer assetRenderer =
            workflowHandler.getAssetRenderer(classPK);
\index{workflow}

        AssetEntry assetEntry = assetRendererFactory.getAssetEntry(
            assetRendererFactory.getClassName(), assetRenderer.getClassPK());
```

```
        List<AssetCategory> assetCategories = assetEntry.getCategories();

        returnValue = "Default Review";

        for (AssetCategory assetCategory : assetCategories) {
            String categoryName = assetCategory.getName();

            if (categoryName.equals("legal")) {
                returnValue = "Legal Review";

                return;
            }
        }
    ]]>
</script>
<script-language>groovy</script-language>
```

Within a workflow, the next task or state is chosen based on the return value. For a complete example a workflow script that uses the above Groovy script, please see the legal-workflow-script.xml file in the User Guide's code folder on Github.[1]

The combination of Liferay's scripting and workflow engines is incredibly powerful. However, since it provides users with the ability to execute code, it can be dangerous. When configuring your permissions, be aware of the potential consequences of poorly, or maliciously, written scripts inside of a workflow definition. For more information on creating workflow definitions with Kaleo workflow, see the chapter on it in this guide.

20.4   Custom Java Tools in the Script Engine

Users of the Script Engine face several challenges, including debugging and logging challenges. One approach to overcome these challenges is to develop custom Java utilities that can be called from your scripts. These utilities can write to a custom log file or the Liferay log file. You can also place breakpoints in your utility code and step through it using your favorite debugger.

Liferay's use of Spring and PortletBeanLocatorUtil makes calling these Java utilities from your script easy, regardless of the scripting language you're using.

Let's begin by creating a Liferay Hook project. If you're using Liferay IDE or Liferay Developer Studio, select *File →New Liferay Project*. Name the project *script-utils* and accept the display name generated by the wizard. Be sure to select *Hook* for the Plugin Type and then select *Finish*.

You're using a Liferay Hook Plugin to deploy your utility, but you're not using any of the typical hook features. You just need a way to make your code available to the portal and the Hook Plugin is the least obtrusive way to do this. This means you don't need to add anything to the liferay-hook.xml file. Instead, you'll begin by adding your utility code.

You'll be following the Dependency Injection design pattern so begin by creating the interface. Right-click on the docroot/WEB-INF/src folder and select *New →Interface*. You'll create your interface in the com.liferay.sample package. Name it ScriptUtil.

Next, add two methods to the interface.

```
package com.liferay.sample;

public interface ScriptUtil {

    public String operationOne();
        public String operationTwo(String name);

}
```

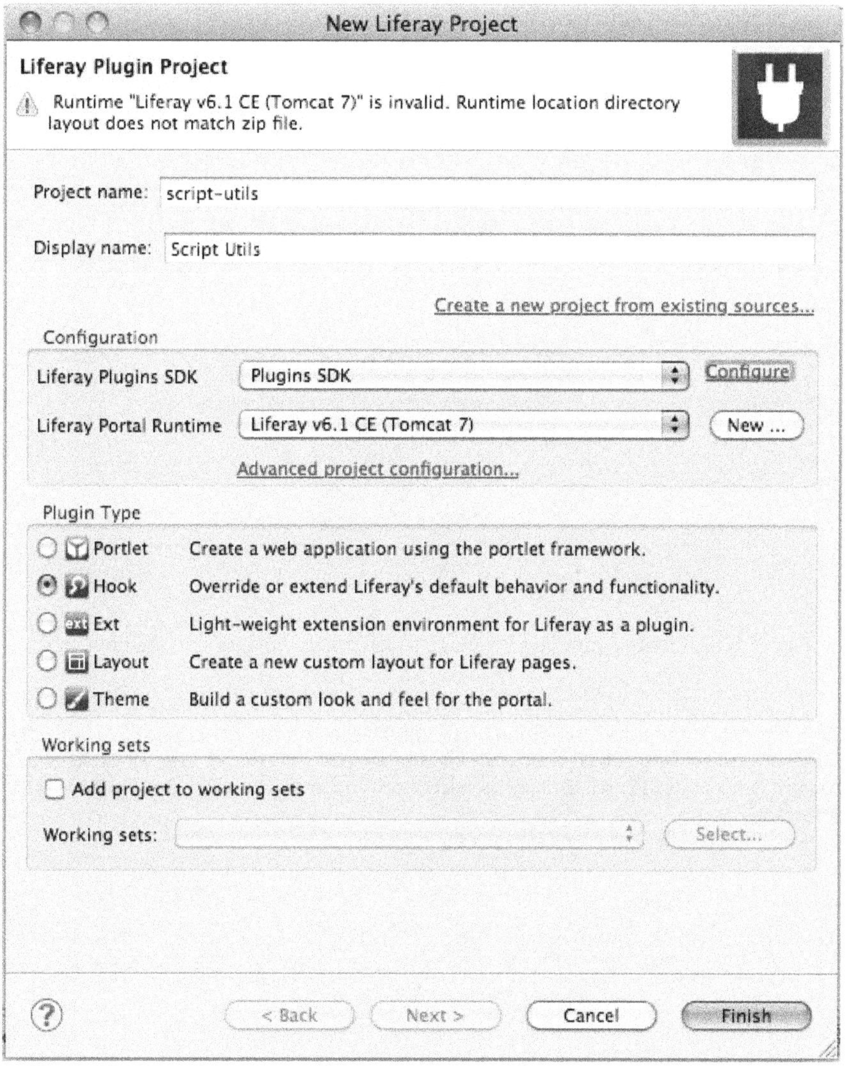

Figure 20.1: Creating a new utilities project is easy if you use Liferay IDE or Liferay Developer Studio.

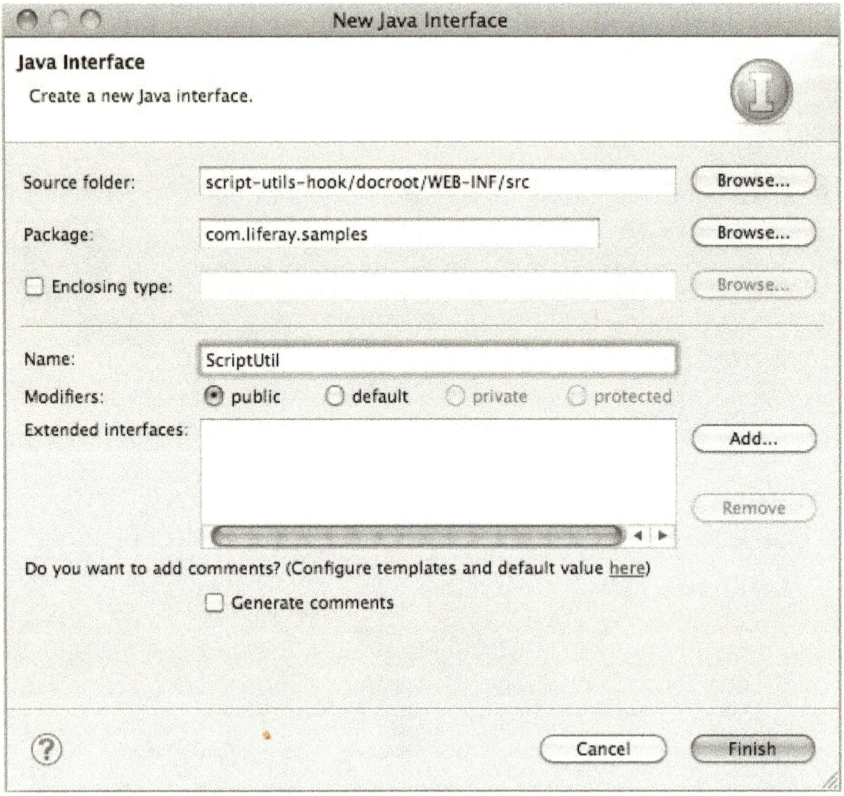

Figure 20.2: Create a new Java interface which you'll implement in the next step.

Next, create the implementation class. Right-click on the docroot/WEB–INF/src folder and select *New Class*. Create the class in the com. liferay. sample package and name it ScriptUtilImpl. Be sure to select com. liferay. sample. ScripUtil as the Interface.

Next, add implementations for the two methods.

```
package com.liferay.sample;

import com.liferay.portal.kernel.log.Log;
import com.liferay.portal.kernel.log.LogFactoryUtil;

public class ScriptUtilImpl implements ScriptUtil {

    @Override
    public String operationOne() {
                return "Hello out there!";
    }

    @Override
    public String operationTwo(String name) {

        _log.debug("Inside of Operation Two");
                    return "Hello " + name + "!";
    }
            private static Log _log = LogFactoryUtil.getLog(ScriptUtilImpl.class);

}
```

Figure 20.3: Create a new Java Class that implements the interface you created earlier.

Liferay makes extensive use of the Spring Framework and you'll be using it here to inject your implementation class into the application. Spring needs a bean definition which you'll declare in an XML file named hook-spring.xml. Create a docroot/WEB-INF-/src/META-INF directory, create the hook-spring.xml file in this folder, and add the following code to hook-spring.xml:

```
<?xml version="1.0"?>

<beans xmlns="http://www.springframework.org/schema/beans"
       xmlns:xsi="http://www.w3.org/2001/XMLSchema-instance"
       default-destroy-method="destroy" default-init-method="afterPropertiesSet"
       xsi:schemaLocation="http://www.springframework.org/schema/beans
       http://www.springframework.org/schema/beans/spring-beans-3.0.xsd">
           <bean id="com.liferay.sample.ScriptUtil" class="com.liferay.sample.ScriptUtilImpl" />
</beans>
```

Upon deployment, you'll need the portal to create a BeanLocator for your plugin. The BeanLocator reads the bean definitions you provided. Create a docroot/WEB-INF-/web.xml file in your project and add the following code to it:

```
<web-app version="2.4" xmlns="http://java.sun.com/xml/ns/j2ee"
    xmlns:xsi="http://www.w3.org/2001/XMLSchema-instance"
    xsi:schemaLocation="http://java.sun.com/xml/ns/j2ee
    http://java.sun.com/xml/ns/j2ee/web-app_2_4.xsd">
        <context-param>
            <param-name>portalContextConfigLocation</param-name>
            <param-value>/WEB-INF/classes/META-INF/hook-spring.xml</param-value>
        </context-param>
</web-app>
```

If your project already contains a docroot/WEB-INF/web.xml file, you can simply add the contents of the <context-param> element inside of the <web-app> element. Save all of the changes you've made and deploy the hook. Once the hook has been deployed successfully, the ScriptUtil can be used in your script engine code.

To see the ScriptUtil code in action, navigate back to the *Control Panel →Server Administration →Script*. Change the script type to Groovy and enter the following script:

```
myUtil = com.liferay.portal.kernel.bean.PortletBeanLocatorUtil.locate(
    "script-utils-hook", "com.liferay.sample.ScriptUtil")

println(myUtil.operationOne())

println(myUtil.operationTwo("Joe Bloggs"))
```

Click *Execute* and you should see the results of your script displayed right under the script console.

20.5   Summary

In this chapter, we saw how Liferay's script engine opens up many exciting possibilities for working with Liferay. You can write and execute scripts from Liferay's Script console in the Control Panel using in a variety of languages including Beanshell, Javascript, Groovy, Python, and Ruby. We learned how you can leverage Liferay's Services Oriented Architecture (SOA) from any of the popular scripting languages that Liferay supports. We also saw how those scripts could be used to simplify administrative tasks by leveraging the Script console. Next, we discovered how you could enhance workflow by using the power of scripts. Lastly, we saw how you could overcome some of the limitations of running scripts in Liferay by creating custom Java utilities that could be executed from within your scripts.

As you can see, Liferay's script engine opens up many exciting possibilities for working with Liferay regardless of your language of choice.

## CHAPTER 21

MANAGING LIFERAY WITH LIFERAY CLOUD SERVICES

Liferay Cloud Services (LCS) is a set of tools and services that lets you manage and monitor your Liferay installations. While Liferay's patching tool lets you apply fix packs and other updates, the install process is still manual. LCS simplifies this process by automatically installing any fix packs that you *choose*. That last point is an important one—LCS won't install anything that you don't specifically choose for installation. You still have control over what gets applied to your Liferay installations. LCS just automates the process by enabling one-click downloading and updating. You can also use LCS to monitor the performance of your Liferay instances. This includes data on pages, portlets, memory usage, JVM performance, and much more. Even better, the features of LCS work regardless of whether your Liferay instance is on a single discreet server, or distributed across a node.

Before going any further, you should make sure that your Liferay instances meet the requirements for LCS—you must be running Liferay Portal 6.1 GA 3, or 6.2 GA 1 or above. Using LCS to apply fix packs and other updates is an EE only feature. The monitoring features of LCS are available to both Liferay CE and EE.

Also, you should take note of a few key terms used throughout this guide:

- *Project*: Represents a group of users belonging to a company or organization. For example, a project can consist of all the users from a project team or business unit, or it can include the entire company.
- *Environment*: Represents a physical cluster of servers, or a virtual or logical aggregation of servers.
- *Server*: Describes a concrete portal instance. It can be a standalone server or a cluster node.

As you go through this guide, you'll cover the following sections on LCS:

- LCS Account Setup
- Portal Preconfiguration (Liferay 6.1 GA3 only)
- Patching Tool Configuration (EE only)
- LCS Client Configuration
- Using LCS

Next, you'll get started by setting up your LCS account.

21.1   Setting up Your LCS Account

To use LCS, you first need to have an account at Liferay.com. You then need to set up an
LCS account at lcs.liferay.com. When creating an LCS account, you're taken through the
steps of accepting the terms of service, setting your password, and setting your password
reminder. You're then taken to the *Projects* screen where you can join an existing project
or create a new one.

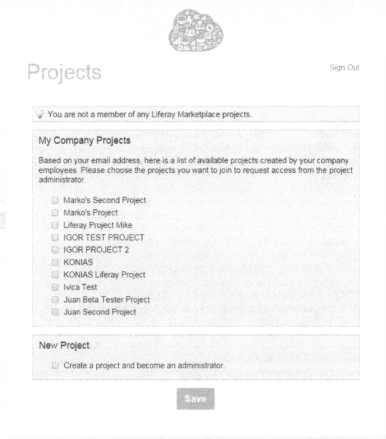

Figure 21.1: When creating your LCS account, you can join an existing project or create
a new one.

The list of existing projects, if present, is the list of projects associated with the domain
of your email address. This is typically the company your email address is associated with.
For example, if your email address is joebloggs@janesblogfactory.com, you're then
presented with a list of existing projects registered to users with the @janesblogfacto-

ry.com domain. This lets you quickly and easily join the LCS projects that are associated with your company. To request access to a project, simply check its checkbox and click *Save*. Your request is then sent to the project administrator for approval. Note that it's possible for the project administrator to pre-assign you a role in a project (more on LCS roles in a moment). In this case, you won't have to wait for approval. For more information on user management in LCS, please see the *Managing LCS Users in Your Project* section of this guide.

Alternatively, you can create a new project and make yourself its administrator. To do so, click the checkbox next to *Create a project and become an administrator* in the New Project section of the Projects screen. The section then expands to let you name the project and choose to go to directly to the project's *Dashboard* (more on the Dashboard later). Give your project a name and then click *Save*.

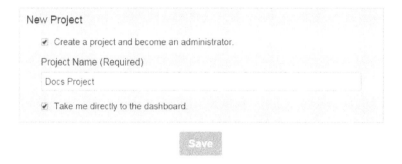

Figure 21.2: You can also create a new project from the Projects screen.

So what exactly can an LCS Administrator do? Fantastic question! As LCS Administrator, you can assign roles to the rest of the users in your project. Each user of LCS needs to have an assigned role. The following roles are available:

- LCS Administrator: All LCS functionality is available to administrators. This is the only role that can manage the roles of other users.
- LCS Environment Manager: All LCS functionality is available in the scope of an environment, with the exception of managing other users.
- LCS Environment Viewer: Has read-only access in the scope of an environment.

You should note that each of these LCS roles assume that the user already has the LCS User role in his or her Liferay.com account. The LCS User role is granted automatically the first time the user enters their LCS account. The actions that can be performed by each of the LCS roles are detailed in the below permissions matrix.

LCS Permissions Matrix

Action	LCS Administrator	LCS Environment Manager	LCS Environment Viewer
Access LCS	true	true	true
Access Any Environment	true	false	false
Access a Particular Environment	true	true	true
Manage Users in Any Environment	true	false	false
Manage Users in a Particular Environment	true	true	false
Invite Users to LCS	true	false	false
Create and Delete Environments	true	false	false
Edit Any Environment	true	false	false
Edit a Particular Environment	true	true	false
Server Registration in Any Environment	true	false	false
Server Registration in a Particular Environment	true	true	false
Install Fix Packs in Any Environment	true	false	false
Install Fix Packs in a Particular Environment	true	true	false

Now that your LCS account has been set up and you have an understanding of the LCS roles, you can get your portal ready for LCS.

21.2 Preconfiguring Your Portal for LCS

If you're running Liferay 6.2, then you can skip this step. If, however, you are running Liferay 6.1 GA3, then there's a small pre-configuration step that you need to take before using LCS: you need to update the spring.configs property in your portal-ext.properties file. This is a workaround for a bug in Liferay 6.1 GA3, where the values for this property are listed in the wrong order. This causes the metrics service in LCS to not be initialized. To fix this, add the following configuration to your portal-ext.properties file:

```
spring.configs=\
    META-INF/base-spring.xml,\
    \
    META-INF/hibernate-spring.xml,\
    META-INF/infrastructure-spring.xml,\
    META-INF/management-spring.xml,\
    \
    META-INF/util-spring.xml,\
    \
    META-INF/jpa-spring.xml,\
    \
    META-INF/executor-spring.xml,\
    \
    META-INF/audit-spring.xml,\
    META-INF/cluster-spring.xml,\
    META-INF/editor-spring.xml,\
    META-INF/jcr-spring.xml,\
    META-INF/ldap-spring.xml,\
    META-INF/messaging-core-spring.xml,\
    META-INF/messaging-misc-spring.xml,\
    META-INF/mobile-device-spring.xml,\
    META-INF/notifications-spring.xml,\
    META-INF/poller-spring.xml,\
    META-INF/rules-spring.xml,\
    META-INF/scheduler-spring.xml,\
    META-INF/scripting-spring.xml,\
    META-INF/search-spring.xml,\
    META-INF/workflow-spring.xml,\
    \
    META-INF/counter-spring.xml,\
    META-INF/mail-spring.xml,\
    META-INF/portal-spring.xml,\
    META-INF/portlet-container-spring.xml,\
    META-INF/staging-spring.xml,\
    META-INF/virtual-layouts-spring.xml,\
    \
    META-INF/monitoring-spring.xml,\
    \
    #META-INF/dynamic-data-source-spring.xml,\
    #META-INF/shard-data-source-spring.xml,\
    #META-INF/memcached-spring.xml,\
    \
    META-INF/ext-spring.xml
```

A server restart is required after updating portal-ext.properties. Next, you need to configure the patching tool.

21.3 Configuring the Patching Tool

Liferay EE's patching tool is leveraged by LCS to apply its updates. If you're running a Liferay EE bundle, then you already have the patching tool installed. If you're not running a bundle, then please see the LDN section on how to install the patching tool. Once you have the patching tool installed, there are a few steps you need to complete before LCS can use it. Note that the commands below apply to Linux, Unix, and Mac systems. If you're running Windows, simply drop the .sh from each command that has it.

1. Navigate to the patching-tool directory on the command line. It's typically located in the Liferay Home folder.

2. Make sure that you have version 10 or higher of the patching tool. To display the version of your patching tool, run patching-tool.sh info.

3. Configure the patching tool by running patching-tool.sh setup.

4. Patches downloaded through LCS are installed by the patching tool agent on server startup. For the agent to start with your server, you need to set the javaagent property in the JVM options. Make sure that you specify the correct file path to the patching-tool-agent.jar. Here's an example of setting the javaagent property:

```
-javaagent:../../patching-tool/lib/patching-tool-agent.jar
```

If your patching tool is installed in a location other than the Liferay Home folder, you must specify the path of the patching-tool folder as a JVM argument for the app server. This is done with the patching.tool.home property. For example:

```
-Dpatching.tool.home=/opt/liferay-portal-6.1.20-ee-ga2/patching-tool/
```

Great! Now you're all set to deploy and configure the LCS client portlet.

21.4   Configuring the LCS Client

You're now ready to configure the LCS client for use in your portal. If your server accesses the web through a proxy, then you need to set a couple of properties inside the WAR file of the LCS client portlet.

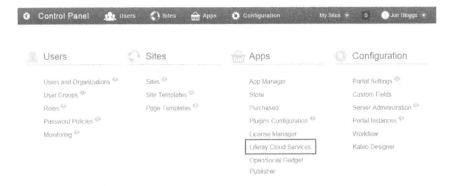

Figure 21.3: LCS appears in your Control Panel as Liferay Cloud Services, in the Apps section.

1. In the WAR file of the LCS client portlet, open the WEB-INF/classes/portlet-ext.properties file.

2. At the end of the file, add the following properties and set them to the appropriate values for your proxy. proxy.host.name= proxy.host.port=

3. Update LCS client WAR with the modified `portlet-ext.properties` file.

4. Deploy the LCS client WAR, or redeploy it if it's already deployed.

The application listed below is requesting access to your account.

Liferay Cloud Services ⊚

If you grant access, this application will be able to do the following:
- Read data on your behalf
- Write data on your behalf

Grant Access   **Deny Access**

Figure 21.4: The LCS client portlet requires access to your LCS account.

Once you deploy the LCS client portlet, you can use it to register your server with your LCS account. Access the portlet by clicking on *Liferay Cloud Services* under the *Apps* section of the *Control Panel*.

After clicking *Authorize Access* on the screen that appears, you are then taken to the LCS website. Log in with your credentials and then click *Grant Access*.

Next, you need to register your server with LCS by filling out the following fields:

1. Cloud Services Project: Choose your project from the menu.

2. Environment: Select an environment from the menu or create a new one by clicking the *Add New Environment* button. An environment should be a logical group of servers. A group of development servers or a cluster are good examples of environments. If you elect to create a new environment, a popup asks you to enter its *Name*, *Location*, and *Description*.

3. Server Name: Give your server a name that you can use to distinguish it in your LCS account.

4. Server Location: This can be a city, location in an office building, or anywhere else that lets you know where the server is physically located.

5. Server Description: Type in any description that you want to give your server. You can use this field to help differentiate the servers you are managing using LCS.

Upon clicking *Register*, your LCS client portlet shows your connection status. Note that it can take up to 10 or 20 seconds to perform the initial handshake with LCS and send the first batch of information to the cloud. If you don't see any change in status after 20

Figure 21.5: The Add New Environment pop-up.

seconds, try refreshing the page. If you see a red symbol indicating no data is being trans-
mitted, please contact the Liferay team for support.

Once a successful connection is established, some statistics and links are displayed.
Here's a description of what's displayed:

- Heartbeat Interval: The communication interval with LCS. For example, if this value
  is 00 : 01 : 00, then the portlet communicates with LCS once every minute.
- Message Task Interval: The message interval with LCS. Messages received from LCS
  let the portlet know about any available updates.
- Metrics Task Interval: The interval at which server statistics and metrics are taken.
- Project: Clicking this link takes you to this server's registered project.
- Environment: Clicking this link takes you to this server's registered environment.
- Server: Clicking this link takes you to the server on LCS.
- Disconnect: Disconnects this Liferay instance from LCS.
- Reset Credentials: Removes the authorizing account from registration with LCS.
  It's important to note that your credentials are not human readable in the portal
  instance. This is because OAuth, which uses tokens, is used for authentication.

Great! Now that you've registered your server with your LCS account, you can dig in to
the features of LCS.

21.5   Using LCS

Once your LCS client is registered with your LCS account, you can get down to the business
that LCS was designed for—managing and monitoring your Liferay instance. If you're
not already there, log in with your account on lcs.liferay.com. This is where you'll apply
updates, view server metrics, manage environments, invite external users to your project,
and more.

Figure 21.6: The server registration screen.

At this point, you might be wondering what information about your servers is stored on the LCS servers. Great question! In order to offer the best service possible, we store the following information about your servers: patches installed on each server, portal.properties (except sensitive data), JVM metrics, portal and portlet metrics, and cache and server metrics. Sensitive data is defined as any key-value pair that contains usernames or passwords. For example, the following properties are considered sensitive and are not stored on the LCS servers:

```
omniadmin.users
ldap.security.credentials.0, ldap.security.credentials.1, ldap.security.credentials.2 ...
facebook.connect.app.secret
auth.token.shared.secret
auth.mac.shared.key
captcha.engine.recaptcha.key.private
amazon.secret.access.key
tunneling.servlet.shared.secret
microsoft.translator.client.secret
dl.store.s3.secret.key
auto.deploy.glassfish.jee.dm.passwd
```

Also, any properties that end in .password and are not stored, with the exception of the following non-sensitive properties:

```
portal.jaas.plain.password
portal.jaas.strict.password
login.create.account.allow.custom.password
```

Now that you know what information is stored on the LCS servers, it's time to get to the heart of LCS—the *Dashboard*.

The LCS Dashboard lets you view and manage your project, environments, and servers. If you're not already at the Dashboard, click it near the upper left-hand corner of your LCS site. Clicking *Dashboard* takes you to the project view. From there, you can get to the environment view and the server view. Each of these views gives you a different look into certain aspects of your LCS project. You'll start with the project view.

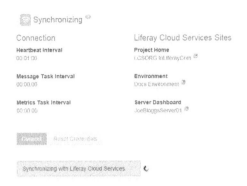

Figure 21.7: The server is connecting to LCS.

Using the Project View

You can get to the project view at any time by clicking the Dashboard tab near the upper left-hand corner of your LCS site. The project view provides you with an overview of your LCS project, including fix packs, alerts, environments, and servers. Fix packs are displayed prominently in a table on the middle of the page. Note that the status, environment, server, and location are listed for each fix pack. If the fix pack is available, you can download it by clicking the Download button to its right. Once a fix pack is finished downloading, an alert appears in the Alerts table below the fix packs table. This notification tells you the download is finished and to restart your server. Restarting your server installs any downloaded fix packs. Note that you must start your server with the privileges required to write to the disk location where patches are stored and processed (the patching-tool folder).

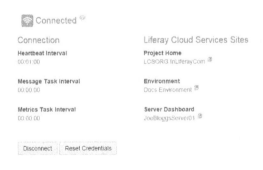

Figure 21.8: The server is connected to LCS.

But what about using LCS to install fix packs across a cluster? Just follow the same procedure! LCS downloads and installs fix packs simultaneously across all nodes—you don't have to handle each one individually.

In addition to displaying fix pack messages, the Alerts table also displays many other kinds of messages. For example, an alert appears whenever a server is offline. Since this

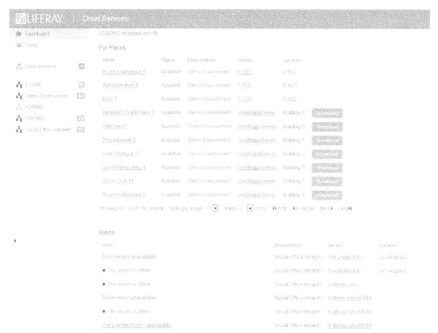

Figure 21.9: The LCS project view shows an overview of your LCS project.

is an important message, it appears with a red dot next to it. Other alerts appear when monitoring is unavailable, the patching tool is unavailable, or other issues are detected.

To the left of the fix packs and alerts are the environments in your project. You can also create new environments here by clicking the blue plus icon. If you look at the icons next to each environment, you'll notice that they're not all the same. In fact, the color and type of the icon tells you something about that environment:

- **Red icon:** Indicates that there is some sort of problem or issue with one or more servers in that environment.
- **Green icon:** Indicates that the servers in that environment are operating properly.
- **Icon with a circle:** Indicates that the servers in that environment are in a cluster.

You can get more information about a specific environment by clicking it. This takes you to the environment view.

Using the Environment View

Clicking an environment on the left-hand side of the project view takes you to the environment view. The environment view, as its name implies, gives you more information about an environment in your LCS project. As with the project view, fix packs and alerts are displayed on the center of the screen. In fact, they behave exactly the same here as they do in the project view. The only difference is that they show fix packs and alerts for the environment instead of the project as a whole. Located above the fix packs, the Environment Details button lets you edit or delete the environment. To the left of the fix packs is the list of servers in the environment. Clicking on one of the servers takes you to the server view for that server.

Figure 21.10: The LCS environment view shows an overview of an LCS environment.

Using the Server View

The server view provides you with detailed information about a server, including statistics and performance metrics. You can get to the server view by clicking a server in the environment view or by clicking a server in the fix pack or alerts tables. Fix packs and alerts are the first thing you see here, as the Fix Packs Alerts button is selected by default when you enter server view. While the alerts table functions the same as it does in the other views, the fix packs table behaves a bit differently. Fix packs are broken down into those that are available for installation and those that are already installed. You can access these through the *Available* and *Installed* tabs at the top of the fix packs table.

To view metrics and statistics of your server's performance, click the *Metrics* button near the top of the page. The metrics are broken down into three main categories: *Application*, *JVM*, and *Server*. Application is selected by default when you click the Metrics button.

The Application category also has three other categories within it: *Pages*, *Portlets*, and *Cache*. Pages lists the frequency with which specific pages are loaded, along with their average load time. Portlets lists the same statistics, but for specific portlets in your server. The Cache category lists Liferay Single VM metrics and Hibernate metrics. In the following screenshot, the statistics in the Portlet category are shown.

The JVM category, as its name indicates, shows statistics about the JVM running on your server. This includes data on the garbage collector and memory. The number of runs,

Figure 21.11: The LCS server view shows an overview of a server registered with LCS.

total time, and average time are listed for each garbage collector item. The memory metrics are presented in a bar chart that shows the usage of the Code Cache, PS Eden Space, PS Old Gen, PS Perm Gen, and PS Survivor Space.

Server is the third category in the Application category. The Server category shows additional information about how your server is running. For example, a horizontal bar graph shows the number of current threads that are running on your server. Similarly, horizontal bar graphs are used to represent the JDBC connection pools.

You can also view the settings for a server by clicking on the *Server Details* button, which is to the right of the Metrics button. The first tab under the Settings button is *LCS Server Settings*. This lets you view or edit your server's name, description, and location. You can also unregister your server from LCS. The second tab under the Settings button is *About Server*. This provides general information about your Liferay instance and hardware. This information is useful to the Liferay support team in the event that you need their assistance.

As you can see, the LCS Dashboard is a powerful tool that greatly simplifies the update process and also gives you extensive information on how your servers are running. Next you'll take a look at how to manage the users in your LCS project.

Managing LCS Users in Your Project

The Users section of LCS is where you manage the LCS users that are part of your project. It's here that you can grant or revoke LCS roles or invite others that aren't yet part of your

Figure 21.12: The LCS application metrics show portlet performance statistics, like frequency of use and average load time.

project. To manage users, first click the *Users* icon just below the Dashboard icon on the upper-left of your screen. You're presented with a table of the users on your project. To the right of each is the Manage button. Clicking *Manage* lets you assign or revoke LCS roles for that user.

To invite external users to your project, click on the *Invite* button. The *Invite User* pop up lets you invite anyone with a valid email address. You can also search for Liferay.com users to invite. Once you've chosen some users, the *Role* selection box lets you preassign LCS roles for when they accept your invitation.

To view sent invitations, click the *Invitations* tab. A table displays invitations, listing invited users' email addresses along with who invited them and the date that the invitation was sent. The table also shoes the preassigned LCS role and environment. You can cancel an invitation by clicking the red *Cancel* button in the *Action* column of the invitation.

As you've now seen, LCS is a powerful tool that simplifies the management of your Liferay servers. You can apply fix packs with just a single click and a server restart—a process that even works across a cluster. You also get a one stop shop for monitoring the performance of your Liferay servers. Metrics like JVM performance, Liferay page and portlet load times, and number of current threads give you an inside look at how your server is running. What's more is that you can do all this collaboratively by inviting others to your project and giving them specific roles in LCS.

Next, you'll learn about Liferay clustering.

Figure 21.13: The LCS JVM metrics show performance data for memory and the garbage collector.

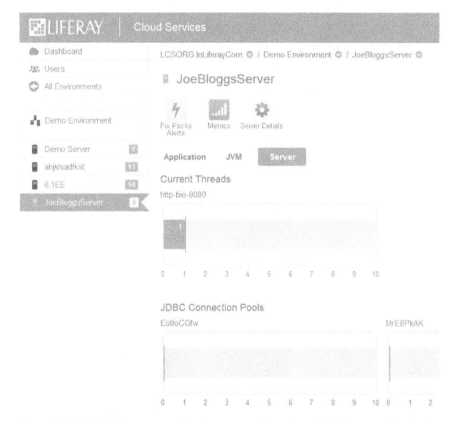

Figure 21.14: The LCS server metrics show current threads and JDBC connection pools.

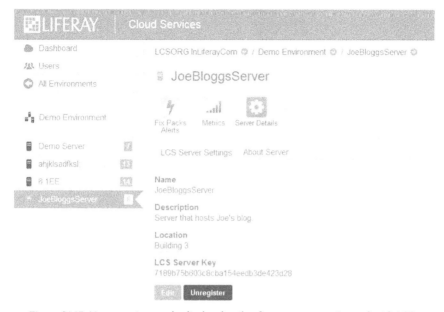

Figure 21.15: You can view and edit the details of your server registered with LCS.

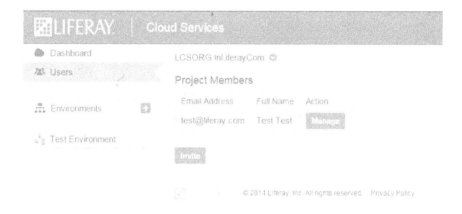

Figure 21.16: The Users tab lets you manage the LCS users in your project.

Figure 21.17: You can invite users to your LCS project and even preassign them roles.

Figure 21.18: The Invitations tab lets administrators view and cancel invitations.

## CHAPTER 22

CONFIGURING LIFERAY FOR HIGH AVAILABILITY

Liferay Portal is a robust, enterprise-ready portal solution. As such, it is fully ready to support mission-critical, enterprise applications in an environment configured for multiple redundancies and 24/7 uptimes. The product, however, like other products of its kind, doesn't come configured this way out of the box, so there are some steps that need to be taken to tune it for your needs.

This chapter covers these topics in detail. Liferay runs on so many different Java EE application servers that we can't cover all the differences between them. For this reason, we'll only discuss Liferay configurations. For example, we'll look at how to configure Liferay to work in a clustered environment, but not how to create the cluster in your application server. The documentation for your particular application server is always a much better place to learn those kinds of things.

This chapter explains how to configure Liferay for a number of advanced scenarios, such as

- Clustering

- Distributed Caching

- Deploying Customized versions of Liferay

- Performance Testing and Tuning

- Content Delivery Network

During the discussion, we'll mention a number of other open source products upon which Liferay relies for much of this functionality. These products all have their own documentation which should be consulted for a fuller view of what these products can do. For example, Liferay uses Ehcache for its caching mechanism. We'll cover how to configure Ehcache to enable caches in Liferay, but will refer you to that product's documentation for further information about that product.

Sometimes Liferay supports multiple products which perform the same function. There are, for example, several single sign-on implementations you can use with Liferay. We'll leave it up to you to select which product best fits the needs of your project without recommending one product over another.

With all of that said, let's get started configuring Liferay for the enterprise.

22.1   Liferay Clustering

Liferay Portal is designed to serve everything from the smallest to the largest web sites. Out of the box, it's configured optimally for a single server environment. If one server isn't sufficient to serve the high traffic needs of your site, Liferay scales to the size you need.

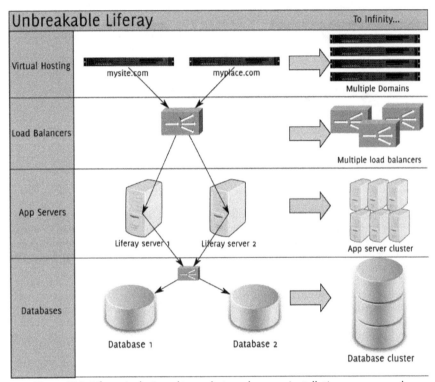

Figure 22.1: Liferay is designed to scale to as large an installation as you need.

Liferay works well in clusters of multiple machines (horizontal cluster) or in clusters of multiple VMs on a single machine (vertical cluster), or any mixture of the two. Once you have Liferay installed in more than one application server node, there are several optimizations that need to be made. At a minimum, Liferay should be configured in the following way for a clustered environment:

- All nodes should be pointing to the same Liferay database or database cluster.
- Documents and Media repositories should be accessible to all nodes of the cluster.
- Search should be configured for replication or should use a separate search server.
- The cache should be replicating across all nodes of the cluster.
- Hot deploy folders should be configured for each node if you're not using server farms.

If you haven't configured your application server to use farms for deployment, the hot deploy folder should be a separate folder for all the nodes, and plugins will have to be deployed to all of the nodes individually. This can be done via a script. If you do have farms configured, you can deploy normally to any node's deploy folder, and your farm configuration should take care of syncing the deployment to all nodes.

Many of these configuration changes can be made by adding or modifying properties in your portal-ext.properties file. Remember that this file overrides the defaults in the portal.properties file. The original version of this file can be found in the Liferay source code or can be extracted from the portal-impl.jar file in your Liferay installation. You can also browse an online version of Liferay's properties file: http://docs.liferay.com/portal/6.2/propertiesdoc/portal.properties.html. It's a best practice to copy the relevant section you want to modify from portal.properties into your portal-ext.properties file, and then modify the values there.

 Note: This chapter documents a Liferay-specific cluster configuration, without getting into specific implementations of third party software, such as Java EE application servers, HTTP servers, and load balancers. Please consult your documentation for those components of your cluster for specific details of those components. Before configuring Liferay in a cluster configuration, make sure your OS is not defining the hostname of your box to the local network at 127.0.0.1.

We'll discuss each of the points above one by one to present a clear picture of how to cluster Liferay.

All Nodes Should Point to the Same Liferay Database

This is pretty self-explanatory. Each node should be configured with a data source that points to one Liferay database (or a database cluster) that all the nodes will share. This ensures all the nodes operate from the same basic data set. This means, of course, Liferay cannot (and should not) use the embedded HSQL database that is shipped with the bundles (but you already knew that, right?). And, of course, it goes without saying that the database server is a separate physical box from the server which is running Liferay.

Beyond a database cluster, there are two more advanced options you can use to optimize your database configuration: a read-writer database configuration, and sharding.

Read-Writer Database Configuration

Liferay allows you to use two different data sources for reading and writing. This enables you to split your database infrastructure into two sets: one that is optimized for reading and one that is optimized for writing. Since all major databases support replication in one form or another, you can then use your database vendor's replication mechanism to keep the databases in sync in a much faster manner than if you had a single data source which handled everything.

Enabling a read-writer database is simple. In your portal-ext.properties file, configure two different data sources for Liferay to use, one for reading, and one for writing:

```
jdbc.read.driverClassName=com.mysql.jdbc.Driver
jdbc.read.url=jdbc:mysql://dbread.com/lportal?useUnicode=true&characterEncoding=UTF-8 \
&useFastDateParsing=false
jdbc.read.username=**your user name**
jdbc.read.password=**your password**
jdbc.write.driverClassName=com.mysql.jdbc.Driver
jdbc.write.url=jdbc:mysql://dbwrite.com/lportal?useUnicode=true&characterEncoding=UTF-8 \
&useFastDateParsing=false
jdbc.write.username=**your user name**
jdbc.write.password=**your password**
```

Of course, specify the user name and password to your database in the above configuration.

After this, enable the read-writer database configuration by uncommenting the Spring configuration file which enables it in your spring.configs property (line to uncomment is in bold):

```
spring.configs=\
META-INF/base-spring.xml,\
META-INF/hibernate-spring.xml,\
META-INF/infrastructure-spring.xml,\
META-INF/management-spring.xml,\
META-INF/util-spring.xml,\
META-INF/editor-spring.xml,\
META-INF/jcr-spring.xml,\
META-INF/messaging-spring.xml,\
META-INF/scheduler-spring.xml,\
META-INF/search-spring.xml,\
META-INF/counter-spring.xml,\
META-INF/document-library-spring.xml,\
META-INF/lock-spring.xml,\
META-INF/mail-spring.xml,\
META-INF/portal-spring.xml,\
META-INF/portlet-container-spring.xml,\
META-INF/wsrp-spring.xml,\
META-INF/mirage-spring.xml,\
**META-INF/dynamic-data-source-spring.xml,\**
#META-INF/shard-data-source-spring.xml,\
META-INF/ext-spring.xml
```

The next time you restart Liferay, it will now use the two data sources you have defined. Be sure you have correctly set up your two databases for replication before starting Liferay.

Next, we'll look at database sharding.

Database Sharding

Liferay, starting with version 5.2.3, supports database sharding for different portal instances. Sharding is a term used to describe an extremely high scalability configuration for systems with massive amounts of users. In diagrams, a database is normally pictured as a cylinder. Instead, picture it as a glass bottle full of data. Now take that bottle and smash it onto a concrete sidewalk. There will be shards of glass everywhere. If that bottle were a database, each shard now is a database, with a subset of the data in each shard.

This allows you to split up your database by various types of data that might be in it. For example, some implementations of sharding a database split up the users: those with last names beginning with A to D go in one database; E to I go in another; etc. When users log in, they are directed to the instance of the application that is connected to the database that corresponds to their last names. In this manner, processing is split up evenly, and the amount of data the application needs to sort through is reduced.

By default, Liferay allows you to support sharding through different portal instances, using the *round robin shard selector*. This is a class which serves as the default algorithm for sharding in Liferay. Using this algorithm, Liferay selects from several different portal instances and evenly distributes the data across them. Alternatively, you can use the manual shard selector. In this case, you'd need to use the UI provided in the Control Panel to configure your shards.

Of course, if you wish to have your developers implement your own sharding algorithm, you can do that. This is a great use of the Ext plugin. You can select which algorithm is active via the portal-ext.properties file:

```
shard.selector=com.liferay.portal.dao.shard.RoundRobinShardSelector
#shard.selector=com.liferay.portal.dao.shard.ManualShardSelector
#shard.selector=[your implementation here]
```

Enabling sharding is easy. You'll need to make sure you are using Liferay's data source implementation instead of your application server's. Set your various database shards in your portal-ext.properties file this way:

```
jdbc.default.driverClassName=com.mysql.jdbc.Driver
jdbc.default.url=jdbc:mysql://localhost/lportal?useUnicode=true&characterEncoding=UTF-8 \
&useFastDateParsing=false
jdbc.default.username=
jdbc.default.password=
jdbc.one.driverClassName=com.mysql.jdbc.Driver
jdbc.one.url=jdbc:mysql://localhost/lportal1?useUnicode=true&characterEncoding=UTF-8 \
&useFastDateParsing=false
jdbc.one.username=
jdbc.one.password=
jdbc.two.driverClassName=com.mysql.jdbc.Driver
jdbc.two.url=jdbc:mysql://localhost/lportal2?useUnicode=true&characterEncoding=UTF-8 \
&useFastDateParsing=false
jdbc.two.username=
jdbc.two.password=
shard.available.names=default,one,two
```

Once you do this, you can set up your DNS so several domain names point to your Liferay installation (e.g., abc1.com, abc2.com, abc3.com). Next, go to the Control Panel and click on *Portal Instances* under the Configuration heading. Create two to three instances bound to the DNS names you have configured.

If you're using the RoundRobinShardSelector class, Liferay automatically enters data into each instance one by one. If you're using the ManualShardSelector class, you'll have to specify a shard for each instance using the UI.

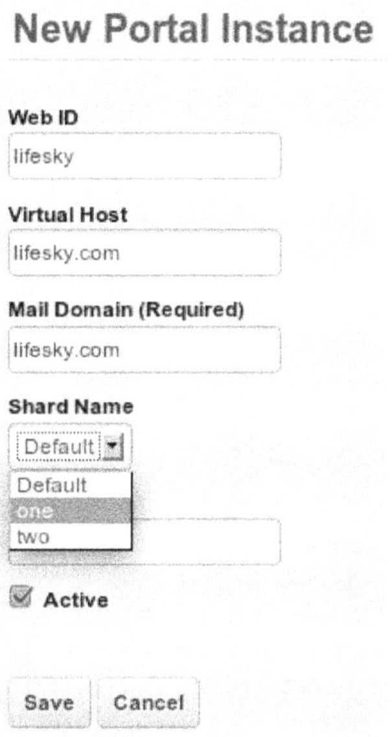

New Portal Instance

Web ID

lifesky

Virtual Host

lifesky.com

Mail Domain (Required)

lifesky.com

Shard Name

Default
Default
one
two

☑ **Active**

Save   Cancel

Figure 22.2: When creating a shard using the manual shard selector, specify the shard you want to use for that instance.

The last thing you need to do is modify the spring.configs section of your portal-ext.properties file to enable the sharding configuration, which by default is commented out. To do this, your spring.configs should look like this (modified section is in bold):

```
spring.configs=\
    META-INF/base-spring.xml,\
    \
    META-INF/hibernate-spring.xml,\
    META-INF/infrastructure-spring.xml,\
    META-INF/management-spring.xml,\
    \
    META-INF/util-spring.xml,\
    \
    META-INF/jpa-spring.xml,\
    \
    META-INF/executor-spring.xml,\
    \
    META-INF/audit-spring.xml,\
    META-INF/cluster-spring.xml,\
    META-INF/editor-spring.xml,\
    META-INF/jcr-spring.xml,\
    META-INF/ldap-spring.xml,\
    META-INF/messaging-core-spring.xml,\
    META-INF/messaging-misc-spring.xml,\
    META-INF/mobile-device-spring.xml,\
    META-INF/notifications-spring.xml,\
    META-INF/poller-spring.xml,\
    META-INF/rules-spring.xml,\
    META-INF/scheduler-spring.xml,\
    META-INF/scripting-spring.xml,\
    META-INF/search-spring.xml,\
    META-INF/workflow-spring.xml,\
    \
    META-INF/counter-spring.xml,\
    META-INF/mail-spring.xml,\
    META-INF/portal-spring.xml,\
    META-INF/portlet-container-spring.xml,\
    META-INF/staging-spring.xml,\
    META-INF/virtual-layouts-spring.xml,\
    \
    #META-INF/dynamic-data-source-spring.xml,\
    *META-INF/shard-data-source-spring.xml,\*
    #META-INF/memcached-spring.xml,\
    #META-INF/monitoring-spring.xml,\
    \
    classpath*:META-INF/ext-spring.xml
```

That's all there is to it. Your system is now set up for sharding. Now that you've got your database set up and optimized for a large installation, let's turn to clustering the Documents and Media Library.

Documents and Media Library Clustering

Beginning with Liferay 6.1, Liferay's Documents and Media Library is capable of mounting several repositories at a time while presenting a unified interface to the user. By default, users can use the Liferay repository, which is already mounted. This repository is built into Liferay Portal and can use one of several different store implementations as its backend. In addition to this, many different kinds of third party repositories can be mounted. If you have a separate repository you've mounted, all nodes of the cluster will point to this repository. Your avenue for improving performance at this point is to cluster your third party repository, using the documentation for the repository you have chosen. If you don't have a third party repository, you can configure the Liferay repository to perform well in a clustered configuration.

The main thing to keep in mind is you need to make sure that every node of the cluster has the same access to the file store as every other node. For this reason, you'll need to take a look at your store configuration.

There are several options available for configuring how Liferay's Documents and Media library stores files. Each option is a *store* which can be configured through the portal-ext.properties file by setting the dl.store.impl= property. Let's consider the ramifications of the various store options.

Using the File System Store

This is the default store. It's a simple file storage implementation that uses a local folder to store files. You can use the file system for your clustered configuration, but you'd have to make sure the folder to which you point the store can handle things like concurrent requests and file locking. For this reason, you need to use a Storage Area Network or a clustered file system.

The file system store was the first store created for Liferay and is heavily bound to the Liferay database. By default, documents are stored in a document_library subfolder of the data folder in a Liferay bundle. Of course, you can change this path to anything you want by using the dl.store.file.system.root.dir= property.

This store creates a folder structure based on primary keys in the Liferay database. If, for example, you upload a presentation with the file name workflow.odp into a folder called *stuff*, the file system store creates a folder structure which looks like the figure below.

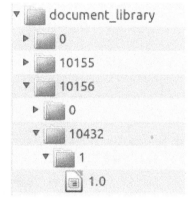

Figure 22.3: Liferay's file system store creates a folder structure based on primary keys in Liferay's database.

The actual folder path that is used by Liferay for storing documents is this:

```
/companyId/folderId/numericFileEntryName/versionNumber
```

The first folder name is the company ID to which the site belongs. The second folder name is the ID of the Documents and Media folder within which the document resides. The third folder name is the numeric file entry name of the document itself. Finally, the fourth name is a version number which is used for storing multiple versions of the document.

 Note: The numeric file entry name of a document is distinct from the document ID; be careful not to confuse the two! Each has an independent counter. The numeric file entry name of a document is used in the folder path for storing the document but the document ID is not. The numeric file entry name of document can be found in the name column of the DLFileEntry table in Liferay's database; the document ID can be found in the fileEntryId column of the same table.

As you can see, the File System Store binds your documents very closely to Liferay, and may not be exactly what you want. But if you've been using the default settings for a while and need to migrate your documents, Liferay provides a migration utility in the Control Panel in *Server Administration →Data Migration*. Using this utility, you can move your documents very easily from one store implementation to another.

Speaking of other store implementations, let's look at some others Liferay provides.

Using the Advanced File System Store

Liferay's advanced file system store is similar to the default file system store. Like that store, it saves files to the local file system—which, of course, could be a remote file system mount. It uses a slightly different folder structure to store files, which is pictured below.

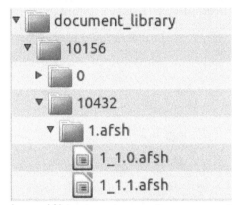

Figure 22.4: The advanced file system store creates a more nested folder structure than the file system store.

So what makes the advanced file system store *advanced*? Several operating systems have limitations on the number of files which can be stored in a particular folder. The advanced file system store overcomes this limitation by programmatically creating a structure that can expand to millions of files, by alphabetically nesting the files in folders. This not only allows for more files to be stored, but also improves performance as there are less files stored per folder.

The same rules apply to the advanced file system store as apply to the default file system store. To cluster this, you'll need to point the store to a network mounted file system that all the nodes can access, and that networked file system needs to support concurrent requests and file locking. Otherwise, you may experience data corruption issues if two users attempt to write to the same file at the same time from two different nodes.

You may decide the advanced file system store for whatever reason doesn't serve your needs. If this is the case, you can of course mount other file systems into the documents and media library. In addition to this, you can also redefine the Liferay store to use one of three other supported protocols. We'll look at these next.

Using the CMIS Store

Though you can mount as many different CMIS (Content Management Interoperability Services) repositories as you like in the Documents and Media library, you may wish also to redefine the Liferay repository to point to a CMIS repository as well. Why? Users might want to create a folder or upload content to the Liferay repository. It would be nice if that Liferay repository was connected to a clustered CMIS repository by the administrator without having to mount it through the UI. The CMIS store allows you to do just that.

If you wish to use the CMIS store, all you need to do is set the following four directives in your portal-ext.properties file:

```
dl.store.cmis.credentials.username=yourusername
dl.store.cmis.credentials.password=yourpassword
dl.store.cmis.repository.url=http://localhost:8080/url/to/your/cmis/repository
dl.store.cmis.system.root.dir=Liferay Home
```

With the configuration above, the Liferay repository is connected to CMIS via the CMIS store. As long as all nodes are pointing to your CMIS repository, everything in your Liferay cluster should be fine, as the CMIS protocol prevents multiple simultaneous file access from causing data corruption.

From here, we'll move on to the JCR store.

Using the JCR Store

Liferay Portal supports as a store the Java Content Repository standard. Under the hood, Liferay uses Jackrabbit, a project from Apache, as its JSR-170 compliant document repository. By default, Jackrabbit is configured to store the documents on the local file system upon which Liferay is installed, in the [Liferay Home]/liferay/jackrabbit folder. Inside this folder is Jackrabbit's configuration file, called repository.xml.

Using the default settings, the JCR store is not very different from the file system stores, except you can use any JCR client to access the files. You can, however, modify Jackrabbit's configuration so it stores files in a database that can be accessed by all nodes, and so that it operates as a cluster within Liferay's cluster.

To move the default repository location to a shared folder, you do not need to edit Jackrabbit's configuration file. Instead, find the section in portal.properties labeled **JCR** and copy/paste that section into your portal-ext.properties file. One of the properties, by default, is the following:

```
jcr.jackrabbit.repository.root=${liferay.home}/data/jackrabbit
```

Change this property to point to a shared folder that all the nodes can see. A new Jackrabbit configuration file is then generated in that location, and you'll have to edit that file to modify Jackrabbit's configuration.

Note that because of file locking issues, this isn't the best way to share Jackrabbit resources, unless you're using a networked file system that can handle concurrency and file locking. If you have two people logged in at the same time uploading content, you could encounter data corruption using this method, and because of this, we don't recommend it for a production system. Instead, if you want to use the Java Content Repository in a cluster, you should redirect Jackrabbit into your database of choice. You can use the Liferay database or another database for this purpose. This requires editing Jackrabbit's configuration file.

The default Jackrabbit configuration file has sections commented out for moving the Jackrabbit configuration into the database. This has been done to make it as easy as possible to enable this configuration. To move the Jackrabbit configuration into the database, simply comment out the sections relating to the file system and comment in the sections relating to the database. These by default are configured for a MySQL database. If you are using another database, you will likely need to modify the configuration, as there are changes to the configuration file that are necessary for specific databases. For example, the default configuration uses Jackrabbit's DbFileSystem class to mimic a file system in the database. While this works well in MySQL, it doesn't work for all databases. For example, if you're using an Oracle database, you'll need to modify this to use OracleFileSystem.

Modify the JDBC database URLs so they point to your database. This, of course, must be done on all nodes of the cluster. Don't forget to create the database first, and grant the user ID you are specifying in the configuration file access to create, modify, and drop tables. After this, be sure to uncomment the <Cluster/> section at the bottom of the file. For further information, it's best to check out the Jackrabbit documentation. Please see the Jackrabbit documentation at `http://jackrabbit.apache.org` for further information.

Once you've configured Jackrabbit to store its repository in a database, the next time you bring up Liferay, the necessary database tables are created automatically. Jackrabbit, however, does not create indexes on these tables, and so over time this can be a performance penalty. To fix this, you'll need to manually go into your database and index the primary key columns for all the Jackrabbit tables.

Note that this configuration doesn't perform as well as the advanced file system store, because you're storing documents in a database instead of on the file system. But it does have the benefit of clustering well. Next, we'll look at Amazon's S3 store.

Using Amazon Simple Storage Service   Amazon's simple storage service (S3) is a cloud-based storage solution which you can use with Liferay. All you need is an account, and you can store your documents to the cloud from all nodes, seamlessly.

This is easy to set up. When you sign up for the service, Amazon assigns you some unique keys which link you to your account. In Amazon's interface, you can create "buckets" of data optimized by region. Once you've created these to your specifications, all you need to do is declare them in `portal-ext.properties`:

```
dl.store.s3.access.key=
dl.store.s3.secret.key=
dl.store.s3.bucket.name=
```

Once you have these configured, set your store implementation to the S3Store:

```
dl.store.impl=com.liferay.portlet.documentlibrary.store.S3Store
```

Consult the Amazon Simple Storage documentation for additional details on using Amazon's service.

We have one more store to go over: the Documentum store.

Using the Documentum Store   If you have a Liferay Portal EE license, you have access to the Documentum hook which adds support for Documentum to Liferay's Documents and Media library. The Documentum hook is included in the Documentum Connector EE app which you can download and install from Liferay Marketplace.

This hook doesn't add an option to make the Liferay repository into a Documentum repository, as the other store implementations do. Instead, it gives you the ability to mount Documentum repositories via the Documents and Media library UI.

There's not really a lot to this; it's incredibly easy. Click *Add →Repository*, and in the form that appears, choose *Documentum* as the repository type. After that, enter a name for the repository, specify the location of the Documentum repository and cabinet, and Liferay mounts the repository for you. That's really all there is to it. If all your nodes are pointing to a Documentum repository, you can cluster Documentum to achieve higher performance.

Now that we've covered the available ways you can configure Documents and Media for clustering, let's move on to configuring search.

Clustering Search

You can configure search for clustering in one of two ways: you can use pluggable enterprise search (recommended) or you can configure Lucene so indexes replicate across the individual file systems of the nodes in the cluster. We'll look at both ways to do this.

Using Pluggable Enterprise Search

As an alternative to using Lucene, Liferay supports pluggable search engines. The first implementation of this uses the open source search engine *Solr*, but in the future there will be many such plugins for your search engine of choice. This allows you to use a completely separate product for search, and this product can be installed on another application server or cluster of servers. Your search engine then operates completely independently of your Liferay Portal nodes in a clustered environment, acting as a search service for all the nodes simultaneously.

This makes it much easier to deal with search indexes. You no longer have to maintain indexes on every node in your cluster, and you get to offload indexing activity to a separate server, so your nodes can concentrate their CPU power on serving pages. Each Liferay node sends requests to the search engine to update the search index when needed, and these updates are then queued and handled automatically by the search engine, independently. It's kind of like having an army of robots ready and willing to do your bidding.

First, you'll need to configure your Solr server, and then you need to install Liferay's Solr plugin to redirect searches over to it.

Configuring the Solr Search Server   Since Solr is a standalone search engine, you'll need to download it and install it first according to the instructions on the Solr web site [1]. Of course, it's best to use a server that is separate from your Liferay installation, as your Solr server becomes responsible for all indexing and searching for your entire cluster. You definitely don't want both Solr and Liferay on the same box. Solr is distributed as a .war file with several .jar files which need to be available on your application server's classpath. Once you have Solr up and running, integrating it with Liferay is easy, but it requires a restart of your application server.

The first thing you need to define on the Solr box is the location of your search index. Assuming you're running a Linux server and you've mounted a file system for the index at /solr, create an environment variable that points to this folder. This environment variable needs to be called $SOLR_HOME. So for our example, we would define:

```
$SOLR_HOME=/solr
```

This environment variable can be defined anywhere you need: in your operating system's start up sequence, in the environment for the user who is logged in, or in the start up script for your application server. If you're using Tomcat to host Solr, modify setenv.sh or setenv.bat and add the environment variable there.

Once you've created the environment variable, you then can use it in your application server's start up configuration as a parameter to your JVM. This is configured differently per application server, but again, if you're using Tomcat, edit catalina.sh or catalina.bat and append the following to the $JAVA_OPTS variable:

```
-Dsolr.solr.home=$SOLR_HOME
```

This takes care of telling Solr where to store its search index. After you have Solr installed and the configuration finished, shut it down, as there is some more configuration to do.

Installing the Solr Liferay Plugin   Next, you have a choice. If you have installed Solr on the same system upon which Liferay is running (not recommended), you can simply go to the Liferay Marketplace and install the *solr-web* plugin. This, however, defeats much of the purpose of using Solr, because the goal is to offload search indexing to another box to free up processing for your installation of Liferay. For this reason, you really shouldn't run

---

[1]http://lucene.apache.org/solr

Liferay and your search engine on the same box. Unfortunately, the configuration in the plugin is set exactly that way, presumably to allow you to experiment with different search configurations. To run them separately—as you would in a production environment—, you'll have to make a change to a configuration file in the plugin before you install it so you can tell Liferay where to send indexing requests. In this case, go to the Liferay Marketplace and download the plugin to your system.

Open or extract the plugin. Inside the plugin, you'll find a file called solr-spring.xml in the WEB-INF/classes/META-INF folder. Open this file in a text editor and you will see the entry which defines where the Solr server can be found by Liferay:

```
<bean class="com.liferay.portal.spring.context.PortletBeanFactoryPostProcessor" />

<!-- Solr search engine -->
\index{Solr}

<bean id="com.liferay.portal.search.solr.server.BasicAuthSolrServer"
    class="com.liferay.portal.search.solr.server.BasicAuthSolrServer">
    <constructor-arg type="java.lang.String" value="http://localhost:8080/solr" />
        </bean>
```

Modify this value so it points to the server where Solr is running. Then save the file and put it back into the plugin archive in the same place it was before.

Next, extract the file schema.xml from the plugin. It should be in the docroot/WEB-INF/conf folder. This file tells Solr how to index the data coming from Liferay, and can be customized for your installation. Copy this file to $SOLR_HOME/conf on your Solr box (you may have to create the conf directory).

Before you start Solr, you should provide Solr with a list of **synonyms** and **stop words**. Synonyms are words that should be equivalent in search. For example, if a user searches for *important information*, you may want to show results for *required information* or *critical information*. You can define these in synonyms.txt. Stop words are defined in stopwords.txt and are words that should not be indexed: articles, pronouns, and other words that have little value in a search. Place these files in your $SOLR_HOME/conf folder. Examples for both of these files are found in the Solr archive in the solr-4.1.0/example-/solr/collection1/conf folder. Additional Solr configuration options, most importantly solrconfig.xml and elevate.xml, are in the $SOLR_HOME/conf folder. Now you can start Solr. After Solr has started, hot deploy the solr-web plugin to all your nodes. See the next section for instructions on hot deploying to a cluster.

Once the plugin is hot deployed, your Liferay server's search is automatically upgraded to use Solr. It's likely, however, that initial searches will come up with nothing: this is because you need to reindex everything using Solr.

Navigate to the Control Panel. Under the Configuration heading, click on *Server Administration*. On the Resources tab, click the *Execute* button next to *Reindex all search indexes*. When you click this button, Liferay begins sending indexing requests to Solr for execution. Once Solr has indexed all your data, you'll have a search server running independently of all your Liferay nodes.

Installing the plugin to your nodes has the effect of overriding any calls to Lucene for searching. All Liferay's search boxes will now use Solr as the search index. This is ideal for a clustered environment, as it allows all your nodes to share one search server and one search index, and this search server operates independently of all your nodes. If, however, you don't have the server hardware upon which to install a separate search server, you can sync the search indexes between all your nodes, as is described next.

Clustering Lucene Indexes on All Nodes

Lucene, the search indexer which Liferay uses, can be configured to sync indexes across each cluster node. This is the easiest configuration to implement, though of course, it's not as "clean" a configuration as using pluggable enterprise search. Sometimes, however, you just don't have another server to use for search indexing, so you need a way to keep all your nodes in sync. By default, Liferay provides a method called Cluster Link which can send indexing requests to all nodes in the cluster to keep them in sync. This configuration doesn't require any additional hardware, and it performs very well. It may increase network traffic when an individual server reboots, since a full reindex will be needed. But this should rarely happen, making it a good tradeoff if you don't have the extra hardware to implement a Solr search server.

You can enable Cluster Link by setting the following property in your `portal-ext.properties` file:

```
cluster.link.enabled=true
```

To cluster your search indexes, you also need to set the following property:

```
lucene.replicate.write=true
```

If you have `cluster.link.enabled=true` but `lucene.replicate.write=false`, you'll enable cache replication but not index replication.

Of course, `cluster.link.enabled=true` and `lucene.replicate.write=true` need to be set on all your nodes. That's all you need to do to sync your indexes. Pretty easy, right? Of course, if you have existing indexes, you'll want to reindex as described in the previous section once you have Cluster Link enabled on all your nodes.

Distributed Caching

Enabling Cluster Link automatically activates distributed caching. Distributed caching enables some RMI (Remote Method Invocation) cache listeners that are designed to replicate the cache across a cluster.

Liferay uses Ehcache, which has robust distributed caching support. This means that the cache can be distributed across multiple Liferay nodes running concurrently. Enabling this cache can increase performance dramatically. For example, suppose that two users are browsing the message boards. The first user clicks a thread to read it. Liferay must look up that thread from the database and format it for display in the browser. With a distributed Ehcache running, this thread is stored in a cache for quick retrieval, and that cache is then replicated to the other nodes in the cluster. Suppose then that the second user who is being served by another node in the cluster wants to read the same forum thread and clicks on it. This time, the data is retrieved more quickly. Because the thread is in the cache, no trip to the database is necessary.

This is much more powerful than having a cache running separately on each node. The power of *distributed* caching allows for common portal destinations to be cached for multiple users. The first user can post a message to the thread he or she was reading, and the cache is updated across all the nodes, making the new post available immediately from the local cache. Without that, the second user would need to wait until the cache was invalidated on the node he or she connected to before he or she could see the updated forum post.

Once you enable distributed caching, of course, you should do some due diligence and test your system under a load that best simulates the kind of traffic your system needs to handle. If you'll be serving up a lot of message board messages, your script should reflect that. If web content is the core of your site, your script should reflect that too.

As a result of a load test, you may find that the default distributed cache settings aren't optimized for your site. In this case, you'll need to tweak the settings yourself. You can modify the Liferay installation directly or you can use a plugin to do it. Either way, the settings you change are the same. Next, we'll discuss a special EE-only optimization that can be made to the cache. After that, we'll explain how to configure Liferay's caching settings.

Enhanced Distributed Cache Algorithm

By default, Liferay's distributed cache uses the RMI replication mechanism, which uses a point to point communication topology. As you can guess, this kind of structure doesn't scale well for a large cluster with many nodes. Because each node has to send the same event to other nodes N − 1 times, network traffic becomes a bottleneck when N is too large. Ehcache also has a performance issue of its own, in that it creates a replication thread for each cache entity. In a large system like Liferay Portal, it's very common to have more than 100 cached entities. This translates to 100+ cache replication threads. Threads are expensive, because they take resources (memory and CPU power). Most of the time, these threads are sleeping, because they only need to work when a cached entity has to talk to remote peers.

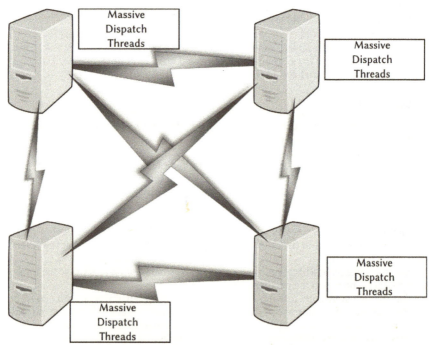

Figure 22.5: The default algorithm requires each node to create massive amounts of dispatch threads to update the cache for each node in the cluster.

Putting heap memory aside (because the amount of memory on the heap depends on the application(s) running), consider the stack memory footprint of those 100+ threads. By default on most platforms, the thread stack size is 2 MB; for 100 threads, that's more than 200 MB. If you include the heap memory size, this number can become as high as 500 MB for just one node. And that massive amount of threads can also cause frequent context switch overhead, which translates to increased CPU cycles.

For large installations containing many nodes, Liferay has developed an enhanced algorithm for handling cache replication that can can fix both the 1 to N − 1 network communication bottleneck, as well as the massive threads bottleneck. The default implementation uses JGroups' UDP multicast to communicate.

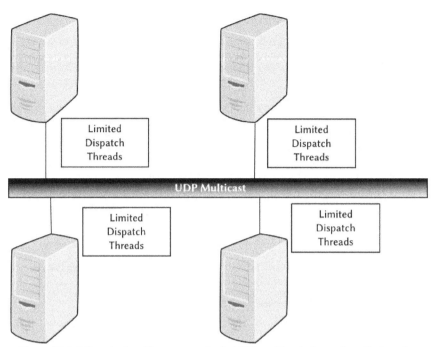

Figure 22.6: Liferay's algorithm uses a single UDP multicast channel, so that nodes don't have to create a thread for each other node in the cluster.

To reduce the number of replication threads, we provide a small pool of dispatching threads. These deliver cache cluster events to remote peers. Since all cache entities' cluster events must go through our pool of dispatching threads to communicate, this gives us a chance to coalesce events: if two modifications to the same cache object happen at almost the same time, we can combine the changes into one, and then we only need to notify remote peers once. This reduces traffic on the network. We should also note that newer versions of Ehcache support the JGroups replicator and can also fix the 1 to N – 1 network communication; however, they cannot fix the massive threads issue and they cannot coalesce cache events.

For EE customers who are interested in this feature, all you have to do to enable the enhanced algorithm is to install a plugin from the Liferay Marketplace and set the following property in the portal-ext.properties files of each of your nodes:

```
ehcache.cluster.link.replication.enabled=true
```

Search Liferay Marketplace for the *Ehcache Cluster EE* plugin, which is free to all EE customers, and install it on each of your nodes. The new algorithm is immediately activated and you can reap the benefits right away.

Next, let's discuss how to modify your Ehache settings. As we've seen, it's easy to use the default Ehcache settings just by enabling Cluster Link. If you need to tweak the cache for your site, you have two options: you can modify Ehcache settings with a plugin or you can modify them directly.

Modifying the Ehcache Settings With a Plugin

A benefit of working with plugins is that you can quickly install a plugin on each node of your cluster without taking down the cluster. Modifying the Ehcache settings with a plugin is recommended over modifying Liferay's Ehcache settings directly. We'll discuss this method first. If you're not a developer, don't worry—even though you'll create a plugin, you won't have to write any code.

Since we're assuming you're an administrator and not a developer, we'll take the easiest route, and use Liferay's graphical development tools, rather than the command line Plugins SDK by itself. If you're a Liferay EE customer, download Liferay Developer Studio from the Customer Portal. Set it up with all the defaults from the first start wizard, and you're good to go (skip the next paragraph).

If you're not a Liferay EE customer, download Eclipse and install Liferay IDE from the Eclipse Marketplace. Download the Plugins SDK for your edition of Liferay from either the Customer Portal (EE) or the Downloads page on liferay.com. Connect Liferay IDE to your Plugins SDK using the instructions found in the *Liferay Developer Network*.[2]

Next, create a hook plugin by selecting *File →New Liferay Project*. Select *Hook* as the project type and give your project a name. Click *Finish* and your project is created.

In your project, create a text file called portlet.properties in the docroot/WEB-INF/src folder. This file can override properties in your portal just like portal-ext.properties. Into this file, add the following three properties:

```
net.sf.ehcache.configurationResourceName=
ehcache.single.vm.config.location=
ehcache.multi.vm.config.location=
```

Liferay's configuration files are, of course, used by default. If you're overriding these properties, it's because you want to customize the configuration for your own site. A good way to start with this is to extract Liferay's configuration files and then customize them. If you're running an application server (such as Tomcat) that allows you to browse to the running instance of Liferay, you can extract Liferay's configuration files from Liferay itself. If you're not, you can extract them from Liferay's .war file or Liferay's source code. In either place, you'll find the files in the portal-impl.jar file, which is in Liferay's WEB-INF/lib folder. The files you want are hibernate-clustered.xml, liferay-single-vm.xml, and liferay-multi-vm-clustered.xml, and they'll be in the /ehcache folder in this .jar. Once you have these, make a subfolder of the docroot folder in your project. Place the files you extracted into this folder and then specify this folder in the properties above.

For example, if you created a folder called custom_cache in your project's docroot folder, you'd copy the three XML configuration files (hibernate-clustered.xml, liferay-single-vm.xml, and liferay-multi-vm-clustered.xml) there. Then you'd edit your portlet.properties and specify your configuration files in the three properties above:

```
net.sf.ehcache.configurationResourceName=/custom\_cache/hibernate-clustered.xml
ehcache.single.vm.config.location=/custom\_cache/liferay-single-vm.xml
ehcache.multi.vm.config.location=/custom\_cache/liferay-multi-vm-clustered.xml
```

Save the file and deploy the plugin (deploying plugins is covered on the Liferay Developer Network), and the settings you've placed in those files will override the default Liferay settings. In this way, you can tweak your cache settings so that your cache performs optimally for the type of traffic generated by your site. The strength of doing it this way is that you don't have restart your server to change the cache settings. This is a great benefit, but beware: since Ehcache doesn't allow for changes to cache settings while the cache is alive, reconfiguring a cache while the server is running will flush the cache.

---

[2]https://dev.liferay.com/develop/tutorials/-/knowledge_base/6-2/liferay-ide

There is, of course, another way to do this if you don't want to create a plugin. It requires you to restart the server to enable the new cache settings, but you don't have to work with any developer tools to do it.

Modifying the Ehcache Settings Directly

This method is pretty similar to the plugin method, except that you have to modify the Liferay installation directly. You'll still need to extract Liferay's configuration files as described in the previous section. Next, shut down your server and find the location in the server where Liferay is installed (this may not be possible on all application servers, and if this is the case, you'll need to use the plugin method described above). For example, suppose you're running Liferay on Tomcat. Tomcat stores the deployed version of Liferay in [Tomcat Home]/webapps/ROOT. Inside this folder is the folder structure WEB-INF/classes. You can create a new folder in here called custom_cache to store the custom versions of the cache configuration files. Copy the files you extracted from Liferay into this folder.

You then need to modify the properties in portal-ext.properties that point to these files. Copy/paste the *Hibernate* section of portal.properties into your portal-ext.properties file and then modify the net.sf.ehcache.configuration-ResourceName property to point to the clustered version of the configuration file that is now in your custom folder:

```
net.sf.ehcache.configurationResourceName=/custom_cache/hibernate-clustered.xml
```

Now that Liferay is pointing to your custom file, you can modify the settings in this file to change the cache configuration for Hibernate.

Next, copy/paste the *Ehcache* section from the portal.properties file into your portal-ext.properties file. Modify the properties so they point to the files in your custom folder. For example:

```
ehcache.multi.vm.config.location=/custom_cache/liferay-multi-vm-clustered.xml
```

You can now take a look at the settings in these files and tune them to fit your environment and application. Let's examine how to do that next.

Customizing Hibernate Cache Settings

By default, Hibernate (Liferay's database persistence layer) is configured to use Ehcache as its cache provider. This is the recommended setting. If you're using the default settings using Cluster Link, you already have this enabled. If, however, you need to customize the settings, you'll have to customize it in one of the ways described above: either in a plugin or in the deployed instance of Liferay. The first thing, of course, is to start off with the clustered version of the file. Copy the hibernate-clustered.xml configuration file to your plugin or to a place in Liferay's classpath (as described above) where you can refer to it. Then change the following property to point to the file:

```
net.sf.ehcache.configurationResourceName=/path/to/hibernate-clustered.xml
```

Next, open this file in a text editor. You'll notice that the configuration is already set up to perform distributed caching through a multi-cast connection. The configuration, however, might not be set up optimally for your particular application. Notice that by default, the only object cached in the Hibernate cache is the User object (com.liferay.portal.model.impl.UserImpl). This means that when a user logs in, his or her User object will go in the cache so that any portal operation that requires access to it (such as permission checking) can retrieve that object very quickly from the cache.

You may wish to add other objects to the cache. For example, a large part of your application may be document management using the Documents and Media portlet. In this case, you may want to cache media objects, such as DLFileEntryImpl to improve performance as users access documents. To do that, add another block to the configuration file with the class you want to cache:

Your site may use the message boards portlet, and those message boards may get a lot of traffic. To cache the threads on the message boards, configure a block with the MBMessageImpl class:

```
<cache eternal=''false'' maxElementsInMemory=''10000''
    name=''com.liferay.portlet.messageboards.model.impl.MBMessageImpl''
    overflowToDisk=''false'' timeToIdleSeconds=''600''>
```

Note that if your developers have overridden any of these classes in an Ext plugin, you'll have to specify the overridden versions rather than the stock ones that come with Liferay Portal. You can customize the other ehcache configuration files in exactly the same way. Refer to Ehcache's documentation for information on how to do this.

As you can see, it's easy to add specific data to be cached. Be careful, however, as too much caching can actually reduce performance if the JVM runs out of memory and starts garbage collecting too frequently. You'll likely need to experiment with the memory settings on your JVM as well as the cache settings above. You can find the specifics about these settings in the documentation for Ehcache.

Configuring Liferay's Caching Settings

To understand how Liferay behaves with various cache configurations, let's consider five different scenarios.

- Scenario 1: The portal administrator does not override the default cache configuration files (i.e., does not override ehcache.single.vm.config.location, ehcache.multi.vm.config.location, or net.sf.ehcache.configuration-ResourceName) but does set cluster.link.enabled=true and ehcache.cluster.link.replication.enabled=true. This is the recommended configuration for a Liferay cluster, as long as the Ehcache Cluster EE app, available from Liferay Marketplace, has been installed. **Important**: The Ehcache Cluster EE app must be installed or cache replication will *not* work with this configuration. In this scenario, Liferay automatically resets cache peer and cache event listers and replaces them with Cluster Link based listeners. This basically activates Cluster Link based cache replication. The configured LiferayCacheManagerPeerProviderFactory, RMICacheManagerPeerListenerFactory, and LiferayCacheEventListenerFactory classes are replaced with Cluster Link based implementations.

- Scenario 2: The portal administrator does not override the default cache configuration files, does set cluster.link.enabled=true, but does not set ehcache.cluster.link.replication.enabled=true. In this case, Liferay utilizes Ehcache's out-of-the-box replication mechanisms (Multicast for discovery and RMI for replication). Lots of replicator threads appear in the log with this configuration.

- Scenario 3: The portal administrator does not override the default cache configuration files and does not set cluster.link.enabled=true. In this case, Liferay does not activate any replication and operates with the assumption that there's no cluster.

- Scenario 4: The portal administrator overrides the default cache configuration files and sets cluster.link.enabled=true and ehcache.cluster.link.replication.enabled=true. In this case, Liferay uses Cluster Link based replication

for any caches configured with the LiferayCacheEventListenerFactory classes. If the portal administrator configured a different CacheEventListener class
for a specific cache (e.g., JGroups), then Liferay uses that listener class. This a basically a hybrid mode that was useful prior to Liferay 6.1 before Liferay supported
cached object replication (and only supported cached event replication). This is *not*
a recommended configuration for Liferay 6.1 or later.

- Scenario 5: The portal administrator overrides the default cache configuration files
  and sets cluster.link.enabled=true but does not set ehcache.cluster-
  .link.replication.enabled=true. In this case, Liferay uses the cache configurations specified in the custom cache configuration files. This is the recommended
  configuration when overriding the default cache configuration files.

As a general rule, we recommend that portal administrators *not* set custom cache configuration files but to set cluster.link.enabled=true and ehcache.cluster.link-
.replication.enabled=true (i.e., we recommend that portal administrators set up
the configuration in scenario 1). If it's necessary to tune the cache configurations, it's better to do it via a plugin than to do it directly. We explained how to do this in the section
above called *Modifying the Ehcache Settings With a Plugin*.

Next, we'll show how to share indexes in a database. This is actually not a recommended configuration, as it's slow (databases are always slower than file systems), but
for completeness, we'll go ahead and tell you how to do it anyway. But you've been fore-
warned: it's far better to use one of the other methods of clustering your search index.

Sharing a Search Index (not recommended unless you have a file locking-aware SAN)

If you wish to have a shared index (and we really hope you don't), you'll need to either
share the index on the file system or in the database. This requires changing your Lucene
configuration.

The Lucene configuration can be changed by modifying values in your portal-ext-
.properties file. Open your portal.properties file and search for the text *Lucene*.
Copy that section and then paste it into your portal-ext.properties file.

If you wish to store the Lucene search index on a file system that is shared by all of the
Liferay nodes (not recommended: you've been warned), you can modify the location of the
search index by changing the lucene.dir property. By default, this property points to
the lucene folder inside the Liferay home folder:

```
lucene.dir=${liferay.home}/data/lucene/
```

Change this to the folder of your choice. You'll need to restart Liferay for the changes
to take effect. You can point all of the nodes to this folder and they will use the same index.

Like Jackrabbit, however, this is not the best way to share the search index, as it could
result in file corruption if different nodes try reindexing at the same time. We do not recommend this for a production system. A better way (though still not great) is to share the
index via a database, where the database can enforce data integrity on the index. This is
very easy to do; it is a simple change to your portal-ext.properties file. Of course, we
also don't recommend this for a production system, as accessing the index from a database
will be slower than from a file system. If, however, you have no other option and want to
do this anyway, keep reading.

There is a single property called lucene.store.type. By default this is set to go to
the file system. You can change this so that the index is stored in the database by making
it the following:

```
lucene.store.type=jdbc
```

The next time Liferay is started, new tables are created in the Liferay database, and the index is stored there. If all the Liferay nodes point to the same database tables, they will be able to share the index. Again, performance on this is not very good. Your DBAs may be able to tweak the database indexes a bit to improve performance. For better performance, you should consider using a separate search server or syncing the indexes on the nodes' file systems.

> **Note:** MySQL users need to modify their JDBC connection string for this to work. Add the following parameter to your connection string:
>
> ```
> emulateLocators=true
> ```

Alternatively, you can leave the configuration alone, and each node will have its own index. This ensures against collisions when multiple nodes update the index. However, the indices will quickly get out of sync since they don't replicate. For this reason, this is not a recommended configuration either. Again, for a better configuration, replicate the indexes with Cluster Link or use a separate search server (see the section on Solr above).

Now we can look at the last consideration when clustering Liferay: hot deploy.

Hot Deploy

Plugins which are hot deployed will need to be deployed separately to all the Liferay nodes. The best way to do this is to configure your application server to support *farms.* This is a feature that enables you to deploy an application on one node and then it replicates automatically to each of the other nodes. This, of course, is configured differently for each application server, so you'll need to consult your application server's documentation to learn how to do this. It's by far the best way to handle hot deploy, and is the recommended configuration. If you have this working, great! You can skip the rest of this section completely.

If for some reason your application server doesn't support this feature or you can't use it, you'll need to come up with a way to deploy applications across your cluster. Each node needs to have its own hot deploy folder. This folder needs to be writable by the user under which Liferay is running, because plugins are moved from this folder to a temporary folder when they are deployed. This is to prevent the system from entering an endless loop, because the presence of a plugin in the folder is what triggers the hot deploy process.

When you want to deploy a plugin to the entire cluster, copy that plugin to the hot deploy folders of all of the Liferay nodes. Depending on the number of nodes, it may be best to create a script to do this. Once the plugin has been deployed to all of the nodes, you can then make use of it (by adding the portlet to a page or choosing the theme as the look and feel for a page or page hierarchy).

All of the above will get basic Liferay clustering working; however, the configuration can be further optimized. We will see how to do this next.

22.2 Performance Tuning

Once you have your portal up and running, you may find a need to tune it for performance, especially if your site winds up generating more traffic than you'd anticipated. There are some definite steps you can take with regard to improving Liferay's performance.

Memory

Memory is one of the first things to look at when you want to optimize performance. If you have any disk swapping, you want to avoid it at all costs: it has a serious impact on performance. Make sure your server has an optimal amount of memory and your JVM is tuned to use it.

There are three basic JVM command switches that control the amount of memory in the Java heap.

```
-Xms
-Xmx
-XX:MaxPermSize
```

These three settings control the amount of memory available to the JVM initially, the maximum amount of memory into which the JVM can grow, and the separate area of the heap called Permanent Generation space.

The first two settings should be set to the same value. This prevents the JVM from having to reallocate memory if the application needs more. Setting them to the same value causes the JVM to be created up front with the maximum amount of memory you want to give it.

```
-Xms1024m -Xmx1024m -XX:MaxPermSize=256m
```

This is perfectly reasonable for a moderately sized machine or a developer machine. These settings give the JVM 1024MB for its regular heap size and have a PermGen space of 256MB. If you're having performance problems, and your profiler is showing that there's a lot of garbage collection going on, the first thing you might want to look at is increasing the memory available to the JVM. You'll be able to tell if memory is a problem by running a profiler (such as Jprobe, YourKit, or the NetBeans profiler) on the server. If you see Garbage Collection (GC) running frequently, you definitely want to increase the amount of memory available to the JVM.

Note that there is a law of diminishing returns on memory, especially with 64 bit systems. These systems allow you to create very large JVMs, but the larger the JVM, the more time it takes for garbage collection to take place. For this reason, you probably won't want to create JVMs of more than 2 GB in size. To take advantage of higher amounts of memory on a single system, run multiple JVMs of Liferay instead.

Issues with PermGen space can also affect performance. PermGen space contains long-lived classes, anonymous classes and interned Strings (immutable String objects that are kept around for a long time to increase String processing performance). Hibernate—which Liferay uses extensively—has been known to make use of PermGen space. If you increase the amount of memory available to the JVM, you may want to increase the amount of PermGen space accordingly.

Garbage Collection

As the system runs, various Java objects are created. Some of these objects are long-lived, and some are not. The ones that are not become *de-referenced*, which means that the JVM no longer has a link to them because they have ceased to be useful. These may be variables that were used for methods which have already returned their values, objects retrieved from the database for a user that is no longer logged on, or a host of other things. These objects sit in memory and fill up the heap space until the JVM decides it's time to clean them up.

Normally, when garbage collection (GC) runs, it stops all processing in the JVM while it goes through the heap looking for dead objects. Once it finds them, it frees the memory they were taking up, and then processing can continue. If this happens in a server environment, it can slow down the processing of requests, as all processing comes to a halt while GC is happening.

There are some JVM switches that you can enable which can reduce the amount of time processing is halted while garbage collecting happens. These can improve the performance of your Liferay installation if applied properly. As always, you will need to use a profiler to monitor garbage collection during a load test to tune the numbers properly for your server hardware, operating system, and application server.

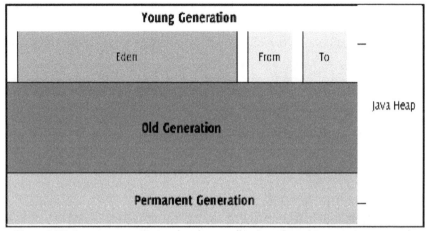

Figure 22.7: Java uses generational garbage collection. If an object survives enough garbage collection events, it's promoted to a new memory pool. For example, an object could be promoted from the young generation memory pool to the old generation memory pool or from the old generation memory pool to the permanent generation memory pool.

The Java heap is divided into sections for the young generation, the old generation, and the permanent generation. The young generation is further divided into three sections: Eden, which is where new objects are created, and two "survivor spaces, which we can call the *From* and *To* spaces. Garbage collection occurs in stages. Generally, it's more frequently done in the young generation, less frequently done in the old generation, and even less frequently done in the permanent generation, where long-lived objects reside. When garbage collection runs in the young generation, Eden is swept for objects which are no longer referenced. Those that are still around are moved to the *To* survivor space, and the *From* space is then swept. Any other objects in that space which still have references to them are moved to the *To* space, and the *From* space is then cleared out altogether. After this, the *From* and the *To* spaces swap roles, and processing is freed up again until the next time the JVM determines that garbage collection needs to run.

After a predetermined number of *generations* of garbage collection, surviving objects may be moved to the old generation. Similarly, after a predetermined number of *generations* of garbage collection in the old generation, surviving objects may be moved to the permanent generation.

By default, the JDK uses a serial garbage collector to achieve this. This works very well for a short-lived desktop Java application, but is not necessarily the best performer for a long-lived, server-based application like Liferay. For this reason, you may wish to switch to the Concurrent Mark-Sweep (CMS) collector.

In CMS garbage collection, rather than halting application processing altogether, this garbage collector makes one short pause in application execution to mark objects directly reachable from the application code. Then it allows the application to run while it marks all objects which are reachable from the set it marked. Finally, it adds another phase called the *remark* phase which finalizes marking by revisiting any objects modified while the application was running. It then sweeps through and garbage collects. Though it sounds more complicated, this has the effect of greatly reducing the amount of time that execution needs to be halted to clean out dead objects.

Just about every aspect of the way memory management works in Java can be tuned. In your profiling, you may want to experiment with some of the following settings to see if any of them can increase your performance.

NewSize, MaxNewSize: The initial size and the maximum size of the New or Young Generation.

+UseParNewGC: Causes garbage collection to happen in parallel, using multiple CPUs. This decreases garbage collection overhead and increases application throughput.

+UseConcMarkSweepGC: Use the Concurrent Mark-Sweep Garbage Collector. This uses shorter garbage collection pauses, and is good for applications that have a relatively large set of long-lived data, and that run on machines with two or more processors, such as web servers.

+CMSParallelRemarkEnabled: For the CMS GC, enables the garbage collector to use multiple threads during the CMS remark phase. This decreases the pauses during this phase.

SurvivorRatio: Controls the size of the two survivor spaces. It's a ratio between the survivor space size and Eden. The default is 25. There's not much bang for the buck here, but it may need to be adjusted.

ParallelGCThreads: The number of threads to use for parallel garbage collection. Should be equal to the number of CPU cores in your server.

A sample configuration using the above parameters might look something like this:

```
JAVA_OPTS="$JAVA_OPTS -XX:NewSize=700m -XX:MaxNewSize=700m -Xms2048m
-Xmx2048m -XX:MaxPermSize=128m -XX:+UseParNewGC -XX:+UseConcMarkSweepGC
-XX:+CMSParallelRemarkEnabled -XX:SurvivorRatio=20
-XX:ParallelGCThreads=8"
```

Again, you should always follow the procedure of adjusting the settings, then testing under load, then adjusting again. Every system is different and these are general guidelines to follow. Next, we'll see some modifications we can make to Liferay's properties to help increase performance.

Properties File Changes

There are also some changes you can make to your portal-ext.properties file once you are in a production environment.

Set this property to true to load the theme's merged CSS files for faster loading for production. By default it is set to false for easier debugging for development. You can also disable fast loading by setting the URL parameter css_fast_load to 0.

```
theme.css.fast.load=true
```

Set this property to true to load the combined JavaScript files from the property javascript.files into one compacted file for faster loading for production.

```
javascript.fast.load=true
```

These are various things the Liferay engineering team has done to increase performance generally. If your developers make use of Liferay's tools and platform, their JavaScript and themes can also take advantage of these properties.

Let's look at one final, general way of increasing Liferay's performance: disabling unused servlet filters.

Disabling Unused Servlet Filters

Liferay comes by default with a number of servlet filters enabled and running. It is likely that for your installation, you don't need them all. Since servlet filters intercept the HTTP request and do some processing on it before Liferay even has a chance to start building the page, you can increase performance by disabling the ones you're not using.

You can disable servlet filters you're not using by using your portal-ext.proper-ties file. Copy the *Servlet Filters* section from the original portal.properties file into your customized file, and then go through the list and see if there are any you can disable, by setting them to false.

For example, if you are not using CAS for single sign-on, disable the CAS Filter. If you are not using NTLM for single sign-ons, disable the NTLM Filter. The fewer servlet filters you are running, the less processing power is needed for each request.

As you can see, there are many things you can do to increase Liferay's performance generally. But don't forget to load test your own applications! It may be that a performance issue comes from a custom-built application that's doing something it shouldn't do. Always load test your system before putting it into production: that's the best way of finding out potential performance problems, and that way, you'll find them during performance testing, and not when your system is in production.

Next, you'll learn how to configure a Content Delivery Network, which can also help with your portal's performance.

22.3   Content Delivery Network

A Content Delivery Network (CDN) is an interconnected system of servers deployed in multiple data centers that use geographical proximity as a criteria to deliver content across the Internet. For more information on CDNs and their general use cases and technical details, visit the Wikipedia article on CDN.[3]

First, you'll discover the perks of using a CDN in Liferay and learn about general guidelines for using a CDN in your Liferay Portal instance. Then, you'll learn the steps to configure a CDN for your portal. It's time to expand your Liferay content around the world!

Using CDN for Performance Enhancements

A CDN serves static content to users in a Liferay Portal instance. These static resources (images, CSS, JavaScript, etc.) from the portal are stored on multiple servers around the world, and when requested, are retrieved by the server nearest to the user.

The CDN functions as a caching proxy, meaning that once static content is copied to a local server, it is stored in a cache for quick and easy retrieval. This drastically improves latency time, because browsers can download static resources from a local server down the street instead of halfway around the world. A user's request to the CDN for content is directed to a server machine using an algorithm. That algorithm attempts to use a server closest to the user. The figure below shows a visual representation of using geographical proximity to improve latency.

Because of the reduced wait time for requests and reduced load on your application server, a CDN is a great option to improve your portal's performance. Using a CDN with Liferay, however, has some restrictions.

Liferay only works with CDNs that can dynamically retrieve requested resources from Liferay. For this reason, you should check with your CDN provider to make sure you don't have to upload anything to them manually in order for it to work. The CDN must fetch the content itself.

---

[3]http://en.wikipedia.org/wiki/Content_delivery_network

Figure 22.8: The red lines on the map represent the required distances traveled by requests from a server to the user. Using CDN allows a user to request static resources from a much closer local server, improving download times.

There are several properties in Liferay that enable you to configure your CDN and tweak it to your portal's needs. You'll cover how to do this next.

Configuring Liferay to Use a CDN

Now that you have a general understanding of what a CDN accomplishes and how it's used in Liferay, it's time to set one up for yourself. You can set your CDN and its properties using two different methods: editing your portal's properties file or using the Control Panel.

To configure your CDN by properties file, you'll need to create a portal-ext.properties file in your Liferay Home directory and set the appropriate CDN properties. You can view the CDN properties and their descriptions by visiting the Content Delivery Network section of the portal.properties HTML document.

Once you configure your CDN host, static assets automatically get uploaded to the CDN, and Liferay generates URLs to them that replace the old host with your new CDN host.

To configure your CDN in the Control Panel, navigate to the Control Panel →*Portal Settings*. In the main configuration, you'll notice three fields related to CDNs:

- *CDN Host HTTP*
- *CDN Host HTTPS*
- *CDN Dynamic Resources Enabled*

These properties are exactly the same as the ones you can specify in your portal-ext-.properties. Make sure to visit the CDN section of the Properties Document referenced previously if you don't know how to fill in the CDN fields. Once you're finished, click *Save* and your old host is replaced with your new CDN host for static content.

As you can see, configuring a CDN is extremely easy, and can drastically reduce latency time and improve your portal's performance.

Figure 22.9: The Control Panel lets you configure your portal's CDN.

22.4 Summary

We've seen how good a fit Liferay Portal is for the enterprise. It can be scaled linearly to grow to whatever size you need to serve your users. Liferay Cloud Services lets you manage and monitor your Liferay instances from a single interface. Clustering is also a snap, and Liferay harmonizes very well with whatever environment you may have.

Liferay Portal is also built for performance. You can take advantage of read-writer database configurations, as well as database sharding. You can tune it to support over 3300 concurrent users on a single server with mean login times under half a second and maximum throughput of more than 79 logins per second. We've seen some tips for tuning Liferay Portal, and we have to keep in mind the adage about tuning: load test and profile, tune, repeat.

Configuring a Content Delivery Network is also advantageous when you want to increase your portal's performance. By accessing static resources from a local server, latency time and your application server's load are drastically reduced.

In all, Liferay Portal gives you all the options you need to build a high-performance, robust environment that supports your enterprise.

INDEX

www.ingramcontent.com/pod-product-compliance
Lightning Source LLC
Chambersburg PA
CBHW051218050326
40689CB00007B/733